Handbook of Small States

This Handbook covers a wide spectrum of issues relating to small states. Chapters in the volume have been grouped under the three main themes of economic, social and environmental issues. The economics sections include chapters dealing with trade, finance and regulatory frameworks, while the social theme covers health, migration and population ageing, as well as overall social wellbeing. The environmental theme examines matters such as measuring environmental performance, natural disasters, the ocean economy, and the validity of the Sustainable Development Goals.

The approaches taken by the authors vary, but in all cases the chapters draw practical policy implications for small states. The book can therefore be considered as a wide-ranging depositary of information on small states with the aim of deriving policy prescriptions, and thus as an excellent resource for academics, students and policymakers.

Lino Briguglio is an Economics Professor at the University of Malta and also directs the Islands and Small States Institute of the same University. He possesses a PhD in Economics from the University of Exeter, UK. He was formerly Head of the Economics Department and of the Banking and Finance Department of the University of Malta, as well as Director of the University Gozo Campus. He also acted as Chief Executive Officer of the Foundation for International Studies of the University of Malta. His main area of interest is islands and small states studies, in particular economic aspects, and he has authored many publications on this subject. He is known internationally for his seminal work on the vulnerability index. He has also pioneered studies on economic resilience.

Handbook of Small States

Economic, Social and Environmental Issues

Edited by Lino Briguglio

Routledge
Taylor & Francis Group

LONDON AND NEW YORK

First published 2018
by Routledge
2 Park Square, Milton Park, Abingdon, Oxon OX14 4RN

and by Routledge
52 Vanderbilt Avenue, New York, NY 10017

First issued in paperback 2020

Routledge is an imprint of the Taylor & Francis Group, an informa business

First edition published 2018

Europa Commissioning Editor: Cathy Hartley

Editorial Assistant: Eleanor Simmons

by Taylor & Francis Books

British Library Cataloguing in Publication Data
A catalogue record for this book is available from the British Library

Library of Congress Cataloging in Publication Data
Names: Briguglio, Lino, editor.
Title: Handbook of small states : economic, social and environmental issues / edited by Lino Briguglio.
Description: Abingdon, Oxon ; New York, NY : Routledge, 2018. | Series: Europa emerging economies
Identifiers: LCCN 2017048622 (print) | LCCN 2017050442 (ebook) | ISBN 9781351181846 (ebook) | ISBN 9781857439281 (hardback)
Subjects: LCSH: Developing countries--Economic conditions. | States, Small--Economic conditions. | Developing countries--Social conditions. | States, Small--Social conditions.
Classification: LCC HC59.7 (ebook) | LCC HC59.7 .H2973 2018 (print) | DDC 330.9172/4--dc23
LC record available at https://lccn.loc.gov/2017048622

ISBN 13: 978-0-367-58070-4 (pbk)
ISBN 13: 978-1-85743-928-1 (hbk)

Typeset in Bembo
by Taylor & Francis Books

Contents

Contents

Contents

Figures

Tables

List of tables

List of tables

Boxes

Contributors

Jihad Alwazir is an Assistant Director at the International Monetary Fund (IMF) Monetary and Capital Markets department in Washington, DC. He was Governor and Chairman of the Board of Directors of the Palestine Monetary Authority (PMA) between January 2008 and November 2015, and founder and Chairman of the Palestine Deposit Insurance Corporation (PDIC) established in 2013. He served in several senior positions in the private and public sectors at various stages in his career: A member of the board of the Palestine Monetary Authority and later Deputy Governor, Acting Minister and Deputy Minister of Finance and Permanent Secretary General of the Ministry of Planning. He holds a PhD in Business Administration from Loughborough University, UK.

Dag Anckar retired in 2005 from the position as Professor of Political Science at the Åbo Akademi University in Finland (1974–2005). In 1994–2003 he was Visiting Professor (political science) at the Mid-Sweden University. He is a former President of the Finnish Political Science Association (1974–76, and 1992–95), of which he is a Honorary Member. He was in 1984–87 President of the Nordic Political Science Association, serving on the Board of that Association in 1975–99, and serving on the Executive Committee of the International Political Science Association in 1988–94. He was in 1998 awarded an Honorary Doctorate from the University of Uppsala (Sweden) and in 2003 awarded an Honorary Doctorate from the University of Turku (Finland). He has published extensively in the field of comparative politics, contributing to journals like *Comparative Politics*, *Democratization*, *European Journal of Political Research*, *International Political Science Review*, and *Scandinavian Political Studies*.

Natasha Azzopardi Muscat qualified as a medical doctor in 1995 and obtained her specialization in public health medicine in 2003. She was awarded a PhD from Maastricht University, having successfully defended her dissertation on the Europeanisation of Health Systems from a Small State Perspective. Between 2001 and 2013 she held various senior positions in the Ministry of Health in Malta including that of Chief Medical Officer. She presently works as a consultant in public health medicine at the Directorate for Health Information and Research in Malta and is a senior lecturer in the Department of Health Services Management at the University of Malta. Her main research interest is health systems and health policy with a particular focus on small states and she has authored several publications. She is also the President of the European Public Health Association.

George R. Barker is currently a Visiting Fellow at the London School of Economics, and at the British Institute of International and Comparative Law London. He is President of the Australian Law and Economics Association, a Fellow of the Law and Economics Association of

New Zealand and on the Editorial Board of the European Journal of Law and Economics. He is also a visiting associate Professor at the Australian National University (ANU), having been Director of the ANU Centre for Law and Economics in 1998–2017. He gained a DPhil in Economics from Oxford University in 1992, and holds both Bachelor of Laws and Master of Economics degrees. In 2010 he was the lead economic advisor on the design of a uniform competition and consumer law, enforcement and dispute resolution mechanism for Pacific Island Forum Countries. He has authored books, articles and given expert economic testimony on a wide range of matters in Asia-Pacific, North America and Europe involving the economic analysis of law.

Jamila Beckles is presently an Economist at the Central Bank of Barbados (CBB) on the Fiscal Unit. She is a past graduate of the University of the West Indies, where she received a BSc in Economics and Accounting, and was also awarded the 2014 CBB Scholarship, and the Wendell McClean prize in Economic Theory. Jamila's recent research interests are focused on issues relating to small open economies, public sector expenditure, and trade analysis.

Richard L. Bernal, possess a PhD in Economics and is currently Pro-Vice Chancellor, Global affairs, University of the West Indies (UWI). He previously served on the Broad of Directors of the Inter-American Development Bank. As Director-General of the Caribbean Regional Negotiating Machinery he was chief trade negotiator for the Caribbean Community (CARICOM). For 10 years he was Jamaica's Ambassador to the United States and to the Organization of American States. He worked in Jamaica's Central Bank, the Planning Agency and as Advisor to the Minister of Finance on external debt management and stabilization policy. He taught International and Development Economics at the UWI. His publications include numerous journal articles, book chapters and three books: *Globalization, Trade and Economic Development. A Study of the CARIFORM-EU Economic Partnership Agreement* (2013). *Dragon in the Caribbean. China's Global Re-Positioning. Challenges and Opportunities for the Caribbean* (2014) and *The Influence of Small States on Superpowers: Jamaica and U.S. Foreign Policy* (2015).

Markand Bhatt is an Assistant Lecturer at The University of the South Pacific (USP), Fiji. He received his MCom in Economics from USP and has been teaching undergraduate Economics courses since 2010. His research interests are in area of development economics.

Lino Briguglio is an Economics Professor at the University of Malta and also directs the Islands and Small States Institute of the same University. He possesses a PhD in Economics from the University of Exeter (UK). He was formerly Head of the Economics Department and of the Banking and Finance Department of the University of Malta, as well as Director of the University Gozo Campus. For a time he was also the Chief Executive Officer of the Foundation for International Studies of the University of Malta. His main area of interest is islands and small states studies, in particular economic aspects, and he has authored many publications on this subject. He is known internationally for his seminal work on the 'vulnerability index' (see for example *World Development*, Vol. 23(9): 1615–1632 (1995) which led to a world-wide interest and to many quantitative studies on Economic and Environmental Vulnerability. He has also pioneered studies on economic resilience.

Marie Briguglio is a resident academic at the University of Malta, lecturing and conducting research in the fields of Behavioural Economics, Environmental Economics and Social Marketing. She completed her PhD (Economics) at Stirling University, an MSc at University

College London (Environmental and Resource Economics, Distinction) and an Honours degree at the University of Malta (Economics, Distinction). Prior to returning to academia, Marie held various senior civil service positions including Deputy Director of the Malta Environment and Planning Authority, responsible, *inter alia*, for negotiation and implementation of the European Union environmental acquis, and as National Focal Point for the United Nations Framework Convention on Climate Change. Throughout her career Marie secured and managed several internationally funded projects in the environmental field and she is currently the Principal Investigator on several international and national research projects. Marie is also an award-winning screen-writer/broadcaster and remains highly active in outreach projects, including as co-Chairperson of the President of Malta's Forum for Active Community Engagement.

Carl Camilleri possesses a Master of Science degree in Econometrics from Queen Mary and Westfield College (University of London) in 1999 with Distinction, and obtained his PhD in Economics from City University (London) in 2015. He is a Lecturer in Econometrics and Health Economics at the University of Malta within the Department of Economics. Prior to joining the Department of Economics, Dr Camilleri served in the public service within the Economic Policy Division (Ministry of Finance) for 10 years and held the position of Senior Economist within the same Division. Dr Camilleri was mainly responsible for macroeconomic forecasting and was directly involved in the modelling and analysis of pension reform systems within the Maltese economy.

Satish Chand is Professor of Finance in the School of Business at the University of New South Wales based at the Australian Defence Force Academy in Canberra. His research interests include labour migration, fragile states and the challenges of development, and he has published works on these subjects.

Chee Keong Choong is Professor and Vice President (Student Development and Alumni relations) at Universiti Tunku Abdul Rahman (UTAR), Malaysia. He currently holds the Tan Sri Dato' Sri Dr Teh Hong Piow Professorial Chair in Banking and Finance at the Faculty of Business and Finance, UTAR. He is actively involved in research, covering the areas of private capital flows (foreign direct investment, aids, remittances), financial system (financial and banking institutions and development), and economic integration (ASEAN Economic Community), Trans-Pacific Partnership Agreement (TPPA) and China's Belt and Road Initiative (OBOR). He has published various studies in national and international journals, book chapters, and conference proceedings.

John Gerard Cozier is a Financial Research Officer in the Policy, Research and Planning Division of the Trinidad and Tobago Securities and Exchange Commission. John completed his Doctorate in Economic Development Policy from the University of the West Indies, St. Augustine in 2015 and his undergraduate studies in Finance at Florida Memorial University. His research interests lie in finance, capital market development and economic development policy. He works as part of a team in developing policies and guidelines which shape the development of the nascent capital markets of Trinidad and Tobago. John is a tutorial instructor in Economics at the University of the West Indies, St Augustine.

Valerio Crispolti is a Senior Economist in the Fiscal Affairs Department (FAD) of the International Monetary Fund (IMF). He graduated from the University of Rome 'La Sapienza' in 1999; and, holds a MA in Economics from the University Pompeu Fabra of Barcelona and a

MA in Economics from the University of Turin (CORIPE). Prior to joining FAD, Valerio worked as an Economist in the Africa Department of the IMF (2009–13), as an Advisor to the Italian Executive Director at the IMF Board (2005–09), and as an Economist in the research department of the Italian Central Bank (2001–05). During his tenure at the Fund, he has worked on various countries – including the Republic of San Marino and the Comoros – and participated in several initiatives aimed at strengthening the IMF engagement with small countries. His research interests extend also to issues related to growth-friendly fiscal policies and international reserves accumulation in low-income countries.

Reginald Darius is an international macroeconomist with over 15 years' experience in Macroeconomic and Fiscal policy design and implementation. Dr Darius is currently the Director for the Economic Policy Division at Commonwealth Secretariat, and prior to that he was Permanent Secretary in the Ministry of Finance, Government of Saint Lucia in 2012–16. Dr Darius also served as Senior Economist at the International Monetary Fund during 2005–12. Dr Darius holds a PhD in Economics from the University of Warwick, and a Master's degree (Economics) from the University of Cambridge. He has published papers in a number of international journals in the areas of fiscal and monetary policy, exchange rate regimes and unemployment.

Omar Dhaher is an Assistant Professor of Management at Al-Quds University, Palestine, Director of the Dual Studies IT Program and Senior Researcher at Research Center Information, Law and Society (CRIDS) at University of Namur, Belgium. He holds a Bachelor degree in Computer Science from Al-Quds University, Palestine in 1999. He won a Clinton's scholarship in 2001 to pursue a dual Master's degree in Business Information and Information Systems Management from Duquesne University, PA, USA (2003) and a PEACE Scholarship in 2009 to pursue a doctoral research project on 'Telecommunications Regulatory Design in Unstable and Small States: The Case of Palestine'. He holds a PhD in Economic Sciences and Management (2017) from University of Namur, Belgium.

Matthew Dornan is the Deputy Director of the Development Policy Centre, Crawford School of Public Policy at the Australian National University. An economist, he leads the centre's research on economic development in the Pacific Islands and has published extensively on infrastructure development and management in the region. Matthew convenes the Energy for Development cluster of the ANU's Energy Change Institute, is the managing editor of the Development Policy Centre's Discussion Paper series, and sits on the editorial board of the Asia and the Pacific Policy Studies journal. He holds a PhD from the Crawford School of Public Policy at ANU and has previously worked for a number of development programs in the Pacific islands.

Rebecca Gookool is currently a PhD student registered with the Department of Economics at the University of the West Indies St Augustine. She currently holds a Bachelor of Science degree in Economics and an MPhil in Agricultural Economics. She has been a part time member of staff at the Department since 2004 and a Researching Consultant with the Trade and Economic Development Unit since 2010. She is one of the Component Coordinators on the Southwest Local Economic Development Project which is funded by the IDB and Atlantic. Her current research is in the area of the economic impact of the Economic Partnership Agreement on the Caribbean region.

Kevin Greenidge holds a BSc in Economics with first class honours from the University of the West Indies, a Master's degree in Economics from the University of Cambridge in the UK and a PhD from the University of Nottingham, also in the UK. He also holds a certificate in Business Management from Columbia University. Apart from this formal education, Kevin also attended a number of training programmes at various international institutions such as the International Monetary Fund (IMF) Institute, the Monetary Study Centre Gerzensee, and the Centre for Latin American Monetary Studies. Dr Greenidge is the former Director of the Research and Economic Analysis Department at the Central Bank of Barbados and is currently Senior Economist at the IMF.

Patrick Guillaumont, President of the Fondation pour les Etudes et Recherches sur le Développement International (FERDI), is Emeritus Professor at the University of Auvergne and founder of the Revue d'Economie du Développement. He was a member of the Committee of Development Policy at the United Nations (CDP), where he chaired various expert groups on the LDCs (Least Developed Countries) and has worked for many international institutions. Patrick Guillaumont has published many books and papers on development. Recent works are focused on development finance, aid allocation and vulnerability. They include *Caught in a Trap, Identifying the least developed countries* (2009), *Out of the trap. Supporting the least developed countries* (2017), *Financing Sustainable Development: Addressing Vulnerabilities* (2015) edited with Matthieu Boussichas, and, as a co-author, *Linking security and development. A Plea for the Sahel* (2016).

Roger Hosein is currently a senior lecturer and coordinator of the Trade and Economic Development Unit (TEDU) at the Department of Economics, University of the West Indies, St Augustine. Dr Hosein was the lead consultant in the technical design of the Government's Dollar for Dollar and GATE programs. He has worked with several organizations including the Caricom Secretariat, the Caribbean Development Bank, the World Trade Organization (WTO), the World Bank and the Inter-American Development Bank (IDB). He has also collaborated with the majority of multinational energy companies operating in Trinidad and Tobago. He has written six (6) books, either directly or with co-authors and has published over 50 peer reviewed papers and chapters in peer reviewed journals. Currently his research includes corporate social responsibility, localized economic development planning, revealed comparative advantage theory, natural trading partner hypothesis and the Dutch Disease in small petroleum exporting countries.

Fazurin Jamaludin is an Economist in the Risk Management Unit of the International Monetary Fund (IMF). Prior to that, he worked in the Small States Division of the IMF's Asia and Pacific Department, where he also served as desk economist for Solomon Islands and Timor-Leste. As part of his work on small states and Pacific island countries, he has conducted research in the areas of financial development, financial inclusion, and linkages between small states and regional and global economies.

T. K. Jayaraman is a Professor of Economics, Fiji National University, Fiji Islands since 2012. Earlier, he was Professor of Economics at the University of the South Pacific for 14 years. Prior to his academic career, he was a Senior Economist with the Manila-based Asian Development Bank for 15 years. He holds BA (Hons) from University of Madras, India; and Master's and Doctoral degrees from the University of Hawaii (Manoa), Honolulu, assisted by an East West Centre Grant and a Fulbright Grant. His leading publications include articles in journals such as *Journal of Policy Modeling* and *International Review of Economics*; and books: *A Single Currency for Pacific Islands* (Nova Science Publishers, New York, 2012); *Issues in Monetary and Fiscal Policies in*

Small Developing States: A Case Study of the Pacific (Commonwealth Secretariat, London, 2011), *Issues in Monetary Economics* (University of the South Pacific, Suva, Fiji Islands, 2003), *Readings in Monetary Economics of Pacific Islands* (University of the South Pacific, 2008) and *Financial Sector Development and Private Investment in Vanuatu* (Macmillan Brown Centre for Pacific Studies, University of Canterbury, New Zealand, 2000).

Tarron Khemraj is Associate Professor of Economics at New College of Florida, the honours college of the State University System of Florida. He is also Research Associate at Central Bank of Barbados and Caribbean Centre for Money and Finance. His research is applied in nature, focusing on monetary economic issues for small open emerging economies and political economy of development. His work tends to be unorthodox in nature. He holds a PhD in Economics from The New School for Social Research in New York, an MA in Development Economics from University of Manchester in England, and a BSocSc in Economics from University of Guyana in Guyana. Before entering academia, he worked as a central bank economist at Bank of Guyana.

Rainer Lanz works as Economic Affairs Officer in the Development Division of the World Trade Organization, which he joined in 2012. His main responsibility is to support the work of the Sub-Committee on Least Developed Countries (LDCs) as its Secretary. Previous to joining the WTO, Mr. Lanz worked for four years at the Organization for Economic Co-operation and Development (OECD), where he was involved in the development of the OECD Services Trade Restrictiveness Index and worked on private sector development in South East Europe. Mr. Lanz holds a PhD in Economics from the Ludwig-Maximilian University of Munich. He has published several articles on trade-related issues.

Evan Lau is Associate Professor within the Department of Economics at the Universiti Malaysia Sarawak (UNIMAS). He is the managing editor of the *International Journal of Business and Society* (IJBS) published by the same university. He possesses a PhD in Economics. He has vast research experience, covering the areas of International Economics with numerous applications of econometrics techniques. Apart from journal publications, he contributes to programmes on national television and radio stations discussing mainly Malaysia's annual budget. He was among the highly cited authors in UNIMAS.

Dongyeol Lee is currently an Economist in the Asia and Pacific Department of the International Monetary Fund. His country assignments include Vanuatu and Korea. He possesses a PhD in Economics from Michigan State University. He was formerly a Senior Economist at the Bank of Korea. His primary research interests lie in the area of industrial organization, economic growth, and international trade. His leading publications include articles in journals such as *Review of Industrial Organization*, *Information Economics and Policy*, *Contemporary Economic Policy*, *Japan and the World Economy*, *Journal of Asian Economics* and *Journal of the Asia Pacific Economy*.

Troy Lorde is a senior lecturer in economics at The University of the West Indies (UWI), Cave Hill Campus. Prior to joining the UWI, he worked at the United Nations Development Programme (UNDP) for Barbados and the Organization of Eastern Caribbean States as Assistant to the Resident Coordinator. He is also a member of the Commonwealth Specialist Pool of Consultants on Small States and Climate Finance. His main research interests are in the fields of international tourism, international trade, and international competitiveness. He has published over 40 papers in peer-reviewed journals, prepared seven technical reports and presented papers at more than 30 conferences. Currently, his research agenda includes the tourism sharing economy, welfare effects of trade agreements, and the legacy of the ICC Cricket World Cup on the Caribbean. He holds a BSc (First Class Honours) from the UWI, an MA from York University, Canada, and a PhD from the University of Surrey, UK, and is a past Commonwealth Scholar.

Meredith Arnold McIntyre, a Grenadian national, received a BSc (Economics) Honours degree from the University of the West Indies (Cave Hill campus; Barbados) in 1982. In 1985 he was awarded a Fulbright Scholarship and completed an MA in Economics at Yale University. He was awarded a PhD in Economics in 1990 from University of Toronto. Dr McIntyre had an extensive career in the region, working for the Caribbean Development Bank, the Organization of Eastern Caribbean States Secretariat, as a consultant with the Caribbean Export Development Agency, and in 1996 joining the CRNM (recently renamed the Office of Trade Negotiations, CARICOM Secretariat) as the lead Technical Adviser. Dr McIntyre joined the International Monetary Fund in February2001 as a senior economist in the Policy Development and Review Department. Dr McIntyre has published articles in academic journals in the areas of macroeconomic policy in small, open economies; regional integration in the Caribbean; trade policy and economic development; fiscal policy and debt management and multilateral trade liberalization in the Doha Round. Dr McIntyre published a book in 1995 entitled *Trade and Economic Development in Small, Open Economies: The Case of the Caribbean Countries*.

Travis Mitchell possesses a Master's degree in Economics from the University of Warwick, UK and a Bachelor in Economics degree from the University of the West Indies, Cave, Hill Campus. He is currently Economic Adviser at the Commonwealth Secretariat, London, and was formerly Senior Economist at the Central Bank of Barbados. He has also held the position of Economist at the European Delegation to Barbados and the Organization of Eastern Caribbean States. Travis's research interest is in the area of debt sustainability but he has published research in the areas of tourism and exchange rates. He is in the midst of completing a PhD Economics degree at Keele University in the UK.

Stefano Moncada graduated in Development Economics from the University of Rome 'La Sapienza' (First Class) and completed a Master of Arts in European Studies at the University of Malta in 2005. He obtained his PhD in Economics from the University of Malta with a focus on the impacts of official Development Assistance (ODA) on health and adaptive capacity in Least Developed Countries (LDCs). As part of his research he developed a new impact evaluation assessment that makes use of participatory qualitative research and quantitative (quasi-experimental) techniques. He has lectured at the University of Malta, based at the Institute for European Studies, since 2008 in the areas of Development Economics, climate change adaptation and health, island studies and sustainable development. His recent research activities include health and economic assessments, in the face of climate change, of urban communities in Africa and in Small Island Developing States (SIDS). Prior to joining academia, Stefano worked in the Italian Parliament as manager and economic policy analyst, in the field of development economics, health economics applied to low-income countries, and the environment. He currently forms part of the Executive Committee of the European Association of Development and Training Institutes (EADI).

Winston Moore is presently Professor of Economics and Head of the Department of Economics at The University of the West Indies, Cave Hill Campus. Prior to this, he held the position of Senior Economist at the Central Bank of Barbados. His recent research has examined the issues surrounding the green economy and private sector development, as well as the economic impact of climate change on tourism. Dr Moore has published more than 80 peer-reviewed papers, books and book chapters. He holds a PhD in Economics from the University of Surrey; a MSc in Economics from the University of Warwick; and, a BSc in Economics from the University of West Indies, Cave Hill.

Cheong Fatt Ng is a lecturer in the Department of Finance, Faculty of Business and Finance, University Tunku Abdul Rahman (UTAR) in Malaysia. He obtained his Bachelor of Economics and Master of Philosophy degrees from UTAR in 2013 and 2016, respectively. His research interest is in the area of environmental economics, energy economics and financial economics.

Vincent Nossek is Research Assistant at the Fondation pour les Etudes et Recherches sur le Développement International (FERDI). His work is focused on International financing for development and the post-2015 Agenda, Sustainable Development Goals, as well as on the Climate and Development Program.

Bonapas Francis Onguglo is a senior economist at UNCTAD. He is the Head of the Trade Analysis Branch in the Division on International Trade in Goods and Services, and Commodities. He has many years' experience in supporting developing countries develop policies, regulations, institutions and capacities to integrate effectively and gainfully into the international trading system. He specializes in international trade and development issues including trade policy formulation, trade regulations, trade negotiations, trade and environment, ocean economy, and trade and creative industries. On these issues he has written articles and policy and analytical reports.

Charumathi Raja holds a Master's degree in International and Development Economics from Yale University and a BSc in Economics from the University of Warwick. She is currently working as a Senior Associate at the Bank of England, focusing on prudential policy frameworks. She has held additional positions at the International Rice Research Institute, the Philippines, and the Centre for Development Finance, India, focusing on economic modelling and forecasting. Her research interests include applied econometrics, development finance, and information and communications technology for development.

Robert Read is Senior Lecturer in International Economics at the University of Lancaster, UK. He is an Economics graduate of the Universities of Essex (BA) and Reading (PhD). After research and teaching positions at the University of Reading, he was an Economist for Unilever plc at its London Head Office monitoring macroeconomic and strategic developments in East Asia, Latin America and Sub-Saharan Africa. He is a leading international authority on the growth performance of small economies and has published numerous articles in leading academic journals, book chapters and reports on this subject (much of it in collaboration with Harvey Armstrong). He has also published extensively on a range of other topics in international economics. He has been an invited expert speaker at many international conferences and has also acted as a consultant to many leading international institutions, including the African, Caribbean and Pacific (ACP) Group of States, the European Commission, the Technical Centre for Agricultural and Rural Cooperation ACP-EU (CTA), the UK Department for International Development (DfID), the Falkland Islands Government, the UK Foreign Office, the Dutch

Foreign Ministry, the Commonwealth Secretariat, the World Bank and its Foreign Investment Advisory Service (FIAS) and the World Trade Organization (WTO).

John Laing Roberts is an international consultant on macroeconomics and sustainable development, working with the Indian Ocean Commission, the Commonwealth Secretariat, the Common Market for Eastern and Southern Africa (COMESA) and the Government of Mauritius. He has Master's and PhD degrees from University of Birmingham, specializing in health economics. During 1962–1989 he worked in the National Health Service, becoming a Regional Administrator in 1981. He has been an adviser to the World Health Organization (WHO), the World Bank, the African Development Bank and the European Union (EU). He has taught in the Universities of Birmingham, Bristol, Cardiff, Manchester and Mauritius. He has contributed to the United Nations Environment Programme (UNEP)'s Global and African Environment Outlook series, publishing case studies on malaria eradication and cyclones. He is a co-author of the Commonwealth Secretariat publications: *Saving Small and Island States*, 2010; *Tools for Mainstreaming Sustainable Development in Small States*, 2011; *Partnerships for Sustainable Development in Small States*, 2011; and *The Big Divide*, 2012, on progress with MDGs in small states. He was Consulting Editor (2013–15) for the Central Bank in Mauritius.

Wendell Samuel, a national of St Vincent and the Grenadines, is Deputy Division Chief in the Eastern II Division of the International Monetary Fund (IMF)'s African Department. Mr Samuel holds Bachelor and Master of Economics degrees from the University of the West Indies, and a PhD in Economics from New York University. Prior to joining the African Department, he held the positions of Deputy Division Chief in the Western Hemisphere Department, Senior Director of Research and Information at the Eastern Caribbean Central Bank, and a lecturer in the Department of Economics at the University of the West Indies. He also served as the IMF's Regional Resident Representative for the Eastern Caribbean Currency Union Countries.

Maurice Schiff was born in Belgium, obtained his Bachelor and Master of Economics degrees from the Hebrew University in Jerusalem and his PhD from the University of Chicago. He spent two years as Professor and Research Director of the Faculty of Economics and Business of the University of Concepcion, Chile. He worked at the World Bank from 1983 to 2011, mostly in the Development Research Department, and was consultant in the World Bank's Office of the Chief Economist for Latin America and the Caribbean. He is a Research Fellow of the Institute of Labor Economics (Germany) and the Center for Research and Analysis of Migration (UK). His work has focused on different aspects of trade, migration and development, including sectoral and economy-wide policies' impact on developing country agriculture; trade, FDI and ICT-related technology diffusion; regional integration; international migration; social capital, migration and trade; nutrition; and natural resources, migration and trade. He has published over ten volumes and over one hundred articles in refereed journals and as volume chapters.

Niamh Sheridan is a Senior Economist in the Strategy, Policy and Review Department (SPR) of the International Monetary Fund (IMF). She holds a PhD from Johns Hopkins University, Baltimore, Maryland and a Master of Economic Science degree from University College Dublin, Ireland. Prior to joining the SPR, Niamh worked in the Asia Pacific Department of the IMF (2010–2017) and worked on Australia, Fiji, Malaysia, and Singapore. During 2015–17 she was mission chief for Samoa and worked extensively on issues relating to corresponding banking. Other work on small states included analysis of the impact of spillovers from advanced economies. She has also worked in the IMF's Institute for Capacity Development, training government officials on a broad range of macroeconomic topics, including open economy macroeconomics, monetary economics, and econometric techniques and forecasting. Her research interests are in monetary economics topics such as inflation targeting in advanced and emerging market economies, the monetary transmission mechanism, forecasting inflation, and models of inflation expectations.

Jonathan Spiteri is a Resident Academic at the University of Malta, and a Visiting Lecturer in Economics at the University of Edinburgh. He graduated with Honours in Economics (First Class) from the University of Malta, a Master of Science in Economics (with Distinction) and, as an ESRC Scholar, a PhD in Economics, both from the University of Edinburgh. Jonathan's current research interests include behavioural economics, environmental economics, health and media economics. He is currently involved in the R2Pi Horizon 2020 project which examines the shift from the concept of Circular Economy to one of Circular Economy Business Models in Europe. He also forms part of the Nudge-It FP7 project which aims to develop and implement novel scientific approaches across various disciplines in order to further understanding of people's nutritional choices and health outcomes.

Patrizia Tumbarello studied Economics at Harvard University and holds a PhD in Economics and Finance from Università di Roma Tor Vergata. She is currently the Chief of the Strategy, Data Standards, and Review Division in the Statistics Department at the International Monetary Fund (IMF). Prior to this position, she was the Unit Chief of the Small States Unit in the Asia and Pacific Department of the IMF. She has been the mission chief for the Solomon Islands and Kiribati. Previous assignments included Australia, Vietnam, Algeria, Morocco and low-income countries such as Albania and Moldova. She also spent time in the IMF's Strategy, Policy and Review and Middle East and Central Asia Departments focusing on emerging markets and economies in transition. Her research interests and publications have focused on studies on enhancing macroeconomic resilience to natural disasters and climate change, on fiscal frameworks, trade, and corporate and banks' vulnerabilities.

Melchior Vella graduated in Commerce, majoring in Economics and Public Policy, then in B. Com. (Honours) in Economics (First Class) from the University of Malta and completed a Master of Science degree in Economics at the University of Essex in 2016 with distinction. He currently serves in the public service as an economist at the Economic Policy Department within the Ministry for Finance.

Arina Viseth was born in Laos and is a French national. A Fulbright scholar, she holds a double PhD in Economics from the University of Delaware and from the Université de Lyon II. She is currently an Economist in the Eastern II Division in the African Department of the International Monetary Fund (IMF). Prior to joining the IMF, she was a consultant in the trade unit of the World Bank Institute.

David Vivas Eugui is Legal Officer at the Trade, Environment, Climate Change and Sustainable Development Branch, DITC, at the United Nations Conference on Trade and Development (UNCTAD). He was also Senior Economic Affairs Officer, Trade Negotiations and Commercial Diplomacy Branch at the same organization; Deputy Programmes Director at the International Centre for Trade and Sustainable Development (ICTSD); Senior Attorney at the Center for International Environmental Law (CIEL); Attaché for Legal Affairs at the

Mission of Venezuela to the World Trade Organization (WTO) and Staff Attorney at the Venezuelan Institute of Foreign Trade. He is an international expert with more than 20 years of experience on legal and economic issues, including in trade and environment, biodiversity, oceans economy and intellectual property. He has a Juris Doctor from the Universidad Católica Andres Bello, Venezuela, a Master of Laws (LLM) degree from Georgetown University in the United States and Master's degree on Transnational Business at Universidad Externado, Colombia. Constant participation in academic activities have been carried out at Strasbourg University, WIPO DL Academy (Geneva), University of Business and International Studies (Geneva), Universidad de Buenos Aires, Universidad Javeriana (Colombia), and Universidad Católica del Peru.

Philip von Brockdorff graduated BA (Hons) Public Administration, MSc Econ. (Wales) and D.Phil. (University of York). He is also a graduate member of the Chartered Institute of Personnel Development (UK). His teaching areas include Macroeconomics, Public Sector Economics and Cost Benefit Analysis, while his research areas are mainly on Transport and Economics of Ageing Populations. He is Head of Department of Economics at the University of Malta and is also a member of the European Economic and Social Committee in Brussels. vice-Chairperson of the the Climate Action Board, and member of the Retail Price Index Board. He has authored several papers relating to pensions and transport. He is currently working on a research project on work-based pensions in conjunction with Prof Iain Clacher from the University of Leeds.

Laurent Wagner is a researcher at the Fondation pour les Etudes et Recherches sur le Développement International (FERDI). He holds a PhD in development economics from Université d'Auvergne. He is the author of several publications in journals such as *World Development, Review of World Economics* or *The World Economy*. Development economist with a strong suit in applied econometrics, he has notably contributed on trade facilitation issues, vulnerability, foreign aid effectiveness and aid allocation.

Yanling Wang was born in China, obtained her PhD at Georgetown University in 2003, specializing in international trade, and is currently Full Professor of Economics at the Norman Paterson School of International Affairs at Carleton University in Ottawa. Her research interests lie in the empirical analysis of issues related to international trade and foreign direct investment, including their impact on international knowledge spillovers. Dr Wang has served as the President of the Canadian Women Economists Network (CWEN) and of the Chinese Economists Society (CES). Dr Wang is currently serving as the Executive Vice President of the Ottawa Association of Chinese Canadian University Alumni.

Patrick Kent Watson is former Professor of Applied Economics and University Director at the Sir Arthur Lewis Institute of Social and Economic Studies of the University of the West Indies. He holds Master's and Doctoral degrees in Mathematical Economics and Econometrics from the Université de Paris I (Panthéon-Sorbonne) and a Bachelor of Commerce degree, with Accounting as a principal subject, from the University of Leeds. He specializes, and is widely published in, empirical studies related to the Caribbean Economy, in particular in the areas of economic modelling, money and finance and climate change. He served on the Board of Directors of the Central Bank of Trinidad & Tobago (2001–04), was Deputy Chairman of the Regulated Industries Commission of Trinidad and Tobago and Chairman of the Trinidad and Tobago Securities and Exchange Commission (2012–16). He was also a Senator in the

Parliament of Trinidad & Tobago (2010–2011) and a Member of the Board of the International Organization of Securities Commissions (2012–16).

Hans-Peter Werner is a former Counsellor with the Development Division of the World Trade Organization (WTO) in Geneva, Switzerland. His main areas of expertise concern international trade challenges for small economies, how aid for trade can serve to build trade capacities in developing and least-developed countries and how the WTO's multilateral trade negotiations relate to the Sustainable Development Goals and Agenda 2030, including follow-up activities for Financing for Development. Throughout his career, Mr Werner has authored numerous reports and articles about the challenges developing countries and small economies face in international trade, especially in the area of non-tariff barriers, e-commerce for development and linking to global value chains. Prior to joining the WTO, he worked as a journalist, a public affairs consultant and as an economist. He holds a Master's degree from the Graduate Institute of International and Development Studies in Geneva, Switzerland.

DeLisle Worrell is a member of the Bretton Woods Committee and the immediate past Governor of the Central Bank of Barbados. He was the Bank's founding Research Director and subsequently served as Deputy Governor. Between 1998 and 2008 Dr Worrell worked with the International Monetary Fund and more recently, he served as the Executive Director of the Caribbean Centre for Money and Finance (CCMF). Dr Worrell has had research fellowships at Princeton University, Yale University, the Peterson Institute, the Smithsonian Institution in Washington, DC, the Federal Reserve and the University of the West Indies. He holds a PhD in economics from McGill University, Montreal.

Hanlei Yun worked as a research analyst in Caribbean Division, West Hemisphere Department in the International Monetary Fund (IMF) for three years, where she had extensive experiences in macroeconomics. She participated in country team missions to IMF programme countries that primarily examine issues of fiscal and external debt sustainability, developed approaches to promote balanced and inclusive growth and contributed to the staff report and selected issue papers about non-performing loans, tourism sector growth and doing business environment. She also authored and co-authored four IMF working papers covering 'structural reforms and growth', 'bank mergers', 'Caribbean energy's macro related challenges' and 'diversity and growth'. Before that, she worked as an evaluation consultant in the World Bank Group and at JP Morgan as a financial analyst. She holds a Master's degree in Applied Economics at Georgetown University and a Bachelor of Economics degree at Peking University

Sanjana Zaman is a broad-based economist with a focus on policy-based research. Her research interests include macroeconomics, public finance, poverty and inclusive growth, and international trade. She has worked extensively on a range of developing and emerging economies in South Asia, East Asia, the Pacific, the Caribbean, and Africa. She is currently working as a Research Officer at the Commonwealth Secretariat's Economic, Social and Sustainable Development Division. Prior to that she worked as a Freelance Analyst at Dun and Bradstreet and as a Research Analyst at the World Bank. She holds a Master's degree in Economics from the University of Warwick.

Foreword

Small states are increasingly in the news, but, as with most newsworthy situations, for their plight rather than their successes. The disadvantages these countries face can be overwhelming. Many of these states are small islands, highly susceptible to events completely outside their control. Natural disasters, global warming and sea-level rise threaten the existence of some. Most of these states are very trade open, and a subtle shift in demand for their exports, which often include tourism, can spell the difference between prosperity and poverty. Because their economic development largely depends on forces outside their control, these small states tend to be highly economically vulnerable, with some burdened with debt contracted to get them through the lean years.

As the global environment shifts, so do the prospects of these countries. At present, many are facing an uncertain future as the world economy retrogresses away from a dynamic open environment to one of increased protectionism and economic nationalism.

In spite of their economic constraints, a number of small states succeed economically in terms of their GDP per capita and economic growth by engaging in trade, mostly in services such as tourism and financial services. Some resort to activities such as tax havens and offshore finance.

While many observers wring their hands in despair, others are developing, positive, innovative solutions. A significant effort in this regard is under way at the University of Malta, where Professor Lino Briguglio heads an interdisciplinary academic entity – the Islands and Small States Institute. This group, set up in the early 1990s, is at the forefront of innovative solutions for small island economies including the so-called economic vulnerability and resilience framework.

This volume, edited by Professor Briguglio, pulls together much of this new cutting-edge research. Its 29 chapters written by the world's foremost authorities on small economies offer a spectrum of new insights to the opportunities opening for such economies.

The volume centres on three principal issues: economic, social and environmental. The economic themes touch on trade, finance and regulatory frameworks. The social issues section covers many aspects including health, migration, population ageing, as well as overall social wellbeing. The environmental stream relates to such matters as measuring environmental performance, natural disasters, the Ocean economy, and the validity of the Sustainable Development Goals. In all cases, the chapters draw practical policy implications for small states.

One finishes the volume with the sense that the future of small states is not as hopeless as often depicted. In many cases, a new generation of leaders is committed to the betterment of their populations through the opening of co-operative agreements with like-minded neighbours. In others, many of the suggestions offered throughout the volume present a ray of fresh hope.

Through their blending of the actual with the possible, Professor Briguglio and his contributors have provided us with the standard work on the subject for years to come.

Robert E. Looney, Series Editor

Acronyms and abbreviations

ACP	African, Caribbean and Pacific Group of States
AOSIS	Alliance of Small Island States
CARICOM	Caribbean Community and Common Market
CARIFORUM	Caribbean Forum
CBRs	Correspondent banking relationships
CET	Common external tariff
ECCAS	Economic Community of Central African States
COMESA	Common Market for Eastern and Southern Africa
ECOWAS	Economic Community of West African States
ECP	Economic Partnership Agreement
EU	European Union
FDI	Foreign direct investment
GDP	Gross domestic product
GNI	Gross national income
GVCs	Global value chains
ICT	Information and communications technology
ICTSD	International Centre for Trade and Sustainable Development
IMF	International Monetary Fund
LDC	Least developed country
MDC	More developed country
MDG(s)	Millennium Development Goal(s)
MTOs	Money transfer operators
ODA	Official development assistance
OECD	Organisation for Economic Co-operation and Development
OECS	Organisation of Eastern Caribbean States
PICs	Pacific island countries
PIF	Pacific Islands Forum
RCA	Revealed comparative advantage
SAARC	South Asian Association for Regional Cooperation
SADC	Southern African Development Community
SAP	Structural adjustment programme
SDG(s)	Sustainable Development Goal(s)
SDS	Small developing states
SIDS	Small island developing states
SMEs	Small and medium-sized enterprises
SOFIEs	Small open financially integrated economies

Acronyms and abbreviations

SVEs	Small vulnerable economies
TFP	Total factor productivity
UN	United Nations
UNCTAD	United Nations Conference on Trade and Development
UNDP	United Nations Development Programme
UNWTO	United Nations World Tourism Organization
VAR	Vector autoregression
WTO	World Trade Organization

Introduction

Lino Briguglio

1 The purpose of this book

The purpose of this book, as its name suggests, is to discuss issues relating to the economy, the environment and society of small states. The book contains 29 chapters, other than this introductory one, with contributions by 53 authors and co-authors, writing on various topics relating to the title of the book, some of which have not been suitably explored before in the literature on small states.

The coverage of the small states included in the studies varies between chapters. Some chapters deal with all small states at the global level, generally in an attempt to compare them with larger states with regard to a particular issue. Others are pitched at the regional level and focus on small states located in the Caribbean and Pacific regions, generally referring to the commonalities and disparities of the small states in these regions. There are no chapters that focus specifically on the African, Asian, European and Indian Ocean regions, but the chapters that overview small states globally do refer to the small states located in these regions.

The style of the studies also differs between chapters. A number of studies, particularly some of those relating to finance, are highly technical, utilizing econometric techniques. Others are descriptive and mostly based on non-mathematical argumentation. However, all chapters derive important implications for small states in terms of economic, social, environmental and political governance, depending on the focus on the particular chapter.

This introductory chapter is organized in five sections. Sections 2 and 3 discuss two important problems faced by authors of studies on small states, namely the issue of measuring the size of countries and the lack of data on small states. The five sections that follow deal with the main themes covered by the chapters, namely trade, finance, regulatory frameworks, social relations, and environmental concerns. Section 9 concludes by synthesising the main messages conveyed by the authors of the chapters.

2 Measuring the size of countries

Almost all chapters in this volume measure country size in terms of their population, which is the most common indicator of countries size used in the literature,[1] although, as we shall explain below, different authors in this book use a different cut-off points to distinguish between small states and large ones.[2] The number of small sovereign states globally therefore depends on the population threshold chosen. A common population limit used is 1.5 million[3] and using this definition there are about 45 such sovereign states.

Country size can also be measured using indicators other than population size, although population size remains the one most widely used. The area of the territory, which is a geographical factor, and the GDP of the country, which has direct economic connotations, have been used. Downes (1988) proposed a method of combining the three indicators to measure country size.

An alternative definition of a small state, used by the World Trade Organization to define 'small vulnerable economies'[4] is the 'share of world trade', following the proposal by Davenport (2001) who suggested a threshold of 0.02% of merchandise trade.[5] One problem, with this classification is that it enables countries with relatively large populations but with a small volume of world trade, to be considered as small (see Hein, 2004).

Different population thresholds

Why do different authors use different population thresholds? Often, the reason is not given expressly, but some authors do try to justify their choice. For example, Read (Chapter 14) states that he adopted a population size threshold of 5 million in order to facilitate the inclusion of the relatively abundant body of empirical research on the effects of FDI in Ireland. Von Brockdorff and Vella (Chapter 24) set a population threshold of 2 million arguing that in any case, even the Commonwealth Secretariat and the World Bank include countries with a population exceeding 1.5 million. Barker (Chapter 24) used the World Bank list of small states, which included a few states with a population exceeding 1.5 million. Worrell (Chapter 8), decided to combine a population and GDP threshold with a population of 1.2 million or less and GDP of US$8 billion (2015) or less, basing his choice on the degree of export concentration. Lanz and Werner (Chapter 1) selected countries according to their share of global trade and note that since the relative volume of trade, and not population, is used as criterion, several 'small vulnerable economies' covered in their chapter do not meet the 1.5 million threshold.[6] Greenidge et al. (Chapter 4) set a cut-off point of 3 million for Caribbean countries considered separately as a group, presumably to include larger 'small states' such as Jamaica.

In some chapters, countries are grouped into a number of size categories (e.g. Von Brockdorff and Vella, Chapter 24; Read, Chapter 19), again basing on population size. Some authors did not commit themselves to a population threshold, but presented all states along a population continuum, observing the slope of the trend line along such a continuum (e.g. Azzopardi Muscat and Camilleri, Chapter 23; Briguglio (M.) and Spiteri, Chapter 18; Briguglio (L.) and Vella, Chapter 2).

'Official' lists of small states

There are at least five lists of small states presented in websites of international organizations (see Appendix 1). The most restrictive one is that proposed by UNCTAD which is confined to 28 small island developing states (SIDS).[7] There are two other lists of SIDS, namely the United Nations list, containing 37 states[8] and the AOSIS list, containing 39 states.[9] These differ from the UNCTAD list in two main ways. They both include seven relatively large states (Cuba, Dominican Republic, Guinea-Bissau, Haiti, Jamaica, Papua New Guinea, and Singapore) and also a few countries that are not islands but have a large proportion of their populations living in the coastal areas (Belize, Guyana, Guinea Bissau and Suriname), while three states are parts of larger islands (Papua New Guinea, Haiti and Dominican Republic).

The Commonwealth Secretariat, which defines small states as those with a population of up to 1.5 million, also presents a list of 30 small states which were formerly British colonies[10] in its website. The list includes non-island states and developed countries (see Appendix 1). Even in this list, we find five states included, namely Botswana, Jamaica, Lesotho, Namibia and Papua New Guinea, with a population size the exceeds 1.5 million.

The World Bank, which also defines small states as those with a population of up to 1.5 million, has a list of 50 small states in is website,[11] eight of which have a population exceeding this population threshold. The list, which includes developing as well as developed small states, for some reason leaves out Luxembourg.

In all 58 countries feature in these five small-state databases, with 20 included in all of them (see Appendix 1).

Unsettled issues

The above all goes to show that in the literature, including this volume, there are different approaches for identifying which territories should qualify as 'small states', and every approach has its merits and demerits. The lack of precise definition of what constitutes a small state has a number of undesirable repercussions, including problems associated with comparing such states with larger ones. However, although there is lack of uniformity in this regard, studies on small states have proliferated during the past three decades, many of which identify the pros and cons of small country size and derive implications for good social, political and economic governance in these states.

3 Data on small states

Many authors in this volume remarked that they encountered problems as a result of lack of data when trying to compare small states with larger ones, and more so when trying to use time-series analysis. For example, Briguglio (M.) and Spiteri (Chapter 18) faced this problem in their attempt to construct indicators of social preferences and Moncada *et al.* (Chapter 25), in trying to find data relating to environmental variables. Roberts (Chapter 26) remarked that such lack of data rendered many Sustainable Development Goals not measurable in the case of small states and therefore not possible to monitor performance in this regard.

The expression that 'due to lack of data many small states are excluded from the analysis' or text to that effect, is often found in studies on small states, particularly in matters relating to the environment. Such 'data deprivation'[12] often limits the ability of authors to conduct studies as deeply or as extensively as they would wish and as a result also limit the ability of policy makers in small states and in international organizations to effectively monitor changes in such states.

The reason for lack of data on small states can be due to two main reasons with the first one pertaining to the database producers and the second to the small states themselves. As Veenendaal and Wolf (2016) argue, small states are often considered not to be 'real' states and not of importance to be included in global databases. However, possibly a more important reason for the lack of data pertaining to small states, is the limited capacity of small states in dedicating resources to national statistical offices for the collection and processing of certain data, particularly when there is no obligation to collect such data or when there is no clear material gain in collecting such data. This is associated with the indivisibility problem, in that certain overhead costs in the provision of government services cannot be downscaled in proportion to the population, and therefore tend to be more costly for smaller countries.

Malta, Cyprus and Estonia, which are small-state members of the European Union, are obliged to produce data for Eurostat,[13] and the latter supports the activities of the national statistics offices of these countries. As a result, data pertaining to these small states are generally as good in terms of quality and coverage as that of larger states. It is however very likely that the cost per capita for collecting data in these small states is likely to be much higher that than it is, say, in Germany, France and Italy.

4 Trade

High dependence on international trade

Small states are characterized by special interconnected features in view of their size, including a small domestic market, limited natural resources endowments, constraints relating to diversification possibilities, and limitations in their ability to reap the benefits of economies of scale, especially when their final sales are mostly directed to their domestic market.

Due to these characteristics, small states tend to be highly dependent on international trade. Their small domestic market forces them to seek external markets so as to produce on a sufficiently large scale to render production viable. Their limited natural resources endowments lead them to depend highly on imports. This, in turn, renders them highly exposed to forces outside their control leading to a high degree of exposure to economic shocks and to GDP growth volatility. The exposure to shocks is discussed in some chapters of this book, with the authors suggesting solutions that could attenuate the downsides of such exposure.

Crispolti (Chapter 6), examining the experience of 36 small states covering the period 1980–2016, assesses the role of international reserves as a cushion against large external shocks, including sharp swings in the terms of trade, abrupt changes in export demand, and a fall in financial inflows, and finds that international reserves do indeed act as a buffer against external shocks but this depends on the structural characteristics of the economy. He argues that typically, reserve holdings above three months of imports prior to a shock event have helped small states navigate through certain types of external shocks, but warns that maintaining a reserve above three months of imports was not a safe haven for countries with a flexible exchange rate regime.

Briguglio (L.) and Vella (Chapter 2) referring to the effect of openness on GDP growth volatility show that openness does indeed give rise to such volatility, but good economic and political governance could dampen down such fluctuations. The authors associate their findings with the vulnerability and resilience framework, proposed by Briguglio et al. (2009), which was used to explain why many small economies succeed economically in spite of (and not because of) the disadvantages associated with small country size.

Economies of scale constraints

Most chapters, when describing the characteristics of small states, refer to their limited ability to reap the benefits of economies of scale, and this constitutes a major disadvantage in their external trade dealings. This is a consequence of their relatively small-sized enterprises, due to the so-called indivisibility problem, where fixed costs cannot be downscaled in proportion to the production runs. This negatively affects the competitiveness of these states in the global market. Some chapters in this volume address this constraint and suggest strategies that could attenuate such a problem.

Lanz and Werner (Chapter 1) examine the opportunities and challenges which 32 small economies face when trying to integrate and upgrade in global value chains. They argue that the value chains relating to selected goods (agrifood and seafood, textiles and clothing) and services (tourism, information technology and business process outsourcing), there is an untapped export potential which could be exploited by small states. The authors also refer to the need for small states to foster backward linkages between tourism and other domestic sectors such as agriculture, fishing and services. Lanz and Werner emphasize the importance for small economies, facing economies of scale constraints, of reforming trade facilitation measures and improving transport and ICT infrastructures. In addition, meeting international standards requires that small states invest in laboratories and testing facilities, and training in related skills.

Bernal (Chapter 5) writing about higher education as an export of services, argues that for small island developing states there is an opportunity to develop higher education as an export and this is best executed by a cluster organized and operating on a regional multi-country template, using modern information and communication technologies. This allows these small countries to overcome the lack of economies of scale and widen the range of course offerings and the diversity of student experiences. However, this needs to be done on a sufficient scale, with vigorous international marketing and with strategic coordination and networking.

Economies of scale constraints also occur in the case of governments services, such as regulatory frameworks. Barker (Chapter 17) contends that small states would benefit if they choose to enter regional cooperation agreements on competition and consumer law. The analysis suggests the benefits of such arrangements are that they allow the relevant parties to exploit scale economies, and overcome inter-jurisdictional externalities.

5 Finance

Financial markets

A characteristic of this volume, compared to other books on small states, is that it contains a relatively large proportion of chapters on financial markets. These chapters tend to be somewhat technical, as the subject lends itself well to econometric testing. The themes investigated include monetary transmission mechanisms (Samuel and Viseth, Chapter 11), exchange rate regimes (Worrell et al., Chapter 8), excess liquid assets in monetary policy (Khemraj, Chapter 9), role of correspondent banking (Alwazir et al., Chapter 7) and the development stock markets (Cozier and Watson, Chapter 10).

A conclusion that frequently emerges in these chapters is that the small size of the countries being investigated calls for special policy considerations. For example, Worrell et al. argue that the policy options implicit in the classical Mundell-Fleming trilemma of exchange controls, an exchange rate peg and independent monetary policy, are not applicable to small open economies in today's world of international financial integration. Samuel and Viseth contend that the financial sector in small states is often under-developed, oligopolistic, and prone to excess domestic currency liquidity, and renders policy prescriptions suitable for large developed states no so useful for small ones. Khemraj, also referring to the imperfectly competitive security market in small economies, proposes a 'compensation strategy' meaning that the central bank of a small economy tend to find it difficult to resort to the classical open market operations which require a liquid and developed secondary money market and should therefore create alternative investment opportunities in national currencies given that the economy faces ongoing foreign exchange and balance of payments constraints.

On the institutional side of financial markets, Cozier and Watson, describe the evolution of the stock exchanges in the Caribbean region, concluding that the stock markets in the region are in a state of underdevelopment. Alwazir *et al.* contend that financial services in the small states of the Pacific are being eroded as a result of the withdrawal of corresponding banking relationships. They call for collective efforts to address the consequences of withdrawal of corresponding banking relationships and outline policy measures to help the affected countries mitigate the impact.

Aid and financial flows

Three chapters deal with financial flows into small states, in the form of official development assistance (ODA) and foreign direct investment (FDI). The chapters on ODA present a totally different opinion regarding financial transfers to small states. Jayaraman and Lau (Chapter 12) examine the resource transfers have led to the so-called Dutch Disease, in that they affected the real exchange rates, and hurting the competitiveness of the limited range of exports of the Pacific island countries. On the other hand, Guillaumont *et al.* (Chapter 12), while agreeing that the ODA received by small states is relatively high, measured in per capita terms or as a ratio to GNI, argue that this is justified in view of the high degree of economic vulnerability of the small developing countries.

Read (Chapter 14) also writing about capital transfers into small states, this time based on the profit motives of the investors, contends that FDI is a key factor promoting economic growth in that it not only represents an additional source of capital but also embodies advanced technology, know-how and market access. The author, basing on an extensive literature review, states that contrary to a priori expectations, small economies have been very successful in attracting high pro-rata inflows of FDI, particularly in tourism and financial services. The primary attractions of these inflows are the openness of small states to international trade in goods and services, as well as the favourable tax treatment for foreign investors. However, the chapter argues that the positive growth effects of FDI inflows are constrained by the narrow and shallow structures of activity in small economies, which may generate adverse competition and crowding-out effects – echoing the Dutch disease arguments put forward in Chapter 12.

6 Regulatory frameworks and structural reform

Dornan (Chapter 15), writing about reform in the electricity sector, which has been widespread since the 1980s, refers to the recent wave of reform focussing on regulatory oversight. The chapter reviews the reform experience of small island states, arguing that the absence of economies of scale in the power sectors of these countries makes many of the reforms advocated for larger states ill-suited for small island states. The chapter discusses the strengths and weaknesses of different reform models in small island states, and highlights the size of the electricity market as an important determinant of what type of regulatory approach is appropriate.

Dhaher (Chapter 16), referring to regulatory arrangements in telecommunications, analyses the viability of competition in small states given their economic and social characteristics and the impact of these characteristics in adopting regulatory frameworks. He emphasizes the point that the small domestic market of small states constrains the degree of competition possible, and therefore an economic policy that promotes competition should identify and use the right regulatory approaches, suitable for such circumstances. Dhaher argues, similarly to Dornan, that regulatory frameworks that were tailored for large developed countries may not be appropriate for small economies unless such frameworks are adapted to take account of the special characteristics of such economies.

Some small states choose to enter regional cooperation agreements on competition and consumer law. The CARICOM and the Pacific Islands Forum are cases in point, where the great majority of members are small states. Barker (Chapter 17) describes these two regional arrangements, as well as others in Africa and Asia, which have small developing states as members. In addition to the possibility of small states enjoying the benefits of economies scale from this form of cooperation, such arrangements help these states minimize inter-jurisdictional externalities, while retaining independence or sovereignty – without fully merging to form larger unified or federated states. According to the author, regional arrangements have further relevance to very small states that are subject to trade isolation.

Competition law and policy are often linked to economic reform, with the underlying rationale being that the introduction of competition and private sector involvement leads to efficiency and performance. Prescriptions for economic reform also include modernization of taxation and trade and financial liberalization. Such reforms are the subject of Chapter 4, authored by Greenidge *et al.* The authors state that since the 1980s, with the introduction of IMF/WB adjustment programs, structural reforms have been a core part of the reform agenda in the Caribbean. The chapter reviews the package of structural reforms in trade liberalization, financial liberalization and tax policy, and gauges their impact on growth in the Caribbean small states. The authors conclude that the benefits of structural reforms are only seen over the long-term and the reform effort needs to assign major importance to strengthening institutional quality.

Trade liberalization is often considered as a major component of economic reform, and assumed to be of benefit to the participating economies. Indeed, this argument formed the basis of the pressures mounted by institutions such as the WTO on developing countries to reduce tariffs, remove non-tariff barriers, and liberalize capital flows. Such trade-liberalising measures form part of the Economic Partnership Agreements (EPAs) between the EU and the ACP group of states. Hosein *et al.* (Chapter 3) undertook a review of the economic welfare impact of the change in the modality of trade interaction between the EU and the Caribbean subsequent to the implementation of the Economic Partnership Agreement between CARIFORUM and the EU. The authors, using three partial equilibrium models, discuss the trade and fiscal implications of the agreement and infer from the simulations that the general level of economic welfare declined for all CARICOM economies in the post-EPA period.

7 Social and political aspects

Social and political issues associated with small states are often given less importance then economic and environmental ones. The reasons for this could be that societies in small states are generally considered to be more cohesive than larger ones and, albeit with many exceptions, democracy seems to work well in such states. In this volume, social and political matters which are examined include social preferences (Briguglio (M.) and Spiteri, Chapter 18) well-being (Read, Chapter 19), migration (Chand, Chapter 20 and Schiff and Wang, Chapter 21), health (Azzopardi Muscat and Camilleri, Chapters 23) aging (Von Brockdorff and Vella, Chapter 24) and political outcomes (Anckar, Chapter 22).

Briguglio (M.) and Spiteri refer to the growing application of psychological principles to Economics that has created an expanding literature in Behavioural Economics, which explores how humans decide and behave in economic situations. A key contribution has been to show that deviations from the assumption of self-interested, cost-benefit maximising individuals with stable preferences are not only common, but systematic. But the application of such ideas to issues faced by small states has received scant attention, even though recent years have witnessed a similarly thriving research agenda in the economics of small states. The authors seek to address this gap by juxtaposing some of the findings from the Behavioural Economics literature on social preferences with those emerging from the economics literature on small states and complementing the insights with fresh data linking social preferences with population size, using four key constructs relating to social preferences, namely trust, inequality aversion, altruism and reciprocity. The authors sought to link these variables with country size. The evidence from the behavioural economics literature, coupled with the analysis conducted in this chapter, demonstrate that social preferences may indeed have a key role to play in shaping the social relations in small countries.

Robert Read investigates the relationship between several dimensions of country size and wellbeing based upon a dataset of 196 sovereign countries stratified into four size quartiles. The evidence suggests that smaller economies tend to have higher levels of wellbeing than larger ones in per capita incomes, human development, life satisfaction and governance, although there were many exceptions. These findings accord with the view of other authors (for example Baldacchino, 2005) that small economies have greater policy flexibility and responsiveness to external shocks, aided by closer proximity between policy-makers and constituents.

Important considerations associated with social development relate to health and aging. Azzopardi Muscat and Camilleri contend that the literature on health in small states is very thin, possibly due to the fact that traditionally the health sector has not been identified as a specific policy priority in the development agenda for small states. The chapter presents an extensive literature review on health systems in small states, which seems to indicate that the main weaknesses in this regard are inherent, namely lack of capacity in the delivery of health services, the inability to provide certain specialized services and a small genetic pool, possibly leading to genetic disorders. Another problem faced by small states is the limited ability to negotiate good prices due to small quantities purchased and this coupled with high transportation costs in the case of islands, pose a problem of access to affordable medicines. The authors, however, note that some small states succeed in delivering relatively good health services in spite of these constraints, possibly because in a small jurisdiction it is easier for the government to identify and address shortcomings in health care and policy makers tend to have a 'helicopter view' of health issues, rendering health-related policies more implementable. Social cohesion, often a characteristic of small states, may permit a more comprehensive population health surveillance. The small population size renders it easier to keep national registers and leads to a 'shorter distance' between research, policy and practice, enabling more rapid uptake of the policy intervention. This is in line with the vulnerability/resilience framework, proposed by Briguglio et al. (2009).

In examining the relationship between life expectancy (a proxy for health outcome), expenditure on health per capita (a proxy for health resources) and the BMI index (a proxy for health determinants) the authors found that although small state health systems exhibit several common challenges, yet their health outcomes and the extent to which they are able to mitigate these challenges appear to be affected mainly by their stage of development (proxied by GDP per capita) and by geographical location, rather than country size per se.

There are not many studies on aging in small states, and the study authored by Von Brockdorff and Vella (Chapter 24) may set the scene for further studies on this social issue. The authors test whether there are significant differences between small states and larger countries in terms of their demographic transitions. The analysis also takes into account the magnitude and speed of ageing in different sized countries, classified by income per capita categories. The main conclusion is that the speed of ageing in larger countries has been different from the experience of small countries during the period 1950 to 2015. Higher migration outflows and higher fertility rates have shaped the demographic transition of small states somewhat differently from that of larger countries.

Two chapters that deal with migration both refer to the issue of brain drain from small states. Chand contends that small island nations have witnessed higher rates of emigration, particularly of professional and skilled workers, compared to their larger and richer metropolitan counterparts. The author states that the economic arguments for emigration of skilled workers from small nations to large rich nations are strong mostly because this raises the incomes of the migrant, suggesting that small nations must learn to live with the reality of skilled emigration and use it as an opportunity to benefit those unable or unwilling to emigrate. Chand argues that the debate on the effects of skilled-emigration on source nation revolve around the question of brain drain, with the positive side being the reverse flow of remittances and diaspora investment. The policy responses by the authorities of the sending small nations, proposed by the author, include trying to maximize the income of the emigrants, possibly by harmonising educational qualifications that will increase employability and income of the emigrants, and encouragement of the circular flow of capital and talent between source and destination. He also suggests scheme of portable pensions to provide the option for emigrants to return home to retire.

Schiff and Wang's study is essentially on technology diffusion but it has important implications relating to migration. The authors find, as a result of their econometric study, that in small states, the share of migrants who are skilled is larger than the share of residents who are skilled, because rich nations select immigrants on the basis of skills, implying that the brain drain has a negative impact on the stock of human capital and thus on total factor productivity growth in these countries, with the impact being larger in small than in large countries. The authors also find that the total factor productivity growth in small states is more sensitive to changes in the brain drain.

The authors make an interesting point regarding the net effect of 'brain drain' and 'brain gain'. They argue that the brain drain might lead people to acquire more education because this would raise their probability of migrating. The return to education would provide an incentive for residents in small states to invest in education. Since only a share of people acquiring more education will be able to migrate, the brain drain would be expected to generate a brain gain.[14] Hence, the loss of human capital associated with the brain drain would be expected to be if one takes into account the educational brain gain.

8 Environmental concerns

A number of chapters in this volume deal with environmental considerations. One chapter (Moncada et al., Chapter 25) tests whether small states exhibit certain specific environmental traits when compared to larger states, while two chapters (Roberts, Chapter 26; Onguglo and Vivas Eugui, Chapter 27) discuss environmental concerns in the context of the Sustainable Development Goals. Two other chapters (Darius et al., Chapter 28; Jayaraman et al., Chapter 29) discuss the effect of natural disasters on the economy.

Moncada et al. position their discussion against the background of environmental economics, as an academic subject, and its application to small island states. The authors state that the environment has emerged as one of the main issues of our times and economics, as a discipline, has responded. The authors also attempt to show empirically whether a number of environmental variables are correlated with country size, obtaining mixed results, leading to the conclusion that country size does not matter significantly in this regard. But, they contend, this does mean the small states are not inherently at higher environmental risk than larger states, as it may be possible that the variables they chose for their analysis may have captured the net effect of vulnerability and resilience. This means that small states may be highly inherently environmentally vulnerable, but pro-environmental community measures may be more effective in a small country, particularly small island states, where the proximity of nature to human life is more immediate than in larger countries.

Environmental aspects relating to small island states are often associated with sustainable development and with the Sustainable Development Goals (SDGs) that have emerged through the UN system. Onguglo and Vivas Eugui focus on SDG 14 which seeks to 'Conserve and sustainably use the oceans, seas and marine resources for sustainable development'. This *oceans goal* has two intertwined aspects, namely conservation and preservation (stewardship) of oceans resources on the one hand, and sustainable use of the marine resources on the other hand, in order to meet the needs of a growing world population. The chapter discusses the economic potential of the oceans or blue economy with a particular focus on fish trade and marine genetic resources. The chapter further explores some of the approaches that could enable SIDS to promote marine-based sustainable growth and development.

Roberts, writing on the SDGs and their usefulness in measuring progress in small states, argues that the SDGs are not appropriate for this purpose, as evidenced by the very high levels of missing data and the weak level of response from SIDS as shown in the UN data base from January 2017 to the end of March 2017. The author also refers to the over-complex UN database both in the compilation and the presentation of entries. Roberts contends that there is also a lack of a clear definition of SIDS which total 51 in the UN database, of which 23 countries are either not small, or not islands, or not developing, or not sovereign states. The chapter proposes a simpler structure of the data requirement for the SDGs pertaining to a more precisely defined set of 28 SIDS, and proposes a short list of seven fundamental indicators for which data could be readily obtained, and which relate to inherent features and policy induced measures.

A major environmental concern for SIDS relates to natural disasters, which is referred to in many chapters but are treated as the focus of the study by Darius *et al.* (Chapter 28 and Jayaraman *et al.*, Chapter 29).

Darius *et al.* discuss the fiscal consequences of natural disasters and conclude that country size matters in this regard, highlighting differences between the fiscal responses in small and larger developing countries, by way of an econometric test. Their results indicate that small states' fiscal policy tends to respond pro-cyclically while larger developing countries respond counter-cyclically to natural disasters, for smaller disasters, but there is evidence of counter-cyclical fiscal responses when both are struck by large disasters. In addition, the chapter demonstrates that benchmark responses are underpinned by a decrease in expenditure and a decrease in revenue in small states, and in contrast, an expansion in expenditure and a decrease in revenue in larger states. Expenditure increases in large states are driven mainly by expansions in wages and salaries, while revenue declines are underlined by lower revenues from goods and services.

Jayaraman *et al.* (Chapter 29) examine the effect of natural disasters, in the form of tropical cyclones, on tourism. They refer to the fact that tourism has emerged as engine of growth in Fiji, but the uncertainties associated with the disastrous impact of tropical cyclones have been causing greater anxieties in recent times with increase in the number of cyclones each year hitting the South Pacific region. Although tourism has now emerged as an engine of growth in Pacific Island Countries (PICS), there are growing uncertainties in regard to its future. There are increasing concerns relating to impacts of cyclones, as they now appear to have become regular, annual occurrences, causing immense loss of lives and damages to infrastructure. The results of the study show that cyclones negatively affect tourism in Fiji. The authors, arguing that the costs of damages from natural disasters are to an extent determined by economic policies and conditions of the countries concerned, use the result of the study to propose corrective mechanisms to counteract the negative effects of cyclones, including early warning systems, building of cyclone resistant roads and other communication facilities.

9 Conclusion

This introductory chapter has given an overview of the other 29 chapters included in this volume. A number of similarities and differences between small states and larger countries, and between the small states themselves, were identified by the various authors. Perhaps the main economic features shared by all small states is their limited human and physical capacity, their inability to reap the benefits of economies of scale in certain forms of production, their relatively high degree of trade openness and their high exposure to external economic conditions beyond their control.

In environmental matters, the results would seem to suggest that size does not matter much, possibly because the variables used to test the correlations with country size might have captured the net effects of the countries' inherent vulnerabilities and the spontaneous and policy-induced measures taken by the community and by the government to build resilience, in which case the inherent environmental vulnerability of small states would not be manifested in the data. This matter however remains to be tested rigorously.

With regard to social issues, several tendencies associated with small country size emerged. A common social feature of small states is that they tend to be more cohesive than larger states, although there are many exceptions. Another common tendency is that emigration from small states is relatively high, giving rise to brain drains and also affecting their demography. The issue of limited capacity and economies of scale constraints were also found to be relevant with regard to the provision of government services by small states, including those relating to health.

An argument that emerged over and over again in this book is that in spite of the constraints and limitations they face, some small states are highly successful in terms of their GDP per capita and their economic growth, as well as in the social and political governance, pointing to the fact that appropriate policies can enable these countries to withstand their vulnerabilities.

However, the analysis presented in this chapter clearly shows that the small states cannot be described as a homogenous group. They differ in many aspects, most notably in their stage of development, their remoteness from main commercial markets, their proneness to natural disasters and their governance arrangements.

It is impossible to summarize the wealth of information, the depth of analysis and the extensive coverage of small states in a single introductory chapter, as this one, which has, by no means, covered all the topics dealt with by the different authors. The chapters that follow will give deeper and more detailed expositions of the issues discussed here.

Notes

1 One reason why population is often the preferred method to measure country size that it is 'intuitively appealing from an economic point of view as it reflects the size of the labour force and therefore the constraints associated with human resources and the potential number of consumers' (Commonwealth Secretariat, 2007). In addition, updated data on population is relatively easy to obtain.
2 In the literature, various population upper limits are proposed. In some studies mostly dealing with politics, higher thresholds, reaching 18 million, are used (see Taylor, 1971; Katzenstein, 1985; Hey, 2003; Crowards, 2002). At the other extreme, the definition of small states is sometimes confined to a maximum of 500,000 and some studies distinguish between small states and microstates or ministates (see Rose, 2002, Table 4.1.)

3 The Commonwealth Secretariat (http://thecommonwealth.org/small-states) and the World Bank (www.worldbank.org/en/country/smallstates) both use a population cut-off point of 1.5 million.
4 See www.wto.org/english/thewto_e/minist_e/min11_e/brief_svc_e.htm/.
5 Lanz and Werner (Chapter 1) state that WTO has no official definition for small economies and refer to the Revised Draft Modalities for Agriculture which describes a small economy as one whose average share for the period 1999–2004 did not exceed (a) 0.16 of world merchandise trade; (b) 0.10% of world non-agricultural market access trade; and (c) 0.40% of world agricultural trade.
6 Lanz and Werner include 32 'small vulnerable economies' (SVEs) economies in their study, representing those SVEs which have been most active under the WTO's Work Programme on Small Economies since its establishment in 2002.
7 http://unctad.org/en/pages/aldc/Small%20Island%20Developing%20States/UNCTAD%C2%B4s-unofficial-list-of-SIDS.aspx. UNCTAD states that this list is for analytical purposes only.
8 https://sustainabledevelopment.un.org/topics/sids/list/. The UN list also includes 20 territories which are not UN members.
9 http://aosis.org/about/members/. The AOSIS list also includes five observers which are non-sovereign islands.
10 The Commonwealth list excludes two small states, namely Maldives and the Gambia, both of which left the Commonwealth, although the Gambia might rejoin.
11 https://data.worldbank.org/region/small-states/.
12 This term was used by Serajuddin *et al.* (2015) with regard to data on poverty.
13 Eurostat, located in Luxembourg, runs the European Statistical System, providing statistical information and promoting the harmonisation of statistical methods across the EU.
14 Chand and Clemens (2008) show this to be the case using Fiji as a case study.

References

Baldacchino, G. (2005). 'The contribution of 'social capital' to economic growth: lessons from island jurisdictions'. *The Round Table*, 94(378): 31–46.
Briguglio, L., Cordina, G., Farrugia, N. and Vella, S. (2009). 'Economic vulnerability and resilience: concepts and measurements'. *Oxford development studies*, 37(3): 229–247.
Chand, S. and Clemens, M. (2008). *Skilled emigration and skill creation: a quasi-experiment*. Working Papers. Crawford School of Economics and Government, Australian National University.
Commonwealth Secretariat (2007). *Small States: Economic Review and Basic Statistics*. Annual Series, Vol. 12. London: Commonwealth Secretariat.
Crowards, T. (2002). 'Defining the category of 'small'states'. *Journal of International Development*, 14(2): 143–179.
Davenport, M. (2001). *A Study of Alternative Special and Differential Arrangements for Small Economies*. Interim Report. Prepared for the Commonwealth Secretariat.
Downes, A. (1988). 'On the Statistical Measurement of Smallness: A Principal Component Measure of Country Size'. *Social and Economic Studies*, 37(3): 75–96.
Hein, P. (2004). 'Small island developing States: origin of the category and definition issues'. In *Is a special treatment of small island developing States possible?* Geneva: UNCTAD.
Hey, J. (2003). *Small states in World Politics: Explaining foreign policy behavior*. Boulder, CO: Lynne Rienner Publishers.
Katzenstein, Peter J. (1985). *Small states in world markets: Industrial policy in Europe*. Ithaca, NY: Cornell University Press.
Rose, E. A. (2002). *Dependency and Socialism in the Modern Caribbean: Superpower Intervention in Guyana, Jamaica, and Grenada, 1970–1985*. Lanham, MD: Lexington.
Serajuddin, U., Uematsu, H., Wieser, C., Yoshida, N. and Dabalen, A. (2015). *Data Deprivation: Another Deprivation to End*. World Bank, Policy Research Working Paper, No. 7252.
Taylor, C. (1971). 'Statistical typology of microstates and territories: towards a definition of a microstate'. In *Small States and Territories: Status and Problems*. New York: Arno Press.
Veenendaal, W. and Wolf, S. (2016). 'Concluding remarks: Achievements, challenges, and opportunities of small state research'. In *State Size Matters: Politik und Recht im Kontext von Kleinstaatlichkeit und Monarchie*. London: Springer.

Appendix 1

Table I.A1 Five databases for small states

	Pop. (2015)	WB	UNCTAD	UN	AOSIS	Com. Sec.
Antigua & Barbuda	0.089	★	★	★	★	★
Bahamas	0.364	★	★	★	★	★
Bahrain	1.294	★				
Barbados	0.280	★	★	★	★	★
Belize	0.366	★		★	★	★
Bhutan	0.779	★				
Botswana	2.129	★★				★★
Brunei Darussalam	0.417	★				★
Cabo Verde	0.525	★	★	★	★	
Comoros	0.799	★	★	★	★	
Cook Islands	0.847				★	
Cuba	11.480			★★	★★	
Cyprus	0.847	★				★
Djibouti	0.966	★				
Dominica	0.071	★	★	★	★	★
Dominican Republic	9.980			★★	★★	
Equatorial Guinea	0.799	★				
Estonia	1.313	★				
Fiji	0.891	★	★	★	★	★
Gabon	1.855	★★				
Gambia	1.991	★★				
Grenada	0.107	★	★	★	★	★
Guinea-Bissau	1.628	★★		★★	★★	
Guyana	0.767	★		★	★	★
Haiti	10.711			★★	★★	
Iceland	0.333	★				
Jamaica	2.814	★★	★	★★	★★	★★
Kiribati	0.114	★	★	★	★	★
Lesotho	1.932	★★				★★
Luxembourg	0.563					
Maldives	0.348	★	★	★	★	
Malta	0.429	★				★
Marshall Islands	0.054	★	★	★	★	
Mauritius	1.263	★	★	★	★	★

Table 1.A1 (continued)

	Pop. (2015)	WB	UNCTAD	UN	AOSIS	Com. Sec.
Micronesia, F.S.	0.102	★	★	★	★	
Montenegro	0.622	★				
Namibia	2.281	★★				★★
Nauru	0.012	★	★	★	★	★
Niue	0.002				★	
Palau	0.018	★	★	★	★	
Papua New Guinea	7.718			★★	★★	★★
Qatar	2.421	★★				
Samoa	0.193	★	★	★	★	★
San Marino	0.034	★				
Sao Tome & Principe	0.203	★	★	★	★	
Seychelles	0.093	★	★	★	★	★
Singapore	5.535			★★	★★	
Solomon Islands	0.588	★	★	★	★	★
St Kitts & Nevis	0.056	★	★	★	★	★
St Lucia	0.173	★	★	★	★	★
St Vincent & Grenadines	0.110	★	★	★	★	★
Suriname	0.556	★		★	★	
Swaziland	1.119	★				★
Timor–Leste	1.167	★	★	★	★	
Tonga	0.104	★	★	★	★	★
Trinidad & Tobago	1.360	★	★	★	★	★
Tuvalu	0.011	★	★	★	★	★
Vanuatu	0.269	★	★	★	★	★
Total	**58**	**50**	**28**	**37**	**39**	**30**
Pop. over 1.5 million	13	8	0	7	7	5

Sources: World Bank: https://data.worldbank.org/region/small-states; UNCTAD: http://unctad.org/en/pages/aldc/Small%20Island%20Developing%20States/UNCTAD%C2%B4s-unofficial-list-of-SIDS.aspx; United Nations: https://sustainabledevelopment.un.org/topics/sids/list; Alliance of Small Island States: http://aosis.org/about/members; Commonwealth Secretariat: http://thecommonwealth.org/small-states/.

Notes: * indicates that the country belongs to the organization/s heading the respective column/s. ** indicates that the country has a population of over 1.5 million.

Part I
Trade

Opportunities and challenges for small economies in global value chains

Rainer Lanz and Hans-Peter Werner[1]

1 Introduction

Small economies face numerous challenges when trying to buy and sell goods and services at globally competitive prices. Many have a small market size and narrow resource base which limits them from exploiting economies of scale. Many too are islands, are situated in remote locations and are highly vulnerable to natural disasters.

Geographic location, economies of scale, air and seaport infrastructure and adequate logistics and inspection systems are all determinants of the ability of small economies to sell products or services abroad, or from becoming partners in global value chains.

This paper discusses the indicators used to identify small economies (Section 2) and examines how small economies can tap into and benefit from global value chains in goods and services trade (Section 3). It does this by identifying some of the main opportunities and challenges. By analysing a number of statistical indicators and responses to the OECD/WTO Aid-for-Trade questionnaires, the paper identifies issues which small economies must address if they are to successfully tap into value chains. These include trade costs related to transport infrastructure and trade facilitation, standards compliance, access to finance and labour skills.

In the case of goods value chains, the paper analyses the integration of small economies in the agrifood, seafood and textiles and apparel sectors (Section 4). It discusses how small economies have used some of their distinct advantages in these value chains. Value chains in services, especially the importance of the tourism sector for small economies, are examined as are information technology (IT) and business process outsourcing services, especially for remote small economies (Section 5).

Trade policy experiences with value chains are also examined and put in a historical context (Section 6). In this regard, the paper looks back some 40 years to examine how the understanding of value chains has evolved and what policy options are available to small economies. Challenges with upgrading and diversification are discussed as well as the role of imports for export competitiveness.

2 Small economies

The size of countries can be measured by different indicators. Population size is often used for this purpose.

The Commonwealth Secretariat uses a cut-off population point of 1.5 million in its definition of small states and includes non-island states as well as a few states with a population over 1.5 million on the assumption that these share similar characteristics with the smaller countries,[2] The World Bank also defines small states as those with a population of 1.5 million or smaller.[3]

The United Nations lists 37 UN members as small island developing states (SIDS)[4], while UNCTAD uses more strict criteria for defining SIDS, and for analytical purposes, proposes a list of 29 SIDS.[5] Population size is here again used as a main criterion for defining small country size.

The WTO has no official definition for small economies. However, in trade negotiations during the Doha Round, the size of trade flows had been the defining criteria of whether countries would be eligible to use flexibilities foreseen for small economies (WTO, 2017). For example, the Revised Draft Modalities for Agriculture describe a small economy as one whose average share for the period 1999–2004 did not exceed (a) 0.16 of world merchandise trade; (b) 0.10% of world non-agricultural market access (NAMA) trade; and (c) 0.40% of world agricultural trade.

While the Agriculture Draft Modalities list 45 countries as meeting the above criteria, this study includes the 32 small economies which have been most active under the WTO's Work Programme on Small Economies since its establishment in 2002 (Table 1.1). It should be noted that since trade, and not population or geography, is used as criterion, several small economies covered in this chapter do not meet other criteria discussed above. For instance, Cuba, Dominican Republic, Papua New Guinea, and Sri Lanka have populations larger than 1.5 million, while Central and South American countries are not islands.

Table 1.1 Small economies included in the analysis

ISO3	Country name	ISO3	Country name	ISO3	Country name
Africa		*Caribbean*		*Central and South America*	
CPV	Cape Verde	ATG	Antigua and Barbuda	BLZ	Belize
MUS	Mauritius	BRB	Barbados	ECU	Ecuador
SYC	Seychelles	CUB	Cuba	SLV	El Salvador
Asia		DMA	Dominica	GTM	Guatemala
BRN	Brunei Darussalam	DOM	Dominican Republic	GUY	Guyana
FJI	Fiji	GRD	Grenada	HND	Honduras
MDV	Maldives	JAM	Jamaica	NIC	Nicaragua
PNG	Papua New Guinea	KNA	Saint Kitts and Nevis	PAN	Panama
WSM	Samoa	LCA	Saint Lucia	PRY	Paraguay
LKA	Sri Lanka	VCT	Saint Vincent and the Grenadines	SUR	Suriname
TON	Tonga	TTO	Trinidad and Tobago		
VUT	Vanuatu				

3 Opportunities and challenges

One of the most important changes in the nature of international trade has been the growing inter-connectedness of production processes across many countries, with each country specializing in a particular stage of a good's production. In the trade literature, these processes are referred to as global supply chains, global value chains, international production networks, vertical specialization, offshore outsourcing and production fragmentation. For the sake of clarity, this paper will refer to 'global value chains' or GVCs with the recognition that international supply chains may often be regional, rather than global (WTO, 2013).

The fragmentation of production processes associated with the rise of GVCs allows firms in small economies and developing countries to participate in international trade without developing the full range of vertical capabilities across a value chain. By opening up access to new and often higher value markets, participation in GVCs can offer smaller and emerging economies an opportunity to add more value within their local industries, expand employment and raise incomes. But this also requires efforts at the national level to mainstream GVC trade into economic development, build greater internal capacity and generate more linkages with the local economy (Bamber *et al.*, 2014a, 2014b).

Many developing countries and small economies alike are trying to support domestic firms to link to GVCs. They are also trying to attract foreign firms and improve border procedures to facilitate trade flows. While some studies urge governments to further reform their trade policies and streamline border clearance measures, they also emphasize that inducing the long-term participation of firms in these competitive value chains can be very challenging. This is true especially since GVCs in today's world are highly dynamic. They place strict demands on participating firms and are increasingly consolidated around a small number of strong global lead firms.

An OECD study, 'Connecting local producers in developing countries to regional and global value chains,' finds that regardless of a firm's position in the value chain, minimum quality, cost, and reliability requirements must be consistently met in order to participate in the chain on an ongoing basis (Bamber *et al.*, 2014a). It finds also that the capacity of firms to consistently meet some of these requirements is affected by the local institutional context in which they operate. These local-level aspects of value chains include 'the skill level of the available human capital, the establishment of local standards systems, specific infrastructure policies and the degree of industry institutionalization'. Joining a GVC, however, does not always translate into positive development gains from trade. Concerns exist that GVCs can increase inequality or have other adverse effects. Therefore, polices to integrate into GVCs should include economic, social and environmental dimensions which could help reduce such potentially negative impacts of GVC participation (Kaplinsky, 2005).

What are the opportunities that GVCs can offer small economies?

Integration into GVCs can help small economies diversify their production and export structure away from natural resources or primary agricultural commodities to manufacturing and services, where labour productivity and wages are higher (WTO, 2014). Typical sectors for an initial integration are apparel and clothing in manufacturing and call centres and IT business process outsourcing in services. Structural change can also be facilitated by the fact that certain tasks or skillsets can be exploited by different GVCs.

A main benefit from integration into GVCs is employment creation. The creation of new jobs does not only result in static gains by reducing underemployment but also allows for dynamic gains such as improved skills and employability of the labour force. However, successful integration into GVCs makes small economies vulnerable to negative shocks, at least in the short term, from potential GVC disintegration due to the decreasing competitiveness of domestic firms or due to the re-location of production by foreign investors.

Small economies, which do not have the endowments to create economies of scale in a broad range of activities, can benefit from GVCs by specializing in specific tasks or products. Integration might be easier in services than manufacturing. In particular, transportation costs of manufacturing products tend to be high for small economies as several of them are islands and remote from potential trading partners. Besides economic development, GVCs can spread international best practices in social and environmental efforts through the use of standards linked to corporate social responsibility (UNCTAD, 2014).

What are the challenges for small economies to integrate into GVCs?

GVCs pose two interlinked challenges. First, small economies need to establish policies and a business environment that allows domestic firms to improve their productivity to the point that they are able to integrate into GVCs, either through exports or by supplying foreign affiliates located in their market. Second, is the challenge of attracting FDI. According to UNCTAD (2013), determinants for investment and GVC activities can be broadly grouped into horizontal determinants that are the same across sectors or production stages, and determinants that tend to be sector or stage-specific.

Horizontal determinants relate to political and economic stability, the business environment, market size, infrastructure and the policy framework. These determinants often 'make or break' investment decisions. Results from Aid-for-Trade questionnaires of firms operating in five different value chains show that they share a number of major obstacles when trying to connect to value chains. In particular, suppliers from small economies and other developing countries and lead firms highlight transportation costs and related infrastructure, access to (trade) finance, customs procedures, labour skills, inadequate standards infrastructure and the regulatory and business environment as major obstacles to the participation of developing country suppliers in GVCs (OECD/WTO, 2013).

Beyond these necessary horizontal conditions for GVC integration, different stages and sectors are characterized by specific requirements to be met by potential suppliers and their host countries. In the case of knowledge creation stages such as research and development (R&D) and design, specific determinants to GVC integration include a developed national innovation system, skilled labour force, sound R&D and innovation policy as well as an intellectual property rights regime. In agrifood value chains, the ability of firms to comply with standards, including sanitary and phytosanitary (SPS) measures, as well as the availability of standards infrastructure for testing and certification, are key to GVC integration (Cattaneo, 2013). In information and communication technology (ICT) value chains, technological and language skills and the regulations of telecommunication providers are GVC specific determinants (Lanz, 2013).

Kowalski et al. (2015) find that the structural and policy determinants of GVC participation can differ significantly by sector and by the development level of countries. For instance, policy determinants such as import tariffs, tariffs faced in export markets and revealed FDI openness seem to be of lesser importance in the case of low-income countries compared to middle- and high-income countries.

Due to their small size and remoteness, small economies might find it particularly difficult to integrate into GVCs. Even though GVCs make it easier for small economies to specialize in specific stages of production, the lack of economies of scale can still constitute a problem for certain manufacturing activities. Furthermore, the small size of the home market reduces the scope to benefit from horizontal, i.e. market-seeking, FDI.

The problem of size is aggravated if a small economy is remote from major markets or hubs of production networks. Closeness to a big market such as the United States, the European Union (EU) or China will attract production that is subsequently exported to these markets. Similarly, closeness to a production hub facilitates the integration into the value chain. Kowalski *et al.* (2015) show that countries which are more distant to manufacturing hubs in Europe, North America and Asia/Pacific are less integrated in GVCs in terms of backward linkages. Examples of relatively small economies that have benefitted from closeness to big markets are the Baltic States and other countries in Eastern Europe, Singapore and Cambodia in Asia or Costa Rica in Central America.

Once an economy has integrated into GVCs, it faces policy challenges related to upgrading. Upgrading in GVCs means that firms move to conducting higher value-added activities resulting in an increased domestic value-added-capture within GVCs. Firms can upgrade by improving processes (process upgrading), by producing new or improved products (product upgrading) or by embarking on new functions within or outside a given GVCs (functional upgrading). Upgrading can also occur through so-called intersectoral upgrading, where acquired capabilities are used to produce new products or engage in new activities pertaining to different GVCs (WTO, 2014).

Table 1.2 shows that trade costs in small economies are, on average, higher than for the average WTO Member. This is particularly true for border compliance costs, which are highest in small economies in the Caribbean (US$590) and in Asia/Pacific (US$576) in the case of exporting. However, with respect to costs for documentary compliance, small economies tend to perform better than the average WTO Member. In terms of time to trade, exporting takes the most time in small economies in Asia/Pacific and Central and South America, while exporting is relatively time-efficient in the Caribbean.

Available data on transport infrastructure reveal that possible bottlenecks are low quality of road infrastructure in small economies in Central and South America, and low quality of port infrastructure in small economies in Africa and Asia/Pacific. To a certain extent, small economies also appear to lag behind in terms of digital connectivity. For example, while 51% of the population in the average WTO Members have access to mobile broadband, only 27% of the population in the average small economy in Central and South America and Asia/Pacific do so.

Table 1.2 also shows that in terms of legal institutions small economies display heterogeneity. Small economies in Central and South America as well in Africa have, on average, weaker legal rights than small economies in the Caribbean and Asia/Pacific, as well as the average LDC country.

As part of the Fourth Global Review of Aid for Trade in 2013, the OECD and the WTO jointly surveyed the public and the private sectors on their views regarding the barriers that developing country firms face when connecting to value chains. From the public sector, 80 partner countries participated, 23 of which are small economies. The private sector questionnaire surveyed lead firms and suppliers from developing countries operating in such value chains as agrifood, ICT, textiles and apparel, tourism, and transport and logistics. Out of 455 suppliers, 103 suppliers indicated that they have their head office in a small economy.

The results show that the public sector in small economies regards access to trade finance and domestic infrastructure as the two main obstacles to the participation of their firms in value chains. These two issues were mentioned by 57% (13 out of 23) and 48% (11 out of 23) of small economies, respectively. According to the survey, small economies and other developing economies face similar obstacles. Noteworthy differences are that other developing economies see domestic infrastructure as being the main obstacle. Meanwhile, border procedures in export markets are perceived as an obstacle by small economies but not by other developing economies.

Table 1.2 Trade cost indicators for small economies, 2016

	Small economies					WTO Members	LDCs
	All	C. and S. America	Caribbean	Africa	Asia/Pacific		
Cost to trade							
Export: border compliance (US$)	521	439	590	422	576	400	519
Export: documentary compliance (US$)	112	75	92	123	179	129	230
Import: border compliance (US$)	620	427	893	434	590	468	648
Import: documentary compliance (US$)	121	80	100	128	195	170	313
Time to trade							
Export: border compliance (hours)	60	71	48	73	55	57	94
Export: documentary compliance (hours)	52	46	36	34	88	52	101
Import: border compliance (hours)	61	56	56	69	71	75	132
Import: documentary compliance (hours)	49	51	37	30	70	65	113
Maritime connectivity							
Liner shipping (max. value in 2004 = 100)	13	17	9	14	13	30	10
Quality of transport infrastructure							
Air transport, 1–7 (best)	4.43	4.26	4.86	4.24	4.35	4.46	3.15
Port infrastructure, 1–7 (best)	4.14	4.09	4.48	3.82	3.96	4.09	2.90
Roads, 1–7 (best)	4.10	3.80	4.18	4.37	4.69	4.09	3.14
Communications infrastructure							
Mobile-broadband subscriptions (% of pop.)	33	27	39	43	27	51	15
Fixed-broadband subscriptions (% of pop.)	9	5	16	11	3	13	1
Mobile telephone subscriptions (% of pop.)	110	112	108	142	97	113	69
Individuals using the internet (% of pop.)	45	36	58	50	38	49	13
Legal institutions							
Legal rights index (0=weak to 12=strong)	5.23	4.70	5.60	3.33	6.13	5.47	4.91

Table 1.2 (continued)

	Small economies					WTO Members	LDCs
	All	C. and S. America	Caribbean	Africa	Asia/Pacific		
Time required to enforce a contract (days)	734	867	739	620	605	647	709
Ease of doing business							
Ease of doing business ranking	105	110	108	90	99	89	151
Time required to start a business (days)	21	30	14	17	20	20	27
Ease of access to loans, 1–7 (best)	3.89	4.08	3.63	3.76	3.86	3.89	3.16

Source: WTO, WT/COMTD/SE/W/34; World Bank World Development Indicators; World Economic Forum Global Competitiveness Index (GCI); International Telecommunication Union (ITU) World Telecommunication/ICT Indicators.

Notes: Cost and time to trade measure the cost in US$ and the time in hours required for documentary and border compliance. Indicators represent simple averages across countries. Depending on the availability of data, averages are based on 31 to 32 small economies (10 in Central and South America, 10 to 11 in the Caribbean, 3 in Africa and 8 in Asia/Pacific), 158 to 163 WTO Members and 43 to 48 LDCs. WEF GCI data allowed only calculating averages for 15 small economies (7 Central and South American, 4 Caribbean and 2 African), 130 WTO Members and 25 LDCs.

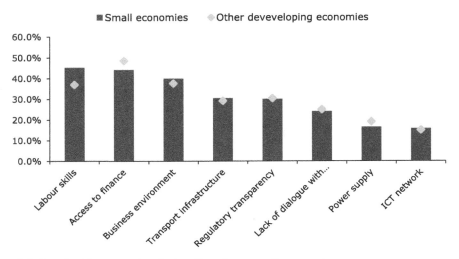

Figure 1.1 Supply-side constraints facing firms from small economies

It also emerged that transport costs and trade facilitation constitute the main difficulties for suppliers from small economies. In particular, 49% and 47% of suppliers regard transportation costs and delays and customs procedures as some of the key difficulties they encounter when trying to connect to value chains. Access to trade finance and inadequate transport capacity are further obstacles highlighted by suppliers from small economies.

Figure 1.1 shows that, according to the private sector, the lack of labour skills, access to finance and the business environment are the three main national supply-side constraints facing firms from small economies. In contrast, hard infrastructure such as ICT networks and power supply appear to be minor issues. An exception is inadequate transport infrastructure, which is mentioned as a constraint by 30% of suppliers from small economies.

The results show that to a large extent, the public and private sector views regarding barriers to GVC integration for small economy firms coincide. Access to (trade) finance, transport infrastructure and related trade costs were most often mentioned. Further barriers highlighted include standards compliance and the business environment. While relatively few public officials consider labour skills as a major obstacle, it was mentioned by about 45% of the responding firms as a main national supply-side constraint.

Results from the Aid-for-Trade monitoring exercise complement the information from the different indicators presented in Table 1.2. The results from the monitoring exercise underscore the need to improve transport infrastructure and improve customs procedures to lower trade costs. Furthermore, while the firms participating in the monitoring exercise do not prioritize ICT infrastructure development, indicators of internet usage further suggest that small economies, particularly in Central and South America as well as in Asia/Pacific, lag behind in this area.

4 Integration of small economies in goods value chains

To analyse the trade participation of small economies in goods value chains, reference is made to the BACI trade database from the French research institute CEPII. It provides bilateral exports at the 6-digit level of the HS 2002 product classification. BACI is based on the UN's

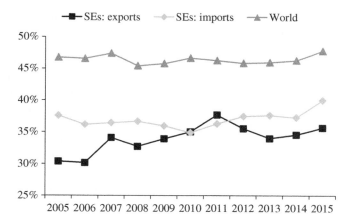

Figure 1.2 Small economies' composition of exports and imports

Comtrade database but uses reconciliation and estimation techniques to increase data coverage and consistency (Gaulier and Zignago, 2010).

The share of intermediate goods in merchandise trade indicates that small economies tend to be less integrated into goods value chains as compared to the world. Figure 1.2 shows that in 2015, non-fuel intermediate goods constituted 36% and 40% of small economies' exports and imports, respectively. Trade in intermediate goods is relatively more important at the world level, where it accounted for 48% of total trade in 2015. This lower share of intermediates exports and imports reflects on the one hand, the relatively lower integration of small economies into GVCs, and, on the other, the product and sector specialization of small economies.

While the distinction between intermediate and final goods is generally an appropriate approximation for value chain participation at the country level, a different approach needs to be taken for certain sectors. In particular, in the case of agrifood and seafood value chains, we analyse the trade patterns of primary and processed products often used for final consumption.

Agrifood and seafood

Agrifood and seafood products are among the main export products of small economies. The integration and upgrading within these GVCs can help economic development and poverty alleviation.

Both value chains have experienced significant changes over the last decades due to population growth, urbanization, changing diets, ICT and structural transformation in retail markets (Cattaneo, 2013). For example, technology improvements such as GPS, satellite monitoring or genetically modified organisms have increased the productivity of wild fishing and boosted aquaculture production. Modern agrifood and seafood value chains are buyer-driven chains where large retailers or food manufacturers constitute the lead firms. These lead firms typically operate either in regional or global markets and vertically coordinate the value chain, also ensuring that products meet food safety as well as private standards.

The most important sector-specific obstacles to participation in agrifood chains are compliance with a myriad of public and private food standards, which become particularly important in the case of upgrading into packaging and processing. According to Bamber *et al.* (2014a), the competitiveness of developing countries in agrifood GVCs depends on five broad factors: availability of both low-cost labour and skilled labour, local SPS standards and their implementation, transportation infrastructure and services, industry maturity and access to finance. Small economies face particular challenges with integrating and upgrading in value chains due to their vulnerability to exogenous demand and supply shocks, their vulnerability to market access conditions and the prevalence of small-scale farmers and fishermen.

The seafood value chain is similar to the agrifood value chain regarding the value distribution along the chain. Primary sectors receive a relatively lower share of the retail value of highly processed products and a higher share in less processed and fresh products (Gudmundsson *et al.*, 2006). When analysing the seafood value chain, it is vital to distinguish between large-scale and small-scale fishery, the latter accounting for about 90% of fishery employment and being particularly relevant in developing countries. In terms of value chain dynamics in small-scale fisheries, small-scale fishers and fish farmers receive relatively less value compared to processors and retailers (Bjorndal *et al.*, 2014). One way to support the viability of small-scale fishery in small economies is through the creation of linkages with the tourism value chain.

Figure 1.3 illustrates the positioning of small economies in agrifood and seafood GVCs through exports of primary and processed products of cocoa, coffee, fruits and nuts, and fish. Among the three product groups pertaining to agrifood value chains, exports of fruits and nuts are highest in value with about US$6.4 billion for primary products and US$0.7 billion for processed products in 2015. Small economies are positioned at the initial stages of the agrifood value chain. For all three agrifood product groups, small economies display a substantially higher share in world exports of primary products compared to processed products. For instance, in 2015, small economies accounted for 12.2% of world exports of primary coffee but only for 0.4% of processed coffee.

In the seafood value chain, small economies have intensified their production of processed fish products. While small economies exported US$0.5 billion worth of primary fish products in 2015, only slightly more than in 2005, their exports of processed fish increased from US$1.9 billion in 2005 to US$3.2 billion in 2015. This increase also reflects an increasing positioning of small economies at processing stages in fish value chains, as their share in world trade of processed fish increased from 5.1% in 2005 to 5.4% in 2015.

We calculate the small economies' revealed comparative advantage (RCA) in primary and processed exports to further assess their specialization and competitiveness in agrifood and seafood value chains. The RCA indicator is calculated as the ratio of a country's world export

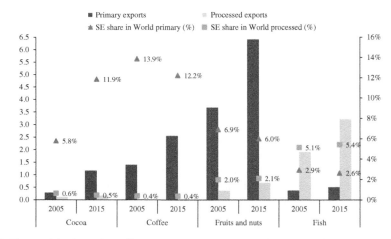

Figure 1.3 The positioning of small economies in primary and processed exports

share in a particular product divided by the country's overall world export share. An RCA measure larger than one indicates that the country has a revealed comparative advantage in a particular product.

Table 1.4 shows that small economies have a strong revealed comparative advantage in primary products of cocoa, coffee and fruits. However, in terms of processed products, small economies have only a comparative advantage in fruits, but not in cocoa and coffee. In the fish value chain, small economies have a revealed comparative advantage in both primary and processed exports.

However, Table 1.4 also reveals differences between regions and between countries. Small economies in Central and South America as well as the Caribbean tend to be more specialized in exports of products. In contrast, for small economies in Africa and Asia, exports of processed products within the fish value chain are of greater importance.

Textiles and clothing

The labour-intensive textile and apparel value chain has served many developing countries as a starting point for export-led development. The value chain is buyer-driven, where the respective lead firms are positioned downstream in the chain close to the consumer (Gereffi, 1999).

Lead firms, such as retailers or brand manufacturers, typically control high-value-added activities such as R&D, design, marketing and distribution and outsource manufacturing activities to suppliers. The manufacturing part of the textile and clothing value chain consists of the following stages. Raw materials in the form of natural (cotton, silk) or synthetic fibres constitute inputs to the production of textile components, i.e. yarn and fabric. These textile inputs are then used to manufacture clothing or other final products for home furnishing or industry. The 'assembly' from textiles to clothing constitutes the lower end of value-added activities in the chain and involves low-skilled, labour-intensive activities such as cutting, making (sewing) and trimming (CMT).

Textile and apparel value chains are of major importance for several small economies, particularly in Central America and the Caribbean, but also in the Asia/Pacific region. Small economies, however, differ in their position in the textile and apparel value chain. For example, Sri Lanka has been able to developed strong linkages to global buyers and its firms have upgraded within the chain by adding design to their functional portfolio and by producing more complex niche products such as women's underwear, intimate apparel and sportswear (Fernandez-Stark et al., 2011). Another example is Nicaragua, which increased its activities in the manufacturing of clothing thanks to trade preferences with the United States and foreign direct investment, including from Asia. However, Nicaragua mainly conducts CMT functions and faces a number of upgrading challenge (Frederick et al., 2014).

Figure 1.4 shows that exports of textiles and clothing amounted to almost US$18 billion in 2015, corresponding to about 15% of total small economies' exports. The share of intermediates in textile and clothing exports of small economies has fluctuated around 10% in recent years, which is significantly lower than the respective 35% at the world level. Hence, in comparison to the rest of the world, small economies tend to be specialized in the assembly stages of clothing production, while other countries tend to produce more intermediate textiles such as yarn and fabrics.

An analysis of the geographic dimension of the chain shows that Europe and North America constitute the main markets for exports of final products (WTO, 2015). While small economies in Africa and in the Asia/Pacific region export more apparel to Europe than to North America, small economies in the Caribbean and Central and South America almost exclusively deliver to the North American market.

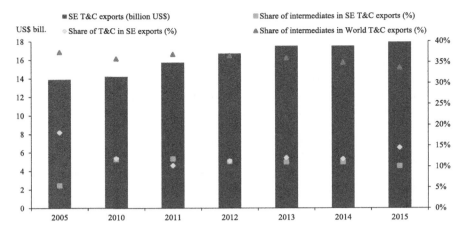

Figure 1.4 Exports of textiles and clothing as a percentage of total small economies' exports

Table 1.3 also confirms that small economies are positioned at the assembly stage of the chain as between 62% and 79% of their imported textiles are intermediate inputs while only 6% to 19% of textile exports constitute intermediates. While both export and imports of textiles have increased between 2005 and 2015, the relative importance of textiles has actually diminished for small economies. For instance, the share of textiles in exports of small economies decreased from 18% in 2005 to 14% in 2015.

Table 1.4 shows that Sri Lanka is the biggest exporter of both intermediate (US$364 million) and final (US$5.268 million) textile and clothing products. Other major exporters include Central American economies (Honduras, El Salvador, Nicaragua, Guatemala), the Dominican Republic in the Caribbean and Mauritius in Africa. It is interesting to note that even though only 10% of exports of textile and clothing products are intermediates, high RCA values indicate that small economies such as Sri Lanka, Honduras, El Salvador, Nicaragua and Mauritius have a strong comparative advantage in these intermediates. In contrast, RCA values are lower for final textiles and clothing exports, and even slightly below one, i.e. 0.95, for the small economies as a group. One likely explanation for the lower 'relative' competitiveness of small economies in final clothing products is the importance of other major exporting countries such as China, Vietnam or Bangladesh.

5 Integration of small economies in services value chains

The proliferation of ICT and the increasing fragmentation of services have blurred the distinction between manufacturing and services. This blurriness has also become apparent in balance of payment (BOP) statistics as they appear in the 6th BOP Manual of the IMF's Balance of Payments and International Investment Position Manual which presents revised and updated standards for concepts, definitions, and classifications for international accounts statistics. For example, services trade now includes the category of goods-related services, which includes 'manufacturing services on physical inputs owned by others' and 'maintenance and repair services n.i.e.' The first category covers essentially manufacturing on a contract basis including activities such as processing, assembly, labelling, packing, etc. The second comprises maintenance and repair work by residents of an economy on goods that are owned by non-residents and vice versa.

Table 1.3 Trade indicators for textile and clothing products by region

Country	Exports				Imports			
2015	US$ (billion)	Share in region total (%)	RCA	Intermediates (%)	US$ (billion)	Share in region total (%)	RCA	Intermediates (%)
Small economies	17.89	14%	3.17	10%	13.20	7%	1.52	69%
Africa	0.94	23%	5.06	12%	0.45	7%	1.50	75%
Asia	5.75	20%	4.42	6%	2.78	8%	1.74	79%
Caribbean	1.50	6%	1.34	19%	1.85	5%	1.03	62%
C. and S. America	9.70	15%	3.20	11%	8.13	7%	1.63	66%
2005								
Small economies	13.90	18%	3.65	5%	10.16	9%	1.84	69%
Africa	0.94	35%	6.96	8%	0.39	9%	1.75	84%
Asia	3.96	25%	4.93	4%	2.11	14%	2.86	88%
Caribbean	2.13	9%	1.89	1%	1.80	6%	1.16	55%
C. and S. America	6.88	20%	3.94	7%	5.86	10%	1.95	66%

Source: CEPII BACI database.

Note: The Broad Economic Categories (BEC) classification is used to distinguish between intermediate and final textile products. Textiles and textile products correspond to HS section XI (chapters 50–63) of the HS 2002 product classification. See footnote 11 (CEPII BACI database) for a definition of RCA.

Table 1.4 Exports and revealed comparative advantage (RCA) by country and value chain

Country	Cocoa				Coffee				Fruits and nuts				Fish				Textiles and clothing					
	Exports (US$ million)		RCA		Exports (US$ million)		RCA		Exports (US$ million)		RCA		Exports (US$ million)		RCA		Exports (US$ million)			RCA		
	Primary	Processed	Primary	Processed	Primary	Processed	Primary	Processed	Primary	Processed	Primary	Processed	Primary	Processed	Primary	Processed	Processed	Interm.	Final	Primary	Interm.	Final
Africa	**0.52**	**0.23**	**0.20**	**0.02**	**0.22**	**0.06**	**0.04**	**0.03**	**7.74**	**0.70**	**0.28**	**0.08**	**9.21**	**816.56**	**1.84**	**0.08**	**52.87**	**112.37**	**829.12**	**1.84**	**6.72**	**1.79**
Cape Verde	0.51	0.07	6.43	0.22	0.21	0.03	1.23	0.40	0.02	0.00	0.02	0.01	0.02	60.53	0.13	0.01	125.82	0.12	5.73	0.13	1.49	0.06
Mauritius	0.00	0.15	0.00	0.02	0.01	0.03	0.00	0.02	6.26	0.58	0.28	0.08	7.76	382.94	1.91	0.08	30.39	111.67	822.91	1.91	8.17	2.18
Seychelles	0.00	0.01	0.00	0.00	0.00	0.00	0.00	0.00	1.47	0.12	0.34	0.09	1.43	373.10	1.86	0.09	157.88	0.59	0.48	1.86	0.03	0.06
Asia	**124.46**	**5.09**	**6.95**	**0.08**	**150.29**	**0.97**	**3.96**	**0.06**	**237.15**	**59.51**	**1.22**	**1.02**	**167.37**	**762.13**	**4.80**	**1.02**	**7.07**	**369.02**	**5376.2**	**4.80**	**6.24**	**0.84**
Brunei Darussalam	0.00	0.01	0.00	0.00	0.04	0.00	0.01	0.00	0.01	0.08	0.00	0.01	0.29	1.54	0.04	0.01	0.06	0.41	15.42	0.04	0.08	0.00
Fiji	0.02	0.14	0.03	0.06	0.00	0.04	0.00	0.07	1.27	9.08	0.19	4.54	25.46	153.22	21.33	4.54	41.51	3.25	88.90	21.33	3.01	0.22
Maldives	0.00	0.00	0.00	0.01	0.00	0.00	0.00	0.02	0.09	0.00	0.06	0.00	55.98	129.01	207.49	0.00	154.62	0.03	2.77	207.49	0.42	0.01
Papua New Guinea	120.46	0.66	21.15	0.03	149.16	0.14	12.37	0.03	0.00	0.04	0.00	0.00	4.33	285.16	0.39	0.00	8.32	0.90	0.35	0.39	0.00	0.01
Samoa	0.11	0.02	2.21	0.12	0.28	0.00	2.53	0.00	0.36	3.72	0.64	22.08	2.17	16.29	21.62	22.08	52.40	0.10	0.26	21.62	0.10	0.08
Sri Lanka	0.10	4.25	0.01	0.16	0.64	0.66	0.04	0.10	234.56	46.49	2.94	1.94	73.88	103.20	5.16	1.94	2.33	364.30	5268.3	5.16	14.90	2.03
Tonga	0.00	0.00	0.00	0.00	0.00	0.00	0.00	0.00	0.74	0.08	9.45	3.38	3.65	0.00	258.83	3.38	0.00	0.03	0.09	258.83	0.25	0.17
Vanuatu	3.76	0.00	44.69	0.01	0.17	0.12	0.95	1.57	0.11	0.02	0.12	0.07	1.61	73.72	9.81	0.07	145.43	0.01	0.11	9.81	0.03	0.00
Caribbean	**283.67**	**32.08**	**18.34**	**0.56**	**39.46**	**6.38**	**1.20**	**0.44**	**525.31**	**74.69**	**3.13**	**1.48**	**63.04**	**27.85**	**2.09**	**1.48**	**0.30**	**277.90**	**1222.9**	**2.09**	**1.64**	**0.73**
Antigua and Barbuda	0.00	1.23	0.00	2.39	0.48	0.00	1.64	0.02	0.20	0.04	0.13	0.10	0.00	1.98	0.01	0.10	2.36	0.28	5.84	0.01	0.87	0.08
Barbados	0.00	0.45	0.00	0.43	0.02	0.01	0.03	0.03	0.33	5.01	0.11	5.42	1.51	0.14	2.74	5.42	0.08	0.90	10.49	2.74	0.77	0.13
Cuba	0.53	1.88	0.60	0.58	3.08	1.32	1.65	1.59	1.52	5.71	0.16	1.98	1.89	0.44	1.10	1.98	0.08	0.46	0.24	1.10	0.01	0.02
Dominica	0.03	0.15	0.50	0.79	0.03	0.00	0.31	0.00	1.92	0.28	3.51	1.71	0.12	0.00	1.21	1.71	0.00	0.42	0.55	1.21	0.22	0.36
Dominican Republic	276.78	19.23	44.79	0.84	6.13	2.50	0.47	0.43	496.47	31.04	7.41	1.54	5.60	5.20	0.47	1.54	0.14	273.39	1200.4	0.47	4.04	1.81
Grenada	3.64	0.24	165.33	2.98	0.00	0.01	0.00	0.45	2.01	0.03	8.42	0.40	5.66	0.01	132.20	0.40	0.05	0.14	0.18	132.20	0.17	0.26
Jamaica	1.06	0.67	1.31	0.23	29.71	2.49	17.45	3.29	11.91	15.02	1.37	5.72	0.04	1.10	0.03	5.72	0.23	1.15	1.71	0.03	0.04	0.06
St Kitts and Nevis	0.00	0.00	0.00	0.00	0.00	0.00	0.00	0.00	0.01	0.00	0.02	0.00	0.00	0.00	0.00	0.00	0.00	0.00	0.09	0.00	0.04	0.00
St Lucia	0.13	0.00	2.46	0.00	0.00	0.01	0.00	0.26	7.90	0.01	13.37	0.07	0.00	0.00	0.00	0.07	0.00	0.02	0.09	0.00	0.04	0.01
St Vincent/Grenadines	0.00	0.14	0.00	0.48	0.00	0.00	0.00	0.00	2.68	0.01	3.10	0.03	0.09	2.44	0.57	0.03	5.07	0.19	0.39	0.57	0.10	0.10

Table 1.4 (continued)

Country	Cocoa				Coffee				Fruits and nuts				Fish				Textiles and clothing				
	Exports (US$ million)		RCA		Exports (US$ million)		RCA		Exports (US$ million)		RCA		Exports (US$ million)		RCA		Exports (US$ million)			RCA	
	Primary	Processed	Primary	Processed	Primary	Processed	Primary	Processed	Primary	Processed	Primary	Processed	Primary	Processed	Primary	Processed	Processed	Interm.	Final	Interm.	Final
Trinidad and Tobago	1.51	8.09	0.22	0.32	0.00	0.04	0.00	0.01	0.36	17.53	0.00	0.01	48.12	16.54	3.57	0.78	0.40	0.95	2.92	0.01	0.01
C. & S. America	**760.63**	**130.11**	**18.21**	**0.84**	**2362.1**	**27.03**	**26.71**	**0.69**	**5641.5**	**544.35**	**12.46**	**0.47**	**268.01**	**1604.4**	**3.30**	**3.99**	**6.38**	**1039.3**	**8662.9**	**4.31**	**1.02**
Belize	0.48	0.06	1.66	0.06	0.19	0.78	0.32	2.87	76.86	50.57	24.72	2.87	1.17	35.89	2.10	54.03	20.78	0.79	2.60	0.19	0.11
Ecuador	749.87	109.25	61.75	2.44	19.61	1.95	0.76	0.17	3367.0	265.31	25.59	0.17	96.15	1142.1	4.07	6.70	15.62	89.00	32.02	0.05	0.30
El Salvador	0.10	7.41	0.03	0.56	150.73	1.25	19.90	0.37	5.71	80.23	0.15	0.37	4.98	90.40	0.71	6.88	4.20	334.16	2258.4	13.13	3.82
Guatemala	0.32	10.60	0.04	0.39	737.36	4.04	47.41	0.58	1347.7	97.31	16.93	0.58	3.92	55.40	0.27	4.06	1.25	273.00	1337.3	3.78	1.52
Guyana	0.00	0.01	0.00	0.00	0.00	0.00	0.00	0.00	9.98	3.04	0.92	0.00	22.20	35.69	11.44	0.93	5.95	0.55	5.25	0.11	0.02
Honduras	0.81	0.39	0.15	0.02	1015.2	1.90	91.69	0.39	489.19	34.54	8.63	0.39	4.27	88.89	0.42	2.02	2.82	242.36	3373.8	13.41	1.90
Nicaragua	7.29	0.16	2.32	0.01	417.60	4.54	62.64	1.53	55.85	2.36	1.64	1.53	19.87	12.18	3.24	0.23	0.64	22.99	1434.1	9.47	0.30
Panama	1.77	2.17	0.59	0.20	21.32	12.57	3.37	4.47	227.61	3.87	7.03	4.47	95.28	86.40	16.39	0.40	4.80	27.03	126.87	0.88	0.37
Paraguay	0.00	0.06	0.00	0.00	0.00	0.00	0.00	0.00	11.53	6.16	0.20	0.00	0.00	0.00	0.00	0.35	0.00	49.43	92.06	0.36	0.38
Suriname	0.00	0.00	0.00	0.00	0.00	0.00	0.00	0.01	50.12	0.96	6.33	0.01	20.17	57.48	14.18	0.40	13.06	0.02	0.50	0.01	0.00
SVEs	**1169.3**	**167.50**	**15.05**	**0.58**	**2552.0**	**34.44**	**15.51**	**0.47**	**6411.7**	**679.24**	**7.61**	**0.47**	**507.62**	**3210.9**	**3.36**	**2.68**	**6.86**	**1798.6**	**16091**	**4.30**	**0.95**

Source: CEPII BACI database.

Notes: The Broad Economic Categories (BEC) classification is used to distinguish between primary (BEC 111, 112, 21) and processed (BEC 121, 122, 22) agrifood products. The products are defined following the HS 2002 product classification: Cocoa – HS chapter 18; Coffee – HS chapter 09; Fruits and nuts – HS chapter 08 and HS headings 2006, 2007, 2008 and 2009. Primary (BEC 112) and processed (BEC 121 and 122) fish products are taken from HS chapters 03 and 16. Ornamental fish, corals and fish fats and oils are not included as they are not categorized as food. The BEC classification is also used to distinguish between intermediate and final textile products. Textiles and textile products correspond to Section XI (chapters 50–63) of the HS 2002 product classification.

Table 1.5 shows that goods-related services are of high importance for several Central American economies. Goods-related services account for a high share of total services exports of Honduras (60%), Nicaragua (44%), and El Salvador (26%), which all have a relative comparative advantage. These high trade flows represent the 'assembly' or services activity of these countries in the textile and clothing value chain.[6] This new services category will reveal further insights into the value chain patterns as data availability improves.

Tourism

Tourism is a sector of major importance for many small economies. In 2013, tourism accounted, on average, for almost 9% of GDP across 30 small economies, as compared to only 3% for the world (WTO, 2015). Small economies differ in their dependency on tourism. For instance, tourism accounts for only 1% in Papua New Guinea, Paraguay and Suriname. In contrast, tourism played an important role in the graduation from LDC status of Cabo Verde and the Maldives in 2007 and 2011, respectively (Honeck, 2012). This important role is reflected in significant travel exports, which accounted for 70% and 89% of Cabo Verde's and the Maldives´ total services exports in 2015, respectively (Table 1.5).

Table 1.5 shows that tourism accounts for about half of small economies' services exports, which also reflects their comparative advantage in the sector. All small economies, except Cuba, Brunei Darussalam and Papua New Guinea, have a revealed comparative advantage in travel exports. The biggest travel exporter is the Dominican Republic (US$6.1 billion), followed by Panama (US$4.1 billion), Sri Lanka (US$3 billion), Cuba (2.6 billion), Maldives (US$2.6 billion) and Jamaica (US$2.4 billion).

The core components of the tourism value chain include travel organization and booking, transportation, accommodation, food and beverage provision, handicrafts, excursions as well as cultural and natural assets (UNWTO, 2013). International linkages in the value chain are mostly related to travel organization and booking as well as international transportation. However, most of the activities in the tourism value chain take place in the destination country and are related to accommodation and food, as well as to the provision of other domestic goods and services for tourists.

Tourism has many backward linkages to other sectors in the domestic economy such as agriculture (e.g. food supply to hotels), construction, communications, utilities (e.g. supply of electricity and water to hotels) and events management. Hence, through the creation of backward linkages to other sectors, tourism can contribute to the economic diversification of small economies and the growth of sectors such as agriculture, fishing and services. However, this requires sound policy planning and co-ordination among different ministries. Furthermore, in order to establish backward linkages and support local employment, firms need to overcome difficulties relating to meeting international hospitality standards as well as food quality and safety standards (Jansen, 2013).

Information technology and business process outsourcing

Advances in information and communication technology have opened up opportunities for small economies to use IT and business process outsourcing (BPO) to diversify their exports. Entry points can include services in areas such as call centres, data entry and processing centres, and back offices (such as purchases, logistics, accounting, claims and payment processing).

Developing country suppliers face a number of specific challenges when trying to enter value chains through IT and BPO services (Lanz, 2013). Determinants of competitiveness include a

Table 1.5 Services export indicators by sector and small economy (2015)

Country	Total		Goods-related			Travel			Computer			Other business		
	US$ million	Growth p.a. (%)	US$ million	% of Total	RCA	US$million	% of Total	RCA	US$ million	% of Total	RCA	US$ million	% of Total	RCA
C. & S. America	**24,696.2**	**9.6**	**2,855.1**	**13.5**	**4.0**	**10,108.7**	**40.9**	**1.7**	**78.9**	**0.5**	**0.1**	**920.1**	**4.1**	**0.2**
Panama	11,969.3	14.3	16.7	0.1	0.0	4,141.0	34.6	1.4	58.7	0.5	0.1	544.4	4.5	0.2
Guatemala	2,703.4	8.3	–	–	–	1,579.7	58.4	2.4	20.1	0.7	0.1	118.6	4.4	0.2
Honduras	2,634.0	4.1	1,572.6	59.7	17.7	650.4	24.7	1.0	–	–	–	59.6	2.3	0.1
El Salvador	2,271.0	4.6	583.2	25.7	7.6	816.9	36.0	1.5	64.5	2.8	0.4	65.3	2.9	0.1
Ecuador	2,221.2	8.9	6.0	0.3	0.1	1,551.4	69.8	2.8	–	–	–	–	–	–
Nicaragua	1,341.9	10.5	587.1	43.8	13.0	528.6	39.4	1.6	–	–	–	10.0	0.7	0.0
Paraguay	776.9	12.7	89.5	11.5	3.4	317.0	40.8	1.6	–	–	–	2.7	0.3	0.0
Belize	468.2	4.9	–	–	–	371.6	79.4	3.2	–	–	–	58.9	12.6	0.6
Suriname	167.4	-0.9	-13.3	-7.9	-2.4	87.6	52.3	2.1	1.8	1.1	0.2	33.4	20.0	0.9
Guyana	142.9	-0.3	–	–	–	64.6	45.2	1.8	0.0	0.0	0.0	27.3	19.1	0.9
Caribbean	**24,626.5**	**3.0**	**78.8**	**1.0**	**0.3**	**13,247.2**	**53.8**	**2.2**	**90.5**	**0.9**	**0.1**	**603.9**	**5.1**	**0.2**
Cuba	11,369.0	4.9	–	–	–	2,600.8	22.9	0.9	–	–	–	–	–	–
Dominican Republic	7,267.1	1.7	78.7	1.1	0.3	6,115.8	84.2	3.4	53.8	0.7	0.1	273.0	3.8	0.2
Jamaica	3,027.4	2.8	–	–	–	2,400.6	79.3	3.2	36.7	1.2	0.2	197.3	6.5	0.3
Barbados	1,376.6	-0.4	–	–	–	965.7	70.2	2.8	–	–	–	–	–	–
Antigua and Barbuda	477.7	0.5	–	–	–	306.7	64.2	2.6	–	–	–	27.2	5.7	0.3
Saint Lucia	454.1	0.4	0.0	0.0	0.0	397.1	87.4	3.5	–	–	–	28.1	6.2	0.3
Grenada	190.2	5.2	–	–	–	146.0	76.7	3.1	–	–	–	13.3	7.0	0.3
St Kitts and Nevis	180.6	1.3	0.1	0.1	0.0	116.9	64.7	2.6	–	–	–	23.3	12.9	0.6

Table 1.5 (continued)

Country	Total		Goods-related			Travel			Computer			Other business		
	US$ million	Growth p.a. (%)	US$ million	% of Total	RCA	US$million	% of Total	RCA	US$ million	% of Total	RCA	US$ million	% of Total	RCA
St Vincent/ Grenadines	150.3	-0.4	0.0	0.0	0.0	95.7	63.7	2.6	–	–	–	30.2	20.1	0.9
Dominica	133.5	4.6	0.0	0.0	0.0	102.0	76.4	3.1	–	–	–	11.5	8.6	0.4
Africa	**4,140.5**	**6.5**	**11.8**	**2.4**	**0.7**	**2,172.0**	**52.5**	**2.1**	**81.1**	**2.9**	**0.4**	**941.6**	**22.7**	**1.0**
Mauritius	2,802.1	5.7	–	–	–	1,432.6	51.1	2.1	81.1	2.9	0.4	701.4	25.0	1.1
Seychelles	839.2	9.2	–	–	–	392.4	46.8	1.9	–	–	–	225.6	26.9	1.2
Cape Verde	499.2	6.7	11.8	2.4	0.7	347.0	69.5	2.8	1.0	0.2	0.0	14.6	2.9	0.1
Asia	**11,701.3**	**11.5**	**26.3**	**1.9**	**0.6**	**6,803.5**	**58.4**	**2.4**	**679.3**	**8.8**	**1.3**	**160.7**	**2.0**	**0.1**
Sri Lanka	6,366.0	15.4	–	–	–	2,980.7	46.8	1.9	676.7	10.6	1.5	42.3	0.7	0.0
Maldives	2,894.0	24.8	–	–	–	2,567.5	88.7	3.6	–	–	–	–	–	–
Fiji	1,173.1	2.6	18.1	1.5	0.5	760.3	64.8	2.6	2.3	0.2	0.0	28.9	2.5	0.1
Brunei Darussalam	640.0	0.4	–	–	–	139.9	21.9	0.9	–	–	–	–	–	–
Vanuatu	277.5	7.5	–	–	–	227.6	82.0	3.3	0.1	0.0	0.0	3.2	1.2	0.1
Samoa	181.9	3.5	8.2	4.5	1.3	125.8	69.2	2.8	0.3	0.2	0.0	7.9	4.4	0.2
Papua New Guinea	109.7	-9.2	–	–	–	1.7	1.6	0.1	–	–	–	78.4	71.4	3.2
Tonga	59.1	7.9	–	–	–	–	–	–	–	–	–	–	–	–
Small economies	**65,164.5**	**6.6**	**2,972.0**	**9.6**	**2.8**	**32,331.4**	**49.7**	**2.0**	**929.7**	**2.6**	**0.4**	**2,626.4**	**5.6**	**0.3**

Source: WTO Statistics Database.

cheap labour force, which is also skilled in terms of language, business skills such as accounting and IT skills such as database administration or programming. Furthermore, sound ICT infrastructure and telecommunications regulations are crucial for a cost-effective and high quality delivery of IT and BPO services.

So far, only few small economies have been relatively successful in developing an IT and BPO sector. Evidence is provided in Table 1.5, which approximates small economies' relevance in outsourcing by providing statistics on computer services exports and other business services exports, the latter including, inter alia, R&D services, professional services, advertising, market research and technical services. For instance, other business services accounted for only US$2.6 billion or 5.6% of services exports in 26 small economies in 2015. However, exports in computer services reveal that Sri Lanka, Mauritius Jamaica and El Salvador have been relatively successful in building an export-oriented IT industry.

With computer services exports of US$676 million, Sri Lanka is by far the biggest exporter of computer services among small economies (Table 1.5). It is also the only small economy which has reached a revealed comparative advantage in the sector. Sri Lanka has therefore made good progress in following India's path to position itself as an offshore destination for IT and BPO services (WTO, 2015). There are over 300 IT and BPO companies that operate in Sri Lanka, mostly small and medium companies and a few large global players. Sri Lanka has developed an export-oriented software industry focusing on telecommunications, banking, financial services and insurance (BFSI) and software testing.

The BPO sector in Sri Lanka focuses on financial and accounting services, investment research, engineering services, call centre services and UK based legal services. Colombo now has the world's largest pool of UK qualified English-speaking accounting professionals outside the UK itself. Success factors for the development of the IT software and BPO industry in Sri Lanka include investment incentives by the Government, low-labour costs and an English-speaking, skilled labour force. Challenges include the lack of a tier-two offshoring location beyond Colombo and the need to further upgrade skilled labour and ICT infrastructure.

Economies in the Caribbean and Central America have also made progress in developing their IT and BPO sectors, albeit at a lower scale. Jamaica has a locational advantage as a 'nearshore' investment location to North America, operating in the same time zone and sharing English as a main language. Supported by the government, the ICT sector grew significantly in the last decade (UNCTAD, 2013). In particular, thanks to government support, Jamaica experienced large FDI inflows into its telecommunications infrastructure, including the development of the IT-focused Montego Bay Free Zone. Similarly, Central American countries such as the Dominican Republic, El Salvador and Guatemala are trying to position themselves as 'nearshore' platforms for offshore services to the Hispanic market in the US (Fernandez-Stark et al., 2011).

In the past, the remoteness of several small economies has hampered their connectivity to telecommunications networks. However, thanks to technological advances and increased demand, a number of projects have built submarine cables to deliver high-speed bandwidth connections to isolated communities thereby supporting socio-economic development. For instance, the Interchange Cable Network linking Vanuatu to Fiji has generated several positive socio-economic impacts in Vanuatu, allowing it to become the most competitive ICT/Telecommunications hub in the South Pacific region (OECD/WTO Aid-for-Trade Case Stories 2015[7]).

6 Policy challenges for small economies with GVCs

This chapter has thus far provided a discussion on some of the evidence of integration of small economies in GVCs and their various experiences, especially in the agrifood, seafood and the textiles and clothing value chains. Some services value chains have also been examined in the tourism and information technology sectors. This section will take a closer look at how understanding value chains has evolved and what small economies can do to secure either a greater share of the production process of a value chain or retain more value in their respective markets.

More than 20 years ago, an often cited 'global value chains' typology was developed by Gary Gereffi (1994). It separated value chains into two major types: the first was buyer driven; the second, production driven. Production driven value chains are run by global companies which coordinate the backward and forward linkages described earlier. Such value chains are usually run by capital and technology-intensive industries active in automobile and aircraft manufacturing and industries related to computer assembly and heavy machinery. Buyer-driven value chains, on the other hand, refer to activities in which large retailers and branded manufacturers play the pivotal roles in setting up decentralized production networks in a variety of exporting countries.

For small economies, it is typically the buyer-driven type which provides access to a value chain. Buyer-driven chains usually exist in more labour-intensive consumer goods industries such as the garments, footwear, toys, housewares and consumer electronics sectors and are more prevalent in developing countries and in small economies.

The ways of thinking about value chains has evolved since the mid-1990s and has expanded to include characteristics such as the level of complexity of inter-firm transactions, the extent to which information can be codified, and finally the degree of capability of the supply base in relation to the requirements of the transaction (Gereffi et al., 2005). These value chain characteristics change over time in an interplay with technological advances and domestic or international regulations. This requires companies, especially those which wish to continue to dominate a particular production component, to manage various types of knowledge and know-how particular to that production sector.

Many suppliers in developing countries produce for lead firms in GVCs. Lead firms are not directly involved in the manufacturing of particular products but do concentrate on downstream and upstream processes such as logistics, finance, design and marketing, areas which are generally more skill intensive (Fernandez-Stark et al., 2011). Already a decade ago, researchers focused on how gains are distributed between parties in a GVC-based business relationship and found that much has to do with the relative bargaining power of each (Gereffi et al., 2005). This can depend on how unique and desirable the supplier is and whether or not a lead firm can do without its services or whether or not its contribution can be performed in another country at a lower price or can be automated or codified. It is often the case that lead firms possess rare capabilities, while suppliers further down the chain stand in increasingly fierce competition with each other to supply these firms. This leads to a large gain capture for the lead firms (WTO, 2014).

Nearly 25 years ago, Stan Shih who owned an IT business proposed 'the smiling curve,' to show the distribution of value-added through the product life cycle. The curve shows that upstream activities, such as research and development, and downstream ones such as marketing and distribution, are characterized by higher value-added creation than manufacturing or assembly activities (Dedrick and Kraemer, 1998).

Since then, the smiling curve (also known as the 'smiley curve') which portrays unit value and not volume, has changed under the forces of increased globalization of manufacturing activities. It has deepened and there are now lower-levels of value-added in the middle stages of the value chain. Much of this is due to offshoring to less expensive production sites, increased competition and competitiveness gains amongst countries offering similar production capabilities and the IT revolution, which further reduces coordination costs (Baldwin, 2012).

Upgrading scenarios are by no means easy for small economies. Diversification along the value chain is much more difficult because of small size. Even small, industrialized economies have tended to specialize in just a small part of the overall chain where a large share of what they export includes a large proportion of imported components. Any further diversification in the gamut of export products would, therefore, also require more imports.

While productivity gains may be realized with the initial shift in labour from agriculture to manufacturing and services, the gains are no longer as large as they were in the past, especially not since the 1970s when such trends began. Recent research (Escaith, 2013; Kowalski *et al.*, 2015) argues that the volume of the activity may matter as much as the domestic value-added share or the level of sophistication. Hence, important benefits can be derived from specializing in less sophisticated assembly activities according to comparative advantages and performing these on a large scale.

Escaith (2013) also argues that while the smiley curve addresses apparent production costs, it does not consider the underlying investments and the risks attached to them. For a firm in a small economy, gains are probably higher at the intensive margin (doing more of what you know) than trying to 'capture' other parts of the GVC such as research and development tasks, which can be both risky and expensive.

In small economies, smaller businesses usually have knowledge of local clients, tastes and needs but can find themselves in weaker positions when they try to integrate or upgrade in a value chain. In the research literature, this has been referred to as 'high road' to competitiveness, contrasting with the 'low road', which is typical of firms which compete by squeezing wages and profit margins rather than by improving productivity, wages, and profits. The key difference between the high and the low road to competitiveness is often explained by the different capabilities of firms to 'upgrade' or the capacity of a firm to innovate to increase the value-added of its products and processes (Humphrey and Schmitz, 2002).

Upgrading over time has been shown to be closely linked to innovation. Enterprises may achieve this by entering higher unit value market niches or new sectors, or by undertaking new productive functions. Humphrey and Schmitz (2002) identified four types of upgrading: (i) process upgrading or transforming inputs into outputs more efficiently by reorganizing the production system or introducing superior technology; (ii) product upgrading by moving into more sophisticated product lines in terms of increased unit values; (iii) functional upgrading by acquiring new, superior functions in the chain, such as design or marketing or abandoning existing low-value added functions to focus on higher-value added activities and; (iv) intersectoral upgrading by applying the competence acquired in a particular function to move into a new sector. For instance, in Chinese Taipei, the competence gained in producing TVs was used to make monitors and then eventually computers (Guerrieri and Pietrobelli, 2004; Humphrey and Schmitz, 2002).

It has also been shown that companies in small economies which are located near each other or in industrial clusters actually have a better chance of upgrading. This has also been found to be true for businesses in larger developing and developed countries because together, companies (especially SMEs) are able to overcome such obstacles as lack of trained workers, inadequate technology and availability of key data to remain informed of market developments. It also facilitates access to credit to expand a business, upgrade equipment or to engage in export activities (Gereffi *et al.*, 2001).

Chinese Taipei, Singapore and Hong Kong, China are good examples of how to achieve production expertise and marketing know-how. There are many SMEs in these economies which co-exist in designated business areas. The high quality products they produce are offered at competitive prices and enable them to enter established markets and to compete with products made by larger companies with more money, more employees and greater economies of scale. Already in the late 1990s, Stiglitz (1996) noted that the success of these East Asian countries resulted from a mix of domestic policies they developed to create competitive markets, promote exports, education and technology and encourage more collaboration between government and industry and among firms.

UNCTAD (2013) points to similar policies which developing countries and small economies used effectively to engage in and upgrade along GVCs. Developing countries could build productive capacities including through technology dissemination and skill building, thereby opening up opportunities for longer-term industrial upgrading. According to UNCTAD, however, reaping the potential benefits of GVCs is not automatic. Therefore, industrial and government policies play a role as does a supporting development strategy. This is all the more important given the dynamic nature of GVCs and the fact that value chains can move quite easily.

The increasing importance of GVCs offers opportunities to small economies as they can specialize in specific stages of the chain or take advantage of new services tasks created through the fragmentation of production. Improvements in transport and ICT infrastructure, the upgrading of laboratories and testing facilities, training to improve the skills of workers, export promotion initiatives or matchmaking between suppliers and buyers typically require both private and public investment. Targeted assistance and sound policy-making can indeed help the governments of small economies make the decisions that will allow SMEs and larger firms to take advantage of the opportunities which value chains offer. Policies for integrating into, moving up and realising additional gains from value chains are key factors given the dynamic nature of GVCs.

7 Conclusions

This chapter presented an overview of both the challenges and opportunities small economies face when trying to integrate into GVCs. While it is not an exhaustive study of this subject, some important areas were examined which provide some new material and analysis in light of the special circumstances small economies face in regard to value chain integration.

By specializing in specific tasks or stages within the value chain, small economies can, to a certain extent, mitigate their lack of economies of scale and realize economic benefits. GVCs can further help small economies diversify their export structure away from primary commodities towards manufacturing and services. As was discussed, this is by no means an automatic process.

In order to benefit as much as possible from goods and services value chains, sustained efforts are required to mainstream GVC trade into the broader national economic development agenda. This requires coordinating diverse elements involving transport and customs clearance issues and managing the general business and investment environment. It also requires a focus on building adequate port and air links as well as transportation and IT infrastructure. Still other issues include governance, rule of law, access to finance, labour policies related to training and skills building, and general national education levels.

Of the 32 small economies in the Asian/Pacific, African, Caribbean and Central and South American regions examined in this report, several have distinct advantages and are actively pursuing value addition in specific GVCs such as textiles, as well as in agrifood and seafood. The services sector provides other possibilities, especially services linked to tourism, call centres and business process outsourcing. These are all areas where small economies have made significant inroads.

Analysing trade patterns of cocoa, coffee as well as fruits and nuts, we find that small economies are more integrated in the first stages of agrifood chains. For example, in 2015, small economies accounted for 12.6% of world exports of primary coffee but for only 0.4% of processed coffee. An analysis of revealed comparative advantage indicators confirms that small economies are more competitive in the exports of primary, as compared to processed products. The gap in export competitiveness in primary versus processed agrifood exports points to untapped export potential and upgrading challenges related to SPS standards, supplier-buyer linkages, the prevalence of small-scale farming, labour skills and access to finance.

Seafood value chains are of major importance to many small economies that have access to the sea or are islands, particularly in Africa and Asia. Small economies increasingly participate in processing stages of fish value chains, where they display a stronger comparative advantage as compared to primary stages. Besides upgrading the technology related to harvesting and processing, a major challenge in seafood value chains is the need for sound fishery management to ensure the sustainability of fish stocks.

The buyer-driven textiles and the clothing value chain has served several developing countries, including small economies, as a starting point for export-led development. Small economies in Central America and also Sri Lanka in Asia have successfully integrated into textile and clothing value chains. We find that small economies are predominantly positioned in the assembly stages of the chain as 69% of their imports are intermediate inputs while 90% of their exports constitute final clothing products. However, the comparative advantage analysis reveals that small economies tend to be more competitive in intermediate stages of the chain, which likely reflects increasing competition of major exporters such as China, Vietnam and Bangladesh in the final stages of the chain.

Small islands are particularly dependent on tourism, which accounts for about 9% of GDP across 30 small economies – three times as much as for the world. Most small economies have a comparative advantage in travel exports. Tourism is particularly important for smaller island small economies such as the Maldives, for which travel exports constituted 89% of services exports in 2015. Tourism has many backward linkages to other sectors in the domestic economy such as agriculture, fishing and services, and therefore plays an important role for employment creation and economic diversification. The exploitation of these backward linkages requires sound policy planning and coordination, as well as the need to address challenges related to meeting hospitality standards as well as food quality and safety standards.

IT and business process outsourcing are other services which offer great potential to small economies as physical distance and economies of scale are of lesser relevance compared to manufacturing. So far, only a few small economies such as Sri Lanka, Mauritius and Jamaica have been relatively successful in developing IT and offshore business services. Success factors and challenges are a low-cost and skilled workforce, both in terms of IT and language skills, as well as a high-quality ICT infrastructure and related services.

Some trade policy experiences and further examples of upgrading in value chains were also examined. Possibilities for more efficient production practices, better technology and moving into higher value–added activities such as marketing and design were discussed. Clearly, there is strength through numbers and there are benefits of clustering. Small companies in industrial clusters have better chances of achieving upgrades in value chains than those which are isolated.

There are several challenges faced by small economies that point to an important role for WTO-related initiatives and policies, such as Aid for Trade and trade facilitation. Improvements in transport and ICT infrastructure, the upgrading of laboratories and testing facilities, training to improve the skills of workers, export promotion initiatives or matchmaking between suppliers and buyers typically require both private and public investment. The implementation of the WTO Trade Facilitation Agreement (TFA) and the related support through the WTO TFA Facility can help small economies lower these costs and thereby contribute to GVC integration.

Industrial and government policies and the role that they play in supporting development are also very important. Policies for integrating into, moving up and realizing additional gains from value chains are key factors given the dynamic nature of GVCs. But small economies, if supported with the right policies, can benefit from value chains in goods and services trade and realize positive economic gains, no matter how small their size or how far away they are from their nearest customer.

Notes

1 The views expressed in this article are those of the authors and do not necessarily reflect those of the WTO, its Secretariat or its members.
2 http://thecommonwealth.org/small-states/.
3 http://www.worldbank.org/en/country/smallstates/.
4 https://sustainabledevelopment.un.org/topics/sids/list/.
5 http://unctad.org/en/Pages/ALDC/Small%20Island%20Developing%20States/UN-recognition-of-the-problems-of-small-island-developing-States.aspx/.
6 It should be noted that there is an overlap in merchandise trade measured by customs statistics and services trade measured by BOP statistics. In other words, the definition of goods in the balance of payments is not one-to-one transferable to merchandise trade.
7 See www.oecd.org/aidfortrade/casestories/.

References

Baldwin, R. E. (2012). *Global Supply Chains: Why They Emerged, Why they Matter, and Where They are Going*. CEPR Discussion Paper No. 9103.

Bamber, P. and Fernandez-Stark, K. (2014a). 'Inclusive value chain interventions in the high-value agrifood sector in Latin America'. In Hernández, R., Martínez Piva, J. M. and Mulder, N. (eds), *Global value chains and world trade: Prospects and challenges for Latin America*. Economic Commission for Latin America and the Caribbean: 137–162.

Bamber, P., Fernandez-Stark, K., Gereffi, G. and Guinn, A. (2014b). *Connecting Local Producers in Developing Countries to Regional and Global Value Chains – Update*. Trade Policy OECD Paper No. 160.

Bjorndal, T., Child, A. and Lem, A. (2014). *Value chain dynamics and the small-scale sector: policy recommendations for small-scale fisheries and aquaculture trade*. Rome: Food and Agriculture Organization of the United Nations (FAO).

Cattaneo, O. (2013). *Aid for Trade and Value Chains in Agrifood*. Paris: OECD/WTO.

Dedrick, Jason and Kraemer, K. L. (1998). *Asia's Computer Challenge: Threat or Opportunity for the United States and the World?* New York: Oxford University Press.

Escaith, H. T. (2013). 'International Supply Chains, Trade in Value-Added and Development: A Small Economy's Perspective'. IDE-JETRO Conference 'Global Value Chains: Quo Vadis?.

Fernandez-Stark, K., Frederick, S. and Gereffi, G. (2011). *The Apparel Global Value Chain: Economic Upgrading and Workforce Development*. Durham, NC: Duke University, Centre on Globalization, Governance and Competitiveness.

Frederick, S.Bair, J. and Gereffi, G. (2014). *Nicaragua and the Apparel Value Chain in the Americas: Implications for Regional Trade and Employment*. Durham, NC: Duke University, Centre on Globalization, Governance and Competitiveness (CGGC).

Gaulier, G. and Zignago, S. (2010). *BACI: International Trade Database at the Product-level The 1994–2007 Version*. CEPII Working Paper 2010-23.

Gereffi, G. (1994) 'The Organization of Buyer-Driven Global Commodity Chains: How US Retailers Shape Overseas Production Networks'. In Gereffi, G.and Korzeniewicz, M. (eds), *Commodity Chains and Global Capitalism*, Westport, CT: Praeger: 95–122. Available at: http://hdl.handle.net/10161/11457

Gereffi, G. (1999). 'International trade and industrial upgrading in the apparel commodity chain'. *Journal of International Economics*, 48(1): 37–70.

Gereffi, G., Humphrey, J. and Kaplinsky, R. (2001). 'Globalisation, Value Chains and Development'. *Institute for Development Studies*, 32(3): 1–8.

Gereffi, G., Humphrey, J. and Sturgeon, T. (2005). 'The governance of global value chains'. *Review of International Political Economy*, 12(1): 78–104.

Gudmundsson, E., Asche, F. and Nielsen, M. (2006). *Revenue Distribution through the Seafood Value Chain*. Rome: Food and Agriculture.

Guerrieri, P. and Pietrobelli, C. (2004). 'Industrial districts' evolution and technological regimes: Italy and Taiwan'. *Technovation*, 24(11): 899–914.

Honeck, D. (2012). *LDC Export Diversification, Employment Generation and the "Green Economy": What roles for tourism linkages?*. Working Paper ERSD-2012–24. Geneva: WTO.

Humphrey, J. and Schmitz, H. (2002). *How does Insertion in GVCs Affect Upgrading in Industrial Clusters*. Sussex: Institute of Development Studies.

Jansen, M. (2013). *Aid for Trade and Value Chains in Tourism*. OECD/UNWTO/WTO.

Kaplinsky, R. (2005). *Globalization, Poverty and Inequality: between a rock and hard place*. London: John Wiley & Sons.

KowalskiP., Gonzalez, J. L., Ragoussis, A. and Ugarte, C. (2015). *Developing Countries' Participation in Global Value Chains – Implications for Trade-Related Policies*. OECD Trade Policy Papers No. 179.

Lanz, R. (2013) *Aid for Trade and Value Chains in Information and Communication Technology*. OECD/WTO.

OECD (2013). *Aid for Trade at a Glance 2013: Connecting to Value Chains*. Paris: OECD.

Stiglitz, J. E. (1996). 'Some lessons from the East Asian Miracle'. *The World Bank Research Observer*, 11(2): 151–177.

UNCTAD (2013). *World Investment Report 2013 – Global Value Chains: Investment and Trade for Development*. Geneva: UNCTAD.

UNCTAD (2014). *World Investment Report 2014 – Investing in the SDGs: An Action Plan*. Geneva: UNCTAD.

United Nations World Tourism Organization (UNWTO) (2013). *Sustainable Tourism for Development Guidebook*. Madrid: UNWTO.

World Trade Organization (WTO) (2013). *World Trade Report: Factors shaping the future of world trade*. Geneva: WTO.

World Trade Organization (WTO) (2014). *World Trade Report: Trade and Development: Recent Trends and the Role of the WTO*. Geneva: WTO.

World Trade Organization (WTO) (2015). *Challenges and Opportunities experienced by Small Economies when linking into Global Value Chains in Trade in Goods and Services*. Background Note by the WTO Secretariat, WT/COMTD/SE/W/31.

World Trade Organization (WTO) (2017). Work Programme on Small Economies: Compilation Paper. WTO Secretariat Note, WT/COMTD/SE/W/22/Rev.8.

2

Trade openness, volatility and governance

Lino Briguglio and Melchior Vella

1 Introduction

It is generally acknowledged that a high degree of trade openness renders a country susceptible to external economic conditions and, as a result, also to be highly exposed to external shocks, possibly leading to GDP growth volatility in the country in question. This chapter will test this hypothesis, subject to a number of control variables, notably political and economic governance. The approach used to test this relationship is the regression method, using panel data.

The confirmation of the hypothesis of this study may help to explain the so-called 'small state paradox' referred to in Briguglio *et al.* (2009), meaning that highly-open economies can and do remain relatively stable in spite of the fact that openness, by itself, tends to generate a high degree of volatility, which is often considered to be economically harmful.

This proposed relationship is an extension of the arguments put forward by Briguglio *et al.* (2009) and Briguglio (2016), where factors that lead to economic vulnerability were juxtaposed against factors that lead to economic resilience in order to assess the risk of a country being harmed by external shocks. These two studies were not based on regression analysis, but on observations of variables that where assumed to lead to economic vulnerability and resilience, and this analysis enabled the authors to classify countries, in terms of the so-called vulnerability and resilience (V&R) framework.

The possibility that GDP growth volatility is influenced by economic and political governance, may also help to explain why some highly-open economies do not exhibit a high degree of GDP growth volatility, while economies which are not highly open to trade exhibit a high degree of volatility – the reason being that good economic, political and social governance may be conducive to the reduction of volatility.

The chapter proceeds as follows. Section 2 presents a brief literature review on the relationship between trade openness and GDP growth volatility. Section 3 explains the methodology utilized in this study to test the relationship between trade openness and GDP growth volatility. Section 4 presents the estimation results and reports on some diagnostic tests relating to the validity of the results. Section 5 concludes the study and puts forward a number of implications that are derived from the results presented in the previous section.

2 Literature review

Openness and economic volatility

Trade openness is often thought to bring real benefits, including improved productivity due to scale-efficiency and enhanced variety of goods at lower cost to consumers. In addition, producers would have a large market for their products, thus earning more than if the same products were sold only on the domestic market (Jensen, 2004). In this sense, it may be argued that trade openness is conducive to economic growth, ceteris paribus.

However, trade openness could also generate volatility which may harm growth. Many authors associate openness with volatility, including Di Giovanni and Levchenko (2009), Easterly et al. (2001), Karras and Song (1996), Krishna and Levchenko (2009) and Loayza and Raddatz (2007). Easterly and Kraay (2000) further argue that in small economies, characterized by high degree of openness, the positive and negative effects of openness may offset each other.

Some authors consider that export concentration exacerbates the effect on trade openness on volatility. This view is echoed by Haddad et al. (2010) who argue that export diversification (the obverse of concentration), both across products and markets, reduces growth volatility. The authors first discuss the mechanisms by which trade openness affects growth volatility, with one of the variables considered being export diversification index. They found evidence that export diversification reduces the effect of trade openness on growth volatility.

Jensen (2004) further argues that the effect of openness on volatility increases if exports are concentrated in certain commodities, including oil, which are characterized by high price fluctuations. A similar view is also expressed in Koren and Tenreyro (2007), who assert that volatility is particularly intense when exports consist mainly of commodities, a characteristic of many developing countries.

Various authors, while admitting that trade openness leads to GDP growth volatility, also acknowledge the importance of domestic factors in attenuating or exacerbating volatility, including governance, institutional frameworks and domestic economic policy. Political institutions and policy mismanagement are also likely to affect the degree to which trade openness generates volatility (Acemoglu et al., 2003; Ahmed, 2003; Chang et al., 2009; Fatás and Mihov, 2013; Gavin and Hausmann, 1998; Malik and Temple, 2009).

The extent to which trade openness affects volatility is also thought to depend on the stage of development. For example, Abubaker (2015) found that trade openness has a more sizeable effect on volatility in developing countries when compared to developed countries. In the same vein, Jensen (2004) contends that GDP per capita has a significant effect on income volatility. This may explain why particularly poor economies, like Least Developed Countries (LDCs), are also characterized by high income volatility, even though they do not tend to be characterized by particularly high levels of openness.

Some studies also distinguish between different types of trade openness, arguing that some forms of openness are highly destabilising compared to other forms. For example, Jackman (2014) investigated the relationship between tourism specialization and output volatility in a sample of 34 small island developing states (SIDS). The conclusion is that there appears to be a positive relationship between tourism and output volatility, and that the impact of tourism on economic volatility depends greatly on the volatility of tourism inflows.

Financial depth is also expected to affect macroeconomic volatility. Dabla-Norris and Srivasal (2013) examine this relationship and find that financial depth could lead to a dampening of output volatility, but only up to a point. They find that at very high levels, such as those observed in many advanced economies, financial depth amplifies volatility.[1]

A number of studies do not confirm the positive effects of trade openness on volatility. A case in point is Cavallo (2008) who presents empirical evidence that suggests that, after appropriately accounting for the likely endogeneity of trade, the net effect of trade openness on output volatility is stabilising. This view is echoed in Cavallo and Frankel (2008).

In the same vein, Bowdler and Malik (2017) argue that trade openness can reduce volatility by shifting consumption and production towards goods for which the terms of trade are relatively stable. Likewise, Hegerty (2014) concludes that trade openness appears to be correlated with a reduction in output volatility for LDCs. Bejan (2006) argues that if one controls for government size and some measures of external risk, such as export concentration index, the effect of openness on the output volatility turns out to be negative.

Openness and economic growth

Although, most studies conclude that trade openness generates GDP growth volatility, which is a downside, openness is generally found to be positively related to GDP growth. Studies that associate openness with growth often base their arguments on the possibility that international trade stimulates competitiveness, leading to increased productivity and innovation, improves resource allocation and lowers prices for consumers. Such an argument is proposed by Winters (2004) and Easterly and Kraay (2000). Some studies show that the positive effect of trade openness on economic growth, is particularly possible when there are conducive institutional frameworks (Dollar and Kraay, 2003).

Many studies show that the quality of institutions is an important consideration in assessing the effects of trade openness. Calderon and Fuentes (2006), for example, argue that countries with strong institutions receive the largest benefit of trade openness.

Some authors, however, refer to the downside of trade openness on growth in the short run, due to adjustment costs of trade openness, possibly leading to poverty and inequality (Goldberg and Pavcnik, 2004).

Yanikkaya (2003), goes as far as to show that openness may actually not be good for growth. The author shows through his estimation that trade barriers are positively and significantly associated with growth, especially for developing countries.

The downsides of volatility

The arguments derived from the literature so far generally point out that while openness may be good for growth, with a few dissenting opinions, it also has negative effects by generating volatility, again with a few dissenting voices. This leads to the question as to why volatility is undesirable.

There are various reasons for this, including that fluctuations can generate a welfare loss (Loayza et al., 2007) through the negative effect of uncertainty (economic, political, and policy-related). This matter is also discussed in Montalbano (2011).

In addition, volatility may usher in a higher risk of policy failure (Gavin and Hausmann, 1998; Rodrik, 1999; Fatás and Mihov, 2013), including fiscal and monetary policies that intensify rather than calm the trade cycle. Furthermore, volatility may also lead to lower growth (Ramey and Ramey, 1995), particularly in the case of poor countries (Easterly et al., 2000). Hnatkovska and Loayza (2005) for example, estimate that a one standard-deviation increase in macroeconomic volatility results in an average loss of 1.3 percentage points in annual per capita GDP growth.

Output volatility is also associated with socially undesirable outcomes like inequality and poverty. Meschi and Vivarelli (2007) find that trade of developing countries with high-income countries are destabilising as they worsen income distribution in these countries, both through imports and exports. This would seem to suggest that technological differentials between trading partners are important factors in explaining the effects of volatility that result from economic openness.

On the other side of the coin, Kose *et al.* (2004) found that trade openness appears to attenuate the negative relationship between growth and volatility. Specifically, they find that the estimated coefficients on interactions between volatility and trade integration are significantly positive, suggesting that countries that are more open to trade appear to be able to tolerate higher volatility without hurting their long-term growth.

García-Herrero and Vilarrubia (2006) building upon the study by Ramey and Ramey (1995), namely that volatility reduces economic growth, showed empirically that a moderate degree of volatility can be growth-enhancing, while very high volatility is clearly detrimental. These results point to the existence of a 'Kuznets curve' type of relationship between volatility and growth.

3 Methodology

Testing the relationship between volatility and trade openness

In the literature, the procedure used to estimate the relationship between openness and volatility is generally the regression method, often utilising panel data. GDP growth volatility is generally measured by the standard deviation of GDP growth,[2] and openness is computed as the average of exports and imports, as a ratio of GDP (e.g. Haddad *et al.*, 2010).

The control variables utilized in the regression equations varied, as indicated in the literature review, and included variables representing policy and institutional frameworks, the stage of development, export concentration, terms of trade, financial liberalization, and geographical dummy variables. Some of these control variables are related to each other, and in our estimation procedure we try to avoid this problem.

To test the hypothesis that trade openness generates GDP growth volatility, we specify the following equation, using annual data for 171 countries spanning the years from 2010 to 2015:

$$\text{VLT}_{i,t} = \alpha + b\ \text{OPN}_{i,t} + c\ \text{EGV}_{i,t} + d\ \text{PGV}_{i,t} + \varepsilon_{i,t}$$

where:

VLT refers GDP growth volatility; OPN refers to trade openness; EGV refers to economic governance; and PGV refers to political governance. The political governance variable may possibly captures the stage of development, given that these two variables are highly positively correlated. The subscripts indicate that all variables refer to country *i* in year *t*. Further, $\varepsilon_{i,t}$ is assumed to be normally distributed with mean zero and constant variance.

The basic assumption underpinning the above equation is that GDP volatility is influenced by trade openness as well as by economic and political governance. A priori, one expects that trade openness (OPN) has a positive effect on growth volatility. On the other hand, good economic governance (EGV) and good political governance (PGV) are expected to have a negative effect on volatility, and therefore good governance could attenuate the effect of trade openness. Conversely, bad governance could exacerbate volatility.

In present study, the use of fixed effects in panel data procedure was preferred over the random effects estimator. In the equation we assume that $\varepsilon_{i,t}$ includes a time-invariant component that captures those country-specific and time-invariant factors that are not otherwise captured by the other observable explanatory variables.

Based on the specifications outlined above, the model is fitted using fixed effects. The estimation is done by using Driscoll and Kraay (1998) standard errors accounting for heteroscedasticity and autocorrelation consistent standard errors.

The methodology is subject to caveats which need to be acknowledged. First, the Driscoll-Kraay standard errors estimation is based on an asymptotic theory. In interpreting the results, cautiousness is advised since the panel used in this study contains a large cross-section of countries but a short-time dimension. Second, the methodology is based on a static model which restricts inertia effects. The model could be improved by considering a dynamic panel data model, however, due to data constraints for some variables we rest on the Driscoll-Kraay estimator.

In addition, there is the possibility that governance may be endogenous, with the ensuing estimation bias that this may create, in that countries that are more prone to shocks may be compelled to improve their governance in order to reduce exposure to shocks.

Data used

VLT is measured by the standard deviation of GDP growth rates, with a rolling window size of 10 years. The data was sourced from the IMF economic outlook database.[3]

OPN is measured as the average of imports and exports of goods and services as a ratio of GDP [(Exports + Imports)/2 /GDP]. The data was sourced from the UNCTAD statistics.[4]

PGV is measured by the Rule of Law indicator of the so-called Kaufman Index,[5] which ranges between −2.5 and +2.5. Negative values are considered as bad political governance, with higher negative values representing higher levels of bad governance, while positive values are considered as indicators of good governance, with higher positive values representing higher levels of good governance. Without good governance in place, it would be relatively easy for adverse shocks to result in economic and social chaos and unrest. Thus the term for the PGV will represent an intensification effect on volatility when it takes a negative value, and an attenuation effect on volatility when it takes a positive value, assuming that its estimated coefficient is negative.

EGV (economic governance) is measured in two alternative ways. First, this variable is measured solely by the debt as a ratio of GDP. Second, we consider the average of the following two indices, namely (i) debt as a ratio of GDP and (ii) current account imbalances as a ratio of GDP. Following Briguglio *et al.* (2009) and Briguglio (2016), these indicators were chosen because they were thought to be policy induced and are therefore closely related to economic governance. It should be noted here that economic governance is likely to be associated with many other factors for which data is sparse or which are difficult to capture quantitatively.

The debt/GDP ratio is thought to be related to economic governance, with high debt ratios indicating weak governance in this regard. Low debt ratios would allow room for manoeuvre in taxation and expenditure in the face of adverse shocks (Briguglio *et al.*, 2009). A country with a high current account deficits may find it more difficult to mobilize resources in order to offset the effects of economic shocks.

The debt/GDP component was considered as representing good economic governance if its value is 60% or lower, with lower values being taken as representing better economic governance. Conversely, ratios higher than 60% were considered as associated with bad economic governance, with higher ratios being associated with worse economic governance.[6] The debt/GDP ratio was rescaled so that 60% was set to equal zero, while values equal to or higher than 60% were rescaled to take values of between 0 and −0.5 and values equal to or lower than 60% were rescaled to take values of between 0 and 0.5. This procedure of assigning negative values for weak economic governance is helpful for drawing Figure 2.1, as will be explained in Section 4.

The current account/GDP component was considered as being associated with good economic governance if its value was 0 or higher, with higher values representing better economic governance.[7] Conversely, negative values of the ratio were associated with bad economic governance with higher negative ratios being associated with worse economic governance. Positive and negative values of the ratio were rescaled to take a value of between +0.5 and −0.5. This rescaling procedure was useful in order to take an average of the debt ratio and the current account balance, since both were rescaled to take a value of between −0.5 and +0.5, with zero being the point of neutrality.[8]

To separate the effects of initial cyclical factors both the debt to GDP and current account imbalances ratio are measured with a 10-year backward average. The data was sourced from the IMF World Economic Outlook database.[9]

4 Estimation results

Using data for 171 countries,[10] and the debt/GDP to measure EGV, the following estimation results were obtained:

$$\text{VLT} = \quad 2.24 + \quad 0.04 \text{ OPN} - 2.71 \text{ EGV} - 1.85 \text{ PGV} \qquad (1)$$
$$\textit{t-statistics} \quad (6.89) \quad (5.14) \quad (-4.17) \quad (-2.93)$$

R-squared = 0.84   Number of observations = 1,026

The estimated parameters are in line with a priori expectations. The numbers in parentheses are the t-statistics and indicate that the estimates of the coefficient on the explanatory variables are statistically different from zero at the 95% level.

The results confirm that, keeping governance constant, trade openness does intensify GDP growth volatility. Nevertheless, this does not automatically imply that more open economies face a higher degree of growth volatility. Indeed, the regression results confirm that well-governed economies could mitigate the effects of openness. It may also be implied that, the stage of development, measured by GDP per capita, could also be associated with a dampening of volatility, given that GDP per capita is closely correlated with political governance.

The equation performed satisfactorily in terms of residual diagnostic tests. Pooled unit root tests were also conducted on the variables, showing that the null hypothesis of having a unit root process is not accepted at 1% level. Regarding multicollinearity, the correlation between OPN, EGV and PGV across countries was not found to be unduly high. A diagnostic test was also conducted to test for fixed effects.

The results of the Hausman test decisively favours the use of the fixed effects estimator over random effects in this analysis. This confirms the use of the fixed effects over random effects in order to account for county's unobserved heterogeneity.

We also estimated an alternative specification where the EGV variable was measured as an average of the ratios debt /GDP and current account balance/GDP. The estimated results are as follows:

$$\text{VLT} = \quad 1.88 + \quad 0.04 \text{ OPN} - 5.39 \text{ EGV} - 1.79 \text{ PGV} \qquad (2)$$
$$\textit{t-statistics} \quad (6.11) \quad (4.97) \quad (-1.75) \quad (-2.77)$$

R-squared = 0.84   Number of observations = 1,026

Lino Briguglio and Melchior Vella

As can be seen by comparing equation (1) with equation (2) the results are very similar, with the only difference that the EGV variable is now only significant at the 90% level.

Implications of the results

The results would seem to suggest that the hypothesis that GDP growth volatility is influenced by trade openness and good governance is confirmed. This implies that volatility can be the result not only by high exposure to external economic conditions but also of internal governance factors.

This implication is illustrated in Figure 2.1.

In this Figure, GDP growth volatility is measured along the vertical axis and trade openness on the horizontal axis. The markers show volatility with and without the governance effect, utilising the estimation results of equation (1).[11] Volatility without governance is estimated by removing the governance terms from the estimated equation (shown by the round grey markers in the diagram, on the straight line trend line) and volatility with governance is estimated by including the governance terms in the estimated equation (shown by the diamond shaped markers in the diagram).

From this chart we can identify four possible scenarios into which countries can be grouped, as explained below.

The right section of the diagram relates to those countries that have a relatively high degree of trade openness, in this case higher than 50%. Some register a volatility score below the trend line, indicating that the governance effect has attenuated their volatility, as shown by a downward-pointing arrow. Others have a volatility score above the trend line, indicating that governance has intensified their volatility, as shown by the upward-pointing arrow. This means that the right side of the diagram has two types of economies, namely (a) highly-open economies with good governance which include Malta, Singapore, and Luxembourg and (b) highly-open economies with weak governance which include Equatorial Guinea, Maldives and Belize.[12]

The left section of the diagram relates to those countries that have a relatively low degree of trade openness. Again, well-governed countries register a volatility score below the trend line,

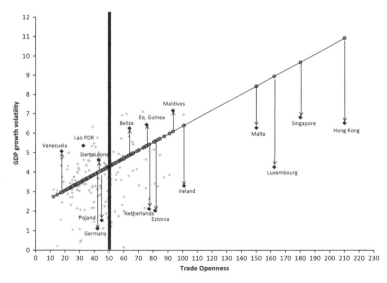

Figure 2.1 How the governance scores attenuate or exacerbate the effect of trade openness on GDP growth volatility

while weakly-governed countries have an intensified volatility score above the trend line. This means that the left side of the diagram has two additional types of economies, namely (c) slightly-open economies (less than 50% of GDP) with good governance, including, Germany and Poland and (d) slightly-open economies with weak governance, including Venezuela, Sierra Leone and Russia.

Volatility and small states

The economies of small states are generally characterized by a high degree of trade openness, meaning that they are likely to be associated with a high degree of to growth volatility. Using the benchmarking exercise proposed in the figure the distinction between attenuated or intensified volatility can be made. Small states with a volatility score below the trend line in the Figure are those that have possibly attenuated their growth volatility through good economic and political governance. Conversely, small states with a volatility score above the trend line are those that possibly exacerbated their volatility as a result of weak governance.

Table 2.1 provides an overview of small states in terms of their growth volatility with and without governance as measured from the estimated regression.[13] Almost all of the small states in Europe are endowed with good governance scores that mitigated volatility associated with trade openness. Similarly, governance scores are also conducive to the reduction of volatility in most of the small states in the Caribbean region. By contrast, the picture is mixed in African, Atlantic/Indian and Pacific regions. Such benchmarking verifies the 'small state paradox' (Briguglio et al., 2009), such that highly-open economies can and do withstand their inherent vulnerability by adopting policies that counteract growth volatility.

It should be recalled that governance captures the effects of political (PGV) as well as economic governance (EGV), and consequently their separate scores could reinforce or counteract each other. By way of example, Cyprus ranked amongst the weakly governed countries because its weak economic governance (high debt-to-GDP ratio and large current account deficit) more than offset the effect of the favourable political governance score. Conversely, Bahrain ranked behind Cyprus with regard to the political governance score, however, it performed very well in terms of economic governance, and that is why it was ranked among the well-governed countries.

5 Conclusions and implications

This study has tested the relationship between trade openness and GDP growth volatility, using a sample of 171 countries. The regression equation was kept as simple as possible,

Table 2.1 Small states classified by degree of openness and governance

Highly-open economies with good governance	*Highly-open economies with weak governance*
Luxembourg, Estonia, Iceland, Mauritius, Malta, Tuvalu, Bahrain, Vanuatu, Saint Lucia, Micronesia Suriname, Antigua and Barbuda, Lesotho, Cape Verde, Solomon Islands, Guyana	Fiji, Cyprus, Seychelles, Maldives, Equatorial Guinea, Belize
Moderately-open economies with good governance	*Moderately-open economies with weak governance*
Brunei Darussalam, Samoa, Bahamas, Barbados, Saint Vincent and the Grenadines, Dominica, Swaziland, Gabon, Saint Kitts and Nevis, Bhutan	Djibouti, Grenada, Comoros, Gambia, Guinea-Bissau, Sao Tome and Principe

reflecting the possibility that GDP growth volatility is influenced by trade openness, economic governance and political governance, the latter variable also possibly proxying the stage of development.

By keeping other relevant variables constant, this study confirms the hypothesis that trade openness exacerbates growth volatility. However, the possibility that growth volatility is mitigated by good economic and political governance is also confirmed. This may explain why some economies do not exhibit a high degree of GDP growth volatility even though they are highly-open.

The main implication of these results is that countries that are highly dependent on international trade, including most small states, would be expected to be associated with growth volatility, which has various downsides, as explained in the literature review. However, it does not necessary follow that highly trade-open economies – small states in particular – are the ones that experience the highest degree of GDP growth volatility. This is because, as our results suggest, countries may adopt appropriate policies to attenuate the effect of openness on volatility. In other words, it is possible that highly-open economies do not exhibit a high degree of GDP growth volatility, while economies which are not highly trade-open may exhibit a high degree of volatility, as a result of weak governance.

A major implication that can also be derived from this study is that highly trade-open countries, in particular small states, are those countries which mostly need to adopt good economic and political governance, if they are to counteract growth volatility, with all its downsides.

This is in line with the vulnerability/resilience framework, proposed in Briguglio *et al.* (2009) and Briguglio (2016), where factors that lead to economic vulnerability were juxtaposed against factors that lead to economic resilience in order to assess the risk of a country being harmed by external shocks. This framework was used to show that small economically vulnerable states, can, and do, adopt policies that enable them to withstand the downsides of economic vulnerability.

Notes

1 On this matter see also Tornell *et al.* (2003).
2 Various other methods of measuring volatility have been proposed (see Cariolle, 2012).
3 Source: www.imf.org/external/pubs/ft/weo/2016/01/weodata/index.aspx/.
4 Source: http://unctadstat.unctad.org/wds/ReportFolders/reportFolders.aspx/.
5 Sourced from: http://info.worldbank.org/governance/wgi/index.aspx#home/.
6 A debt-to-GDP ratio of 60% is considered as a prudential limit for the EU member states, and a higher ratio is considered be fiscally unsustainable. However, there is considerable debate on this threshold value of the Debt/GDP ratio (see Chowdhury and Islam, 2014).
7 Although a current account surplus is generally considered to be a better situation than a current account deficit, one could question whether such a surplus is a sign of good economic governance, as such a situation may signify that a country could improve its standard of living, by, for example, stimulating demand and encouraging imports. In addition, a current account surplus may push up the exchange rate of a floating domestic currency. On the other hand, a current account deficit may be an indication that a country is living beyond its means, and therefore not sustainably – thus associating it with weak economic governance. In addition, a deficit reflects relatively lower national savings in relation to investment. On this issue see Ghosh and Ramakrishnan (2006).
8 The cut-off value of zero is somewhat arbitrary, but it will not affect the statistical significance of the estimated coefficients. It will however be of some importance when interpreting the results, given that a value of less than zero will be interpreted as an indicator of bad economic governance, with higher negative values suggesting a higher degree of bad governance.
9 Source: www.imf.org/external/pubs/ft/weo/2016/01/weodata/index.aspx/.

10 The IMF database, from which the volatility data was sourced, contained 187 politically independent states. Sixteen countries were omitted due to missing data. These are Afghanistan, Chad, Eritrea, Iraq, Kiribati, Kosovo, Liberia, the Marshall Islands, Mongolia, Montenegro, Palau, Sudan, Syria, Timor-Leste, Tonga, Turkmenistan.

11 Similar results were obtained when applying the results of equation (2).

12 It should be noted, with regard to the classification of countries discussed above, that the choice of cut-off value of openness of 50% is subjective and the classification of countries would change if a different cut-off point is chosen. Irrespective of this threshold, however, this does not change our results that good governance is likely to attenuate the effect of trade openness on volatility.

13 Small states are defined here as sovereign countries with a population of at most 1.5 million people. This is in line with criteria adopted by the World Bank criteria (see: www.worldbank.org/en/country/smallstates) and the Commonwealth Secretariat (http://thecommonwealth.org/small-states).

References

Abubaker, R. (2015). 'The asymmetric impact of trade openness on output volatility'. *Empirical Economics*, 49(3): 881–887.

Acemoglu, D., Johnson, S., Robinson, J. and Thaicharoen, Y. (2003). 'Institutional causes, macro-economic symptoms: volatility, crises and growth'. *Journal of Monetary Economics*, 5(1): 49–123

Ahmed, S. (2003). 'Sources of economic fluctuations in Latin America and implications for choice of exchange rate regimes'. *Journal of Development Economics*, 72(1): 181–202.

Bejan, M. (2006). 'Trade openness and output volatility'. Instituto Tecnologico Autonomo de Mexico.

Bowdler, C. and Malik, A. (2017). 'Openness and inflation volatility: Panel data evidence'. *The North American Journal of Economics and Finance*, 41: 57–69.

Briguglio (2016). 'Exposure to external shocks and economic resilience of countries: evidence from global indicators'. *Journal of Economic Studies*, 43(6): 1057–1078.

Briguglio, L., Cordina, G., Farrugia, N. and Vella, S. (2009). 'Economic vulnerability and resilience: concepts and measurements'. *Oxford Development Studies*, 37(3): 229–247.

Calderon, C. and Fuentes, R. (2006). 'Complementarities between Institutions and Openness in Economic Development: Evidence for a Panel of Countries'. *Cuadernos de Economía*, 43: 49–80.

Cariolle, J. (2012). *Measuring macroeconomic volatility: applications to export revenue data, 1970–2005*. FERDI working paper No I14. Clermont Ferrand, France: FERDI.

Cavallo, E. A. (2008). 'Output volatility and openness to trade: a reassessment'. *Economia*, 9(1): 105–138.

Cavallo, E. A. and Frankel, J. A. (2008). 'Does openness to trade make countries more vulnerable to sudden stops, or less? Using gravity to establish causality'. *Journal of International Money and Finance*, 27(8): 1430–1452.

Chang, R., Kaltani, L., and Loayza, N. V. (2009). 'Openness can be good for growth: The role of policy complementarities'. *Journal of Development Economics*, 90(1): 33–49.

Chowdhury, A. and Islam, I. (2014). 'Is there an optimal debt-to-GDP ratio?'. *VoxEU Debate on the Global Crisis*, 9.

Dabla-Norris, M. E., and Srivisal, M. N. (2013). *Revisiting the link between finance and macroeconomic volatility*. Washington, DC: International Monetary Fund.

di Giovanni, Julian and Andrei A. Levchenko (2009). 'Trade openness and volatility'. *Review of Economics and Statistics*, 91(3) (August): 558–585.

Dollar, D., and Kraay, A. (2003). 'Institutions, trade, and growth'. *Journal of Monetary Economics*, 50(1): 133–162.

Driscoll, J. C. and Kraay, A. C. (1998). 'Consistent covariance matrix estimation with spatially dependent panel data'. *Review of economics and statistics*, 80(4): 549–560.

Easterly, W. and Kraay, A. (2000). 'Small States, small problems? income, growth, and volatility in small states'. *World Development*, 28(11): 2013–2027.

Easterly, W., Islam, R., and Stiglitz, J. E. (2001). 'Shaken and stirred: explaining growth volatility'. *Annual World Bank conference on development economics*, 2000: 191–211

Fatás, A. and Mihov, I. (2013). 'Policy volatility, institutions and economic growth'. *Review of Economics and Statistics*, 45(2): 362–376.

García-Herrero, A. and Vilarrubia, J. (2006). *The Laffer curve of macroeconomic volatility and growth: can it be explained by the different nature of crises?* Paper prepared by A. García-Herrero and J. Vilarrubia presented at the XI Meeting of the Network of America Central Bank Researchers hosted by Banco Central de la República Argentina, in Buenos Aires, November 22–24.

Gavin, M. and Hausmann, R. (1998). 'Macroeconomic Volatility and economic development'. In *The Political Dimension of Economic Growth*. Basingstoke: Palgrave Macmillan, 97–116.

Goldberg, P. J. and Pavcnik, N. (2004). Trade, inequality, and poverty: what do we know? Evidence from recent trade liberalization episodes in developing countries. NBER Working Paper 10593 Growth Volatility. In Boris Pleskovic and Nicholas H. Stern (eds), *Annual World Bank Conference on Development Economics*: 191–211. Washington, DC: The World Bank.

Ghosh, A. and Ramakrishnan, U. (2006). 'Current account deficits: is there a problem?'. *Finance and Development*, 43(4).

Haddad, M., Lim, J. J. and Saborawski, C. (2010). *Trade openness reduces growth volatility when countries are well diversified*. World Bank Policy Research Working Paper No. 5222.

Hegerty, S. W. (2014). *Openness and macroeconomic volatility: do development factors drive such ambiguous results?*. Department of Economics, Northeastern Illinois University.

Hnatkovska, V. and Loayza, N. (2005). 'Volatility and growth'. In Aizenmann, J. and Pinto, B. (eds), *Managing Economic Volatility and Crises*. Cambridge: Cambridge University Press.

Jackman, M. (2014). 'Output volatility and tourism specialization in small island developing states'. *Tourism Economics*, 20(3): 527–544.

Jensen, M. (2004) *Income volatility in small and developing economies: export concentration matters*. Geneva: World Trade Organization.

Karras, G. and Song, F. (1996). 'Sources of business-cycle volatility: An exploratory study on a sample of OECD countries'. *Journal of Macroeconomics*, 18(4): 621–637

Koren, M. and TenreyroS. (2007). 'Volatility and development'. *The Quarterly Journal of Economics*, 122(1): 243–287.

Kose, M. A., Prasad, E. and Terrones, M. (2004). 'How do trade and financial integration affect the relationship between growth and volatility?' Washington, DC: International Monetary Fund. Mimeographed document.

Krishna, P. and Levchenko, A. (2009). *Comparative advantage, complexity and volatility*. NBER Working Paper No. 14965.

Loayza, N. V., Ranciere, N. and Serven, L. and Ventura, J. (2007). 'Macroeconomic volatility and welfare in developing countries: an introduction'. *The World Bank Economic Review*, 21(3): 343–357.

Loayza, N. V. and Raddatz, C. (2007). 'The structural determinants of external vulnerability the structural determinants of external vulnerability'. *The World Bank Economic Review*, 21(3): 359–387.

Malik, A. and Temple, J. (2009). 'The geography of output volatility'. *Journal of Development Economics*, 90(2): 163–178.

Meschi, E. and Vivarelli, M. (2007). *Trade openness and income inequality in developing countries*. Working Paper. Coventry: University of Warwick, Centre for the Study of Globalisation and Regionalisation. Working Papers No. 232.

Montalbano, P. L. (2011). 'Trade openness and developing countries' vulnerability: concepts, misconceptions, and directions for research'. *World Development*, 39(9): 1489–1502.

Ramey, G., Ramey, V. (1995). 'Cross-country evidence on the link between volatility and growth', *The American Economic Review*, 85(5): 1138–1151.

Rodrik, D. (1999). 'Where did all the growth go? external shocks, social conflict, and growth collapses'. *Journal of Economic Growth*, 4(4): 385–412.

Tornell, A., Westermann, F., Martinez, L. (2003). Liberalization, growth and financial crises: lessons from Mexico and the developing world. *Brookings Papers on Economic Activity* No. 2.

Winters, L. A. (2004). 'Trade liberalisation and economic performance: An overview'. *The Economic Journal*, 114(4–F21).

Yanikkaya, H. (2003). 'Trade openness and economic growth: a cross-country empirical investigation'. *Journal of Development Economics*, 72(1): 57–89.

3

Trade, fiscal and welfare considerations of the CARIFORUM-EU Economic Partnership Agreement: a CARICOM perspective

Roger Hosein, Rebecca Gookool and Troy Lorde

1 Introduction

The economies of the Caribbean region have long maintained a trading relationship with the economies of the European Union (EU), emanating no doubt from the colonial history between the two regions. Indeed, since colonial times to the post-independence period, preferential trading arrangements have existed between the EU and its former hinterlands. These arrangements were articulated in the various dispensations of the Yaounde Convention (1963, 1969) and the Lomé Convention (1975, 1979, 1984, 1990, 1995).[1]

In the 1990s, the nature and mode of trading relations between the EU and the Caribbean began to change with the establishment of the World Trade Organization (WTO) in 1995. The conditional necessity of requesting and obtaining waivers for preferences from the latter, enlargement of the EU trading bloc, and the agitation of the US banana producers operating in Central America compounded the pressures towards more liberalized trading regimes. This led to the Cotonou Agreement, the successor of the various Lomé Conventions, which included articles of trade reciprocity and allowances for region-specific agreements between the EU and the geographical blocs of the ACP countries. As the section of the Cotonou Agreement that dealt with trade was deemed incompatible with the rules of free trade of the WTO, this necessitated the signing of Economic Partnership Agreements (EPAs) between the EU and specific blocs of ACP countries (Mandelson, 2007).[2] CARIFORUM (a bloc comprising CARICOM, excluding Montserrat, and the Dominican Republic) negotiated the Caribbean-specific regional EPA with the EU. The primary objective of the CARIFORUM-EU EPA, which came into effect in 2008, was to establish improved trading opportunities for CARIFORUM economies with the EU, and thereby encourage diversification and economic development in the region.

In this chapter, the authors analyse the trade, fiscal and welfare impacts of the EPA to date within the context of the initial five-year period, 2008–2015, of the Agreement. It provides analysts and policy makers with a robust discussion on the trade displacement, trade diversion and trade creation impacts of the Agreement, the possible implications of the same and permits more efficient policy responses. Trade displacement is treated here as the substitution of imports from a regional partner with imports from an extra regional partner. Trade diversion is explained as the substitution of imports from an efficient extra regional partner with imports from a less efficient partner and trade creation is explained as the increase in imports from a partner in the context of a trade agreement. The chapter utilizes three permutations of the partial equilibrium approach; specifically, the Greenaway and Milner (2004), SMART and the TRIST frameworks (these methods are elaborated below).

The discussion proceeds as follows. Section 2. presents the literature review followed by a detailed overview of the methods in Section 3. The results of the simulations will be presented in Section 4. The chapter then concludes with some generalized policy directives.

2 Literature review

Since the mid-1990s, amidst the push towards greater liberalization of trade, several studies (Andriamananjara et al., 2009; Brenton et al., 2007; Gomez, 2007; Greenaway and Milner, 2004; Hosein, 2008; Hosein et al., 2013; Lorde and Alleyne, 2016; Mahabir, 2011; Marshall et al., 2009; Preville, 2006; Thomy et al., 2013) have examined the potential impact of EU EPAs on various geographical blocs of the ACP including the Caribbean region. Indeed, these studies profile the impact of the same on trade, welfare and government revenues considering the potential loss in tariff revenues. The models applied in these studies can be generally categorized either as general equilibrium models or partial equilibrium models.

General equilibrium models can be used to simulate the simultaneous effect of a change in trade policy on several related and interrelated markets or industries. This type of approach captures the multi-sectoral interaction of a specific shock and provides a comprehensive outlook of its impact. Although the general equilibrium model has comprehensiveness as an advantage, the data required to utilize such a model is extensive. Consequently, the application of such models to developing country cases, where data availability is a major challenge, is infrequent. As such, the partial equilibrium model is used more frequently.

Partial equilibrium models are sufficiently versatile to provide the static impacts of trade policy reform on trade trends and tariff revenues. In this regard, partial equilibrium models are well suited to provide indicators of the short-term impact of a given shock on a particular market (Zgovu and Kweka, 2007). Partial equilibrium models compare trade creation and trade diversion effects as a basis for the measurement of welfare. The generalized assumption is that tariff reductions will be translated into reductions in the price of the final product to consumers.[3] Although partial equilibrium approaches do admit some challenges,[4] their application provides a basis for conjecture, in comparing the impact of liberalization across countries, or over time for a single economy. A brief overview of the literature that applies specifically to the impact (potential and actual) of the CARIFORUM-EU EPA will therefore be discussed against this background.

Several studies investigate the EPA's impact at a regional level. Nicholls et al. (2001) use the Almost Ideal Demand System (AIDS) to forecast the fiscal effects of potential Free Trade Area (FTA) forces between the EU and CARICOM. These researchers conclude that CARICOM members would lose fiscal revenues if an FTA were formed with the EU. In particular, the authors estimate that the OECS bloc would be more significantly affected than the rest of CARICOM, projecting that the extent of the loss would be approximately 33% of tax revenue earned. Nicholls et al. (2001) recommend that CARICOM members should implement specific mechanisms for distributing the gains from any agreement in a manner that would mitigate the potential fiscal fallout. Such mechanisms would also have to be complemented by revenue-generating alternatives as a means of reducing dependence on trade tariffs. Mahabir (2011) uses a gravity model approach to assess how the EPA could affect CARICOM exports to the EU. The author finds that the region as a whole would not experience a significant increase in exports to the EU as a consequence of the EPA; however, members classified as less developed might have some success in penetrating the EU market.

Other researchers conducted country studies to assess the EPA. Gomez (2007) examined its implications for Belize. The primary method of analysis was a general assessment of documents and reports complemented by a series of focus groups and in-depth interviews with public and private sector stakeholders. The paper also developed two liberalization scenarios using 2004 data extracted from the ASYCUDA system in Belize's Customs Department for every national tariff line disaggregated at the HS 8-digit level, along with both the volume and value of imports. Results suggested that Belize should use a phased approach to liberalization, as this would allow the country to protect its main revenue earners and domestic industries from import competition (Gomez, 2007). Marshall et al. (2009), using a dynamic partial equilibrium model applied to the Jamaican case, find that trade liberalization under the CARIFORUM-EU EPA had no significant impact on GDP growth, inflation, imports and fiscal revenues. The authors conclude, however, that challenges would arise for Jamaica in taking advantage of the benefits on offer from the EPA. Meyn et al. (2009) focused on the development component of the EPA to ascertain the extent of support that might be needed. The simulated revenue effects revealed that significant losses could occur. Meyn et al. (2009) estimate that by 2013 annual revenue losses for Barbados would be approximately €2–6 million, €3 million for Suriname, and €0.5–2 million for Guyana. By 2023, annual losses are expected to more than double: €6–18 million for Barbados, €11–12 million for Suriname, and €1–5 million for Guyana. Likewise, Stevens et al. (2009) projects that by 2033, when all liberalization schedules are to have been completed, annual revenue losses will be €3.1 million for Dominica, €186.3 million for the Bahamas, and €41.3 million for Trinidad and Tobago (T&T). Table 3.1 provides the summary findings from this study.

Welfare changes are likely to result from implementation of free trade agreements. One of the seminal works on the concept of welfare within the context of the CARIFORUM-EU EPA is provided by Greenaway and Milner (2004). The authors developed two frameworks for the evaluation of welfare effects, one under conditions of perfect import source substitution and the other under conditions of imperfect import source substitution. Dodson (2013) apply the partial equilibrium model, as proposed by Greenaway and Milner (2004), to assess the static welfare effects of the EPA on the Guyanese economy; the imperfect substitution framework was used in this case. The author concludes that intra-regional and non-EU extra-regional trade diversion effects are likely to be significant, especially given that the EU is not a traditional trade partner of Guyana. Hosein (2008) in evaluating the impact of the EPA on the Trinidad and Tobago economy with the Greenaway and Milner framework, estimates that in 2005, trade creation amounted to EC$266.8 million (US$98.81 million), while trade displacement and trade diversion were EC$86.1 million (US$31.89 million) and EC$5,507.7 million (US$2,039.89 million) respectively. For 2008, trade creation was estimated at US$161 million, and trade displacement and trade diversion at US$37.69 million and US$3,278.3 million respectively. Khadan and Hosein (2014) also employed the Greenaway and Milner (2004) approach to evaluating the impact of the EPA on the selected CARICOM economies. They conclude that CARICOM economies would experience negative welfare changes emanating from a fall in fiscal revenues associated with the EPA, corroborating earlier findings by Greenaway and Milner.

Table 3.1 Hypothetical annual revenue loss (€000)

	2011–2013	*By 2033*
Antigua and Barbuda	7625	19241
Bahamas	133379	186303
Barbados	54	22016
Belize	383	5856
Dominica	30	3117
Grenada	162	4219
Guyana	22	5168
Haiti	0.02	4113
Jamaica	251	26845
St Kitts and Nevis	44	3861
St Lucia	13	32680
St Vincent and the Grenadines	2511	40068
Suriname	1239	16741
Trinidad and Tobago	152	41295

Source: Stevens *et al.* (2009).

In 2013, Hosein *et al.* evaluated the impact of the EPA using a host of complementary methods, one of which focused on the impact on trade and welfare using the SMART application, a partial equilibrium model.[5] The findings are summarized in Tables 3.2 and 3.3. In the first instance, Hosein *et al.* show that for the countries listed, while trade with the EU is expected to increase, trade with the non-EU rest of the world is expected to decline. Notably, the magnitude of the decline in trade with the non-EU rest of the world is less than the magnitude of the increase in trade with the EU (Table 3.2). Fiscal revenues are expected to decline and so too welfare in the post-EPA period (Table 3.3).

Lorde and Alleyne (2016) applied TRIST,[6] an excel-based partial equilibrium model developed by the World Bank, to the Barbados case. The research concludes that the overall welfare effects on the Barbados economy are likely to be relatively small. The authors used 2013 data and found that trade diversion from CARIFORUM amounted to Bds$0.44 million (US$0.22 million) and from the rest of the world Bds$7.62 million[7] (US$3.81 million). By way of comparison, in this paper, the authors also estimated that in 2013, Barbados' trade diversion from CARIFORUM would be US$0.22 million and from the rest of the world at US$5.5 million.

Table 3.2 Change in export revenue of specific CARICOM economies (US$ million)

Country	*Non- EU Rest of the Word*	*EU*
Guyana (2011)	−10.41	37.75
St Kitts and Nevis (2009)	−1.84	4.11
St Lucia (2007)	−4.63	12.48
Barbados (2007)	−21.24	56.94

Source: Hosein *et al.* (2013).

Table 3.3 Change in fiscal revenue and welfare (US$ million)

	Change in Revenue	*Change in Net Welfare*
Guyana (2011)	−12.983	−11.039
St Kitts and Nevis (2009)	−1.809	−1.483
St Lucia (2007)	−10.699	−9.525
Barbados (2007)	−29.579	−23.468

Source: Hosein *et al.* (2013).

Table 3.4 provides a summary of different impact assessment studies of the CARIFORUM-EU EPA on CARIFORUM economies.

The landscape on the assessment of the EPA literature, as discussed above, is based on a series of conjecture, assumptions and simulations to estimate the impact of the Agreement in the narrow case and of trade liberalization in the wider context on the region. Though applied to select countries in some cases, the analyses reviewed are not an adequate explanation of the existing trends in trade or welfare for several reasons: not all aspects of the Agreement have been fully implemented by all countries[8] and up-to-date data is not readily available for review in some cases; and, the majority of the region-specific cases discussed used partial equilibrium models, which focus on the impact of only one agreement which is part of the regional landscape.

In the next section, the partial equilibrium empirical approaches used in the chapter are described. This is followed by the empirical results. The chapter then concludes with a discussion of the policy relevance and implications.

3 Methods

Analysis of adjustment outcomes caused by trade policy reform is critical to policy makers, especially in developing economies, as they seek to navigate the global trade landscape and better negotiate for incentive structures bilaterally or multilaterally. Specifically, such analysis informs the policy response at the domestic level in relation to sector-specific and even macroeconomic concerns. An immediate concern, especially for lower-income economies, is the impact of trade reform on fiscal revenues; in particular, tariff revenues in many small developing economies constitute a major source of government revenues. Moreover, trade reform also affects domestic employment and prices, which in turn affect households, particularly the most vulnerable. In this regard, understanding the adjustment implications of trade reform can contribute to the efficient design of the same, as well as to the implementation of support mechanisms to reduce the negative externalities associated with adjustment.

Consequently, this chapter employs three partial equilibrium approaches to evaluate the trade and welfare effects of the EPA on CARICOM economies. The authors propose that such an approach is versatile enough to capture the static effects of the impact of liberalization on import quantities, tariff revenues, and hence welfare. The models also permit a high level of aggregation such as applied by Greenaway and Milner (2004). A high level of aggregation allows for the analysis of sector-specific and country-specific impacts of tariff changes.

There is wide consensus that the results of partial (and general) equilibrium models are sensitive to elasticities. Indeed, this is underpinned by the principle of Armington elasticities, that is, the degree of substitution between different import sources. This key behavioural parameter

Table 3.4 CARIFORUM-EU impact assessment studies on CARIFORUM economies

Author/Study	Methods	Trade bloc/Country	Main findings
Nicholls *et al.* (2001)	Almost Ideal Demand System (AIDS)	CARICOM	The conclusion of the research is that the smaller economies within the Caribbean Basin would experience greater loss in fiscal revenues than the MDCs in the region.
Greenaway and Milner (2004)	Partial equilibrium analysis	CARICOM	CARICOM economies are expected to experience intra and extra regional trade diversion effects which negatively impact of overall welfare levels.
Preville (2006)	Mixed methods – assessment of reports and documents. Stakeholder interviews and focus groups	Windward Islands	Windward islands are likely to experience a fall un tariff revenues if trade with the EU is liberalized.
Gomez (2007)	Mixed methods – assessment of reports and documents. Stakeholder interviews and focus groups. Institute of Development Studies methodology	Belize	Belize is expected to experience some degree of welfare loss as a result of intra-regional trade diversion but this is expected to be low given that CARICOM is not a major trading partner of Belize.
Hosein (2008)	Partial equilibrium model	T&T	The T&T economy experienced a loss in welfare in the EPA environment. Between 1998 and 2005 the welfare loss declines.
Marshall *et al.* (2009)	Dynamic partial equilibrium model	Jamaica	Simulation impact on GDP, imports, inflation and revenues were minimal.
Mahabir (2011)	Gravity model	CARICOM	The LDCs within CARICOM have been able to benefit from the EPA. The MDCs within CARICOM however have not been able to use the preferential access under the Agreement to effectively penetrate the EU market.
Hosein *et al.* (2013, unpublished study)	Mixed methods – trade competitiveness, variance decomposition and partial equilibrium analysis	CARIFORUM	The results of this study indicate that the Dominican Republic is more likely to benefit from the EPA than the CARICOM economies.
Lorde and Alleyne (2016)	Partial equilibrium model using TRIST	Barbados	The overall trade and development impacts of the EPA on Barbados are expected to be small.

Source: Authors' compilation.

drives the quantitative and qualitative results used by policy makers (McDaniel and Balistreri, 2002). Models which evaluate the impact of trade policy are often premised on the conversion of that policy into price effects. Such models use the extent of these price shifts to determine how indicators, such as trade flows, output, government revenues and hence welfare, are impacted by various reforms. The direction and magnitude of the impact depends on the size and nature of the shock emanating from the policy change, as well as the behavioural relationships which are assumed by the model.

The aforementioned behavioural relationships are generally represented as elasticities, reflecting the responsiveness of one set of variables to changes in another set. Hence, knowledge of elasticities is critical for considering the impact of policy changes. Armington elasticities are therefore an important component of this set of parameters. Each of the various frameworks utilized, applies the Armington principle, empirically. Despite being widely applied throughout the literature, there is no single set of accepted specifications of Armington elasticities. The most widely used estimates, though, are drawn from Deardorff and Stern's (1986) research or from the various general equilibrium models such as the Global Trade Analysis Project.[9]

This study, utilizes the following frameworks employed extensively in the literature as the preferred tools of applied partial equilibrium analysis, as complementary tools for evaluating the impact of the EPA on CARICOM countries: Greenaway and Milner's (2004) imperfect substitution case, the SMART Analysis (from the World Integrated Trade Solution (WITS) software) and the Trade Reform Impact Simulation Tool (TRIST) Analysis. TRIST is the most recent iteration of the framework and provides a comprehensive model which enables the researcher to identify the impact on multiple markets.

Comparison of Frameworks

Table 3.5 presents a comparison of the basic model assumptions, input data, markets considered, import and trade source substitution elasticity measures as well as the elasticity of supply.

Simulations: trade and fiscal analysis

Greenaway and Milner (GM) (2004)

To evaluate the trade and fiscal impacts of the EPA using the Greenaway and Milner (2004) framework, SITC 2-digit data was obtained for all CARICOM economies (excluding Haiti) for 2008 and 2014.[10] Import demand and substitution elasticities are not readily available for CARICOM and accordingly these parameters were drawn from the work of Greenaway and Milner.[11] Elasticities for a particular product group were assumed to be the same for all CARICOM countries. The current 2-digit tariff levels were also obtained from Greenaway and Milner. The authors adjusted the Greenaway and Milner elasticity assumptions to obtain the various estimates presented below.

Following the research of Thomy et al. (2013), trade source substitution estimates of 1, 0.75 and 0.5 respectively were employed.[12] Additionally, based on the default of 1.5 used by both the WITS and TRIST frameworks, the authors also applied this elasticity assumption to the GM framework. The authors report the results based on a trade source substitution elasticity of 0.5.[13] This estimate is much lower than that assumed by Greenaway and Milner (2004). Further, the application of a single trade source substitution elasticity effectively restrains the model to two rather than three markets, that is, the EU and the non-EU rest of the world. In particular, the system treats the EU as the market in which the trade reform occurs, holding the original conditions constant in all other markets.

Table 3.5 Comparison of methods and assumptions

	Greenaway and Milner (2004)	*WITS / SMART*	*TRIST*
Model	Imperfect substitution based on Armington Theory	Imperfect substitution based on Armington Theory	Imperfect substitution based on Armington Theory
Input data	SITC 2 digit	HS data (up to 6 digit)	HS data (up to 8 digit) ISIC data can also be used
Number of markets considered	3 – Partner Country, EU and Non-EU Rest of the World	2 – EU and the Non-EU Rest of the World	The system can consider up to 14 trade blocs (including ROW)
Import demand elasticities	Estimates were obtained from a study by Stern (1976)	Empirically estimated for each country up to HS 6-digit level – (Kee *et al.*, 2008)	Use a default of 0.5
Import source substitution elasticities	Global Trade Analysis Project (GTAP) behavioural parameters (Hertel and Tsigas, 1997)	Uses a default of 1.5	Uses a default of 1.5
Elasticity of supply	Not empirically considered by Greenaway and Milner but the model framework assumes that supply is infinitely elastic	Uses a default of 99 representing infinite elasticity of supply	Not explicitly considered but implicitly assumes infinite supply

Source: Authors' compilation.

SMART

Observations to run the SMART simulation were obtained from TRAINS, which can also be accessed via WITS. TRAINS contains annual tariff structures at the MFN Applied and Preferential rates, some information on non-tariff barriers (since 1988) and the national tariff line levels. The national tariff structure provided is country-specific and contains as much as 15,000 distinct tariff lines. TRAINS also contains import statistics by country of origin up to the HS-6-digit level. SMART automatically imports data from TRAINS based on the scenario designed by the analyst.

TRIST

The input data for TRIST was also obtained from TRAINS. While the framework allows for the inclusion of actual data collected at the various ports of entry, practical reasons prevent the authors from doing so in each of the countries under study (e.g. length of time, resources). The assumptions applied were therefore the following:

1   the statutory tariff is equivalent to the tariff received;
2   VAT was applied to imports at the going national rates; and
3   imports were not subject to excise duties.

4 Results

This section presents the results and analysis from each of the frameworks discussed previously. The estimates vary in terms of scale; however, the general trend identified by each method is consistent. The variations in the estimates are due in particular to the application of varying tariff levels, different levels of product aggregation and different substitution elasticities. The GM framework applies the model parameters provided by Greenaway and Milner (2004). The SMART analysis uses in-built parameters. The data sourced to undertake SMART was also used in the TRIST model. TRIST is a more advanced comprehensive framework than SMART.

Trade effects

Table 3.6 provides comparative estimates of the trade effects due to the EPA using the Greenaway and Milner (2004), WITS and TRIST methods. Results show that the extent of trade displacement across all three methods increases over the time period captioned for Antigua and Barbuda, Bahamas, Barbados, Dominica, Guyana, Jamaica and Suriname, while trade diversion increases over the period for Bahamas, Belize, Guyana, Jamaica and Suriname.

Under each permutation also, there is a significant amount of trade displacement and trade diversion. This is a significant finding, especially given that one of the main goals of the EPA is to boost the level of intra-regional trade.[14] Further, the potential loss in welfare as a result of trade diversion must be considered within the context of other bilateral and multilateral trade and development agreements to which the region is party.

Fiscal and welfare effects

The fiscal effects of the EPA, as shown in Table 3.7, reveal that in each case, CARICOM countries experienced a decline in fiscal revenues. In addition, each model indicates that losses would increase over time for Barbados, Belize, Dominica, Jamaica and Suriname.

In terms of welfare, unlike GM and SMART, TRIST does not explicitly calculate this variable. As such the authors present the estimates generated using the GM and WITS frameworks only. The welfare position of the economy is evaluated as a function of the change in trade and fiscal positions. The results for the impact on welfare are presented in Table 3.8. Results indicate that in all cases the economic welfare of the identified economies declines. This is a critical finding which should inform the nature of the parameters of the negotiations of the EPA in the current five-year review. Indeed, what is needed is more targeted, deliberate, mechanisms which can reduce the impact of the losses being experienced by CARICOM economies.

5 Conclusion

Non-reciprocal preferential market access has been a feature of the trade policy landscape for the greater part of the 20th century; however, this trend has been changing, becoming less pervasive and more targeted to special cases, especially in the last decade. In the context of the EPA, the EU has been pressing for the shift away from preferences to a 'freer' form of trade relations with ACP countries. This is one of the main motivations for the region-specific negotiations of EPAs. The literature, however, remains unclear as to the net impact of reciprocity in the first case of a more liberalized trade platform in the wider context.

This chapter contributes to the literature by providing a more robust application of the concept of the customs union and its potential economic and welfare impact on participating economies. The chapter reviewed the trade and fiscal impacts of the EPA on CARICOM

Table 3.6 A comparison of the trade effects from the EPA, using various partial equilibrium models ('000 US$)

		Trade displacement effect(change in M1)			Trade diversion(change in M2)			Trade creation(change in M3)		
		GM	WITS	TRIST	GM	WITS	TRIST	GM	WITS	TRIST
Antigua and Barbuda	2009	(3,552.50)	(720.20)	(420.80)	(16,782.40)	(4,312.10)	(2,492.70)	2,679.40	2,320.78	5,989.21
	2015	(3,106.20)	(831.30)	(471.60)	(19,350.70)	(4,197.60)	(2,378.80)	2,660.60	1,288.95	5,716.54
Bahamas	2010	(3,278.50)	(17.90)	(12.50)	(124,860.40)	(12,031.40)	(5,462.50)	2,306.10	312.06	11,562.45
	2014	(7,707.70)	(53.40)	(36.30)	(155,359.80)	(12,987.30)	(6,812.00)	5,477.70	(1,996.01)	13,178.12
Barbados	2010	(6,439.40)	(1,175.80)	(719.10)	(35,945.40)	(14,139.50)	(8,196.30)	7,399.00	6,312.54	17,754.79
	2013	(24,137.20)	(1,708.00)	(220.50)	(38,884.10)	(10,412.20)	(5,545.70)	8,134.00	7,059.95	14,391.94
Belize	2008	(639.00)	(60.10)	(37.90)	(23,824.60)	(1,970.90)	(1,161.50)	1,604.10	172.64	2,333.21
	2014	(2,105.00)	(8.30)	(2.40)	(43,238.20)	(3,557.10)	(2,076.60)	2,387.20	7,608.36	6,515.59
Dominica	2010	(2,790.20)	(235.10)	(141.10)	(6,963.60)	(1,240.20)	(719.10)	920.50	287.18	1,697.19
	2012	(3,202.60)	(287.20)	(173.80)	(6,208.60)	(1,310.90)	(736.80)	987.00	263.58	1,790.82
Grenada (2009 for GM est.)	2008	(4,347.20)	(635.10)	(369.70)	(7,823.40)	(2,708.90)	(1,561.40)	1,485.20	473.67	3,738.18
	2010	(4,327.20)	(379.80)	(217.40)	(7,994.60)	(943.10)	(533.30)	1,485.20	757.32	1,722.40
Guyana	2008	(15,523.70)	(913.50)	(574.40)	(29,030.40)	(4,484.20)	(2,595.70)	5,090.50	8,445.41	7,179.01
	2015	(19,099.00)	(1,307.50)	(758.30)	(47,705.70)	(4,486.50)	(2,705.80)	5,431.60	5,795.22	6,959.99
Jamaica	2010	(43,003.60)	(1,514.80)	(939.60)	(185,347.40)	(26,781.90)	(14,983.80)	16,279.00	7,541.31	31,496.11
	2013	(51,070.00)	(2,397.10)	(1,456.80)	(213,443.90)	(36,423.10)	(20,978.80)	17,852.40	8,520.95	42,262.47
St Kitts	2008	(2,098.80)	(242.20)	(120.60)	(12,201.20)	(1,550.80)	(841.30)	1,099.30	339.80	1,954.71
	2011	(1,612.10)	(146.10)	(91.50)	(9,891.80)	(1,307.50)	(751.30)	818.30	(6.07)	1,575.17
St Lucia (2008 for GM est.)	2010	(9,899.50)	(823.80)	(467.50)	(20,913.30)	(2,442.50)	(1,377.80)	2,880.10	2,227.46	4,221.93
	2014	(8,862.10)	(297.60)	(162.90)	(18,482.30)	(2,259.20)	(1,243.60)	3,346.90	1,424.66	3,289.75
St Vincent	2010	(6,305.90)	(610.40)	(358.70)	(9,768.20)	(2,474.40)	(1,469.20)	1,821.60	811.08	3,491.80
	2011	(7,141.10)	(594.80)	(353.00)	(9,379.90)	(2,361.90)	(1,384.70)	1,717.80	608.59	3,255.68

Table 3.6 (continued)

		Trade displacement effect(change in M1)			Trade diversion(change in M2)			Trade creation(change in M3)		
		GM	WITS	TRIST	GM	WITS	TRIST	GM	WITS	TRIST
Suriname	2009	(14,068.30)	(3,119.50)	(1,771.00)	(28,528.60)	(14,812.80)	(8,682.60)	13,301.60	14,974.74	25,074.18
	2013	**(24,198.90)**	**(3,371.50)**	**(1,899.30)**	**(42,228.70)**	**(15,553.40)**	**(9,050.30)**	21,166.10	15,940.27	26,582.59
Trinidad /Tobago (2008 for GM est.)	2010	(7,853.70)	(1,168.00)	(639.80)	(333,307.90)	(39,687.10)	(22,373.70)	40,410.30	58,396.51	49,280.23
(2010 for GM est.)	2012	(7,851.50)	(843.20)	(516.90)	(244,093.60)	(38,548.80)	(23,033.60)	20,893.00	9,977.46	45,166.59

Source: Authors' compilation.

Table 3.7 Change in fiscal revenue ('000 US$)

		GM	Direction	WITS	Direction	TRIST	Direction
Antigua and Barbuda	2009	(8,785.27)	←	(7,853.00)	→	(8,079.04)	→
	2015	(9,067.25)		(7,265.62)		(7,487.39)	
Bahamas	2010	(22,583.72)	←	(20,114.20)	→	(17,468.67)	→
	2014	(33,762.80)		(11,170.16)		(17,062.07)	
Barbados	2010	(22,951.25)	←	(23,026.27)	←	(23,928.09)	←
	2013	**(25,021.00)**		**(25,318.48)**		**(25,992.54)**	
Belize	2008	(6,766.44)	←	(2,870.43)	←	(2,868.03)	←
	2014	**(11,470.84)**		**(11,212.78)**		**(11,243.66)**	
Dominica	2010	(3,064.01)	←	(2,160.46)	←	(2,215.52)	←
	2012	**(3,131.65)**		**(2,237.27)**		**(2,298.91)**	
Grenada (2009 for GM est.)	2008	(4,505.51)	←	(4,401.24)	→	(4,441.41)	→
	2010	(4,517.32)		(2,363.88)		(2,480.73)	
Guyana	2008	(15,068.25)	←	(10,119.69)	→	(10,556.93)	→
	2015	(17,540.18)		(8,757.84)		(9,266.96)	
Jamaica	2010	(65,399.85)	←	(40,622.06)	←	(41,687.30)	←
	2013	**(71,571.08)**		**(50,094.95)**		**(51,746.41)**	
St Kitts	2008	(4,382.14)	→	(2,699.88)	→	(2,563.73)	→
	2011	(3,336.73)		(1,840.29)		(1,892.31)	
St Lucia (2008 for GM est.)	2010	(9,706.44)	←	(6,120.42)	→	(5,809.07)	→
	2014	(10,365.63)		(4,815.86)		(4,989.00)	
St Vincent	2010	(5,522.27)	→	(4,201.07)	→	(4,314.20)	→
	2011	(5,231.86)		(3,843.98)		(3,940.12)	

Table 3.7 (continued)

		GM	Direction	WTTS	Direction	TRIST	Direction
Suriname	2009	(33,900.17)	↑	(36,392.78)	↑	(37,080.05)	↑
	2013	**(52,900.83)**		**(38,501.82)**		**(39,491.83)**	
Trinidad and Tobago (2008 for GM est.)	2010	(128,453.93)	→	(73,832.36)	→	(75,678.34)	→
(2010 for GM est.)	2012	(77,023.45)		(51,720.30)		(53,655.15)	

Source: Computed.

Note: bold type indicates increasing fiscal losses.

Table 3.8 Change in welfare ('000 US$)

		GM	WITS
Antigua and Barbuda	2009	(8,575.56)	(6,851.40)
	2015	(8,841.76)	(6,429.26)
Bahamas	2010	(22,425.61)	(16,488.98)
	2014	(33,348.98)	(9,074.61)
Barbados	2010	(22,328.06)	(19,611.60)
	2013	(24,348.26)	(21,164.70)
Belize	2008	(6,645.30)	(2,556.07)
	2014	(11,280.95)	(10,238.79)
Dominica	2010	(2,994.09)	(1,897.73)
	2012	(3,056.21)	(2,001.67)
Grenada	2008	(4,399.73)	(3,971.71)
(2009 for Greenaway and Milner estimate)	2010	(4,411.55)	(2,564.63)
Guyana	2008	(14,741.41)	(8,246.89)
	2015	(17,157.03)	(7,052.22)
Jamaica	2010	(64,108.06)	(35,662.99)
	2013	(70,145.59)	(55,835.16)
St Kitts	2008	(4,292.58)	(2,438.18)
	2011	(3,271.49)	(1,657.18)
St Lucia (2008 for Greenaway and Milner estimate)	2010	(9,485.34)	(5,377.91)
	2014	(10,110.38)	(4,290.43)
St Vincent	2010	(5,385.04)	(3,651.21)
	2011	(5,102.62)	(3,300.88)
Suriname	2009	(32,986.57)	(32,765.36)
	2013	(51,538.59)	(34,934.30)
Trinidad and Tobago (2008 for Greenaway and Milner estimate)	2010	(126,277.05)	(62,099.67)
(2010 for Greenaway and Milner estimate)	2012	(75,694.00)	(46,647.57)

Source: Computed.

economies utilising 3 methods for evaluating the same; the Greenaway and Milner (2004) imperfect substitution model, the SMART framework from WITS, and the TRIST simulation. Though the results vary in terms of magnitude across methods, the simulation results in general, point to the same conclusions; that is, while trade with the EU is expected to rise, imports from CARIFORUM and the non-EU ROW are expected to fall.

Simulations from each method indicate a falloff in fiscal revenues for all countries under study. The results show explicitly that the EPA is welfare-reducing for CARICOM economies, and that interventions to mitigate the losses are urgently needed. In particular, the findings of this chapter reveal that states with increasing welfare losses are Barbados, Belize, Dominica, Jamaica and Suriname, under the assumptions of duty-free and quota free market access.

It may be argued that the Agreement has not delivered the broad-based benefits in terms of trade and welfare gains that were advanced by its proponents. This position, though, should be considered against the background that not all CARICOM economies have fully implemented the Agreement, even though resources under the Agreement have been allocated to support EPA implementation units in each country.[15] Indeed, this was one of the major conclusions of the joint select committee adjourned to review the first five-year period of the agreement. In particular, the report acknowledged the difficulties that the CARIFORUM private sector has in converting the market access under the EPA into meaningful market presence. This situation no doubt exists due to the limited production capacity and structural constraints which face the regional private sector. In this regard therefore, CARICOM economies must consider other revenue-generating interventions for the medium to long term. In this regard, local development production planning is critical for these countries, which must consider the diversification of markets (exports and imports) as a deliberate strategy to strengthening the long-term prospects of their respective economies.

The findings from this and several other studies on the topic, such as those listed in Table 3.4, point to the diversity of effects and therefore a need for continuous engagement of stakeholders, who may be affected by the adjustments associated with EPA. The projected losses in fiscal revenues, to the extent identified in Table 3.7, provide the impetus for the region to collectively address its development issues. Indeed, development interventions such as a regional trade policy, which would include standard protocols for investing and attracting investments, can be beneficial to the regional integration process in the first instance, and to the region's growth prospects over time in the second instance. In addition, continuous engagement of the regional private sector is critical to ensuring that the benefits on offer from the Agreement are fully realized, in the context of an increasingly liberalized trade environment. Under the Agreement, the first round of liberalization took place in 2008. To date, the liberalization experiences, in relation to the specific requirements of the EPA, differ among individual CARICOM economies. Consider in particular that the exports of most CARIFORUM economies are concentrated in mineral- and other traditional commodity-based sectors. Trade in new sectors have for the most part been limited given that these economies have not diversified to the extent anticipated by Article 8 (IV) of the Agreement. It should be noted though that the Dominican Republic has had some success in terms of market access for exports of textiles, medical supplies and electronic equipment to the EU.

EPAs are indeed very detailed instruments and since their signing, developing countries, such as those in the Caribbean, have experienced some undesirable adjustment costs. With the CARIFORUM-EU EPA under review, there is room for flexibility in the discussions with the EU in order to mitigate some of the negative impacts experienced thus far. With particular reference to the likely fall off in trade among CARIFORUM members, one of the goals of the EPA, which is to stimulate intra-regional trade, can be questioned, especially in the context of the investments made to support the regional integration process.[16] Further, regional development may be compromised if trade is diverted away from non-EU natural trading partners.

There is therefore also much scope for country-specific work in terms of the implications of the Agreement on the social and economic climate of a given country. The scope of the EPA is wide and the legislative and trade adjustments at the local and regional level are numerous. As a result, delays in full implementation have come from the need to align local frameworks to that required under the Agreement. Indeed, this asymmetry in reform, biased against the region is also contributing to the significant adjustment costs being experienced. EPAs do provide benefits to participating countries; however, the access to these benefits in many regards is qualified or conditional. There is also much room to evaluate the benefits on offer from the Agreement at the individual country level. At the country-specific level, therefore, what is required is the adoption of tools for prospective analysis, supported by continual, detailed surveillance of the productive sectors to determine which may contract in the context of further liberalization under the EPA. This would permit the design of effective policies to support these sectors where deemed nationally appropriate. Sectors that have growth and export-earning potential must be identified or cultivated and intensively developed.

The region as a whole can also leverage the support facilities on offer as part of the EPA itself. In particular, the Agreement provides facilities for 'aid for trade' and other development assistance; for example, the resources on offer from the various European Development Funds to prioritize trade and development interventions for the region, such as addressing the capacity of regional firms to better target extra-regional markets, including the EU. Interventions can also be targeted towards developing niche market opportunities that can be leveraged by the region. To this end, under the Agreement, the EU has allocated funding to the tune of €47 million for the period 2012 to 2015, to support Governments in the modernization of their respective taxation regimes, and for regional businesses to build capacity to meet EU health, safety and environmental standards. These funds are also geared towards supporting the diversification of economies and the development of the regional services sector.

Apart from the EPA, the region as a whole must also deliberately pursue other bilateral and multilateral agreements that are a part of the regional and global landscape. In addition to EPA-specific interventions, CARICOM must recognize that its own legislative and productive frameworks may require restructuring in order to avail the region of opportunities on offer from trade agreements in general. In this regard, CARICOM governments must reduce the time taken to complete such restructuring. Delays are costly in terms of missed opportunities. This includes, regulatory reform, especially in property rights and enforcement, institutional strengthening, cost of business reductions, ease of doing business improvements, diversification of the production base, investment promotion and protection strategies, and coherent, consistent financial and communications platforms. Interventions to support domestic competition, productivity and exports will no doubt benefit the economy on all fronts, to better enable regional economies to engage sustainable trading relationships.

Notes

1 These agreements articulated the relationship between EU (formally the European Economic Community—EEC) and ACP countries towards the aim of strengthening the growth prospects of the ACP economies. They included specific outreach strategies for aid, economic cooperation and political support. A key characteristic of these agreements was that they granted non-reciprocal market access to the EU market by ACP countries. ACP is an organization is composed of 79 African, Caribbean and Pacific states. Information about the ACP is available at www.acp.int/content/secretariat-acp/.

2 Mandelson, Peter, 'Mandelson urges final push in EPA talks', Remarks to the INTA Committee, Brussels, 11 September 2007.

3 This does not always happen in reality as the reduction in tariffs is often appropriated by the importer (or exporter) due to a situation of asymmetries regarding the pass through of tariff changes to consumers (Gasiorek and Winters, 2004). The models used by the authors in this chapter assume that the full change in the tariff is passed on to the consumer as a price adjustment.

4 A criticism of this approach is that it ignores the other welfare effects on an economy such as the resource reallocation process or the changes in the terms of trade, which often occur in an economy subsequent to a liberalization exercise. The partial equilibrium model also generally assumes a common price elasticity demand for imports and substitutability between goods from different import sources. Brenton *et al.* (2007; 2009) reiterates this warning that partial equilibrium models are not "all encompassing" and cannot be used to provide a holistic picture of the macroeconomic cost or benefit of a particular trade reform action.

5 SMART is the simulation framework provided by the World Integrated Trade Solution facility.

6 TRIST – Trade Reform Impact Simulation Tool – The system is geared towards simulating the impact of tariff reforms on fiscal revenues, and imports and protection. The framework also is used to evaluate which sectors in the domestic economy would likely be most affected in terms of employment and output by the change.

7 Refer to Table 10 in Lorde and Alleyne (2016).

8 To date, not all CARIFORUM countries have fully ratified the CARIFORUM-EU EPA. ECDPM (2014) notes that around half of EU and CARIFORUM Member States have ratified the Agreement, and ten out of 15 CARIFORUM countries have given effect to the agreed tariff reductions.

9 Saito (2004) discusses two versions of Armington specifications, defined as weakly separable and strongly separable. The basket of goods defined as weakly separable assumes that the marginal rate of substitution between two goods in the same basket (or the same country) is separable from the rest. For example, the rate of substitution of between two domestically produced goods is not dependent on foreign produced goods (Armington, 1969). Saito (2004) explains this as the intergroup elasticity. Bergstrand (1985) and Feenstra (1994) assume that goods are strongly separable, implying that the marginal rate of substitution between two goods (not only from the same country, but also from different countries) is separable from the rest. For example, the substitution between US and Canadian goods does not depend on German produced goods. This, Saito refers to as the intragroup elasticity.

10 Data from 2008 is available for most countries. For those countries for which 2008 data is unavailable, the next available year is used. The most up to date data for each country is also evaluated. For the majority of countries, the most up to date data is 2014.

11 Greenaway and Milner originally obtained import demand elasticities from Stern (1976) and substitution elasticities from the Global Trade Analysis Project behavioural parameters (Hertel and Tsigas, 1997). The import demand elasticities for 2-digit HS code were matched to SITC 2-digit commodity groups in order to develop the model applied in this chapter.

12 The authors used varying elasticities to show that impact on welfare of differing assumptions, concluding that in the case of Botswana, the EPA was improving.

13 The authors are of the view that a smaller trade source substitution elasticity is relevant especially given that on average, for the period 2000–2014, less than 10% of imports originated from the EU. This trend provides some indication that non-EU markets are a more significant import source for the region. For this reason, also, the demand elasticity for EU goods was reduced to 0.5.

14 According to Article 1 of the Economic Partnership Agreement, one of the main objectives of the agreement is to, promote regional integration, economic cooperation and good governance.... for trade and investment between the Parties and in the CARIFORUM region and to promote the gradual integration of the CARIFORUM states into the world economy, in accordance with their political choices and development priorities. Further, Article 4 of the Agreement states that, The parties recognize and reaffirm the importance of regional integration among CARIFORUM states as a mechanism for enabling these States to achieve greater economic opportunities, and enhanced political stability and to foster their effective integration to the world economy.

15 For many of the CARICOM economies, these units are lodged in the respective Ministries of Trade.

16 EC (2012) noted that for the period 2012–2015 €46.5 million was allocated to support the implementation of the Agreement, €28.3 million allocated to supporting Caribbean businesses to access the benefits of the EPA, €27.5 million allocated to consolidating the CSME, €22.5 million to fostering corporation between Haiti and the Dominican Republic, €8.6 million to promoting integration between Eastern Caribbean states.

References

Andriamananjara, S., Brenton, P., von Uexkull, E. and Walkenhorst, P. (2009). Assessing the Economic Impacts of an Economic Partnership Agreement on Nigeria. *World Bank Policy Research Working Paper* 4920.

Armington, P. S. (1969). A theory of demand for products distinguished by place of production. *Staff Papers*, 16(1): 159–178.

Bergstrand, J. H. (1985). 'The gravity equation in international trade: some microeconomic foundations and empirical evidence'. *The Review of Economics and Statistics*: 474–481.

Brenton, P., Hoppe, M. and von. Uexkull, E. (2007). *Evaluating the Revenue Effects of Trade Policy Options for COMESA Countries: The Impacts of a Customs Union and an EPA with the European Union*. Washington, DC: World Bank.

Deardorff, A. V. and Stern, R. M. (1986). *The Michigan Model of World Production and Trade*. Cambridge, MA: The MIT Press.

Dodson, L. (2013). 'The EU-CARIFORUM Economic Partnership Agreement (EPA): An assessment of the static welfare impacts on Guyana'. *World Journal of Entrepreneurship, Management and Sustainable Development*, 9(4): 272–284.

Feenstra, R. C. (1994). 'New product varieties and the measurement of international prices'. *The American Economic Review*: 157–177.

Gasiorek, M. and Winters, L. A. (2004). 'What Role for the EPAs in the Caribbean?'. *The World Economy*, 27(9): 1335–1362.

Gomez, D. (2007). *Implications of EU-CARIFORUM Economic Partnership Agreement for Belize – A Forward Assessment. Trade Capacity Building for Enhanced Private Sector Engagement Project*. Belize: Belize Chamber of Commerce & Industry.

Greenaway, D. and Milner, C. (2004). A Grim REPA?. *GEP Research Paper* 30(30).

Hertel, T. W.and Tsigas, M. E. (1997). *Structure of GTAP. Global Trade Analysis: modeling and applications*: 13–73. Cambridge: Cambridge University Press.

Hosein, R. (2008). 'EU-Caribbean EPA – The Welfare Impact and Implications for Trinidad and Tobago'. *Business, Finance & Economics in Emerging Economies*, 3(1).

Hosein, R., Khadan, J. and McClean, S. (2013). Preliminary study on the status of implementation of the EU-CARIFORUM Economic Partnership Agreement. Unpublished study prepared for the United Nations Economic Commission on Latin America and the Caribbean.

Kee, H. L., Nicita, A. and Olarreaga, M. (2008). 'Import demand elasticities and trade distortions'. *The Review of Economics and Statistics*, 90(4): 666–682.

Khadan, J. and Hosein, R. (2014). Trade, Economic and Welfare Impacts of the CARICOM–Canada Free Trade Agreement. *MPRA Paper* 54836.

Lorde, T. and Alleyne, A. (2016). Estimating the Trade and Revenue Impacts of the European Union-CARIFORUM Economic Partnership Agreement: A Case Study of Barbados. *Working Paper* 16(1). Department of Economics, Cave Hill Campus,

Mahabir, R. (2011). Early Signals of the CARIFORUM-EU Economic Partnership Agreement. *Central Bank of Trinidad and Tobago, Working Papers* 03.

Marshall, S., Stennett, R. and Williams, K. (2009). Simulating the Dynamic Macroeconomic Effects of the EU/CARIFORUM EPA on Jamaica. *Bank of Jamaica Working Paper*, March 23.

McDaniel, C. A. and Balistreri, E. J. (2002). A Discussion on Armington Trade Substitution Elasticities. *Working Paper* 2002–01-A. U.S. International Trade Commission Office of Economics.

Meyn, M., Stevens, C., Kennan, J., Highton, N., Bilal, S., Braun-Munzinger, C., van Seters, D., Campbell, C. and Rapley, J. (2009). *The CARIFORUM–EU Economic Partnership Agreement (EPA): The Development Component*. Brussels: European Parliament.

Nicholls, S., Christopher-Nicholls, J. and Colthrust, P. (2001). *Evaluating the Fiscal Impact of REPA between the European Union and CARICOM*. Nottingham: University of Nottingham.

Preville, C. (2006). *Mid-Term Review of the Negotiation of an Economic Partnership Agreement (EPA) between CARIFORUM and the EU: Implications for Agriculture and Farmers of the Windward Islands*. Saint Vincent and the Grenadines: WINFA.

Saito, M. (2004). 'Armington elasticities in intermediate inputs trade: a problem in using multilateral trade data'. *Canadian Journal of Economics/Revue canadienne d'économique*, 37(4): 1097–1117.

Stern, R. (1976). *Price elasticities in international trade: An annotated bibliography*. London: Springer.

Stevens, C., Meyn, M. and Kennan, J. (2009) The CARIFORUM and Pacific ACP Economic Partnership Agreements: Challenges Ahead?. *Commonwealth Secretariat Economic Papers* 87.

Taylor, T. G., Antoine, P. A. and Liu, H. (2007). *An Analysis of the Potential Trade and Fiscal Impacts on the OECS of a Reciprocal Trade Agreement with the European Union*. Gainesville: Department of Food and Resource Economics, University of Florida.

Thomy, B., Tularam, G. A. and Siriwardana, M. (2013). 'Partial Equilibrium Analysis to Determine the Impacts of a Southern African Customs Union-European Union Economic Partnership Agreement on Botswana's Imports'. *American Journal of Economics and Business Administration* 5(1).

Zgovu, K. and Kweka, J. (2007). Empirical Analysis of Tariff Line-level Trade, Tariff Revenue and Welfare Effects of Reciprocity Under an Economic Partnership Agreement with the EU: Evidence from Malawi and Tanzania. *AERC Research Paper* 184.

4

The effects of structural reforms on economic growth in the Caribbean small states[1]

Kevin Greenidge, Meredith Arnold McIntyre and Hanlei Yun

1 Introduction

In the 1980s and 1990s there was a marked shift in the development policy paradigm in the Caribbean away from the emphasis on the protection of domestic markets and significant state involvement in the economy. The new outward oriented strategy emphasized export competitiveness, the adoption of liberal policies to facilitate the more efficient functioning of markets and reduce the role and interventions of the state in the economy.

The shift to liberal economic policies involved the adoption of a general set of structural reforms and these underpinned the policy advice and conditionality in adjustment programmes supported by the international financial institutions, such as the IMF, the World Bank and the Inter-American Development Bank.

We can summarize the general package of reforms as: (1) trade reforms – pursuit of trade liberalization involved the removal of import quotas; tariff reductions; and improved export incentives; (2) exchange rate policy – to ensure a real exchange rate that would improve international competitiveness and restructure economic incentives to expand the production of exports; (3) tax reforms – aimed at neutrality and administrative simplification including a shift from trade taxes to other taxes e.g. VAT; (4) financial liberalization – set positive real rates to encourage domestic savings and promote investment including through interest rate policy reform; (5) product pricing policies – removal of subsidies, including agricultural subsidies; elimination of price controls; and (6) privatization – the transfer of public companies to the private sector to improve efficiency and resource allocation.

Despite the importance of structural reforms to promoting growth in the Caribbean there has been no systematic attempt to measure what has been reformed or what still remains to be reformed in the various structural policy areas as well as the importance of institutional quality to growth in small states. Caribbean research has been focused on assessing the effectiveness of stabilization policies adopted in IMF programmes in the region. Hilaire (2000) examined the Caribbean approach to stabilization through looking at the experiences of Barbados, Guyana, Jamaica and Trinidad and

Tobago with IMF stabilization programmes in the 1980s and 1990s. Similarly, Fontaine (2005) and Greenidge *et al.* (2011) analyze the impact of Fund programmes in specific countries in the region.

The chapter assesses the impact of structural reforms on growth in the Caribbean. It builds a set of indices to measure the extent of structural reforms in the region, and employs these to estimate both short-run and long-run effects of structural reforms on growth, controlling for other possible growth determinants using panel dynamic OLS estimation. Also, in recognizing the importance of institutional quality to growth in developing countries, but given the very limited data specific to the Caribbean, the paper widens the sample to include other small states to gauge the effects of institutional quality.[2]

2 Stylized facts on structural reforms in the Caribbean

Trade reforms

Up to the 1980s trade regimes in the Caribbean were comparable to those of many developing countries. They were characterized by high and widely dispersed tariffs and considerable use of non-tariff barriers (NTBs), including quantitative restrictions such as discretionary licensing requirements. Protectionist policies in the region also included high import duties being imposed on imports from within the region and this severely impeded the growth of intraregional trade.

Trade liberalization took root in the region in the 1980s as part of the structural conditionality of IMF and World Bank adjustment programmes. Trade was liberalized with quantitative restrictions being phased out and replaced by temporarily higher import duties that were themselves lowered over time. Baumann (2008) estimated that non-tariff barriers which affected an estimated 40% of imports in the mid-1980s affected only 11% by 1997.

Membership in the Caribbean Community (CARICOM) brought a commonality to trade policy as all countries subscribed to the common external tariff (CET) on extra-regional imports. To initiate the process of liberalization in line with global trends, CARICOM countries agreed to a schedule of phased reductions in the CET starting in 1991. In February 1991, the rate structure was brought down from a range of 0–70%, to one of 0–45%, and in 1993 to 5–20% to be implemented over a five-year period. The CET tariff structure was to be 0–5% to 20%.

Tariff rates imposed under the CET depend on the nature of the taxable commodity. Most commodities are grouped as competing (if regional production satisfies at least 75% of regional demand) or noncompeting, and then each group is subdivided into inputs (primary, intermediate, and capital) and final goods. The rate structure is 0 or 5% on noncompeting inputs, 10% on competing primary and capital inputs, 15% on competing intermediate inputs, and 20% on all final goods. The CET agreement also allows for a special rate on agricultural products, limited duty exemptions related to economic development, and some additional national discretion in the setting of tariff rates. About half of the countries in the region – which account for the majority of CARICOM trade – have implemented the final reductions of the CET. Despite delays in implementation all the countries in the region with the exception of Antigua and Barbuda, Montserrat and St Kitts and Nevis have completed the four phases of the CET.

Between the late 1990s and early 2000s, every country, except for the Bahamas,[3] had a nearly 10-point reduction in average import tariff rates (Figures 4.1 and 4.2). Tariffs dropped from average levels of 22% in 1998 to 13% in 2001 but stagnated since then as some countries have not fully adopted the CET. The Bahamas maintained relatively high tariffs with an average tariff of 30% in the period 1996 to 2013. Also, Montserrat was permitted a 'slow track' of CET implementation and as a result the average tariff was 21% in 1996 and 18% in 2013.

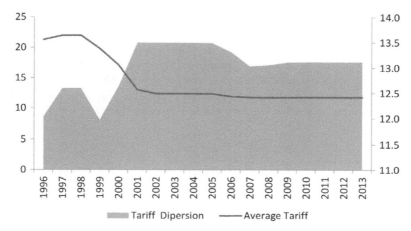

Figure 4.1 Tariff rate and dispersion, 1996–2013 (%)
Data applies to Antigua and Barbuda, the Bahamas, Barbados, Belize, Dominica, Grenada, Guyana, Jamaica, Montserrat, St Kitts and Nevis, St Lucia, St Vincent and the Grenadines, Suriname, Trinidad and Tobago.
Source: World Integrated Trade Solution (WITS) database and IMF staff calculations.

Figure 4.2 Average tariff rates, 1998 and 2013 (%)
Source: WITS database and IMF staff calculations.

Financial liberalization

Following the establishment of the various central banks in the region in the early 1960s and early 1970s, a wide range of policy instruments were employed to maintain monetary stability. These included primary and secondary reserve ratios, interest rate controls and moral suasion. Also in keeping with objectives of currency stability, virtually all of the Caribbean central banks at one point or another have utilized exchange controls as a general policy tool. However, coming into the 1980s, these economies, faced with growing balance of payments problems and rising fiscal deficits, were forced to seek ways to improve their domestic financial systems to achieve more efficient mobilization and allocation of resources.

The process of financial liberalization in the Caribbean is most evident during the early 1990s, mainly as a result of the countries engaging in IMF stabilization and structural adjustment programmes, which were designed to restore economic growth. The adoption of such policies was in an effort to liberalize the domestic financial systems and, in some cases, included the lifting of restrictions on capital flows and the floating of exchange rates.

Credit controls

All the countries reviewed abolished credit controls during the early 1990s, but have placed greater reliance on reserve requirements, which continue to be an active policy tool today. In this regard, while Guyana, Jamaica and Trinidad and Tobago have abandoned secondary reserve requirements and only maintain the cash reserve requirement, Barbados, The Bahamas and the Organization of Eastern Caribbean States (OECS) have retained both instruments.

Interest rates

One of the first monetary measures adopted by central banks in the region was the control of interest rates on deposits which was subsequently extended to loans. However, the deregulation of interest rates has been a common feature of the liberalization process, as the countries adopted more indirect instruments of monetary policy. Only OECS currently have controls on interest rates in the form of a floor on the deposit rates, which is argued as complementary policy in support of their fixed exchange rate regime. Barbados recently abolished the minimum savings rate on deposit which was in place for over 40 years.

Privatization

There has been a general trend towards the privatization of commercial banks in the region. Currently, there are very few state-owned banks and they are concentrated in the ECCU sub-region. The most recent privatization occurred in Barbados, where the Barbados National Bank was partially privatized in 2003 after 30 years of state control; the state retained a significant interest in the Bank until 2013 when it was totally privatized.

Exchange controls

The area of exchange controls was perhaps the most emphasized dimension of the financial liberalization programmes undertaken by Caribbean countries in the 1990s. This is because such controls were viewed as a hindrance to the inflow of much-needed capital for economic growth. Also, financial liberalization is seen as an essential part of the proposed CSME which makes provisions for the free movement of goods, services, capital, selected categories of skills and the right of CARICOM nationals to set up business in any CARICOM country. Thus, the movement to the CSME has encouraged CARICOM countries to speed up the liberalization process. Guyana, Jamaica and Trinidad and Tobago have removed all restrictions on both the current and capital accounts, albeit at different paces. While Jamaica fully liberalized both accounts simultaneously, Guyana phased the process over a five-year period, starting with current account transactions and then moving to the capital account. Trinidad and Tobago sequenced the liberalization efforts over a three-year period. Fixed-exchange rate countries of Barbados,

The Bahamas and the OECS have liberalized current account transactions, while choosing to gradually remove restrictions on capital accounts.

Barriers to entry

Not much has changed in this dimension since the establishment of the various central banks in the early 1960s and early 1970s. The legislation governing the operations of regional central banks (Central Bank Act) details the necessary criteria for entry to the respective banking systems and this is complemented by a Financial Institutions Act. It is not clear whether or not these criteria are restrictive. Nevertheless, there are very few documented cases of an application for a banking license being refused, although there are several cases of licenses being revoked.

Bank autonomy (government regulation of operations)

From the inception of the various central banks the focus has been on prudential regulation and supervision as opposed to direct involvement in the day-to-day operations of banks. So, except for the Government of Jamaica's direct intervention in the operations of some banks following the financial crisis of the 1990s as part of the restructuring programme, this has not been an area of concern in the region.

In summary, the Caribbean countries have made significant progress in the implementation of financial liberalization programme over the last three decades. All countries have eliminated controls on credit allocation, deregulated interest rates, embarked on a path of privatization and reduced or abolished exchange controls. However, they have all kept reserve requirements as part of their monetary policy programmes. Another interesting feature of the process is that those countries with fixed exchange rate regimes have, up to December 2005, all maintained significant restrictions on the capital account and have also continued to administer a minimum deposit rate, while those with floating rate regimes have fully liberalized those areas.

Tax reforms

With a greater commitment to liberal economic policies, tax reform took root in Caribbean countries. The common feature of the reforms in the tax area has been the pursuit of neutrality, legal and administrative simplification with greater collection. The reforms had the effect of replacing taxes on foreign trade with domestic taxes, and the extreme marginal rates that some countries applied to personal and company income taxes have been lowered since the value-added tax has gained wider acceptance. Nevertheless, the effectiveness of taxes in most countries in the region remains weak due to the widespread use of tax exemptions resulting in a significant narrowing of the tax bases and problems of evasion and administration. Indeed, all Caribbean countries have fiscal incentive regimes that provide generous tax concessions to encourage investments in the main economic sectors. In addition, in many countries discretionary tax exemptions are also pervasive further reducing the tax base.

The taxation of income that is levied in the Caribbean countries varies considerably (Figures 4.3 and 4.4). Countries such as Antigua and Barbuda, the Bahamas, and St Kitts and Nevis did not levy any taxes on personal income for most of the last two decades.[4] Although St Kitts and Nevis does not have explicit taxes on personal income, Housing and Social Development Levy has been introduced in 1996 on all wages and salaries; the structure and the rate of the levy have since changed.[5] At the other end of the spectrum are countries that levy taxes on income.

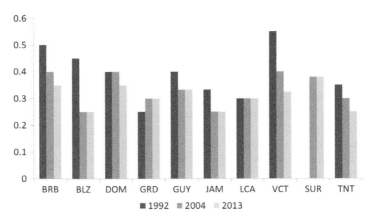

Figure 4.3 Personal income tax (%)
Source: International Bureau of Fiscal Documentation (IBFD) tax survey of KPMG and IMF staff calculations.

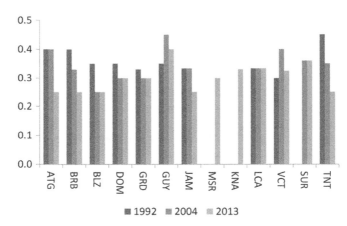

Figure 4.4 Corporate income tax (%)
Source: IBFD tax survey of KPMG and IMF staff calculations.

Income taxation in the Caribbean countries has undergone two rounds of reforms since 2000. From the early to mid-2000s, reforms focused on the consolidation of direct taxation: the PIT (personal income tax) was introduced in Antigua and Barbuda, and a 3% levy on salaries was introduced in Grenada to aid the reconstruction effort after Hurricanes Ivan and Emily, propping up income tax collections until it was repealed in 2009. For Suriname, the available data is from 2004 and the personal income tax rate has not changed since then (rate=0.38). Corporate income tax (CIT) revenue also increased during that period, particularly in St Kitts and Nevis primarily as a result of a new tax audit programme and increased profitability of the indigenous bank. Toward the end of the decade, the second round of reforms focused on reducing income tax rates, along with some widening of the base and a reduction in the number of PIT brackets. Except for St Lucia, the high marginal rates of personal income tax rate applied in the 1990s on personal income were cut substantially in the 2000s in our sample group, from an average of 42% to 30%.[6]

Tax reform in the Caribbean is designed to create a tax system that is efficient, equitable and administrable, moreover, provides adequate and stable revenues. The highest priority is to replace existing domestic consumption taxes with a value-added tax (VAT). The introduction of the VAT reshaped the revenue structure. It is applied to certain goods that have been highly taxed, including petroleum products, alcoholic beverages, tobacco, passenger cars and services such as telecommunications. The introduction of a VAT also facilitated the reduction of import duties associated with trade liberalization. Economic theory has shown that a value-added tax is superior to a system with non-zero tariffs in that it is possible to increase revenue and consumer welfare by replacing tariffs by consumption taxes. Tariffs lead to distortions of factor use in production as domestic prices are no longer equal to international prices. Therefore, replacing tariffs by consumption-based taxes can lead to more efficient production and in particular a wider tax base as consumption taxes can be levied on all goods consumed whereas tariffs only apply to imports.

To moderate the distorting effects of taxation on production and investment decisions and to compensate from the expected revenue losses from trade liberalization, in the 1990s and 2000s, most Caribbean countries adopted value added tax systems on consumption. The introduction of the VAT reshaped the revenue structure. For ECCU, most of the countries adopted the standard rate of 15% with a lower rate of 10% applied to tourism industries. There were reversals in Grenada (1995) and Belize (1999) due to weak design and administration or policy reasons. In Grenada, many goods and services were zero-rated; the value-added tax was essentially unable to significantly broaden the tax base.

The implementation of the VAT during 2006–2012 was the cornerstone of the successful tax reform in Caribbean countries, especially for ECCU countries. In addition, there was an increase in the coverage or efficiency of the VAT in most countries. Despite the failure of value-added taxation to gain a permanent foothold in Grenada and Belize in the 1990s, the more recent experience in Barbados, St Kitts and Nevis and St Lucia was quite successful, reflected in higher VAT Productivity, also known as c-efficiency ratios (Table 4.1).[7]

Table 4.1 Caribbean countries: VAT rates, mid-2013 (%)

	Date VAT introduced	*Standard rate at introduction*	*Current standard rate*	*VAT productivity at introduction*	*VAT productivity in 2013*
Antigua and Barbuda	Jan. 2007	15.0	15.0	0.55	0.51
Bahamas	Jan. 2015	7.5	7.5		
Barbados	Jan. 1997	15.0	17.5	0.13	0.72
Belize[a]	Jul. 2006	10.0	12.5	1.12	0.82
Grenada	Feb. 2010	15.0	15.0	0.54	0.56
Dominica	Mar. 2006	15.0	15.0	0.70	0.76
Jamaica[b]	Oct. 1991	10.0	16.5	0.72	0.55
St Kitts and Nevis	Nov. 2010	17.0	17.0	0.10	0.75
St Lucia	Oct. 2012	15.0	15.0	0.37	0.80
St Vincent/ Grenadines	May 2007	15.0	15.0	0.13	0.26
Trinidad and Tobago	Jan. 1990	15.0	15.0	0.49	0.43

Sources: International Bureau of Fiscal Documentation, 2013; Deloitte, Global Indirect Tax Rates, 2013.

Notes: [a] Only telephone services are subject to GCT at a rate of 20 percent. And motor vehicles are subject to GCT at rates up to 113.95 percent.
[b] A 10% rate applies on goods; an 8% rate also applies on services; 25.0% and 50.0% are reserved for luxury goods like yachts.

Privatization

Following their independence in the 1960s and early 1970s most Caribbean countries embarked on a process of nationalization of what they considered to be the key institutions to support their long-term growth and development, particularly utility companies and banks. These actions were guided by the dominant ideology of that period. As independent countries they aimed to assert their sovereignty and economic independence, including through ownership of the country's main economic sectors. However, coming in to the 1990s, this process began to unwind as one by one these countries became involved in structural adjustment programmes (SAP) supported by the IMF and World Bank. For example, as part of its 1989 SAP, Guyana privatized 14 public enterprises between 1989 and 1992 including the telecommunications and transportation companies, and its largest bank. In Trinidad and Tobago the process got under way in 1987 under the newly elected National Alliance for Reconstruction government and by 1995 roughly 30 companies had either been fully or partially privatized. Jamaica's privatization programme began in 1981 with support from both the IMF and World Bank and by 1991 close to 200 companies were diversified. This pattern of privatization was consistent throughout the different countries in the region, to varying degrees.

3 Literature review on structural reforms

A number of empirical analyses highlighted the importance of structural reforms. Easterly, et al. (1997) measured econometrically the impact of macroeconomic policy reforms on growth using a world-wide panel of 70 countries during 1961–1993 including 16 from Latin America. They found that stabilization and reforms in Latin America have raised the region's average long-term economic growth by 1.9–2.2 points. However, ELM the same authors did not address the issue of the impact of structure reform.

Fernandez-Arias and Montiel (1997) added an index of structural reforms to the basic Easterly et al. model (for 69 countries, 18 in Latin America) and found that macro reforms in recent years added an additional 0.5% to the average growth rate. Lora and Barrera, (1997) estimated a standard long-run growth model using 19 countries' observations, which suggested that reforms had a quite powerful effect on growth, measured either directly or indirectly through investment and productivity. A recent IMF paper (Dabla-Norris et al., 2013) indicated that structural reforms gave greater play to market forces, better policymaking and greater trade and financial openness, which are keys to sustained growth.

However, according to a recent published IMF World Economic Outlook (IMF, 2016), product market liberalization-reforms that increase competition in the sale of goods and services have a positive effect on productivity, especially in the service sectors, but the short-term effect is negative. Meanwhile, labour market deregulation does not help productivity at all, and even has negative effects in the short-run.

There is a broad consensus in the literature based on influential theoretical models that indicated trade openness can lessen market restrictions and accelerate the diffusion of technology, which is an important component of a strategy to invigorate economic growth.[8] The literature does not only provide support for the importance of structural reforms in the growth process. Ros (2000), Rodriguez and Rodrik (1999) cast serious doubt on the supposedly robust positive relationship between trade reform and growth. They pointed out it is in highly sensitive to the way trade reform is measured and there are data problems.[9]

There is considerable empirical analysis that provides strong evidence indicating that a higher initial level of financial development is associated with higher subsequent rates of economic growth and improvements in economic efficiency after controlling for a wide variety of economic factors.[10]McKinnon (1973) and Shaw (1973) argued that financial repression in developing countries may prevent an efficient allocation of capital, and that financial liberalization, by unifying domestic capital markets, would boost financial development and economic growth.

Most of the studies consider one broad type of reform in isolation, while there exists a smaller literature that jointly assessed effects of different reforms and focused on interactions between subsets of reforms in the areas of international trade, capital account and domestic finance. Hauner and Prati (2008) conducted research on the sequencing of capital account, trade and domestic finance reforms and found that trade is a leading indicator, but they cannot detect a clear sequencing pattern between the latter two and provided a normative assessment. McKinnon (1973) argued that trade liberalization and domestic financial reforms should precede capital account liberalization, as capital account liberalization may exacerbate existing trade distortions or destabilize highly regulated domestic financial markets. In a panel setting, Braun and Raddatz (2007) found that domestic financial development has a smaller effect on growth in countries that are open to trade and with free capital flows. More recently, a 2015 IMF staff report pointed out that structural reforms on the fiscal side are top priority, but the benefits of reform tend to become more pronounced when reforms are bundled together.

4 Measuring the impact of reforms: methodology and indices

In order to measure the effects of structural reforms on growth, quantified indexes were constructed so that one could compare the extent of reforms between countries or the progress of the reform in a single country. Several studies have made valuable contributions to the index. Lora (2012) developed a set of reform indices to measure the effect of region-wide structural reforms in 19 Latin America countries during the period 1985–1995 through five policy areas: trade policy, financial policy, tax policy, privatization and labour legislation. He updated the index in 2012 to measure the evolution of structural reforms in the period from 1985–2009.

Another important effort is the study by Burki *et al.* (1997), focussing the reform agenda for Latin America and the Caribbean. The study concentrated on five areas of structural reform: international trade openness, financial development, labour market flexibility, proper use of public resources and efficiency of public revenue generation, and good governance.

In addition, there are other databases and indexes related to structural reform. Some of them covered a variety of policy reforms (Morley *et al.*, 1999; World Bank, 2004; Ostry *et al.*, 2009), while others focused on specific areas such as financial regulation and supervision (Abiad and Mody, 2005; Barth *et al.*, 2008) and labour legislation (Aleksynska and Schindler, 2011; Rama and Artecona, 2002).

In this chapter, we extend Lora's trade and tax index to Caribbean countries and adopt the methodology utilized by Greenidge and Milner (2007) to quantify financial liberalization. Annual data was collected for 13 Caribbean countries from 1970 to 2014. The countries are Antigua and Barbuda, the Bahamas, Barbados, Belize, Dominica, Jamaica, Montserrat, St Kitts and Nevis, St Lucia, St Vincent and the Grenadines, Suriname, and Trinidad and Tobago. The index reflects the evolution of the three reform areas: trade reform, financial liberalization and tax reform. Each sub-index was normalized between zero and one, where zero is the least liberalized while one is the opposite. The difference between raw data and the least liberalized country observation is expressed as a percentage of the difference between the maximum and minimum observations for all the countries over the entire period. Instead of using a simple average of the sub-indexes to compute the reform index as was done by Lora, the chapter used

Principal Component Analysis. The index measured each country's performance relative to the most liberalized country in the region so that it was only intended to measure the neutrality of the policies rather than the quality. However, indices are not strictly comparable across sectors.

In formal terms the index value for the country i at time t is

$$I_{it} = (R_{it} - Max)/(Min-Max)$$

where I_{it} is the index value for country i at year t, R_{it} is raw value for country i at year t, Max is the maximum value of the measure for all countries over all years, and Min is minimum value of the measure for all countries over all years.[11]

Trade reform

The trade index includes two subcomponents: the average level of tariff rates and the dispersion of tariffs (Figures 4.5 and 4.6).[12] Dates are taken from the World Integrated Trade Solution (WITS) database of the World Bank for the period 1996 to 2013. Principle component analysis is used to calculate the combined indices; the index is on a scale of 0–1 where 0 is the highest tariff level and largest dispersion while 1 is the opposite. 1 also means most liberalized trade regime.

One problem with the index is lack of data. There is neither adequate historical data for ECCU countries, nor continuous series with common methodologies. Given these considerations, the latest available tariff rates have been imputed to represent the value of previous missing data. In addition to tariffs, there could also have been quantitative restrictions on imports, such as quotas and licensing requirements for which there are no tariff equivalents and cannot be reflected in the trade reform database.

In the trade area, as discussed earlier, the reform process was very intense between 1998 and 2001 as the trade index surges. However, except for Barbados, there were no major changes thereafter, the reform was halted since some Caribbean countries did not fully adopt CET and finish the programme.

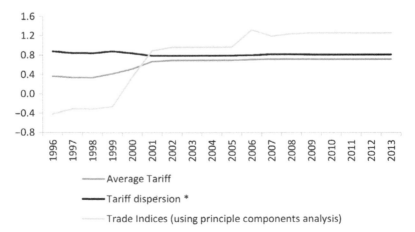

Figure 4.5 Trade reform indices (average of 13 Caribbean countries)
Note: * Tariff dispersion is the standard deviation of tariff rate.
Source: WITS database and IMF staff calculations.

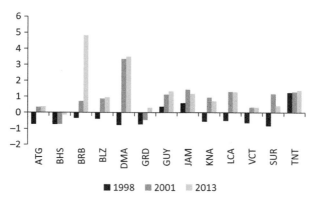

Figure 4.6 Index of tax reform, 1998, 2002, 2013
Source: WITS database and IMF staff calculations.

International financial liberalization

Measuring financial liberalization (IFL) is not an easy task, primarily given its multifaceted nature. We adopted the approach designed by Greenidge and Milner (2007), subdivided the various restrictions on the free flow of international finance into controls on payments and transfers and controls on capital transactions. The categorization was based on the IMF's annual report on Exchange Arrangements and Exchange Restrictions (1971–2015), which contained detailed information on each member country's exchange arrangements, administration of controls, prescription of currency, regulations on imports an import payments, payments for invisibles, exports and export proceeds, proceeds from invisibles, capital account transactions, and gold.

The constructed indices were based on the decision rules sets out in Table 4.2. Table 4.3 demonstrates the process of constructing the indices using 1991 as an example. Capital Receipts and Payments are measured by 'Capital' which is scored on a 0–4 scale. Inward and outward current account transactions are based on a scale of 0–8 (note that current account transactions include both goods and services, each of which is on a scale of 0–4). Finally, there is a category of 'international agreement' which is scored on a 0–2 scale. The resulting 0–14 scale gives a measure of IFL. Higher numbers indicate more financial liberalization.

The IFL index is then calculated on a scale of 0 to 1 where 0 corresponds to the lowest IFL and 1 to the highest. In constructing the indices, the major concern is that the conversion of the qualitative text to a quantitative measure is somewhat subjective, although in a consistent way. Another restriction comes from lack of measurement on the domestic financial liberalization, such as freedom of interest rate, state ownership and regulations, entry barriers and the credit controls due to insufficient data in ECCU.

The IFL indices cover 12 CARICOM countries for the period 1979–2013 (see Figures 4.7 and 4.8).[13] Clearly, central banks made certain efforts to liberalize financial controls during this period. Nevertheless, even within the ECCU, there are noticeable differences in the indices. The index for Antigua and Barbuda shows that this economy is far more liberalized than any other ECCU country. It was almost fully financially liberalized from the early 1980s (index=0.8) while the other member countries were not. One view expressed by market participants is that precarious fiscal policies pursued by the government caused the opening up to foreign capital to close the saving-investment gap.

Table 4.2 Decision rules coding

Value	Descriptions
	Goods and invisibles payments and receipts
x=0	All receipts and payments are blocked
x=0.5	All receipts and payments are necessarily surrendered
x=1	All receipts and payments require approval from the Central Bank.
	Receipts and payments heavily taxed
x=1.5	Authorized banks are allowed to provide foreign exchange for transactions within a certain limit.
	Transfers do not require approval but are taxed
x=2	Transfers are free
	Capital Payments and Receipts
x=0	Approvals are rare
x=0.5	Surrender of receipts is required
x=1	Approval is required from the Central Bank or Minister of Finance.
	Approval is not required but transfers are heavily taxed
x=1.5	Approval is required but liberally or routinely given
	Approval is not required but transfers are taxed
x=2	Approval is not required and transfers are not taxed
	International Agreements
x=0.5	Member of CARICOM
	Country is a member of a currency zone
x=1	IMF Article VIII Status

Trinidad and Tobago had active government interventions in the financial sector since 1980s, the movement of the index from 5.5 to 6.5 in the late 1980s and then to 7.5 in 1992 reflects the government's decision to move to a dual exchange rate in the 1980s and remove exchange controls on trade services and capital flows in early 1990s. In 1993, Trinidad and Tobago introduced a floating exchange rate and removed all restrictions on the capital account; this is captured in the IFL index, which spiked from 7.5 to 13.

In the 1980s, Jamaica had one of the most complicated financial systems in the Caribbean region, consisting of a number of restrictions and regulations. The IFL index for Jamaica was 5.5 in the early 1980s highlighting the fact that restrictions on current account payments and capital flow controls were used extensively. Jamaica began its financial sector reform in 1985 and undertook an extensive process to achieve macroeconomic stability in 1991. Currently, the index of Jamaica is 13 emphasizing the fact that Jamaica is one of the most financially liberalized economies in CARICOM.

Tax reform

For tax liberalization, four indices have been constructed, by year and country, computed on a scale of 0 to 1 (see Figures 4.9, 4.10 and 4.11).

Table 4.3 An example for the construction of the indices using 1991 IMF data

	Capital payment	Capital receipts	Payment for imports	Payment for invisibles	Receipts for exports	Receipts for invisibles	Agreement	Score	
								C	IFL
Antigua and Barbuda	2.0	2.0	1.5	1.5	2.0	2.0	2.0	4.0	13.0
Barbados	1.0	1.0	1.5	1.5	0.5	0.5	0.5	2.0	6.5
Belize	1.5	1.5	1.5	2.0	0.5	0.5	1.5	3.0	9.0
Dominica	1.0	1.0	1.5	1.5	0.5	0.5	2.0	2.0	8.0
Grenada	1.0	1.0	1.5	1.5	0.5	0.5	1.0	2.0	7.0
Guyana	1.0	1.0	1.5	2.0	1.0	0.5	1.5	2.0	8.5
Jamaica	2.0	2.0	1.5	2.0	2.0	2.0	1.5	4.0	13.0
St Kitts and Nevis	1.0	1.5	1.5	1.5	0.5	0.5	2.0	2.5	8.5
St Lucia	1.0	1.0	1.5	1.5	0.5	0.5	2.0	2.0	8.0
St Vincent/ Grenadines	1.0	1.5	1.5	2.0	0.5	0.5	2.0	2.5	8.5
Suriname	1.0	1.0	1.5	1.5	0.5	0.5	1.0	2.0	7.0
Trinidad and Tobago	1.0	1.0	1.0	1.5	1.0	0.5	1.5	2.0	6.5

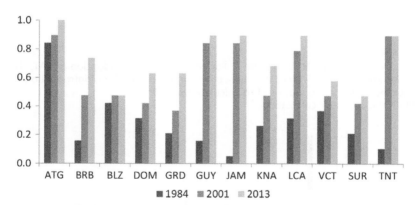

Figure 4.7 Index of financial reform, 1984, 2001, 2013
Source: AREAER Report by IMF and IMF staff calculations.

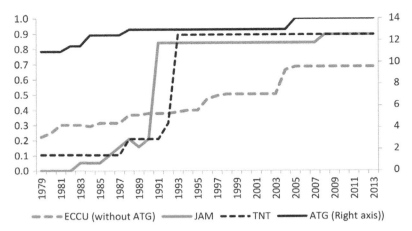

Figure 4.8 Indices of international financial liberalization
Source: IMF staff calculations.

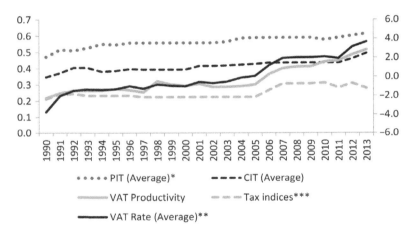

Figure 4.9 Indices of tax reform
Notes: * PIT excludes ATG, BHS and KNA. ** For years prior to the adoption of VAT, the value of the index was imputed as 0.5 times the value of the index in the year of introduction of VAT. *** Principal component analysis was used to calculate tax indices.
Source: IBFD and IMF staff calculations.

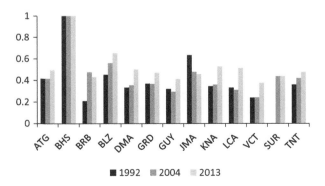

Figure 4.10 Index of tax reform, 1992, 2004, 2013
Source: IBFD and IMF staff calculations.

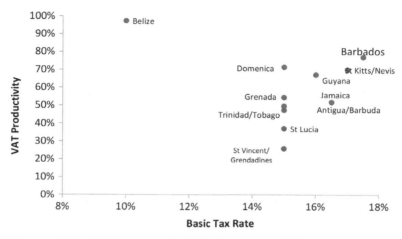

Figure 4.11 Productivity of VAT compared with basic tax rate, 2012
Source: IMF staff calculations.

a   The maximum marginal tax rate on personal income where 0 is the highest rate.
b   The maximum marginal tax rate on corporate income where 0 is the highest rate.
c   Basic VAT rate on a scale of 0 to 1, where 0 is the highest tax rate, for years prior to adoption of VAT, the value was imputed as 0.5 times the value of the index in the year of introduction of VAT.
d   VAT productivity (calculated as the ratio between the tax revenue and private consumption times the basic VAT rate) on the same scale, where 0 represents the lowest productivity. The latest available data were imputed for the initial years.[14] For some countries there is no VAT but consumption taxes, for example, in Antigua and Barbuda, there is the Antigua and Barbuda Sales Tax (ABST); in Jamaica there is General Consumption Tax (GCT); and for Belize, there is General Sales Tax (GST).

Tax data was collected from various sources such as (i) *International Bureau of Fiscal Documentation, IBFD*; (ii) *Individual Income Tax and Social Security Rate Survey* and (iii) *Corporate and Indirect Tax Survey* of KPMG in addition to IMF data provided by country authorities. Some of the data was reported on a fiscal year basis and in these cases, for comparative purposes, it was converted to calendar year.

The justification for using the top marginal rates of income tax instead of average is that the former influences labour and investment decisions. We consider the productivity rates of taxes to be the indicators of the degree of effective neutrality of the taxes, which in turn is the result of the neutrality established in the tax regulations and of the efficiency of collection, which depends on evasion and the collection efforts of the tax administration. Therefore, the higher ratings of tax policy correspond to countries with the lowest, flattest tax rates with most effective collection. Tax reforms were quite intense in the 2000s with the reduction of both personal and corporate income tax and introduction of VAT. Two rounds of strong reforms can be observed from the tax indices especially due to the increase in VAT productivity. Except for the Bahamas, Jamaica and Suriname, tax reform went smoothly in the region. Although tax rates have been homogenized, the effective collection of VAT (measured as c-efficient) differs due to the exclusion of many final goods and services, especially in countries that apply higher rates. Also, it reflects the performance of a government's revenue administration. For Belize, a wide range of domestic supplies is zero-rated and a number of supplies of goods and services are exempt which negatively affect the recent revenue performance.

5 Model specification, methodology and results

Based on the above discussion, most empirical studies on structural reform and growth begin with the standard growth regression, often referred to as the Barro regression following the pioneering work of Barro and Sala-i-Martin (1995), and add to this baseline model a measure of structural reforms and perhaps a number of interaction terms depending on what is being investigated (see Equation below). The idea is to estimate the effects of structural reforms on growth, controlling for other possible growth determinants. Note that this workhorse regression model of the growth literature, the Barro regression, was first proposed in the seminal work of Mankiw *et al.* (1992), but with additional explanatory variables.

$$Y_{i,t} = \beta_i X_{i,t} + \varepsilon_{i,t} + \gamma_i Z_{i,t} + \varphi_i SR_{i,t} + \emptyset\left(SR_{i,t} * ?_{i,t}\right)$$

The ? indicates that different variables can be used to interact with the indicator of structural reforms.

Here, Y is growth in real GDP per capita and, as noted by Durlauf *et al.* (2004), X can be seen as representing those growth determinants suggested by the Solow growth model (namely: capital accumulation and population growth), while Z captures those determinants that lie outside the original Solow theory. In addition, whereas the X variables are quite common in empirical studies, the Z variables vary considerably across studies and also by country (Kenny and Williams, 2001). Moreover, there is an extensive list of such Z variables. The Durlauf *et al.* (2004) survey identifies 145 different regressors, the vast majority of which have been found to be statistically significant in at least one study using conventional standards. They note that one of the main reasons why so many alternative growth variables have been identified is due to questions of measurement, and attribute the high percentage of statistically significant growth variables to publication bias and data mining.

Specification of the equation to be tested

Remaining with the empirical literature and accepting the Equation as an appropriate framework for examining the growth effects of structural reforms, the question is how to choose among the vast number of possible growth determinants. This is far from an easy task as Durlauf *et al.* (2004) point this out when they argue that the absence of consensus is one of the fundamental problems of the empirical growth literature.

The choice of variables is arrived at by a survey of the literature as it relates to developing countries, in particular work done on the Caribbean region.[15] The following variables are revealed from the survey: fiscal policy, openness to international trade, financial development, inflation, and capital accumulation.[16]

Since we are not only interested in the long-run effect of structural reforms on growth but also on the dynamics of the various channels, we opted for a panel co-integration approach, specifically dynamic OLS estimation (DOLS). The choice for panel DOLS versus other alternative estimations procedures such as bias-corrected OLS (BCOLS) or fully modified OLS (FMOLS) is that DOLS is the superior estimator in small samples as discussed in McCoskey and Kao and Chiang (2000). The long-run estimates from the DOLS are then embodied in a short-run error-correction model.

Results

The results, presented in Appendix 2, suggest that in the long-run, foreign direct investment, gross domestic investment, trade openness and the real effective exchange rate exert a positive impact on the level of real GDP, while government consumption expenditure and financial development have a negative effect.

The finding that investment, both domestic and foreign, is significant in raising output in the long-run is consistent with the central role given to investment in physical capital in the growth literature. Moreover, a 1% rise in domestic (foreign) investment accumulation leads to approximately 0.5 (0.1) percentage point increase in output over time.

The positive coefficient on openness suggests that greater openness to international trade has allowed these economies to raise output levels over the years. The caveat is that this is an outcome indicator and as such may be capturing other policy actions that encourage trade but that are unrelated to openness. For instance, in many Caribbean countries, exports of services are mainly tourism and have little to do with actual openness to trade in the traditional sense. It is possible to have trade controls in place but invest heavily in tourism product development and marketing. It is more likely that the proxy is capturing such effects.

The negative impact of government consumption expenditure on the long-run level of output is not surprising and one explanation is that government spending in the region has occurred at the expense of private investment and to the extent that this spending is not productive, fiscal policy will have a negative impact on growth. However, it does not necessarily imply that all categories of government spending reduce output but that in the aggregate it does.

The results suggest that capital accumulation is found to be the main driver of growth in the short-run, while government consumption and the real effective exchange rate have no impact.

It appears that the benefits of structural reforms are only seen over the long term (Figure 4.12) Specifically, these reforms have been effective in raising output levels over time. We find that lowering average tariff rates, removing restrictions on the flow of international finance, and increasing the productivity of the VAT have boosted the long-run level of real GDP. However, there is no evidence that structural reforms have any impact in the short-run.[17]

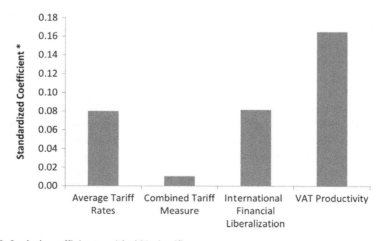

Figure 4.12 Scaled coefficients with 1% significance
Note: * Standardized coefficient = standard deviation of dependent variable/standard deviation of regressor coefficient.
Source: IMF calculations.

6 Other considerations: institutional quality

Besides reforms in trade and financial sector, a voluminous literature established the correlation between institutions and economic performance (Lewis and Martin, 1956; North, 1990). Developed countries have laws that provide incentives to engage in productive economic activity. Investors rely on secure property rights, facilitating investment in human and physical capital; government power is balanced and restricted by an independent judiciary; contracts are enforced effectively, supporting private economic transactions.

The institutional framework defines the incentives and wealth-maximization opportunities of individuals and organizations. Typically, institutions in lower-income countries are far weaker than they are in high-income countries and often weaken the impact of reform initiatives, a point emphasized by Kuczynski and Williamson (2003). They claimed that this significantly impeded the positive impact of liberal economic policy reforms in Latin America. Mauro (1995) demonstrated that there is a negative correlation between corruption and economic growth, Knack and Keefer (1995) found that different institutional measures, such as quality of the bureaucracy, property rights, and the political stability of a country have a positive statistically significant relationship with economic performance. Similarly, Cukierman *et al.* (1992) argued that a lack of correlation between the central bank's constitutional autonomy and low inflation in developing countries is likely due to weakness of the judiciary in enforcing autonomy.

In addition, the literature highlights the simultaneous relationship between growth, investment and institutions, in that not only will higher institutional efficiency result in higher rates of economic growth, but higher rates of growth will enable the country to improve the quality of its existing institutions. Rosenberg and Birdzell (1986) explained that systems that protect property rights, such as the judiciary, required development commerce at first, before instituting actual mechanisms and regulations. Eggertson (1990), Mauro (1995) and Clague *et al.* (1996) all suggested that a good economic performance increases institutional efficiency.

An IADB (2009) study on the quality of institutions supporting business development (and competitiveness) found that the Caribbean did not rank highly in comparative institutional quality.[18] The study found that the region did best when comparing the effectiveness of the legal system with comparators. In particular, Barbados was ranked highly in the ratings and is approximately equivalent to the high-income OECD average; although the court system is notoriously slow, albeit fair, in rendering verdicts.

To measure the government's efforts to improve the quality of institutions, the chapter utilizes the World Bank's 'Worldwide Governance Indicators' for the 13 sample countries in the period 1996–2013. The Worldwide Governance Indicators aggregate indicators of six broad dimensions of governance: political stability and absence of violence/terrorism, government effectiveness, regulatory quality, rule of law, and control of corruption. The indicator ranges from −2.5 to 2.5 where −2.5 is the weakest governance performance while 2.5 is the strongest.

The six institutional quality sub-indexes are:

a. *Political stability and absence of violence/terrorism* (PS), which reflects perceptions of the likelihood that the government will be destabilized or overthrown by unconstitutional or violent means, including politically-motivated violence and terrorism.

b. *Government effectiveness* (GE), which reflects perceptions of the quality of public services, the quality of the civil service and the degree of its independence from political pressures, the quality of policy formulation and implementation, and the credibility of the government's commitment to such policies.

c. *Regulatory quality* (RQ), which reflects perceptions of the ability of the government to formulate and implement sound policies and regulations that facilitate and promote private sector development.

d. *Rule of law* (RL), which reflects perceptions of the extent to which agents have confidence in and abide by the rules of society, and in particular the quality of contract enforcement, property rights, the police, and the courts, as well as the likelihood of crime and violence.

e. *Control of corruption* (CC), which reflects perceptions of the extent to which public power is exercised for private gain, including both petty and grand forms of corruption, as well as 'capture' of the state by elites and private interests.

f. *Voice and accountability* (VA), which reflects perceptions of the extent to which a country's citizens are able to participate in selecting their government, as well as freedom of expression, freedom of association, and a free media.

Institutional quality matters for economic growth. Not only will higher institutional efficiency result in higher rates of economic growth, but higher rates of growth will enable the country to improve the quality of its existing institutions.

In 2000, the tourism-based Caribbean small states[19] outperformed both of the other groups[20] shown in Figure 4.13a especially in voice accountability, government effectiveness and regulatory quality. Political stability was relatively the same in all small states. In 2013, the Caribbean still outperformed the other groups, as shown in Figure 4.13b, there is improvement in government effectiveness and corruption control, but regulatory quality deteriorated as well as rule of law. A similar outcome was also found for the other small states.

In 2000, relative to small economies, tourism-based Caribbean countries did better in regulatory quality, corruption control and voice and accountability as measured by the Worldwide Governance Indicators (Figures 4.14a and 4.14b). The sound policies facilitated and promoted private sector development, which would help the countries to attract more tourism and create growth opportunities. However, Caribbean commodity-based countries (Guyana, Suriname and

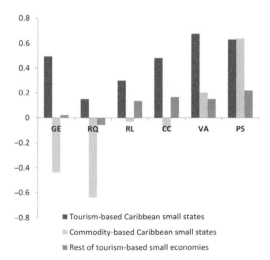

Figure 4.13a Relative institutional quality index, 2000
Note: the abbreviations on the horizontal axis stand for the six institutional quality sub-indexese, as indicated above.
Source: World Bank governance indicator and IMF staff calculation.

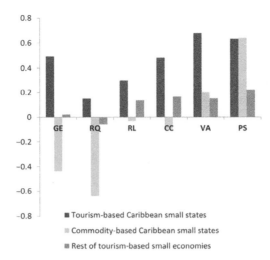

Figure 4.13b Relative institutional quality index, 2013
Note: the abbreviations on the horizontal axis stand for the six institutional quality sub-indexes, as indicated above.
Source: World Bank governance indicator and IMF staff calculation.

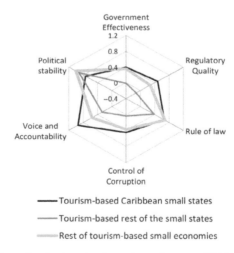

Figure 4.14a Institutional quality for tourism-based small states, 2000

Trinidad and Tobago), had a much lower institutional quality score and did not perform as well on the rule of law in society and political stability as the rest of small economies.

Tourism-based Caribbean countries outperform the small economies in regulatory quality, corruption control and voice freedom.

Overall, commodity-based Caribbean countries have worse institutional quality with a lower score compared to tourism-based economies.

Significant improvement had been made by tourism-based Caribbean economies in political stability, control of corruption and government effectiveness, which enhanced business environment in these countries compared to the rest of small economies (Figures 4.15a and 4.15b).

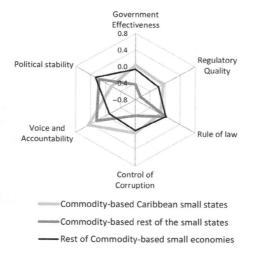

Figure 4.14b Institutional quality for commodity-based small states, 2000

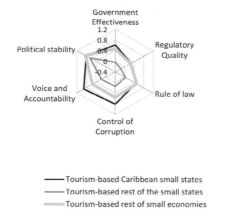

Figures 4.15a Institutional quality for tourism-based small states, 2013

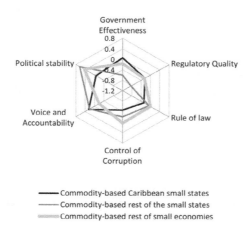

Figure 4.15b Institutional quality for commodity-based small states, 2013

Although the absolute value of the index is relatively low (0.91 compared to 2.5, the maximum), the governments of tourism-based Caribbean countries, especially St Kitts and Nevis, St Lucia and St Vincent and the Grenadines performed better.

In contrast, commodity-based economies performed worse in 2013 compared to 2000, especially in voice and accountability, anti-corruption and political stability. The unhealthy institutional quality environment in these commodity-based Caribbean countries may have contributed to the economic growth gap in these economies (see Appendix 4).

Researchers have shown that long-term sustainable growth depends on the quality of a country's institutions. Ideally, we would have liked to have included a measure of institutional quality in the earlier econometric analysis to ascertain the impact of institutional quality on growth. However, the indicators of institutional quality are only available from 1996 which would question the reliability of any estimates derived.

To quantity the effects of institutional quality, we widened the sample to include 24 other small states to compensate for the reduction in the number of years, and utilized the same model, to estimate the effects of institutional quality on growth.

The results (presented in Appendix 3 and in Figure 4.16) indicate that government regulatory quality, political stability and voice and accountability are significant in raising output over the long-run while anti-corruption can have a short-run effect to boost the economy. Additionally, improvements to government effectiveness can contribute to higher economic growth in both the short-run and long-run. Political stability, on the other hand, has no direct effect on growth. In summary, from a long-time perspective, institutional quality is essential to achieve stronger growth.

7 Conclusion

Overall, the region has made some progress in structural reforms, particularly in 1990s, but reform momentum has stalled. There is still much more that needs to be done to support

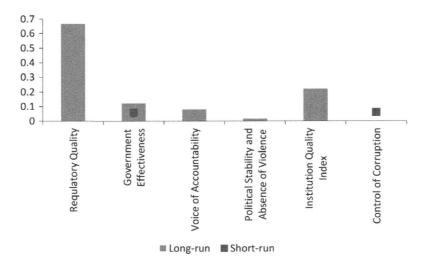

Figure 4.16 Scaled coefficients with 5% significance
Note: * Standardized coefficient = standard deviation of dependent variable/standard deviation of regressor coefficient.
Source: IMF calculations.

growth. One conclusion of this chapter is that the benefits of structural reforms are only seen over the long-term and we found no evidence of short term gains. There have been gains from lowering average tariff rates, removing restrictions on the flow of international finance, and increasing the productivity of the VAT. However, special attention should be paid to reducing the wide-ranging tax concessions. Caribbean authorities are encouraged to make sustained efforts to improve the productivity of the VAT and further liberalize the trade regime via full implementation of the CET by all countries (reduce tariff exceptions) and remove remaining quantitative restrictions (QRs). The remaining restrictions on the flow of international finance, including on FDI, should be removed over the medium to long-run.

Institutional quality is important for promoting growth, especially for small states. Structural reforms can be undertaken to make government more effective, such as improving the quality of the civil service and the speed of policy formulation and implementation. Country authorities can focus on rationalizing economic regulations and improving administrative efficiency to reduce the transactions costs of doing business. In addition, they can make efforts to incorporate regulations that facilitate and promote private sector development, and reduce the perception of corruption.

Finally, future research could attempt to gauge the contribution of structural reforms to total factor productivity and potential growth by employing growth accounting decomposition before and after reform episodes. Moreover, domestic financial and capital market reforms, privatization and labour market reforms are all worth including if data is available.

Notes

1 The views expressed in this chapter are those of the author(s) and do not necessarily represent the views of any institution they may be affiliated with including the International Monetary Fund.
2 Refer to Appendix 1 for the list of countries included in the analysis.
3 The Bahamas, although in CARICOM, did not sign up to the CARICOM Single Market and Economy.
4 Antigua and Barbuda had no personal income tax up to 2005 when PIT was reintroduced. Recently the government announced plans to eliminate the PIT in two stages by 2017.
5 The Housing and Social Development Levy Act was amended multiple times, the latest of which was in early 2011 requiring contributions of 3% on wages and salaries by all employers and a progressive marginal rate schedule (from 3.5% to 12%) applicable to different brackets of wages, payable by employees.
6 The change of the sample group comes from IMF staff calculations. Tax rate data were sourced from: (i) International Bureau of Fiscal Documentation, IBFD; (ii) Individual Income Tax and Social Security Rate Survey and (iii) Corporate and Indirect Tax Survey of KPMG; in addition to the Global Indirect Tax Rate from Deloitte.
7 C-efficiency ratio is a measure of revenue productivity, and equals total VAT revenue as percentage of consumption or GDP, divided by the VAT standard rate.
8 McKinnon (1973), Krueger (1997), Dollar (1992), Sachs and Warner (1995) and Henry (2007) are among the several studies supporting this view.
9 Rodriguez and Rodrik (1999) pointed out that data sets covering relatively short time spans will reveal a positive relationship between trade restrictions and output growth.
10 Beck et al., 2000a and 2000b, Aghion et al., 2005.
11 The approach adopted in this chapter to gauge structural reforms is the most commonly used method in literature.
12 We took the standard deviation of tariff rate from WITS database as the measurement of tariff dispersion.
13 Montserrat and Anguilla not included.
14 The tax revenue data comes from IMF staff estimates, and consumption data comes from the World Economic Outlook database, IMF.

15 Specifically, works by Williams and Daniel (1991), the World Bank (1994), Boamah (1997), Lewis and Craigwell (1998), Peters (2001), and Downes (2003). Note that a wider review of the literature on these variables is contained in Greenidge and Milner (2007).

16 In the regression, capital accumulation includes domestic investment (both in real and nominal terms) and foreign direct investment; trade openness is the sum of export and import in percent of GDP; for fiscal policy, additional indicators include government public consumption (both in real and nominal terms), primary fiscal balance, public investment (both in real and nominal terms); for financial development, indicators such as claims on the private sector, broad money and private credit. All regressions use annual data from 1960 to 2014, the data comes from IMF World Economic Outlook database, World Development Indicators and IMF staff calculation.

17 The short-run estimates are in the Appendix 3

18 The study plotted public institutions score from the World Economic Forum's *Global Competitiveness Report* (WEF, 2006) against the overall Global Competitiveness Index. The relationship between institutions and competitiveness is strong and positive but the Caribbean countries in the sample (Barbados, Guyana, Jamaica, Suriname and Trinidad and Tobago) did not perform well.

19 Tourism-based Caribbean small states are Antigua and Barbuda, Bahamas, Barbados, Belize, Dominica, Grenada, Jamaica, St Kitts and Nevis, St Lucia, St Vincent and the Grenadines.

20 The two other groups are (a) 'Commodity-based Caribbean small states' and (b) 'Other tourism-based small economies'. The former group includes Guyana, Suriname and Trinidad and Tobago. The second group includes Maldives, Mauritius, Cabo Verde, Fiji, Seychelles and Vanuatu, Commodity-based small states include Palau, Tonga, Tuvalu, Bhutan, Solomon Islands, Timor-Leste, Kiribati, the Marshall Islands, Micronesia, Samoa, Montenegro, Comoros, Swaziland, Djibouti and Sao tome and Principe.

Appendix 1

Table 4.A1 Countries included in the analysis

Caribbean Countries	Rest of the small states	Rest of the small economies		Small states used in the regressions	
Antigua and Barbuda	Bhutan	Bahrain	Mauritius	Antigua and Barbuda	Tonga
Bahamas, the	Cabo Verde	Bhutan	Mongolia	Bahamas, The	Fiji
Barbados	Comoros	Botswana	Montenegro	Barbados	Solomon Islands
Belize	Djibouti	Brunei Darussalam	Namibia	Belize	Vanuatu
Dominica	Fiji	Cabo Verde	Qatar	Dominica	Kiribati
Grenada	Kiribati	Comoros	Samoa	Grenada	Marshall Islands
Guyana	Maldives	Cyprus	Sao Tome/Principe	Guyana	Mauritius
Jamaica	Marshall Islands	Djibouti	Seychelles	Jamaica	Cape Verde
St Kitts and Nevis	Mauritius	Equatorial Guinea	Slovenia	St Kitts and Nevis	Seychelles
St Lucia	Micronesia	Estonia	Solomon Islands	St Lucia	Comoros
St Vincent/Grenadines	Montenegro	Fiji	Timor Leste	St Vincent/Grenadines	Swaziland
Suriname	Palau	Gabon	Tonga	Suriname	Djibouti
Trinidad and Tobago	Samoa	Gambia	Tuvalu	Trinidad and Tobago	Sao Tome/Principe
	Sao Tome and Principe	Guinea-Bissau	Vanuatu	Maldives	
	Seychelles	Iceland			
	Solomon Islands	Kiribati			
	Swaziland	Latvia			
	Timor Leste	Lesotho			
	Tonga	Luxembourg			
	Tuvalu	Macedonia, FYR			
	Vanuatu	Maldives			
		Malta			

Note: we define a small economy as one with a population of less than 3 million people.

Appendix 2

Table 4.A2 Results re long-run estimates for structural reform and growth

Sample	1979–2014	1979–2014	1979–2014	1979–2014	1980–2013	1979–2014	1979–2014	1982–2014
Countries	12	12	12	12	11	11	11	11
No. of observations	395	395	395	395	352	360	360	333
Foreign investment	0.103 ***	0.103 ***	0.101 ***	0.089 ***	0.146 ***	1.015 ***	0.802 **	0.089 **
Domestic investment	0.534 ***	0.566 ***	0.647 ***	0.307 ***	0.547 ***	0.532 ***	0.529 **	0.338 *
Government consumption	−0.345 ***	−0.324 ***	−0.347 ***	−0.251 ***	−0.174 ***	−0.313 **	−0.247 **	−0.228 *
Broad money	−1.039 ***	−1.127 ***	−1.151 ***	−0.906 ***	−1.067 ***	−1.062 ***	−1.079 ***	−0.986 ***
OPEN	0.118 **	0.118 **	0.117 **	0.100 **	0.104 **	0.118 ***	0.103 **	0.100 *
REER	−0.056 ***	−0.049 ***	−0.051 ***	−0.057 ***	−0.057 ***	−0.056 ***	−0.052 ***	−0.051 ***
Constant	10.21 ***	10.05 ***	9.49 ***	8.83 ***	9.61 ***	10.232 ***	8.852 ***	8.64 ***
Average tariff rates	0.635 ***							0.598 ***
Tariff dispersion		0.103						
Combined tariff measure			0.224 ***					
International fin. lib.				0.835 ***				0.844 ***
Personal income taxes					0.117			
VAT						0.044		
Productivity of VAT							1.983 ***	

Note: *, **, *** indicates significance at the 10%, 5% and 1% level, respectively.

Appendix 3 Long-run estimates for institutional quality and growth

Table 4.A3 Short-run estimates for institutional quality and growth

Constant	0.077***	0.032***	0.041***	0.039***	0.046***	0.186***	0.034***
Lagged growth	0.254***	0.260***	0.245***	0.245***	0.257***	0.243***	0.257***
Dlog (domestic investment)	0.026***	0.016***	0.017***	0.017***	0.016***	0.011***	0.017***
Dlog (domestic investment)	0.013***	0.014***	0.015***	0.014***	0.015***	0.012***	0.014***
Dlog (domestic investment)	0.012**	0.011***	0.010***	0.011***	0.011***	0.012***	0.009***
Dlog (foreign investment)	0.017*	0.101***	0.127***	0.097***	0.108***	0.361***	0.143***
Dlog (foreign investment)	0.143**	0.172***	0.154***	0.180***	0.168***	0.092***	0.152***
Dlog (government consumption)	−0.053***	−0.050***	−0.049	−0.053	−0.050	−0.067	−0.045
Dlog (government consumption)	−0.038***	−0.022	−0.019	−0.023	−0.026	−0.048	−0.021
REER	−0.011**	−0.001***	−0.003***	−0.003***	−0.005***	−0.034***	−0.002***
Open	0.031**	0.061***	0.065***	0.065***	0.065***	0.080***	0.063***
Open	0.030***	0.017***	0.015***	0.018***	0.014***	0.007***	0.014***
Equilibrium correcting term	−0.031***	−0.037**	−0.038**	−0.028**	−0.038**	−0.033**	−0.033**
Regulatory quality		−0.024					
Regulatory quality		0.036					
Government effectiveness			0.013**				
Government effectiveness			0.009				
Voice of accountability				0.014			
Voice of accountability				0.013			
Political stability					0.004		

Table 4.A3 (continued)

	(1)	(2)	(3)	(4)	(5)	(6)	(7)
Constant	0.077 ***	0.032 ***	0.041 ***	0.039 ***	0.046 ***	0.186 ***	0.034 **
Political stability					0.006		
Rule of law						-0.012	
Rule of law						0.012	
Control of corruption							0.014
Control of corruption							0.008
R-squared	0.356	0.383	0.39	0.38	0.38	0.37	0.39
Adjusted R-squared	0.317	0.313	0.32	0.31	0.31	0.30	0.32
S.E. of regression	0.036	0.033	0.03	0.03	0.03	0.03	0.03
Sum squared residuals	0.723	0.345	0.34	0.35	0.34	0.34	0.34

Note: *, **, *** indicates significance at the 10%, 5% and 1% level, respectively.

Table 4.A4 Long-run estimates for institutional quality and growth

Sample	1996–2013	1996–2013	1996–2013	1996–2013	1996–2013	1996–2013	1996–2013	1996–2013
Countries	24	24	24	24	24	24	24	24
No. of observations	406	396	406	406	395	384	401	406
Foreign investment	0.103***	0.103***	0.103***	0.101***	0.089***	0.146***	1.015***	
Dif. foreign investment	0.659**	0.603***	0.557***	0.608**	0.777***	0.795**	0.608**	0.781**
Domestic investment	0.042***	0.015***	0.038***	0.028**	0.043***	0.015**	0.042***	0.042*
Government consumption	0.061*	−0.047	0.061***	0.048**	0.041**	−0.012**	0.047**	0.002
Broad money	0.633***	0.449***	0.612***	0.644***	0.652***	0.609***	0.629***	0.592***
REER	−0.222***	−0.117***	−0.207***	−0.158**	−0.207***	−0.217***	−0.245***	−0.230***
Open	0.171**	0.262***	0.211***	0.195***	0.186***	0.175***	0.181***	0.203***
Constant	0.32	1.74	0.35	0.12	0.28	0.95	0.530	1.02***
Regulatory quality		0.861***						
Government effectiveness			0.104**					
Voice of accountability				0.045**				
Political stability					0.012			
Rule of law						0.076***		
Control of corruption							0.018	
Institution quality index								0.211***

Note: *, ** , *** indicates significance at the 10%, 5% and 1% level, respectively.

Appendix 4: the institutional quality in the Caribbean, 1996–2013

The institutional quality, as measured by the Worldwide Governance Indicators, in most countries in the Caribbean is weak with a relative low score compared to the highest 2.5 margin. Anguilla stands out in the region.

Political stability and absence of violence: most of the countries in the region have a positive index value in 2013 except Guyana. Overall, improvement in the ratings took place in the region, especially after 2006–07. Prior to 2006, the ratings of Belize, Grenada and Suriname showed a marked shift down but stabilized thereafter. In sum, the region maintains a good rating for political stability and security which is supportive to growth.

Government effectiveness: there is a large divergence of the index in the region. Anguilla and Barbados have strong positive ratings, which reflect efficient government structures while Belize and Guyana have consistently negative ratings which indicate weak public policy. St Kitts and Nevis, St Lucia and St Vincent and Grenadines showed strong improvement after 2004 while Grenada and Trinidad and Tobago maintained a positive rating.

Regulatory quality: the region showed a very weak pattern. In 2013, the average index value of the region was as low as 0.23 and for countries such as Grenada, Guyana and Barbados; the quality index fell to its lowest level. St Kitts and Nevis, St Lucia and St Vincent and the Grenadines displayed significant variation in their indices with a sharp improvement in 2004 followed by an almost completely reversal from 2005 to 2013. Anguilla has the best quality of governance in the region.

Rule of law: Anguilla has the highest rating in the region and Guyana, Jamaica and Suriname maintained a negative rating overtime. There was a significant decline in Trinidad and Tobago from 2002 to 2007. The Bahamas also experienced a sharp deterioration after 2009, which indicated the need for policy actions to strengthen the legal and judicial systems to support an improved environment for investment and growth.

Control of corruption: most OECS members (except Dominica and Grenada) had significant improvement after 2004 and maintained a rating around 1.5. While larger countries like Belize and Guyana compares unfavourably with the rest of the Caribbean. Suriname's score deteriorated significantly over the period. The index suggests that part of the region needs to decisively tackle corruption as important part of the structural reform agenda.

Voice and accountability: Barbados has freer government participation while Guyana has the most conservative political environment. A significant v-shape of the index for St Vincent, St Lucia, St Kitts and Guyana appeared from 2004 to 2006.

References

Abiad, A. and Mody, A. (2005). *Financial Reform: What Shakes It? What Shapes It?*. IMF Working Papers, No. 3–70. Washington, DC: International Monetary Fund.

Aghion, P., Howitt, P. and Mayer-Foulkes, D. (2005). 'The Effect of Financial Development on Convergence: Theory and Evidence'. *Quarterly Journal of Economics*, 120: 173–222.

Aleksynska, M. and Schindler, M. (2011). Labor Market Regulations in Low-, Middle- and High-Income Countries: A New Panel Database. *IMF Working Papers*, No. 1–76, Washington, DC: International Monetary Fund.

Barro, R. J. and Sala-i-Martin, X. (1995). *Economic Growth*. New York: McGraw-Hill.

Barth, J. R., Caprio, G. and Levine, R. (2008). 'Bank regulations are changing: for better or worse?' *Comparative Economic Studies*, 50(4): 537–563.

Baumann, R. (2008). Integration in Latin America: Trends and Challenges. In *ECLAC Studies and Research*. Brasilia: Economic Commission for Latin America and the Caribbean.

Beck, T., Demirguc-Kunt, A., Levine, R. and Maksimovic, V. (2000a). Financial structure and economic development: firm, industry, and country evidence. *World Bank, Policy Research Working Paper*, 2423. Washington, DC: World Bank.

Beck, T., Levine, R. and Loayza, N. (2000b). 'Finance and the sources of growth'. *Journal of Financial Economics*, 58: 261–300.

Boamah, D. (1997). The effect of human capital on economic growth in the Caribbean. *Central Bank of Barbados Working Papers*, Vol. II: 103–117.

Braun, M. and Raddatz, C. (2007). 'Trade liberalization, capital account liberalization and the real effects of financial development'. *Journal of International Money and Finance*, 26: 730–761.

Burki, S. J., and Perry, G. (1997). *The Long March: A Reform Agenda for Latin America and the Caribbean in the Next Decade*. Washington, DC: World Bank Publications.

Clague, C., Keefer, P., Knack, S. and Olson, M. (1996). 'Property and contract rights in autocracies and democracies'. *Journal of Economic Growth*, 1: 243–276.

Cukierman, A., Webb, S. and Neyapti, B. (1992). 'Measuring the independence of central banks and its effect on policy outcomes'. *The World Bank Economic Review*, 6(3): 353–398.

Dabla-Norris, E., Ho, G., Kochhar, K., Kyobe, A. and Tchaidze, R. (2013). Anchoring growth: the importance of productivity-enhancing reforms in emerging market and developing economies. *IMF Staff Discussion Note*, No. SDN/13/08. Washington, DC: International Monetary Fund.

Dollar, D. (1992). 'Outward-Oriented Developing Economies Really Do Grow More Rapidly: Evidence from 95 LID'S, 1976–1985'. *Economic Development and Cultural Change*, 40: 523–544.

Downes, A. S. (2003), 'Economic Growth in a Small Developing Country: The Case of Barbados'. *The Latin American and Caribbean Economic Association*. Online, available at: http://lacea.org/country_studies/barbados.pdf/.

Durlauf, S. N., Johnson, P. A. and Temple, J. R. W. (2004). Growth Econometrics. *Wisconsin Madison Social Systems Working Paper*, No. 18. University of Wisconsin-Madison.

Easterly, W., Loayza, N., Montiel, P. (1997). 'Has Latin America's post reform growth been disappointing?'. *Journal of International Economics*, 43: 287–311.

Eggertson, T. (1990). *Economic Behavior and Institutions*. Cambridge: Cambridge University Press.

Fernandez-Arias, E. and Montiel, P. (1997). Reform and growth in Latin America: All pain, no gain?. *OCE Working Paper*, 351. Washington, DC: Inter-American Development Bank.

Fontaine, T. (2005). Caribbean country experiences with IMF stabilization programs within the context of globalization. *IMF Working Paper*. Washington, DC: International Monetary Fund.

GreenidgeK. and Milner, C. (2007). The nature and measurement of financial liberalisation: an application to the Caribbean. In Craigwell, R. (ed.) *Aspects of Financial Liberalisation and Capital Market Development in the Caribbean*. Barbados: Central Bank of Barbados: 5–53.

GreenidgeK., Boamah, D. and Mapp, S. (2011). 'The macroeconomic impact of IMF-supported programmes in small open economies: the case of Barbados'. *Journal of Business, Finance and Economics in Emerging Economies*, 6(1): 90–135.

Hauner, D. and Prati, A. (2008). 'Openness and domestic financial liberalization: which comes first?' Presented at the IMF conference On the causes and consequences of structural reforms. Washington, DC, February 28–29.

Henry, P. B. (2007). 'Capital account liberalization: Theory, evidence, and speculation'. *Journal of Economic Literature*, 45(4): 887–935.

Hilaire, A. D. L. (2000). *Caribbean approaches to economic stabilization. IMF Working Paper*, No. 00/73. Washington, DC: International Monetary Fund.

IADB (2009). *Institutions and the Legal Framework for Business Development in the Caribbean*. Washington, DC.

IMF (2016). 'Time for a supply-side boost? Macroeconomic effects of labour and product market reforms in advanced economies'. *World Economic Outlook* (Chapter 3), April. Washington, DC: IMF.

Kao, C. and Chiang, M. H. (2000). 'On the estimation and inference of a cointegrated regression in panel data'. In *Advances in Econometrics*, 15: 179–222.

Kenny, C. and Williams, D. (2001). 'What Do we know about economic growth? Or, why don't we know very much?'. *World Development*, 29(1): 1–22.

Knack, S., and Keefer, P. (1995). 'Institutions and economic performance: cross-country tests using alternative institutional measures'. *Economics and Politics*, 7(3): 207–227.

Krueger, A. (1997). 'Trade Policy and Economic Development: How We Learn'. *The American Economic Review*, 87(1): 1–6.

Kuczynski, P. P. and Williamson, J. (eds) (2003). *After the Washington Consensus: Restarting Growth and Reform in Latin America.* New York: Columbia University Press.

Lewis, D. and Craigwell, R. (1998). 'The Determinants of Growth in a Small Open Economy: Barbados'. *Journal of Eastern Caribbean Studies*, 23(2): 1–29.

Lewis, W. A. and Martin, A. (1956). 'Patterns of public revenue and expenditure'. *Manchester School of Economic and Social Studies*, 24: 203–244.

Lora, E. (2012). Structural reforms in Latin America: What has been reformed and how to measure it. *IDB Working Paper Series* No. IDB-WP-346. Washington, DC: Inter-American Development Bank.

Lora, E., and Barrera, F. (1997). A decade of structural reforms in Latin America: Growth, productivity and investment are not what they used to be. *Research Department Working Paper* 350. Washington, DC: Inter-American Development Bank, Research Department.

Mankiw, N. G., Romer, D., and Weil, D. N. (1992). 'A contribution to the empirics of economic growth'. *Quarterly Journal of Economics*, 107(2): 407–437.

Mauro, P., 1995, 'Corruption and growth'. *Quarterly Journal of Economics*, 110: 681–712.

McCoskey, Suzanne and Kao, Chihwa (1998). 'A Residual-based Test of the Null of Cointegration in Panel Data'. *Econometric Reviews*, 17: 57–84.

McKinnon, Ronald I. (1973). *Money and Capital in Economic Development.* Washington, DC: Brookings Institution.

Morley, S. A., Machado, R. and Pettinato, S. (1999). Indexes of Structural Reform in Latin America. *Reformas económicas series*, No. 12. Santiago, Chile: ECLAC.

North, D. (1990). *Institutions, Institutional Change and Economic Performance.* Cambridge: Cambridge University Press.

Ostry, J. D., Prati, A. and Spilimbergo, A. (2009). Structural Reforms and Economic Performance in Advanced and Developing Countries. *IMF Occasional Paper Series*, 268.

Peters, A. C. (2001). 'Determinants of Growth in the English Speaking Caribbean'. *Savings and Development*, 25(3): 312–330.

Rama, M. and Artecona, R. (2002). *A Database of Labor Market Indicators Across Countries.* Washington, DC: World Bank. Manuscript.

Rodriguez, F. and Rodrik, D. (1999). Trade policy and economic growth: A Skeptic's Guide to the cross-national evidence. *NBER Macroeconomics Annual*, 15: 261–325.

Rodrik, D. (1999). *The New Global Economy and Developing Countries: Making Openness Work.* Washington, DC: Overseas Development Council.

Ros, J. (2000). *Development Theory and the Economics of Growth.* Ann Arbor: University of Michigan Press.

Rosenberg, N. and Birdzell, L. (1986). *How the west grew rich: The economic transformation of the industrial world.* New York: Basic Books.

Sachs, J. D. and Warner, A. M. (1995). Economic reform and the process of global integration. *Brookings Papers on Economic Activity*, No. 1: 1–95.

Shaw, E. (1973). *Financial Deepening in Economic Development.* New York: Oxford University Press.

Williams, M. and Daniel, C. (1991). 'Government activity and economic performance in a small developing economy', *Economia Internazionale*, 44(2–3): 269–281.

World Bank (1994). Jamaica: A strategy for growth and poverty reduction. *World Bank Country Economic Memorandum* No. 12702-JM.

World Bank (2004). *Doing Business "Understanding Regulation".* Washington, DC: World Bank.

5

The export of higher education services from small island developing states: the Caribbean potential

Richard L. Bernal

1 Introduction

This chapter argues that the export of higher education services is a viable option for small developing countries located in the Caribbean region. This region has a number of advantages for attracting foreign students, including affordability, accessibility, security and language. The region also enjoys the advantage of being located close to the largest and most expensive market for higher education, namely the USA. However, the universities in the Caribbean have not included themselves in international ranking schemes and this reduces the ability of prospective students to conduct a comparative evaluation.

This chapter argues that one way to enhance the competitiveness of the Caribbean is through the establishment of a higher-education cluster, which involves trans-border collaboration for research, studying and teaching, possibly with the support of or in partnership with the government and the private sector. In this way higher education could form the basis of a new export sector with the potential to be an engine of economic growth for the region. The main advantage of a cluster is that it could enable small universities to respond collectively to the challenges and opportunities of a world which is increasingly one of knowledge and technology without borders. The prospects are good because there is a rapid growth in the globalization of higher education as reflected clearly in the increased international mobility of students and faculty.

This chapter is organized in five sections. Section 2 describes the characteristics of small island developing states (SIDS) referring to the universities in these states and the reasons why students would choose to study in these states. Section 3 discusses the global market for higher education which has expanded as a result of information and communication technology (ICT). The fourth Section makes a case for further collaboration between the universities in the Caribbean region in the form of a cluster. The fifth section concludes the chapter.

2 Small island developing states (SIDS)

The meaning of SIDS

Since this chapter focuses on small island developing states, it is useful to discuss the definition of this term.

There is no single formally accepted definition of a small island developing state because, amongst other things, size is a relative concept. A variety of criteria has been applied for measuring country size including population size or a combination of various indicators including population size, GDP and land area (Bernal, 1998).

The Alliance of Small Island States (AOSIS) has 39 SIDS as members (see Appendix 2), some of which are not very small (e.g. Cuba, Dominica Republic, Haiti, and Papua New Guinea). The list also includes countries that are not islands such as Suriname, Guinea-Bissau and Belize and even some such as Guyana, Cuba and Papua New Guinea, which have relatively large land areas.

The Commonwealth Secretariat employs a population threshold of 1.5 million to designate small states but include larger countries such as Jamaica because they share many of the characteristics of small country size.[1]

Often countries, classified as small island developing states (SIDS), are considered to have similar structural characteristics, including a small domestic market, limited ability to reap the benefits of economies of scale, a high degree of openness, concentration on a few exports and poor natural resources endowments (Briguglio, 1995). Some SIDS are also highly susceptible to natural disasters (Pelling and Uitto, 2001) and to being highly harmed by climate change (Nurse *et al.*, 2014; United Nations, 2010). Various studies associate these characteristics with economic and environmental vulnerability (Commonwealth Secretariat, 1997, Briguglio, 1995, United Nations, 2010).

Universities in small island developing states

Many SIDS have a university located on the island itself (e.g. the University of Mauritius) or, in the case of the Caribbean and the Pacific SIDS, an intergovernmental university (UWI – the University of the West Indies and USP – the University of the South Pacific) situated in various locations within these two regions with campuses in different islands. However, in some of the SIDS in these two regions there are also universities which are independent of the UWI and the USP (see Appendix 1 for a description of the higher education institutions in the Caribbean).

Universities operating in small island developing states (SIDS) can benefit from increased participation in the global market for higher education. These potential benefits include increasing the scale of operations and thereby realizing economies of scale and scope allowing for cost savings and increased revenue. In order to take advantage of the growing global market for higher education, investment in state-of-the-art ICT is of paramount importance. Lendle and Olarreaga (2017) show that technology has "significantly reduced the cost of entry into international markets for small and medium sized firms, which can now reach far away consumers and create global reputation as a seller at very low costs".

Another potential benefit for universities with a global outlook is that this enables the institutions to better prepare their students for the global labour market by providing a global standard education and the experiential learning as a result of exposure to the global practices, contact with foreign students and faculty of many nationalities on their own campuses, as well as opportunities for international travel.

Foreign students and sale of courses and degrees over the Internet can be a source of foreign exchange earnings, which can be valuable to public universities as they seek to be more entrepreneurial (Thorp and Goldstein, 2013).

The gravamen of the entrepreneurial university, particularly those located in SIDS, trying to expand their engagement in the provision of education at the global level, is probably the ability to form and sustain partnerships (Etzkowitz, 2008, Thorp and Goldstein, 2013), with governments, the private sector and multinational development finance institutions.[2]

Why choose a SIDS university?

There are several reasons why students, and their parents, would choose universities in small island developing states, including those located in the Caribbean.

In many instances the reason for choosing one university rather than another is some perception of the domestic environment which encourages students to go abroad. Many foreign students in the Caribbean have a good experience in this regard, which is not surprising given that most Caribbean countries have thriving hospitality/tourism industries, and a salubrious climate and beautiful natural environment.

Social and political realities are also relevant. This applies to all students when comparing alternative locations across the world. An example from the United States will illustrate this point. There has been a 39% decline in the number of applications from foreign students to study at American universities since the election of Trump (Redden, 2017a; Altbach and de Wit, 2017: 3–5). At the same time the number of applicants to study at Canadian universities has increased (Redden, 2017b).

Another factor relates to the difficulty of gaining entry to certain programmes, such as the requirements to join programmes for training medical doctors in the US, which has provided an opportunity for the growth of in the medical schools in the Caribbean, such as St George's University in Grenada and Ross University in St Kitts.

Comparative cost of admission is another important determinant of student mobility (Varghese, 2008). The escalating costs of university education in the United States has led students to go to foreign countries where costs are lower, such as Germany, where the cost of university education is subsidized by the state. The increase in tuition fees in public universities during 2008–2014 in the US were as high as 72% in Arizona, 69% in Georgia, 66% in Louisiana and over 50% in California, Colorado, Florida, Hawaii and Washington (Wang, 2016). The affordability of the cost of living in the location of the university could be another consideration in this regard (CEDA, 2011).

The language of instruction could be a factor relating to the choice of a university. English being the main language in many Caribbean countries is obviously an advantage.

The quality of education is a major determinant of the willingness to study abroad. The quality of education provided by universities in SIDS must be of comparable quality to that available elsewhere in the world. Very often such quality is measured by the ranking of the institution offering the educational services.

The Caribbean can be considered as having a comparative advantage in most of these factors. However, the fact that the Caribbean universities are not highly ranked may give the impression that their quality of education may not be sufficiently high, and this is where these universities need to improve their image.

The experience of private medical schools in the Caribbean

A number of private medical schools in the Caribbean have managed to successfully take advantage of the global market in this type of education.

It is estimated that there are 70 medical schools operating in the Caribbean (McFarling, 2017) of which 39 are for-profit medical schools (Eckhert and van Zanten, 2014 – Faimer Report). Offshore medical schools in the Caribbean illustrate the demand in the global market for this type of education and that private universities have succeeded in responding to this demand. The 2014 Faimer Short Report (ibid.) indicates that a number of U.S. international medical graduates (IMGs) who achieved Educational Commission for Foreign Medical Graduates

(ECFMG) certification has increased fivefold from 527 in 1995 (9% of ECFMG certifications) to 2,963 or 30% of certifications in 2013. 'The majority of USIMGs are enrolled in for-profit, privately owned medical schools located in the Caribbean' (ibid.). Eckhert and van Zanten (2014) report that in 2013, nearly all of the students that attained ECFMG certifications were from 8 medical schools located in Caribbean islands. Almost 1800 medical graduates that obtained such certification attended St George's University School of Medicine in Grenada and the Ross University School of Medicine in Dominica.

The success of these medical schools would seem to suggest that the small size of university and value of its financial endowment need not be a deterrent to being visible and competitive in the global market for higher education, given the willingness of the institution to take advantage of the expanding demand for higher education. The experience of St George's Medical School in Grenada and the Veterinary School at Ross University in St Kitts demonstrate that small universities in small island developing states can be financially viable, indeed, profitable and provide students, nearly all foreign, with an education recognized in the United States.

Experience of public universities in the Caribbean SIDS

There are indications of the encouraging potential demand from foreign institutions and students for courses and degrees offered by Caribbean public universities. The experience of the University of the West Indies since the middle of 2016 is instructive. The UWI has established a joint centre with State University of New York[3] with its student base of over 500,000 and a joint degree in software engineering through Global Institute of Software Technology (GIST) in Suzhou, China.[4] This is remarkable as Vice-Chancellor Sir Hilary Beckles stated: "One of the largest nations of the world has now partnered with one of the smallest nations. This is truly significant!"[5] The UWI has also reached joint centre agreements with University of Johannesburg and University of Lagos. The demand from Africa is evident in the experience, for example, the University of the West Indies mid-2017 offered one scholarship for postgraduate studies and received 364 qualified applicants of which 320 were from Africa.

Unmet demand for higher education from Caribbean SIDS

In spite of the successes just mentioned, there is considerable room and opportunities for expanding educational services as an export from the Caribbean. As will be explained in another section of this chapter, the demand for higher education online on a global scale is enormous and certainly all universities, including the Caribbean ones, have considerable scope for participating in this global market.

The 6,449 online students which the UWI serviced in 2013/14 is a small share of the Caribbean demand for online higher education (Longsworth, 2014). A clear indication of this is that approximately 66 UK higher education providers operating in the Caribbean had a combined enrolment in the same academic year of 21,940 students of which 12,814 (58%) were located in Trinidad and Tobago (QAA, 2015).

Universities in the Caribbean have not moved as quickly as some universities in North America, Western Europe and parts of Asia in seizing the opportunities of the global market for several reasons, primarily because they are mostly publicly owned, established to obviate the need and expense of sending students to overseas institutions and to educate the nationals to replace colonial administrators and managers of foreign-owned enterprises (Cobley, 2000).

In the case of the UWI, the mission of educating Caribbean nationals in Caribbean territory remains an overarching objective. This mission remains the priority because only 10% of the 20–34 age cohort was enrolled in university compared to 35% in Latin America and 50% in North America (Beckles *et al.*, 2002: 18).

The pressure to explore the global market for higher education gained momentum in the Caribbean relatively recently. It arose mainly from the necessity to be less reliant on government funding because several stakeholder governments were facing fiscal challenges. In addition, there was a growing encroachment by foreign universities in the Caribbean market for higher education, both by physical presence and on the internet. Moreover, the benefits of serving the global market were evident from the growth and financial viability of private foreign-owned institutions operating in the Caribbean.

The alacrity with which Caribbean universities involved themselves in the global market for higher education was tempered by several factors, principally their small size (Bacchus and Brock, 1987), limited resources and limited brand recognition. It was only in recent years that the paucity of government contributions made entrepreneurial initiative urgent. Emblematic of this was when the government of Barbados decided to cut back on free higher education for all.

Another matter that might have diminished the eagerness of the Caribbean higher education system from going global was the concern that seeking more foreign students could be at the expense of Caribbean student enrolment. Earnings from higher education over the internet was not considered as important as servicing and overcoming the 'locational' disadvantage of some Caribbean students.

There was also the reality that entrepreneurial verve and profit-driven culture did not come naturally or easily to the Caribbean public universities and small local tertiary institutions supplying a 'public good' on the basis of predictable financial subventions from stakeholder governments.

In addition, purist notions of the role of public universities led to the belief in some quarters that the pursuit of profit involved sacrificing academic standards. This is an issue not confined to the Caribbean (Cottom, 2017).

3 Global market for higher education

Growing global market

Higher education, like other aspects of modern living, has become globalized and, as a result, international mobility of people, technology, information and ideas has increased exponentially. These trends have been evident for the last 10–15 years (Odin and Manicas, 2004).[6] Concurrently, there has been a process of "massification" in which the number of degree granting institutions has increased from 3,703 in 1944 to approaching 19,000 in 2015 (Zeleza, 2016: 3). This environment poses challenges and opportunities for all universities particularly those which are located in small island states.

The premise on which any university decides to enter the global market for higher education relates to the possibility of attracting some of the millions of internationally mobile students (British Council, 2012). As already argued one way of succeeding in the competitive environment is by moving up in the world rankings of universities and offer courses at competitive rates. This is true even for the universities that have traditional been the highest rated e.g. Oxford, Cambridge and Harvard.[7] The ranking race is one area where the Caribbean universities need to improve their performance in order to succeed in expanding the exports higher education.

The modern global economy is a knowledge-driven one and to succeed in this constantly changing global education market, a university must have a culture and leadership which is innovative, agile and entrepreneurial.

New technology as a key driver for higher education export

There are two main modes of exporting higher education services, first, attracting fee-paying foreign students and second, sale of courses or degrees over the internet. The first mode of delivery has been going on since the existence of universities and the second mode is more recent and growing rapidly as universities supply an increasing number of massive open online courses (MOOC).

There has been a paradigm shift in global higher education towards massive open online courses (MOOC) in a veritable revolution allowing unlimited participation via the internet. Modern information and communications technology makes it possible to deliver lectures (live and recorded) and interactive discussions and increased global access at inexpensive rates. MOOC are rapidly transforming learning and distance teaching (Bradshaw, 2014) and they are being developed and propagated by virtually all universities including the most highly rated universities. A number of companies are now entering the market for higher education such as Coursera and Udacity. Universities are moving aggressively for example, edX, a non-profit MOOC established by Harvard University and the Massachusetts Institute of Technology (MIT).

This rapidly changing environment can enable the universities of SIDS to overcome the major constraints associated with operating in a small national or regional market, namely lack of economies of scale and physical remoteness.

The first condition would no longer be a binding constraint in a globalized setting because economies of scale constraints can be overcome by recourse to the global market, attracting foreign students and selling of courses and degrees online through the internet. Modern computer technology has gone a long way to providing efficiencies and cost saving opportunities.

The downsides of physical remoteness can be reduced through electronic means for online students. In the case of the Caribbean travel connections are satisfactory for foreign students wishing to study in the Caribbean, as nearly all SIDS have vibrant tourist sectors accompanied by good air transport.[8]

ICT and strategic international marketing

ICT is not only useful for universities to offer courses online but also to market their products so as to attract prospective undergraduates and postgraduate students from all over the world. Students who wish to study abroad search globally via the Internet and a presence on the web by the universities of SIDS highly improves their visibility.

Like all universities, those in SIDS need to assure prospective students that they will be prepared to join the global labour market by what the students will learn and by being given a 'global exposure' such as by spending a semester or two in foreign countries. An example of marketing this type of service provision is the slogan: 'preparing you for today's global economy' used by the world-renowned School of Oriental and African Studies (SOAS) at London University a well-established top brand in higher education. This advertisement placed in *The Economist* goes on to assure the prospective student of a global approach when it states that its MSc in Finance will encompass the mature economies of the United States and Japan as well as the emerging market economies and China.[9] As a further reassurance to the prospective students it points out that SOAS is 'Ranked 6th in the UK and 1st in London for Business and

Management by the Guardian University League Table 2016.'[10] Not lost on the prospective applicants is that London is one of the world's leading financial centres.

The international marketing of educational services from the Caribbean SIDS should be based not only on the perceived demand of existing and potential international students, but on creating innovative products. This can be done by, for example, inventing entirely new courses, in line with emerging issues, thereby positioning the Caribbean universities at the leading edge. This, in turn, requires foresight and forecasting skills.

4 Higher education as a regional export cluster

All institutions, including universities, have to continually innovate to survive in changing local, regional and global circumstances. One potentially viable response by the universities of the Caribbean to the new conjuncture is the establishment of a regional export cluster of higher education institutions.

The meaning of a regional cluster

Clusters are collaborative systems, which according to Porter (1990: 148–153; 1998: 77–90) can increase productivity of companies operating in close proximity, increase innovation and stimulate the formation of new businesses within the cluster. Clusters, in the case of universities, can also attract academic talent and researchers.

The term 'cluster' is different from a regional education 'hub' (Knight, 2010: 20–21) because the latter term implicitly connotes location in one physical location and the markets the hub seeks to tap are countries in the same region. The term cluster as used in this paper is located in and operates across several, not necessarily contiguous, small island developing states and seeks opportunities in the global, as against only regional, market for higher education.

Clustering, as a form of collaborative endeavour, could permit institutions of higher education in the region to work together and circumvent the problem of indivisibility of overhead costs and help these universities to attain some of the scale and diversity which universities in large developed countries have as natural advantages (Yusuf and Nabeshima, 2007).[11]

For a cluster of higher educational institutions to be successful, extensive international networking is necessary. As Shields and Edwards (2010) concluded: 'the degree to which most universities are competitive in recruiting international students will increasingly be shaped by the scope and character of their global network rather than any intrinsic characteristics of their individual courses, culture, or campuses'. The establishment and operation of a regional cluster can be international networking initiatives aided and promoted by regional governments and other stakeholders as well as by international organizations.

It should be noted here that multi-campus institutions like the UWI are not clusters in the true sense because the UWI is a government owned university operating three land-based campuses in three countries. These are not as subject to competitive market forces as private institutions are. Being part of a cluster, competing internationally, could improve the operations of the UWI.

Advantages of a Caribbean cluster

A cluster of Caribbean universities will have a number of advantages. It will allow the realizing of economies of scale and scope through more intensive use of plant and infrastructure and other overhead costs.

In addition, there are several benefits beyond those from enlargement and aggregation. It will facilitate offering an increased number and diversity of courses for example the UWI does not offer architecture but it is strong in tropical medicine.

The collaboration between public and private universities will allow a cross-fertilization of institutional cultures and practices for example exposing public higher education institutions to a more entrepreneurial approach to operation and to international marketing.

The exchange and collaboration of research and teaching from a larger combined pool of talent, expertise and experience can enhance the academic reputation of participating universities and open the possibility to attract large research projects thereby improving their ranking at the same time. Such an arrangement could also generate ancillary and support industries such as publishing and international conferences.

A regional cluster could also allow more intra-regional and extra-regional double degrees which is of considerable interest to those planning to live and work outside the Caribbean.

In addition, a Caribbean cluster could provide a very wide variety of courses and degrees and could offer a variety of multi-lingual, multi-cultural experiences delivered in the classroom and by osmosis. The region already offers nearly 500 undergraduate degrees and almost 600 graduate degrees as well as numerous certificates and diplomas (Rochester, 2015: 14). A student in a three-year undergraduate degree could live in three or four countries, experience different cultures and live in a variety of language zones.

Favourable existing pre-conditions in the region

There exist favourable conditions for building a higher-education cluster in the Caribbean region. There is a tradition of collaboration in the region which can be built upon to form a cluster. The Caribbean is already at the centre of various regional associations of tertiary institutions. One such organization is the Association of Caribbean Tertiary Institutions (ACTI) which was registered and incorporated in November, 1990 in Kingston, Jamaica. It was established after a series of discussions among Caribbean tertiary institutions during the late 1980s. Its genesis was the recognition that a mechanism was needed to assist most tertiary institutions within the Caribbean and urged the need for a mechanism designed to assist in the strengthening of tertiary level institutions and to effect better articulation between their programme offerings and those of the University of the West Indies.

There is also the Association of Caribbean Higher Education Administrators (ACHEA)[12] which was launched in July 2001 at the Mona Campus of the University of the West Indies. Among its objectives are to establish and promote networking opportunities and mentoring support for administrators in higher educational institutions in the Caribbean and to foster links and exchanges with similar organizations in higher education overseas.[13] There are also Latin American networks such as the Association of Universities of Latin America and the Caribbean (UDUAL), a nongovernmental organization which consists of 200 affiliated universities and colleges, both public and private, from 21 countries in Latin America and the Caribbean region.[14]

The Association of Caribbean Universities and Research Institutes (UNICA) was established in 1967, with membership spanning the English, Spanish, French and Dutch Caribbean. The Association has partnered with international higher education organizations and associations to strengthen the capacity of education institutions in the region to achieve sustainable development goals. The UWI as the largest and best known global brand and is a member of all of the associations of universities as best placed to be the core of an export cluster of higher education institutions.

The education export cluster and overall economic development

The establishment of an export cluster for higher education has the potential to be transformative to the Caribbean region. Such an initiative would be instrumental in promoting a new impetus for sustainable development.

It is accepted wisdom that achieving sustainable economic development requires substantial investment in human capital thereby increasing productivity. Education also has a positive social and economic effect on many aspects of the quality life and education is accepted as a public good which improves individuals and countries. This connection was firmly established in the early 1960s by empirical studies on the returns of education to economic growth (Schultz, 1961) and the impact of the quality of education on economic growth. This recognition has led many countries to establish ambitious targets relating to the percentage of their population being university educated. In the Caribbean region, a minimum participation rate of 35% has been mooted (Kassim *et al.*, 2013).

The promotion of educational services as an export, through the establishment of a higher-education cluster, could be the catalyst for the long overdue process of strategic global repositioning (Bernal, 1996). The region has suffered low and fluctuating rates of economic growth since the start of the global economic crisis. This cyclical disturbance compounded the economic malaise emanating from the decline of primary agricultural export production, notably sugar and bananas in many of the countries especially the smaller ones. The high dependence on one sector, particularly tourism for many SIDS and petroleum products for Trinidad and Tobago, reveals the vulnerability of these economies, emanating from having too many eggs in one basket.

This higher-education cluster could also contribute to a transformational change in the Caribbean region, which is urgently needed, through a coordinated continual flow of new knowledge which is the fundamental requirement for economic development. This type and amount of knowledge, which can only come from universities, would be enhanced as a result of a higher degree of collaboration between the region's universities. There are no developed countries without the knowledge foundation which comes from great universities producing the research and teaching for a highly-educated cadre of human resources capable of continuous reinvention of international competitiveness.

Therefore, in addition to its direct contribution as an export of services, the cluster would enhance the universities' capacity for policy based research which will support innovation in the private sector and furnish governments and regional institutions with pragmatic and timely policy advice.

5 Concluding remarks

This chapter has argued that for small island developing states there is a largely untapped opportunity to develop higher education as an export and, in the case of the Caribbean SIDS, this is best executed by a higher-education cluster, organized and operating on a regional multi-country template, using modern information and communication technologies, with vigorous international marketing and with strategic coordination and networking.

The Caribbean is well suited to bring to fruition such a cluster because it already has the institutional components, experience and a demonstrated capacity at the regional and national levels from both public and private universities. The success of the Caribbean medical schools would seem to suggest that Caribbean institutions of higher learning can compete successfully with those of larger countries.

The regional cluster, driven by ICT in the delivery of the services and marketing, has an internal competitive logic for the participating institutions as it can mitigate to a certain extent the disadvantages of small size and insularity.

This chapter has also argued that such a development will be good for education and good for economic development. With a well-designed strategy of marketing and global repositioning, education could become a major contributor to incomes and employment as well as earnings of foreign exchange in the region.

Notes

1 http://thecommonwealth.org/small-states. The World Bank uses a similar population threshold for defining small states (see www.worldbank.org/en/country/smallstates).
2 This type of collaboration can transform economically depressed areas into research driven 'innovation hotspots' (van Agtmael and Bakker, 2016).
3 See article 'SUNY, UWI establish Center for Leadership and Sustainable Development' in *Jamaica Observer*, September 24, 2016. www.jamaicaobserver.com/magazines/career/SUNY–UWI-establish-Center-for-Leadership-and-Sustainable-Development-_74760/.
4 See "New Institute of Information Technology Established from UWI-China Partnership" February 26, 2016. www.mona.uwi.edu/marcom/newsroom/entry/6317/.
5 See 'UWI goes global, establishing new institute with China', February 29, 2016. http://sta.uwi.edu/news/releases/release.asp?id=1527/.
6 See 'Higher Education Market worth 70.62 billion USD by 2020', retrieved from www.marketsandmarkets.com/PressReleases/higher-education.asp/.
7 See www.timeshighereducation.com/news/which-universities-could-challenge-higher-education-elite/.
8 In the case of the Caribbean SIDS there is an additional constraint related to the limited ability of the state to fund higher education would probably remain a constraining condition because even when the government allocates a sizeable share of its budget to education the absolute amount in dollars will remain small (Warrican, 2015: 210).
9 It is to be noted here that the global market for higher education is likely to follow the trend of the centre of gravity of the world economy shifting towards the East (Bernal, 2014; Rachman, 2017; Jacques, 2012) with China as the largest both supplier and source of students. The rush for the Chinese market began some time ago but has now reached the point that every university needs to acknowledge the global rise of China and that a modern university education is not complete without some exposure to China.
10 Refer to advertisement of London University in *The Economist*, May 28 2016, p. 78.
11 This a dilemma for universities from small and developing countries compared to the 'sale and diversity of the United States or its ready access to a huge global pool of scholarly talent or to ample research funds from private as well as state sources'. Refer to Fong and Lim (2015).
12 The Association of Caribbean Higher Education Administrators, www.acheacaribbean.org/.
13 Ibid.
14 UDUAL (the Association of Universities of Latin America and the Caribbean): www.groningendeclaration.org/signatories/udual-association-universities-latin-america-and-caribbean-1/.

Appendix 1: Higher education in the Caribbean

There are over 150 universities and colleges in the Caribbean (Rochester, 2015). The dominant feature of the higher education sector in the Caribbean is the large number of very small institutions, usually nationally based in each island. These institutions are so small that even amalgamation will not sufficiently enlarge them to enhance their institutional viability and therefore cooperation and collaboration would be advantageous in several respects to the smaller institutions.

There are four kinds of universities supplying higher education in the Caribbean: (1) resident public universities, (2) resident private for-profit universities, (3) foreign universities both private and public that deliver content through branch campuses in the Caribbean and (4) local resident private universities franchising courses and degrees from foreign universities. International branches campuses are a very limited part of the higher education sector in the Caribbean as it is internationally (Lane and Kinser, 2011). Franchising of content from foreign universities is well developed. The latter two categories do not export higher education, they purvey the educational products of foreign public and private universities. Since 2000 there are at least 60 universities selling into the Caribbean market for higher education (Howe, 2002; Thomas, 2007: 13–56). A list of the major universities in the Caribbean region is presented below.

Resident public universities and resident private universities export higher education services in two main modes of delivery namely (i) cross-border trade via the internet which is a new and relatively underdeveloped aspect of the export of higher education; and (ii) consumption abroad which relates to foreign students coming to campuses physically located in the Caribbean. These are the dominant modes of service delivery at present but this could change in the future. Another mode could develop if there are double degrees delivered in two or more locations, one of which outside of the Caribbean. Another mode would involve movement of persons.

The institutions of higher education

Public universities

University of the West Indies. The UWI is one of two regional cross-country universities in the world. Since its inception in 1948, the University of the West Indies (UWI) has evolved from a fledgling college in Jamaica with 33 students to a full-fledged, regional University with over 50,000 students. Today, the UWI is the largest, most longstanding higher education provider in the Commonwealth Caribbean, with three residential campuses in Barbados, Jamaica, Trinidad and Tobago, and the Open Campus (Brandon, 1999) operating from 12 sites. The UWI has faculty and students from more than 40 countries and collaborative links with 160 universities globally; it offers undergraduate and postgraduate degree options in Food and Agriculture, Engineering, Humanities and Education, Law, Medical Sciences, Science and Technology and Social Sciences. the UWI's seven priority focal areas are linked closely to the priorities identified by CARICOM and take into account such over-arching areas of concern to the region such as environmental issues, health and wellness, gender equity and the critical importance of innovation.

University of Technology (Jamaica). The University of Technology, Jamaica was accorded university status in1995. It was formerly the College of Arts, Science and Technology which was established in 1958 with just over 50 students enrolled in four programmes. It now has a student body of over 13,000 pursuing over 100 programmes at certificate, diploma and degree levels.

University of Guyana (Guyana). Established in 1983 it offers 60 undergraduate and graduate programmes and has an enrolment of 8,000 students.

Mico University College (Jamaica). Founded in 1836 as Mico College it the oldest teacher training college in the Western Hemisphere, and one of the oldest in the world. It has about 3,000 students.

University of Trinidad and Tobago (Trinidad). The University of Trinidad and Tobago (UTT) is a state-owned university in Trinidad and Tobago established in 2004. Its main campus is located at Wallerfield in Trinidad. It was formed by an amalgamation of several former technological colleges and has 12 locations throughout the country.

Private universities

The profitable operation of private universities in the Caribbean that rely almost entirely on non-regional students primarily Americans is proof that (1) there is a market for higher education services in the form of demand from the United States, (2) Americans paying US dollars are willing to live and study in the Caribbean and (3) that this business can be profitable. There is a demand for studying medicine in these off-shore universities as indicated by the fact that there are an estimated 3,500 Canadians studying medicine overseas, compared to about 10,500 in Canada (Sheppard, 2011). The numbers are probably higher for Americans studying abroad. Where they studied is not an issue because to practice in the US they must be board-certified by completing a residency programme at an accredited institution and passing at a certain grade, written and, depending on the specialty, oral examinations. Two such institutions were start-ups and did not have the advantage of being established brand-names but were innovative in the approach to teaching medicine (Howard, 2017). It suggests that the University of the West Indies which was established almost seventy years ago, and is well regarded brand-name could meet some of the demand and earn foreign exchange from the provision of such services.

St George's University. St George's University is a privately-owned university established in 1976 in Grenada, West Indies, offering degrees in medicine, veterinary medicine, public health, the health sciences, nursing, arts and sciences, and business at both the under-graduate and graduate levels. From an inauspicious initiative, the institution has grown by starting the School of Medicine in January, 1977. Courses in international business, life sciences, medical sciences, pre-medical and pre-veterinary medicine were added in 1997. In 1999 The School of Veterinary Medicine and the Department of Public Health and Preventive Medicine were established. Currently there are 2,300 faculty and 6,022 students.

Ross University. Ross University School of Veterinary Medicine (RUSVM) was founded in 1978 by DeVry Medical International, Inc. and established in St Kitts and Dominica. It offers a Doctor of Veterinary Medicine degree in St Kitts which is accredited by the American Veterinary Medical Association Council on Education and in 2014, it began offering Master of Science and PhD degrees in Public Health and Global Animal Health. Ross University School of Medicine is located in Dominica. Ross has graduated over 11,000 practicing physicians.

Northern Caribbean University (Jamaica). Northern Caribbean University (NCU) is a private, liberal-arts university located in Jamaica that is owned and operated by the Seventh-day Adventist Church. It offers professional, pre-professional and vocational programmes. The main campus in Mandeville and three regional campuses situated in Kingston, Montego Bay and St Anne, serve just under 6,000 students.

University of the Southern Caribbean. University of the Southern Caribbean was previously the Caribbean Union College. It is a private, coeducational institution operated by the Seventh-day Adventist Church. It has three locations in the twin-island Republic of Trinidad and Tobago along with sites in Antigua, Barbados Guyana and St Lucia.

Appendix 2

Table 5.A1 List of 39 members of the Alliance for Small Island States

Antigua and Barbuda	*Mauritius*
Bahamas	Nauru
Barbados	Niue
Belize	Palau
Cape Verde	Papua New Guinea
Comoros	Samoa
Cook Islands	Singapore
Cuba	Seychelles
Dominica	Sao Tome and Principe
Dominican Republic	Solomon Islands
Fiji	St Kitts and Nevis
Grenada	St Lucia
Guinea-Bissau	St Vincent and the Grenadines
Guyana	Suriname
Haiti	Timor-Leste
Jamaica	Tonga
Kiribati	Trinidad and Tobago
Maldives	Tuvalu
Marshall Islands	Vanuatu
Micronesia, Federated States of	

Information about AOSIS is available at http://aosis.org/. There is also a United Nations list of 37 SIDS available at http s://sustainabledevelopment.un.org/topics/sids/list, which is similar to the AOSIS list, but leaves out the Cook Islands and Niue.

References

Altbach, P. G., and de Wit, H. (2017). 'Trump and the Coming Revolution in Higher Education Internationalization'. *International Higher Education*, 89: 3–5.

Bacchus, K. and Brock, C. (1987). *The Challenge of Scale. Educational Development in the Small States of the Commonwealth*. London: Commonwealth Secretariat.

Beckles, H., Perry, A. and Whiteley, P. (2002). *The Brain Train. Quality Higher Education and Caribbean Development*. Kingston: University of the West Indies.

Bernal, R. L. (1996). Strategic Global Repositioning and the Future Economic Development of Jamaica. *North South Agenda Paper* No. 18. Miami, FL: North South Center, University of Miami.

Bernal, R. L. (1998). The Integration of Small Economies in the Free Trade Area of the Americas. *CSIS, Policy Paper on the Americas*, Vol. IX, Study No.1. Washington, DC: Center for Strategic and International Studies.

Bernal, R. L. (2014). *Dragon in the Caribbean: China's global redimensioning Challenges and Opportunities for the Caribbean*. Kingston: Ian Randle Publishers.

Brandon, E. (1999). The Open Campus evolved from a long experience with long distance teaching. In Harry, K. *Higher education through open and distance learning*. London: Routledge.

Briguglio, L. (1995). 'Small island developing states and their economic vulnerabilities'. *World Development*, 23(9): 1615–1632.

British Council (2012). *The shape of things to come: higher education global trends and emerging opportunities to 2020*. London: British Council.

Bradshaw, D. (2014). Teaching revolution gathers pace. Available at www.ft.com/content/88757cba
-9979-11e3-b3a2-00144feab7de. Accessed on 1 June 2017.

Caribbean Export Development Agency (CEDA) (2011). *Towards a strategy for the Cariforum Higher Education Sector*. Barbados: Bridgetown.

Cobley, A. (2000). The Historical Development of Higher Education in the Anglophone Caribbean. In Howe, G. (ed.), *Higher Education in the Caribbean: Past, Present and Future Directions*. Kingston: University of the West Indies Press: 1–23.

Commonwealth Secretariat (1997). *A future for small states: Overcoming vulnerability*. London: Commonwealth Secretariat.

Cottom, T. M. (2017). *Lower Ed: The Troubling Rise of For-Profit Colleges in the New Economy*. New York: The New Press.

Eckhert, L. and van Zanten, M. (2014). *Faimer Short Report. Overview of For-Profit Schools in the Caribbean*. Philadelphia, PA: Faimer.

Etzkowitz, H. (2008). *The triple helix: University-industry-government innovation in action*. London: Routledge.

Fong, P. E. and Lim, L. (2015). 'Evolving Great Universities in Small and Developing Countries'. *International Higher Education*, 33: 9–10.

Howard, B. (2017). *Training for the Future*. Best Grad School, U.S. News & World Report: 40–43.

Howe, G. D. (2002). *Contending with change: Reviewing tertiary education in the English-speaking Caribbean*. Caracas: International Institute for Higher Education in Latin America and the Caribbean.

Jacques, M. (2012). *When China rules the world: The end of the western world and the birth of a new global order*. London: Penguin Books.

Kassim, H. S., Dass, A., and Best, T. (2013). *Higher Education and Statistical Review: Issues and trends in Higher education 2013*. University of the West Indies, Office of Planning and Development.

Knight, J. (2010). 'Regional Education Hubs – Rhetoric or Reality'. *International Higher Education*, 59 (Spring): 20–21.

Lane, J. and Kinser, K. (2011). 'The cross-border education policy context: Educational hubs, trade liberalization, and national sovereignty'. *New Directions for Higher Education*, 2011(155): 79–85.

Lendle, A. and Olarreaga, M. (2017). *Can Online Markets Make Trade More Inclusive?*. ADBI Working Paper742. Tokyo: Asian Development Bank Institute.

Longsworth, L. (2014). *Bringing the UWI to You. A Community approach to Online and Distance Education*. Kingston: University of the West Indies Open Campus.

McFarling, U. L. (2017). Why the United States is no longer turning up its nose at Caribbean medical schools. Available at www.statnews.com/2017/02/17/caribbean-medical-schools/. Accessed on 1 June 2017.

Nurse, L. A., McLean, R. F., Agard, J., Briguglio, L. P., Duvat-Magnan, V., Pelesikoti, N., Tompkins, E. and Webb, A. (2014). *Climate Change 2014: Impacts, Adaptation, and Vulnerability*. Geneva: Intergovernmental Panel on Climate Change: 1613–1654.

Odin, J. K., and Manicas, P. T. (2004). *Globalization and higher education*. Honolulu: University of Hawaii Press.

Pelling, M., and Uitto, J. I. (2001). 'Small island developing states: natural disaster vulnerability and global change'. *Global Environmental Change Part B: Environmental Hazards*, 3(2): 49–62.

Porter, M. E. (1990). 'The Competitive Advantage of Nations'. *Harvard Business Review*, 68(2): 73–93.

Porter, M. E. (1998). 'Clusters and the new economics of competition'. *Harvard Business Review*, 76(6): 77–90.

QAA (2015). *Review of UK Transnational Education Caribbean 2014*. Southgate: Quality Assurance Agency for Higher Education.

Rachman, G. (2017). *Easternization: Asia's rise and America's decline from Obama to Trump and beyond*. New York: Other Press.

Redden, E. (2017a). Canada's Moment. Available at https://continuingedupdate.blogspot.kr/2017/04/canadas-moment-elizabeth-redden-inside.html/.

Redden, E. (2017b). Will International Students Stay Away? Available at www.insidehighered.com/news/2017/03/13/nearly-4-10-universities-report-drops-international-student-applications/.

Rochester, N. (2015). *Internationalization of Higher Education Services and Institutional Partnership*. Paper for the 3rd CARIFORUM-European Union Business Forum, Montego Bay, Jamaica.

Schultz, T. W. (1961). 'Investment in Human Capital'. *American Economic Review*, 51(1): 1–17.

Sheppard, M. (2011). Too many Canadians studying medicine overseas. More medical schools opening but no residency positions. Available at www.cbc.ca/news/health/too-many-canadians-studying-medicine-overseas-1.993980/.

Shields, R. and Edwards, R. M. (2010). Student Mobility and Emerging Hubs in Global Higher Education. In L.M. Portnoi, V. D. Rust and S. Bagley (eds), *Higher Education, Policy and Global Competition Phenomenon*. New York: Palgrave McMillan: 235–248.

Thomas, M. (2007). The Liberalization of Higher Education: Its Impact and Implications for the UWI and Tertiary Education in the Anglophone Caribbean- Potentials and Risks for the Delivery of Cross-border Education. In Watson, E. F., and Grant, J. M. A. (eds), *New directions in university education: Perspectives from the developing world*. Bridgetown, Barbados: Learning Resource Centre, UWI.

Thorp, H. and Goldstein, B. (2013). *Engines of innovation: The entrepreneurial university in the twenty-first century*. Chapel Hill, PA: UNC Press Books.

United Nations (2010). *Trends in sustainable development. Small island developing states (SIDS)*. New York: United Nations.

Varghese, N. V. and Institut international de planification de l'éducation (2008). *Globalization of higher education and cross-border student mobility*. Paris: UNESCO, International Institute for Educational Planning.

Van Agtmael, A. and Bakker, F. (2016). *The smartest places on earth: Why rustbelts are the emerging hotspots of global innovation*. New York: PublicAffairs Books.

Wang, A. (2016). Tuition is increasing at alarming rates at US public universities. Available at https://qz.com/588920/tuition-is-increasing-at-alarming-rates-at-us-public-universities/.

Warrican, S. J. (2015). Building a Quality Institution of Higher Learning in a Small State: Issues, Considerations and Challenges. In A. K. Perkins (ed.), *Quality in Higher Education in the Caribbean*. Kingston: University of the West Indies Press.

Yusuf, S., and Nabeshima, K. (2007). *How universities promote economic growth*. Washington, DC: World Bank.

Zeleza, P. (2016). *The transformation of global higher education: 1945–2015*. New York: Palgrave MacMillan.

Part II
Finance

6

Do small states need large external buffers? Evidence from an event-study analysis

Valerio Crispolti[1]

1 Introduction

Small states, compared to other groups of countries, are more vulnerable to a wide range of exogenous shocks such as natural disasters, sharp swings in the terms of trade, abrupt changes in export demand, or sudden stop of financial flows (Briguglio, 2016; Cabezon *et al.*, 2015; Auguste and Cornejo, 2015). Such vulnerability arises, to a large extent, from the intrinsic economic structural characteristics of small states. These are well documented and include: high trade openness due to limited natural resource endowments and a small domestic market – which make small states extremely dependent on foreign exchange to finance their imports; a narrow production base that reflects the small size of the economy and the limited scope for economic diversification and import substitution; lack of domestic competition because of the small size of the market, and remoteness (Briguglio, 2016; IMF, 2013a). However, vulnerability can also be related to home-grown factors related to policy mismanagement such as large fiscal and external imbalances, high inflation, and unsustainable debt ratios, which amplify the impact of exogenous shocks (IMF, 2006, 2013b and 2015). In addition, policy mismanagement is positively correlated with the quality of institutions (Acemoglu *et al.*, 2001).

Although small states are intrinsically more vulnerable than other countries to external shocks, they can reduce the risk of being adversely affected from such shocks by increasing the resilience of their economies (Briguglio *et al.*, 2009; Briguglio, 2016). This is done by adopting sound macroeconomic policies aimed at building policy buffers (e.g., lower debt, higher fiscal balances and international reserves), which could help the economy withstand and counter economic shocks. For example, broadening the tax base and reducing the rigidity of public spending, while improving access to finance, would allow building fiscal buffers for countercyclical fiscal policies during downturns and stepping up infrastructure spending to boost potential output. Similarly, policies aimed at diversifying the export base and trade partners would reduce the vulnerability of the economy to abrupt changes in the external environment (e.g. swings in the terms of trade, a fall in demand from export-destination markets) and favour the accumulation of foreign exchange needed to finance imports. Resilience can also be strengthened by arranging conditional financing in the form of self-insurance (e.g. contingency funds), plans to tap borrowed or grant resources, and risk-transfer arrangements through private or sovereign insurance as well as multilateral risk-sharing mechanisms (e.g. international safety net).

While sound macroeconomic policies are the first line of defence for limiting a country's vulnerability (Becker *et al.*, 2007), international reserves constitute an important form of self-insurance against shocks, as these can be mobilized rapidly to avoid a disorderly macroeconomic adjustment. In particular, countries typically hold international reserves to limit volatility in the exchange rate, cushion the domestic economy against shocks, and provide liquidity to domestic financial markets and the banking sector, especially if there is significant dollarization (Jeanne and Wyplosz, 2003). Country experience suggests that indeed reserves have proven useful during crises, as countries with higher reserve holdings were better able to smooth consumption and expand fiscal policy to help offset the effects of the crisis, compared to those with lower reserve levels (IMF, 2011). However, accumulating reserves is costly due to the opportunity cost of immobilizing resources and foregoing returns on alternative investments. Hence, countries need to trade off the costs of holding reserves against the consumption-smoothing benefits of having a ready stock of reserve assets.

This study examines the experience of 36 small states[2] covering the period 1980–2016 in order to assess the role of international reserves as a cushion against large external shocks, such as natural disasters, sharp swings in the terms of trade, abrupt changes in export demand, and a fall in financial inflows, including foreign direct investment (FDI) and remittances. As in Crispolti and Tsibouris (2012), this chapter gauges the macroeconomic impact and costs associated with different external shocks that hit small states over the last four decades using an event-study analysis. The macroeconomic impact of shocks is expressed in terms of key macroeconomic indicators such as per-capita gross domestic product (GDP) growth, current and fiscal account ratios to GDP, and international reserve accumulation; while, the costs of shocks are measured in terms of forgone real per-capita GDP and absorption growth with respect to pre-shock trends. The chapter also compares macroeconomic costs of shocks across countries to determine whether such costs vary according to the level of international reserves held prior to a shock event.

The main finding of this study is that the effectiveness of international reserves as a buffer against external shocks depends on the type of shock that is experienced as well as on the structural characteristics of the economy. Typically, reserve holdings above three months of imports prior to a shock event have helped small states buffer per-capita GDP growth against natural disasters and shocks relating to remittances and FDI, but less so in the case of terms-of-trade shocks and external demand. In addition, countries with higher reserve coverage generally suffered smaller absorption losses in the face of most external shocks. However, maintaining a reserve cover above three months of imports was not a safe haven for countries with a flexible exchange rate regime in the year preceding the shock and for micro states, particularly when the cost associated with shocks are expressed in terms of forgone real per-capita absorption growth.

The study is structured as follows: Section 2 provides a brief summary of the existing literature on reserve adequacy. Section 3 describes the methodology used to identify shock episodes and assess related macroeconomic costs, while Section 4 presents some stylized facts pertaining small states during the period 1980–2016. Sections 5 and 6 discuss the results of the event-study analysis for small states, and the potential role played by international reserve holdings in cushioning the economy from external shocks. Finally, Section 7 presents some concluding remarks.

2 Literature review

A significant strand of literature focuses on the role of reserves as an insurance mechanism against external shocks in advanced and emerging economies. Aizenman and Lee (2007) look at main drivers of the reserve accumulation and find evidence supporting the view that countries hoard reserves as self-insurance against costly output contractions induced by sudden stops (i.e., an abrupt reduction of capital inflows) and capital flight. In particular, they conclude that current trends of growing trade openness and greater exposure to financial shocks account for a large share of observed accumulation of international reserves. Durdu *et al.* (2009) test the hypothesis that countries accumulate reserves to self-insure against external shocks and conclude that financial globalization and sudden-stop risk explain the observed surge in reserves in many countries in recent decades. Interestingly, they find that business cycle volatility is not a major factor behind recent trends in reserve accumulation.

Jeanne and Ranciere (2006, 2008) develop a model of optimal level of international reserves for emerging economies that are vulnerable to sudden stops in capital flows. They find that reserves help countries smooth domestic absorption after a shock to capital flows, and derive a closed-form formula for the optimal level of reserves that weighs the benefits (e.g. crisis mitigation) and the opportunity costs (e.g. differential between domestic and foreign real interest rates) of holding reserves. The optimal level of reserves suggested by their model is close to the 'Greenspan-Guidotti' rule (i.e., full coverage of total short-term external debt)[3] and consistent with the order of magnitude observed in many emerging market countries over the last decades, for plausible calibrations of the model.

More recently, Calvo *et al.* (2012) developed a model of optimal stock of international reserves in which reserves affect both the probability of a sudden stop and associated output costs. They find that generally policymakers' decision on the amount of international reserves held are influenced by considerations on currency denomination mismatches and current account deficits. However, there are other idiosyncratic factors that may play a role in explaining reserve accumulation, such as the perceived presence of a lender of last resort, being a large oil producer, or potential credit lines from institutions such as the International Monetary Fund (IMF) or the Federal Reserve.

A significantly smaller number of studies focused on the determinants of reserve accumulation in low-income countries (LICs) with limited access to foreign capital markets.

These studies primarily discuss the risks stemming from the current account of the balance of payments. Barnichon (2009) develops an intertemporal model to determine the optimal level of reserves in a small open economy that holds costly foreign reserves to smooth import fluctuations in the face of large external disturbances, such as a natural disaster or a terms-of-trade shock. He finds that the popular rule of thumb of maintaining reserves equivalent to three months of imports gives only an imprecise benchmark.[4]

Drummond and Dhasmana (2008) extend the Jeanne-Ranciere framework to examine the implications of aid and terms-of-trade shocks in Sub-Saharan countries. They find that the optimal level of reserves depends on the size and probability of shocks as well as the output cost associated with such shocks. They conclude that Sub-Saharan countries do not carry reserves consistent with the expected output costs associated with terms-of-trade or aid shocks.

Crispolti *et al.* (2013) develop a simple cost-benefit analytical framework of precautionary reserve holdings and find that the optimal reserve holdings depend crucially on country characteristics and policy fundamentals. In this context, calibrated optimal reserves vary from about one to seven months of imports, with higher estimated reserves for fragile states, and commodity exporters than for other countries. In addition, optimal reserves are generally higher for countries with fixed exchange rate regimes and not receiving support from the IMF in the event of a shock, and for countries facing a lower cost of reserves. Consequently, they conclude that the standard metric of a level of reserves equivalent to three months of imports can be considered a lower bound at best.

While the literature on reserve accumulation in advanced and emerging economies is well established, studies on small states have been limited. Dehesa *et al.* (2009), using a model similar to that used by Jeanne and Ranciere (2008), find that international reserves held by the Eastern Caribbean Currency Union are generally adequate for a variety of external current and capital account shocks. However, greater international integration through capital account liberalization and rapid financial deepening suggests that reserve coverage may need to further increase to help insure against adverse capital flows.

Mwase (2012) investigates the drivers of reserve accumulation in small islands and derives an operational metric to determine the optimal level of reserves based on small states' unique characteristics (e.g. high trade openness, limited financial structures). Following the approach discussed in IMF (2011), the proposed metric is a weighted function of broad money, short-term debt and exports. Based on this new metric, Mwase (2012) concludes that holding about 75% to 100% of this metric reduces the probability of a crisis to less than 2% in small islands.

More recently, Moore and Glean (2016) extended the methodology developed by Crispolti *et al.* (2013) to assess the adequacy of reserve holdings in small states by performing a cost-benefit analysis based on the inherent vulnerabilities of small states (e.g. to natural disasters and terms-of-trade shocks) and computing the cost of holding reserves as the output loss associated with an over-investment in reserves. Their results suggest that in small states, the optimal holding of foreign exchange reserves is approximately six months of imports, approximately thirteen weeks higher than the international rule of thumb of three months of imports. In addition, they find that the estimate of optimal reserve holdings is interrelated with the economic characteristics of the country, particularly its fiscal stance.

To sum up, the assessment of reserve adequacy in small states remain an area for further research. The few studies available adopt standard approaches that were developed to gauge reserve holdings in advanced and emerging economies and that are only partially accounting for the unique characteristics of small states. These studies generally find that small states are more vulnerable than larger countries to external shocks and consequently would benefit from higher level of international reserves. In addition, such studies conclude that the appropriate reserve cover also depends on the structural characteristics of small states.

3 Methodology and data

Identifying external shocks

Following the methodology developed by Crispolti *et al.* (2013), an external shock is identified by a 'significant worsening' in a country's climatic conditions, terms of trade, external demand (proxied by real GDP growth in trading partners), foreign direct investment (FDI) inflows, or remittances. A significant worsening of the shock variable is defined as an annual percentage change that falls below the bottom 10th percentile of the country-specific distribution of annual changes, as shown in Figure 6.1.[5]

Importantly, shock events are derived independently from each other (i.e., the matrix of variances and co-variances of shocks is assumed to be diagonal), and shock episodes that are contiguous or less than three years apart are recorded as one shock event occurring in the earliest available year. While alternative definitions of a shock event exist in literature, this one presents several advantages as it (i) allows to control for heterogeneity among small states by using country-specific distributions; (ii) captures rare events by focusing on the

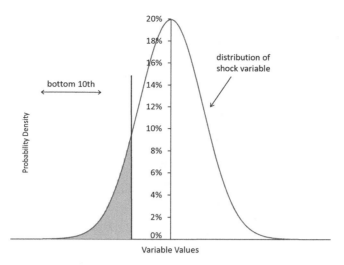

Figure 6.1 Definition of shock episodes

bottom 10th percentile of the shock variable's distribution of annual changes; and, (iii) focuses the analysis on the reaction to the shock by assuming the same frequency of shocks for each country.

Measuring the economic impact and cost of a shock

For each shock event, the analysis identifies its economic impact and measures its cost in terms of forgone growth of real per-capita GDP and absorption (i.e., consumption plus investment). Specifically, the economic impact of a shock was evaluated by means of a five-year event window capturing the behaviour of the relevant macroeconomic variables from one year before the shock episode to three years after. A worsening of the relevant macroeconomic variables within the five-year event window would suggest a negative correlation between the occurrence of an external shock and economic performance.[6] Conversely, the economic cost associated with a shock is computed by comparing the actual growth rates of per-capita GDP or absorption with their respective pre-shock trends—proxied with the average growth rate in the three years preceding a shock episode. More specifically, the comparison is made by quantifying the annual differences between a 'shock' growth index—based on actual growth—and a 'no-shock' growth index—reflecting trend growth, as illustrated in Figure 6.2.

By construction, both indices take a value of 100 in the year preceding a shock. Subsequently, the 'shock' index changes in line with realized growth, while the 'no-shock' index increases at a constant rate given by the variable's pre-shock trend growth. The difference between the two indices can be positive or negative in any given year: if negative, it represents an annual loss in terms of percentage points of per-capita GDP or absorption growth. Accordingly, the cost associated with a shock is provided by the cumulative sum of annual losses over the period following a shock episode. In addition, the number of years in which a country experiences a loss may be interpreted as a measure of duration of the economic cost associated with a shock. Importantly, the economic impact and costs of shocks are assessed without controlling for the presence of combined-shock episodes (i.e., instances in which two or more

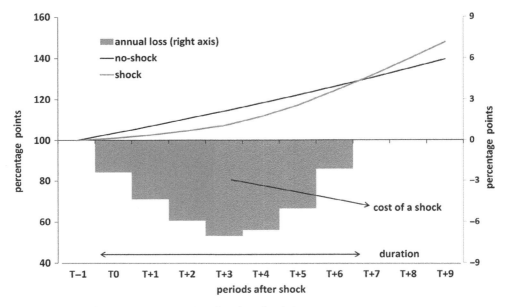

Figure 6.2 Identifying the cost associated with a shock *
Note: * The cumulated sum of the annual losses represents the cost in percentage points associated with a shock. In this example, the duration is seven years.

shocks of different nature strike simultaneously). While this may lead to overemphasizing annual
losses associated with shock events, combined shocks are not very frequent in the sample as one
out of five shock years featured two simultaneous shocks and one out of hundred featured three
simultaneous shocks.

Controlling for the structural characteristics of the economy

After computing the impact and cost of shocks, these are examined by controlling for a number
of structural characteristics of the economy, including its level of development (e.g. low-income
countries or otherwise), its exchange rate regime (i.e. fixed, intermediate, flexible),[7] the composition of exports (i.e. non-oil primary commodities, services), the level of indebtedness, and
the presence of a financial arrangement with the IMF. With respect to the latter, the existence
of a financial arrangement is assessed during the period ranging from a year prior to the shock
episode to three years after. A distinction was made between countries that had a financial
arrangement with the IMF (i.e. either in the year of the shock or the one before) or no
arrangement at all.

4 Stylized facts

Integration in the global economy

Over the past four decades, small states have steadily increased their ties with international
markets. Trade openness, measured as the sum of imports and exports over gross domestic
product (GDP), has increased from an average of 101% in the 1980s to 103% in 2010–16, as

Table 6.1 Small states and international markets (in % of GDP; average values)

		1980–89	*1990–99*	*2000–09*	*2010–16*
	Trade openness	80.7	80.1	93.5	105.1
Africa	FDI	1.4	2.0	6.0	34.7
	Remittances	1.6	2.8	4.4	7.0
	Trade openness	99.2	100.7	100.2	114.7
Asia	FDI	5.9	2.1	3.4	4.3
	Remittances	9.2	7.7	8.4	8.0
	Trade openness	109.6	108.0	98.3	94.5
Caribbean	FDI	3.3	6.5	9.4	8.7
	Remittances	4.7	4.5	6.4	6.4
	Trade openness	101.0	100.7	98.2	103.6
Small States	FDI	3.7	4.3	6.7	11.5
	Remittances	5.7	5.2	6.9	7.1

Source: World Economic Outlook 2017; World Bank; estimates.

shown in Table 6.1. This marginal change, however, masks stark differences in regional patterns: small states in Africa and Asia increased their trade openness from respectively 80 and 99% on average in 1980–89 to 105 and 114% in 2010–16; whereas, small states of the Caribbean became less open with trade openness falling from 110% on average in the 1980s to 95% in 2010–16. These trends were more pronounced in African and Caribbean micro states (defined here as countries with population below 200,000 people). Over the same period, small states were also exposed to increasing inflows of FDI and remittances. In the 1980s, on average, FDI and remittances accounted for a little more than 4 and 6% of GDP, respectively. With the turn of the century, such inflows gained prominence reaching an average of about 12 and 7% of GDP in 2010–16. The experience of micro states is somewhat different as the increase in FDI was less pronounced, and remittances as share of GDP declined markedly between 1980–89 and 2010–16.

While greater integration in the global economy has brought several advantages to small states – including bigger markets for their products, diversification into new sectors, economies of scale, and better risk sharing, it has also increased their exposure to events over which these economies have little, if any, influence. Since 1980, small states have been confronted with significant and increasing volatility in external demand, relative prices, and FDI (Table 6.2). For example, the volatility (measured as the average standard deviation) of small states' external demand (proxied by real GDP growth in small states' major trading partners) increased by about 10% between the 1980–89 and 2010–16. Over the same period, the volatility of the percentage change in the relative prices of imports of goods in terms of exports of goods (i.e., terms of trade) increased from an average of 12 in the 1980s to an average of 13 after 2010. This is also the case when the terms of trade are computed weighting the prices of exports and imports by the relative importance of imports and exports of goods in the economy, as suggested by Easterly and Kraay (2000). The rise in the volatility of FDI was dramatic with the standard deviation of the FDI-to-GDP ratio increasing eight-fold between the 1980s and recent years (Table 6.2).

Table 6.2 Small states and volatility in the external environment (in standard deviations; average values)

		1980–89	1990–99	2000–09	2010–16
	Terms of trade	17.6	16.3	23.5	12.3
Africa	Terms of trade (weighted)	5.6	3.6	5.7	4.6
	External demand	0.1	0.3	0.4	0.5
	FDI	0.5	1.5	4.6	82.2
	Terms of trade	3.5	14.6	10.0	22.6
Asia	Terms of trade (weighted)	1.8	4.2	1.6	8.0
	External demand	0.4	1.2	0.3	0.5
	FDI	7.8	1.3	1.6	2.5
	Terms of trade	4.7	8.3	4.9	4.2
Caribbean	Terms of trade (weighted)	2.5	3.2	2.0	2.5
	External demand	0.4	0.8	0.5	0.3
	FDI	3.6	2.9	3.1	2.3
	Terms of trade	12.0	11.7	15.0	13.2
Small States	Terms of trade (weighted)	4.1	3.4	3.5	4.8
	External demand	0.4	0.9	0.4	0.4
	FDI	4.8	2.5	3.1	33.7

Source: World Economic Outlook 2017; World Bank; estimates.

Exposure to significant external changes

Over the last three decades, small states in the sample have been frequently confronted with significant changes in their external environment. Using the definition of a significant change, discussed further in Section 3, and taking all the mentioned types of shocks into consideration, small states were hit by an external shock approximately every ten years (Table 6.3).[8] The likelihoods of natural disasters and external-demand shocks were slightly higher, about one every eight to nine years, while the probability of a shock to the terms of trade ranged between one every eight to one every ten years depending on whether the terms of trade are weighted or not by a country's imports and exports. In contrast, shocks to remittances were somewhat less frequent (one every eleven years). Compared to other small states, micro states were stormed more frequently by natural disasters (one every eight years) and less frequently by terms-of-trade shocks (one every eleven years).

The size of external shocks also varied depending on the type of shock (Table 6.3). Typically, shocks to external demand and the terms of trade had a magnitude of just less than two standard deviations from the sample mean, while remittances and FDI shocks registered more than two standard deviations. This implied subdued growth in main small states' trading partners, a fall in relative prices of about 12% under a terms-of-trade shock, and a decline in the FDI and remittances ratios to GDP by 9% and 3%, respectively.

The geographical distribution of shocks showed noteworthy differences (Table 6.3). While shocks to external demand occurred with a similar frequency in all regions,

Table 6.3 Frequency and size of external shocks (average values)

		Terms of trade[1]	External demand	FDI	Natural disasters[2,3]	Remittances
Africa	Frequency	17.0	19.0	16.0	47.0	14.0
	Frequency (country years)	7.7	8.6	8.2	9.9	17.8
	Size (% change)	−18.8	0.8	−23.5	n.a.	−1.1
	Size (in st. deviations)	−2.2	−1.9	−1.9	n.a.	−2.1
Asia	Frequency	19.0	29.0	41.0	87.0	33.0
	Frequency (country years)	11.3	8.7	11.1	7.9	11.9
	Size (% change)	−14.5	1.5	−5.6	n.a.	−3.4
	Size (in st. deviations)	−1.6	−1.6	−2.2	n.a.	−2.0
Caribbean	Frequency	59.0	46.0	62.0	133.0	34.0
	Frequency (country years)	11.2	8.3	10.4	9.5	7.8
	Size (% change)	−10.1	−0.4	−7.3	n.a.	−2.3
	Size (in st. deviations)	−1.8	−2.0	−2.2	n.a.	−2.3
Small States	Frequency	95.0	94.0	119.0	267.0	81.0
	Frequency (country years)	10.4	8.5	10.3	9.0	11.2
	Size (% change)	−12.5	0.5	−8.9	n.a.	−2.5
	Size (in st. deviations)	−1.9	−1.8	−2.1	n.a.	−2.2

Source: World Economic Outlook 2017; World Bank; EM-DAT; estimates.
Notes: [1] Terms of trade are for goods only and are weighted by a country's imports and exports.
[2] Data on natural disasters were kindly provided by the Centre for Research on the Epidemiology of Disasters at the School of Public Health of the Université Catholique de Louvain, Belgium (see Guha-Sapir *et al.*, 2015).
[3] Given the heterogeneity of indicators used to identify natural disasters (Appendix 1), it was not possible to estimate the sample size of a natural disaster shock.

significant changes in the terms of trade and FDI inflows were more likely to happen in small states in Africa (one shock every eight years). At the same time, the likelihood of a natural disaster striking was significantly higher in small states in Asia (one shock every eight years) than in those in Africa (one shock every eighteen years). By contrast, drops in remittances were significantly less common in small states in Africa (one shock every seventeen years) than in the Caribbean (one shock every eight years). In micro states, the most common external shocks were natural disasters and large swings in external demand (about one shock every eight years).

In terms of size, small states in the Caribbean were confronted with the largest external-demand shocks (2 standard deviations from the mean), while the size of shocks did not exceed 1.6 standard deviations from the mean in small states in Asia. At the same time, small states in Africa witnessed the largest drops in the terms of trade (more than two standard deviations), and small states in the Caribbean faced the deeper drop in FDI and remittance. Compared to other country groups, micro states experienced slightly larger terms-of-trade and FDI shocks (about two standard deviations).

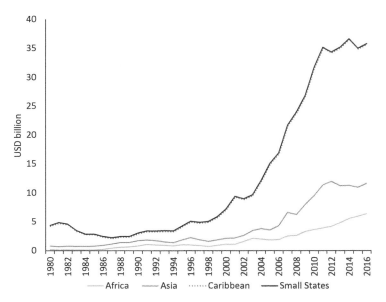

Figure 6.3 International reserve holdings in small states
Source: World Economic Outlook 2017; World Bank; estimates.

Against the backdrop of heightened exposure to external shocks, many small states have seen a significant increase in their holdings of international reserves over the last two decades as shown in Figure 6.3.

Changes in external reserves

In 2016, small states held just over US$35 billion in reserves, almost US$30 billion more than in 2000. This rapid increase in reserves possibly reflects policy the choice among small states to build precautionary reserves to insure against external shocks, and may have been facilitated by the favourable long-term trends in commodity prices, including oil and agricultural products (Erten and Ocampo, 2012; Erdem and Ünalmış, 2016). The build-up of reserves holdings was remarkable in the Caribbean small states with the region accounting for about two thirds of the total increase and Trinidad and Tobago alone for about US$7 billion. Small states in Africa and Asia increased their stock of international reserves to the tune of US$5 billion since 2000. Differentiating small states by their structural characteristics confirms that the recent trends in reserve accumulation were broad based.

The accumulation of international reserves in small states appears noticeable also when examined through the lens of traditional metrics for reserve adequacy, such as coverage in terms of imports, broad money, and short-term debt (Figure 6.4).[9] The import cover, measuring the number of months of imports that can be financed if foreign exchange inflows were to cease, is typically applied to countries with less open capital accounts. In this case, the traditional rule of thumb for an adequate cover is three months of imports. For countries with large banking sector and very open capital accounts, the broad money cover (i.e., the ratio of reserves to broad money, typically M2) provides a measure of the potential for resident-based capital flight and is particularly relevant for dollarized economies. Typically, the benchmark for a prudent

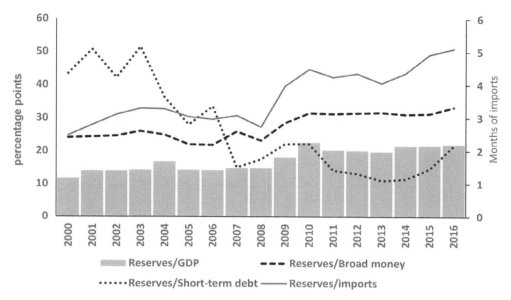

Figure 6.4 Indicators of reserve coverage in small states

range for reserve holdings is 20% (IMF, 2011). The short-term debt cover (i.e., the ratio of reserves to short-term external debt with one-year or less maturity) is an indicator of crisis risk for market-access countries with large short-term cross-border financial transactions. The 'Greenspan-Guidotti' rule of 100% cover of short-term debt is commonly used as benchmark for assessing reserve adequacy in emerging market economies.

Regional trends confirm a significant build up in international reserves over the last two decades (Figure 6.5).

The median import cover of small states in Africa was persistently above three months of imports, increasing up to about seven months in 2016. Small states in Asia and the Caribbean also experienced a rise in the import cover, although less pronounced. A similar picture emerges when small states' reserve holdings are expressed in terms of broad money, with Caribbean small states showing a more gradual increase and economies in Asia experiencing a significant drop in the median reserve cover after the onset of the global financial crisis. Importantly, the build-up of reserves in recent years has also reflected the Special Drawing Right (SDR) allocation agreed by the members of the IMF in response to the global financial crisis in 2009.[10]

Structural characteristics of different country groups

Breaking down reserve accumulation by various structural characteristics of the economy provides further insights. During the last two decades, low-income small states had persistently higher reserve cover than other small states, with the difference somewhat increasing in most recent years (Figure 6.6). This may reflect the fact that low-income small states usually have limited or no access to financial markets and are therefore more in need of resources to self-insure against external shocks.

The increase in reserve coverage was particularly sharp in oil exporting small states which, benefiting from high petroleum prices, maintained a median import cover of about eight

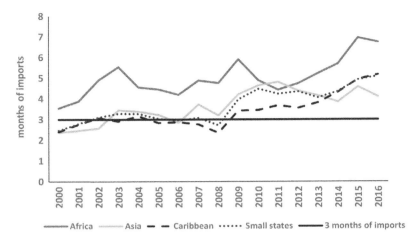

Figure 6.5a Regional trends in reserve holdings
Source: World Economic Outlook 2017; World Bank; estimates.

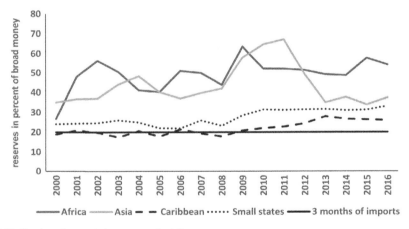

Figure 6.5b Regional trends in reserve holdings
Source: World Economic Outlook 2017; World Bank; estimates.

months (Figure 6.7). Such an increase was more gradual in small states exporting non-oil commodities or services, with the reserve-to-import ratio hovering around four months.

Reserve accumulation also outpaced the conventional rule of thumb of three months of import both in economies with fixed and floating exchange rate regimes (Figure 6.8). However, small states with a peg generally tended to have less reserve coverage, possibly reflecting access to pooled reserves or contingent financial support, which reduce the need for piling up large international reserves. On the contrary, countries with a managed exchange regime saw a reduction in their reserve cover from about five months of imports in 2010 to about four months in 2016 – possibly indicating the use of reserves to smooth the exchange rate movements in the aftermath of the global financial crisis. In terms of coverage of broad money, countries with a peg had a median reserve cover consistently below that of the whole sample and significantly lower than that of countries with a managed float regime.

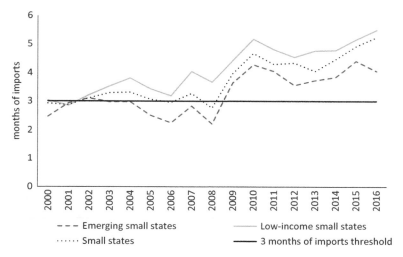

Figure 6.6a Reserve cover in months of imports by income level
Source: World Economic Outlook 2017; World Bank; estimates.

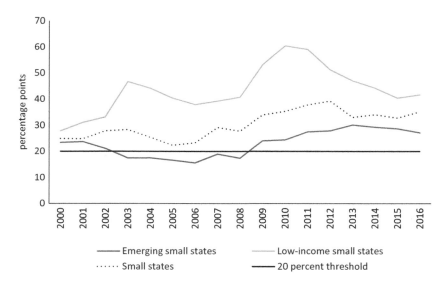

Figure 6.6b Reserve cover in terms of broad money by income level
Source: World Economic Outlook 2017; World Bank; estimates.

5 Event-study analysis

Macroeconomic impact of external shocks

Table 6.4 summarizes the estimates of the macroeconomic impact of external shocks on small states between 1980 and 2016. It can be seen that shock episodes have been accompanied by a visible deterioration of the macroeconomic situation in small states in the sample (Table 6.4).

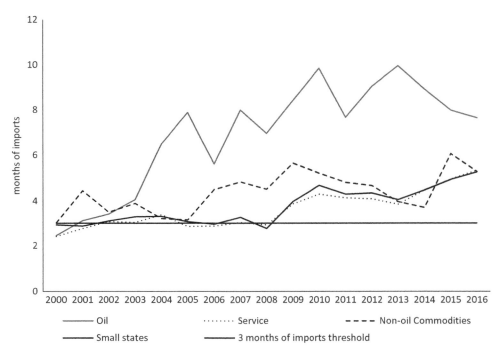

Figure 6.7a Reserve holdings by structural characteristics of small states
Source: World Economic Outlook 2017; World Bank; estimates.

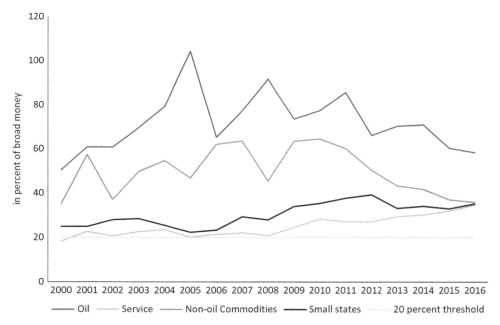

Figure 6.7b Reserve holdings by structural characteristics of small states
Source: World Economic Outlook 2017; World Bank; estimates.

Figure 6.8a Reserve holdings by structural characteristics of small states
Source: World Economic Outlook 2017; World Bank; estimates.

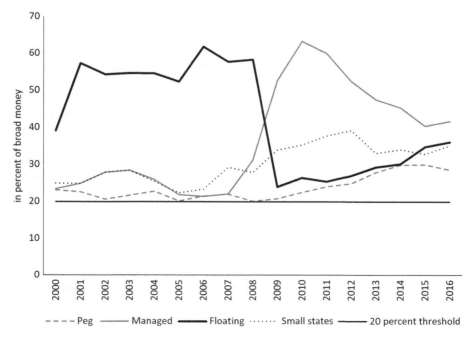

Figure 6.8b Reserve holdings by structural characteristics of small states
Source: World Economic Outlook 2017; World Bank; estimates.

External-demand shock

External-demand shock episodes are found to be associated with a more persistent weakening in main macroeconomic indicators when compared to other shocks. For example, after significant fall in external demand, both median real per-capita GDP and absorption growth rates continue to remain below pre-shock levels after three years from the shock episode. Similarly, the median deficit of the current and fiscal accounts deteriorated markedly during the three years following an external-demand shock.

Terms-of-trade shocks

In the case of a terms-of-trade shock, the median real per-capita GDP growth rate slowed down by about 1 percentage point in the year of the shock episode and remained below the pre-shock trend in the following two years. On the other hand, median real per-capita absorption growth, fell by about 2 percentage points in the year after a terms-of-trade shock, and remained subdued in the following years.

Against this background, the median current account deficit widened by more than 1 percentage point of GDP in the shock year, possibly reflecting the lags with which quantities adjusted to new relative prices.

Table 6.4 also shows that as quantities adjust to the new relative prices, the deficit on the current account of the balance of payments gradually narrowed until it reached a stronger position than that prevailing before the shock year.

The overall fiscal balance also deteriorated by about 0.3 percentage points of GDP in the year the shock hit. The median reserve coverage in months of imports remained fairly stable hovering around 2.8 months of imports and reflecting a contemporaneous slowdown in the accumulation of international reserves and growth of imports.

Natural disasters

The macroeconomic impact associated with natural disasters appears to be short-lived on economic activity and more durable on fiscal and the current account balances. The median real GDP per-capita growth was dented in the year of the shock but recovered thereafter, while the median per-capita real absorption growth first accelerated in the shock year and then gradually weakened in the following two years. The dynamics of the median current account deficit appeared u-shaped with a noticeable deterioration in the first two years and a strong improvement by the end of the third year after a shock episode.

Natural disasters appeared to be associated with a long-lasting deterioration of the median overall fiscal account, pointing to significant budgetary costs related to the reconstruction.

FDI and remittances shocks

Table 6.4 indicates that the macroeconomic impact associated with significant changes in the FDI and remittances-to-GDP ratios is somewhat mixed. The median real per-capita growth started decelerating only in the year following a shock, while per-capita absorption weakened as soon as a shock hit the economy, especially in the case of a FDI shock. Similarly, the median deficit of the fiscal account deteriorated markedly in comparison with pre-shock levels, while the median current account balance of the balance of payments improved – particularly in the

Table 6.4 Macroeconomic impact of external shocks (% change unless specified otherwise)

	External demand					Terms of Trade					Natural disasters					FDI					Remittances				
	T-1	T0	T+1	T+2	T+3	T-1	T0	T+1	T+2	T+3	T-1	T0	T+1	T+2	T+3	T-1	T0	T+1	T+2	T+3	T-1	T0	T+1	T+2	T+3
Real per-capita GDP	1.95	1.33	0.87	1.92	1.28	1.87	0.73	1.10	1.24	1.92	1.65	0.99	2.77	1.71	1.69	2.04	2.07	1.57	1.99	1.51	1.88	2.14	1.05	1.74	2.00
Real per-capita consumption	0.77	0.69	0.09	2.03	0.97	1.34	2.01	0.19	0.71	1.80	1.53	2.02	1.73	2.19	1.40	3.83	0.06	0.28	3.46	2.95	3.14	1.00	3.05	2.09	2.46
Real per-capita absorption	2.04	-0.79	-0.44	2.16	1.57	1.55	1.27	-1.57	0.86	0.24	1.28	2.39	2.35	1.42	1.74	4.00	-0.43	0.85	2.43	1.94	3.03	2.95	1.99	1.93	0.61
Current account (% of GDP)	-6.79	-8.36	-7.55	-8.16	-7.38	-9.08	-10.28	-9.81	-8.08	-8.31	-6.96	-7.19	-7.72	-6.96	-5.51	-9.08	-7.28	-7.97	-8.01	-6.35	-5.39	-6.08	-5.59	-5.31	-7.38
Overall fiscal balance (% of GDP)	-1.36	-2.52	-3.38	-2.74	-2.72	-2.85	-3.21	-3.02	-2.77	-3.12	-2.21	-2.38	-2.55	-2.54	-3.35	-1.97	-2.55	-3.30	-3.04	-2.73	-1.02	-1.93	-1.72	-2.17	-2.17
Reserves	4.87	7.31	9.14	3.46	8.97	13.11	8.45	7.55	0.97	9.31	7.31	11.88	7.60	6.20	9.51	11.03	6.65	5.77	7.96	3.83	10.18	8.24	11.93	9.50	8.96
Reserves (in months of imports)	2.80	3.26	3.38	3.19	3.11	2.81	2.78	2.81	2.76	2.88	2.62	2.60	2.61	2.76	2.95	2.60	2.89	3.16	3.09	2.94	2.85	2.99	3.10	3.38	3.39

Source: World Economic Outlook 2017; World Bank; EM-DAT; estimates.

face of a large change in FDI – suggesting that foreign financing flows may have large import content. Against this backdrop, the median import cover improved noticeably.

A significant worsening in FDI and remittances flows had a prolonged impact on most countries' per-capita GDP growth and absorption.

The effect of structural characteristics

The structure of the economy also affected the impact of shocks (Table 6.5). For example, after a terms-of-trade shock, low income states and non-oil primary commodity exporters suffered a sizable slowdown in the median real per-capita GDP growth, likely reflecting their greater dependence on exports as sources of financing.[11]

Interestingly, micro states and those that had a financial arrangement with the IMF around the time of the shock episode exhibited a modest (i.e., less than 0.5 percentage points of GDP) deceleration in the median per-capita GDP growth in the in the year of a terms-of-trade shock.

Highly-indebted countries and those with a fixed exchange rate regime in the year prior to the shock episode experienced a protracted fall in the per-capita absorption in the years following a shock event.

External-demand shocks had a significant macroeconomic impact on micro states and economies with a fixed exchange rate regime in the year preceding the shock, with median per-capita absorption falling for two consecutive years.

On the other hand, the macroeconomic consequences of natural disasters were more visible in service exporting small states where per-capita GDP and absorption growth remained below pre-shock periods three years after a shock stroke, possibly reflecting the heightened vulnerability of such countries to natural disasters.

FDI shocks were associated with a dramatic fall in per-capita absorption in low income and micro states as well as in countries with a peg at the eve of the shock episode. On the other hand, shocks to remittances were accompanied with a weakening of economic activity in small states that did not have any financial arrangement with the IMF in the year preceding the shock episode and in the four years that followed.

Macroeconomic costs of shocks

The macroeconomic costs associated with external shocks were large and persistent in the 36 small states analysed in this study (Figure 6.9 and Figure 6.A1). With regard to FDI and external-demand shocks, cumulative losses expressed as forgone per-capita GDP growth were, respectively, as high as 50 and 30 percentage points over the ten years following a shock episode.

Costs in terms of foregone growth of real per-capita absorption were significantly larger. While these results seem to overstate the cost of FDI and external-demand shocks – possibly because the period under review covers the global financial crisis and its aftermath – they are broadly consistent with previous analysis emphasizing the heightened vulnerability of small states to changes in trade and financial flows (IMF, 2013a and 2015). Shocks to the terms of trade were also accompanied with output and absorption losses, although less severe. By contrast, the macroeconomic costs related to natural disasters were typically modest, approximately 0.3 percentage points of per-capita GDP growth in a year and nil in terms of per-capita absorption growth.

Detailed analysis indicates that the magnitude and persistence of costs varied significantly, reflecting differences in the structural characteristics of the economy (Figure 6.A1). External demand shocks were generally associated with larger and more persistent costs in terms of real

Table 6.5 Macroeconomic effects of different external shocks by country groups (median values; in %; T0 is the shock year)

Effects on per-capita GDP growth

Country group	External demand					Terms of Trade					FDI					Natural disasters					Remittances				
	T-1	T0	T+1	T+2	T+3	T-1	T0	T+1	T+2	T+3	T-1	T0	T+1	T+2	T+3	T-1	T0	T+1	T+2	T+3	T-1	T0	T+1	T+2	T+3
Small States	1.9	1.3	0.9	1.9	1.3	1.9	0.7	1.1	1.2	1.9	2.0	2.1	1.6	2.0	1.5	1.7	1.0	2.8	1.7	1.7	1.9	2.1	1.0	1.7	2.0
Fixed Exchange Rate	1.9	1.2	0.7	1.4	0.7	1.7	0.7	1.0	1.3	1.5	1.8	1.5	1.4	1.4	1.1	1.4	0.4	2.2	1.3	1.7	1.9	1.9	0.7	1.7	1.6
Flexible Exchange Rate	3.1	1.2	1.5	1.9	1.0	1.6	-0.1	1.5	2.1	1.6	3.4	2.9	2.3	3.0	2.5	2.3	2.5	4.3	3.6	3.9	-0.7	1.5	3.8	1.7	1.2
Non-oil Commodity Exporters	1.9	1.3	1.0	2.0	1.4	1.9	0.7	1.2	1.6	1.9	1.9	2.0	1.6	1.8	1.6	2.2	1.2	2.9	1.7	1.7	1.6	2.0	1.4	1.7	1.9
Service exporters	2.1	1.3	1.4	1.9	1.7	1.7	1.0	1.0	2.3	2.0	2.0	1.9	1.4	2.5	1.7	1.5	2.1	2.9	1.8	1.2	1.4	2.1	1.5	1.7	1.9
Low Income States	1.8	1.3	0.6	1.9	1.3	2.1	0.0	1.2	2.2	3.2	1.9	1.6	1.2	1.7	1.2	2.3	2.6	2.9	1.1	1.7	1.6	2.0	1.2	2.2	1.3
Micro States	3.1	1.7	-0.9	1.8	2.3	2.1	1.8	0.6	3.0	1.9	1.5	1.9	1.5	1.4	1.5	1.6	1.9	2.7	1.7	2.1	2.6	1.9	1.7	1.7	1.6
Highly Indebted States	1.9	1.3	1.0	1.9	1.2	1.7	0.7	1.2	1.2	1.8	1.9	2.0	1.6	1.8	1.3	2.2	0.9	3.1	1.6	1.6	1.4	2.1	1.0	1.7	2.0
No IMF Programme	2.9	1.6	1.8	3.1	2.0	1.9	0.9	1.4	1.3	2.6	2.2	2.2	2.0	2.6	1.8	2.4	1.7	3.1	1.7	1.7	2.6	2.4	1.5	2.8	1.9
Early IMF Programme	1.0	0.8	0.5	1.9	1.2	0.9	0.6	0.4	2.1	1.7	1.8	1.5	1.5	1.7	1.3	2.4	0.7	2.0	3.0	1.7	0.7	1.9	1.5	1.6	1.4

Effects on per-capita absorption growth

Country group	External demand					Terms of Trade					FDI					Natural disasters					Remittances				
	T-1	T0	T+1	T+2	T+3	T-1	T0	T+1	T+2	T+3	T-1	T0	T+1	T+2	T+3	T-1	T0	T+1	T+2	T+3	T-1	T0	T+1	T+2	T+3
Small States	2.0	-0.8	-0.4	2.2	1.6	1.6	1.3	-1.6	0.9	0.2	4.0	-0.4	0.8	2.4	1.9	1.3	2.4	2.3	1.4	1.7	3.0	2.9	2.0	1.9	0.6
Fixed Exchange Rate	0.4	-1.7	-0.4	0.3	-0.1	1.1	0.4	-1.5	0.7	0.0	4.0	-2.4	-1.1	3.0	2.7	-0.3	1.6	2.9	-1.2	0.8	2.4	2.4	0.9	1.7	-0.9
Flexible Exchange Rate	0.3	-2.1	1.1	9.6	0.8	2.1	-0.9	0.5	3.4	1.7	2.2	2.1	1.7	2.2	1.7	3.2	1.8	1.1	1.8	4.9	0.6	2.9	0.0	2.1	5.9
Non-oil Commodity Exporters	1.9	-0.9	-0.4	2.2	1.6	1.9	1.5	-1.5	1.4	0.4	3.8	-0.8	0.4	2.8	2.4	1.5	2.0	2.9	1.8	1.7	2.4	3.4	2.0	1.9	0.6
Service exporters	2.0	-1.5	-0.3	2.2	1.7	2.4	1.5	-1.5	1.6	1.7	3.5	-0.8	0.4	3.2	2.7	2.6	2.4	3.0	1.1	1.6	2.1	3.6	-0.1	1.9	1.0
Low Income States	1.4	-0.9	1.2	0.6	1.1	2.1	1.3	-2.3	1.5	0.5	4.2	-2.2	-2.3	2.2	2.0	2.1	3.9	2.1	-0.8	2.1	2.8	2.7	0.3	2.4	-0.9
Micro States	5.9	-0.1	-2.3	2.3	1.7	3.3	2.6	-2.5	1.8	2.9	4.7	-3.4	-0.4	3.4	3.5	2.8	2.4	5.0	-1.6	0.0	3.9	5.0	0.2	1.8	1.6
Highly Indebted States	1.8	-1.2	-0.6	2.2	0.4	1.4	1.3	-1.5	1.1	0.1	4.1	-1.9	-0.1	2.9	2.2	0.4	1.6	2.9	1.6	1.4	2.4	2.9	2.0	1.9	0.6
No IMF Programme	1.8	0.8	0.3	1.3	1.9	1.1	0.9	0.2	0.7	-0.1	4.0	-0.8	1.3	3.1	3.3	2.2	2.5	3.0	1.5	1.0	5.5	3.6	4.4	0.8	2.4
Early IMF Programme	2.1	-0.9	-1.4	1.4	0.1	2.1	0.3	-3.0	1.8	1.7	2.5	-0.4	-0.7	1.6	0.6	-1.7	-0.9	-1.6	2.0	3.1	1.8	-0.4	0.0	2.7	0.6

Source: World Economic Outlook 2017; World Bank; EM-DAT; estimates.

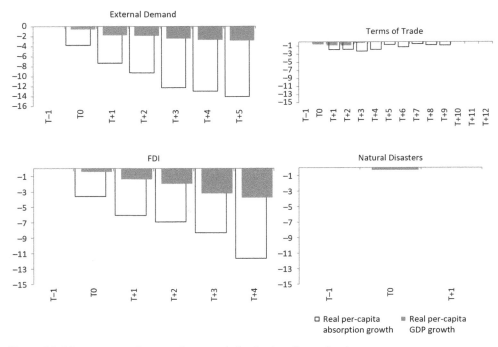

Figure 6.9 Macroeconomic cost of external shocks (median values)
Source: World Economic Outlook 2017; World Bank; EM-DAT; estimates.

per-capita GDP growth in micro states, small states with a peg in the year prior the shock episode, and countries under external-demand shocks without a financial arrangement with the IMF.

Highly-indebted and service exporting small states also experienced significant per-capita GDP losses, exceeding two percentage points of GDP per year. Countries with a flexible exchange rate regime prior to a shock event did not experience any loss, highlighting the role of exchange rate as shock absorber. Interestingly, an early programme engagement with the IMF was generally associated with very limited losses, pointing to the importance of having access to additional external financing in the proximity of a shock event.

The analysis in terms of real per-capita absorption growth supports some of the previous findings (Figure 6.A1). For example, under term-of-trade shocks small states with a fixed exchange rate regime normally suffered larger absorption losses than economies with a flexible exchange rate regime – confirming earlier results on the role of the exchange rate. Also, in the case of services-exporting small states, costs associated with a significant worsening in the terms of trade led to a decrease of over 20 percentage points of absorption in ten years.

However, highly-indebted economies experienced a the sharpest and most prolonged drop in per-capita absorption growth compared to pre-shock trends. In addition, in this case, the presence of an IMF financial arrangement did not produce tangible benefits in shielding absorption against terms-of-trade shocks, perhaps reflecting the role played by fiscal consolidation in such arrangements. Finally, the loss in terms of per-capita absorption growth compared to pre-shock trends was fairly small and short-lived (less than one percentage point of absorption in ten years) in micro states and non-oil primary commodity exporters.

6 The role of international reserve holdings

The role of international reserves is examined by grouping small states according to whether their reserve coverage was strictly above or below three months of imports in the year preceding the shock event and by comparing losses between the two groups. The assessment was performed only in terms of import cover (i.e., reserves expressed in months of imports) due to data limitations relating to the other traditional reserve metrics (i.e., broad-money and short-term debt covers). In addition, given the lack of consensus in the literature on an appropriate benchmark for the import cover of small states, the analysis was performed using the standard threshold of three months of imports that is widely used as rule of thumb in many developing economies. It has been argued that higher levels of the import cover may be more appropriate for some small states in light of their vulnerabilities (Mwase, 2012; Moore and Glean, 2016). The reader, therefore, should interpret the findings discussed in the reminder of this chapter with caution.

International reserves holdings helped contain the macroeconomic impact and costs associated with several external shocks. Table 6.6 summarizes the cumulative losses in terms of per-capita GDP and absorption growth associated with various types of shocks in small states with different economic structures and different reserve cover. The tendencies shown in Table 6.6 are derived from a detailed analysis on the annual losses over a 10- year period after a shock episode, which is presented in the Appendix (Figures 6.A2 and 6.A3). The Appendix also documents the behaviour of main economic indicators over a five-year event window around a shock episode differentiating by the structural characteristics of a country and its level of international reserve holdings prior to the shock event (Table 6.A5).

Small states with levels of international reserves above three months of imports in the year preceding a shock event were generally able to better cushion economic activity in the face of natural disasters and shocks to FDI and remittances flows. By contrast, holding three months or less of reserves' imports coverage prior to external-demand and terms-of-trade shocks did not undermine small states' ability to mitigate the impact of adverse shocks on economic activity

Also, small states with higher reserve cover typically experienced a smoother adjustment in real per-capita absorption growth than those holding a shallow level of reserves. Except for the case of natural disasters, average annual median loss in terms of forgone absorption growth ranged generally between two and nine percentage points in countries with more than three months of imports over ten years (Figure 6.A3). By contrast, countries with lower reserve coverage presented an average annual median loss between 1 and 25 percentage points for the last ten years. In the case of FDI shocks, cumulative losses were more than twelve times larger than those of economies with more than three months of imports, suggesting that benefits of entering a shock episode with higher reserve holdings may be substantial.

The role of international reserves as a cushion against external shocks also varied depending on the structural characteristics of the economy (Table 6.6). In terms of real per-capita GDP losses, a reserve cover above three months of imports at the eve of a shock episode was not a safe haven for small states with a flexible exchange rate regime in the year preceding the shock. Cumulative GDP losses were also significant in non-oil primary commodity exporters and small states that did not have a financial arrangement with the IMF. By contrast, reserves holdings above three months of imports provided a cushion against most shocks in low-income and micro states, in countries with a peg prior to a shock event, in service exporting economies, and highly-indebted states. Interestingly, except for economies with a flexible exchange rate arrangement, all other countries facing a terms-of-trade shock suffered larger per-capita GDP losses in connection with a shock episode with reserves holdings higher than three months and the opposite was the case with remittances shock (Figure 6.A2).

Table 6.6 Macroeconomic costs of exogenous shocks by country group and reserve coverage (cumulative losses with respect to pre-shock trends in percentage points (pp) over ten years after the shock episode; median values)

Country groups	Type of shock									
	External demand		Terms of Trade		FDI		Natural disasters		Remittances	
	≤ 3 m	>3 m	≤ 3 m	>3 m	≤ 3 m	>3 m	≤ 3 m	>3 m	≤ 3 m	>3 m
Per-capita GDP costs										
Whole sample	VLNE	VH	VLNE	M	VH	M	VLNE	VLNE	H	VLNE
Flexible exchange rate	VLNE	VH	M	VLNE	VLNE	H	VLNE	VLNE	VLNE	VH
Fixed exchange rate	H	VH	VLNE	M	VH	VLNE	M	VLNE	VH	VLNE
Non-oil commodity exporters	VLNE	VH	VLNE	M	VLNE	VLNE	VLNE	VLNE	VLNE	VLNE
Service exporters	H	M	VLNE	VH	VH	H	VLNE	VLNE	VH	VLNE
Low income states	M	M	VLNE	H	VH	M	VLNE	VLNE	H	VLNE
Micro states	VH	M	VLNE	VLNE	VH	H	VLNE	VLNE	VH	M
Debt-to-GDP>50%	VLNE	VH	M	VH	VH	M	VLNE	VLNE	H	VLNE
No-IMF programme	VLNE	VH	VLNE	VLNE	VLNE	VH	VLNE	VLNE	H	VLNE
IMF programme	L	M	VLNE	M	VH	VLNE	VLNE	VLNE	VLNE	VLNE
Per-capita absorption costs										
Whole sample	VH	VH	M	M	VH	M	VLNE	VLNE	H	M
Flexible exchange rate	VH	M	VLNE	VH	VLNE	H	VLNE	VH	VLNE	VLNE
Fixed exchange rate	VH	VH	VLNE	VH	VH	VH	VH	VLNE	VH	VH
Non-oil commodity exporters	VH	L	VLNE	M	M	VH	VH	VLNE	VH	VLNE

Table 6.6 (continued)

Country groups	Type of shock									
	External demand		Terms of Trade		FDI		Natural disasters		Remittances	
	≤ 3 m	>3 m	≤ 3 m	>3 m	≤ 3 m	>3 m	≤ 3 m	>3 m	≤ 3 m	>3 m
Service exporters	VH	VH	VLNE	VH	VH	VH	M	VLNE	M	VH
Low income states	VH	VH	VLNE	M	VH	VH	VH	VLNE	VH	VH
Micro states	VH	VH	VLNE	VH	VH	VH	VH	VLNE	VH	VLNE
Debt-to-GDP>50%	VH	VH	VH	M	VH	VH	M	VLNE	VLNE	H
No-IMF programme	VH	VH	VH	VLNE	VH	L	VLNE	VLNE	VH	VLNE
IMF programme	VH	VH	VLNE	VH	VH	VH	VH	VLNE	VLNE	VH

Note: VH=Very High (larger than 50 pp); H= high (between 30 and 50 pp); M =medium (between 10 and 30 pp); L = low (between 5 and 10 pp); VLNE = Very low or negligible (below 5 pp).

In terms of real per-capita absorption losses, international reserves appeared to have helped smoothing the adjustment in low-income states and economies with a fixed exchange rate regime, suggesting that countries with partial access to financial markets and limited exchange rate flexibility can improve their resilience to external shocks by building up international reserve buffers (Table 6.6).

Among countries with reserve coverage above three months of imports, absorption losses were also generally smaller in non-oil primary commodity exporters, highly-indebted economies, and countries without a financial arrangement with the IMF, or with one before or during a shock episode (Figure 6A.3). On the other hand, higher reserve holdings did not seem to have helped contain absorption losses in micro states and countries with a flexible exchange rate regime prior to a shock episode. Remarkably, all countries facing either a natural disaster or an external-demand shock showed smaller absorption losses when they entered the shock episode with higher reserve holdings, with the exception of countries with a flexible exchange rate regime and exporting non-oil primary commodities in the case of natural disasters, and micro states in the case of external-demand shock.

7 Conclusions

Small states, compared to other groups of countries, are more vulnerable to a wide range of exogenous shocks such as natural disasters, sharp swings in the terms of trade, abrupt changes in export demand or sudden stop of financial flows. Despite such vulnerabilities, small states can reduce the risk of being adversely affected from external shocks by increasing the resilience of their economies.

While sound macroeconomic policies are the first line of defence for limiting a country's vulnerability, international reserves constitute an important form of self-insurance against shocks, as they can be mobilized rapidly to avoid a disorderly adjustment.

Although a significant strand of literature has focused on the role of reserves as a self-insurance mechanism against external shocks in advanced and emerging economies, only a few studies have focused on the determinants of reserve accumulation in small states.

This study examines the experience of 36 small states over the period 1980–2016 with the view to assess the role of international reserves as a cushion against large external shocks (i.e., natural disasters, sharp swings in the terms of trade, abrupt changes in external demand, and a fall in financial inflows, including foreign direct investment and remittances). Following the methodology developed by Crispolti *et al.* (2013), it identifies relevant shock episodes, assesses their economic impact, and measures associated cost in terms of forgone real per-capita GDP and absorption growth rates. The economic impact and costs associated with each type of shock are also computed controlling for a number of structural characteristics of the economy, including the level of development, the exchange rate regime, the composition of exports, the level of indebtedness, and the presence of a financial arrangement with the IMF.

The results of this study suggest that shock episodes are typically accompanied by a visible deterioration of the macroeconomic situation, which may be exacerbated by structural vulnerabilities. Accordingly, the role of international reserves as a buffer against external shocks depends on the type of the shock that is faced as well as on the structural characteristics of the economy.

Typically, reserve holdings above three months of imports prior to a shock event are associated with smaller per-capita GDP costs in small states confronted with natural disasters and shocks to remittances and FDI, while this is not the case with regard to terms-of-trade and external-demand shocks. Moreover, countries with reserves above three months of imports generally suffered smaller costs in terms of per-capita absorption in the face of most external shocks. However, maintaining a higher reserve coverage was not a safe haven for micro states and countries with a flexible exchange rate regime in the year preceding the shock particularly when the macroeconomic costs associated with shocks are expressed as forgone real per-capita absorption growth.

Notes

1 The views expressed in this chapter are those of the author and do not necessarily represent the views of the International Monetary Fund, its Executive Board, or management.
2 The definition of small states used in this study is that of Small Island Developing States (SIDS), which the United Nations consider a distinct group of developing countries facing specific social, economic and environmental vulnerabilities (https://sustainabledevelopment.un.org/topics/sids/list). Due to data limitation, this study focuses only on the following 36 SIDS: Anguilla, Antigua and Barbuda, Bahamas, the, Barbados, Belize, Cabo Verde, Comoros, Dominica, Dominican Republic, Fiji, Grenada, Guinea-Bissau, Guyana, Haiti, Jamaica, Kiribati, Maldives, the Marshall Islands, Mauritius, Micronesia, Montserrat, Palau, Papua New Guinea, Samoa, São Tomé and Príncipe, Seychelles, Solomon Islands, St. Kitts and Nevis, St. Lucia, St. Vincent and the Grenadines, Suriname, Timor-Leste, Tonga, Trinidad and Tobago, Tuvalu, and Vanuatu. While Anguilla and Montserrat are not politically independent small states, their inclusion in the analysis was decided on account of the United Nations list of SIDS and the availability of data.
3 www.federalreserve.gov/BoardDocs/Speeches/1999/19990429.htm/.
4 For a discussion on the origin of this rule of thumb see www.imf.org/external/pubs/ft/wp/2001/wp 01143.pdf/.
5 The threshold of the 10th percentile was derived from the country-specific distribution of the shock variable excluding the 1st and 99th percentiles to limit the impact of outliers on the analysis.
6 The reader should not interpret negative correlations as evidence of a direction of causality because the analysis does not control for the numerous factors other than external shocks that might have affected economic performance within the five-year window.
7 The exchange rate classification follows Ghosh *et al.* (2015) and the relevant regime is the one prevailing the year before the shock event.
8 While this result is a consequence of the definition of shock used in the present analysis, the actual frequency of shocks in the sample may have differed from 10% (i.e. a shock every ten years) because of the adjustments mentioned in Section 3.
9 Short-term debt is not reported here because of the poor quality of short-term external debt data in many small states. For countries with reliable short-term debt data, reserve holdings were found to be significantly above the rule of thumb of three months of imports, possibly reflecting their limited market access and reliance on concessional longer-term financing from official sources.
10 See www.imf.org/external/np/sec/pr/2009/pr09283.htm/.
11 See the Appendix for a list of the countries included in each group.

Appendix 1

Data sources and definition (Table 6.A1)

The event-study analysis is based on a panel of 36 small states. The sample period spans from 1980 to 2016 for the analysis of shock episodes. The data used for the event-study analysis mainly come from the IMF April 2017 World Economic Outlook and the World Bank World Development Indicators databases with a few exceptions that are documented below. To reduce the number of missing observations, historical data on per-capita GDP and absorption were reconstructed using growth rates from the Penn World Tables (version 7).

Shock variables (Table 6.A2)

Remittances flows are expressed in billions of US dollars. Data are available from the World Bank database at http://data.worldbank.org/.

A natural disaster is defined according to the Centre for Research on the Epidemiology of Disasters (Guha-Sapir *et al.*, 2015). Its occurrence is triggered by at least one of the following: (i) ten or more people reported killed; (ii) hundred or more people reported affected; (iii) declaration of a state of emergency; (iv) call for international assistance. Data are available at www.emdat.be/database.

External demand conditions are proxied with real GDP growth in trading partners as reported in the April 2017 Global Economic Environment database (IMF internal database).

FDI inflows are expressed in billions of US dollars and taken from the April 2017 World Economic Outlook database, available at www.imf.org/external/pubs/ft/weo/2010/01/index. htm. To reduce the number of missing observations, historical data were reconstructed using the World Bank database (World Development Indicators).

The terms-of-trade index is for goods only and weighted by a country's imports and exports as in Easterly and Kraay (2000). Data comes from the April 2017 World Economic Outlook database.

Macroeconomic variables (Tables 6.A3 and 6.A4)

The dummy for the exchange rate regime is taken from the Ghosh *et al.* (2015). To reduce the number of missing observations, historical data on exchange rate regimes were reconstructed using Reinhart and Rogoff's database on exchange rate regimes available at www.carmenreinha rt.com/data/browse-by-topic/topics/11/.

The series capturing the presence of a financial programme with the IMF comes the MONA database available at www.imf.org/external/np/pdr/mona/index.aspx. To reduce the number of missing observations, historical data on programme arrangements were reconstructed using historical data on IMF financial arrangements with member states (IMF internal database)

External variables (such as current account, imports, stock of international reserves) are expressed in billions of US dollars and come from the April 2017 World Economic Outlook database.

Domestic variables such as real per-capita GDP growth, real per-capita consumption growth, real per-capita absorption growth, imports, the current account of balance of payments, trade openness, overall fiscal balance, and public debt are all taken from the April 2017 World Economic Outlook database and complemented with the World Bank database (World Development Indicators). The overall fiscal balance variable is expressed in millions of national currency.

Table 6.A1 Country groups

Country	ISO code	Region	Low-income small states	Micro states	Fragile states	Service exporters	Non-oil primary commodity exporters	Heavily-indebted
Anguilla	312	WHD	0	1	0	0	0	0
Antigua and Barbuda	311	WHD	0	1	0	1	0	1
Bahamas, the	313	WHD	0	0	0	1	0	1
Barbados	316	WHD	0	0	0	1	0	1
Belize	339	WHD	0	0	0	0	0	1
Cabo Verde	624	AFR	1	0	0	1	0	1
Comoros	632	AFR	1	0	1	1	0	1
Dominica	321	WHD	1	1	0	1	0	1
Dominican Republic	243	WHD	0	0	0	1	0	1
Fiji	819	APD	0	0	0	1	0	1
Grenada	328	WHD	1	1	0	1	0	1
Guinea-Bissau	654	AFR	1	0	0	0	1	1
Guyana	336	WHD	1	0	0	0	1	1
Haiti	263	WHD	1	0	0	1	0	1
Jamaica	343	WHD	0	0	0	1	0	1
Kiribati	826	APD	1	1	1	1	0	0
Maldives	556	APD	1	0	0	1	0	1
Marshall Islands	867	APD	0	1	1	0	1	1
Mauritius	684	AFR	0	0	0	1	0	0
Micronesia	868	APD	0	1	1	0	0	0
Montserrat	351	WHD	0	1	0	0	0	0
Palau	565	APD	0	1	0	1	0	0
Papua New Guinea	853	APD	1	0	0	0	1	1
Samoa	862	APD	1	1	0	1	0	1

Table 6.A1 (continued)

Country	ISO code	Region	Low-income small states	Micro states	Fragile states	Service exporters	Non-oil primary commodity exporters	Heavily-indebted
São Tomé and Príncipe	716	AFR	1	1	0	1	0	1
Seychelles	718	AFR	0	1	0	1	0	1
Solomon Islands	813	APD	1	0	1	0	1	1
St Kitts and Nevis	361	WHD	0	1	0	1	0	1
St Lucia	362	WHD	1	1	0	1	0	1
St Vincent and the Grenadines	364	WHD	1	1	0	1	0	1
Suriname	366	WHD	0	0	0	0	1	1
Timor-Leste	537	APD	1	0	1	0	0	0
Tonga	866	APD	1	1	0	1	0	1
Trinidad and Tobago	369	WHD	0	0	0	0	0	0
Tuvalu	869	APD	0	1	1	0	1	1
Vanuatu	846	APD	0	1	0	0	0	0

Source: World Economic Outlook 2017; World Bank; EM-DAT; estimates.

Table 6.A2 Summary statistics, shock variables (% changes unless indicated otherwise; average values)

Country	External demand	Terms of trade (goods only, weighted)	Terms of trade (goods only)	FDI (in % of GDP)	Remittances (in % of GDP)
Anguilla	n.a.	n.a.	n.a.	22.3	n.a.
Antigua and Barbuda	2.8	0.2	−0.7	10.1	2.3
Bahamas, the	3.2	−1.5	−0.8	6.5	n.a.
Barbados	2.9	−1.4	−0.6	3.8	2.4
Belize	2.8	−0.9	−0.3	5.0	4.7
Cabo Verde	3.0	−1.6	6.4	4.4	10.8
Comoros	3.9	0.4	4.0	0.8	9.7
Dominica	2.4	−0.9	1.2	6.8	6.7
Dominican Republic	2.5	−0.9	−0.7	2.6	6.0
Fiji	3.0	n.a.	n.a.	3.3	3.1
Grenada	4.0	0.0	3.8	7.4	7.0
Guinea-Bissau	5.9	1.2	3.7	0.8	3.2
Guyana	2.5	−0.6	0.8	5.2	8.2
Haiti	2.7	−0.8	−1.1	0.7	20.2
Jamaica	2.6	−1.0	−0.8	2.9	9.9
Kiribati	4.9	−3.1	−0.8	0.5	9.5
Maldives	3.3	−0.7	1.4	14.6	0.6
Marshall Islands	n.a.	n.a.	n.a.	2.5	14.9
Mauritius	2.6	0.7	1.7	33.9	1.2
Micronesia	n.a.	n.a.	n.a.	0.1	4.3
Montserrat	n.a.	n.a.	n.a.	8.1	n.a.
Palau	n.a.	−2.5	3.4	4.5	0.9
Papua New Guinea	4.1	−0.2	1.8	3.5	0.2
Samoa	3.7	n.a.	n.a.	1.6	20.4
São Tomé and Príncipe	2.7	−3.3	2.4	8.3	2.8
Seychelles	2.4	−0.4	2.6	9.6	0.9
Solomon Islands	7.4	−1.5	−3.4	4.0	1.7
St. Kitts and Nevis	2.9	−0.5	0.7	13.5	5.3
St. Lucia	3.1	−0.9	0.4	9.4	3.5
St. Vincent and the Grenadines	2.8	−1.7	−0.4	10.8	5.0
Suriname	2.8	1.1	0.8	−3.7	0.4
Timor-Leste	n.a.	n.a.	n.a.	1.9	5.9
Tonga	3.0	−6.8	−1.0	2.6	23.5
Trinidad and Tobago	2.8	1.4	0.9	9.5	0.4
Tuvalu	3.3	n.a.	n.a.	0.9	19.3
Vanuatu	4.1	n.a.	n.a.	7.3	5.0

Table 6.A2 (continued)

Country	External demand	Terms of trade (goods only, weighted)	Terms of trade (goods only)	FDI (in % of GDP)	Remittances (in % of GDP)
Memorandum:					
Small states	3.3	−0.8	1.0	6.5	6.2
Africa	3.4	−0.5	3.4	9.9	4.0
Asia	4.1	−1.9	0.0	4.0	8.4
Caribbean	2.9	−0.6	0.3	6.8	5.3
Low-income small states	3.7	−1.1	1.4	5.0	8.0
Micro states	3.2	−1.5	1.1	7.3	8.2
Fragile states	4.9	−1.4	−0.1	1.6	9.3
Service exporters	3.1	−1.1	1.1	7.3	7.1
Non-oil primary commodity exporters	4.3	0.0	0.7	1.9	4.8
Heavily-indebted	3.3	−0.8	1.0	5.2	6.7

Source: World Economic Outlook 2017; World Bank; EM-DAT; estimates.

Table 6.A3 Summary statistics, macroeconomic indicators

Country	Real per-capita GDP	Real per-capita consumption	Real per-capita Absorption	Current account balance (in % of GDP)	Overall fiscal balance (in % of GDP)
Anguilla	1.6	1.7	1.5	−27.0	−3.0
Antigua and Barbuda	2.7	3.4	3.4	−13.2	−6.6
Bahamas, the	0.3	1.6	2.1	−7.1	−2.7
Barbados	0.8	0.9	0.8	−3.8	−3.5
Belize	2.5	2.2	1.7	−6.3	−4.3
Cabo Verde	3.5	0.9	1.9	−9.2	−7.6
Comoros	−0.2	−0.4	0.1	−6.0	−2.0
Dominica	2.6	2.2	2.2	−15.2	−2.6
Dominican Republic	2.8	3.4	3.2	−3.2	−2.4
Fiji	1.5	1.5	1.0	−5.4	−2.9
Grenada	3.1	3.2	2.9	−15.4	−3.9
Guinea-Bissau	−0.1	0.3	−0.4	−10.7	−2.3
Guyana	1.7	n.a.	n.a.	−14.8	−4.0
Haiti	−0.9	−1.6	−1.4	−3.2	−2.5
Jamaica	0.4	1.1	0.8	−7.4	−2.9
Kiribati	−0.7	n.a.	n.a.	2.4	−5.2
Maldives	5.3	6.5	7.0	−6.0	−7.5
Marshall Islands	1.1	n.a.	n.a.	−9.9	2.9
Mauritius	3.7	4.0	3.7	−3.5	−3.9
Micronesia	0.0	n.a.	n.a.	−12.5	−0.5
Montserrat	2.3	9.5	4.0	−25.8	−0.3
Palau	1.3	1.2	1.2	−16.5	−2.6
Papua New Guinea	0.8	n.a.	n.a.	−3.2	−0.8
Samoa	1.6	n.a.	n.a.	−3.8	−3.1
São Tomé and Príncipe	−0.2	1.5	0.6	−24.0	4.3
Seychelles	2.6	2.7	2.6	−12.4	−1.7
Solomon Islands	0.1	−1.8	−1.3	−6.6	0.5
St Kitts and Nevis	3.2	2.8	2.7	−14.8	−2.9
St Lucia	2.2	1.1	1.4	−12.7	−2.1
St Vincent and the Grenadines	2.7	3.2	3.0	−15.9	−1.5
Suriname	1.3	1.9	3.9	−1.9	−3.1
Timor-Leste	3.8	1.7	4.0	18.9	18.6
Tonga	3.6	n.a.	n.a.	−5.0	1.3
Trinidad and Tobago	1.6	2.6	1.4	4.4	−1.2
Tuvalu	0.3	n.a.	n.a.	−6.7	−5.1
Vanuatu	0.4	0.8	2.4	−1.6	−1.7

Table 6.A3 (continued)

Country	Real per-capita GDP	Real per-capita consumption	Real per-capita Absorption	Current account balance (in % of GDP)	Overall fiscal balance (in % of GDP)
Memorandum:					
Small states	1.7	2.0	1.9	−8.1	−2.1
Africa	1.5	1.5	1.4	−10.9	−2.3
Asia	1.5	1.9	2.4	−4.2	−0.9
Caribbean	1.8	2.3	2.1	−9.6	−2.9
Low-income small states	1.6	1.4	1.5	−8.5	−1.7
Micro states	1.8	2.8	2.4	−11.8	−2.1
Fragile states	0.3	−0.6	0.2	−3.4	0.6
Service exporters	1.9	2.1	2.1	−8.9	−3.0
Non-oil primary commodity exporters	0.7	0.0	0.4	−7.6	−1.4
Heavily-indebted	1.7	1.7	1.8	−9.1	−2.6

Source: World Economic Outlook 2017; World Bank; EM-DAT; estimates

Table 6.A4 Summary statistics, reserves indicators (% changes unless indicated otherwise; average values)

Country	Reserves holdings (in billions of US$)	Imports	Reserves (in months of imports)	Reserves (in % of broad money)	Reserves (in % of short-term debt)
Anguilla	8.4	8.1	2.3	n.a.	n.a.
Antigua and Barbuda	11.5	6.7	1.9	15.1	n.a.
Bahamas, the	8.2	5.3	1.7	13.8	n.a.
Barbados	7.9	4.3	3.1	22.0	n.a.
Belize	14.5	7.2	2.2	22.3	54.6
Cabo Verde	19.0	7.7	4.1	34.5	0.3
Comoros	10.8	7.2	5.9	86.5	27.9
Dominica	16.9	5.9	2.5	17.8	32.9
Dominican Republic	30.1	7.8	1.5	12.0	167.3
Fiji	8.5	6.1	3.8	34.0	10.7
Grenada	9.8	6.0	2.8	20.1	45.9
Guinea–Bissau	21.8	5.5	6.3	120.1	211.8
Guyana	20.8	5.1	2.1	27.0	1785.7
Haiti	45.4	7.8	2.3	21.2	176.0
Jamaica	19.9	5.1	2.5	37.6	114.2
Kiribati	1.8	12.1	47.2	n.a.	n.a.
Maldives	35.2	13.8	2.0	34.2	107.5
Marshall Islands	−0.6	3.3	0.3	n.a.	n.a.
Mauritius	25.0	7.6	3.9	24.8	16.2
Micronesia	2.3	2.2	0.1	n.a.	n.a.
Montserrat	11.1	3.8	4.3	n.a.	n.a.
Palau	−0.3	9.4	0.2	n.a.	n.a.
Papua New Guinea	10.6	7.0	3.4	40.1	31.7
Samoa	13.0	5.0	4.7	n.a.	1.9
São Tomé and Príncipe	18.1	7.8	4.2	57.4	93.5
Seychelles	20.6	8.0	1.5	21.2	n.a.
Solomon Islands	16.5	7.0	4.0	62.6	22.5
St Kitts and Nevis	14.9	6.8	3.3	19.1	n.a.
St Lucia	11.9	6.4	2.3	20.1	53.9
St Vincent and the Grenadines	12.2	5.5	2.5	24.1	22.8
Suriname	54.1	6.5	2.4	23.7	n.a.
Timor-Leste	40.6	12.7	3.6	n.a.	n.a.
Tonga	9.8	8.0	4.7	51.8	2.5
Trinidad and Tobago	10.7	6.0	7.3	59.7	n.a.
Tuvalu	12.0	6.9	6.6	n.a.	n.a.
Vanuatu	12.8	5.8	4.2	n.a.	42.6

Table 6.A4 (continued)

Country	Reserves holdings (in billions of US$)	Imports	Reserves (in months of imports)	Reserves (in % of broad money)	Reserves (in % of short-term debt)
Memorandum:					
Small states	17.4	6.9	3.5	33.9	153.9
Africa	19.2	7.3	4.3	54.4	77.1
Asia	14.5	7.8	4.5	43.7	32.1
Caribbean	18.4	6.1	2.7	23.7	274.7
Low-income small states	18.5	7.5	4.2	41.8	192.0
Micro states	12.1	6.7	3.7	24.5	34.4
Fragile states	13.9	7.6	6.5	73.7	25.2
Service exporters	17.0	7.3	3.5	28.2	62.0
Non-oil primary commodity exporters	23.5	6.0	3.7	52.1	531.4
Heavily-indebted	18.3	6.7	3.1	33.2	167.7

Source: World Economic Outlook 2017; World Bank; EM-DAT; estimates.

Table 6.A5 Economic impact of shocks by structural characteristics and reserve coverage (% change unless specified otherwise; median values)

Group	Reserves	variables	External demand					Terms of Trade					FDI					Natural disasters					Remittances				
			T-1	T0	T+1	T+2	T+3	T-1	T0	T+1	T+2	T+3	T-1	T0	T+1	T+2	T+3	T-1	T0	T+1	T+2	T+3	T-1	T0	T+1	T+2	T+3
Small States	>3 months	Real per-capita GDP	2.6	1.6	0.9	1.9	1.5	2.0	0.2	0.3	1.2	1.5	2.0	1.5	1.2	2.1	1.2	1.7	2.0	2.9	1.7	1.2	1.0	2.0	0.2	1.9	1.5
		Real per-capita consumption	1.2	2.5	-0.4	2.4	0.6	2.4	2.4	-3.4	0.7	1.5	2.4	0.8	0.0	3.0	2.2	2.5	3.3	2.9	2.2	2.5	3.5	1.8	-0.2	6.3	-0.9
		Real per-capita absorption	2.1	2.7	1.3	2.2	-0.3	3.5	0.9	-2.5	1.5	-0.4	3.5	0.3	1.4	2.0	1.0	2.6	4.4	2.6	0.8	3.8	3.7	-1.0	-0.8	1.9	-2.1
		Current account (% of GDP)	-5.4	-6.7	-7.5	-8.2	-7.7	-6.3	-9.2	-9.8	-5.7	-7.7	-6.3	-3.3	-7.5	-7.3	-5.5	-4.5	-6.4	-7.7	-6.3	-6.7	-5.1	-7.3	-5.7	-6.5	-8.1
		Overall fiscal balance (% of GDP)	-1.3	-2.9	-3.6	-3.4	-3.5	-2.8	-3.7	-3.6	-3.3	-3.7	-3.3	-3.6	-3.1	-3.1	-2.9	-2.0	-2.3	-3.0	-3.3	-3.3	-0.6	-1.3	-1.3	-2.2	1.7
		Reserves	9.2	3.9	5.8	4.5	6.6	14.1	2.0	4.0	0.4	9.6	3.2	4.7	2.1	8.6	2.0	9.6	5.6	7.4	3.8	4.4	14.9	4.8	8.7	9.5	1.7
		Reserves (in months of imports)	4.3	4.8	5.1	5.6	5.6	1.3	0.8	1.9	1.7	2.1	2.1	2.6	2.0	1.7	2.1	5.1	4.4	4.7	5.1	4.5	5.3	2.7	2.6	1.7	5.6
	≤3 months	Real per-capita GDP	1.3	-0.8	0.2	1.8	1.0	4.0	3.0	2.1	1.9	2.0	-0.5	0.4	2.0	4.0	1.7	1.8	0.4	2.6	2.2	1.4	1.0	2.1	5.1	2.4	3.3
		Real per-capita consumption	0.2	-0.8	0.2	1.8	1.0	2.1	3.0	1.4	0.3	1.8	0.4	-0.5	-0.1	4.0	3.4	0.3	0.8	1.4	2.2	0.7	2.1	1.0	5.1	1.9	3.3
		Real per-capita absorption	1.4	-1.7	-0.7	0.5	1.9	4.2	-0.8	-0.5	0.5	1.8	-0.8	-0.1	4.1	2.7	2.4	-0.9	0.7	2.2	1.4	0.7	2.4	3.8	2.3	1.9	3.9
		Current account (% of GDP)	-10.8	-10.6	-7.9	-8.2	-4.3	-10.0	-10.7	-9.6	-8.3	-9.3	-9.1	-9.7	-8.0	-9.7	-9.0	-8.2	-7.7	-7.8	-7.4	-4.3	-7.3	-5.1	-4.9	-4.6	-6.4
		Overall fiscal balance (% of GDP)	-1.5	-2.3	-3.0	-1.6	-2.4	-1.7	-2.4	-2.7	-2.2	-2.7	-2.2	-2.2	-3.0	-3.0	-2.4	-2.2	-2.9	-2.3	-2.2	-3.5	-2.5	-3.1	-2.0	-2.0	-2.2
		Reserves	-1.8	7.9	13.1	6.2	11.4	9.1	16.2	8.4	4.9	8.0	7.8	7.8	10.1	7.5	4.4	5.9	13.8	7.8	8.4	19.4	8.6	9.6	20.9	9.4	14.9
		Reserves (in months of imports)	1.7	1.8	2.1	2.2	2.3	1.5	2.1	1.9	1.9	2.3	1.9	1.9	1.9	2.0	2.0	1.7	1.6	2.0	1.8	2.0	1.7	1.5	1.9	1.9	2.0
Fixed Exchange Regime	>3 months	Real per-capita GDP	1.9	1.2	0.7	0.5	-0.2	1.1	0.8	1.1	1.0	1.1	1.1	-0.7	0.0	1.5	0.5	1.2	0.7	2.3	0.1	1.0	0.8	1.0	0.0	1.3	0.5
		Real per-capita consumption	-2.2	1.2	0.2	0.4	-1.2	0.5	-2.6	-0.7	2.5	0.4	-0.7	-2.6	0.0	2.5	0.4	1.7	3.2	1.7	0.8	0.2	0.3	0.7	0.3	-0.4	-3.6
		Real per-capita absorption	-2.1	-1.0	-0.1	-0.4	-3.0	1.5	-2.0	1.2	1.2	-0.6	1.9	0.0	1.5	1.5	0.5	1.9	4.4	6.0	-0.5	1.0	2.4	-0.4	-3.4	1.5	-1.7
		Current account (% of GDP)	-2.6	-4.8	-5.7	-3.6	-4.4	-13.3	-5.0	-3.3	-3.0	-8.6	-10.1	-3.6	-3.6	-2.5	-2.9	-5.8	-9.3	-10.6	-11.7	-10.8	-8.2	-1.3	-5.3	-7.4	-8.9
		Overall fiscal balance (% of GDP)	12.6	5.2	5.8	-0.6	7.5	-5.0	-3.6	8.0	8.3	-3.0	-3.6	-3.6	6.0	8.6	-2.5	-0.6	-2.1	-2.6	-3.1	-3.4	-1.3	-1.3	-1.4	-2.5	-3.4
		Reserves	4.0	4.7	4.3	3.8	4.5	14.7	4.8	6.0	8.6	17.3	4.0	4.3	4.5	4.1	3.9	5.6	5.6	3.0	5.7	7.4	21.3	3.0	6.0	12.3	4.1
		Reserves (in months of imports)	2.1	1.3	1.2	3.2	1.2	2.5	2.6	1.6	1.6	1.9	1.8	1.8	1.8	1.8	2.0	-0.1	5.6	4.9	4.2	2.0	5.6	3.2	6.4	6.3	5.9
	≤3 months	Real per-capita GDP	-0.4	0.2	0.2	2.5	0.9	6.6	3.0	1.0	-0.2	0.6	2.6	-1.8	-1.9	4.8	3.5	2.7	1.0	1.4	0.7	1.4	2.5	3.2	2.5	3.1	2.2
		Real per-capita consumption	1.6	-1.7	-0.4	0.3	1.9	8.4	2.6	1.6	0.3	1.8	6.6	-1.8	-1.9	4.8	3.7	1.6	1.0	1.4	0.7	0.6	1.6	0.7	5.9	3.4	4.2
		Real per-capita absorption	-10.6	-1.7	-0.4	0.3	1.9	8.4	1.7	-0.6	0.3	1.8	8.4	-2.7	-1.2	4.9	3.7	3.7	0.8	2.8	-1.5	0.6	3.7	4.3	2.2	2.3	-0.1
		Current account (% of GDP)	-10.6	-11.5	-8.4	-8.2	-7.7	-18.7	-14.6	-10.5	-10.1	-11.5	-12.4	-9.9	-9.9	-12.1	-12.0	-8.9	-9.6	-10.2	-9.5	-7.3	-8.9	-8.2	-9.4	-8.7	-10.8
		Overall fiscal balance (% of GDP)	-1.6	-2.3	-4.0	-3.3	-2.4	-1.8	-2.6	-3.0	-3.6	-3.1	-2.1	-3.3	-3.3	-4.4	-2.5	-3.0	-3.2	-2.4	-2.1	-2.5	-3.0	-4.1	-2.5	-2.1	-2.2
		Reserves	4.4	7.3	9.0	4.3	7.9	5.3	16.3	5.7	4.4	6.1	5.7	5.7	7.0	7.1	4.4	5.8	8.6	10.2	5.2	16.7	5.8	4.1	24.6	5.4	4.8
		Reserves (in months of imports)	1.6	1.5	2.1	2.0	2.2	1.6	2.3	2.2	2.1	2.3	1.6	1.7	1.7	2.0	2.0	1.7	1.8	2.0	1.8	2.0	1.5	1.6	1.6	1.8	2.0

Table 6.A5 (continued)

Group	Reserves	variables	External demand					Terms of Trade					FDI					Natural disasters					Remittances				
			T-1	T0	T+1	T+2	T+3	T-1	T0	T+1	T+2	T+3	T-1	T0	T+1	T+2	T+3	T-1	T0	T+1	T+2	T+3	T-1	T0	T+1	T+2	T+3
Flexible Exchange Rate Regime	>3 months	Real per-capita GDP	6.2	2.8	3.9	7.1	2.9	1.6	-0.1	2.1	3.7	1.0	5.1	2.8	3.0	3.7	3.5	2.3	3.7	5.3	5.1	3.9	4.3	3.9	4.2	6.0	2.1
		Real per-capita consumption	-1.2	-7.1	10.9	19.4	8.5	5.7	7.6	-8.7	-0.2	2.6	4.8	2.5	2.5	2.4	3.6	2.8	2.1	2.9	3.6	8.4	11.5	-2.2	-5.0	6.7	7.1
		Real per-capita absorption	0.0	-6.2	9.2	19.2	5.4	6.1	8.6	-3.7	3.5	0.6	3.9	3.8	3.8	1.0	1.7	3.0	0.9	1.0	-4.2	6.6	8.2	-0.5	2.1	8.4	3.2
		Current account (% of GDP)	2.7	5.0	-8.4	-13.8	-7.3	-3.9	-7.4	-10.3	-9.5	-8.4	-5.0	-4.8	-6.3	-9.2	-7.3	-4.8	-7.7	-9.5	-7.2	-9.0	0.4	7.7	2.0	1.8	7.4
		Overall fiscal balance (% of GDP)	0.3	-1.7	-3.3	1.8	1.8	-0.6	-3.6	-3.2	-3.2	-5.5	-3.2	-1.8	-3.5	-3.2	-1.8	-2.8	-0.9	-5.6	1.3	0.4	-3.6	1.0	0.0	-3.5	2.3
		Reserves	46.2	29.2	13.0	17.4	32.6	9.7	28.6	13.0	6.8	9.4	2.5	9.6	14.6	12.3	9.6	-3.8	23.6	28.1	10.3	22.7	23.8	16.4	34.0	28.9	13.1
		Reserves (in months of imports)	4.5	5.0	5.7	4.6	4.9	3.2	4.3	4.6	4.6	4.4	4.6	5.0	5.7	4.6	4.9	4.2	5.3	5.4	6.6	7.1	4.5	4.0	5.2	5.7	6.0
	≤3 months	Real per-capita GDP	-1.5	-0.3	0.6	-1.7	-0.4	1.0	0.7	1.5	1.5	3.3	2.9	3.6	1.0	2.1	1.9	1.9	0.2	2.8	3.3	2.9	-2.4	1.0	1.0	0.0	-0.2
		Real per-capita consumption	0.0	-1.4	-4.3	12.8	-1.7	-1.3	-3.3	4.6	1.3	5.2	4.0	3.6	5.4	3.2	6.3	3.7	0.8	0.8	7.9	-4.7	-4.7	1.0	0.7	5.2	3.3
		Real per-capita absorption	0.3	-2.1	-2.1	9.6	-1.2	-0.7	-3.1	7.4	3.4	5.7	0.7	1.6	3.5	4.2	1.7	3.5	2.9	1.1	3.5	0.1	3.0	0.0	0.0	2.1	5.9
		Current account (% of GDP)	-3.3	-2.6	-1.0	0.1	-0.1	1.5	0.6	-1.7	-1.8	-2.9	-1.5	-1.5	-0.4	-1.9	-1.4	-6.0	-7.0	-5.4	-3.4	-1.7	-1.6	-2.5	-3.0	-1.5	-3.1
		Overall fiscal balance (% of GDP)	0.5	-0.7	-1.8	0.2	0.4	2.1	1.4	0.5	-1.2	-2.5	-1.2	0.3	-1.3	-1.4	-3.1	-0.2	-3.0	-5.0	-3.9	-3.5	-2.4	-1.4	-1.4	-2.6	-3.0
		Reserves	48.3	-5.0	23.0	48.4	36.5	62.3	14.3	23.6	44.6	11.1	29.9	48.3	23.8	4.7	20.3	53.4	29.9	10.9	28.7	46.6	34.2	8.6	39.0	-7.4	26.9
		Reserves (in months of imports)	1.8	2.0	2.0	2.5	3.1	1.9	1.9	1.8	2.3	2.6	1.7	2.3	3.0	2.3	2.7	1.3	1.4	1.2	1.6	2.2	2.0	1.9	2.2	1.7	2.7
Non-oil Primary commodity Exporters	>3 months	Real per-capita GDP	2.5	1.6	1.1	3.0	1.7	1.9	0.2	0.7	1.7	1.6	1.9	1.5	1.3	1.3	1.4	2.2	2.6	3.0	1.7	1.2	0.5	1.5	0.4	1.6	1.3
		Real per-capita consumption	2.2	2.5	0.2	2.1	0.6	0.9	0.0	-3.3	1.6	1.8	3.2	-0.4	0.5	3.0	2.1	2.6	3.3	3.4	0.7	2.2	2.8	2.8	-0.7	0.4	-3.0
		Real per-capita absorption	2.1	2.9	1.4	2.3	1.3	1.1	1.1	-2.1	1.9	-0.2	2.9	-0.4	1.2	2.1	1.4	2.6	3.4	3.9	0.8	3.3	3.1	-0.4	-1.1	1.9	-2.3
		Current account (% of GDP)	-5.7	-6.7	-7.5	-9.1	-8.5	-9.7	-10.2	-8.6	-8.0	-8.0	-7.4	-7.4	-8.6	-8.6	-6.3	-5.0	-8.8	-7.9	-6.3	-6.7	-5.4	-8.2	-8.3	-7.2	-8.2
		Overall fiscal balance (% of GDP)	-2.0	-3.6	-5.5	-3.5	-3.9	-2.9	-3.8	-3.8	-3.3	-3.8	-3.0	-3.3	-3.7	-3.1	-3.2	-3.5	-3.0	-3.1	-3.3	-3.4	-0.3	-1.9	-1.3	-2.2	-3.4
		Reserves	9.4	7.4	6.0	-0.4	7.4	17.9	2.6	7.6	0.6	9.5	12.4	2.4	2.0	9.0	2.0	9.4	8.5	5.0	5.7	4.0	13.3	3.0	8.7	12.3	0.3
		Reserves (in months of imports)	4.3	4.7	4.8	4.4	4.5	4.1	4.0	4.1	4.1	4.2	4.4	4.5	4.8	4.6	4.5	4.2	4.7	4.6	5.1	4.5	5.2	5.4	5.1	5.6	5.6
	≤3 months	Real per-capita GDP	1.3	1.3	0.8	1.9	1.2	1.7	1.8	1.4	1.6	2.0	2.0	2.1	2.0	1.8	1.8	2.1	0.7	2.6	1.7	2.1	2.7	2.7	2.6	1.7	2.1
		Real per-capita consumption	0.2	-0.8	0.2	1.8	1.0	1.7	1.7	0.8	0.0	1.8	4.0	-0.4	0.5	4.0	3.6	0.3	0.7	1.4	2.3	3.3	0.9	0.9	5.4	2.3	3.3
		Real per-capita absorption	1.4	-1.7	-0.7	0.5	1.9	2.4	1.8	-1.0	0.3	1.8	4.2	-1.0	-0.2	4.7	3.5	-0.7	0.6	2.8	1.8	0.7	3.1	4.4	3.2	1.9	4.2
		Current account (% of GDP)	-10.8	-10.6	-7.9	-8.2	-4.3	-10.1	-10.9	-10.2	-8.2	-9.2	-10.3	-9.3	-8.0	-3.1	-9.0	-9.1	-8.2	-7.9	-8.5	-4.5	-8.1	-5.6	-5.8	-5.1	-6.4
		Overall fiscal balance (% of GDP)	-1.5	-2.3	-3.0	-1.6	-2.4	-3.0	-2.6	-2.9	-2.5	-2.6	-1.9	-2.2	-3.1	-3.1	-2.6	-2.4	-2.9	-2.3	-2.2	-4.1	-2.5	-3.6	-2.1	-2.1	-2.2
		Reserves	-1.8	7.9	13.1	6.2	11.4	9.9	16.3	8.0	4.4	7.3	5.3	6.0	8.0	6.6	4.2	5.7	13.8	7.4	7.6	19.4	8.6	8.2	21.2	9.4	13.1
		Reserves (in months of imports)	1.7	1.8	2.1	2.2	2.3	2.1	2.1	2.1	1.9	2.2	1.4	1.7	1.7	1.9	1.8	1.5	1.6	1.7	1.7	1.9	1.7	1.6	1.5	1.9	2.0
Service Exporters	>3 months	Real per-capita GDP	1.9	1.6	1.1	2.4	1.7	1.7	0.8	-0.2	3.1	1.5	1.5	1.5	1.1	2.4	1.7	2.7	2.7	3.1	1.9	1.2	0.1	1.7	0.4	1.8	0.6
		Real per-capita consumption	3.5	2.4	0.2	2.1	0.4	0.4	1.3	-3.2	0.7	2.2	3.2	2.1	0.5	3.3	0.4	2.6	3.2	5.4	-0.5	2.4	-0.4	2.8	-2.4	1.3	-1.0
		Real per-capita absorption	2.1	1.6	1.4	2.2	-0.3	1.4	1.3	-1.9	1.8	0.4	2.2	-0.4	2.2	2.2	0.5	3.2	3.2	5.4	-7.4	-8.5	2.4	2.4	-3.9	1.9	-0.6
		Current account (% of GDP)	-6.1	-8.7	-7.5	-10.6	-9.1	-11.4	-3.8	-3.4	8.3	-3.0	-7.4	-7.4	-9.3	-3.6	-3.4	-5.8	-9.1	-8.3	-7.4	-8.5	-5.8	-8.2	-7.2	-8.2	-10.6
		Overall fiscal balance (% of GDP)	-2.2	-3.6	-4.9	-3.6	-4.0	-3.8	3.9	8.3	12.0	8.7	-3.4	-3.1	-3.6	-3.6	-3.4	-3.4	-3.6	-3.0	7.0	3.0	-0.3	-0.6	-0.5	-3.3	-3.6
		Reserves	9.0	7.4	9.3	-0.4	7.9	19.6	3.9	8.3	12.0	8.7	3.1	3.1	3.1	8.6	4.3	12.8	4.6	7.0	5.9	3.0	23.1	3.5	11.8	10.7	-2.0
		Reserves (in months of imports)	4.3	4.8	4.7	4.3	4.4	3.7	3.9	4.3	4.5	4.2	4.0	4.4	4.6	4.8	4.3	4.6	4.6	4.7	5.1	4.4	5.4	5.4	5.5	5.5	5.6
	≤3 months	Real per-capita GDP	2.5	1.3	1.7	1.5	1.3	1.3	1.6	1.4	1.6	2.0	2.1	2.1	2.0	3.0	2.0	3.0	0.8	2.7	1.8	2.0	2.4	2.4	2.5	1.7	2.0
		Real per-capita consumption	-0.5	0.1	-0.3	3.0	1.6	1.7	1.7	0.8	0.8	1.9	4.1	4.2	4.1	0.8	4.2	2.1	0.5	2.1	2.2	1.8	1.8	2.5	4.2	1.7	3.3
		Real per-capita absorption	1.8	-1.5	-1.0	2.4	2.0	2.7	1.7	-1.3	1.4	4.9	4.2	-1.0	-0.2	4.9	3.6	5.0	0.5	2.9	1.6	0.5	5.0	5.0	2.3	1.9	3.9
		Current account (% of GDP)	-10.9	-10.7	-7.9	-8.8	-7.6	-11.9	-10.2	-8.7	-10.4	-14.3	-10.2	-10.2	-9.6	-3.2	-10.1	-8.4	-2.9	-8.4	-2.4	-4.6	-8.8	-6.2	-8.0	-5.3	-8.8
		Overall fiscal balance (% of GDP)	-1.8	-3.0	-3.5	-2.7	-2.4	-2.6	-2.4	-2.5	-2.6	-2.0	-2.5	-2.5	-3.2	-4.3	-3.8	-2.9	-2.9	-2.4	-2.2	-4.2	-2.5	-2.5	-1.9	-2.6	-2.6
		Reserves	0.1	8.2	19.3	8.3	10.7	16.2	11.6	4.9	7.3	5.3	13.0	7.9	13.0	10.3	7.6	18.9	1.8	4.4	7.8	21.1	8.8	9.6	23.5	9.4	13.1
		Reserves (in months of imports)	1.7	1.8	2.2	2.4	2.3	2.1	2.2	2.1	2.3	1.5	2.1	2.1	2.1	2.1	2.1	1.8	1.7	1.7	1.7	2.0	1.7	1.7	1.6	1.9	2.0

Table 6.A5 (continued)

Group	Reserves	variables	External demand T-1	T0	T+1	T+2	T+3	Terms of Trade T-1	T0	T+1	T+2	T+3	FDI T-1	T0	T+1	T+2	T+3	Natural disasters T-1	T0	T+1	T+2	T+3	Remittances T-1	T0	T+1	T+2	T+3
Low-income Small States	>3 months	Real per-capita GDP	2.2	1.2	0.7	2.4	1.5	2.6	-0.5	1.0	2.2	1.7	1.9	1.4	1.1	1.0	1.0	1.6	2.7	2.7	1.0	1.0	0.9	1.7	0.4	1.6	1.3
		Real per-capita consumption	1.7	2.4	1.4	0.7	-0.8	1.1	0.6	-4.0	3.2	2.1	3.2	-2.4	-0.7	2.8	2.1	2.8	3.6	4.3	-0.7	-3.6	2.6	1.6	-0.2	0.8	-3.6
		Real per-capita absorption	1.3	0.7	2.1	1.3	-1.1	1.4	0.4	-2.5	1.5	-0.4	3.8	-2.3	-1.1	1.7	-0.2	2.7	5.5	4.3	-0.6	1.4	3.7	-1.0	-1.3	2.3	-2.8
		Current account (% of GDP)	-5.8	-8.3	-8.7	-14.7	-11.1	-9.0	-8.0	-10.1	-5.2	-8.3	-13.3	-6.3	-8.6	-7.4	-6.2	-6.2	-9.2	-9.0	-8.5	-8.6	-5.4	-8.1	-6.5	-7.4	-8.5
		Overall fiscal balance (% of GDP)	-1.2	-3.5	-3.6	-3.7	-4.4	-2.3	-3.9	-4.0	-3.3	-5.4	-2.8	-3.5	-4.0	-1.8	-2.3	-2.0	-2.1	-3.2	-3.5	-3.4	0.3	-1.3	-1.1	-2.2	-2.4
		Reserves	9.0	4.8	15.5	-0.5	8.7	17.4	2.3	8.0	0.4	5.9	16.6	-0.2	2.0	9.0	0.2	9.1	-0.8	-1.1	5.6	5.7	17.8	2.7	11.8	10.7	-0.8
		Reserves (in months of imports)	4.6	1.3	5.2	4.4	4.5	4.2	4.3	4.4	4.0	3.8	4.6	4.9	4.9	5.3	4.9	4.3	4.6	4.6	5.1	4.9	5.3	5.4	5.1	5.6	5.6
	≤3 months	Real per-capita GDP	0.8	1.3	0.2	1.6	1.3	1.7	1.3	1.4	2.2	3.8	3.0	2.5	1.6	1.9	1.5	1.0	2.1	3.0	1.2	3.2	2.1	4.4	2.5	3.6	0.8
		Real per-capita consumption	-0.7	0.1	0.1	1.5	1.4	0.0	2.8	1.0	-1.2	6.3	4.3	-0.5	-3.4	5.1	3.7	0.3	-0.7	1.7	2.6	2.2	0.1	4.1	6.8	3.4	6.0
		Real per-capita absorption	1.6	-0.9	-0.1	0.6	2.4	2.4	5.0	-0.8	1.4	6.5	4.3	-0.5	-2.5	4.1	4.2	1.5	1.5	1.1	-1.5	3.4	1.0	4.2	5.3	2.4	3.0
		Current account (% of GDP)	-12.4	-12.2	-10.5	-10.6	-8.6	-11.0	-14.2	-12.8	-9.1	-14.5	-10.7	-10.6	-9.8	-9.4	-9.5	-10.2	-10.5	-8.3	-8.7	-5.7	-9.0	-5.6	-9.6	-6.3	-8.4
		Overall fiscal balance (% of GDP)	-2.5	-2.6	-3.0	-1.6	-2.3	-3.2	-2.9	-2.5	-2.5	-2.6	-1.6	-1.5	-3.0	-3.5	-1.9	-2.4	-3.2	-2.5	-2.2	-3.9	-1.4	-1.2	-3.4	-2.3	-1.8
		Reserves	-3.8	7.9	11.3	1.5	13.5	16.1	16.3	8.4	4.4	8.5	13.5	7.8	8.0	6.6	11.3	-6.8	13.8	10.0	8.4	20.3	1.0	13.2	12.8	7.2	16.5
		Reserves (in months of imports)	2.1	2.1	2.2	2.5	2.7	2.3	2.3	2.3	2.4	2.3	1.8	2.0	2.0	2.0	2.2	1.6	1.7	1.7	1.8	2.3	1.9	1.7	2.1	2.0	2.0
Micro States	>3 months	Real per-capita GDP	2.2	2.0	-1.2	1.2	1.8	-1.3	1.4	-1.5	3.1	1.0	1.1	0.7	0.9	1.1	1.5	1.7	1.7	2.9	1.6	0.9	1.4	1.5	1.0	1.9	1.1
		Real per-capita consumption	8.4	2.7	-1.6	6.3	-2.1	-1.0	2.8	-6.3	3.6	2.5	0.6	0.7	-0.6	6.7	2.2	2.8	-0.2	5.6	3.6	0.8	-2.9	4.6	-8.5	2.6	2.1
		Real per-capita absorption	6.6	0.8	2.4	-2.9	-3.4	0.5	-0.7	-5.5	4.1	0.0	3.5	-2.4	6.4	0.8	1.0	2.9	2.9	13.9	-3.5	1.7	-0.1	2.7	4.1	2.2	-1.1
		Current account (% of GDP)	-8.6	-8.5	-8.3	-14.7	-9.8	-23.2	-24.7	-20.6	-20.8	-22.1	-15.5	-9.9	-11.9	-8.9	-6.2	-7.1	-9.2	-9.9	-7.6	-8.5	-6.2	-9.9	-11.4	-9.9	-8.6
		Overall fiscal balance (% of GDP)	-1.2	-2.0	-2.5	-3.7	-5.3	-5.8	-4.1	-2.4	-3.6	-3.0	-3.0	-3.0	-3.6	-1.3	-2.3	-1.9	-0.6	-3.0	-2.9	-3.4	-1.0	-2.6	-3.3	-3.7	-3.6
		Reserves	9.5	2.8	13.1	-0.2	6.6	22.2	15.3	11.5	22.0	8.0	15.3	4.3	1.7	9.5	4.6	10.0	8.9	5.2	5.9	6.6	16.3	2.8	5.9	14.7	10.5
		Reserves (in months of imports)	4.4	4.7	5.0	5.1	4.5	3.4	3.9	4.6	5.0	4.5	4.5	4.7	4.7	5.1	4.9	3.9	4.5	4.9	5.2	5.1	5.1	3.2	4.7	5.1	5.9
	≤3 months	Real per-capita GDP	3.3	1.4	1.0	3.3	3.1	2.3	1.8	1.7	2.4	3.1	1.7	3.0	1.9	1.7	1.5	3.0	2.2	2.9	1.8	2.3	2.7	3.2	3.1	1.7	1.9
		Real per-capita consumption	1.2	0.3	-1.8	3.0	2.2	2.1	2.6	1.2	0.0	1.9	5.9	-3.7	-1.8	6.3	3.7	0.3	1.2	4.6	3.1	0.1	7.1	0.3	5.9	2.9	3.2
		Real per-capita absorption	5.5	-0.9	-4.8	2.5	3.5	4.2	1.6	-1.6	0.6	5.7	6.2	-4.5	-1.5	4.7	3.6	2.7	0.9	4.2	-0.8	-1.2	5.5	5.1	3.2	1.4	7.3
		Current account (% of GDP)	-16.9	-14.5	-13.1	-14.2	-11.4	-13.8	-15.9	-14.2	-12.2	-13.8	-21.0	-14.1	-12.7	-14.1	-16.6	-10.4	-12.1	-16.1	-12.3	-10.8	-9.3	-8.5	-9.4	-10.3	-14.6
		Overall fiscal balance (% of GDP)	-2.1	-0.5	-3.3	-0.8	-1.8	-3.4	-1.7	-1.7	-2.2	-2.6	-1.9	-2.0	-3.3	-4.3	-2.1	-2.3	-2.9	-1.7	-2.1	-3.0	-2.1	-3.6	-2.1	-2.0	-1.8
		Reserves	0.1	5.3	30.1	4.6	8.7	5.6	15.0	8.4	2.7	6.0	5.3	5.7	5.5	8.7	5.5	6.1	16.3	4.8	10.2	20.3	5.9	7.4	23.8	6.2	6.9
		Reserves (in months of imports)	1.9	1.9	2.3	2.4	2.5	2.2	2.3	2.3	2.3	2.3	1.8	1.8	1.8	1.9	2.0	1.6	1.9	2.0	1.8	2.6	1.5	1.5	1.7	1.7	2.0

Table 6.A5 (continued)

Group	Reserves	variables	External demand T-1	T0	T+1	T+2	T+3	Terms of Trade T-1	T0	T+1	T+2	T+3	FDI T-1	T0	T+1	T+2	T+3	Natural disasters T-1	T0	T+1	T+2	T+3	Remittances T-1	T0	T+1	T+2	T+3
Highly-indebted small states	>3 months	Real per-capita GDP	2.2	1.6	0.9	2.9	1.5	1.9	0.1	0.4	1.2	1.5	1.9	1.5	1.3	0.9	0.7	1.6	2.4	2.5	1.1	1.1	0.2	1.6	0.2	1.6	1.3
		Real per-capita consumption	1.7	2.5	-0.6	1.2	-0.4	1.3	1.2	-3.7	0.5	1.1	-2.3	-1.7	-0.7	2.8	0.4	2.6	3.8	1.7	-0.5	0.4	2.8	-0.7	0.4	1.6	-3.0
		Real per-capita absorption	2.0	2.5	0.5	2.3	-1.1	2.9	0.9	-2.4	1.6	-0.5	2.9	-1.7	0.5	2.0	-0.2	4.9	2.6	-0.5	2.0	2.0	-0.4	-1.1	3.1	1.9	-2.3
		Current account (% of GDP)	-5.6	-6.7	-7.5	-8.9	-9.5	-9.8	-10.6	-10.1	-9.2	-8.4	-9.8	-9.8	-9.1	-7.8	-6.7	-9.1	-8.4	-8.6	-7.4	-8.6	-8.3	-8.5	-5.4	-3.4	-8.2
		Overall fiscal balance (% of GDP)	-1.6	-3.5	-5.5	-3.5	-3.9	-2.9	-3.7	-3.6	-3.2	-3.9	-3.3	-3.3	-3.6	-1.9	-3.2	-2.4	-2.9	-3.0	-3.0	-3.4	-2.2	-1.6	-0.5	-3.4	-3.4
		Reserves (% of GDP)	9.7	3.9	5.8	-0.2	7.0	12.4	8.0	17.4	8.0	9.4	2.0	2.0	2.0	9.0	1.1	2.4	4.7	4.6	5.1	4.5	5.4	8.7	14.3	12.3	0.3
		Reserves (in months of imports)	4.1	4.6	4.7	4.3	4.4	4.4	4.2	4.0	3.8	4.0	4.5	4.5	4.5	4.4	4.0	4.7	4.6	5.1	4.5	5.6	5.1	5.1	5.2	5.6	5.6
	≤3 months	Real per-capita GDP	0.8	1.2	1.0	1.8	1.2	2.0	1.8	1.4	1.3	2.0	0.4	2.0	0.4	2.0	1.7	0.4	0.4	2.8	1.4	2.0	3.1	2.5	2.1	2.4	2.3
		Real per-capita consumption	0.6	-1.2	0.1	2.0	0.9	4.0	0.5	1.3	-0.3	1.4	4.5	4.2	0.4	4.0	2.1	4.6	4.7	4.6	3.8	5.1	5.4	6.2	2.5	2.9	3.2
		Real per-capita absorption	1.6	-1.9	-1.0	0.6	1.7	4.3	1.7	-0.5	0.5	1.7	2.0	3.0	-0.1	4.9	3.1	2.8	3.0	1.4	2.7	1.1	3.1	4.6	6.2	1.4	5.0
		Current account (% of GDP)	-10.7	-10.8	-7.9	-8.8	-5.9	-10.6	-10.7	-10.2	-7.8	-7.7	-8.0	-9.1	-8.0	-7.8	-6.7	-9.1	-8.4	-7.9	-8.6	-5.4	-5.1	-6.4	-6.4	-5.0	-6.4
		Overall fiscal balance (% of GDP)	-1.5	-2.3	-3.0	-2.4	-3.2	-1.9	-3.0	-2.7	-2.4	-2.2	-3.1	-2.4	-3.1	-3.6	-2.7	-2.9	-2.1	-2.2	-2.2	-4.1	-2.0	-2.0	-2.2	-2.3	-2.2
		Reserves (% of GDP)	0.1	8.2	15.7	4.9	11.4	8.2	16.7	8.4	4.9	8.6	9.0	9.0	10.6	7.5	5.8	13.8	7.6	7.8	5.9	19.4	8.6	23.8	9.0	15.0	13.1
		Reserves (in months of imports)	1.7	1.8	2.1	2.3	2.4	1.5	2.2	2.2	2.0	2.3	1.9	1.9	1.9	2.0	1.9	1.6	1.7	1.7	2.0	2.0	1.6	1.5	2.0	2.0	2.0
No-IMF Financial Arrangement	>3 months	Real per-capita GDP	2.9	1.7	0.7	3.1	2.0	2.1	0.1	1.6	1.7	3.3	1.6	2.1	1.6	3.1	1.5	2.4	3.0	3.0	3.3	1.2	2.4	0.6	2.2	2.2	1.6
		Real per-capita consumption	0.6	2.7	0.8	2.1	1.4	3.7	1.1	-0.9	1.6	0.8	2.0	2.4	2.0	2.8	3.0	2.6	2.3	2.0	2.0	2.6	5.2	4.8	0.0	1.5	1.5
		Real per-capita absorption	2.0	3.8	1.3	2.4	1.7	2.8	0.6	0.2	0.8	-0.4	1.9	2.7	1.9	2.3	3.3	3.4	3.2	3.5	2.2	3.5	4.9	4.6	0.8	0.8	-1.6
		Current account (% of GDP)	-5.4	-6.2	-5.7	-7.9	-7.5	-4.2	-7.7	-6.7	-4.8	-6.3	-8.0	-7.3	-8.0	-5.7	-5.3	-4.1	-6.7	-7.2	-5.9	-5.8	-5.7	-5.7	-4.8	-4.8	-1.1
		Overall fiscal balance (% of GDP)	-1.1	-3.0	-4.0	-3.4	-3.6	-2.6	-3.0	-3.4	-3.3	-3.0	-3.6	-3.3	-3.6	-3.0	-2.7	-2.8	-3.5	-3.3	-3.3	-2.2	-2.5	-2.5	-3.2	-3.2	-1.9
		Reserves (% of GDP)	9.8	6.0	5.6	4.5	4.4	10.1	16.1	-2.2	3.3	13.4	2.0	4.5	2.0	9.5	4.6	8.2	12.0	8.2	3.8	0.6	11.1	1.7	14.7	14.7	6.3
		Reserves (in months of imports)	4.2	4.9	5.0	2.4	2.3	4.4	4.1	4.0	4.1	4.1	4.5	4.5	4.5	4.6	4.4	4.6	4.4	4.6	5.1	4.5	4.7	4.7	5.4	5.4	5.6
	≤3 months	Real per-capita GDP	2.3	1.4	1.9	0.8	1.4	2.5	0.7	2.4	1.3	1.9	3.0	3.0	2.2	2.0	2.1	3.1	1.3	3.1	1.3	2.0	2.7	2.1	3.1	3.1	2.2
		Real per-capita consumption	1.1	-3.3	1.0	0.8	1.7	4.9	0.7	2.4	-0.2	0.8	-0.8	-0.8	0.2	4.2	3.7	2.2	1.0	2.1	2.1	0.3	0.3	5.6	2.1	2.1	4.2
		Real per-capita absorption	1.6	-2.5	0.1	-0.2	1.9	4.3	1.2	0.2	0.5	0.6	-2.5	-2.5	0.3	4.4	3.1	1.7	3.0	3.0	0.9	-0.4	3.4	3.4	4.1	0.9	6.2
		Current account (% of GDP)	-10.6	-10.3	-7.9	-3.4	-9.8	-12.1	-10.0	-9.6	-3.5	-11.1	-9.1	-10.3	-9.1	-10.4	-9.6	-7.9	-7.2	-7.9	-8.5	-2.5	-7.9	-7.9	-8.7	-8.7	-6.4
		Overall fiscal balance (% of GDP)	-1.6	-2.3	-3.0	-2.4	-3.4	-1.9	-2.9	-2.4	-3.5	-3.1	-3.3	-2.2	-3.3	-3.9	-2.5	-7.0	-2.9	-2.4	-2.4	-2.5	-3.9	-3.9	-2.5	-2.3	-2.2
		Reserves (% of GDP)	4.4	8.6	8.2	8.4	8.0	7.1	13.1	3.5	0.9	6.2	11.3	7.6	11.3	9.7	4.0	6.2	13.4	9.4	5.9	16.7	13.4	13.8	6.2	6.2	10.3
		Reserves (in months of imports)	1.6	2.1	2.2	2.0	2.1	1.6	2.2	2.0	1.8	2.2	2.1	1.9	2.1	2.0	2.0	1.6	1.9	2.0	1.9	2.0	1.6	1.5	2.1	2.1	2.1
Early IMF Financial Arrangement	>3 months	Real per-capita GDP	1.9	1.0	1.4	1.9	1.5	2.0	-1.2	-1.7	0.7	1.3	1.5	1.4	1.4	0.2	0.5	2.6	5.2	0.6	1.0	1.4	1.0	0.5	1.2	1.2	-0.2
		Real per-capita consumption	5.1	4.4	-0.4	6.3	-0.7	0.5	2.8	-6.4	-2.1	2.4	-0.4	-5.5	-0.4	3.1	2.2	6.0	9.6	-1.0	-1.0	3.0	0.4	-0.7	1.3	1.3	-3.6
		Real per-capita absorption	2.1	0.8	2.4	3.5	1.0	2.9	-1.1	-6.5	1.6	0.2	-0.4	-4.6	-4.6	1.9	-0.9	7.2	6.4	-1.0	3.7	3.1	-1.7	-3.4	1.9	1.9	-1.7
		Current account (% of GDP)	-15.9	-12.7	-13.8	-22.6	-17.2	-13.0	-12.0	-12.2	-9.3	-9.9	-7.5	-7.4	-5.7	-8.1	-8.1	-6.3	-8.9	-6.9	-9.1	-9.1	-8.1	-6.0	-8.9	-8.9	-8.6
		Overall fiscal balance (% of GDP)	-1.2	-2.5	-3.0	-5.5	-6.3	-3.0	-4.6	-4.5	-5.8	-5.8	-3.3	-1.8	-2.4	-1.8	-4.1	-4.1	-2.4	-2.2	-1.1	-0.5	-2.4	-1.4	-2.1	-2.1	-3.5
		Reserves (% of GDP)	19.1	4.8	22.5	-0.4	14.7	18.6	2.7	8.3	5.5	9.3	7.6	8.0	5.6	5.7	-5.2	0.6	3.9	7.4	9.3	4.9	6.1	13.4	7.6	7.6	-0.7
		Reserves (in months of imports)	6.4	5.7	4.7	4.3	4.6	5.5	4.2	4.1	3.8	3.8	5.3	5.6	5.6	5.7	5.1	3.9	3.8	4.5	4.9	4.9	6.1	6.7	6.9	6.9	6.4
	≤3 months	Real per-capita GDP	0.2	-0.2	0.3	1.6	1.1	1.1	0.7	1.5	2.5	2.0	1.7	2.9	2.9	2.1	1.6	0.2	1.0	3.8	2.0	2.0	2.7	6.7	1.7	1.7	2.0
		Real per-capita consumption	-0.1	-0.3	-0.9	3.5	0.2	1.3	3.3	1.5	5.8	3.9	1.3	1.9	1.9	2.5	3.0	-0.4	0.2	1.0	3.4	3.1	1.8	4.3	6.6	6.6	3.2
		Real per-capita absorption	0.8	-0.9	-2.5	0.6	3.5	0.3	1.7	0.5	6.3	4.2	2.3	2.3	2.3	1.1	2.1	-2.5	-1.8	2.3	3.1	0.5	5.8	5.6	7.1	7.1	2.9
		Current account (% of GDP)	-10.9	-11.5	-7.6	-8.5	-5.0	-5.3	-9.4	-7.2	-5.0	-5.3	-4.1	-7.4	-7.4	-7.0	-4.0	-12.1	-2.5	-4.3	-3.9	-3.9	-3.5	-4.1	-5.0	-5.0	-4.0
		Overall fiscal balance (% of GDP)	0.1	-0.3	-1.1	-0.2	-0.9	-1.4	-0.3	-0.9	0.0	-0.7	-1.1	-2.0	-2.0	-0.8	-1.9	-0.2	-0.4	-3.6	-3.5	-3.5	-3.5	-2.8	-0.4	-0.4	-1.5
		Reserves (% of GDP)	0.1	20.9	23.0	17.6	16.0	-3.1	53.4	28.2	9.0	11.4	35.2	11.4	11.4	8.6	14.9	32.2	-0.2	-1.0	21.9	19.2	10.6	38.3	8.9	8.9	14.9
		Reserves (in months of imports)	1.7	1.8	2.1	2.3	2.7	1.7	2.1	2.3	2.3	2.3	1.9	2.5	2.5	2.3	2.1	1.3	1.3	1.7	2.0	2.0	1.9	2.0	1.7	1.7	1.8

Source: World Economic Outlook 2017; World Bank; EM-DAT; estimates

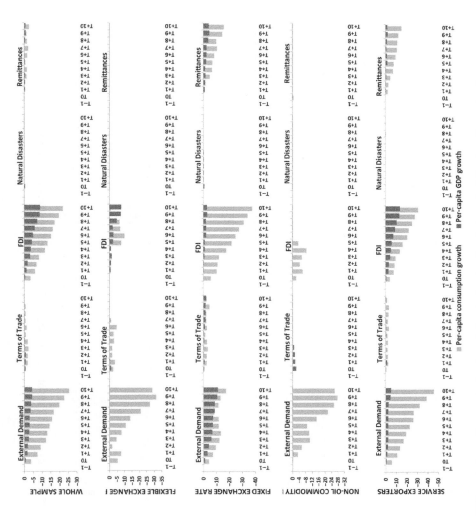

Figure 6.A1 Per-capita GDP and absorption cost of external shocks by structural characteristics (median values)

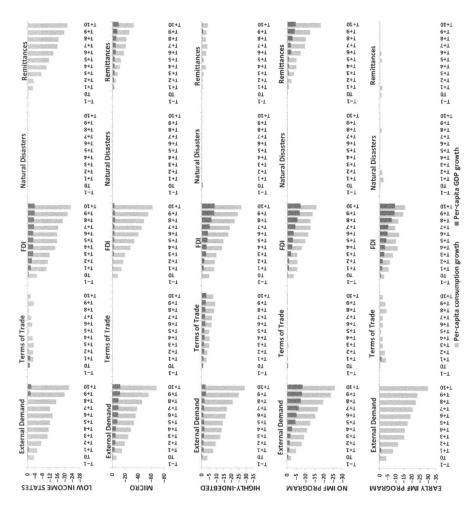

Figure 6.A1 Per-capita GDP and absorption cost of external shocks by structural characteristics (median values)

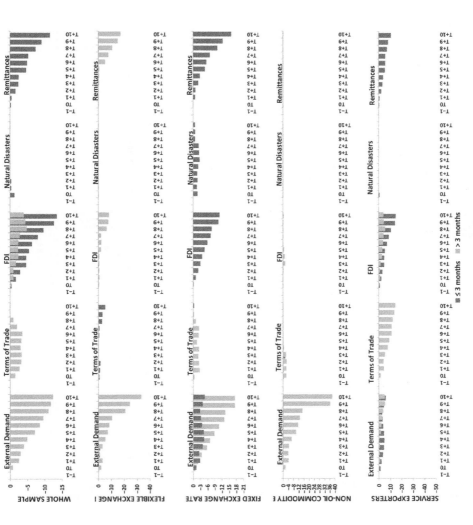

Figure 6.A2 Per-capita GDP cost of external shocks by structural characteristics (median values)

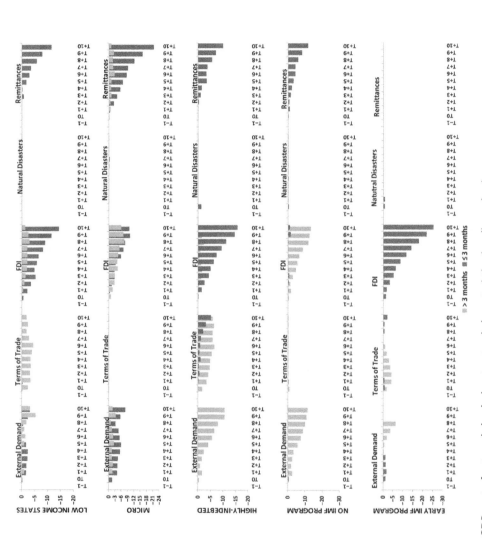

Figure 6.A2 Per-capita GDP cost of external shocks by structural characteristics (median values)

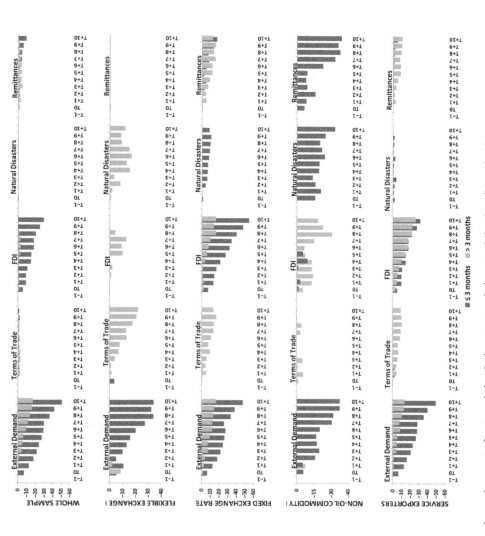

Figure 6.A3 Per-capita absorption cost of external shocks by structural characteristics (median values)

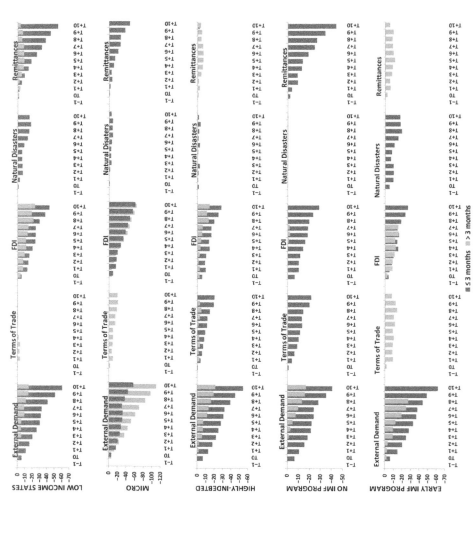

Figure 6.A3 Per-capita absorption cost of external shocks by structural characteristics (median values)

References

Acemoglu, D., Johnson, S. and Robinson, J. A. (2001). 'The Colonial Origins of Comparative Development: An Empirical Investigation'. *American Economic Review*, 91(5): 1369–1401.

Aizenman, J. and Lee, J. (2007). 'International reserves: precautionary versus mercantilist views, theory and evidence'. *Open Economies Review*, 18(2): 191–214.

Auguste, S. and Cornejo, M. (2015). *Vulnerability in Small Island Economies. The case of the Caribbean*. Caribbean Future Forum.

Barnichon, R. (2009). The optimal level of reserves for low-income countries: Self-insurance against external shocks. *IMF Staff Papers*, 56(4): 852–875.

Becker, T. I., Mauro, P., Ostry, J. D., Ranciere, R. and Jeanne, O. D. (2007). *Country Insurance; The Role of Domestic Policies*, No. 254. Washington, DC: International Monetary Fund.

Briguglio, L. (1995). 'Small island developing states and their economic vulnerabilities'. *World Development*, 23(9): 1615–1632.

Briguglio, L. (2016). 'Exposure to external shocks and economic resilience of countries: evidence from global indicators'. *Journal of Economic Studies*, 43(6): 1057–1078.

Briguglio, L., Cordina, G., Farrugia, N. and Vella, S. (2009). 'Economic vulnerability and resilience: concepts and measurements'. *Oxford Development Studies*, 37(3): 229–247.

Cabezon, E. R., Hunter, L., Tumbarello, P., Washimi, K. and Wu, Y. (2015). Enhancing Macroeconomic Resilience to Natural Disasters and Climate Change in the Small States of the Pacific, *WP/15/125*. Washington, DC: International Monetary Fund.

Calvo, G., Izquierdo, A. and Loo-Kung, R. (2012). Optimal Holdings of International Reserves: Self-insurance against Sudden Stops. *NBER Working Paper* No. 18219, July.

Crispolti, V. and Tsibouris, G. (2012). International reserves in low income countries: Have they served as buffers?. *Working Paper* 12/7. Washington, DC: International Monetary Fund.

Crispolti, V., Dabla-Norris, E., Kim, J., Shirono, K. and Tsibouris, G. (2013). Assessing reserve adequacy in low-income countries. *Occasional Paper* No. 276. Washington, DC: International Monetary Fund.

Dehesa, M., Pineda, E. and Samuel, W. (2009). Optimal Reserves in the Eastern Caribbean Currency Union. *Working Paper* 09/77. Washington, DC: International Monetary Fund.

Drummond, P. and Dhasmana, A. (2008). Foreign Reserve Adequacy in Sub- Saharan Africa. *Working Paper* 08/150. Washington, DC: International Monetary Fund.

Durdu, C. B., Mendoza, E. and Terrones, M. (2009). Precautionary demand for foreign assets in Sudden Stop economies: An assessment of the New Mercantilism. *NBER Working Paper* No. 13123.

Easterly, W. and Kraay, A. (2000). 'Small states, small problems? Income, growth, and volatility in Small States'. *World Development*, 28(11): 2013–2027.

Erdem, F. P. and Ünalmış, İ. (2016). 'Revisiting super-cycles in commodity prices'. *Central Bank Review*, 16(4):137–142.

Erten, B. and Ocampo, J.A. (2012). *Super-Cycles of Commodity Prices Since the Mid-Nineteenth Century*. New York: Columbia University Academic Commons.

Ghosh, A. R., Ostry, J. D. and Qureshi, M. S. (2015). 'Exchange rate management and crisis susceptibility: A reassessment'. *IMF Economic Review*, 63(1): 238–276.

Guha-Sapir, D., Below, R. and Hoyois, P. (2015). *EM-DAT: International disaster database*. Brussels, Belgium: Catholic University of Louvain.

IMF (2006). *Country Insurance: The Role of Domestic Policies*. Washington, DC: International Monetary Fund.

IMF (2011). *Assessing Reserve Adequacy*. Washington, DC: International Monetary Fund.

IMF (2013a). *Macroeconomic Issues in Small States and Implications for Fund Engagement*. Washington, DC: International Monetary Fund.

IMF (2013b). *2013 Low-Income Countries Global Risks and Vulnerabilities Report*. Washington, DC: International Monetary Fund.

IMF (2015). *Macroeconomic Developments and Selected Issues in Small Developing States*. Washington, DC: International Monetary Fund.

Jeanne, O. and Ranciere, R. (2006). The Optimal Level of International Reserves for Emerging Market Countries: Formulas and Applications. *IMF Working Paper* 06/229.

Jeanne, O. and Ranciere, R. (2008). The Optimal Level of International Reserves for Emerging Market Economies: A New Formula and Some Applications. *CEPR Discussion Papers* No. 6723.

Jeanne, O. and Wyplosz, C. (2003). The International Lender of Last Resort: How Large Is Large Enough? In Michael Dooley and Jeffrey Frankel (eds), *Managing Currency Crises in Emerging Markets*. Chicago, IL: University of Chicago Press: 89–118.

Moore, W. and Glean, A. (2016). 'Foreign exchange reserve adequacy and exogenous shocks'. *Applied Economics*, 48(6): 490–501.

Mwase, N. (2012). How much should I hold? Reserve Adequacy in Emerging Markets and Small Islands. *IMF Working Paper* 12/205.

7

Declines in correspondent banking in the small states of the Pacific[1]

Jihad Alwazir, Fazurin Jamaludin, Dongyeol Lee, Niamh Sheridan and Patrizia Tumbarello

1 Introduction

The objective of this chapter is to present evidence relating to the erosion of access to financial services, money laundering compliance and related matters in the Pacific island countries (PICs)[2] as well as the potentially negative impact of these developments on the financial sector and macroeconomy of these countries. The chapter also attempts to identify the collective efforts needed to address the consequences of withdrawal of corresponding banking relationships and outline policy measures to help the affected countries mitigate the impact.

A large-scale withdrawal of correspondent banking relationships (CBRs) is occurring in many regions and jurisdictions, including the small states of the Pacific (Commonwealth Secretariat, 2016). The termination of corresponding banking relationships, or, in some cases, pressures on existing ones, is contributing to the closure of bank accounts of money transfer operators (MTOs), particularly for those heavily engaged in remittance transfers.[3] As Erbenová *et al.* (2016) note, banks' decisions are driven by several considerations, including cost-benefit analysis; re-evaluation of business models amid an evolving regulatory and enforcement landscape with regard to prudential requirements; economic and trade sanctions; policies to combat money laundering and the financing of terrorism (AML/CFT – Anti-Money Laundering and Combating the Financing of Terrorism); and tax transparency.

Several features of small states heighten their vulnerability to the withdrawal of CBRs and the reduction in other banking services. The main causes are weaknesses in AML/CFT regimes and poor compliance by some money transfer operators in small states that rely heavily on remittances (originating in Australia, New Zealand, and the United States).[4] CBRs are under strain where there are direct linkages with global banks, and where linkages are more indirect, correspondent banks have stepped up their scrutiny of respondent banks' interaction with the remittance sector (Box 7.1). This added scrutiny has led banks to close MTO bank accounts in both sender and receiver countries. The presence of offshore financial centres in some jurisdictions is also adding to CBR strains. In some instances, non-compliance with the U.S. Foreign Account Tax Compliance Act (FATCA) has led to the withdrawal of CBRs.[5]

Box 7.1   Correspondent banking relationships

Correspondent banking is a bilateral arrangement, often involving a reciprocal cross-border relationship in multiple currencies. A correspondent banking arrangement involves one bank (the *correspondent*) providing a deposit account or other liability accounts, and related services, to another bank (the *respondent*), often including its affiliates. The arrangement requires the exchange of messages to settle transactions by crediting and debiting those accounts.

Correspondent banking enables domestic and cross-border payments. These relationships facilitate a range of transactions and services, including the execution of third-party payments, trade finance, the banks' own cash clearing, liquidity management and short-term borrowing, or funding investment needs in a particular currency.

In the most traditional form of correspondent banking, a respondent bank enters into an agreement with the correspondent bank to execute payments on behalf of the respondent bank and its customers (see diagram). For example, a French travel agent needs to send a

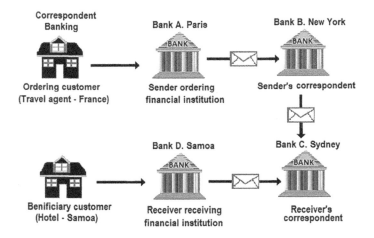

payment to a hotel operator in Samoa. This payment could be sent in several ways but in the diagram the payment is sent from a French bank to a US bank, on to an Australian bank, and then to a bank in Samoa.

A second example illustrates the interaction between migrants' remittances, MTOs, domestic banks in the sender and receiver markets, and correspondent banks. In this example, migrants based in Australia bring their remittances to the MTO, which has an account with an Australian bank. Similarly, small businesses in Samoa use the MTO to send payments for imports, and Samoan families send money to university students. The MTO nets out these amounts and transfers between Australian and Samoan bank accounts in Australian dollars, using a CBR. The MTO may also make transfers elsewhere in the world and these flows could be transmitted using a US CBR relationship. In addition, the Australian banks will use their U.S.-based CBRs for many other transactions other than remittances.

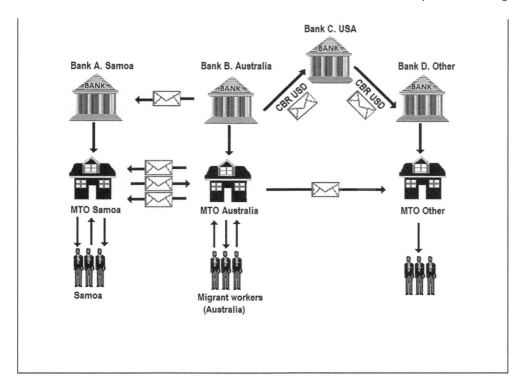

The consequences of CBR withdrawal can be serious. The typically small number of banks and other financial service providers in the domestic banking sectors of small states implies that reduced financial services by one entity can give rise to increased concentration in the provision of services. This could raise systemic risks for the financial sector and heighten the risk of disruption to remittance flows. Loss of CBRs can also limit other financial services, such as those facilitating trade. Furthermore, reduced competition is likely to raise the already-high cost of financial services, including remittances.

In the small states of the Pacific, the consequences of CBR withdrawal show up mainly in the remittance sector, increasing the fragility of remittance systems. In many of the small states, MTOs are an important channel for remittances but many MTOs have had their bank accounts unilaterally closed by banks. As a result, some MTOs are now operating with a single bank account or, in some instances, with no bank accounts. Looking ahead, MTOs could cease operating entirely or shift operations outside formal banking channels: indeed, remittances are already being diverted to less transparent hand-carry of cash across borders or to costlier banking channels. Efforts to increase financial inclusion across the small states of the Pacific were bearing fruit but are now facing setbacks. Closure of MTOs could leave parts of the population without ready access to financial services. The broader macroeconomic impacts have been limited so far, as payment flows can still be re-directed. But without corrective policy actions, the consequences of continued withdrawal of CBRs could undermine the functioning of the financial system, weaken growth prospects, and reduce resilience to shocks.

The rest of the chapter is organised as follows: In Section 2 we examine recent developments in CBRs and focus on the consequences of strained CBRs for remittance channels. We draw on findings from extensive discussions in Australia, New Zealand, and

Samoa with regulators, banks and banking associations, and MTOs. In Section 3, we discuss the impact to date – and the potential effects – on the financial system and the economies of the small states of the Pacific. In the policy discussion of Section 4, we review the main strategy, emphasizing the need for collective action and steps by global, regional, and domestic regulators and standard-setters. We also identify measures that affected countries can adopt to help maintain and ease the strain on CBRs. These measures, however, may not be sufficient. Therefore, we explore options for alternative remittance systems and discuss the prospects for a combination of 'blockchain' technology, a Know-Your-Customer utility, and mobile phone networks.[6] Although the digital economy, through new financial-sector technologies, can be part of the solution, the timeframe for implementation is likely to be lengthy and a key challenge will be avoiding macroeconomic disruption in the interim.

2 Vulnerabilities, drivers and evidence in the PICs

Survey results and overview of drivers

The consequences and challenges posed by CBR withdrawal in the small states of the Pacific are becoming apparent, according to a survey of IMF country teams and the authorities of the Asia and Pacific region, carried out in June-October 2016 (and summarized in Table 7.1). Survey responses[7] suggest that many countries are having greater difficulty in either maintaining CBRs, or are experiencing rising costs and complexities in transferring money and repatriating

Table 7.1 Survey on the consequences of CBR withdrawal: authorities' views

	Are relationships with correspondent banks becoming more difficult?	*Are money transfers becoming more costly and complex to execute? /1*	*Is repatriation of remittances to your country becoming more costly and burdensome?*
Fiji	CBRs have remained broadly intact. The main challenge lies in the local banks' ability to generate sufficient transaction volumes to warrant a continuation of CBRs.	Pricing and execution of money transfers have remained reasonable despite the termination of relationships with remittance agents by the two major banks.	The cost of remittances to Fiji, especially from New Zealand, has increased since mid-2015.
Kiribati	No, but anecdotal evidence points to increased compliance costs.	No	No
Marshall Islands	The country's sole domestic commercial bank is at risk of losing its US correspondent banking relationship.	No, but the loss of the CBR will have strong negative consequences as the MTO operators rely on the domestic bank for remittances.	No
Palau	The loss of CBRs has not been an issue in Palau as the three U.S. FDIC-insured banks conduct all foreign transactions in the country.	No	No. The remittance sector is very small in Palau.

Table 7.1 (continued)

	Are relationships with correspondent banks becoming more difficult?	Are money transfers becoming more costly and complex to execute? /1	Is repatriation of remittances to your country becoming more costly and burdensome?
Papua New Guinea	The level of compliance to maintain CBRs is increasing and continues to do so annually, hence, the higher costs. Certain institutions lost CBRs, others have had difficulties securing them, and others had to close or impose stringent requirements on remittance service providers to maintain their CBRs.	Money transfers are mainly done by commercial banks and authorized dealers and are becoming costly. This is due to costs associated with compliance requirements as CBRs and compliance requirements by the local regulator. Also, remittance services are provided by two commercial banks and apply stringent requirements.	The amount of remittances coming into PNG would be less than outbound payments and not considered costly.
Samoa	Although CBRs have largely been maintained, they are increasingly at risk. Non-compliance with FATCA has also led to loss of a CBR for one local bank.	The environment for money transfer operators has become more difficult, with MTOs facing account closures and imposition of complex requirements by banks.	Yes, the cost of remittance has increased recently. MTOs whose accounts have been closed are unable to serve their customers as quickly or as cost effectively as before.
Solomon Islands	The number of CBRs has declined. In addition, a major regional bank exited and was subsumed by a local bank, which increased CBR concentration.	A few small money transfer operators have ceased operations.	The closure of some MTOs is beginning to affect the cost of sending remittances.
Tonga	Establishing CBRs with U.S. banks has become more difficult. One Australian bank has agreed to open US dollar correspondent bank accounts for local banks.	Most of the bank accounts of money remitters' agents in Australia and New Zealand have been closed.	The cost of remittances from New Zealand to Tonga has risen.
Tuvalu	Tuvalu's largest bank, the NBT, has maintained the key working international CBRs, but access to some currency clearing services is complicated.	Yes	No
Vanuatu	Though the loss of CBRs is not a serious issue, inclusion in the FATF list may pose some difficulties in cross-border payments and trade finance.	The cost of money transfers had been increasing until ANZ lowered the cost. But the cost remains high as receiving banks also charge some fees.	The repatriation of remittances to Vanuatu has been costly for seasonal workers and those providing financial assistance to families in Vanuatu.

Sources and Methodology: IMF survey of country authorities (2016), including discussions with IMF surveillance teams during Article IV consultations and missions.

Note: 1/ Refers to all money transfers, including trade-related transfers and remittances.

remittances, or all of these things. The increased complexity and cost of money transfers and remittances reflect the closure of bank accounts of MTOs, not only in the small states but also in migrant host countries, including Australia and New Zealand. MTO account closures in Fiji, Samoa, and Tonga, both at home and in Australia and New Zealand, are increasing. In other countries – such as Kiribati, the Marshall Islands, Samoa, Tonga, and Tuvalu – survey responses indicate that CBRs have been withdrawn or are increasingly strained.

Vulnerabilities and drivers

The relative importance of the remittance sector and the linkages with global banks help explain difference in recent experiences across the small states and provide insights as to the causes. In countries with higher integration with the global financial system strains in the CBRs appear more likely to occur. In other Pacific small states with stronger financial linkages to Australia and New Zealand, and where remittances are sizable, MTOs are facing account closures in both sender and receiver markets. Weaknesses in AML/CFT frameworks and compliance are also contributing to strains in CBRs and to the closure of MTO accounts. In addition, the presence of offshore financial sectors in several jurisdictions heightens perceived AML/CFT risks. Non-compliance with the U.S. Foreign Account Tax Compliance Act has also contributed to the termination of CBRs.

The high volume of remittance transfers adds to concerns about AML/CFT risks and associated reputational risks for banks. In 2015, remittances averaged about 10% of GDP in the Pacific islands relative to 5% on average for low-income countries (Figure 7.1). Among the small Pacific states, Kiribati, the Marshall Islands, Samoa, Tonga, and Tuvalu depend heavily on remittances – this dependency peaked at 27% of GDP in Tonga.

In terms of US dollars – relevant from the perspective of assessing risks by the global banks – total remittances to the small states are about US$600 million annually, with Fiji, Samoa, and Tonga representing the largest markets (Figure 7.2).

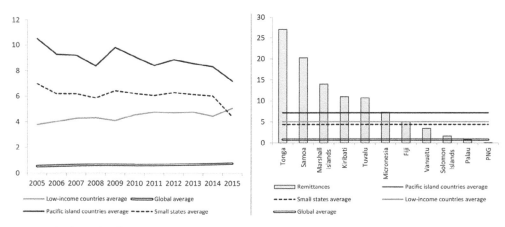

Figure 7.1 The role of remittances in the small states of the Pacific
Source: World Bank, World Development Indicators. Data is for 2014 for the Marshall Islands, Papua New Guinea, Tonga, Tuvalu and Vanuatu and 2015 for Samoa, Kiribati, Micronesia, Fiji, Solomon Islands and Palau.

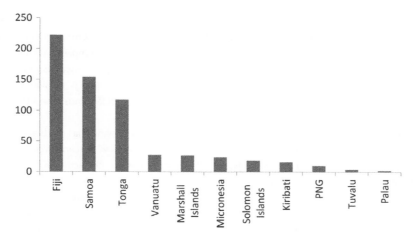

Figure 7.2 Remittances to the Pacific island countries US$ million, 2015
Source: World Bank, World Development Indicators.

In remittance markets dominated by banks, CBRs are strained. But where MTOs dominate the remittance market, concerns by both correspondent and respondent banks about MTOs' AML/CFT compliance are triggering the closure of MTO bank accounts. For example, in the Marshall Islands, where remittances are sent mainly through the domestic bank, its CBR relationships with global banks are under pressure (Box 7.2). In other counrtries such countries as Fiji and Samoa, where MTOs are important for remittances, MTO bank accounts are facing closure both in the domestic economy and in remittance-source countries (Australia and New Zealand).

Box 7.2   Marshall Islands: correspondent banking relationship challenges

Prepared by Serkan Arslanalp.

The Marshall Islands' sole domestic commercial bank has faced the risk of losing its CBR with a U.S.-based bank. Losing this relationship could result in loss of access to U.S. payment and settlement services, which could disrupt economic activity in the Marshall Islands, given the use of the U.S. dollar as legal tender.

Background. The Marshall Islands' only domestic commercial bank, Bank of the Marshall Islands (BOMI), has a CBR with a U.S.-based bank (First Hawaiian Bank, a subsidiary of BNP

Marshall Island banks: corresponding banking relations

Currency	Bank of Marshall Islands	Bank of Guam
US$	First Hawaiian Bank	
AU$	Westpac Banking	
EUR		Wells Fargo
GBP		Wells Fargo

Paribas). Through this relationship, BOMI has access to U.S. settlement and payment services. In 2015, the U.S.-based bank notified BOMI that it may terminate its correspondent banking accounts with BOMI by end-2016, owing to concerns about the cost of complying with new U.S. regulations, especially after penalties stemming from the violations of U.S. sanctions laws by BNP Paribas (its parent company). The authorities informed the IMF 2016 Article IV mission team that the U.S.-based bank had agreed to continue its CBR with BOMI until BOMI finds a new U.S.-based correspondent bank or resolves outstanding compliance issues

Remittances. The cost of transferring remittances to the Marshall Islands has not been affected, as almost all the remittances come through two large operators (MoneyGram and Western Union) that have partnerships with domestic banks. Small money MTOs are not active in the Marshall Islands, unlike in other Pacific islands.

Authorities' response. The authorities are drafting a new AML legislation in line with FATF standards and United Nations Convention Against Corruption rules. Deficiencies identified in the 2011 Mutual Evaluation Report for the Marshall Islands conducted by the Asia-Pacific Group are also being reviewed and rectified, including strengthening the Domestic Financial Intelligence Unit (DFIU). The authorities have begun working with a team of consultants from the U.S. Financial Services Volunteer Corps, which is helping draft the new legislation. The authorities have also met with relevant U.S. regulators – including the U.S. Federal Reserve in April 2016 – to seek guidance on how to strengthen their bank supervisory framework. Furthermore, senior managers of the Banking Commission have attended a workshop on implementing the international AML/CFT standards in April 2016, organized jointly by the IMF's Legal Department and the Singapore Training Institute.

Policy advice. During the 2016 Article IV consultation mission, IMF staff encouraged the authorities to strengthen their AML/CFT framework, particularly relative to Know-Your-Customer (KYC) requirements. Staff also urged the authorities to have an open and regular dialogue with U.S. regulators to flag any new concerns on AML/CFT risks (IMF, 2016).

Differences in the source of remittances also help explain divergent recent experiences. The main sources of remittances are Australia, New Zealand, and the United States, with about 25% for each country on average (Figure 7.3, left-hand side). Some countries (e.g. the Fiji, Solomon Islands, Samoa, and Tonga), are more dependent on remittances from Australia and New Zealand, while others (e.g. Kiribati, the Marshall Islands, Micronesia, and Palau) receive more remittances from other countries, including the United States (Figure 7.2, right-hand side). Respondent banks appear to face CBR challenges with regional correspondents that have closer connections with global banks.

Weak compliance by some MTOs with AML/CFT requirements also contributes to banks' decisions to close accounts. At times, MTOs' compliance with formal Know-Your-Customer (KYC) requirements is weak or absent. But in small communities, customers are often known personally to the proprietor of the small MTO. KYC compliance is also hampered by the lack of formal means of identification in many small states that do not issue national IDs and many individuals do not have driver's licenses or passports.

The operational structural of some MTOs also raises AML/CFT compliance concerns. MTOs vary widely in operational models, size, and level of sophistication, both across and within the small states. But in some markets, MTOs are very small and the only employee may be the owner who operates in partnership with another single operator in a different country,

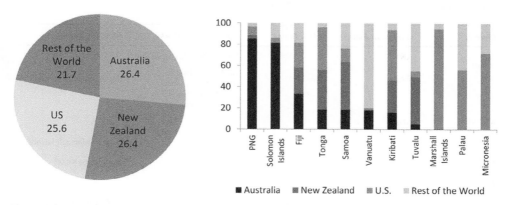

Figure 7.3 Remittance source-countries for the small states of the Pacific (%)
Source: World Bank migration and remittances data.

implying no separate compliance officer. The MTO business model also raises concerns: MTOs accumulate a large number of two-way transfers that are then netted out; a low fee is charged to the customer and profits are determined by the volume of transactions. For example, in Samoa, MTOs handle just over half a million inward money transfers a year, with an average size of just US$270. Typically, an MTO uses its bank accounts for bank-to-bank cross-border transfers of the net amounts (first shopping around for the lowest cost transfer on any given day). From the banks' perspective, the bundling of cross-border transfers into a single transaction complicates monitoring. Banks are not required to perform due diligence on their customer's customer, referred to as 'Know Your Customers' Customer (KYCC).[8] But in applying the risk-based approach, and with uncertainty about the strength of an MTO's systems, a given bank may be concerned about its ability to respond to requests for information. Banks have argued that KYCC is, for all intents and purposes, a requirement. This perceived obligation is the result of banks' understanding of the consequences of U.S. regulatory requirements; their concerns about reputational risks; the increased oversight by correspondent banks; or the need to satisfy domestic legislation. Rather than take this risk or bear the compliance cost, banks opt to close MTO bank accounts.

The Pacific is home to many foreign-owned banks, including from the United States and Australia. The outsized role of foreign banks in the financial sector in many Pacific small states heightens their vulnerability to operational decisions of global and regional banks (Table 7.2).[9] Marshall Islands, Micronesia, and Palau have direct banking relationships with the U.S. banking sector through U.S.-owned banks. In the Marshall Islands, the country's sole domestic commercial bank faced the risk of losing its U.S. correspondent banking relationship. The Marshall Islands depends heavily on remittances, which are channelled through two large MTOs that have partnerships with the domestic bank (Box 2). CBRs in Palau appear to be less affected, probably because of the lower level of remittances. In other countries, Australian banks play a key role and among those with significant remittances flows – Fiji, Samoa, and Tonga – MTOs based in these countries are facing account closures both at home and in remittance-source countries.

Weaknesses in AML/CFT compliance is straining CBR relationships and leading to withdrawal, as is the presence of offshore financial centres (located in the Marshall Islands, Samoa, and Vanuatu). In many of the small states, AML/CFT regimes are lagging both in terms of

Table 7.2 Survey on the consequences of CBR withdrawal: authorities' views

Country	Australian Banks	U.S. Banks[1]	Other Foreign Banks	Domestic Banks
Fiji	ANZ Westpac		Bank of Baroda (India) Bank South Pacific (Papua New Guinea) Bred Bank (Banque Populaire, France)	Home Finance Company
Kiribati	ANZ			
Marshall Islands		Bank of Guam		Bank of Marshall Islands
Micronesia		Bank of Guam		Bank of the FSM[2]
Nauru	Bendigo Bank			
Palau		Bank of Guam Bank of Hawaii Bank Pacific		Asia Pacific Commercial Bank Palau Construction Bank
Papua New Guinea	ANZ Westpac			Bank South Pacific Kina Bank
Samoa	ANZ		Bank South Pacific (Papua New Guinea)	National Bank of Samoa Samoa Commercial Bank
Solomon Islands	ANZ		Bank South Pacific (Papua New Guinea)	Pan Oceanic Bank
Timor-Leste	ANZ		Caixa (Portugal) Bank Mandiri (Indonesia)	National Commercial Bank of Timor-Leste
Tonga	ANZ		Bank South Pacific (Papua New Guinea) MBf (Malaysia)	Tonga Development Bank
Tuvalu				National Bank of Tuvalu Development Bank of Tuvalu
Vanuatu	ANZ		Bred Bank (Banque Populaire, France) Bank South Pacific (Papua New Guinea)	National Bank of Vanuatu

Sources: Jamaludin, et al. (2016) and authors' adaptation.

Notes: 1 Covers banks with physical presence in the respective countries.
2 Insured under the Federal Deposit Insurance Corporation scheme.

framework and effectiveness. Mutual Evaluation Reports for Samoa (Box 7.4) and Vanuatu were published in 2015 by the Asia/Pacific Group on Money Laundering (APG). Other small states face similar shortcomings. The authorities in many of the small states are making progress in addressing deficiencies, including through by establishing and strengthening financial intelligence units.[10] In Papua New Guinea, legislation has been passed that has substantially addressed the AML/CFT deficiencies and has facilitated removal from the Financial Action Task Force's (FATF's) grey list.

Although the consequences of CBR withdrawal vary across the small states, regional banks cite pressure from global correspondent banks as the main cause (Box 7.3).

Box 7.3 Key findings from IMF Staff Discussion Note

'The withdrawal of correspondent banking relationships: a case for policy action'

Correspondent banking relationships enabling the provision of domestic and cross-border payments were terminated in some jurisdictions after the 2008 financial crisis. In recent years, several countries have reported a reduction in CBRs by global banks. Pressure on CBRs has been associated with restricted access to financial services by certain categories of customers, business lines, jurisdictions, or regions. Survey and other available evidence indicates that smaller emerging markets and developing economies in Africa, the Caribbean, Central Asia, Europe, and the Pacific, as well as countries under sanctions, may be the most affected.

Individual banks may decide to withdraw CBRs for a number of reasons. Generally, such decisions reflect banks' cost-benefit analysis, shaped by the re-evaluation of business models in the new macroeconomic environment and changes in the regulatory and enforcement landscape– notably with respect to more rigorous prudential requirements, economic and trade sanctions, anti-money laundering, and combating the financing of terrorism (AML/CFT) and tax transparency. These factors inform banks' risk and reputational cost perceptions. Further pressures to withdraw CBRs may arise where regulatory expectations are unclear, risks cannot be mitigated, or legal impediments interfere with cross-border information sharing. These factors operate concurrently, although their relative significance varies case-by-case.

While the withdrawal of CBRs has reached a critical level in some countries–and can have a systemic impact if unaddressed–macroeconomic consequences have yet to be identified at the global level. Pressure on CBRs could disrupt financial services and cross-border flows (including trade finance and remittances), potentially undermining financial stability, inclusion, growth, and development. The current limited economic consequences partly reflect the ability of affected banks to rely on other CBRs, find replacements, or use alternative means to transfer funds. Still, in a few jurisdictions, pressure on CBRs can become systemic in nature if unaddressed.

Coordinated efforts by the public and private sectors are needed to mitigate the risk of financial exclusion and the potential negative impact on financial stability. An enhanced understanding of the phenomenon, improved data collection, and continued dialogue among stakeholders are imperative to developing appropriate responses tailored to individual country circumstances. Timely implementation of the Financial Stability Board's 2015 action plan endorsed by the G20 Summit will be critical. Home authorities of global banks should communicate their regulatory expectations and affected countries should continue strengthening their regulatory and supervisory frameworks to meet relevant international standards–with the help of technical assistance where needed. Clarifying these standards, including on AML/CFT, could help promote a baseline for regulatory expectations. Industry initiatives could be pursued to facilitate customer due diligence and help reduce compliance costs. In countries facing a severe loss of CBRs and diminishing access to the global financial system, the public sector may consider the feasibility of temporary mechanisms ranging from regional arrangements to public-backed vehicles to provide payment clearing services. IMF staff has been supporting member countries in addressing the CBR withdrawal to promote financial inclusion and ensure financial stability.

Source: Erbenová et al. (2016)

The remittance sector is generally viewed as high risk from the perspective of AML/CFT, and, in addition to penalties for non-compliance, global banks are concerned about reputational risk. Australian and New Zealand banks report that U.S. correspondent banks have increased the frequency and intensity of their due diligence of Australian banks, and the operations of MTOs and remittances are an important focus of their surveillance. The response of banks in Australia is differentiated; at least one bank cut services to remitters across the board while other banks, taking a more risk-based approach, are making decisions on a case-by-case basis. However, Australian banks view the risk-based approach as giving them a pseudo-regulatory role, which is costly from a compliance perspective; they also argue that a risk-based approach transfers non-compliance risks to the banks. The Reserve Bank of New Zealand has responded to closure of MTO accounts by clarifying that compliance with AML/CFT obligations does not require banks to cease providing services to an entire category of customer (Reserve Bank of New Zealand, 2015). The Reserve Bank has emphasized that 'if banks are de-risking to avoid rather than manage and mitigate those risks, then that would be inconsistent with the intended effect of the AML/CFT Act. It seems unlikely, but if banks are using blanket de-risking itself to manage and mitigate those risks, then the Reserve Bank would consider that an inadequate means of complying with their obligations under the AML/CFT Act.'

Evidence: withdrawal of correspondent banking relationships

Information gained by the IMF through its bilateral surveillance points to the withdrawal of correspondent banking relationships for some Asia-Pacific small states. The Marshall Islands' sole domestic commercial bank has faced the risk of losing its CBR with a U.S.-based bank (Box 7.2). In Tonga, the authorities have reported that establishing CBRs with U.S. banks has become more difficult. But one Australian bank has agreed to open USD correspondent accounts for the local banks. On the other hand, other small states in the Pacific – including Fiji, Kiribati, and Palau – have reported limited impact on CBRs to date. Non-compliance with FATCA resulted in termination of a CBR in Samoa.

SWIFT data indicate the trends in CBRs but some caveats suggest caution in using these data to draw firm conclusions about their termination (Bank for International Settlements, Committee on Payments and Market Infrastructures, 2016). From a global perspective, these data show that the number of active correspondents declined between 2012 and 2015 while at the same time the volume of transactions grew and, as a result, the concentration in CBRs increased. Changes in global, regional, and local volumes of CBR transactions can have many causes, including fluctuations in economic activity and other financial sector developments. Furthermore, increases in volumes could still be consistent with strains in CBRs as payments are diverted to other channels following account closures. For example, if payments are rerouted through a third country, correspondent banking activity increases (by creating two transactions instead of one). If two-way remittances and money transfers were previously channelled through MTOs (which then transfer only net amounts through the banks), increased use of banks by migrants and for money transfers could raise the volume and value of CBR transactions. In addition, as these data compare 2015 with 2012, the full impact is likely to be underestimated. Discussions with country authorities in some of the small states suggests that withdrawals of CBRs, and their consequences, began in the latter half of the sample and continued to escalate in 2016.

Bearing these caveats in mind, the Committee on Payments and Market Infrastructures of the Bank for International Settlements (BIS-CMPI) analysis of the SWIFT data suggests that the sharpest fall in active correspondents has occurred in Oceania. The BIS evidence (using BIS

Table 7.3 Trends in CBRs and transactions in selected small states of the Pacific, 2012–15

Country	Change in number of active correspondents	Change in transaction volume	Change in transaction value
Fiji	–1.5	18.8	114.2
Kiribati	10.6	8.3	8.5
Papua New Guinea	–11.6	31.6	–13.4
Samoa	4.5	25.5	44.5
Solomon Islands	–18.3	8.7	–8.7
Tonga	–8.3	3.2	–15.9
Tuvalu	–15.5	47.7	12
Vanuatu	–4.2	–1.7	–33.2

Source: Bank for International Settlement Committee on Payments and Market Infrastructure (2016), Correspondent Banking, Table 1.

country grouping classifications)[11] shows that between 2012 through 2015, Melanesia, Micronesia, and Polynesia experienced declines in active CBRs in almost all years, with net losses of more than 10% in 2012 in Australia and New Zealand, and in Melanesia, and Micronesia. Analysis of country-by-country data for the small states of the Pacific (Table 7.3) shows that the loss of CBRs is largest in Papua New Guinea, the Solomon Islands, and Tuvalu, with smaller losses in Fiji, Tonga, and Vanuatu. Interpreting the data on transactions value and volume is not straightforward, and in some small states, the volume and value of transactions have actually increased. For example, in Samoa, the rise in transactions volume and value partly reflect improvements in domestic macroeconomic conditions but also the diversion of remittances into bank-to-bank transfers. In Fiji, although the number of CBRs fell marginally, the relaxation of exchange controls has contributed to large gains in the volume and value of transactions.

Evidence: disruption in remittances

The closure of MTO bank accounts has added to the fragility of the remittance sector. Current account data for affected countries does not suggest a fall in remittances and a 2015 study by the Australian Transaction Reports and Analysis Centre (AUSTRAC) finds no overall reduction in remittance transfers. But evidence from several sources points to an increasingly fragile remittance sector in which the costs of remittances are once again rising, reversing an earlier declining trend. Other sources of evidence on MTO closure include IMF bilateral surveillance of country authorities; roundtable discussion with MTOs in Samoa; a World Bank survey; AUSTRAC; and a survey conducted by the Australian Remittance and Currency Providers Association. These sources all point to widespread closure of MTO accounts. Data on the cost of remittances, along with analysis of the cost structure, underscore the importance of MTOs in reducing the cost of remittances; they also highlight the potential for increased remittance costs.

The IMF survey of Asia-Pacific countries (Table 7.1) shows that money transfers and remittances are becoming more expensive and complex (Table 7.2). Bilateral surveillance suggests that this is due largely to the closure of MTO bank accounts in both home and host countries. In Tonga, the authorities report that most bank accounts of MTOs in Australia and New Zealand have been closed, necessitating the use of other avenues. One Tongan money transfer operator has unsuccessfully taken a New Zealand bank to court after the closure of the

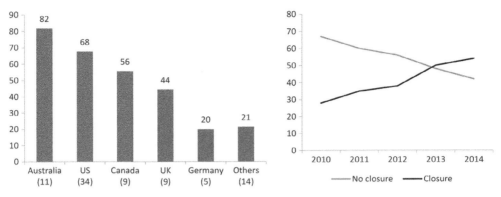

Figure 7.4 Closure of money transfer operator accounts

operator's bank account. Similarly in Samoa, the authorities report major challenges facing MTOs in maintaining bank accounts. A roundtable discussion with Samoan-based MTO owners and managers (with 8 of the 11 MTOs that report to the Central Bank of Samoa) revealed that most now had at most one bank account, compared with several across many banks previously. Moreover, a few MTOs without a business bank account were using personal accounts. Other MTOs were facing new restrictions on account usage, including caps on amounts and frequency of transfers.

The 2015 World Bank survey (World Bank, 2015) shows that the closure of MTO accounts has intensified since 2010 (Figure 7.4). The survey on MTO account access was carried out at the request of the G20 Global Partnership for Financial Inclusion and the Development Working Group. A large share of the MTOs responding to the World Bank survey in both the United States and Australia report closure of at least one bank account.

A survey conducted by the Australian Remittance and Currency Providers Association (is there a reference for this?) reveals the scale of stress in the remittance market. This small-scale survey was conducted in October 2015, with just 63 responses (compared with 538 independent remitter businesses at the end of August 2015).[12] Of these, 60% now have just one account and 20% no accounts. This is consistent with data from the Australian Transaction Reports and Analysis Centre (AUSTRAC), which shows that at least 719 bank accounts belonging to remittance businesses were closed by banks in Australia between January 2014 and April 2015 (AUSTRAC, 2015). Together these surveys help illustrate the greater fragility of the remittance sector in the small states in the Pacific.[13]

The cost of remittances seems to be rising again, reversing the trend of gradual decline owing to efforts by the authorities to lower costs. The cause of the recent uptick in the cost of remittances – which was already high – is not clear. The average cost for sending remittances to Pacific island countries from Australia has been about 12–13%, and from New Zealand, 10–11%. This is well above the G20 target of 5% by 2020 and is much higher relative to other Asian countries. The pricing of remittance transfers is not transparent, with fixed fees and foreign exchange margins that vary significantly depending on the destination, product, and whether the migrant is using a bank for transfers or a money transfer operator.

Costs are much lower for remittances by MTOs than those by banks, with lower fees and smaller foreign exchange margins.[14] The significance of this is that the closure of MTOs could push up the average cost of remittances if access to MTOs is reduced. Cost differences are also the result of the product used by the migrant. Account-to-account services are the most

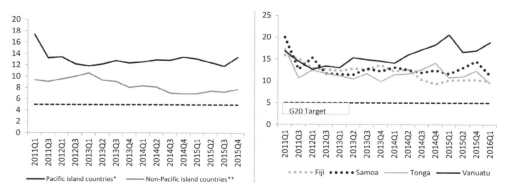

Figure 7.5 Cost of sending US$200 to the Pacific islands
Notes: ** Non-Pacific island countries are island counties in East and South Asia.
Source: World Bank Remittance Prices Worldwide Database

expensive means of transferring money. On the other hand, online, mobile, and card services charge much less to send remittances than other product types. These latter services are largely offered by MTOs. The authorities may wish to consider the feasibility of a payments cost study, which could help policymakers understand the relative costs of different payment systems and the main drivers of changes in charges for banking services.

3 What are the potential consequences?

The potential consequences of withdrawal of CBRs or continued closure of MTO accounts on the small states of the Pacific are significant. At present, much of the strain is being felt in the remittance sector but further withdrawal of CBRs and the resulting exclusion from the global financial system could impact trade in goods and services. A potentially higher-cost, less transparent, and more fragile remittance sector could have far-reaching effects for poverty, financial inclusion, and ultimately, macroeconomic resilience, including the following consequences:

Increase in systemic risk in the financial system. The small number of banks implies that losses of CBRs or closure of MTO bank accounts can quickly create a systemic risk as services become concentrated in a single entity. Furthermore, the banks are small and cannot provide a wide range of services and therefore rely on correspondent banks to offer clients a broader range of services. Loss of a CBR in this situation could leave local businesses without access to some types of financial services.

A more fragile remittance sector. Closures of MTOs' bank accounts and ultimately of MTOs would increase the fragility of the remittance corridors to the Pacific islands. While the level of remittances is holding up, this metric is deceptively reassuring as remittances can be diverted through alternative channels, including through banks and other MTOs that remain operational. From the perspective of the resilience of the system, the number of MTOs has fallen and the ability of MTOs to offer reliable service has declined.

Increased use of more expensive or non-transparent remittance channels. Looking ahead, an increasing share of remittances could also be sent through unregulated channels, which could reduce transparency and the authorities' ability to monitor and investigate transactions. Evidence suggests that there has been a shift in the methods used to transfer money to the Pacific islands, with less reliance on MTOs or increased hand-carry of cash as reported by MTOs.

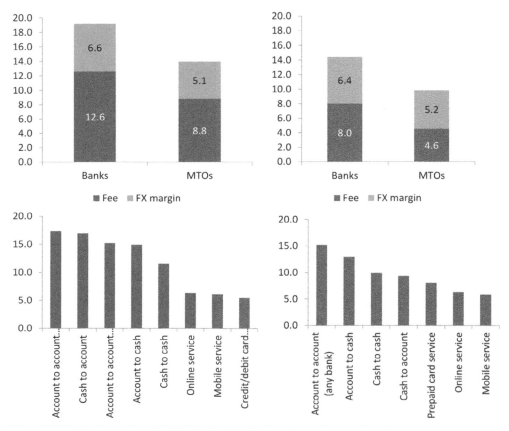

Figure 7.6 Cost of sending US$200 to the Pacific islands by firm and product type
Note: Pacific island countries are Fiji, Samoa, Tonga and Vanuatu
Source: World Bank Remittance Prices Worldwide Database

Increase in the cost of remittances. Without intervention, continued strains in CBRs could result in higher remittance costs. Weaker competition in the remitter market could further raise the already-high cost of remittances. In addition, closure of MTOs bank accounts limits their ability to find the lowest transfer cost, which pushes up their average cost. Furthermore, a shift in flows into the banks will further boost average costs.

Negative consequences for financial inclusion. Enhancing financial inclusion to support growth is a key policy priority for the authorities in many of the small states in the Pacific islands (Sahay *et al.*, 2015). Closure or curtailment of MTOs could have a significant impact on financial inclusion. For example, Samoa is a cash-based society and about 85% of remittances are channelled through money transfer operators (MTOs). The MTOs reach into the community is much greater than that of banks, with the largest MTO having 30 branches outside of Apia, the capital city, compared with 15 for the four banks combined.

Decline in growth and reduced resilience to shocks. Many of the small states are highly dependent on remittances, which play an important role in supporting household consumption. For example, in Samoa, where remittances amount to 20% of GDP, any decline could have a significant impact on GDP. Looking ahead, lower financial inclusion could reduce longer-term growth prospects. A well-functioning and inclusive financial system – now under threat – is essential for long-term growth. The role of remittances in bringing immediate assistance in the aftermath of natural disasters cannot be overstated.

4 Policy recommendations

Broad strategy and the role of collective action

Collective action is needed to mitigate a breakdown in banking relationships. Addressing the withdrawal of CBRs to prevent detrimental macroeconomic impacts in the small states in the Pacific will entail policy actions by authorities in the small states, in remitter countries, and in the home of global correspondent banks. The small states of the Pacific are currently working to upgrade their AML/CFT frameworks to meet more stringent evaluation of the effectiveness in implementing international standards. But these efforts might not be sufficient to halt or reverse the consequences of withdrawal. Regulators and correspondent banks will also have a role to play.

Affected countries must upgrade their regulatory and supervisory frameworks to comply with international standards with regard to both AML/CFT and tax transparency. Ongoing donor support will be needed in many cases to meet these objectives. Practical solutions are needed to maintain the flow of remittances while ensuring compliance with AML/CFT as the current business model of many MTOs may not be sustainable given the increased compliance requirements.

Regulators can continue to play an important role through further outreach and dialogue with global banks and, in addition, regulators in affected jurisdictions (and with regulators in countries whose banks serve as intermediaries for affected jurisdictions). The objective of this outreach is for regulators in affected jurisdictions to continue to clarify their compliance framework and ease the concerns of correspondent banks, and for correspondent banks' home country regulators to consistently communicate their regulatory expectations. In particular, regulators should encourage correspondent banks to upgrade their information gathering to ensure that a well-informed risk-based assessment drives the termination of bank accounts.

The financial industry could play a role in engaging with small countries, as outlined in Lagarde (2016). New tools, such as KYC utilities, can be developed and deployed to help lower compliance costs for banks. Industry efforts to support the training of bankers in implementing AML/CFT in remote jurisdictions will help with consistent application of standards.

Policy actions for affected countries

Policy advice focuses on measures to alleviate the concerns of correspondent banks in the short-term while at the same time, developing new remittance channels for countries that rely on remittances. Measures fall into several categories including upgrading legislation, improving implementation, and increasing capacity. Improved compliance is necessary but might not be sufficient: compliance cost considerations are also factoring into banks' decisions and it will be necessary to reduce these costs. Establishing a national database – a KYC utility – could go a long way to reduce costs, while at the same time enhance compliance. Looking to the future, the digital economy through new financial technologies may offer possible solutions to creating low-cost remittance channels while at the same time ensuring integrity of the payments system. Upgrading payments systems, along with the legal acceptance of electronic signatures, can help create an environment supportive of new financial innovations or Fintech. A payments cost study could also help identify key drivers of higher costs of some financial services in some small states of the Pacific and suggest ways to lower costs, especially in the remittance sector.

Efforts to upgrade the domestic compliance framework should focus on:

- *Addressing shortcomings in domestic AML/CFT frameworks and effectiveness.* For those countries that have completed a Mutual Evaluation Assessment by APG, a key priority will be to implement the recommendations in that report (Box 7.4). Improved compliance by MTOs is also needed.

- *Increasing awareness and capabilities for AML/CFT compliance.* Many of the small states will need to develop a broad-based national approach to the AML/CFT regime and considerably scale up the number of AML/CFT specialists (including at the central bank, Ministry of Finance, Customs, the judiciary, the Attorney General's Office, police, financial sector, and MTOs). Local capacity AML/CFT Specialists Certification Program should be developed through cost-effective training-for-trainers program; donor assistance may also be needed. Such a program will help increase the effectiveness of AML/CFT compliance regimes, helping to ensure buy-in by other government departments, and raise national awareness.

- *Increasing dialogue with key stakeholders.* The authorities should communicate with relevant foreign regulators, financial intelligence units, and correspondent banks on the progress made in the AML/CFT regime. In some cases, and where appropriate, the authorities should emphasize the limited links between the MTO remittance channel to small states and the off-shore financial sector and other companies. Such an assurance could help ease correspondent bank concern over MTO remittances.

- *Upgrading the sanctions regime.* Authorities will need to upgrade the legal framework, as needed, to ensure that UN Security Council resolutions and financial sanctions are properly enforced. The risks of terror financing in the Pacific islands appear to be limited, for example, APG (2015) discusses the low risks of terrorism-related activities in Samoa. Nevertheless, implementing a terrorism financing sanctions framework could support foreign bank confidence in the jurisdiction with minimal effort and cost.

- *Ensuring compliance with FATCA.* One option is for domestic authorities, namely, the central bank, to communicate with the U.S. government and negotiate an intergovernmental agreement (IGA) with the U.S. Treasury on FATCA implementation. FATCA compliance has become a prerequisite for global financial transactions and is essential to ensure continued correspondence relationships in U.S. dollars and to avoid, among other things, a 30% automatic withholding by U.S. banks of any non-compliant bank's U.S. dollar transfers. By signing an IGA, the domestic central bank could reduce the risks, complexity, and cost for local banks. Such a step will also help lower the risks of foreign bank exit and correspondence withdrawal. Samoa has begun negotiations on such an IGA.

Box 7.4   Samoa anti-money laundering and counter-terrorist financing measures*

Overview. Samoa has improved its AML/CFT framework since the 2006 assessment, including through the Money Laundering Prevent Act 2007 and subsequent regulations in 2009. These better align Samoa's framework with the FATF's recommendations under the third round of mutual evaluations. The FATF recommendations were revised for the fourth round in 2012 and, in 2015, Samoa's AML/CFT regime was assessed by the Asia Pacific Group on Money Laundering

(APG) under the revised 2012 FATF standard. APG assessors found significant shortcomings in Samoa's AML/CFT regime, rating it low or moderately effective in 10 out of 11 immediate outcomes assessing effectiveness, and non-compliant or partially compliant with more than half of the 40 FATF recommendations. Hence, the authorities were encouraged to work toward substantial improvements of the AML/CFT framework, both on strategic and operational levels.

Money laundering risks. Samoa faces a range of money laundering risks but terrorist financing risks appear relatively low. Money laundering risks are related mainly to its international (offshore) sector, although domestic risks include the large remittance sector, cross-border movement of cash, and the domestic banking sector.

- The international (offshore) sector presents the main money laundering risk, given its relative anonymity, concerns regarding transparency of ownership and control information, complexity, and tax-exempt status. At the end of 2014, there were 34,000 international business companies, along with 155 international trusts and 7 international banks. Samoan international business companies are created only through Samoan trust and company service providers (TCSPs), which capture beneficial ownership information when the international business company is created. The international trusts are domiciled in Asia, including Hong Kong SAR, China, and Singapore, primarily for asset protection and tax advantages. Samoa's TCSPs have limited ability to detect and report suspicious transactions and supervision of TCSPs is limited in depth and scope. Information on beneficial ownership is not publicly available, except with the permission of the client. While there is little evidence of the proceeds for foreign predicate crimes being laundered through Samoa or its offshore sector, lack of evidence may reflect a system unable to detect money laundering, rather than the absence of it. Steps have been taken to mitigate risks; strengthened provisions implemented at the end of 2015 should significantly increase the capacity of TCSPs to conduct ongoing due diligence.
- The MTO sector is largely responsible for channelling remittances, which, from a global perspective, are generally viewed as a high risk area for money laundering and terrorism financing. Nevertheless, the MTO sector is reasonably aware of money laundering/terrorist financing risks. Large MTOs have implemented reasonably robust measures to identify and verify customer identity, obtain originator and beneficiary information, and scrutinize transactions. The level of suspicious-transaction-reporting is lower than expected given the size of the sector. The government does not require financial institutions to include full beneficiary information with cross-border wire transfer messages; but ordering financial institutions are required to obtain and retain the originator information with the wire transfer.
- Cross-border movement of cash is also identified as an area of risk. Customs is responsible mainly for enforcing the border declaration regime, which is broadly sound in technical terms. The SFIU, Customs, and Immigration coordinate on border currency reports but further coordination – including with police – would improve monitoring and the ability to investigate and prosecute predicate crimes and money laundering.
- Money laundering risks associated with the domestic banking system arise mainly out of its materiality. Domestic proceeds-generating crimes appear to be low.

The high-priority recommended actions include:

- Offshore Sector. Amend International Companies Act, Trust Act, Companies Act, Money Laundering Prevention Act and regulations to address the technical deficiencies and issue additional, updated guidance; Increase the scope and intensity of AML/CFT supervision of the offshore sector, including international banks and insurance companies and TCSPs; Enhance the accuracy and timeliness of beneficial ownership information held by trust and company service providers for international business companies.

- AML/CFT Supervision. Ensure that AML/CFT supervision of financial institutions (i.e., banks and MTOs) and designated non-financial businesses and professions is based on risk; Strengthen the frequency and intensity of on-site inspections of key financial sectors; Increase engagement by supervisors with financial institutions and designated non-financial businesses and professions.
- Enhanced Implementation. Strengthen resources of the Central Bank of Samoa and Samoa Financial Intelligence Unit to undertake AML/CFT supervision; Pursue money laundering investigations as a matter of policy and pursue confiscation action in more serious/complex cases; Improve the effectiveness of the cross-border declaration system.

* Note: This box summarizes the key findings of the Asia Pacific Group on Anti-Money Laundering Mutual Evaluation Report on Anti-Money Laundering and Counter-terrorist Financing Measures, September 2015.

Establishing a centralized national KYC utility by island authorities and actively seeking to KYC remittance recipients could be a viable option for small states to pursue. Collecting KYC Data on individuals receiving or sending remittances through money transfer operators and possibly including KYC data on bank customers as well beneficial ownership information for companies is possible given the relatively small population sizes of the islands. By having the utility within the Financial Intelligence Units, already established in many of these jurisdictions would help satisfactorily address correspondent banks AML/CFT compliance issues as well as address privacy protection concerns as the financial intelligence unit would have the necessary legal authority and responsibility to collect and protect the data. Recognizing that "Know Your Customers' Customer" approach is not a regulatory requirement and noting recent clarifications by U.S. regulators and FATF that it is not a requirement[15], the utility, nevertheless, could also serve as a tool for verifying bank customers' information and could potentially be an important component of financial inclusion efforts, contributing to credit extension, and support banking supervision. It could also serve as the building block for a national ID system.

Coupled with FATF compliant AML/CFT regime applied to MTOs, the utility would include verified KYC information on remittance recipients and senders easing correspondent bank concerns. The financial intelligence unit should take the lead in developing the database, and financial and technical assistance for the implementation of such a system by donors is likely to be needed. The database would help increase compliance and ease the cost of customer due diligence by improving the information available on the customer. This database along with other components of the CDD process, such as ongoing monitoring of the business relationship, will help reassure regulators and correspondent banks. Subject to existing legal requirements, access to the database could be provided to compliant sender and receiver MTOs, correspondent banks, and other financial intelligence units, thus reducing the cost of compliance to the MTOs and ensuring satisfactory AML/CFT vetting of beneficiaries in an electronically secured environment.

Can the digital economy help? The role of Fintech

Technology can be better leveraged to mitigate the consequences of CBR withdrawal on access to financial services, particularly for money transfers. Many technology-based solutions – with the exception of blockchain technology (He *et al.*, 2016) – still need to rely to some degree on existing banking infrastructure for the clearing and settlement of funds, and are thus not completely immune to further withdrawal of CBRs or account closures.[16] However, given the specific challenges faced by many small states of the Pacific, some technology-based solutions could provide viable alternatives. One potential option involves the combination of an adequate mobile phone network, a KYC utility, and blockchain technology.

Given the large distances and geographical dispersion that characterize many small states in the Pacific, wider use of mobile money can allow greater access to financial services and foster more financial inclusion. In contrast to mobile banking, which provides on-line access to an existing bank account, mobile money consists of customers' stored funds maintained by mobile network operators, obviating the need for an underlying bank account. Although large portions of the population in the Pacific small states remain unbanked, mobile telephone networks offer greater coverage, as shown in Figure 7.7, suggesting that mobile money can be a viable tool to further widen access to financial services, including in cross-border transactions.[17] Mobile money facilities can potentially be expanded to allow cross-border mobile money transfers as an alternative to traditional money transfer operators and banks, as demonstrated in some countries in West Africa.[18] This would provide alternatives to conventional channels of cross-border money transfers. In addition, the use of technology to connect with a KYC database would help ensure the integrity of the payments system.

Platforms for the transfer of funds using blockchain technology/distributed ledgers have the potential to reduce the reliance on the banking system for the clearing and settlement of financial transactions (Center for the Edge, 2016). Although still in its early stage of development, blockchain technology Fintech applications promise to reduce the time, cost, and complexity of financial transactions – including cross-border money transfers (Tapscott and Tapscott, 2016). Developments in Fintech and its potential disruption of existing banking models have not gone unnoticed by global banks, and many, including regional Pacific banks,

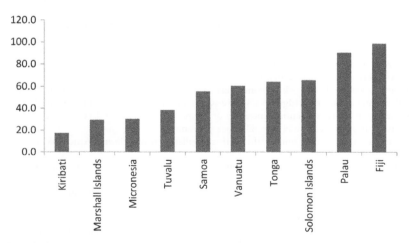

Figure 7.7 Mobile phone subscriptions per 100 inhabitants, 2014
Source: International Telecommunications Union.

are partnering with Fintech companies to explore the use of blockchain distributed ledgers on their mobile banking platforms. The use of blockchain technology will need to take into account the technology gap in many small states of the Pacific as well as challenges posed for market supervision. Plans to tap blockchain technology will need to build on ongoing efforts to address gaps in access to mobile technology in some small states. Central banks and financial supervisors will also need to strengthen and adapt the regulatory framework accordingly in light of concerns about potential vulnerabilities arising from blockchain technology.[19]

5 Conclusion

Collective action will be needed to help mitigate the potentially negative consequences of correspondent banking relationship withdrawal on the small states of the Pacific. We have outlined measures for affected countries to implement that can help ease concerns of the correspondent banks in the short run while laying the foundation for a payments system in the small states that is more cost effective yet fully AML/CFT compliant.

In many cases, donor support will be needed. But these measures may not be sufficient as cost-benefit analysis or risk assessment by correspondent banks could continue to limit their engagement with the small states of the Pacific. In such a scenario, a combination of blockchain technology, with a Know-Your-Customer utility for senders and receivers, along with the mobile phone networks, could provide a platform for cross-border transactions that would not rely on traditional correspondent banking.

Notes

1 This chapter is a revised and updated version of IMF Working Paper WP/17/90. Nothing contained in this chapter should be reported as representing the views of the IMF, its Executive Board, member governments, or any other entity mentioned herein. The views in this chapter belong solely to the authors.
2 The Pacific island nations examined in this chapter includes Fiji, Kiribati, the Marshall Islands, Micronesia, Palau, Papua New Guinea, Samoa, the Solomon Islands, Tonga, Tuvalu, and Vanuatu.
3 Money transfer operators are an important part of shadow banking in the Pacific islands.
4 While high levels of remittances per se do not pose an AML/CFT risk, the large volume of typically small transactions increases the monitoring costs. In a number of instances, the remittance sector has been associated with terrorism financing; in applying the risk-based approach banks are subjecting the remittance sector to enhanced scrutiny.
5 The Foreign Account Tax Compliance Act (FATCA) is a U.S. law designed to prevent tax evasion by U.S. citizens using offshore banking facilities.
6 A blockchain is a data structure that makes it possible to create a digital ledger of transactions and share it among a distributed network of computers. It uses cryptography to allow each participant on the network to manipulate the ledger in a secure way without the need for a central authority. A Know-Your-Customer utility is a central repository or database that stores the data and documents needed for a financial institution's customer due diligence procedures.
7 These surveys were carried out by the IMF surveillance teams during Article IV consultations and missions in 2016.
8 The US authorities clarified this position and issued the joint Foreign Correspondent Banking Fact-sheet in August 30, 2016.
9 See Jamaludin *et al.* (2016) for more information on the banking system in the small states of the Pacific.
10 See Box 7.2 for recent activities taken by the Marshallese authorities.
11 IMF member countries in the Melanesia region are Fiji, Papua New Guinea, the Solomon Islands, and Vanuatu; Micronesian members are: Kiribati, the Marshall Islands, Federated States of Micronesia and Palau; and Polynesian member countries are Samoa, Tonga, and Tuvalu.

12 Most respondents had been in operation for more than 5 years (65%); money transfers were their core activity (85%); had no adverse AUSTRAC opinion/conditions (94%); and had conducted an independent review of their business (63%).

13 Buckley and Ooi (2014) also point out that there is ample anecdotal evidence on the closure MTO accounts by banks across both Australia and the Pacific island countries (PICs); and these account closures have been reported on and criticized by industry professionals, regulators, academics, and industry experts.

14 The analyses on remittance cost use the Remittance Prices Worldwide database (World Bank). More information available at http://remittanceprices.worldbank.org.

15 See Joint Fact Sheet on Foreign Correspondent Banking, https://www.treasury.gov/press-center/p ress-releases/Documents/Foreign%20Correspondent%20Banking%20Fact%20Sheet.pdf; www.occ. gov/news-issuances/bulletins/2016/bulletin-2016-32.html/.

16 As discussed in Erbenová *et al.* (2016).

17 The Pacific islands registered the fastest growth rate in unique mobile telephone subscribers during 2009, at 13%, second only to Sub-Saharan Africa (15%). See GSMA Intelligence (2015).

18 See Scharwatt and Williamson (2015).

19 Financial Stability Oversight Council 2016 Annual Report.

References

Australian Transaction Reports and Analysis Centre (AUSTRAC) (2015). Bank De-risking of Remittance Businesses. *Strategic Analysis brief.*

Bank for International Settlements (2016). *Correspondent Banking.* Basel: Bank for International Settlements, Committee on Payments and Market Infrastructures.

Buckley, R. P., and Ooi, K. C. (2014). 'Pacific injustice and instability: bank account closures of Australian money transfer operators'. *Journal of Banking and Finance Law and Practice*, 25: 243–256.

Center for the Edge (2016). *Bitcoin, Blockchain, and Distributed Ledgers: Caught Between Promise and Reality.* Australia: Deloitte.

Commonwealth Secretariat (2016). *Disconnecting from Global Finance. De-risking: The Impact of AML/CFT Regulations in Commonwealth Developing Countries.* London.

Erbenová, M., Liu, Y., Kyriakos-Saad, N., López-Mejía, A., Gasha, G., Mathias, E., Norat, M., Fernando, F. and Almeida, Y. (2016). The Withdrawal of Correspondent Banking Relationships: A Case for Policy Action, Staff Discussion Note, *SDN/16/06.* Washington, DC: International Monetary Fund.

GSMA Intelligence (2015). *The Mobile Economy: Pacific Islands 2015.* London: GSMA.

International Monetary Fund (IMF) (2016). Republic of Marshall Islands: 2016 Article IV Consultation Staff Report, *IMF Country Report* No. 16/260. Washington, DC: International Monetary Fund.

He, D., Habermeier, K., Leckow, R., Haksar, V., Almeida, Y., Kashima, M., Kyriakos-Saad, N., Oura, H., Saadi Sedik, T., Stetsenko, N. and Verdugo-Yepes, C. (2016). Virtual Currencies and Beyond: Initial Considerations, *Staff Discussion Note* 16/03. Washington, DC: International Monetary Fund.

Jamaludin, F.Sheridan, N., Tumbarello, P., Wu, Y., and Zeinullayev, T. (2016). Global and Regional Spillovers to Pacific Island Countries. In Khor, H. E., Kronenberg, R. and Tumbarello, P. (eds), *Resilience and Growth in the Small States of the Pacific.* Washington, DC: International Monetary Fund: 97–130.

Lagarde, C. (2016). 'Relations in Banking – Making it Work for Everyone'. Speech delivered at the New York Federal Reserve Bank, July 18.

Reserve Bank of New Zealand (2015). Statement about Banks Closing Accounts of Money Remitters.

Sahay, R., Cihak, M., N'Diaye, P., Barajas, A., Mitra, S., Kyobe, A., Mooi, Y. N. and Yousefi, S. R. (2015). Financial Inclusion: Can it meet Multiple Macroeconomic Goals, *IMF Staff Discussion Note* 15/17.

Scharwatt, C. and Williamson, C. (2015). *Mobile Money Crosses Borders: New Remittance Models in West Africa.* London: GSMA.

Tapscott, D. and Tapscott, A. (2016). *Blockchain Revolution.* New York: Portfolio/Penguin.

World Bank (2015). *Withdrawal from correspondent banking: where, why, and what to do about it.* Washington, DC: World Bank.

8

A new approach to exchange rate management in small open financially integrated economies[1]

DeLisle Worrell, Winston Moore and Jamila Beckles

1 Introduction

This chapter focuses on small open financially integrated economies (SOFIEs)[2], which are characterized by (a) high export concentration; (b) a limited range of competitive tradeable production, compared with import needs; and (c) a domestic financial system which is fully integrated into world financial markets. We explain why these structural characteristics render exchange rate adjustment ineffective as a tool for increasing international competitiveness. We provide evidence that confirms the widespread conviction that SOFIEs that have successfully anchored their exchange rates have achieved greater economic prosperity. And we describe a framework for anchoring the exchange rate through the use of fiscal policy to manage aggregate demand.

The disconnect between the views of economists and ordinary folk with respect to exchange rate policy is one of the most universal and enduring characteristics of small open economies. Ordinary folk are preoccupied with maintaining the value of local money in terms of US dollars or whatever is the international trading currency that matters most to them; economists see the exchange rate primarily as the price of foreign currency, to be adjusted flexibly in order to clear the foreign exchange market. A higher price of foreign exchange, in this view, provides an incentive to switch from imports to cheaper domestic goods and services, and increases the returns to exporting, stimulating the export sector. Devaluation of the local currency leads to reduced demand for foreign exchange, increased demand for local substitutes, and, with time, increased capacity in export activity, bringing with it an increased supply of foreign exchange.

Devaluation therefore seems the appropriate action for a slowly growing economy, boosting output of import substitutes and exports, and bringing the demand and supply of foreign exchange into equilibrium.

However, this conclusion depends on three crucial assumptions that cannot be fulfilled in small economies that are integrated into the world of international finance and commerce: one, that there exists the domestic capacity to produce substitutes for imports in sufficient quantity at an internationally competitive price; two, that there is a relatively low pass-through from import prices to domestic inflation and production costs; and three, that foreign currency inflows and outflows on the financial account are unaffected by the volatility of the exchange rate.

This chapter defines a category of economy where these three conditions do not hold, and we show empirically that countries with small populations which have economies below a certain size fall within that category. We then develop a measure of exchange rate volatility for these small economies based on the international currency of greatest interest to them – for most this turns out to be the US dollar, but that is not the case for small European countries. We compare the volatility of local currencies, measured in terms of the dollar or euro as appropriate, against indices of economic performance over time, for all the countries that fall within the SOFIE category. If currency flexibility does provide a tool for growing the economy through import substitution and increased export capacity, then countries with more flexible exchange rates will be expected to show better performance; conversely, if the popular view is indeed the correct one, then the countries with little or no volatility will be the best performers.

We then go on to explain how the three structural features of small open economies modify the expected effects of exchange rate changes, and what are the implications for economic policies for stabilization and development. The analysis will demonstrate that, in economies with these characteristics, an exchange rate peg, with zero volatility, is the ideal to which policy makers should aspire.

If that is the case, why have so many small economies embraced exchange rate flexibility? The answer, we argue, is that they did not find a policy framework that afforded them a decisive influence over the balance of inflows and outflows of foreign exchange. We conclude with a description of the policy framework used in Barbados, which is designed to equip economic policy makers with the tools to achieve the external balance that is crucial to the stability of the exchange rate and the maintenance of investor confidence.

2 The literature

In recent years, the economics community has come to appreciate the reasons why small economies cannot be indifferent to volatility of their exchange rates. In a policy paper issued by the IMF in 2010, the Fund's then Chief Economist Olivier Blanchard and two colleagues wrote: 'For smaller countries, however, the evidence suggests that, in fact, many of them paid close attention to the exchange rate and also intervened on foreign exchange markets to smooth volatility and, often, even to influence the level of the exchange rate. ... Their actions were more sensible than their rhetoric.' The paper acknowledged that exchange rate volatility could occasion disincentives for exportables (in case of unwanted appreciation), as well as financial and economic instability due to the impact on the balance sheets of firms with contracts in foreign exchange.

This view is already a considerable advance on the prevailing opinion of only a few years earlier, reflected in Frankel (2003); Obstfeld and Rogoff (1995). However, it does not fully represent the reality of the small economies which are our concern. The record shows that countries that are defined by the characteristics that are typical of SOFIEs all clung to an exchange rate peg for as long as they were able. In every case the peg was abandoned very reluctantly, and in the face of the uncontrollable growth of an informal foreign exchange market with a heavily depreciated exchange rate. In these circumstances the adoption of a flexible rate regime is seen as symptomatic of economic policy failure, a failure which depresses investor confidence and inhibits potential growth.

The conventional interest rate defence of the exchange rate in the face of speculative currency attack seldom is effective in small economies. The case of Thailand in the mid-1990s is instructive: rather than stimulate the intended inflow of foreign currency, interest rate increases led to a shift of capital flows towards unhedged short-term debt, and inflation in the prices of real estate and other nontradables (Furman *et al.*, 1998). All too often, resort to the interest rate defence is seen as a desperation measure, which undermines public confidence and leads to capital flight, the opposite of what was intended.

The earliest failures among small economies attempting to sustain exchange rate pegs were seen in the 1970s and 1980s, when small economies in many developing countries attempted to ration foreign exchange using controls on current account transactions. These were a universal failure, and by the 1990s it was widely accepted that foreign exchange rationing was not feasible for most, if not all, open economies.

However, the notion persisted that controls on the financial account of the balance of payments were effective, and offered an avenue for the central bank to insulate the domestic money supply from unwarranted or destabilizing foreign exchange flows, occasioned by misinformation, misinterpretation, inadequate information and other market frictions. The existence of restrictions on financial flows is often given as the explanation of the persistence of long-standing exchange rate pegs in such small economies as Barbados and the countries of the Eastern Caribbean Currency Union (Frankel, 2003; Obstfeld and Rogoff, 1995).

The effectiveness of controls on the financial account of the balance of payments is not borne out by the evidence, however. A majority of the very small countries which have unequivocally pegged exchange rates in fact have no exchange restrictions of any kind (Bermuda, Cayman, Turks and Caicos), and in all others the restrictions are loosely applied, for good reason. Apprehension about profit and capital repatriation is a sure way to deter foreign direct investment in countries that always need foreign capital to finance the import content of fixed capital formation. What is more, the trading conglomerates which have a prominent role in every small economy can very easily affect inflows and outflows through Treasury management of the several currencies they deal in daily. This point is made in Worrell (2000). In effect, the well-known Mundell-Fleming trilemma (free capital flows, a fixed exchange rate, and independent monetary policy cannot coexist) reduces to a dilemma: monetary independence is impossible if the exchange rate is pegged.

This fact is now widely recognized, and it is accepted that, in the context of currency unions such as the Euro Area and the Eastern Caribbean Currency Area, monetary policy cannot be used to stabilize the individual economies. We will argue that small very open economies are no different, even if they are not formally part of a larger currency area.

Does this mean that small open economies have no prospect of a combination of monetary and exchange rate policies that will stabilize their economies and promote growth? We argue that such is in fact the case. Economies such as Barbados and Greece must react to international economic downturns by procyclical adjustment of aggregate expenditure, except to the extent that they have the capacity for additional foreign borrowing. Even in that case, foreign borrowing that is not directed to increasing productive capacity should be used to buy time to effect the needed adjustment measures in a less disruptive manner (Worrell, 2012).

The consensus among economists does not yet go this far. It is reflected in Ghosh *et al.* (2016), who argue that for countries with significant currency mismatches, high pass-through of devaluation to inflation, and limited inter-sectoral factor mobility, dual inflation-exchange rate targeting is recommended, using sterilized exchange intervention to stabilize the exchange rate and inflation targeting via monetary policy. Their rationale is that if target inflation is consistent with a zero output gap, under inflation targeting, the policy interest rate would fall if there is capital inflow (with exchange rate appreciation) or with a negative aggregate demand shock (along with a depreciation of the exchange rate). However, policymakers may want to avoid an appreciation which makes exports less competitive. Therefore, they would lower the interest rate in the case of the negative demand shock, and would intervene in the case of a capital inflow.

However, in practice there remains the problem of fiscal dominance, the ever present danger that inappropriate fiscal policy will derail monetary policy (BIS, 2012). In that case, the apparent conflict between monetary and exchange rate policy undermines the overall credibility of the monetary and exchange authorities, and may provoke a flight of capital, frustrating both monetary and exchange objectives.

We know of only two ways of anchoring the exchange rate in circumstances of small very open economies, where the impossible trilemma is reduced to a dilemma between the exchange rate anchor and monetary policy. One of these is a strict currency board arrangement, where the central bank does no lending of any kind from its own resources. It advances only such funds as are deposited on the accounts it holds with the government and financial institutions which are its clientele, whether those deposits are in domestic money or foreign exchange. There is no money creation by the central bank (Hanke, 2002).

The second option, which we will illustrate by drawing on the policy framework in use in Barbados, is to actively use fiscal policy to secure the external balance of the economy at the target exchange rate. In this framework, the central bank's store of foreign reserves is used as a buffer, to buy the time needed to make fiscal adjustments in line with the expected capacity to import.

3 How are SOFIEs different?

The defining characteristic of SOFIEs is the fact that their physical and human resources permit only a limited range of internationally competitive production. We use this characteristic, matched against population and economic size, to categorize the economies that are considered 'small'. Figures 8.1 and 8.2,[3] show the relation between population size and size of GDP on the horizontal axis, and the percentage of total exports accounted for by the five largest items on

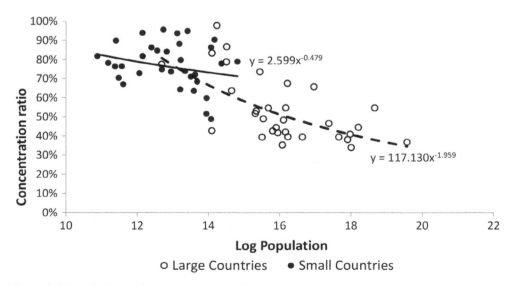

Figure 8.1 Population and export concentration

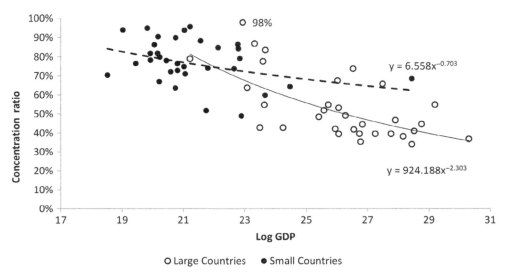

Figure 8.2 GDP and export concentration

the vertical axis. It is apparent that SOFIEs have higher concentration ratios and that the relationship between size and concentration is less variable than for larger economies.

This distinction allows us to define thresholds for small size, based on the apparent relationship between size and export concentration. Based on the relationships shown in Figures 8.1 and 8.2, we arrived at thresholds for small size of populations of 1.2 million or less, and GDP of US$8 billion or less. Figures 8.3 and 8.4 show that the small economies so defined have relatively high import ratios, compared with large economies.

The SOFIE's high import propensity is reflected in a high pass-through of import prices, both of consumption goods and via imported intermediate and capital goods. Figures 8.5–8.7 illustrate small countries' higher sensitivity of domestic prices to foreign prices. They compare domestic price responses of small economies to those of large economies, for changes in world food prices, international oil prices, and changes in the value of the domestic currency.

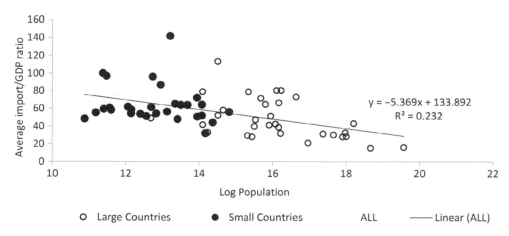

Figure 8.3 Import ratio relative to population size

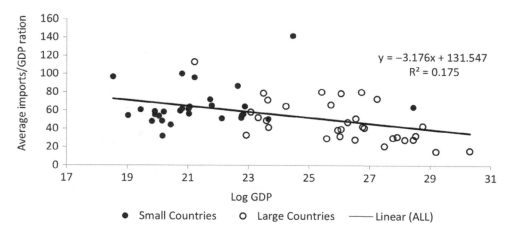

Figure 8.4 Import ratio relative to GDP

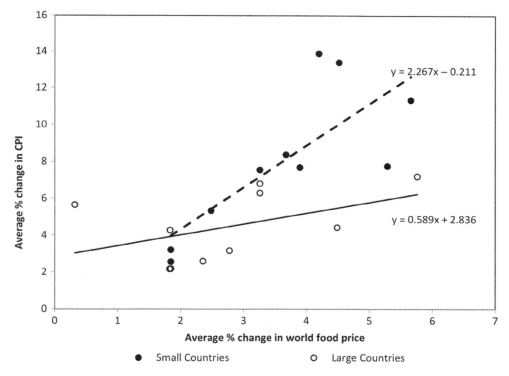

Figure 8.5 Import pass-through of world food prices for selected countries

The SOFIEs' limited range of internationally competitive production means that there is little substitutability between local production and imports, or between local consumption and imports or exports. Domestic producers may not switch from exporting to supplying the local market, because the local market is too small in relation to their production capacity. There are

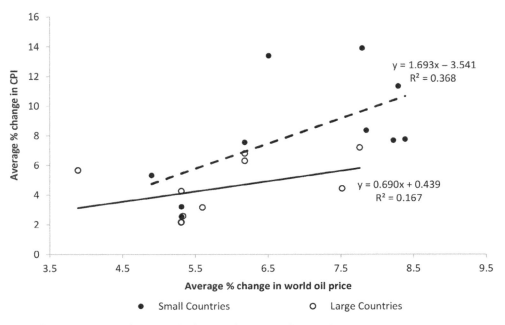

Figure 8.6 Import pass-through of oil prices for selected countries

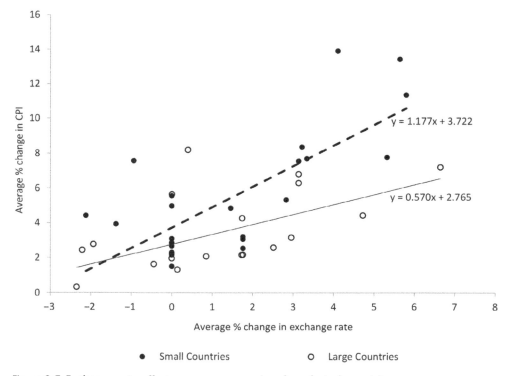

Figure 8.7 Exchange rate effects on consumer prices for selected countries

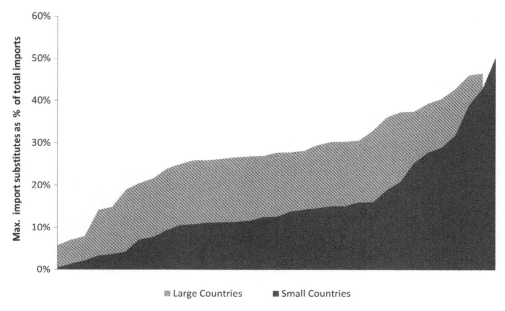

Figure 8.8 Maximum import substitutes as % of imports

no domestic substitutes for the overwhelming majority of imports. And the small country does not have the capacity to produce a range of import substitutes at internationally competitive prices.

Table 8.1 and Figure 8.8 are a first crude attempt to explore the limits to production and expenditure switching from foreign to local sources. We compared the values of imported items with the values of domestic production of comparable items, to gain a rough approximation of the extent of possible import substitution. The mean values and ranges for large and small countries are reported in Table 8.1. In Figure 8.8 large and small countries are ranked by size, to illustrate the fact that import substitution possibilities for large countries are greater, throughout the range.

Because of the structural features that define the SOFIE, there is little substitutability between domestic and foreign goods, in either consumption or production. Very few of the items imported can be produced at home under any circumstance, and of the handful that it is physically possible to produce domestically, those that can be produced at competitive prices form an even smaller set. The domestic market is so small in relation to the capacity of the export sector that a switch from domestic demand adds nothing significant to the supply of exports. Exporters of goods and services will see no change in the demand for their output, which is priced in foreign currency. They may see an improvement in their profitability, to the extent that domestic costs rise by less than the amount of devaluation. Since the main domestic cost is for labour, this profitability improvement is at the expense of worsening inequality, with a

Table 8.1 Crude indicators of maximum import substitution potential (percentage of imports)

	Range	*Weighted average*
Small countries	1%–43%,excluding Bahrain	12%
Large countries	6%–47%	14%

transfer of some portion of labour's share of the national income to the owners of capital. The improvement can therefore be expected to erode over time, and may not provide the anticipated incentive for investment in export capacity.

4 Why do SOFIEs prefer an exchange rate anchor?

Exchange rate variability in SOFIEs

In order to investigate whether SOFIEs do have a preference for predictable exchange rates, we need first to infer what each country regards as their international reference currency, i.e the currency that people think of when they consider the long-term value of their savings. Do Icelanders worry about the value of their currency in terms of the euro or the US dollar? Are Fijians more preoccupied with the value of the Australian or the US dollar? We make inferences about the answer for each country by comparing the volatility of their local currency with the US dollar and the most obvious alternative. The comparison is illustrated using the example of Luxembourg in Figure 8.9. The volatility of the local currency is plotted against the US dollar and against the deutschemark and later the euro, using the same volatility scale. A preference for alignment with the euro is clear.

A similar exercise was carried out for other countries, and the results are summarized in Figure 8.10, which compares, for each country, the local currency volatility with respect to the US dollar and with respect to the largest neighbouring currency of importance in world trade. A clear preference for the US dollar is present in all countries, except for SOFIEs in Europe, where there is a preference for the euro everywhere, apart from Montenegro.

Exchange rate variability in SOFIEs and economic performance

Our next task is to investigate whether countries that have a stable exchange rate anchor show evidence of better economic performance than those that do not. For this we use the Human Development Index as our measure of material well-being. The deficiencies of the more commonly used GDP measure are well known, and the HDI is often considered as the only superior indicator which is available on a comparable basis for countries worldwide.

An exercise of this kind will not produce definitive results; there are, for every country, too many omitted factors which have a greater impact on overall economic performance and welfare than does policy with respect to the exchange rate. However, if the popular sentiment in favour of the exchange rate anchor has merit, we should expect to see an inverse relationship, however weak, between the volatility of the exchange rate and the country's HDI score. That is indeed what we observe in Figure 8.11. We do take account of just a handful of the omitted variables in the econometric test which is reported in Table 8.2. Here we include inflation rate and an indicator of the trade openness of the economy, along with exchange rate volatility, as factors influencing the HDI score. It may be seen that there is the expected negative relationship between exchange rate volatility and HDI performance, suggesting that countries with lower exchange rate volatility are observed to have somewhat better HDI scores. The relationship is statistically credible, lying within the bounds of probability, which suggests there is an underlying relationship. However, the size of that impact is trivial, as measured by our test.

That result is not unexpected, because there are many other variables of which we were not able to take account that would have had a material impact. Interestingly, the negative impact of exchange rate volatility on HDI performance does not show up if we do not recognize that the reference currency for European countries is the euro. The authors have

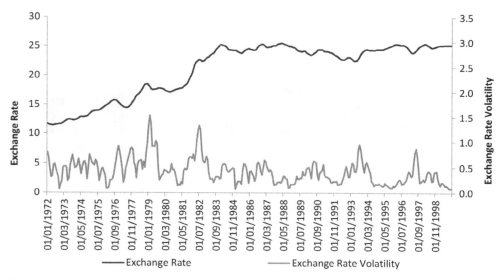

Figure 8.9a Luxembourg (1972–1999) – denominated in Euro

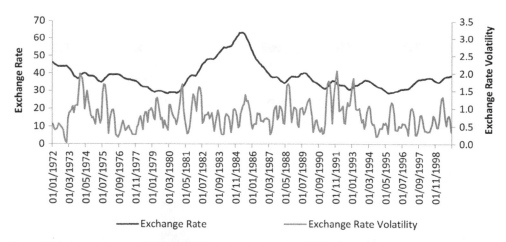

Figure 8.9b Luxembourg (1972–1999) – denominated in US Dollars

replicated the results of Table 8.2, using the US dollar as the reference for all countries, including European countries and the negative relationship between exchange rate volatility and the HDI score did not appear.

The preference for an exchange rate anchor is economically sound, because devaluation is not likely to make the SOFIE more competitive, and integration with the international financial market robs the SOFIE of an independent monetary policy. The standard policy suite of a flexible exchange rate and independent central bank with an inflation mandate is therefore not on offer. Fiscal policy is the sole tool of economic management in the government's armoury.

The foreign exchange markets of SOFIEs are driven overwhelmingly by financial flows in the short run, and not by the settlement of payments for traded goods and services. Trade volumes depend on decisions on investment in productive capacity and on contracts for

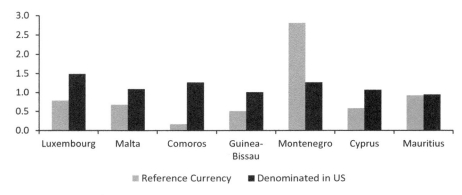

Figure 8.10a Euro exchange rate volatility

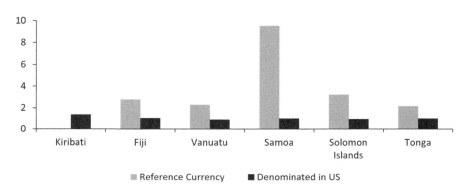

Figure 8.10b A$ exchange rate volatility

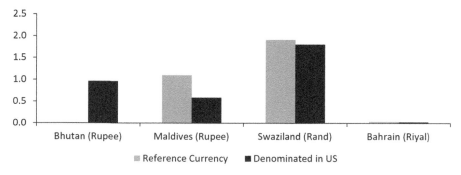

Figure 8.10c Rupee, rand, riyal exchange rate volatility

delivery whose terms are agreed in advance. The critical factor for these transactions is the exchange rate which rules at the time of settlement, which may be months or years after the contract is signed or the investment decision made. What matters most for the volume of trade, therefore, is the predictability of the exchange rate. The observed preference for an exchange rate anchor has a sound economic basis on these grounds (Pindyck, 1991).

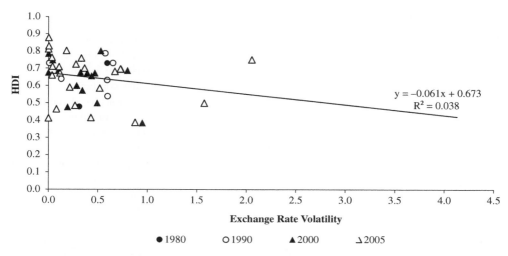

Figure 8.11 Exchange rate volatility and HDI (1980–2015) for selected countries

Table 8.2 Exchange rate volatility and other factors affecting the HDI score

	(1)	*(2)*	*(3)*	*(4)*
	HDI	*HDI*	*HDI*	*HDI*
Exchange rate	−0.007	−0.003	−0.003★★	−0.002★
	(0.004)	(0.002)	(0.001)	(0.001)
Inflation			0.001	0.002
			(0.001)	(0.001)
Trade openness				−0.000★★
				(0.000)
Constant	0.675★★★	0.506★★★	0.495★★★	0.590★★★
	(0.001)	(0.042)	(0.045)	(0.033)
N	201	138	136	135
R–sq	0.011	0.243	0.275	0.231

Standard errors in parentheses

Notes: *$p<0.05$, **$p<0.01$, ***$p<0.001$.

The daily demand and supply of foreign exchange depends, not on price and income elasticities, but on financial arrangements, such as the volume of trade credits, the extent of central treasury management by multinational corporations, the degree of financial integration with the wider world at the corporate and personal levels, and the extent to which domestic and foreign currencies are regarded as adequate inflation hedges. Whenever there is widespread apprehension about the possibility of devaluation, the supply of foreign exchange drains from the domestic market through these channels, and devaluation becomes a self-fulfilling prophecy, unless there is a credible framework for sustaining the exchange rate anchor.

5 Tools for anchoring the exchange rate

The key to successfully anchor the exchange rate of SOFIEs is to recognize that the foreign exchange market of this category of countries is a fixed-price market, which achieves equilibrium by adjusting quantities rather than prices. The supply of foreign exchange is augmented by investment in the tradable goods in which the country is internationally competitive, and the demand is adjusted by reducing the fiscal deficit as needed, and by the choice of domestic and foreign financing of the deficit. There is the obvious problem that the supply-augmenting policies yield results three to five years into the future, and even the fiscal adjustment of demand takes some months to have its full impact. In the framework proposed in this chapter, which is based on that actually applied in Barbados, monetary policy is used to fill the gaps, using a combination of foreign exchange intervention at the announced exchange rate, and intervention on the domestic market for treasury debt instruments, to provide market guidance on interest rates.

The process begins with a forecast of the supply of foreign exchange, based on productive capacity in exported goods and services, and policy measures to bring these activities up to full capacity. The forecast demand for foreign exchange depends on national income, with the addition of a novel variable, the increase in national wealth. The reason is that it is plausible to argue that if there is an exogenous increase in wealth (not produced by an increase in income), aggregate expenditure will increase by some proportion of this exogenous gain. The source of the exogenous wealth increase is additional domestic money issued by the central bank, which may come from two sources: an accumulation of foreign reserves, when foreign currency receipts are sold to the central bank in exchange for domestic money; and central bank credit to commercial banks (rarely) and the government.

In a growing economy we may expect remunerative opportunities in the competitive tradable activities to attract investment to increase capacity, but the resulting increase in foreign exchange supply will not appear in the current policy period, usually the fiscal year. If the forecast demand for foreign exchange exceeds the supply, therefore, the fiscal deficit must be cut, and government borrowing requirements adjusted, so as to achieve the necessary reduction in aggregate demand and, as a result, imports. If the foreign reserves of the central bank are at levels that are considered adequate, this is the extent of fiscal adjustment that is required. If reserves are at excessively high levels, there is room for fiscal expansion, if that is appropriate to the economic circumstances. Conversely, if foreign reserves are considered to be at uncomfortably low levels, a target must be set to increase reserves to the required level, and an additional amount of fiscal contraction programmed in order to achieve that target.

The next element in the framework is a daily monitoring system for tracking the central bank's foreign reserves, to judge whether they are on course to meet the target for the end of the fiscal year. For this the Central Bank of Barbados uses a unique chart, illustrated in Figure 8.12, which allows policy makers to detect very easily when the foreign exchange market is out of equilibrium, and the foreign reserves target is unlikely to be met. Since the Central Bank always sells foreign exchange at the fixed rate whenever the market is short, a persistent foreign exchange shortage causes a depletion of the Bank reserves, as may be observed in 2013, in Figure 8.12. In these circumstances fiscal tightening was called for, and the Central Bank used a portion of its reserves to fund the foreign currency market until the expenditure-tightening measures could take full effect.

6 Conclusion

It has become increasingly evident that the policy options implicit in the classical Mundell-Fleming trilemma of exchange controls, an exchange rate peg and independent monetary

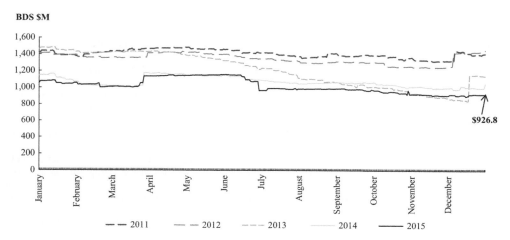

BDS $M

Figure 8.12 Monitoring system used by the Central Bank of Barbados for tracking the central bank's foreign reserves

policy, are not applicable to small open economies in today's world of international financial integration. SOFIEs the world over find themselves struggling unsuccessfully to use the tools developed for use in relatively closed economies and countries with large diversified economies. Small countries purport to allow market-determined exchange rates in circumstances where there is little or no demand for local currency as store of value, meaning that the demand for foreign currency on the financial account is infinite, for all practical purposes. The only agents who will use local currency are those who have no access to foreign exchange. These countries develop monetary tools to target inflation, when in fact in the order of 80 percent of inflation is imported. The elephant in the room, which does not appear in the conventional policy equation, is fiscal policy.

In this chapter, we presented a simple alternative framework for policy formulation which integrates fiscal policy tools, which are known to be the most powerful instruments available to open economies – some would argue to all economies – with monetary and exchange rate objectives. By calibrating the fiscal stance (the magnitude and direction of the fiscal balance, and how fiscal deficits are financed) to ensure external balance in a forward-looking policy framework, with up-to-date monitoring of targets and coordinated arrangements for policy implementation and correction, SOFIEs may attain a high degree of control over their economic fortunes, whatever the international economic circumstances they might encounter.

Notes

1 This chapter has evolved out of ideas presented at seminars hosted by the IMF, the Bank of England, the Peterson Institute, the Chinese Academy of Social Sciences, and the Central Bank of Barbados. We are grateful to our colleagues for their comments and suggestions. We are fully responsible for the views in this paper.

2 The authors owe this term to Mar Gudmundsson, Governor of the Central Bank of Iceland. I first heard it from him at a meeting of the Official Monetary and Financial Institutions Forum (OMFIF) in London, April 2017.

3 See Appendix 1, Chapter 1 for the list of countries included featuring in this chapter's figures.

D. Worrell, W. Moore and J. Beckles

References

Bank for International Settlements (BIS) (2012). Fiscal Policy, Public Debt and Monetary Policy in Emerging Market Economies. *BIS Papers* No. 67. Basel: BIS.

Blanchard, O., Giovanni, D. and Paolo, M. 'Rethinking macroeconomic policy'. *Journal of Money, Credit and Banking* 42(1): 199–215.

Frankel, J. A. (2003). Experience of and lessons from exchange rate regime in emerging economies. *National Bureau of Economic Research Working Paper* No. 10032. Cambridge, MA: National Bureau of Economic Research.

Furman, J., Stiglitz, J. E., Bosworth, B. P. and Radelet, S. (1998). Economic crises: evidence and insights from East Asia. *Brookings papers on economic activity*, 2: 1–135.

Ghosh, A. R., Ostry, J. D. and Chamon, M. (2016). 'Two targets, two instruments: monetary and exchange rate policies in emerging market economies'. *Journal of International Money and Finance*, 60: 172–196.

Hanke, S. (2002). 'On Dollarization and Currency Boards: Error and Deception'. *Journal of Policy Reform*, 5 (4): 206-222.

Obstfeld, M. and Rogoff, K. (1995). 'The Mirage of Fixed Exchange Rates'. *Journal of Economic Perspectives*, 9(4): 73–96.

Pindyck, R. S. (1991). 'Irreversibility, Uncertainty, and Investment'. *Journal of Economic Literature*, XXIX: 1110–1148.

Worrell, D. (2000). Monetary and Fiscal Coordination in Small Open Economies. *IMF Working Paper* WP/00/56. Washington, DC: International Monetary Fund.

Worrell, D. (2012). Small Open Economies Have to be Managed Differently: Devaluation is Contractionary in Both the Short and Long Run. Available at http://voxeu.org/article/why-devaluation-isn-t-viable-option-greece-insights-small-open-economy.

9

Monetary policy and excess liquid assets in small open developing economies

Tarron Khemraj

1 Introduction

This paper analyses the implementation of monetary policy in economies with an exchange rate anchor and imperfectly competitive foreign exchange and money markets. It explains how the monetary authority's tool used for compensating commercial banks also contributes to financial stability by diminishing the volatility of the portfolio of assets.[1] For the purpose of this paper, a small open economy is defined as a country that a price taker in international trade and has a high percentage of trade to GDP.

There are several structural realities that make an exchange rate anchor more likely to be chosen as the primary monetary policy framework in small open developing economies. First, it was recognized a long time ago that the financial system of the Caribbean and the Pacific where many small open economies are located is oligopolistic (Moore and Craigwell, 2002; Blackman, 1998). Second, there is the persistence of non-remunerated excess reserves and interest earning excess liquid assets that reflect oligopolistic interest rate mark-up over a foreign benchmark interest rate (Khemraj, 2006). Third, any central bank which targets the exchange rate must demand an appropriate level of international reserves for the purpose of macroeconomic and exchange rate stability (Blackman, 2006).

The three structural realities are typically not integrated in the conventional views of the monetary transmission mechanism.[2] This paper shows why they are important in shaping a heretofore ignored transmission channel, which I call the 'compensation transmission mechanism'.

The existing literature, taken from the advanced capitalist economies, often imply the central bank controls an instrument of monetary policy – typically a benchmark interest rate as in the case of the Taylor rule – that it reacts in different stages of the business cycle. For us to appreciate why these three structural facts are crucial to the operation of monetary policy in small open economies we have to move away from the conventional explanations of transmission process which are meant for the advanced capitalist economies.[3]

The question must be asked whether the central bank's demand for foreign exchange reserves is important in maintaining exchange rate stability and a stable portfolio of assets in the banking system. In addition, does the accumulation of international reserves affect excess bank liquidity and other assets of the banking system? There is sparse empirical evidence making the connection between central banks' demand for international reserves and commercial bank assets and liabilities. The mainstream literature often emphasizes sterilization as a way of insulating the monetary base from the accumulation of international reserves. Several notable authors also argue that sterilized interventions are mainly 'smoke and mirror' as they exert modest, if any, long-term effect on exchange and interest rates (Obstfeld and Rogoff, 1995). The latter argument no doubt stems from the notion of the impossible trinity, referring to the incompatibility between fixed currencies, monetary autonomy and capital mobility are incompatible and the money neutrality thesis in the context of an open economy.

Invoking the importance of national pride and political economic forces, a few Caribbean economists have noted the importance of a fixed exchange rate as a nominal anchor even with de facto capital mobility (Williams, 2006; Worrell et al., 2000). In so doing, they have indirectly questioned the applicability of the impossible trinity when thinking about the implementation of monetary policy. Khemraj and Pasha (2012) emphasize the tendency of some Caribbean economies – owing to oligopolistic banking and imperfect foreign exchange markets – to circumvent the straightjacket imposed by the impossible trinity. Over the years, other researchers have noted that sterilization is merely endogenous, reflecting offsetting changes on the liability side of the central bank's balance sheet (Lavoie, 2001; Lavoie and Wang, 2012). Instead of active exogenous sterilization, these authors argue in favour of a compensation mechanism.

The chapter is organized as follows. Section 2 discusses the central bank's demand for foreign exchange reserves. Section 3 discusses and reinterprets the emerging literature on excess bank liquidity. Section 4 outlines the notion of compensation and Section 5 looks at its cost. Section 6 shows how compensation contributes to financial stability, while Section 7 concludes.

2 International reserves

A considerable amount of research went into explaining why the large emerging economies demand foreign exchange reserves. The consensus appears to have settled on the need for hold precautionary balances after the Asian crisis (Aizenman and Marion, 2003). However, what happens during the accumulation of foreign reserves is important for our purposes. In small open developing economies, the long-term trend level of international reserves has to be upward sloping – to reflect the proportionate expansion of GDP and imports – even though there will be short-term deviations from the trend. This implies that over a long enough period, the central bank's purchases of foreign currency from exporters will be greater than sales. These purchases will impact on domestic financial assets and bank liquidity (Khemraj, 2006; Khemraj, 2009; Shrestha, 2013). We should also note that the national currencies of small economies are not globally traded; hence, the long-term net purchase is done in the context of the domestic financial system.

For developing and emerging economies the level of foreign exchange reserves is often constrained by the output gap and recurring exchange market pressures (Downes and Moore, 2007; Gevorkyan, 2017). In addition, Thirlwall (1979) shows that the balance of payments explains growth rate differences among countries. These studies imply that notwithstanding the desire for precautionary balances, the economies may not possess the real sectors to generate sufficient precautionary balances. This fact moved former Central Bank of Barbados Governor DeLisle Worrell (2012: 6) to argue that the small very open economy (SVOE) is 'an economic engine that runs of foreign exchange.' The persistent foreign currency constraint, therefore, restricts the policy options, according to Worrell. This requires balancing aggregate demand through fiscal policy with the requirement of holding a corresponding amount of international reserves consistent with the central government's stance. In his approach, economic policy makers are required to think in terms of the tradable versus non-tradable sectors. If the SVOE is to stand a chance of maintaining an upward trend in foreign reserves, then special attention has to be given to the competitiveness of the tradable sector, which is the sector that earns the foreign exchange to ease the long-term foreign currency constraint.

3 Excess liquidity

For the purpose of understanding the compensation hypothesis that is proposed in this chapter, we must first take note of how the long-term accumulation of international reserves determines the level of financial assets and liquidity in the overall financial system. There is an immediate connection between excess liquid assets (demanded in local currency) and foreign exchange reserves held by central bank. Recall, excess liquidity takes two forms. First, there is the component that earns a rate of interest – the excess liquid assets. These are often securities used for monetary policy purposes. Often these are reported as Treasury bills used to 'mop up' excess reserves. However, their role is much more fundamental, being part of a system of compensation in the post-liberalized period. There might also be special securities created for the purpose of monetary policy. Second, there is the non-remunerated component of excess reserves. There are some instances in which excess reserves pay a low rate of interest, but in most economies they carry zero rate of nominal interest.

Often the term liquidity is used in another context that is more relevant to financial structures with well-developed money and capital markets. In this framework, banks supply liquidity (overdraft loans) to firms facing a short-term liquidity shock (Kashyap et al., 2002). According to this view, commercial banks demand liquid assets for two primary purposes: (i) meet unpredictable withdrawals of demand deposits and (ii) supply overdraft loans to firms that have short-term liquidity needs. This interpretation requires that there are deep and liquid markets that allow banks to sell their liquid assets to meet the two needs. However, in the context of small open developing economies, this mechanism would not work as outlined by Kashyap et al. (2002). For example, when firms face a liquidity shock, banks could choose to invest in a safe foreign asset instead of extending overdraft.

There is, on the other hand, an established literature that focuses on explaining bank liquidity preferences beyond the reasons proffered by Kashyap et al. (2002). Often this literature does not make the distinction between excess bank liquidity which earns interest and that which does not. This distinction is crucial because as is argued later, the build-up of excess liquidity reflects the deeper structural feature of the foreign currency constraint and the requirement that the central bank manages around it. The popular approach to modelling the demand for excess liquidity is to specify an Autoregressive Distributed Lag (ARDL) econometric model with various control variables, including several proxies for volatility. One of the early examples is Saxegaard (2006) who tried to determine whether the banks' demand for excess liquidity is involuntary or voluntary (the precautionary motive). This paper was comprehensive taking into account the Monetary and Economic Community of Central Africa (CEMAC) region, Nigeria and Uganda. The author shows that the monetary transmission mechanism weakens in the presence of excess liquidity.

Another well-known attempt to disentangle the voluntary and involuntary nature of excess liquidity was Agénor et al. (2004). The authors put forward the novel idea that the stability of the demand for excess liquidity determines whether the slowdown of credit reflects a supply-side credit crunch or was it demand-induced. If the empirical demand is unstable it reflects the possibility the demand is involuntary, thus being consistent with a demand slowdown. The ARDL approach has found wide applications. For a more comprehensive review of the literature see the paper by Primus *et al.* (2014). The latter authors examine the dynamic evolution of involuntary liquidity for Trinidad and Tobago. Their empirical strategy was quite novel. First, they estimate a model taking into account various estimates of volatility. The first stage allows the authors to simulate voluntary and involuntary excess liquidity. In their second stage, they use a vector error correction model (VEC) to analyse the dynamics of involuntary liquidity given a shock to government expenditure. They found that a shock to the government fiscal balance will increase involuntary liquidity. The implicit assumption of this research project is non-remunerated excess reserves could potentially stimulate the supply of loans in an involuntary regime of excess liquidity.

Other researchers, however, question whether excess reserves determine the supply of loans. In so doing this literature questions the relevance of excess reserves to the bank lending channel of the transmission mechanism (Lavoie, 2007: Chapter 3). Using the method of vector auto-regression, Khemraj (2007) shows that excess reserves have virtually no effect on the quantity of bank loans. Instead, the quantity of excess reserves responds negatively given a positive shock in the quantity of loans. In other works, the author introduces a different interpretation of voluntary and involuntary excess liquidity (see Khemraj, 2006). Voluntary excess liquidity occurs when the commercial bank's liquidity preference curve – drawn in the space of loan interest rate and excess reserves – is horizontal. This implies the demand for excess reserves is perfectly elastic at a nominal interest rate substantially above zero, unlike the established interpretation of a liquidity trap in which the curve is flat at the zero lower bound.

One interpretation of involuntary demand is when the market interest rate rises above the rate at which the demand for excess liquidity is perfectly elastic. This rate is interpreted as a minimum rate or a mark-up lending rate by an oligopolistic commercial bank (Khemraj, 2006; Khemraj, 2014). Since excess reserves and loans are perfect substitutes at the mark-up, the banks will seek to invest the non-remunerated asset into an interest earning one, such as foreign assets. This they could do even in the voluntary or involuntary regimes once there is sufficient foreign exchange. However, they are prevented from doing so in the current time period because of the foreign exchange constraint. The constraint forces commercial banks to first meet the foreign currency needs of established customers – primarily those with loans in national currency – before making a proprietary trade. The constraint also emerges from the fact that the central bank has to quarantine a credible amount of international reserves consistent with the fiscal position of the central government.

The alternative interpretation of voluntary versus involuntary excess reserves has two primary implications. First, it implies the ARDL functions – modelling the demand for excess liquidity (E) – suffer from omitted variable bias.

$$E = L(x_V, 1/r, \Omega) \tag{1}$$

ARDL time series models often include controls for volatility, which is derived from some underlying variable such as demand deposits or a series representing the nominal exchange rate. This is indicated by the variable x_V. The symbol Ω indicates other control variables. The omitted variable is $1/r$, which implies an asymptotic liquidity preference curve. The asymptote occurs at a rate substantially above zero reflecting a mark-up interest rate (Khemraj, 2006; Khemraj, 2014). The latter is not included in the typical ARDL model which is popular for estimating voluntary and involuntary excess liquidity. As these models are estimated by least squares, the omitted variables bias the estimated coefficients.

Second, excess reserves could be invested in other profit-making assets instead of being extended into domestic currency loans. In particular, once established customers are served, the banks could invest in an interest-earning foreign asset. It is for this reason, the central bank needs to sell another domestic profit-making asset to the banks and other financial investors in place of the option of investing scarce foreign currencies in a foreign financial asset. Excess reserves and the foreign currency constraint make it necessary for the central bank to intervene in one-sided sales of national securities for the purpose of stabilising the exchange rate, and by extension the macro economy.

4 Compensation transmission mechanism and the trilemma

Compensation is defined as the one-sided sales of national-currency sovereign securities (such as Treasury bills) to commercial banks and other financial institutions as an incentive system in the presence of the foreign exchange constraint. The sales of these securities should not be misplaced for classical open market operations which require a liquid and developed secondary money market. Open market operations imply the central bank buys or sells securities depending on the economic environment. Compensation, on the other hand, means that the central bank has to create an alternative investment opportunity in national currencies given that the economy faces a perpetual foreign exchange constraint or growth is constrained by the balance of payments in the long run.[4] The existence of the foreign exchange constraint and the fact that the central bank has to demand a credible level of international reserves require that there is a persistence of excess reserves, which banks could in theory invest in foreign currency assets. Later in the chapter, I show how the one-sided sales of national securities are related to the bid-ask spread in the foreign exchange market.[5]

There is however another form of the compensation hypothesis in the literature and it has a long history. Marc Lavoie and his co-authors have done a tremendous amount of research explaining and testing their idea of the compensation thesis at the theoretical and empirical level. The basic hypothesis holds there are endogenous adjustments taking place on the central bank's balance sheet when there are capital inflows. The adjustments are seen as automatic and reflect private decision making. For this reason, Lavoie and Wang (2012) interprets the mainstream notion of sterilization as an endogenous endeavour resulting from offsetting changes on both the asset and liability sides of the monetary authority's balance sheet. In addition, the central bank could create special monetary policy securities that are held as liabilities. Government deposits at the central bank could also allow this endogenous compensating system to occur when foreign currencies flow into the economy. Therefore, capital inflows result in simultaneous changes on the asset and liability sides of the balance sheet without any change in the monetary base. Accompanying the compensation thesis is the reflux mechanism that is explained in detail in Lavoie (2001). Suffice to say, the reflux principle implies banks will use all excess reserves to repay their debt to the central bank. Excess reserves are not loaned out since banks make loans and 'search for reserves later' (Lavoie, 2001: 228).

Banks, however, are unlikely to repay debt with excess reserves because they are interested in buying foreign interest-earning securities. Furthermore, since excess reserves are a much more persistent and recurring feature in the banking system, commercial banks often do not borrow reserves from the central bank, unless there is a severe financial crisis. The excess reserves are injected into the system when the central bank accumulates foreign exchange reserves, which are at least maintained at a specified number of months of import cover. Commercial banks cannot invest all excess reserves in foreign currencies because the central bank's demand for international reserves creates a foreign exchange constraint, a friction preventing all non-remunerated excess reserves from being invested in foreign assets. Therefore, the central bank conducts one-sided sales of official securities to commercial banks in order to encourage them not to increase the bid-ask spread or invest in foreign assets. This compensation system results because of the foreign currency constraint that is created when the central bank demands foreign reserves, a process which creates non-remunerated excess reserves (Khemraj, 2006; Khemraj, 2009).

Examining the compensation hypothesis

Let us examine the compensation hypothesis within the context of an oligopolistic banking sector. It is assumed a commercial bank is a major institutional trader of foreign currency, buying and selling the hard currencies in the domestic market. The bank not only has market power in loan and deposit markets, but also in the foreign exchange market. The bank, of course, uses domestic currency for the making purchases and sales. The market power in the foreign exchange market implies the bank can maintain a wide bid-ask spread. In the short term, owing to sustained shortages of foreign exchange, the dominant bank would be tempted increase the selling rate (the rate importers pay), thus depreciating the currency and widening the spread. In this case, the monetary authority has to respond by offering an alternative asset in which the banks can make money. Here the central bank is forced to sell Treasury bills or a special monetary policy instrument to the commercial banks. Since the banks do not use the excess reserves to make loans at the risk-adjusted marginal cost of lending, they are more likely to purchase the liquid assets at a rate that is profitable.

However, the banks can even collude to bid at a high Treasury bill rate, thus preventing the central bank from having a true benchmark interest rate. Nevertheless, the central bank controls the quantity of Treasury bills it sells to preserve the bid-ask spread at which the banks are already making profits. In other words, the monetary authority compensates the commercial bank by selling them sovereign liquid assets, thereby engendering the build-up of interest earning excess liquid assets, while diminishing non-remunerated excess reserves.

In the next period, however, non-remunerated excess reserves will again increase as the central bank increases international reserves around its trend level, thus requiring another round of liquid assets. The compensation system is necessary because of the long-term foreign exchange constraint and the need to hold foreign currency reserves to defend the peg, a crawling peg or some other system of managed exchange rate.

Let us explain this idea using an imperfect competition model of the foreign exchange market. Typically the market is seen as a flexible price market closer to pure competition. That may very well be true for a globally traded currency that trades at all the main centres of global finance. However, our small very open developing economy does not possess a globally traded currency or a vehicle currency. This economy earns a finite quantity of foreign exchange through exports, capital inflows and remittances. The imperfect competition model is different in that it allows for the persistence of the foreign exchange bid-ask spread in the local market. Since the market is local and the constraint is consistent, triangular arbitrage will not always exist to drive the bid-ask spread towards zero as would tend to be the case in the global foreign exchange market. There are just not sufficient quantities of all the main hard currencies for continual triangular arbitrage to take place. In the typical localized market, there tends to be larger quantities of US dollars than the other main currencies like Japanese yen or Euros.

Figure 9.1 – first presented by Khemraj (2014) – shows a model of compensation within the context of an imperfect foreign exchange market. Both the buying and the selling sides of the market are given. On the buying side the dominant foreign exchange trader – possibly a

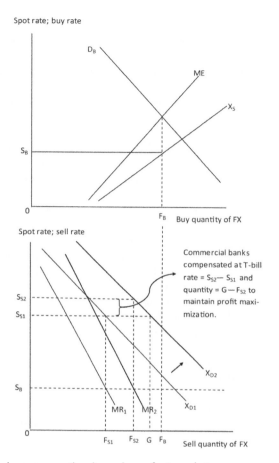

Figure 9.1 Central bank compensation in an imperfect market

price leader – purchases the hard currency as it enters the market through capital inflows, export earning or remittances. The quantity bought is F_B. The dominant bank trader would need to fulfil the requests by its clients for foreign exchange. Therefore, it will sell hard currencies equal to the amount F_{S1}. This allows it to hoard some for the purpose of buying foreign assets to meet the foreign exchange needs of its domestic customers. The quantity it hoards is given by $F_B - F_{S1}$. At this initial equilibrium the buying rate is S_B and the selling rate is S_{S1} (with the bid-ask spread = $S_{S1} - S_B$). The central bank, however, needs a cut of the amount hoarded since it has to maintain a credible level of international reserves. Therefore, it buys foreign exchange from the domestic market by crediting excess reserves at the commercial banks. The demand curve shifts outward from X_{D1} to X_{D2}, thereby potentially causing the selling rate to depreciate from S_{S1} to S_{S2} (assume the exchange rate is quoted as local currency/one US$). Note that the quantity hoarded by the commercial bank declines from $F_B - F_{S1}$ to $F_B - F_{S2}$.

For the central bank to maintain the exchange rate at S_{S1}, it will have to sell another asset to the commercial banks to compensate for the fact that it has increased its demand for international reserves, thereby quarantining from the private sector a quantity of foreign currency. Let us assume it sells Treasury bills to the dominant bank or a few systemically important banks. Maintaining the exchange rate at S_{S1} requires that the central bank compensates or sells G

amount of Treasury bills to the banks at a rate of interest that depends on the elasticity of demand for imports. The more inelastic the demand for imports the higher will have to be the compensation interest rate. The rate of interest offered by the central bank would also need to be commensurate with the banks' desired increase in the bid-ask spread from $S_{S1} - S_B$ to $S_{S2} - S_B$.

Moreover, while the central bank does not exercise full control over the rate of interest, it can exert control over the amount of Treasury bills it sells, thus controlling the level of excess liquid assets in the banking system. This implies excess liquidity and excess reserves are intricately connected to the system of compensation, which is furthermore associated with the fact that a central bank in small open economies has to hold sufficient foreign exchange reserves. When the monetary authority purchases hard currencies it pays with excess reserves, but this process simultaneously worsens the foreign exchange constraint faced by the private sector. Therefore, it sells Treasury bills as compensation for the lost profits the banks would have made by increasing the bid-ask spread.

This action of monetary policy is independent even if there is open capital mobility and a fixed exchange rate. Here monetary policy is conducted with a compensating security and not a monetary aggregate. Therefore, it is possible for the central bank to pursue an independent monetary policy of compensation in spite of having an exchange rate anchor and operating under free capital mobility. Seen from this angle, monetary management circumvents the Trilemma and results in dual anchors – an exchange rate anchor and a monetary anchor. This idea of circumventing the Impossible Trinity is central to Khemraj and Pasha (2012) and Khemraj (2014).

A similar argument with respect to getting around the Trilemma is found in the work of Lavoie and Wang (2012) under which the inflows of foreign exchange results in endogenous and simultaneous compensating adjustments on the liability side of the central bank's balance sheet without influencing the monetary base. Another recent paper by Serrano and Summa (2015) makes the point that the central bank can have an independent interest rate policy even with free capital mobility.

5 Cost of compensation

Analyzing the cost of compensation requires comparing the interest rate an imperfectly competitive buyer of the government security will pay versus where the competitive interest rate would normally exist. The buyer could be a large commercial bank, a major pension fund or the domestic national insurance agency looking for a stable rate of return. Figure 9.2 indicates the model of a monopsony buyer of Treasury bills or some other official security used for this purpose. The marginal expenditure (ME) curve lies above the supply curve (S_G). As usual the demand for the security is downward sloping. The central bank sells the security as it quarantines foreign exchange for the purpose of meeting its target for international reserves.

In a purely competitive market the interest rate will be r_C and the quantity which has to be sold G_C. Here the cost of compensation is the area of the rectangle $0G_Cr_C$. However, the monopsony or oligopsony will prefer to purchase the government security at a lower rate of interest, r_M, because it can. This is likely because it has the capacity to purchase large quantities. Also the central bank only needs to sell the quantity G_M, a lower level of compensation than previous case. Therefore, the cost of compensation when there is imperfect competition in the market for sovereign securities is the area $0G_Mr_M$, clearly smaller than the area representing compensation under pure competition.

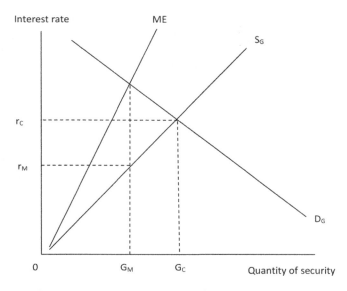

Figure 9.2 The cost of compensation in imperfect and pure competition

6 Financial stability

In recent years, a major focus of the literature has been to combine monetary policy with financial stability within the context of an inflation targeting framework. A comprehensive review of this research agenda was given by Agénor and Pereira da Silva (2013). Previous empirical studies have also shown that excess liquid assets promote relatively more stable banking systems (Moore, 2007; Deléchat *et al.*, 2012). Earlier it was argued that the central bank could simultaneously have an independent monetary instrument – the quantity of excess liquid assets – and also target the nominal exchange rate. This section examines the effect of excess liquidity on the variance and expected return of a stylized bank's portfolio.

The exposition that follows draws heavily from Khemraj (2014). The bank is assumed to hold four assets that when expressed in percentage form can be written as follows $h + r + l + g = 1$. The assets are foreign currency assets (let us call these hoardings) converted into local currency $h = H/A$, excess liquid assets or government securities ($g = G/A$), excess reserves ($r = R/A$) and loans in domestic currency ($l = L/A$). The expected return on each asset takes into consideration a probability of losing money on that asset. Therefore, the expected return on loans includes a discount representing the probability that some borrowers will not repay (this probability is denoted by ρ). Similarly, the expected return on the government security is discounted by the probability the national government will not repay or default (ψ_1). The expected return on hoarding foreign currency takes into account the movements in the foreign exchange rate. When the nominal exchange rate depreciates ($\Delta S>0$) the bank makes money on hoarding foreign exchange assets. When the nominal exchange rate appreciates, however, ($\Delta S<0$) the bank loses money on its stock of foreign exchange.[6] Therefore, we must take into consideration the probability the exchange rate will depreciate (ψ_2) and the probability it will appreciate: ($1 - \psi_2$).

The expected return on domestic currency loans is given as $E_L = (1 - \rho)r_L$. The expected return on the government security is $E_G = (1 - \psi_1)r_G$. When the exchange rate is flexible the expected return on hoarding is given by $E_H = Er_F = \psi_2 \Delta S - (1 - \psi_2) \Delta S$, where Er_F represents the forecast or expected foreign benchmark rate. In a fixed exchange rate regime, return on hoarding foreign asset is just Er_F. Note that if the commercial bank merely holds foreign currency in its vault its return on hoarding is 0% in the case of a fixed exchange rate. Given the ratio of each asset and the individual returns, the expected return on the portfolio can be expressed as:

$$E_P + E_L l + E_G g + E_H h \tag{2}$$

Substituting into equation (2) the asset ratio constraint $h = 1 - r - l - g$ and rearranging the formula will give us the expected return in deviations from the expected return on hoarding as shown by equation (3).

$$E_P = (E_L - E_H)l + (E_G - E_H)g + (1 - r)E_H \tag{3}$$

In a completely fixed exchange rate system, the expected return is simply deviations from the benchmark foreign interest rate. The benchmark foreign rate (r_F) could be, for example, the US Treasury bill rate. The stronger the oligopoly power in the loan market implies that the bank can make more money in national currency. For the fixed exchange rate economy the expected return is given as:

$$E_P^f = (E_L - r_F)l + (E_G - r_F)g + (1 - r)r_F \tag{4}$$

Notice how bank excess reserves in domestic currency play a crucial role in reducing the influence of hoarding or the foreign asset on the portfolio return. Higher levels of excess reserves act as a constraint on bank demand for foreign asset. How would this situation emerge? The answer: by compensating the banks with government securities that pays the compensation interest rate (e_G). The difference between the loan rate and the foreign rate and the Treasury bill rate and the foreign rate is determined by the oligopolistic mark-up. As the banking structure tends towards monopoly we can expect the mark-up to increase, thus increasing the portfolio return. However, increase in excess reserves reduces the effect of hoarding on the return of the portfolio even in an oligopolistic banking structure.

For the purpose of financial stability we must examine the variance of the portfolio of assets. The variance of the portfolio can be expressed as follows:

$$\sigma_P^2 = E(r_P - E_P)^2 = E[l(r_L - E_L)^2 + g(r_G - E_G)^2 + h(r_H - E_H)^2] \tag{5}$$

As usual E represents the expectations operator. The expression $r_H - E_H$ indicates the deviation of actual returns from expected returns on hoarding. The formula suggests that volatility results from the appreciation and depreciation of the exchange rate, increase in the default probability of borrowers, and the probability the government will default, since these are built into the respective expected returns. The equation further suggests that a fixed exchange rate would remove some of the volatility in the bank's portfolio. A completely flexible rate results in more volatility. In a fixed exchange rate economy the portfolio variance becomes:

$$\sigma_P^2 = E[l(r_L - E_L)^2 + g(r_G - E_G)^2 + h(r_F - Er_F)^2] \tag{6}$$

The best forecast of the foreign rate reduces volatility further (that is $r_F = Er_F$). It was observed above that the oligopolistic mark-up increases the return on the portfolio. Let us now examine how the variance is affected by the mark-up. Taking account of $h = 1 - r - l - g$ into equation (6) (the case for the fixed exchange rate) and rearranging will result in:

$$\sigma_P^2 = E\left\{l[(r_L - E_L)^2 - (r_F - Er_F)^2] + g[(r_G - E_G)^2 - (r_F - Er_F)^2] + (1 - r)(r_F - Er_F)^2\right\} \quad (7)$$

If the expression $(r_L - E_L)^2 - (r_F - Er_F)^2$ is expanded it becomes obvious that the square of the spread $(r_L - r_F)^2$ is embedded within the measure of portfolio volatility. Therefore, we can conclude that after controlling for the fixed exchange rate regime, volatility will increase as the markup rises. The $(r_G - E_G)^2 - (r_F - Er_F)^2$ can also be simplified to $(r_G - r_F)^2$.

Equation (7) can be seen as the decomposition of the volatility (or variance) when the banks possess oligopoly market power in the loan and Treasury bill markets. Therefore, it provides an insight into how policy might reduce the variance of the portfolio in the aggregate banking sector. First, throughout the Caribbean the spread between the loan rate and foreign rate $(r_L - r_F)$ is often greater than the spread between the compensating interest rate and the foreign rate $(r_G - r_F)$. In other words, to the extent the central bank's policy shifts the portfolio towards interest earning liquid assets from loans, it will diminish the variance.

Second, to the extent the central bank can wrestle some of the market power away from the commercial banks in the Treasury bill market, the volatility will decline. In other words, the central bank might be able to excise some control over the compensating interest rate and let the banks decide the quantity of G; in which case the spread $(r_G - r_F)$ declines. However, the ability of the central bank to control the rate depends on the elasticity of import demand (as seen in Figure 9.1). Third, an increase in excess reserves – often caused by the long-term accumulation of foreign reserves – will diminish the portfolio volatility, thereby enhancing the stability of the banking system (Moore, 2007). Fourth, anticipating foreign financial and macroeconomic conditions will result in a convergence between $r_F \to Er_F$, thus reducing the variance. Research, forecasting and the dissemination of the information to the commercial banks become important.

7 Conclusion

This chapter observed that bank liquidity – excess or otherwise – is an important aspect of the workings of exchange rate policy and concomitant monetary policy in small open developing economies. Since the foreign exchange market is domestic, the central bank credits the commercial banks with excess reserves (as it accumulates a long-term level of foreign reserves) that are non-remunerated in most countries. Therefore, excess reserves and liquidity have little to do with monetary policy at the zero lower bound and more to do with compensation (one-sided sales) under formidable foreign exchange constraint.

The upward long-term trend of international reserves (which grows as GDP and imports expand) takes away foreign exchange from the private sector in economies that already face the long-term balance of payments or foreign exchange constraint. Therefore, the excess of liquid assets reflects a compensation transmission mechanism at work, whereby the commercial banks are sold an interest-earning asset to replace non-remunerated excess reserves and foreign assets.

The chapter explained algebraically that this compensation system could also diminish the variance of the portfolio of bank assets, thus helping to promote financial stability. This argument, furthermore, calls for a reinterpretation of the voluntary and involuntary nature of excess reserves since the latter does not engender excessive – if any – loan expansion, but could potentially allow for purchasing foreign currency assets, thereby draining the domestic market of scarce foreign currencies.

Notes

1 According to the IMF's de facto exchange rate classification, there are 79 economies with exchange rate anchors and their own national currencies (IMF 2013: 5). The number 79 is obtained from the IMF (2013) report on exchange rate classification. In order to obtain 79, subtract the number of 'dollarized' economies from the total number of countries with an exchange rate anchor.

2 A detailed review of the literature on the monetary transmission mechanism, focusing on developing economies, found little evidence that the conventional explanations of the transmission channels have little or no applications to developing economies (Mishra and Montiel, 2013).

3 Khan (1998) tests some of the conventional transmission mechanisms in the Caribbean context. On the other hand, using vector autoregressions, Khemraj (2007) argues that excess reserves do not appear to determine loans and are actually determined by loans.

4 An important class of growth models in the Post Keynesian tradition that explicitly takes into account the foreign exchange constraint which relates to the balance of payments [see for example Thirlwall (1979) and Ribeiro et al. (2016)].

5 Empirical studies have found evidence consistent with the view that greater exchange rate volatility is negatively associated with economic growth in small open economies (Schnabl, 2008; Vieira et al., 2013).

6 Note, a depreciation that results in a significant pass-through to inflation could cause the commercial banks to lose money on the assets denominated in domestic currency, for example their loans made in the national currency.

References

Agénor, P., Aizenman, J. and Hoffmaister, A. (2004). 'The Credit Crunch in East Asia: What can Bank Excess Liquid Assets tell us?' *Journal of International Money and Finance*, 23(1): 27–49.

Agénor, P. and Pereira da Silva, L. (2013). *Inflation targeting and financial stability: a perspective from the developing world*. Washington, DC: Inter-American Development Bank.

Aizenman, J., Chinn, M. and Ito, H. (2012). The financial crisis, rethinking of the global financial architecture and the trilemma. In Kawai, M., Morgan, P. and Takagi, S. (eds) *Monetary and Currency Policy in Asia*. Cheltenham and Northampton, MA: Edward Elgar.

Aizenman, J. and Marion, N. (2003). Foreign exchange reserves in East Asia: why the high demand?. *FRBSF Economic Letter*, No. 2003–2011, April.

Blackman, C. N. (2006). Finance, investment and economic development: towards an investment-friendly financial environment. In Birchwood, A. and Seerattan, D. (eds) *Finance and Real Development in the Caribbean*. St Augustine, Trinidad and Tobago: Caribbean Centre for Money and Finance, University of West Indies.

Blackman, C. N. (1998). *Central Banking in Theory and Practice: A Small State Perspective*. Trinidad and Tobago: Caribbean Centre for Money and Finance, University of West Indies.

Deléchat, C., Henao, C., Muthoora, P. and Vtyurina, S. (2012). The determinants of banks' liquidity buffers in Central America. *Working Paper* 12/301. Washington, DC: International Monetary Fund.

Downes, D. and Moore, W. (2007). 'Does the exchange rate regime influence the relationship between the output gap and current account?'. *Applied Economics*, 39(15): 1955–1960.

Gevorkyan, A. V. (2017). 'The exchange market regime in a small open economy: Armenia and beyond'. *Journal of Economic Studies*, 44(5): 781–800.

IMF (2013). *Annual Report on Exchange Rate Arrangements*. Washington, DC: International Monetary Fund.

Kashyap, A., Rajan, R. and Stein, J. (2002). 'Banks as liquidity providers: an explanation of the coexistence of lending and deposit-taking'. *Journal of Finance*, 57(1): 33–73.

Khan, G. (1998). *Monetary transmission mechanisms: their operation under fixed and floating rate regimes: the experience of a group of countries*. Occasional Paper Series No. 6. St Augustine, Trinidad and Tobago: Caribbean Centre for Money and Finance, University of West Indies.

Khemraj, T. (2014) *Money, Banking and the Foreign Exchange Market in Emerging Economies*. Cheltenham and Northampton, MA: Edward Elgar.

Khemraj, T. (2009). 'Excess liquidity and the foreign currency constraint: the case of monetary management in Guyana'. *Applied Economics*, 41(16): 2073–2084.

Khemraj, T. (2007). 'Monetary policy and excess liquidity: the case of Guyana'. *Social and Economic Studies*, 56(3): 101–127.

Khemraj, T. (2006). *Excess Liquidity, Oligopoly Banking and Monetary Policy in a Small Open Economy.* Unpublished PhD Dissertation. New York: New School for Social Research.

Khemraj, T. and Pasha, S. (2012). 'Dual nominal anchors in the Caribbean'. *Journal of Economic Studies,* 39 (4): 420–439.

Lavoie, M. (2007). *Introduction to Post-Keynesian economics.* London and New York: Palgrave Macmillan.

Lavoie, M. (2001). The reflux mechanism and the open economy. In Rochan, L. and Vernengo, M. (eds), *Credit, Interest Rates and the Open Economy.* Cheltenham: Edward Elgar.

Lavoie, M. and Wang, P. (2012). 'The 'compensation' thesis, as exemplified by the case of the Chinese central bank'. *International Review of Applied Economics,* 26(3): 287–301.

Mishra, P. and Montiel, P. (2013). 'How effective is monetary transmission in low-income countries? A survey of the empirical evidence'. *Economic Systems,* 37(2): 187–216.

Moore, W. (2007). 'Forecasting domestic liquidity during a crisis: what works best?'. *Journal of Forecasting,* Vol. 26(6): 445–455.

Moore, W. and Craigwell, R. (2002). 'Market power and interest rate spread in the Caribbean'. *International Review of Applied Economics,* 16(4): 391–405.

Obstfeld, M. and Rogoff, K. (1995). 'The mirage of fixed exchange rates'. *Journal of Economic Perspectives,* 9 (4): 73–96.

Primus, K., Birchwood, A. And Henry, L. (2014). 'The dynamics of involuntary commercial banks' reserves in Trinidad and Tobago'. *Journal of Developing Areas,* 48(2): 63–84.

Ribeiro, R., McCombie, J. and Tadeu Lima, G. (2016). 'Exchange rate, income distribution and technical change in a balance-of-payments constrained growth model'. *Review of Political Economy,* 24(4): 545–565.

Saxegaard, M. (2006). Excess liquidity and the effectiveness of monetary policy: evidence from Sub-Saharan Africa. *IMF Working Paper* 06/115. Washington, DC: International Monetary Fund.

Schnabl, G. (2008). 'Exchange rate volatility and growth in small open economies at the EMU periphery'. *Economic Systems,* 32(1): 70–91.

Serrano, F. and Summa, R. (2015). 'Mundell-Fleming without the LM curve: the exogenous interest rate in an open economy'. *Review of Keynesian Economics,* 3(2): 248–268.

Shrestha, P. K. (2013). 'Banking systems, central banks and international reserve accumulation in East Asian economies'. *Economics: The Open Access, Open Assessment E-Journal,* 7: 1–28.

Thirlwall, A. (1979). 'The balance-of-payment constraint as an explanation of international growth rate difference'. *Banca Nazionale del Lavoro Quarterly Review,* 128: 45–53.

Vieira, F., Holland, M., Gomes da Silva, C. and Bottecchia, L. (2013). 'Growth and exchange rate volatility: a panel data analysis'. *Applied Economics,* 45(26): 3733–3741.

Williams, M. (2006). Predictors of currency crises in fixed exchange rate regimes: lessons for the Caribbean from the case of Argentina. In Birchwood, A. and Seerattan, D. (eds), *Finance and Real Development in the Caribbean.* St Augustine, Trinidad and Tobago: Caribbean Centre for Money and Finance, University of West Indies.

Worrell, D. (2012). Policies for stabilization and growth in small very open economies. *Occasional Paper* 85. Washington, DC: Group of Thirty.

Worrell, D., Marshall, D. and Smith, N. (2000). The political economy of exchange rate policy in the Caribbean. *Research Network Working Paper* R-401. Washington, DC: Inter-American Development Bank.

10

The evolution of stock markets in the CARICOM region (1969–2010): lessons for other small emerging economies

John Gerard Cozier and Patrick Kent Watson

1 Introduction

The objectives of this chapter are to present a comprehensive analysis of the development of the regional stock exchanges over time; to put forward policy recommendations for the further development of these exchanges; and to offer lessons to other small emerging economies in the process of developing their own equity markets. The underlying motivation of the chapter is that such financial development goes hand in hand with all-round economic development. Worldwide, the stock exchange has become a major hub of activity, capable, arguably, of stimulating overall economic development (Schumpeter, 1911; Goldsmith, 1969; Shaw, 1973; King and Levine, 1993; Levine and Zervos, 1998; Mohtadi and Agarwal, 2001; Levine, 2001; 1996; and de la Torre and Schmukler, 2007).

The CARICOM region, which is a grouping of 15 Caribbean states[1], has had stock exchanges since 1969 in some of its member states. In this chapter, three exchanges are singled out for attention because they are the most developed in the CARICOM region: the Barbados Stock Exchange (BSE), the Jamaica Stock Exchange (JSE), and the Trinidad and Tobago Stock Exchange (TTSE). Currently, there are ten stock exchanges and seven bond markets in existence within the wider Caribbean.[2] While they have made strides, they are still embryonic when compared to developed markets such as the New York Stock Exchange (NYSE) (see Sebastian, 1989 and Pemberton *et al.*, 2004). The markets do not offer investors the required levels of liquidity to make them attractive. Additionally, there is evidence of a pervasive culture within the Caribbean business community that views equity financing as a last resort.

The idea of a single CARICOM stock exchange has received attention. The Grand Anse Declaration of 1989 first enunciated the concept, which is viewed by some as a vital component of the regional integration process. It is not yet a physical entity, although steps have been taken towards its implementation. There exists, in particular, a Caribbean Exchange Network (CXN), based on an electronic trading platform that allows for simultaneous real-time securities trading on the three stock exchanges. By November 2008, US$150,000 were invested into the CXN by the

BSE, the JSE and the TTSE (Yarde, 2008). Additionally, the three exchanges have also taken steps towards regulatory harmonization. However, there are mixed views on whether the establishment of the single stock exchange is best suited for regional development.

The state of development of the CARICOM Exchanges is compared to selected benchmark markets:[3] the New York Stock Exchange (NYSE), the London Stock Exchange (LSE), the Singapore Stock Exchange (SGX), the Oslo Børs (OB) of Norway, the Johannesburg Stock Exchange (JBSE) of South Africa and the BM&FBOVESPA of Brazil. Relevant market ratios and indicators are used to highlight important areas such as market size, depth and liquidity, as well as risk and return.

The remainder of this chapter is structured as follows. There follows a review of some background material and stylized facts related to equity markets in emerging economies, in particular to the three CARICOM equity markets. This is followed by sections on data and methodology, empirical analysis, policy recommendations and lessons for other small emerging economies and, finally, a section that concludes.

2 Background and stylized facts

Stock markets in the CARICOM region

Stock exchanges in the CARICOM region are relatively new when compared to developed markets (like the NYSE and the LSE). The first, the Jamaica Stock Exchange (JSE), was not established until 1969. The Trinidad and Tobago Stock Exchange (TTSE) followed in July 1970 as a matter of policy to localize the foreign owned commercial banking and manufacturing sectors of the economy. The thrust of the policy was to get such companies to divest and sell a majority of their shares to nationals.[4] The Barbados Stock Exchange (BSE) first opened its doors, and later re-incorporated on August 2, 2001 with the enactment of the Securities Act 2001–13, which repealed and replaced the original Act of 1982.

There is now a total of seven exchanges in the CARICOM region, but only the Eastern Caribbean Stock Exchange (ECSE) comes close to matching the size of the three major regional exchanges in terms of market capitalization.[5] Even so, it continues to be overshadowed by the BSE, the JSE and the TTSE.

The Barbados Stock Exchange

Craigwell and Murray (1998) analysed the capital structure of firms on the BSE to determine the factors that influence the choices that firms make between debt and equity financing. They concluded that the more established firms in Barbados preferred debt financing as postulated by Myers (1984) in his pecking order theory. Additionally, the stock market had yet to establish itself as a viable source of capital financing and that the investment had not risen according to expectations in proportion to the country's Gross Domestic Product. There were hidden factors to be addressed that hindered the market's development. They also argued for modifying the market's structure to promote the required confidence for future growth; and subscribed to James' (1996) view that inefficiency in the market could undermine the financial system, thereby increasing capital costs. This was a warning that inefficiency in the BSE may have dire repercussions for the economic prospects of the country including lower investment, cutbacks in production capacity, higher unemployment, a decreased incentive for innovation and recession. Haynes (1997) reports that, as at the end of 1995, only 18 companies were listed on the exchange (that figure has since risen to 23) and that investors closely hold the shares. The volume of transactions averaged 47 per month, compared to 53 in 1991 (its peak year) and 33 in 1988 (its first full year of operations).

The Jamaica Stock Exchange

The literature on the JSE is a bit more abundant. Kitchen (1986) intimated that the JSE was 'a quiet backwater, very much on the fringe of the financial sector', while Jackson (1986) wrote that 'the stock market is an integral part of the mobilization of long-term capital in Jamaica'. Jackson supported this assertion through tables on three key indicators of stock market development. From a closing value of 41.59 on December 1978, the JSE Market Index began an upward trend (at first gradually) until it eventually reached a high of 1,491.87 in December 1986. This represents a staggering increase of 3,487.09% over a nine-year period! Jackson also reported that the volume of stocks traded had fluctuated over the same period. During the period 1978–1983, trading fluctuated cyclically, with downturns occurring in 1979, 1981 and 1983, followed immediately by upswings in years 1980, 1982 and 1984. From 1984; however, the volume of stocks traded continued its upward trend and reached its high of 50,841,000 during 1986. Consequently, the value of the stocks traded also displayed a cyclical pattern throughout the same period. It is interesting to note that the JSE experienced growth during 1984 and 1985, despite the fact that there was a major devaluation of the Jamaican dollar, relatively high inflation and contraction in consumption in many areas of the economy.

Jackson (1986), Kitchen (1986) and Koot et al. (1989) point to a number of structural changes in the JSE over the period 1983–1984 that allowed for the development of an efficient market, including a large number of new investors, a large increase in trading (both in volume and in value), a more effective use of information by market agents and a tendency for stock prices to more readily reflect important market information. Batchelor et al. (1997) highlight the objectives and operational aspects of the market and delineate the exchange's evolution from 1986 to 1996. They note that growth in market capitalization is much more pronounced than in the number of listings and that the JSE was the region's best performer in 1992 in terms of growth in the market index.

The Trinidad and Tobago Stock Exchange

Bourne (1998) notes that stock ownership in Trinidad and Tobago was highly concentrated, resulting in a stock market of limited size due to factors such as low personal incomes; relative financial naïveté among the general population; and a strong preference towards 'cheap' commercial bank credit. This preference is further enhanced by the fact that many established enterprises are usually guaranteed a ready supply of bank credit because of credit criteria and partly because of interlocking directorates.

Another factor highlighted is the great reluctance to dilute family ownership, which would result in relinquishing control of family-owned firms due to the strong preference towards commercial bank credit among firms and the reluctance to dilute family ownership. The desire to minimize public availability of information about company operations, finance and profitability and 'the small size and limited investment horizons of many local businesses' in less developed countries are also highlighted as significant factors limiting the size of the TTSE and its trading. Finally, Bourne observes that the markets are narrow and thin based on the criteria of volume of transactions, the number of market participants and the degree of price volatility.

Forde et al. (1997) observed the development of an extremely buoyant market, especially at the time of its inception. This buoyancy was fuelled by the government's divestment programme during that time and a willingness by investors to pay high premia in order to capitalize on opportunities. However, the creation of the TTSE did not result in any substantial mobilization of new investment funds. During the period 1982–1986, $52.6 million in new capital was raised, two-thirds of which was raised in its first year of operation. From 1986 to 1995, there was a total of four new issues, and all of these occurred during the period 1991–1995. Forde *et al.* (1997) also note that the TTSE was established at the same time of a major economic downturn following the Oil Boom of 1973–1981, which did not help its fortunes.

The TTSE's strength in 1996 was the high liquidity in the financial system, which forced the depression of bank deposit interest rates and enhanced the stock market's attractiveness. Wainwright Iton noted in a 2008 interview that it was extremely challenging to inveigle private enterprises to list (Burnett, 2008). Watson (2009) notes, however, that market capitalization in the BSE, the JSE and the TTSE, though by no means large even by emerging market standards (as noted in Robinson, 2001), grew phenomenally over the lifetime of the exchanges. This growth was most evident since the 1990s.

Characteristics of the Caribbean stock exchanges

Sergeant (2006) observes that the regional stock exchanges are illiquid compared with exchanges in other jurisdictions, which may be partly explained by the relatively limited range of investment offerings available. Robinson (2005) postulates that the presence of inefficiency in the JSE may be causing uninformed investors to be hesitant to participate in the stock market adversely affecting the market's depth and liquidity. Lorde *et al.* (2009) view market liquidity on the CARICOM markets as being low by international standards.

Craigwell and Murray (1998) summarized the state of the markets as follows:

> The major stock markets in the region, Barbados, Trinidad and Jamaica, are undoubtedly still in their development stage. The three still display the characteristics of emerging markets. The total market capitalisation is relatively small, a very small number of stocks dominate trading, stock ownership is highly concentrated...

Much of this may still be valid in 2017, the time of the writing of this chapter.

3 Data and methodology

The analysis uses the available annual data from the stock exchanges' websites and other statistical databases, such as the World Bank Global Indicators database and the World Federation of Exchanges statistics section. The variables used in the analysis are: a) the composite market indices for the BSE, the JSE and the TTSE, b) volume of shares traded, c) value of shares traded and d) the number of listings at each exchange.

These statistics are then compared with corresponding figures from 1990–2010 for the following six stock exchanges: NYSE, LSE, SGX, BM&FBOVESPA, JBSE and OB. The NYSE and the LSE represent benchmarks by which all markets are judged while the remaining three exchanges represent emerging exchanges. The data provides visual evidence of trends occurring within the markets.

The methodologies used by Haynes (1997), Jackson (1986), Kitchen (1986) and Sergeant (1995) are replicated here since this chapter is partly an update of these works. Additionally, the four market indicators, recommended by Yartey and Adjasi (2007), are employed to determine the levels of stock market development for each exchange,[6] including the number of company listings, market capitalization as a percentage of Gross Domestic Product, the value of shares traded as a percentage of Gross Domestic Product and the turnover rate.[7] The number of listed companies and the turnover rates are well-known measures of stock market size and growth, and are indicative of management's success in achieving administrative and operational objectives. The value of shares traded as a percentage of the Gross Domestic Product is a measure of the population's propensity to invest in equities and may also provide insight into the risk tolerance profile and financial sophistication of the population.

The holding period return (HPR) is calculated to develop a return profile from the data collected. The HPR is determined using a methodology similar to Hallerbach (2003) which combines the 'discretely compounded price return' (capital appreciation or 'price relative') and the 'discretely compounded dividend yield' to estimate the 'discretely compounded total return' ('value relative'). The capital appreciation, p_t as well as the dividend yield, y_t over the period t are defined by equations (1) and (2), respectively:

$$1 + p_t = \frac{PI_t}{PI_{t-1}} \tag{1}$$

where and represent the price index at the end of period t and t − 1, respectively.

$$y_t = \frac{D_t}{PI_{t-1}} \tag{2}$$

where D_t is the cash dividend paid at the end of period t. The combination of the two equations results in the total return as denoted by:

$$1 + r_t = 1 + p_t + y_t = (1 + p_t)(1 + d_t) \tag{3}$$

where d_t denotes the dividend ratio:

$$d_t = \frac{y_t}{1 + p_t} = y_t \left(\frac{PI_{t-1}}{PI_t} \right) = \frac{D_t}{PI_t} \tag{4}$$

Ideally, the dividend yield aspect of the HPR, calculated in both Sergeant (1995) and Hallerbach (2003), should also be included. However, the focus is placed on capital appreciation in this chapter. Even an abridged version of the HPR represents an important aspect of the regional stock market development as it allows comparisons of the rates of return for each market so that informed investment decisions are made when determining investment portfolio strategies and allocations. It becomes decidedly more useful when combined with fundamental and technical investment analysis techniques.

An additional indicator of market return calculated in this chapter was the Sharpe Ratio.

The Sharpe Ratio is also known as the reward-to-variability ratio (Sharpe 1966). It has been used by fund managers to determine the excess return of an investment portfolio. It is defined as 'a measure of the excess return (or Risk Premium) per unit of risk in an investment asset or a trading strategy.' It is calculated as follows:

$$Sharpe\ Ratio = \left(\frac{Asset's\ rate\ of\ return - Risk\text{-}free\ return\ rate}{Standard\ deviation\ of\ asset's\ rate\ of\ return} \right) \tag{5}$$

Volatility is usually measured as the standard deviation of the continuously compounded returns of a financial instrument with a specific time horizon. The measure is often used to quantify the risk of the instrument over that period. The generalized volatility for time horizon T in years is denoted by the formula:

$$\sigma_t = \sigma\sqrt{T} \tag{6}$$

σ is equal to the standard deviation of the index over the period and T is the number of years in question

4 Empirical analysis

Market size

Number of company listings

The empirical data suggests that not much has changed as deficiencies such as a lack of market depth and liquidity still exist. The three exchanges have not attracted many new listings over the years. The JSE has only just begun to inch closer to its high of 51 listings of 1995 with a mean of 43 and a standard deviation of 5. Indeed, the JSE has had many more de-listings than listings despite achieving an absolute increase (of 11) in its listings throughout its lifespan.

The BSE and the TTSE have not fared any better. The BSE's listings increased from 12 in 1987 to 25 in 2010 while the TTSE's rose from 32 in 1981 to 39 in 2010. The average number of companies listed on the BSE is 20 with a standard deviation of 5, as compared to the TTSE's 30 and 5, respectively. The BSE's maximum number of listings of 27 was achieved in 2006 while the TTSE achieved its maximum of 38 in 2009. Further, both exchanges have had difficulty in surpassing their high limit markers: the TTSE has yet to surpass 40 listings while the BSE has not surpassed the 30 mark. Even the JSE has had difficulty in this regard as it has only surpassed the 50-listings mark three times in its over 40 years of existence. Figure 10.1 shows the number of listings over the period 1969–2010 for the three exchanges.

Clearly, work needs to be done in attracting firms onto the stock exchanges which becomes clearer when comparisons are made with the benchmarks (see Appendix 1). The regional exchanges are woefully undersized in comparison but perform reasonably well on the when the growth rates in company listings are compared. The BSE have an average growth rate of 3.57% from 1990 to 2010 with only the SGX and the OB having higher rates. The TTSE's average growth rate of 1.22% is slightly lower than the NYSE (1.78%) but is higher than the LSE's

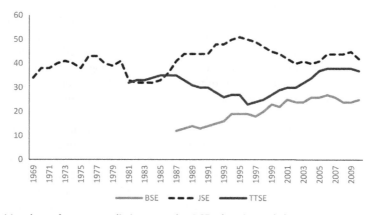

Figure 10.1 Number of company listings on the BSE, the JSE and the TTSE, 1969–2010

Table 10.1 Average growth rate in the number of company listings, 1969–2010

Market	Growth rate (%)
BSE (1989–2010)	3.57
JSE (1969–2010)	−0.15
TTSE (1981–2010)	1.22
SGX (1990–2010)	7.99
BM&FBOVESPA (1990–2010)	−1.96
OB (1990–2010)	3.82
JBSE (1990–2010)	−2.97
NYSE (1990–2010)	1.78
LSE (1990–2010)	0.33

Source: Authors' calculations from market data.

(0.33%). BM&FBOVESPA, the JSE and JBSE all recorded negative growth rates during that period. Table 10.1 below provides a summary:

One possible obstacle is the minimum listing requirements for each exchange and its associated costs. There are also those expenses that are associated with the adherence to the exchanges' reporting standard regulations. These may all prove to be formidable deterrents to a company, especially the small and medium-sized one, which is seeking new capital for expansion projects. The management of these companies may find it is easier to acquire bank financing for their projects.

Volume of shares traded

The volume of shares traded on the JSE rose from 7,450,000 in 1969 to 2,641,537,840 by the end of 2010; an increase of 35,357%. The estimated annual average percentage increase over the lifetime of the JSE is 54.5%, with trading gains in 25 out of the 42 years. Trading over the period 2000–2010 is characterized as one of growth and instability for the JSE with fluctuating volumes of trading activity. The market still managed an impressive 280% increase from its 2000 total, which was achieved in spite of the country's financial sector meltdown in 1997 as well as the onset of the global financial crisis in 2008.

Similarly, the TTSE has seen its volume traded increase from 16,100,000 in 1980 to a high of 436,467,500 in 2003. Since then, the TTSE's volumes have steadily declined with trading in 2010 being 77,562,330, an 82% decline. Overall, the TTSE expanded its trading volume by 382% since its inception and the annual average percentage change was 27.1%, with increases in trading volumes experienced in 14 out of the 31 years. The lower volumes may indicate that the TTSE may be less prone to speculative trading and, consequently, be less volatile than the JSE.

Trading volumes on the BSE have fluctuated wildly from an initial trading volume of 1,536,900 in 1987. Trading has been marked by intermittent periods of growth and decline. In 2002, the BSE experienced a massive trading volume of 514,495,800 shares while trading in the first half of 2009 (2,918,458) was relatively muted when compared to the relatively heavy volumes experienced in 2007 (154,894,700) and 2008 (71,832,300). Trading volume increased in both the latter half of 2009 and in 2010. A number of companies were the targets of take-overs in 2007 and 2008, which may explain the elevated volumes. The drastic drop-off in trading volume for the half-year in 2009 may be the result of investors becoming risk-averse due to the global recession at that time. The improved second half performance in 2009 may most likely have resulted from increased optimism that the world economy was recovering from the recession.

Overall, the region recorded total trading volume of 45,624,696,800 shares from 1969 to 2010. There is a vast disparity between the three regional equity markets in terms of the lifetime average trading volumes. The JSE experienced more extensive trading volumes when compared to the other two exchanges.

Market capitalization

Figure 10.2 below shows market capitalization growth on the three exchanges from their inceptions to 2010. It provides evidence of some degree of volatility in the growth rates which mirror each other, except during the 1999–2000 period when the BSE was the only subject market to contract. The other two markets simply had a slowdown in the growth rate, which could be explained by the number of listings and de-listings that occurred. Another possible explanation may be the economic fortunes of the listed companies, its home base and its export markets. As these fluctuated over time, so did the market prices for the listed securities.

This may be especially true for Jamaica that has suffered socio-economic instability and currency devaluations. The TTSE was arguably a 'victim of poor timing' as some turbulent events occurred during its nascent years. Firstly, it came into being just as the economy entered a decade-long recession, following the oil boom of 1973–81. The recession resulted in a period of strict fiscal discipline (1986–1991) which included a wage cut and freeze for public servants and the introduction of the Value Added Tax. These events, combined, may have severely restricted the population's ability to save and disincentivized them from investing in the fledgling equity market. The lack of market progress may have been compounded even further by the coup attempt in July 1990. One could imagine that the political instability experienced during that time severely hampered the growth prospects of the TTSE. Ironically, the TTSE's market capitalization increased by 152% in 1990 which contradicts the literature (such as Erb

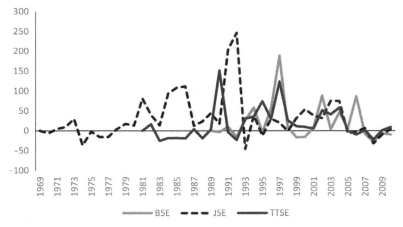

Figure 10.2 Growth in market capitalization, BSE, JSE and TTSE, 1969–2010
Source: Authors' calculations based on data from the stock exchanges' websites.

et al. 1996) that a high level of political risk within a country negatively impacts market development.

The BSE's instability stems from a dependence on tourism. When developed countries experience economic downturns, the revenues for many of the BSE's listed companies are adversely affected by cut-backs in tourist spending. Potential capital gains appreciation and the revenue streams/profitability of the listed companies were negatively impacted. This is highly evident in the case of Cave Shepherd & Co. Limited which experienced lower revenues and profits in 2009 and 2010 than the years prior to the financial crisis (2007 and 2008).

All three economies were severely affected by the global financial meltdown as each market recorded declines in 2008. The TTSE and the BSE posted smaller declines in capitalization than the JSE The market capitalization for the JSE and the TTSE both posted gains in 2010 while the BSE's capitalization fell by a further 9.9% (see Figure 10.2).

The Market Capitalization Ratio (MCR) has been referred to as the 'Buffett Indicator',[8] and also shows the relative significance of the stock exchange to its national economy (see Demirgüç-Kunt and Levine, 1996; Sergeant and Stephen, 2006; and Yartey, 2008). Sergeant, and Stephen (2006) noted that the MCR would have a theoretical value of 100%, if a stock exchange accounts for all of the domestic production. Non-domestic production would then account for MCRs that were in excess of the benchmark while unaccounted domestic production would result in MCRs lower than 100%.

The regional markets had a collective lifetime average MCR of 54%, well below the 100% benchmark. In particular, the JSE and the TTSE have underperformed which suggest that these markets were undervalued. This is particularly troubling for the TTSE as it resides in arguably one of the stronger regional economies. A possible explanation for the TTSE's low ratio may be the fact that there are no company listings from its economy's energy sector, its main source of revenue.[9]

The BSE maintained an average MCR of 96.6%, just slightly short of the benchmark. Indeed, the regional exchanges experienced recent improvements in their MCRs. The JSE achieved its all-time high MCR of 165.9% in 2004 while the TTSE and the BSE achieved theirs in 2004 and 2006 respectively with MCRs of 129.8% and 321.5%.[10]

The global financial crisis had a significant impact on the MCR in the CARICOM region. The value at the JSE declined from 102.95% in 2007 to 47.04% in 2010, and the TTSE's MCR from 71.8% to 57.2%. During the same timeframe, the BSE's MCR declined from 276.6% in 2007 to 133.04% in 2010.

The MCRs of the CARICOM exchanges outperformed those of the BM&FBOVESPA and Norwegian markets but were, however, outperformed by the SGX and the JBSE. Interestingly, the three regional exchanges' ratios compared favourably with those of the NYSE and the LSE with the BSE achieving higher MCRs since 2002. The JSE and the TTSE's ratios lagged slightly behind those of the NYSE and the LSE, but the disparity was not overwhelming.

Market depth and liquidity

Market turnover ratio

Historically, the regional exchanges each suffered from low market turnover rates. Low market turnover ratios have afflicted the BSE, which the ratio averaging 3.68% during the period 1989

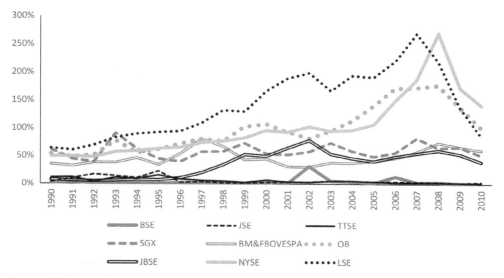

Figure 10.3 Market turnover ratios
Source: Authors' calculations based on market data from the regional stock exchanges and the World Federation of Stock Exchanges.

to 2010. There were significant spikes in the ratios that occurred in 2002 and 2006,[11] which results in an adjusted average turnover ratio of 1.82%.

In comparison, the JSE was 'a montage of peaks and valleys' during 1969 to 1996 with little variance afterwards. There was little market liquidity especially within the decade 2001 to 2010 with an all-time low of 0.57% recorded in 2009. The JSE's market turnover from 1969 to 2010 averaged 5.9%.

The TTSE's market turnover averaged 7.3% from 1981 to 2010. Its ratios for 2009 and 2010 suggest that the local equity market suffered from the global financial crisis and the resulting recession. Investor confidence was also affected as evidenced by the erosion of capital gains the last economic boom achieved. Figure 10.3 below gives a clearer picture of how the CARICOM markets compare in terms of market turnover and they are extremely illiquid based on the evidence.

The LSE, the OB and the NYSE have the highest average market turnover ratios among the selected benchmark markets. Surprisingly, the average for the OB was higher than the NYSE's. The average turnover ratio for the six benchmarks from 1990–2010 (79.3%) is approximately 14 times larger than a similar ratio calculated for the three CARICOM exchanges (5.61%). This is revealing about the illiquidity in the latter.

Ratio of value of shares traded to Gross Domestic Product

The regional markets' ratios suggest that stock market investment does not factor prominently into the majority of financial decisions as evidenced by each market's average ratio being under 10%. When compared with the benchmark markets over the period 1990–2010, the three CARICOM stock markets were dwarfed by all.

Among the benchmark markets, BM&FBOVESPA registered the lowest average ratio over the timeframe while the LSE and the SGX had the highest ratios. Indeed, the LSE had ratios

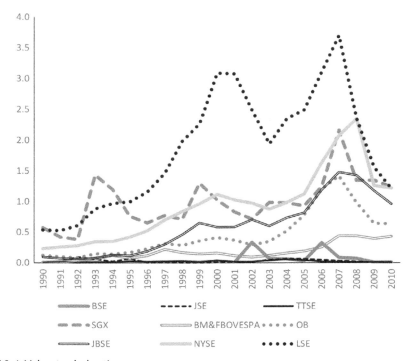

Figure 10.4 Value traded ratios
Source: Authors' calculations based on market data from the regional stock exchanges and the World Federation of Stock Exchanges.

of over 100% since 1996. The NYSE has an average ratio of 92.92%, which ranks third among the selected markets. Figure 10.4 below shows that BM&FBOVESPA had similar ratios to those of the three Caribbean markets in 1990 but reached 44.91% by December 2008. Perhaps a look at the strategies implemented by the Brazilian authorities can provide an operational model that can be followed by the Managers of the CARICOM exchanges (see Figure 10.4).

Market risk and return

Stock market returns

Figure 10.5 shows the cyclical pattern up until 1978 at the JSE can be clearly seen. After 1978, its market return pattern became more jagged, which could be because the JSE was becoming more volatile perhaps as a result of the changing preferences of the market makers. It could also be evidence of market inefficiency as noted by Koot *et al.* (1989) and Agbeyegbe (1994). The TTSE and the BSE have similar return patterns throughout their respective lifetimes. From 1993, all three markets mirrored each other in their index movements which may suggest that financial integration may be occurring within the region.

Table 10.2 below shows that BM&FBOVESPA is clearly the best performer. Interestingly, both the JSE and the TTSE outperformed all the other markets for each of the time periods highlighted in the information notes of Table 10.2 below. Both the JSE and the TTSE each had the highest

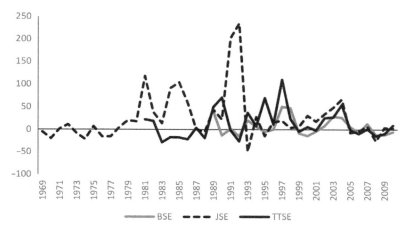

Figure 10.5 Market returns
Source: Authors' calculations based on data collected from the stock exchanges.

average market return during the period (1990–2001) with figures of 43.2% and 25.2%, respectively. Of special interest is the fact that all three CARICOM stock markets achieved higher average returns than those of the NYSE and the FTSE (London) All Share Indices.

Sharpe Ratio

Preliminary evidence shows little movement in the Sharpe Ratios, especially for the JSE where its ratios also clustered around zero as shown in Tables 10.3 and 10.4 below. In 1977, the JSE experienced an 'aberration' with a ratio of −162.98.[12] As a result, the average Sharpe Ratio (from 1969–2010) with its inclusion was −2.95. The outlier's exclusion results in an average ratio of 0.94, which is higher than the 0.75 benchmark.

The average Sharpe Ratio for the TTSE from 1981–2010 was −1.28. The TTSE experienced three years in which its Sharpe Ratio spiked over (and under) its traditional range: 1983, 1985 (a significant drop to −40.76) and 2003. The exclusion of these three years shows the TTSE with a Sharpe ratio of −0.23. Besides those three years, the TTSE's pattern closely resembles that of the JSE.

Surprisingly, the BSE was the only stock market with a positive ratio (1.04) attributable to the spikes in 1998 and 2004. Their exclusion show the BSE possessing a ratio of −0.60. Table 10.4 shows that the BSE's Sharpe Ratio also fluctuated around zero like its two Caribbean counterparts. It can therefore be deduced that investors would possess portfolios that performed better than the relatively safe U.S. 90-day Treasury bond if they invested in equities from the JSE and the BSE while a portfolio of TTSE-listed stocks arguably underperformed.

Tables 10.3 and 10.4 reveal possible regional stock market integration. The literature, which supports the use of the Sharpe Ratio as evidence of integration, is readily available. Table 10.4 shows that the TTSE and the BSE almost mirror each other during 2005–2010, while the JSE only differs from these two markets by an infinitesimal amount. The ratios of the regional markets are relatively much smaller as compared to those of the benchmarks albeit with a few exceptions during the period 1991–2010. The data suggests that the regional markets all outperformed the U.S. 90-day Treasury bill during this time frame.

Table 10.2 Annual market returns (exclusive of dividends)

Year	BSE	JSE	TTSE	SGX	BM&FBOVESPA	OB (a)	OB (b)	JBSE	NYSE	LSE
1990	-13.2	22.3	70.7	-36.8	N/A	-13.5	–	N/A	-7.5	N/A
1991	1.6	202.5	-1.6	28.2	N/A	-9.4	–	26.5	27.1	15.1
1992	-15.4	235.2	-26.4	2.1	N/A	-10	–	-5.3	4.7	14.8
1993	19.9	-49.1	37	68.2	N/A	64.8	–	50.1	7.9	23.4
1994	6.3	27.3	7.5	-11.2	N/A	7.1	–	19.9	-3.1	-9.6
1995	-5.4	-14.5	69.6	3.4	N/A	11.6	–	6.2	31.3	18.5
1996	-0.03	16.5	11.4	3.9	N/A	32.1	28.9	6.9	19.1	11.7
1997	50.5	19.4	110.4	-24.3	N/A	31.5	29.3	-6.8	30.3	19.7
1998	47.6	3.8	23.9	-7.6	N/A	-26.7	-28.4	-12.4	16.6	10.9
1999	-8.4	6.3	-4.3	78	N/A	45.5	46	57.3	9.2	21.3
2000	-14.2	30.9	5.8	-22.3	N/A	-1.7	1.1	-2.5	1	-8
2001	-4.1	18.1	-1.7	-15.7	N/A	-17.2	-16.2	25.4	-10.2	-15.4
2002	8	34.4	25.7	-17.4	-17	–	-32.7	-11.2	-19.8	-25
2003	29	48.5	27.2	31.6	97.3	–	42.5	12	28.8	16.6
2004	26.4	66.9	54.8	17.1	17.8	–	32	21.9	12.6	9.2
2005	5.8	-7.2	-0.7	13.6	27.7	–	34.2	43	7	18.1
2006	-6.8	-3.7	-9.2	27.2	32.9	–	28.4	37.7	17.9	13.2
2007	12.6	7.2	1.3	16.6	43.7	–	8.1	16.2	6.6	2

Table 10.2 (continued)

Year	BSE	JSE	TTSE	SGX	BM&FBOVESPA	OB		JBSE	NYSE	LSE
						(a)	(b)			
2008	-11.9	-25.8	-14.2	-49.4	-41.2	–	-55.7	-25.7	-40.9	-32.8
2009	-6.9	0.9	-7.5	32.5	37.1	–	83.5	2.5	2.6	-1.7
2009	-11.9	4	-9.2	64.5	82.7	–	60.1	28.6	24.8	25
2010	-5.2	2.3	9.2	10.1	1	–	14.2	16.1	10.8	10.9
Avg. A	5.3	30.7	18.4	8.6	193.3	N/A	N/A	N/A	8.3	N/A
Avg. B	6.2	31.2	15.8	10.8	187.6	N/A	N/A	15.2	9.1	7
Avg. C	5.4	43.2	25.2	5.5	318	9.5	N/A	N/A	10.5	N/A
Avg. D	6.9	13.9	13.9	9.9	30.5	N/A	17.2	13.1	7.3	4.7
Avg. E	1.7	14.7	6.8	9	21.7	N/A	16.6	13.7	3.4	1

Table 10.3 Sharpe Ratios, 1991–2010)

Jurisdiction	Ratio	Jurisdiction	Ratio
BSE	1.11	OB TI	0.37
JSE	1.63	OB BPI	0.13
TTSE	1.14	JBSE	0.5
SGX	0.2	NYSE	0.28
BM&FBOVESPA	0.33	LSE	0.18

Market volatility

The market volatility measures[13] confirm that the JSE was the most volatile while the BSE was the lowest of the three: the JSE was 2.31, the BSE 0.84 and the TTSE 1.46. A comparison for the period (1989–2010) provides some interesting results. The JSE (1.89) and the Bo Vespa (1.81) were the most volatile while the BSE (0.84), the NYSE (0.87) and the FTSE (0.83) are among the lowest. The TTSE's Composite Index (1.22) compares favourably with OB's Total (0.94) and Benchmark (1.17) Indices, although SGX's Strait Times Index, OB's All Share Index, as well as FTSE/JBSE's All Share Index each possess higher volatility measures.

Table 10.5 again shows that the JSE was the most volatile as investors routinely had the opportunity to earn returns of nearly 10% on their investments prior to 2000 but were also likely to lose their gains the next day! Meanwhile, a look at the BSE shows a market that was largely inactive and is among the least volatile stock markets among those studied in this chapter.

The three regional stock markets each went through moments of convulsion[14] which usually dissipated quickly and equilibrium restored. The Bo Vespa Index possessed the widest range of volatility in its market returns (between +50% and − 250%), which suggests that it is the riskiest market among the benchmarks. However, it has become more settled since that precipitous decline in the late 1990s. The regional markets' ranges of volatility are like those of the remaining benchmark markets.

5 Policy recommendations and lessons for small developing states

Policy recommendations

There are various avenues for improvement. Firstly, the various administrations need to widen their products offerings. Feasibility studies into the introduction of options, derivatives, and futures contract trading are necessary. There needs to be greater collaboration between the various administrations and the government by first encouraging the divestment of State Enterprises onto the Stock Exchange, especially holdings held within the energy sector. Secondly, the establishment of various fiscal policies (e.g. tax moratoriums for listing and tax credits and/or allowances for individuals that have invested in the Stock Exchange) would make the stock market more attractive.

Executives should also establish strategic alliances with more developed markets. One such example is the reported alliance between the TTSE and the Toronto Stock Exchange. This should provide regional investors with access to a wider range of investment options if it ever comes to fruition. There is also a need to encourage regional conglomerates to cross-list on the regional stock exchanges.

Table 10.4 Sharpe Ratios, 1990–2010

Year	BSE	JSE	TTSE	SGX	BM&FBOVESPA	OB (a)	OB (b)	JBSE	NYSE	LSE
1990	-0.53	1.01	4.42	-0.36		-0.47			-0.8	
1991	-0.24	1.56	-0.11	0.28	4.2	-0.5		1.01	1.29	0.67
1992	-1.55	10.04	-1.69	0.02	1.84	2.13		-0.42	0.03	0.65
1993	0.68	-0.26	0.76	0.68	-0.09	0.11		2.09	0.21	1.17
1994	0.07	0.4	0.09	-0.11	0.02	0.26		0.72	-0.4	-0.83
1995	-1.28	-0.66	1.47	0.03	-0.01	0.99		0.09	1.53	0.88
1996	-1.31	0.53	0.16	0.04	0.11	0.97	0.75	0.13	0.84	0.46
1997	1.27	6.78	1.5	-0.24	0.07	-1.08	0.76	-0.49	1.47	0.95
1998	20.79	-0.06	0.32	-0.08	-0.07	1.46	-0.98	-0.75	0.7	0.42
1999	-0.34	0.62	-0.48	0.78	0.27	-0.2	1.27	2.41	0.28	1.04
2000	-4.82	1.45	-0.002	-0.22	-0.03		-0.09	-0.3	-0.17	-0.73
2001	-0.8	1.81	-0.64	-0.16	-0.03		-0.61	0.97	-0.8	-1.18
2002	0.8	2.87	1.27	-0.17	-0.04		-1.11	-0.69	-1.34	-1.76
2003	1.89	4.77	23.51	0.32	0.17		1.16	0.36	1.39	0.76
2004	12.74	4.98	2.7	0.17	0.02		0.84	0.81	0.48	0.31
2005	0.13	-0.21	-0.12	0.14	0.04		0.91	1.76	0.16	0.85
2006	-1.3	-3.38	-2.33	0.27	0.05		0.74	1.52	0.77	0.55
2007	0.7	0.55	-0.22	0.17	0.07		0.12	0.55	0.14	-0.12
2008	-0.69	-1.11	-1.3	-0.49	-0.08		-1.81	-1.35	-2.52	-2.24
2009	-3.4	0.18	-2.68	0.64	0.14		1.7	1.11	1.16	1.27
2010	-1.13	1.77	0.69	0.1	-0.01		0.31	0.54	0.38	0.42

Table 10.5 Average daily volatility

Jurisdiction	Average daily change (%)	Maximum gain (%)	Maximum loss (%)
BSE Local Index (January 1999–December 2010)	0.005	23.97	−20.94
JSE Main Index (June 1987–December 2010)	0.078	21.45	−18.08
TTSE Composite Index (October 1981–December 2010)	0.059	21.75	−20.43
SGX Strait Times Index (January 1990–December 2010)	0.014	12.87	−9.22
BM&FBOVESPA BOVESPA Index (April 1993–December 2010)	0.129	28.83	−228.72
OB Total Index (January 1990–December 2001)	0.024	8.93	−9.21
OB Benchmark Index (December 1995–December 2010)	0.039	10.14	−10.48
JBSE FTSE/JSE (Africa) Index (June 2002–December 2010)	0.051	6.83	−7.58
NYSE Composite Index (January 1990–December 2010)	0.025	11.53	−10.23
LSE All Share Index (January 1990–December 2010)	0.017	8.81	−8.71

Source: Authors' calculations from market data.

The financial literacy program in Trinidad and Tobago is also a step in the right direction as it will educate the public about the range of available investment options. However, the deeply engrained culture of risk aversion is difficult to overcome. Thus, the program's benefits may not bear fruit until well into the future. There is no sure-fire path to stock market development as it is a matter of developing strategies that encourage greater company participation in the capital markets. Additionally, the creation of an attractive wealth creation vehicle easily accessed by a wider cross-section of the population is also crucial.

Some lessons for other small developing states

While the development of fair and efficient capital markets is an objective for most, there are questions about whether there are suitable for economic development in developing states. Singh (1993) argued that emerging economies should foster bank-based financial systems similar to those of Japan, Germany, and France in lieu of stock markets as these systems had *'a proven record of successfully promoting industrial development'*. He postulated that banks have the means and the incentive to collect the necessary information for monitoring management activities, thus taking a long-term view of firms' prospects. This was vital to encouraging industrialization in emerging economies (Singh, 1993: 23). Robinson (1952) argued that financial development does not promote economic growth but are merely responses to developments within the real sector. Levine and Zervos (1996) asked whether stock markets were merely 'burgeoning casinos' or were linked to economic growth. These are some examples within the literature that either deemphasizes the importance or, at the very least, highlights the negative impacts of stock markets on economic development.

This does not mean that all developing states should eschew the establishment of stock markets for Bank-based systems. Even Singh (1993) admitted that bank-based finance degenerated into *'inflationary/inefficient finance'* in countries with high macro-economic instability during the past two decades due to three main factors: (1) The prevalence of 'crony capitalism;'[15] (2) The development of monopolistic positions in product markets which can thwart new firm entry thereby hindering efficient industrial development; and (3) Imprudent or inadequate government regulation of the banks which can jeopardize the integrity of the financial system.[16] The literature on the positive links between stock market and economic development is just as abundant.

Policymakers in emerging economies must identify the objectives to be achieved with the type of financial system being implemented including advancing the industrialization process and wealth creation. Emerging economies should ask how stock markets help in the industrialization process and these questions have been identified for careful deliberation:

1 What are the channels through which the establishment of a stock market fosters economic and industrial development in a country?
2 How well do such channels operate in practice in countries which have well-functioning stock markets?
3 How are stock markets likely to function in the particular circumstances of emerging economies?
4 If stock markets are established, can the emerging economies avoid their negative effects as Zhao (1987) was suggesting?
5 Are there feasible alternatives to stock market-based financial systems? Will the emerging economies be better off with such alternatives systems? (Singh, 1993: 9).

Wealth creation for the population should be an important consideration by policymakers. Divestment of profitable state-owned corporations is an effective tool for improving incomes and a first step to be taken towards the development of that state's stock market.

The experiences of the CARICOM stock markets are divergent and can provide numerous insights for similar states now embarking on this process. One key area of concern even today is the illiquid states of many of the regional exchanges, which has resulted in thin trading environments. Risk aversion among the population will be an obstacle especially for those populations with no previous interactions with stock market investing. Finally, hesitation by family-owned/privately held companies to list is another important obstacle that policymakers will face. This will only improve through the fostering of measures which engender greater investor confidence and ensuring that any proposed fee framework for market access is not considered onerous and burdensome by prospective registrants.

Care must be taken in developing a healthy investment climate. Transparency, fairness and full disclosure must become vital characteristics in the regulatory process and, by extension, the equity markets. Regulators must also take an active role in clamping down on illegalities within their markets. The prevalence of insider trading and other market manipulation practices only result in deteriorating investor confidence, a greater divide in the wealth gap. We conclude by encouraging all interested parties wishing to establish stock markets to engage with the International Organization of Securities Commissions (IOSCO) to make use of the numerous resources at its disposal.

6 Conclusion

The CARICOM equity markets still suffer from inadequacies that hamper development. Lack of market liquidity and inadequate market size (as evidenced by low market turnover ratios and company listings) are serious hindrances to be addressed by the relevant authorities. Illiquidity in the markets only serves to discourage investors who may require more immediate access to their funds.

The dilemma of the small market sizes become increasingly exacerbated when one realizes that the listed companies mostly come from a limited range of industries. For example, Banking and Financial institutions represent almost one-third of the listings held on the TTSE with Manufacturing and Trading accounting for another 27%. While these may be safe investments, they may not whet the appetites of savvy investors. However, there have been some encouraging signs when one looks at the region's market capitalization ratios and (ex-dividend) returns. They compared favourably with many of the benchmark markets in these areas. There remains much to be done for there to be progress made.

Notes

1 The 15 Caribbean states comprising the CARICOM are Antigua and Barbuda, Bahamas, Barbados, Belize, Dominica, Haiti, Jamaica, Grenada, Guyana, Montserrat, St. Lucia, Suriname, St. Kitts and Nevis, St. Vincent and the Grenadines, and Trinidad and Tobago.
2 Existing stock exchanges are the Bahamas Stock Exchange, the Barbados Stock Exchange, the Bermuda Stock Exchange, Bolsa de Valores de la República Dominicana, the Cayman Islands Stock Exchange, the Eastern Caribbean Securities Exchange, the Guyana Stock Exchange, the Haitian Stock Exchange, the Jamaican Stock Exchange, the Latin American International Financial Exchange and the TTSE. Harripaul (2008) reports on the existence of bond markets in the Bahamas, Barbados, Belize, Dominican Republic, Jamaica, the OECS, and Trinidad and Tobago.
3 The Singapore Stock Exchange was chosen because Singapore is a prime example of how a Small Island Developing State (SIDS) can progress from a 'Third World, Developing' economy to Developed. The BM&FBOVESPA has also had success throughout its tenure, which may provide lessons to small stock exchanges such as those in the CARICOM region. The Oslo Børs and the Johannesburg Stock Exchange may also provide useful insights into the further development of CARICOM markets.
4 See the article on the TTSE's website entitled, 'History of the Trinidad Stock Exchange' – www.stockex.co.tt/stockex/about/profile.aspx.
5 Gitman and Joehnk (2004) defined market capitalization within the context of a firm but their definition can be broadened to the stock market.
6 These were used to evaluate the stages of development attained by a number of stock markets on the African continent.
7 This refers to the value of shares traded in a year as a percentage of the average market capitalization of each stock exchange.
8 The MCR is 'the best single measure of where valuations stand at any given moment'. See www.forbes.com/sites/robertlenzner/2014/02/22/the-stock-markets-valuation-is-at-a-dangerous-115-2-of-the-gdp/. Typically, a result of greater than 100% shows that the market is overvalued, while a value of around 50%, which is near the historical average for the U.S. market, shows undervaluation. However, the determination of the level for both undervaluation and overvaluation of the stock market has been hotly debated: www.investopedia.com/terms/m/marketcapgdp.asp#ixzz3gjDHwSNi.
9 This was at the time of writing. The Trinidad and Tobago NGL Limited was the exchange's first energy listing.
10 These maxim scenarios would have been argued to denote periods when these markets were overvalued if one was to use the 100% benchmark.
11 Its 2002 market turnover ratio spiked due to heavy mergers and acquisitions activity and the demutualization of Barbados Life Assurance Society to become Sagicor Life Inc: www.bse.com.bb/YearEnd/Pdf/Dec2002.pdf. The 2006 performance is attributable to increased mergers and acquisitions activity, such as Neal and Massy's purchase of Barbados Shipping and Trading Company.

12 This is attributable to the political and economic upheaval that occurred at the time. The Manley administration alienated foreign investors by nationalising large, privately held companies. Additionally, the violent clashes between supporters of the ruling People's National Party and the Jamaica Labour Party did not promote a conducive investment environment (McKenzie, 1987).
13 This is based on annual market return figures.
14 These occurred during 2002–2003 for the BSE; 1992–1993 for the JSE and April 1993 for the TTSE.
15 This occurs when the banks finance schemes of particular individuals and families with political connections, rather than promote long-term industrial development.
16 Singh provides the example of Chile following its exercise in financial liberalization during the early 1980s.

Appendix 1

Number of company listings (comparison)

Year	BSE	JSE	TTSE	Singa-pore	Brazil	Norway	South Africa	NYSE	London
1990	13	44	30	172	579	121	769	1,774	2,559
1991	14	44	30	182	570	112	728	1,989	2,572
1992	15	48	28	195	565	123	671	1,750	2,440
1993	16	48	26	216	551	135	631	1,945	2,412
1994	19	50	27	251	549	146	624	2,128	2,416
1995	19	51	27	272	544	165	638	2,242	2,502
1996	19	50	23	296	551	172	626	2,476	2,623
1997	18	49	24	334	545	217	642	2,626	2,513
1998	20	47	25	358	535	235	669	2,670	2,423
1999	23	45	27	408	487	215	658	3,025	2,274
2000	22	44	29	480	467	214	606	2,468	2,374
2001	25	42	30	492	441	212	532	2,400	2,332
2002	24	40	30	501	412	203	451	2,366	2,824
2003	24	41	32	560	391	178	411	2,308	2,692
2004	26	40	34	633	388	188	389	2,293	2,837
2005	26	41	37	686	381	219	373	2,270	3,091
2006	27	44	38	708	350	229	389	2,280	3,256
2007	26	44	38	762	404	248	411	2,297	3,307
2008	24	45	39	767	392	259	411	1,963	3,096
2009	24	45	38	773	386	238	396	2,327	2,792
2010	25	42	37	782	381	237	407	2,317	2,612

Source: Annual reports and the World Federation of Exchanges website, www.world-exchanges.org/home/index.php/statistics/annual-statistics/.

References

Agbeyegbe, T. (1994) (2015). 'Some Stylized facts about the Jamaican Stock Market'. *Social and Economic Studies*, 43(4): 143–156.

Batchelor, P., Foga, C., Lim, G.Sue and Panton, N. (1997). The Evolution of the Financial Sector in Jamaica (1970–1996). In Clarke, L. and Danns, D. (eds) *The Financial Evolution of the Caribbean Community*. St Augustine: Caribbean Centre for Monetary Studies, University of the West Indies: 408–482.

Bourne, C. (1998). Economic Aspects of the Trinidad & Tobago Stock Market. In Bourne, C. and Ramsaran, R. (ed.) *Money and Finance in Trinidad and Tobago*. Jamaica: Institute of Social & Economic Research, The University of the West Indies.

Burnett, V. (2008). 'Iton takes Charge as general manager, CEO at T&T Stock Exchange'. *Trinidad Business Guardian*, January 17: 4–5.

Craigwell, R. and Murray, A. (1998). *The determinants of the capital Structure of listed companies on the securities exchange of Barbados*. July. Central Bank of Barbados.

de la Torre, A. and Schmukler, S. (2007). *Emerging Markets and Globalization: The Latin American Experience*. Washington, DC: Stanford University Press for the World Bank.

Demirgüç-Kunt, A. and Levine, R. (1996). 'Stock Market Development and Financial Intermediaries: Stylized Facts'. *The World Bank Economic Review*, 10(2): 291–321.

Erb, C., Harvey, C. and Viskanta, T. (1996). *Emerging Stock Markets in Middle Eastern Countries*. World Bank Conference on Stock Markets, Corporate Finance and Economic Growth. Washington, DC: World Bank, February 16–17.

Forde, P., Joseph, A., Bruce, C., Nicholls, J., Seepersad, S., Swan-Daniel, A., DeSilva, S., Samuel, G., Rambaran, A. and Sargeant, K. (1997). Financial Evolution in Trinidad & Tobago. In Clarke, L. and Danns, D. (eds) *The Financial Evolution of the Caribbean Community*. St Augustine: Caribbean Centre for Monetary Studies, University of the West Indies: 407–482.

Gitman, L. and Joehnk, M. (2004). *Fundamentals of Investing*. Ninth edition. Boston, MA: Addisson Wesley.

Goldsmith, R. (1969). *Financial Structure and Development*. New Haven, Connecticut: Yale University Press.

Hallerbach, W. (2003). Holding Period Risk-Return Modelling: Ambiguity in Estimation. *Working Paper* No. 63, ERIM Report Series Reference.

Harripaul, A. (2008). *Caribbean Bond Markets – Characteristics, Recent Developments & Role of Ratings*. Paper presented at Caribbean Investor Conference. Hyatt Regency, Port-of-Spain, May 27–28.

Haynes, C. (1997). The Evolution of the Financial Sector in Barbados 1970–1996. In Clarke, L. and Danns, D. (eds) *The Financial Evolution of the Caribbean Community*. St Augustine: Caribbean Centre for Monetary Studies, University of the West Indies: 143–168.

Investopedia (2015). Stock Market Capitalization to GDP Ratio. Available at: www.investopedia.com/terms/m/marketcapgdp.asp#ixzz3gjDHwSNi. Accessed July 17, 2015.

Jackson, J. (1986). 'The Stock Market in the Caribbean: The Jamaican Experience'. *Caribbean Finance and Management*, 2(1): 61–68.

James, E. (1996). 'Providing better protection and promoting growth: A defence of "Averting the old age crisis"'. *International Securities Review*, 49(3): 3–17. Accessed August 15, 2008.

King, R. and Levine, R. (1993). 'Finance and Growth: Schumpeter may be right'. *The Quarterly Journal of Economics*, 108(3): 713–737.

Kitchen, R. (1986). 'The Role of the Jamaican Stock Exchange in the Capital Market: An Historical Analysis'. *Caribbean Finance and Management*, 2(2): 1–23.

Koot, R., Miles, J. and Heitmann, G. (1989). 'Security Risk and Market Efficiency in the Jamaican Stock Exchange'. *Caribbean Finance and Management*, 5(2): 18–33.

Levine, R. (1996). 'Stock Markets: A Spur to Economic Growth'. *Finance & Development*, 33: 7–10.

Levine, R. (2001). 'International Financial Liberalization and Economic Growth'. *Review of International Economics*, 9(4): 688–702.

Levine, R. and Zervos, S. (1996). 'Stock Market Development and Long-Run Growth'. *The World Bank Economic Review*, 10(2): 323–339.

Levine, R. and Zervos, S. (1998). 'Stock Markets, Banks and Economic Growth'. *American Economic Review*, 88(3): 537–558.

Lorde, T., Francis, B. and Greene, A. (2009). 'Testing for Long-Run Comovement, Common Features and Efficiency in Emerging Stock Markets: Evidence from the Caribbean'. *Economic Issues*, 14(2): 55–80.

McKenzie, A. (1987). 'Jamaicans Fuel a Skyrocketing Market'. *Black Enterprise*, December: 93–94.

Mohtadi, H. and Agarwal, S. (2001). *Stock Market Development and Economic Growth: Evidence from Developing Countries*. Minneapolis: University of Minnesota.

Myers, S. (1984). 'The Capital Structure Puzzle'. *The Journal of Finance*, 39(3): 575–592.

Pemberton, C., Vaugirard, V. and Watson, P. (2004). *Stock Market Indices in the CARICOM sub-region: Construction and Use*. The University of the West Indies, St Augustine – The Inaugural International Conference on Business, Banking and Finance. April 27–29.

Robinson, C. (2001). 'Stock Price Behaviour in a Small Emerging Market: Tests for Predictability and seasonality on the Barbados Stock Exchange'. *Savings and Development*, 25(1): 103–115.

Robinson, C. (2005). 'Stock Price Behaviour in Emerging Markets: Tests for Weak Form Market Efficiency on the Jamaica Stock Exchange'. *Social and Economic Studies*, 54(2): 51–69.

Robinson, J. (1952). The Generalization of the General Theory. In Robinson, J. (ed.) *The Rate of Interest and Other Essays*. London: Macmillan: 67–146.

Schumpeter, J. (1911). *A Theory of Economic Development*. Cambridge, MA: Harvard University Press.

Sergeant, K. (1995). The Trinidad and Tobago Stock Exchange: Market Performance and Suggestions for Further Development. In Ramsaran, R. (ed.) *Insights into an Emerging Financial Structure: The Experience of Trinidad & Tobago*. St Augustine: Caribbean Centre for Monetary Studies: 189–226.

Sergeant, K. (2006). *Issues in equities market development and integration*. Caribbean Connect: a high level symposium on the CARICOM Single Market and Economy. Barbados, CARICOM.

Sergeant, K. and Stephen, K. (2006). 'Securities Market Development in Trinidad and Tobago: Contemporary Issues and Challenges'. *Journal of Business, Finance and Economics in Emerging Economies*, 1(1): 1–22.

Sharpe, W. (1966). 'Mutual Fund Performance'. *Journal of Business*, 39(1): 119–138.

Shaw, E. (1973). *Financial Deepening in Economic Development*. Vol. 39. New York: Oxford University Press.

Singh, A. (1993). 'The stock market and economic development: should developing countries encourage stock markets?'. *UNCTAD Review*: 1–74. Accessed July 3, 2016.

Sebastian, S. B. J. (1989). 'The Role of the Securities Market in Mobilizing Resources for the Region'. *Social and Economic Studies*: 115–132.

Watson, P. (2009). 'The Efficiency of the Stock Market in the CARICOM Sub-region: An Empirical Study'. *Applied Financial Economics*, 19(23): 1915–1924.

Yarde, M. (2008). *Update on the Implementation of Caribbean Exchange Network (CXN)*. The Caribbean Group of Securities Regulators 5th Annual Conference). Barbados: The Caribbean Group of Securities Regulators, November 10–11.

Yartey, C. (2008). *The Determinants of Stock Market Development in Emerging Economies: Is South Africa Different?* International Monetary Fund Working Paper, No. 08/32 (February 2008). Washington, DC: International Monetary Fund.

Yartey, C. and Adjasi, C. K. (2007). *Stock Market Development in Sub-Saharan Africa: Critical Issues and Challenges*. International Monetary Fund Working Paper, No. 07/209 (August 2007). Washington, DC: International Monetary Fund.

Zhao, Z. (1987). *Report to the 13th National Congress of the Communist Party of China*. Congressional Report. Beijing: Beijing Review Publications.

11

Monetary transmission mechanisms in selected small island developing states with floating exchange rates

Wendell Samuel and Arina Viseth

1 Introduction

The aim of this study is to examine the effectiveness of the monetary transmission mechanism in the small states that have some amount of monetary policy independence. We examine, in particular, which policy instruments are used and which transmission channels or combination of channels are likely to be the most effective in transmitting policy changes to output and prices for relevant small states. For this purpose, we selected four small island developing states (SIDS)[1] in which the exchange rate regime is floating or managed floating, as classified by the IMF annual exchange rate arrangement (AREAER) database, and for which data was available. Our sample includes Jamaica, Mauritius, Seychelles, and Trinidad and Tobago.[2]

Small states face unique vulnerabilities, often subject to minimal diversification against external shocks and procyclical fiscal policy due to expenditure rigidity and revenue volatility in the face of limited fiscal buffers. In particular, the effectiveness of the monetary transmission mechanism may be limited by low financial inclusion, credit market imperfections and structural liquidity. Accordingly, estimating the effectiveness of monetary transmission mechanisms in small countries with floating exchange rate regimes, may be useful for policy making. To the best of our knowledge, this is the first study that looks at this issue.

The rest of the study is organized as follows: Section 2. describes the theoretical background underlying monetary transmission mechanisms in small open economies. Section 3. gives a broad review of the empirical literature on monetary transmission mechanisms. Section 4. presents the context in which our group of small states' monetary policy operates. Section 5. empirically assesses the effectiveness of the monetary transmission mechanism in the small states with floating exchange rates. Section 6. concludes and provides policy recommendations.

2 Theoretical background

Economic adjustment in small states generally takes place through quantity adjustments rather than price. Markets are usually less well developed and price discovery is more difficult, when compared to the situation in larger states. In addition, there is significant market imperfection because the size of the markets constrains competitive outcomes. For example, the small size of the market limits the number of banks and other financial institutions that might exist leading to oligopolistic pricing behaviour. Accordingly, there tends to be more price rigidity in small open economies which, along with other market imperfections, would normally mean more robust monetary transmission as most monetary transmission mechanisms (MTMs) rely on market imperfections and/or nominal rigidities for monetary policy to affect real output. However, empirically, MTMs in SIDS tend to be weak as less developed financial markets limit the range and efficiency of channels through which monetary impulses are transmitted to the real sector. In essence, some nominal price rigidity is good for monetary transmission but too much unduly restricts it.

There are other characteristics that make monetary transmission in small states different from similar mechanisms in larger states. Mishra *et al.* (2010) identify underdeveloped financial markets in low-income countries (LIC) as a key factor limiting the strength of the transmission of monetary impulses. Underdeveloped financial markets limit the range of assets through which monetary transmission could potentially operate. In addition, financial markets lack depth and liquidity, essential attributes for efficiency of transmission processes. Small market size militates against the existence of certain types of products and institutions. For example, hedging instruments are almost non-existent in many small states, along with some non-bank institutions which are commonplace in more advanced economies. IMF (2016) shows that the strength and efficiency of transmission mechanism across countries could be significantly affected by the type and extent of nonbank institutions in the country. They serve either to amplify or dampen transmission of monetary impulses depending on the transmission channels.

Monetary transmission mechanisms are not immutable; they change with time as the structure of the financial system evolves and the regulatory environment is strengthened. Nevertheless, the balance sheet of financial intermediaries is one of the main channels through which monetary policy is transmitted. Other channels include the monetary channel, credit channel, and risk-taking channels. It therefore stands to reason that transmission mechanisms would vary across countries depending on their structure and even for the same country across time as the structure of the financial system changes. Also, some channels may complement each other, while other may counteract each other. Accordingly, the conduct of monetary policy will need to adopt with the evolution of the monetary transmission mechanism (IMF, 2016).

The balance sheet channel

Monetary policy affects the supply of financing for non-financial firms by causing changes in the balance sheet of financial intermediaries. A tighter monetary policy stance results in the contraction of the balance sheet of these intermediaries reducing their capacity to lend. Such contraction will have asymmetric effects of financial firms depending on their characteristics. The rise in short term interest rates occasioned by the contraction in monetary policy lowers the net worth of banks and other financial intermediaries because their assets usually have longer maturities than their liabilities. Accordingly, their liabilities are re-priced more quickly than their assets, raising funding costs (Bernanke, 2007).

The impact on the net worth of banks is larger because they hold significant amounts of debt on their balance sheet. Financial institutions that do not have access to capital markets and other sources of financing would experience a larger contraction in their balance sheet because of their inability to switch to alternative sources of financing. The shrink in financial firm's balance sheet would be larger depending on the size of the institution, private ownership, access to alternative sources of finances, and access to external capital markets (IMF, 2016). Moreover, if a firm is required to mark-to-market (a fair value method of accounting) as required under US

GAAP, the contraction of their balance sheet will be greater the larger its portfolio subject to this type of reporting.

Banks in small states will generally see some shrinkage in their balance sheet following tighter monetary policy, but on balance the contraction in loan supply should be less than their counterparts in more advanced economies. The rise in short-term rates would lower the net worth of banks because of the mismatch in the maturity of their assets and liabilities. The bulk of their liabilities are deposits which are usually short term, while their assets, mainly loans have longer maturity. As a consequence, banks in many small states have loan repricing clauses in their longer-term assets like mortgages even if such options are only exercised infrequently.[3] Thus, the balance sheet effects are likely to be less acute in SIDS. In most SIDS access to other sources of funding like bonds and quasi equity is limited which would tend to exacerbate the balance sheet contraction. On the other hand, while many banks in SIDS mark to market, the dominance of most basic or standard (plain vanilla) deposits on their balance sheets limits the extent of balance sheet contraction due to this effect.

The risk-taking channel

Contractionary monetary policy can reduce financial firms' ability to absorb losses resulting in diminution in their demand for risky assets, thereby lowering the supply of loans to non-financial firms. A tightening of monetary policy can push up the funding costs of financial intermediaries reducing their profits and their loss absorbing capacity (Adrian and Shin, 2011). In response, they would lower their holdings of risky assets including riskier loans to firms. Reduced lending and asset purchases would lower asset prices helping to contract the economy. In addition, where financial firms focus on fixed nominal yields, a tightening of monetary policy that raises short-term yields would allow firms to achieve the same nominal yield by investing in less risky assets. Similarly, financial intermediaries that are compensated on the basis of relative yields can more easily achieve their benchmarks without investing in more risk assets.

The risk channel is also likely to be less effective in SIDS as bank loans are the major risk assets. Tighter monetary policy could indeed choke off incremental risky loans as bank profitability decline but given the limited range of financial assets the effects that flow through asset prices should be negligible. Moreover, Bolton *et al.* (2016) find that these effects are likely to be less important for banks because they tend to minimize fluctuations in credit as interest rates change to maintain long-term relationships with their customers. In addition, the transmission processes that go through the risk apply to more sophisticated nonbank financial intermediaries like broker dealers that are normally not seen in SIDS.

The regulatory capital channel

Monetary tightening could also reduce loan supply if banks do not have sufficient regulatory capital. As discussed earlier tighter monetary policy could reduce profits for banks, especially retail banks that do a significant amount of maturity transformation. Their funding cost would increase while returns on asset would not vary as quickly. In these circumstances, banks would usually reduce assets limit or even reduce lending. The impact of such lending restrictions on the real economy depends on how easily their customers can substitute other sources of financing for bank lending (Bernanke and Blinder 1992). In addition, the effect of repricing the longer-term assets could also have an important effect on the demand side, as borrowers' debt capacity would become lower while some borrowers no longer qualify for credit, resulting in lower consumption and investment spending.

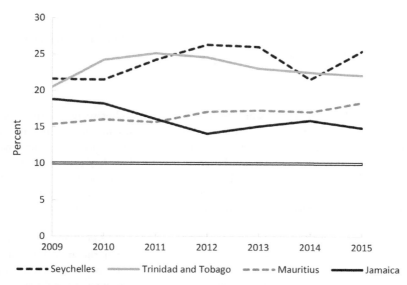

Figure 11.1 Capital adequacy ratio in selected small states
Source: IMF International Financial Statistics database and IMF staff calculations.

In many countries, especially small states with bank centric financial systems, such alternatives are not available and the impact on real activity could be significant. However as discussed above, banks that are heavily involved in maturity transformation would usually find ways to limit the interest rate exposure like allowing for some repricing of their longer-term assets. The extent of loan supply reduction would also be limited by banks trying to keep long term-relationships. Accordingly, banks in many SIDS, on paper, hold regulatory capital far in excess of the minimum capital requirements.

Credit channel

The credit channel (financial accelerator) is based on asymmetric information between borrowers and lenders and imperfections in financial markets which amplify the effects of real economic shocks on firms' perceived ability to repay, leading to a contraction in loan supply (Bernanke and Gertler, 1995). Financial intermediaries lend to non-financial firms based on their net worth, which determines the amount of collateral that can be posted against loans. Monetary tightening reduces the firm's net worth as rising interest rates lower the expected future profits of the firm thereby reducing the value of its equity. Lower equity signals that the firm has lower collateral available and potential lenders would perceive lending to the firm as a more-risky proposition reducing the available supply of loans. Similarly, for households, monetary tightening reduces the net worth of household assets with a negative effect on the supply of loans available to them. These balance sheet effects on borrowers could magnify the effects of monetary policy changes on the real economic activity.

In many small states banks lend on the three Cs, collateral, character and creditworthiness with a strong emphasis on collateral. With limited credit underwriting skills, many banks depend disproportionately on collateral. Hence any action that reduces the perceived value of collateral could have a significant effect on credit. For this reason, it has been suggested that the credit channel would be very important in small states. The development of credit bureaus could however mitigate the effects of collateral on credit. Furthermore, as discussed below, with small and inefficient equity markets, the monetary policy signal provided by equity markets is likely have a low signal to noise ratio.

The money channel

The money channel is a direct transmission of monetary impulses to real output and prices, based on a stable multiplier between reserve money and broad money, the intermediate target. Mishkin (1995) argues that a stable relationship between monetary aggregates and output and prices allows the monetary authority to set broad money (intermediate target) to be consistent with output and inflation. Broad money targets are achieved by manipulating reserve money which is under the control of the monetary authority. Changes in reserve money are translated into broad money changes through the money multiplier which affects real output and prices.

Many SIDS set broad money, an intermediate target, to be consistent with output and inflation. Such a policy framework permits transmission through the monetary channel by affecting directly, spending on goods services and assets, which in turn, affects real output and prices. Not requiring developed asset and financial markets, the money channel may potentially be the most effective. However, instability of the money multiplier and in the velocity of money might reduce the effectiveness of the monetary channel. For example, Davoodi *et al.* (2013), show that there was significant variability in the velocity and money multiplier in East African Community (EAC) countries. In this study, we also find some variability in the money multiplier and velocity of money.

The following monetary transmission mechanisms focuses on how changes in interest rates, asset prices and exchange rates affect investment and consumption decisions. These channels operate through the user cost of capital, inter-temporal substitution effects, wealth effects and knock on effects of interest rate changes on real exchange rates that affect the external current account.

Interest rate channel

The interest rate channel is one of the most traditional channels of monetary transmission and operates through several processes. For households, a rise in interest rates caused by tightening monetary policy affects their choice between saving and consumption. The marginal rate of time preference determines the urgency with which households prefer to consume now. In a typical inter-temporal consumer maximization problem, the household equates the interest rate with his rate of time preference. If interest rates rise they would forego current consumption in favour of future consumption, i.e. save more. Changes in interest rates also have wealth effects. A rise in interest rates reduces the present value of household wealth which in turn could lower their current consumption. Short term-interest rates can also affect long-term interest rates which determine investment decisions, through the effect of expectations on the yield curve. Changes in long-term interest rates affect the user cost of capital thereby affecting investment decisions.

Lending rates are relatively unresponsive to short term variations in monetary policy rates in many SIDS. This means that neither the effect on consumption or investment will be realized. Commercial banks in many developing countries tend to keep lending rates fairly stable absorbing shocks within the ample spread over their cost of funds. In a similar vein, Samuel (2015) argues that banks in the Caribbean SIDS try to maintain stability and predictability in the

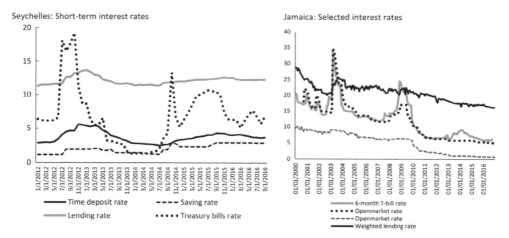

Figure 11.2 Selected interest rates in Seychelles and Jamaica
Source: IMF International Financial Statistics database and Bank of Jamaica.

cost of funds for their long-term clients. In highly bank centric financial systems, banks can maintain roughly stable lending rates because the rate of interest on savings deposits, their most reliable source of funding, does not vary much

Asset prices channel

This channel recognizes that changes in the money supply affect the prices of all financial assets. For example, monetary tightening increases the demand for money and a reduction in demand for other financial assets causing their prices to fall. The rise in interest rates would increase the demand for bonds relative to equities causing the price of equities to fall. Viewed in terms of tightening money supply, it reduces real cash balances available for the purchase of all assets including financial assets causing their prices to fall. For households, this reduces their wealth which as discussed earlier would reduce their consumption. The effects on non-financial firms can be discussed in the context of the Tobin (1969) q theory. Tobin defines q as the ratio of the present value of the firm to its user cost of capital. If q is high, then the firm will invest more because it can issue equity to make investment. On the other hand, if q is low then investment will be lower. Tightening monetary policy affects both the numerator and denominator of q. A rise in interest rate reducing the market value of the firm and increases it replacement cost both of which would lower q and hence investment and thereby real output and prices.

In the less developed financial markets in SIDS the effectiveness of this channel is limited. With fewer asset classes, the household wealth effects of monetary policy are likely to be insignificant, hence the impact on consumption and real output would be similarly small. In bank-centric financial systems like those in SIDS lending rates approximate closely the cost of capital. The channel through the equity market is largely nonexistent in many SIDS and where they exist the lack of depth and liquidity precludes them having a significant effect on investment decisions. In many developed countries, the zero lower bound for interest rates (the liquidity trap) limits the ability to stimulate the economy with monetary policy. This results in money supply having no effect on either interest rates or output. In most SIDS interest rates are well above the zero lower bound, however most experience periods of structural excess liquidity which similarly limits the effectiveness of monetary transmission mechanisms.

Exchange rate channel

Monetary policy changes will cause interest rates to move resulting in exchange rate changes that would affect net exports. The exchange rate channel is usually discussed in the context of the uncovered interest parity (UIP). UIP assumes that there is capital mobility which, in part, drives changes in the nominal exchange rate. If UIP holds then the expected exchange rate change should be equal to the difference between domestic interest rates between two countries. A tightening of monetary policy in the home country would result in an appreciation in the nominal exchange rate. If this nominal exchange rate change translates into some real exchange rate change, net exports could decline causing a contraction in real output.

The assumption that nominal exchange rate changes translate into real exchange rate (RER) changes is important for the transmission mechanism. For many small states this might not be the case as relative prices might not change following a change in the nominal exchange rate leaving the RER unchanged (Cebotari *et al.*, 2015). The RER is defined as the domestic relative price on non-tradable goods to tradable goods, an indicator of the relative incentives to consumption and production in the tradable on non-tradable sectors. It is usually assumed that the prices of non-tradables are determined by domestic factors, while for small open economies the prices of tradables are determined by international prices and the nominal exchange rate. Therefore, a decline in the relative price of non-traded goods – an appreciation in the real exchange rate signals a fall in domestic production cost and by extension an increase in the profitability of traded goods. Samuel (2015) argues that in many small states there is large range of non-traded goods that can be regarded quasi-traded goods for which depreciation in the nominal exchange rate would leave prices constant in foreign currency. In these cases, exchange rate changes affect net exports, and thereby real output only via import compression and not through changes in relative prices. Accordingly, the exchange rate channel is expected to be less effective than in larger states.

The expectations channel

The expectations channel has grown in importance as both policy and business decisions have become more evidence based taking into consideration current and future values of key economic variables. While expectations provide a channel for the transmission of monetary impulses to the real sector in their own right, they also affect how the other channels work. For example, Walsh (2010) shows that monetary transmissions are more effective when expectations are explicitly included in policy models.

The expectations channel is unlikely to be well developed in many SIDS. Expectations formation is rather unsophisticated. In tandem with the level of development of financial markets, expectation formation is also not fully developed which could either exacerbate the effects of the variables or attenuate them. On balance the tendency to attenuate the effects is likely to dominate given the relatively small proportion of market actors who actively generate expectations.

Recognizing the importance of expectations channel, central banks have tried to use this channel by providing forward guidance on the likely path of policy rates and inflation. This allows these expectations to be incorporated into decision making thereby increasing the effectiveness of monetary policy. While the central bank can control the nominal interest rate, consumption and investment decisions are based on real interest rates, thus information about the future path of inflation would be key for these decisions. Price expectations also affect labour market decisions for which the real wage is central. An important ingredient for forward guidance to work is the credibility of the central bank. If the central bank has little credibility then forward guidance would be less effective, even counterproductive.

In Many SIDS, forward guidance is at a rudimentary stage as monetary policy frameworks are evolving. In this regard, forward guidance very much depends on the communication strategy for monetary policy decisions, and whether the actions of the central bank are consistent with the mental model held by economic agents on how the economy functions. Indeed, even if forward guidance is practiced it requires significant credibility on the part of central banks. Absence of credibility reduces the effectiveness of the transmission process making it harder to stabilize the economy Bodenstein *et al.* (2010).

Theoretical analysis of the strength of transmission mechanisms in SIDS is inconclusive. The discussion in this section points to many instances where the strength of monetary transmission channels could be greater or less in small states than they are in larger, deeper financial markets. On balance, indications for weaker transmission mechanisms in small states appear to dominate. However, this is a matter for empirical investigation which is taken up in the next few sections of this chapter.

3 Review of the empirical literature

Studies on the monetary transmission mechanisms have focused on developed economies, and only recently on low income countries. Studies on developed economies have shown evidence of both the money channel (King, 1986; Romer and Romer, 1990; Ramey, 1993) and the credit channel (Bernanke, 1986, 1993; Gertler and Gilchrist, 1994). By contrast, the literature on low income countries (LICs) is relatively more recent, dating from the late 1990s (Azali and Matthews, 1999; Mishra and Montiel, 2012). The latter branch of the literature underlines the challenges LICs countries face, including underdeveloped financial markets and institutional issues that often result in the credit channel being more important than the money channel. Other studies have looked at the transmission mechanisms within a monetary union (Toolsema *et al.*, 2002; Angeloni *et al.*, 2003; Sander and Kleimeier 2004, 2006) and at the transmission mechanism within a single market (Davoodi *et al.*, 2013; Haughton and Iglesias, 2012).

Studies on small states cover country case studies that essentially focused on the Caribbean or Pacific regions, and did not differentiate countries by types of exchange rate regimes (Baksh and Craigwell, 1997; Craigwell and Leon, 1990). In the Caribbean, empirical studies tend to show a weak interest rate channel and some evidence of the credit, money and exchange rate channels, whereas in the Pacific region, studies find both interest rate and credit channels are weak but there is some evidence pointing the existence of money and exchange rate channels.

Studies for the Caribbean show that the exchange rate channel and credit channels can be effective. Allen and Robinson (2004) examine the monetary transmission mechanisms in Jamaica using a small-scale macroeconomic model for the Jamaican economy. The simulation of the impact of different shocks on the inflation and output reveals that there is a direct transmission from interest rates to exchange rates through portfolio substitution and that the exchange rate channel is found to be the channel through which inflation stabilization is achieved. Moore and Williams (2008) use vector error correction models to examine the credit channel of monetary policy transmission using data on Barbados. They test the assumption that monetary policy can still work in a fixed exchange rate regime by raising the financial costs faced by firms, leading to a reduction in the real wage and employment and ultimately leading to a reduction in real credit and consumption. Results show that monetary policy changes do have an impact on both deposits and credit as commercial bank lending falls in response to a tightening in monetary policy.

By contrast, the monetary channel appears to be more effective in Pacific small states. Jayaraman and Choong (2008) examined the monetary transmission mechanisms in Fiji using variance decomposition and impulse response functions, and find that money channel has been the most important. The finding is consistent with other studies on monetary transmission in developing countries where money markets are underdeveloped. Jayaraman and Dahalan (2008) use VAR to look at the monetary policy transmission in Samoa and find that money and exchange rate channels are important. The weak interest rate channel is due to the money markets' early stage of development.

Studies that look at the monetary transmission mechanism within a group of countries were motivated by common characteristics, such as common language, under-developed financial markets, or undertaking financial reforms. Ramlogan (2004) used a VAR analysis to investigate the transmission mechanism in four Caribbean countries: Jamaica, Trinidad and Tobago, Barbados and Guyana. The findings show that credit and exchange rates channels dominate the money channel. The countries are the four largest English speaking Caribbean countries which share the common challenge of an underdeveloped financial system. Yang *et al.* (2012) examine the monetary policy transmission in pacific island countries and find that the interest rate pass-through and credit growth channels are weak, identifying the main challenge to monetary policy being the under-developed domestic financial markets. Primus (2016) used a VAR with exogenous variables to examine the effectiveness of the use of indirect (interest rate) and direct (required reserve ratio) monetary policy instruments in three Caribbean countries that are undertaking financial sector reforms, Jamaica, Trinidad and Tobago and Barbados. The author finds that there is a weak transmission of the policy interest rate but an increase in the required reserve ratio leads to a reduction of private sector credit and excess reserves while alleviating pressures on the exchange rate, therefore concluding that direct instruments should complement the use of indirect instrument.

4 Monetary policy context

This section discusses the context in which Monetary Policy operates. It focuses on the degree of Capital Mobility, Evolution of Exchange Rate Regime and Structure of the Financial Sector.

Country background

As already stated in the introduction, our sample is comprised of the following countries: Jamaica, Mauritius, Seychelles, and Trinidad and Tobago. Table 11.1 provides information on characteristics of these economies, relating to the theme of this chapter.

This section aims at identifying key components of the context in which monetary policy is evolving in the group of small states under study. As emphasized in the theoretical background, monetary transmission mechanisms depend on the country's linkages between the domestic and foreign financial markets (degree of capital mobility), its exchange rate regime, as well as the structure of its financial sector.

- All four countries have gone through a period of capital account and financial sector liberalization and shifted to floating exchange rate regimes, which Jamaica being the earliest to do so and Seychelles the most recent (2009).
- While all four countries have de jure floating regimes, the de factor regimes vary. Mauritius and Seychelles are classified as floating, while Jamaica is classified as a crawl-like arrangement and Trinidad and Tobago, a stabilized arrangement.
- Money and capital markets are at various stages of development in the four countries. All four countries are aspiring to develop deep and liquid financial markets by

Table 11.1 Small states sample and exchange rate regimes

	Jamaica	*Mauritius*	*Seychelles*	*Trinidad and Tobago*
GDP (2015, US$ billion)	14.42	11.51	1.36	25.32
GDP per capita (2015, US$ billion)	5.05	9.11	14.55	18.14
De jure exchange rate	Floating	Floating	Floating	Floating
De facto exchange rate	Crawl-like arrangement	Floating	Floating	stabilized arrangement
M3/GDP (2015, %)	29.95	108.54	67.24	64.14
Monetary policy regime	Other: inflation targeting lite (ITL)	Other: hybrid inflation targeting (conduct monetary policy and manage the exchange rate)	Monetary aggregate target	Exchange rate anchor vís-á-vis the US dollar
Capital market access	Yes	Yes	Yes	Yes

Source: Annual report on exchange arrangements and exchange restrictions, 2016.

strengthening domestic debt markets, including through auction-based mechanism for primary issuances to enhance price transparency and financial market liquidity. Mauritius and Trinidad and Tobago to a lesser extent are seen as financial centres in their respective regions. Foreign exchange markets remain shallow despite efforts by the authorities to enhance them.

- Monetary policy regimes are evolving in these countries. Jamaica and Mauritius are moving to inflation targeting regimes with Jamaica described as inflation targeting 'lite' and Mauritius as 'hybrid' inflation targeting. For the period under consideration Seychelles and Trinidad and Tobago practiced traditional money targeting but Seychelles is moving to establish and interest rate corridor.

Common challenges

Small states are characterized by a lack of diversification, making stabilization policies even more relevant. The lack of diversification has implied that in many of these countries a dependence of revenues from a few sectors, resulting in high volatility of revenues and making the efficiency of monetary stabilization policies even more important.

As explained earlier, monetary policy transmission mechanisms are likely to be hampered by challenges arising from under-developed financial sectors and low financial inclusion. The lack of diversification has often been accompanied by a reliance on foreign exchange, the unsterilized inflows of which result in excess domestic currency liquidity. Because of the lack of depth in the financial sector, one could expect that monetary policy transmission will rather be through quantity and availability of credit rather than the price of credit. Moreover, sterilized intervention in the foreign exchange market in an effort to reduce excess domestic currency liquidity may in turn weaken the exchange rate channel.

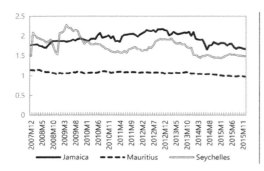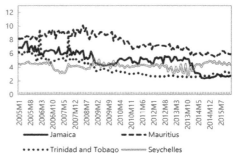

Figure 11.3 Velocity and money multiplier in selected small states
Source: IMF IFS database and staff calculations.

Stability of money multiplier and velocity

In this section, we examine movements in velocity and multipliers using annual, quarterly and monthly data that we compiled for our sample, with 2007 as the starting date.[4] Velocity was derived from broad money and GDP quarterly data for Jamaica, Mauritius, and Seychelles, but not for Trinidad and Tobago, since the quarterly GDP index did not allow for the derivation of quarterly or monthly velocity.

The following results emerge from Figure 11.3:

- The stability of both velocity and money multipliers vary across countries.
- Mauritius appears to have the most stable velocity. For the other countries, velocity varies across time and broadly follows a downward trend, possibly reflecting an increase in monetization.
- Mauritius as well as Trinidad and Tobago seem to have the most stable money multiplier. This is not the case for Jamaica and Seychelles where money multiplier shows significant variability.

From these results, we therefore expect transmission mechanism to be relatively stronger in Trinidad and Tobago and Mauritius.

5 Empirical analysis

Model specification

We follow the widely used structural VAR methodology. To measure the effect of monetary policy, we need to identify purely exogenous shocks to the variables of interest and see how the economy reacts to them. The advantage of a VAR is that it isolates purely exogenous shocks to monetary policy and allows tracing out the dynamics of the variables after the shocks hit the economy. For these reasons, VAR and its variant has been the most commonly used approach adopted in the monetary transmission mechanisms (MTM) literature, both in the context of developing as well as of developed countries. Studies of MTM in developed countries have commonly used VAR and its variants (Christiano *et al.*, 2011, for the US; Weber *et al.*, 2009, for the euro area). Most studies of MTM in LICS have also used VARs (Mishra *et al.*, 2010; Mishra and Montiel, 2012).

Formally, the structural VAR model is as follows:

$$X_t = \beta_0 + \beta_n X_{t-n} + \lambda Y_t + u_t \qquad (1)$$

Where t = 1, …,T and n = 1, …, N;

X_t is a vector of endogenous time series variables, contains the intercept, time trend and other deterministic terms;

Y_t is a vector of contemporaneous exogenous variables;

u_t represents independent events/shocks.

We assume the following endogenous and exogenous variables[5]:

- Endogenous variables: real GDP (y), price level (p), reserve money (m), policy rate (r), credit to the private sector (c), and nominal effective exchange rate (e).
- Exogenous variables: global oil price index, global food price index, the US federal funds rate, and US industrial production. These variables are assumed to be proxies for global demand.
- The ordering assumes that reserve money is the principal monetary policy instrument, which responds to output and prices. This is indeed the case for our sample. While Seychelles has an explicit reserve money targeting framework, Jamaica, Mauritius, and Trinidad and Tobago are in the process of transitioning towards inflation targeting frameworks. Under these circumstances, interest rate, as measured by the policy rate, therefore follows reserve money. Because all the countries in our sample assume a de jure flexible exchange rate, the nominal effective exchange rate is placed last.

A formal explanation of the estimation method of this VAR model is given in Appendix 1.

The identification and ordering of the VAR model utilized in this study implies the following:

- Shocks to real GDP and price level result in contemporaneous responses of reserve money.
- Reserve money is assumed to be the main monetary policy instrument, with shocks to reserve money considered as monetary policy shocks.
- Policy rates are assumed to be used as instruments to signal changes in monetary policy stance
- Commercial banks react with a delay to the policy rate.
- Exchange rates are determined by market forces.

Data and diagnostic testing

We use monthly measures of real GDP, CPI, reserve money, credit to the private sector, interest rates and nominal effective exchange rates. Because only quarterly real GDP data was available monthly estimates of real GDP were derived by interpolating quarterly GDP data using a cubic spline, and then seasonally adjusted using the X13 ARIMA method. Trinidad and Tobago has a quarterly GDP index rather than quarterly GDP.[6] Due to the absence of policy rates in Seychelles and Trinidad and Tobago, t-bill rates were used instead for those countries. Quarterly GDP data were collected from IMF country teams. CPI, reserve money, credit to the private sector, interest rates and nominal effective exchange rates come from the IMF IFS database. Global oil and food indices, US federal funds rate and the US industrial production were from the IMF GAS database. Variables are in log levels, except for interest rates.

The stationarity of the variables was assessed. All variables were tested for stationarity using the Phillips-Perron test. The results reveal that all the variables are non-stationary in levels but the first differences are stationary.

Residuals were tested for serial correlation. In order for a stationary VAR to be correctly specified, residuals need to be completely random or white noise. We tested for residual auto-correlation, and excluded the numbers of lags for which serial correlation were found.

The optimality of the lag order was tested. We investigated the lag structure of the VAR using lag length criteria. Based on the Likelihood ratio test, a lag of 2 was chosen for both Jamaica and Mauritius, a lag of 3 was chosen for Seychelles, and a lag of 5 was chosen for Trinidad and Tobago.[7]

The stability of the VAR system was assessed. We checked the stationarity of the system as a whole by looking at the inverse roots of the characteristics AR polynomial, and all roots lie inside the unit circle, resulting in the VAR being stationary.[8]

Before estimating the structural VAR, we also conducted a granger causality test to check for the joint significance of the policy variables for GDP and prices. The null hypothesis is that the policy variable jointly cannot cause GDP or prices. All p-values for both GDP and prices as dependent variables were found to be above 5%, leading us to conclude that we cannot reject the null hypothesis, i.e. each policy variable cannot jointly cause GDP or prices.

Because operating targets differ across the small states with floating exchange rate regimes, we conducted country-specific analyses. We run the above model as an unrestricted VAR in first differences of the variables (in logs) for each country from December 2005 to December 2015, except for Seychelles, where due to availability of quarterly GDP, the estimated period was January 2006 to September 2015.

Results

The results of the above structural VARs presented in this section are derived from the impulse functions in Appendix 2. The main findings are the following:[9]

- Monetary transmission is weak throughout the small states with a floating exchange rate regime. Monetary shocks explain at most a third of the variation in income and prices and in most cases less than 15%.
- Trinidad and Tobago appears to have comparatively the most efficient transmission mechanisms, with all four transmission channels present.
- Mauritius seems to have comparatively the strongest money channel. The exchange rate channel is weakly present.
- In Jamaica and Seychelles, there is some evidence of the credit and exchange rate channels.

The results are broadly consistent with the evidence for both small states and non-small states. In particular, the finding that monetary shocks explain only a small percentage of the variation of income and prices echoes the results of other studies (see for example Uhlig, 2005; Mishra *et al.*, 2012). The results confirm our earlier hypothesis that monetary policy transmission is likely to be weak in small states, reflecting the structural context in which monetary policy in these countries operate, namely, (i) underdeveloped financial markets, (ii) excess liquidity and (iii) lack of diversification and dependence of foreign exchange. The finding that Mauritius and Trinidad and Tobago appear to have better transmission mechanism is also not surprising given that both countries have a relatively more developed financial system compared to other small states. Weak evidence of the credit and exchange rate channels Jamaica and Seychelles also confirm our earlier expectation that transmission would take place through quantity rather than the price of credit, given the lack of depth in the financial sector and sterilization impact.

Finally, our results suggest that contrary to the predictions of the Mundell-Fleming textbook model, the extent to which monetary policy impacts output and prices depends on the exchange rate regime is not clear cut. These results corroborate previous studies that find that

Table 11.2 De facto exchange regimes: variance decomposition results

GDP

	NEER	Self	CPI	Reserve Money	Interest Rate	Credit
Jamaica	3.9	69.2	5.2	0.8	18.4	2.6
Trinidad and Tobago	14.7	58.4	3.8	6.2	14.2	2.6

CPI

	NEER	GDP	Self	Reserve Money	Interest Rate	Credit
Jamaica	6.0	6.4	79.9	0.3	1.2	6.1
Trinidad and Tobago	4.5	6.2	79.3	5.5	1.6	2.9

the exchange rate regime context in which monetary policy operates may not be what standard textbook describes, i.e. monetary policy turns out to have some effects even in countries with a fixed exchange rate regime (see for example Moore and Williams, 2008).

Variance decomposition

The variance decomposition of the estimated VARs allows us to quantify the relative importance of shocks in variability of inflation and output.

In Jamaica, shocks to interest rate, exchange rate and credit account for most of the variations in GDP and in CPI attributed to monetary shocks. Shocks to interest rate, credit and the exchange rate respectively account for 5.1%, 0.9% and 0.5% variation in GDP. On the other hand, shocks to credit, interest rate, and the exchange rate, respectively, account for 6%, 1.7% and 1.7% variation in CPI.

In Mauritius, shocks to the exchange rate and reserve money accounts for most of the variation in GDP and in CPI from monetary shocks. Shocks to the exchange rate and reserve money account respectively explain 2.7% and 2.4% variation in GDP. Meanwhile, shocks to reserve money and the exchange rate respectively explain 12.6 and 1.7% variation in CPI.

In Seychelles, while exchange rate and interest rate explain most of the variation in GDP, exchange rate and credit explain most of the variation in CPI due to monetary shocks. Shocks to the exchange rate and interest rate account respectively for 5.3% and 3.5% of the variation in GDP, and shocks to credit and exchange rate account for respectively for 4.9% and 2.6% of the variation in CPI.

In Trinidad and Tobago, all variables contribute to the variation in GDP and CPI, with interest rate explaining a much larger proportion of GDP. Shocks to the interest rates and exchange rates explain respectively 24.5% and 7.6% of the variation in GDP. Meanwhile, shocks to reserve money and the exchange rates explain respectively 5.6% and 3.7% of the variation in CPI.

Impulse responses

This section examines the impulse response functions (IR) of the estimated VARs.

Jamaica and Seychelles (Appendix 2, panels 1 and 2):

- *Credit channel.* In both Jamaica and Seychelles, a one standard deviation positive shock to credit would increase CPI. However, reserve money and interest rate were not found to have an impact on credit.
- *Exchange rate channel.* In Jamaica, a one standard deviation positive shock to NEER[10] (appreciation) would result in a reduction of credit to the private sector in the first two periods and NEER seems to be responsive to shocks to interest rates. However, there were no influence of NEER on either price or output. In Seychelles, a one standard deviation positive shock to the exchange rate result in a weak increase in GDP. However, NEER was not found to be responsive to either reserve money or interest rate.

Mauritius (Appendix 2, panel 3):

- *Money channel.* A one standard deviation positive shock to reserve money result in increases in both GDP and CPI during the first two periods.
- *Exchange rate channel.* A one standard deviation positive shock to the exchange rate results in an increase in GDP. Interest rate was found to have some impact on the exchange rate.

Trinidad and Tobago (Appendix 2, panel 4):

- *Money channel.* A one standard deviation positive shock to reserve money result in an increase in both GDP and CPI in the first two periods. The response of CPI to reserve money is however not significant.
- *Interest rate channel.* A one standard deviation positive shock to interest rate result in an increase in GDP over the first four months. However, CPI was not found to be influenced by interest rate shocks.
- *Exchange rate channel.* A one standard deviation positive shock to the exchange rate (appreciation) results in a sustained decrease in GDP over five months. CPI was not found to be influenced significantly by the exchange rate. Neither reserve money nor interest rate were found to have an impact on the exchange rate.
- *Credit channel.* A one standard deviation positive shock to credit results in an increase in GDP (although weakly statistically significant) over the first three months. Although credit was not found to be responsive to reserve money it responds to interest rates in the first period.

De jure versus de facto exchange rates

We attempted an alternative specification of our VAR model in order to consider the de facto exchange rate regimes in Jamaica and Trinidad and Tobago. Although Jamaica and Trinidad and Tobago have a de jure floating exchange rate regimes, their de facto regimes are not. For these reasons, we modified our VAR identification, so as to have NEER, real GDP, CPI, reserve money, policy rate, and credit, in this order. Having the exchange rate first now implies that it is the least endogenous variable of the VAR.

The results[11] indicate that in the case of Jamaica shocks to interest rate, exchange rate and credit account for most of the variations in GDP and in CPI. In the case of Trinidad and Tobago, interest rates and exchange rate shocks explain most of the variation in GDP, but fluctuation in CPI is largely explained by shocks in reserve money and the exchange rate. The results of the impulse responses were broadly similar to the first model: while only the credit channel appears to be present in Jamaica, there is partial evidence of all four channels in Trinidad and Tobago.

6 Conclusion and policy implications

The main contribution of this paper was to assess the monetary transmission mechanisms in SIDS with a floating exchange rate regime. Standard textbook models indeed assume monetary transmission is the most efficient in countries with a floating exchange rate regime, however, no previous studies have specifically looked at this group of SIDS countries. This is surprising as SIDS economies present unique challenges that could hamper transmission mechanisms.

Results show that, monetary transmissions in SIDS with a floating exchange rate regimes are generally weak. In particular, we find that (i) the credit and exchange rate channels appear weakly present in Seychelles and Jamaica, (ii) the money channel appears strongest in Mauritius, and (iii) all four transmission channels seem present in Trinidad and Tobago.

These results indicate, among other things, underdeveloped money markets, structural excess liquidity, high variability in money multipliers and velocities, strong financial market segmentation and high exchange rate pass-through to inflation. The size of the economies implies that the domestic market is too small to accommodate enough firms to create contestable financial markets and in many cases, essential markets do not exist. Accordingly, many transmission channels that exist in larger economies are either insignificant in SIDS or are totally absent. Even though the small states considered in this study have some degree of monetary policy independence, it was insufficient to offset the effects of the factors identified above.

Underdeveloped money markets coupled with lack of contestability limits the strength of monetary transmission mechanisms. Transmission mechanisms appear to be more efficient in Mauritius and Trinidad and Tobago which serve as financial centres, suggesting that deepening financial markets could strengthen monetary transmission. For some SIDS, a shift to interest rate focused monetary policy frameworks could help to strengthen money markets and interbank markets reducing the quasi fiscal cost of issuing more monetary debt. The development of interbank markets is frustrated by structural excess liquidity and inefficient price discovery mechanisms. Better communication between policy makers and market players could also improve the functioning of financial markets and promote more effective monetary policy implementation.

Structural excess liquidity appears to put non-zero lower bounds on interest rates in SIDS. Excess liquidity limits the effectiveness of monetary policy as lowering policy interest rates would elicit very little response from banks that already have all the liquidity they need. Some countries have tried to address this through sterilization but the quasi fiscal costs could be very high. Structural excess liquidity constrains both the interest rate and credit channels. Small states that are prone to excess liquidity could strengthen their analysis of the banking system's liquidity position. In this regard, training additional staff for liquidity forecasting would be helpful, including government cash flow forecast.

Money multipliers and velocity of money appear to be unstable. Unstable money multipliers and velocity imply that the assumed stable relationship between money and income breaks down, limiting the effectiveness of monetary policy. While deepening financial markets as discussed above could lead to further instability in the short run, it would help improve the stability of monetary aggregates over the medium term.

There appears to be strong market segmentation in some countries. This makes it difficult for policy rates to affect the interest rates on which the bulk of consumption and investment decisions are made. In bank-centric financial systems, commercial banks are able to hold lending rates fairly constant because their cost of funds remain fairly stable despite drastic changes in the policy rate. The rate of interest on savings, the largest source of bank funding remains remarkably stable even when policy rates are moving around. The general deepening of financial markets would improve their efficiency over time and help reduce market segmentation.

Because the role of the exchange regime on monetary transmission mechanism is not as clear cut as described in textbook models, one possible extension of this study could be to investigate transmission mechanisms for SIDS with fixed exchange rate regimes. Previous studies were indeed more country specific but more insights on the role of exchange rates in monetary transmission in small states could be drawn from a panel of countries.

Notes

1 SIDS are a category of countries so defined by the United Nations Department for Economic and Social Affairs. See https://sustainabledevelopment.un.org/topics/sids/list/.
2 Guyana, Haiti, Suriname and Papua New Guinea are also SIDS classified as flexible exchange rate regime in the IMF AREAER database, but were excluded from our sample due to the absence of quarterly GDP data.
3 For example, in Eastern Caribbean banks reserve the right to adjust the interest rate on most mortgage contracts, but have generally chosen not to raise rates when liquidity tightens.
4 2007 was chosen to be the starting date due to data availability.
5 In selecting our variables we followed Davoodi *et al.* (2013).
6 See www.central-bank.org.tt/content/output-quarterly-0.
7 The final prediction error tests also confirm these results.
8 Had a solution of the characteristic polynomial had a root equal to one, then this would have revealed that there is cointegration between the variables, and a VECM model rather than an unrestricted VAR would have been more appropriate to estimate.
9 We also ran the structural VAR model using M2 and M1 instead of reserve money, results were not substantially different.
10 Although Jamaica has a de jure floating exchange rate regime, it has de facto a crawl-like arrangement.
11 Results available on request from the authors.

Appendix 1 The VAR model

Formally, the structural VAR model is as follows:

$$X_t = \beta_0 + \beta_n X_{t-n} + \lambda Y_t + u_t \tag{1}$$

X_t is a vector of endogenous time series variables, contains the intercept, time trend and other deterministic terms;
Y_t is a vector of contemporaneous exogenous variables;
u_t represents random independent structural shocks.

$$X_t = G_0 + G_1 X_{t-n} + e_t \tag{2}$$

$$e_t = \mathbf{A^{-1}} \cdot u_t \tag{3}$$

However, because the number of estimated parameters in the reduced form is smaller than the number of parameters in the structural form, restrictions on matrix A are needed to identify the structural model.

$$
\begin{bmatrix} \varepsilon^y_t \\ \varepsilon^p_t \\ \varepsilon^m_t \\ \varepsilon^r_t \\ \varepsilon^c_t \end{bmatrix} =
\begin{pmatrix}
1 & 0 & 0 & 0 & 0 & 0 \\
g_{21} & 1 & 0 & 0 & 0 & 0 \\
g_{31} & g_{32} & 1 & 0 & 0 & 0 \\
g_{41} & g_{42} & g_{43} & 1 & 0 & 0 \\
g_{51} & g_{52} & g_{53} & g_{54} & 1 & 0
\end{pmatrix}
\begin{bmatrix} u^y_t \\ u^p_t \\ u^m_t \\ u^r_t \\ u^c_t \end{bmatrix}
$$

Appendix 2

Panel 4: Trinidad and Tobago

In T&T credit seems to have a weak positive impact on GDP... ...while being briefly responsive to interest rate.

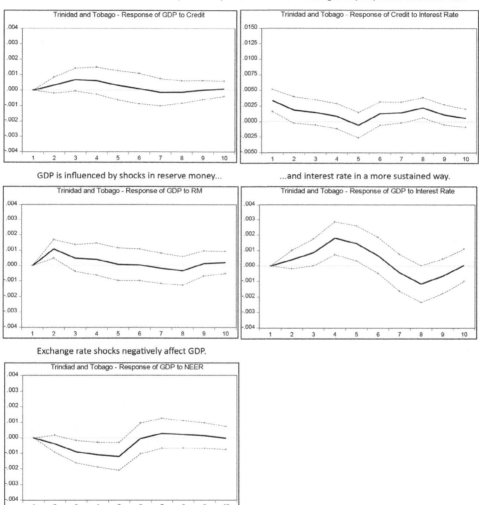

GDP is influenced by shocks in reserve money...   ...and interest rate in a more sustained way.

Exchange rate shocks negatively affect GDP.

Figure 11.A1 Impulse response functions

References

Adrian, T. and Shin, H. S. (2011). Financial Intermediaries and Monetary Economics. In Friedman, B. M. and Woodford, M. *Handbook of Monetary Economics*, Vol. 3. Amsterdam: Elsevier.

Allen, C. and Robinson, W. (2004). *Monetary Policy Rules and the Transmission Mechanism in Jamaica*. Bank of Jamaica Working Papers.

Angeloni, I., Kashyap, A. and Mojon, B. (2003). *Monetary Policy Transmission in the Euro Area*. Cambridge: Cambridge University Press.

Azali, M. and Matthews, K. (1999). 'Money-Income and Credit-Income Relationship During Pre and Post Liberalization Periods: Evidence from Malaysia'. *Applied Economics*, 31(10): 1161–1170.

Baksh, Sherman C. and Craigwell, Roland (1997). The Monetary Transmission Mechanism in Small Open Economies: A Case Study of Barbados. *Savings and Development*: 179–193.

Bernanke, B. S. (1986). Alternative Explanations of the Money-Income Correlation. *Carnegie-Rochester Conference Series on Public Policy*, 25 (Autumn): 49–99.

Bernanke, B. S. (1993). How important is the credit channel in the transmission of monetary policy?: A comment. In *Carnegie-Rochester Conference Series on Public Policy*, 39: 47–52. North-Holland.

Bernanke, B. S. (2007). 'The Financial Accelerator and the Credit Channel'. Remarks at The Credit Channel of Monetary Policy in the Twenty-first Century Conference, Federal Reserve Bank of Atlanta, June 15.

Bernanke, B. S. and Blinder, A. S. (1992). 'The Federal Funds Rate and the Channels of Monetary Transmission'. *American Economic Review*, 82(4): 901–921.

Bernanke, B. S. and Gertler, M. (1995). 'Inside the Black Box: The Credit Channel of Monetary Policy Transmission'. *Journal of Economic Perspectives*, 9(4): 27–48.

Bodenstein, M., Hebden, J., Nunes, R. (2010). Imperfect Credibility and the Zero Lower Bound on the Nominal Interest Rate. *Federal Reserve Board Working Paper*.

Bolton, P., Freixas, X., Gambacorta, L. and Mistrulli, P. E. (2016). 'Relationship and transaction lending in a crisis'. *The Review of Financial Studies*, 29(10): 2643–2676.

Cebotari, A., Acevedo, S., Greenidge, K. and Keim, G. (2015). External devaluations: Are small states different. *Working Paper*, 240. Washington, DC: IMF.

Christiano, L. J., Eichenbaum, M. and Evans, C. L. (1999). Monetary Policy Shocks: What have we Learned and to what End?. In Taylor, J. and Woodford, M. (eds), *Handbook of Macroeconomics*, Vol. 1a. Amsterdam, New York and Oxford: Elsevier Science, North-Holland: 65–148.

Craigwell, R. C. and Leon, H. (1990). 'Causality Testing and Sensitivity to Detrending: The Money-Income Relationship Revisited'. *North American Review of Economics and Finance*, 1.1(1990): 117–133.

Davoodi, H., Dixit, S. and Gabor, P. (2013). Monetary Transmission Mechanism in the East African Community: An Empirical Investigation. *IMF Working Paper*, No. 13/39.

Gertler, M. and Gilchrist, S. (1994). 'Monetary Policy, Business Cycles and the Behavior of Small Manufacturing Firms'. *Quarterly Journal of Economics*, 109 (May): 309–340.

Haughton, A. Y. and Iglesias, E. M. (2012). 'Interest rate volatility, asymmetry interest rate pass through and the monetary transmission mechanism in the Caribbean compared to US and Asia'. *Economic Modeling*, 29: 2071–2089.

International Monetary Fund (IMF) (2016). *Global Financial Stability Report*, October 2016. Washington, DC: IMF.

Jayaraman, T. K. and Dahalan, J. (2008). 'Monetary policy transmission in an undeveloped South Pacific Island country: a case study of Samoa'. *International Journal of Monetary Economics and Finance*, 1(4). Inderscience Enterprises Ltd: 380–398.

Jayaraman, T. K. and Choong, C. (2008). 'Monetary policy transmission mechanism in Fiji: An empirical analysis of the Quarterly Model'. *International Journal of Business and Management*, 3(11): 11–26.

King, Stephen R. (1986). 'Monetary Transmission: Through Bank Loans or Bank Liabilities?'. *Journal of Money, Credit and Banking*, 18(3): 290–303.

Mishkin, Fredrick S. (1995). 'Symposium on the Monetary Transmission Mechanism'. *Journal of Economic Perspectives*, 9(4): 3–10.

Mishra, P., Montiel, P. and Spilimbergo, A. (2010). Monetary Transmission in Low Income Countries. *IMF Working Paper*, No. 10/223.

Mishra, P. and Montiel, P. (2012). How Effective Is Monetary Transmission in Low-Income Countries? A Survey of the Empirical Evidence. *IMF Working Paper*, No. 12/143.

Moore, W. R. and Williams, M.L. (2008). 'Evidence on the Sectoral Monetary Transmission Process under a Fixed Exchange Rate Regime'. *International Economic Journal*, 22: 387–398.

Primus, K. (2016). The Effectiveness of Monetary Policy in Small Open Economies: An Empirical Investigation. *IMF Working Paper*, No. 16/189.

Ramey, V. (1993). How Important is the Credit Channel in the Transmission of Monetary Policy?. *Carnegie-Rochester Conference Series on Public Policy*, 39 (December): 1–45.

Ramlogan, C. (2004). 'The Transmission Mechanism of Monetary Policy'. *Journal of Economic Studies*, 31(5): 435–447.

Romer, C. D. and Romer, D. (1990). New evidence on the monetary transmission mechanism. *Brookings Papers on Economic Activity*, I: 149–213. Washington, DC: Brookings Institution.

Samuel, W. (2015). Fiscal Policy and Competitiveness in the Caribbean. In Yartey, Charles Amo (ed.) *Fiscal Policy: International Aspects, Short and Long Term Challenges, Macroeconomic Effects*. Nova: 197–218.

Sander, H. and Kleimeier, S. (2004). 'Convergence in euro-zone retail banking? What interest rate pass-through tells us about monetary policy transmission, competition and integration'. *Journal of International Money and Finance*, 23(3): 461–492.

Sander, H. and Kleimeier, S. (2006). 'Convergence in interest rate pass-through in a wider euro zone?' *Economic Systems*, 30: 405–423.

Tobin, J. (1969). 'A General Equilibrium Approach to Monetary Theory'. *Journal of Money, Credit and Banking*, 1(1): 15–29

Toolsema, L., Sturm, J. and Dehaan, J. (2002). Convergence of pass-through from money market to lending rates in EMU countries: New evidence. *CCSO Working Papers*. Groningen, The Netherlands: University of Groningen, Centre for Economic Research.

Walsh, C. E. (2010). *Monetary Theory and Policy*. Boston, MA: MIT Press.

Uhlig, H. (2005). 'What are the effects of monetary policy on output? Results from an agnostic identification procedure'. *Journal of Monetary Economics*, 52: 381–419.

Yang, Y., Davies, M., Wang, S., Dunn, J. and Wu, Y. (2012). 'Monetary policy transmission and macroeconomic policy coordination in Pacific island countries'. *Asian-Pacific Economic Literature*, 26(1): 46–68.

Weber, A., Gerke, R. and Worms, A. (2009). Has the monetary transmission process in the euro area changed? Evidence based on VAR estimates. *BIS Working Papers*, No. 276.

Part III
Aid and foreign direct investment

12

Improving aid allocation for small developing states

Patrick Guillaumont, Vincent Nossek and Laurent Wagner

1 Introduction

There seems to be a consensus that small developing states (SDS), and the island ones in particular (the so-called SIDS)[1], should receive a relatively high level of aid, when compared to larger states. However, the validity of this consensus depends on what is meant by small states as well as on what is meant by a relative level of aid. Here we utilize, as is often done, a population threshold of 1.5 million under which countries are said to be 'small' and consider the level of aid they receive either relative to their population or to their income.

The present chapter examines the relative level of aid allocated to small developing states, the rationale behind a relative high level of such aid, and the possible shortcomings of the present modalities of aid allocation to small states.

2 Do small states receive relatively more aid?

Precisely because they are small, small countries receive a small share of the total ODA disbursements, as shown in Figure 12.1. It can be seen that the two curves corresponding respectively to SIDS and to small developing states (SDS) are very close. Indeed, the two groups strongly overlap.[2] It can be seen from Figure 12.1 that the share of aid to SIDS and SDS slightly differ only in 2010 due to the large inflow of aid to Haiti after the earthquake.

Figure 12.1 also shows the larger share of ODA received by other (more populated) groups of countries, such as the least developed countries (LDCs), the landlocked developing countries (LLDCs), or the so-called fragile states (according to the harmonized definition of the multilateral development banks and the OECD).

During the 2006–2015 period both groups (SIDS and SDS) received an average of approximately 3% of the total ODA disbursements. This share can be assessed with respect to the population of the receiving countries, then to their income.

The ODA per capita received by small states

As shown in Figure 12.2, during the period 2006–2015 the level of ODA per capita has been significantly higher for SDS than for the whole set of developing countries, but the gap has recently narrowed.

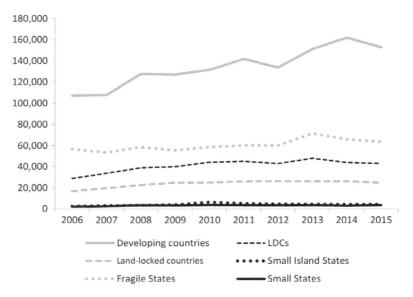

Figure 12.1 ODA total disbursements volume, all donors (in million, US$)
Source: OECD, DAC.

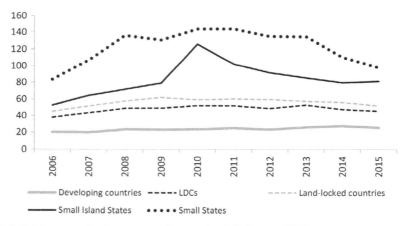

Figure 12.2 ODA per capita by groups of countries (all donors, US$)
Source: OECD, DAC.

ODA per capita received by SIDS peaked in 2010 after Haiti's earthquake at a level of 126 US$ per capita. ODA per capita was in 2015 at 81 US$ in SIDS, against 45 US$ in LDCs, and 25 US$ for all developing countries.

When we consider only the ODA from Development Assistance Committee (DAC) donors and from multilateral donors, as shown in Figures 12.3 and 12.4, the picture does not differ much: multilateral ODA per capita is 4.5 times higher for SDS than for the whole set of developing countries, and three times higher for SIDS.

It is worth noting that the share of the various multilateral institutions in the ODA disbursements going to SDS and SIDS has significantly changed over the last years, as shown in the

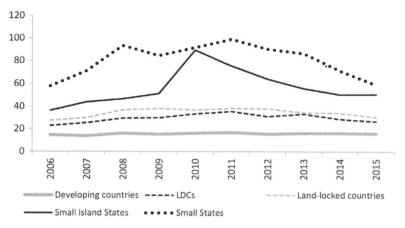

Figure 12.3 ODA per capita by groups of countries (DAC donors, US$)
Source: OECD, DAC.

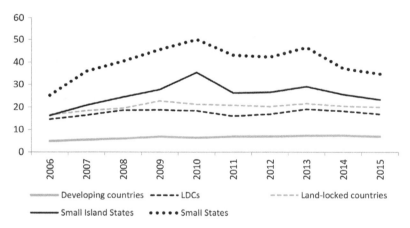

Figure 12.4 ODA per capita by groups of countries (multilateral donors, US$)
Source: OECD, DAC.

Figure 12.5. The share of the EU institutions is relatively high but has decreased, while that of the MDBs (World Bank and regional development banks) has increased. Some of the factors explaining these changes are discussed below.

It is important to note that the ratios of ODA per capita shown in Figures 12.2, 12.3 and 12.4, are population-weighted averages, where the weights are the populations of the recipient countries. They differ from the simple average of the country ratios, as shown in Table 12.1. In this table, which presents data between 2006 and 2015, ODA per capita is calculated as a simple average and as a population-weighted average. It can be seen that the weighted average of both for the SIDS and LDCs is relative lower than the simple average ratio, More so for SIDS, due to significantly higher ratios in the smaller countries.

ODA to small developing states in relation to their GNI

Figures 12.6 and 12.7 show the percentage ratio of ODA to GNI.

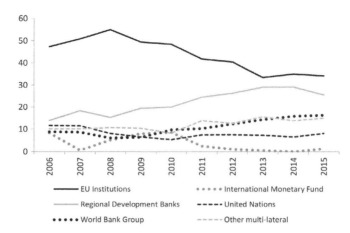

Figure 12.5 Share of multilateral ODA (net disbursements) to SIDS by institution (%)
Source: OECD, DAC.

Table 12.1 ODA per capita, simple averages and population-weighted averages

	2006	*2007*	*2008*	*2009*	*2010*	*2011*	*2012*	*2013*	*2014*	*2015*
LDCs simple averages	106	115	134	131	142	193	162	163	175	208
LDCs population–weighted averages	38	43	49	49	52	52	49	53	47	45
SIDS simple averages	516	347	400	312	371	525	479	493	416	510
SIDS, population–weighted averages	53	65	72	79	126	102	92	85	80	81

Source: OECD, DAC.

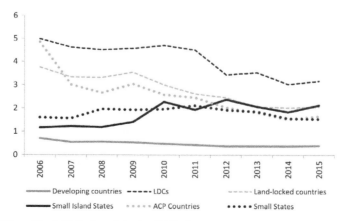

Figure 12.6 ODA as % of GNI of recipients, DAC donors
Source: OECD, DAC.

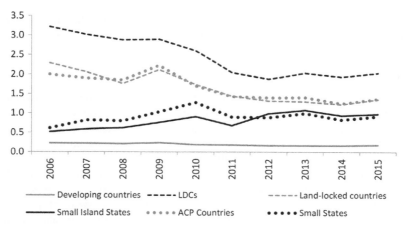

Figure 12.7 ODA as % of GNI of recipients, multilateral donors
Source: OECD, DAC.

Table 12.2 ODA as % GNI, simple averages and GNI-weighted averages

	2006	2007	2008	2009	2010	2011	2012	2013	2014	2015
LDCs simple averages	15	16	17	14	16	14	12	11	12	11
LDCs GNI-weighted averages	8	8	8	8	7	7	5	6	5	5
SIDS simple averages	10	10	10	11	12	13	11	11	10	5
SIDS, GNI-weighted averages	2	2	2	2	3	3	3	3	3	3

Source: OECD, DAC.

Table 12.2 shows the ODA/GNI changes between 2006 and 2015 calculated as a simple average and as a GNI-weighted average. It can be seen that the gap between the ratios pertaining to small countries on one hand and LDCs on the other hand is smaller than the gap between the levels of ODA per capita.

It can be noted also that the trends of the ODA to GNI ratio from 2006 to 2015 diverge, declining for LDCs as well as for the whole set of developing countries, but rather stable for small states, and increasing for SIDS. As for multilateral ODA, still as a percent of recipient GNI, the differences in trends are even more pronounced, as shown in Figure 12.7.

Differences between the simple average and GNI-weighted average (GNI of the recipient countries) of the ODA/GNI ratio may be substantial, in particular for the assessment of the trends (see Table 12.2). For example, in the case of SIDS, while the simple average of the ODA/GNI ratio decreased by half between 2006 and 2015, the weighted average increased by around 50%.

3 The rationale behind the preference given to small states

The preference given to small states in aid allocation is sometimes explained in terms of political economy considerations, in particular by the equal weight of countries in the votes at the UN General Assembly. Thus allocating a higher level of aid per capita to small states would have a higher (potential) political return. If this argument is valid it would normally lead to a stronger preference from bilateral donors than from the multilateral ones, since the latter are supposed to be less sensitive to political considerations, but this does not seem to be case.

Structural handicaps associated to smallness

A more valid reason for giving preference to small states in aid allocation is that smallness can be seen as a structural handicap to growth and development. Since the countries themselves cannot be blamed for their structural handicaps, foreign aid could be a means to compensate these states for such handicaps and thus to enhance the equality of opportunities among nations, in other words to promote international justice (Guillaumont et al., 2017a).

There are several handicaps linked to smallness (Guillaumont, 2009). The first one is the limited ability to benefit from economies of scale that impact the productivity and the potential of diversification. Another important and related handicap is that smallness is a factor of structural vulnerability, evidenced by a high level of instability. It should be noted that instability of exports and instability of agricultural production, are components of the UN Economic Vulnerability Index (EVI). Moreover, smallness is often associated with remoteness from the world markets, which generates high transportation costs. Remoteness is another component of the EVI.[3]

Many small developing countries are remote islands located in tropical areas. These tend to be highly vulnerable to climate change, as indicated by the Physical Vulnerability to Climate Change Index (PCVVI) developed by Ferdi (see Guillaumont, 2015a, 2015b and Guillaumont et al., 2017b).

Figure 12.8 presents three indicators of vulnerability, showing that small developing states tend to be more vulnerable than other groups of developing countries.

To sum up, the structural handicaps faced by small states due to their smallness and other aspects of vulnerability support the rationale for giving a relatively high level of ODA to these states, in addition to that based on income per capita criterion.

4 Evidence from a simple allocation model

It is possible to estimate a general function of aid allocation using the usual explanatory variables to assess the effect of smallness on the level of aid received by countries. For this purpose we estimated the following equation, for 149 countries and the period 2002 to 2015, with all variables measured in logs:

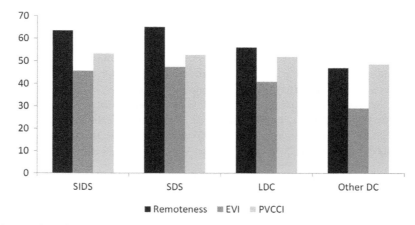

Figure 12.8 Vulnerabilities of small developing states
Note: Each indicator is normalized along a 0–100 scale.

Aid Allocation = f (Population, GDP per capita, Quality of governance).

The estimation results are presented in Table 12.3. The table provides estimates of the revealed allocation rule for bilateral, multilateral and total aid and focuses on the differences of mean of residuals between SDSs and non-SDSs.

There are 22 SDS out of the 149 developing countries that constitute our sample: Antigua and Barbuda, Belize, Cape Verde, Comoros, Dominica, Fiji, Grenada, Guyana, Kiribati, Maldives, the Marshall Islands, Mauritius, Micronesia Fed. States., Palau, Sao Tome and Principe, Seychelles, Solomon Islands, St Lucia, St Vincent and the Grenadines, Suriname, Tonga, Vanuatu. Other small islands as St Kitts & Nevis or Barbados were not included since their GNI per capita is above the threshold for aid recipients.

From Table 12.3 it can be observed that the allocated amount of aid for country i is a positive function of the population size and governance and a negative function of GDP per capita of the same country. As can be seen in columns (2) and (5) compared to (3) and (6), the role of

Table 12.3 Do small states escape general aid allocation rules? Pooled OLS estimations for 149 countries over 2002–2015

Net ODA in millions of constant US$ (log)	(1) Total aid	(2) Bilateral Aid	(3) Multilater-al aid	(4) Total aid	(5) Bilateral aid	(6) Multilater-al aid
Population	0.458★★★	0.484★★★	0.443★★★	0.547★★★	0.526★★★	0.553★★★
	(0.013)	(0.015)	(0.018)	(0.009)	(0.009)	(0.010)
GDP per capita (constant US$)	−0.640★★★	−0.537★★★	−0.901★★★	−0.504★★★	−0.472★★★	−0.736★★★
	(0.031)	(0.030)	(0.031)	(0.026)	(0.025)	(0.025)
Governance index	0.333★★★	0.034	0.667★★★	0.447★★★	0.087	0.806★★★
	(0.125)	(0.127)	(0.108)	(0.126)	(0.126)	(0.107)
Number of observations	1836	1828	1795	1836	1828	1795
Constant set to zero:	No	No	No	Yes	Yes	Yes
t test of average residuals for SDS (means and standard errors)	−0.066 (0.047)	−0.089* (0.060)	−0.041 (0.061)	0.117** (0.049)	−0.003 (0.061)	0.187★★★ (0.058)
Two-sample mean t test of residuals between SIDS and non SDS (differences of means and standard errors)	0.086* (0.054)	0.117** (0.061)	0.054 (0.066)	−0.131★★★ (0.056)	0.015 (0.061)	−0.216★★★ (0.067)

Source: OECD, DAC and the World Bank.
Notes: All variables are measured in logs. The Governance Index is the average of the 6 components of the Worldwide Governance Indicators database of the World Bank. Indicators have been rescaled to range from 1 to 6 instead of -2.5 to 2.5 as in the original data to allow take logs Robust standard errors in parentheses. Each specification includes year dummies. *** $p<0.01$, ** $p<0.05$, * $p<0.10$, + $p<0.15$.
Positive values of the two-sample t test indicate that residuals for non-SIDS are higher than residuals for SIDS.

governance or *performance* is stronger for multilateral institutions as they often give a relatively high weight to governance issues in their allocation formulas.

It should be noted that the elasticity of aid allocation with respect to population size is lower than one, with values of between 0.45 and 0.55, which reveals that a given percentage increase in the population is associated with a lower percentage increase in aid allocation, indicating a strong preference for small states. The constant term may reflect such preference since when this term is retained (columns 1 to 3) the value of the elasticities are lower than when the constant term is dropped (columns 4 to 6).

In most of their allocation formulas the Multilateral Development Banks (MDBs) introduce a fixed minimum amount of aid allocation, independently of the variables used in the above formula. The influence of those minimal amounts or floors is stronger in principle for small states and is possibly reflected in the constant term of the estimate equation, as evidenced by comparing columns (1) to (3) where the constant term is retained with columns (4) to (6) where the constant term is dropped. In addition, once the constant term dropped, as shown in columns (4) to (6), the model is far less able to adequately predict aid allocations in small states. Average residuals for SDSs are strongly negative notably for multilateral aid. Therefore, to a large extent, aid allocation in small states is not driven by the core components of traditional formulas but by the presence of special dispositions such as minimum allocations or floors. This is particularly true for multilateral aid.

4 Improving aid allocation to small states

Although the process of aid allocation seems to be biased in favour of small states, it may still not be well adapted to address the disadvantages associated with smallness. Here we mainly consider multilateral aid allocation, in particular that of the MDBs, since it is often determined by transparent formulas, while the allocation of bilateral aid is very often discretionary.

The current system applied by multilateral development banks (MDBs)

The MDBs have expressed and recently increased their preference for small states. Such a preference has been revealed in the regression results presented in Table 12.3. Two methods have principally been used. One is to set a *basis allocation* for each country before the application of the Performance Based Allocation (PBA) formula, the other is to retain a *minimum allocation* when the application of the PBA formula leads to a lower level than such a minimum.

The first solution leads to lower the relative weight of the traditional criteria of the PBA, all the more as the size of the country decreases. The second solution would cancel any impact of these traditional criteria when the minimum allocation applies. The first solution is applied by the African Development Bank (ADB) for the countries eligible for the African Development Fund (ADF). The second solution is applied by the World Bank for the countries eligible for IDA. Strikingly, the recent decision of both institutions to increase the amount of either the basis allocation or the minimum allocation has eroded the importance of the PBA criterion (Guillaumont and Wagner, 2015).

An alternative approach: non-linear treatment of population

The way smallness is measured in aid allocation may lead to anomalies in such allocation to small developing countries. In the case of the minimum allocation scheme the risk of a threshold effect would lead to all small or very small countries receiving the same amount whatever their respective size, But the respective size of these countries may vary from one to more than

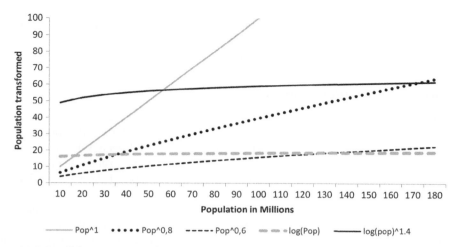

Figure 12.9 Possible treatments of population size

one hundred[4] so that a not-so-small country with a very poor performance may then receive nearly the same 'minimum' amount as a smaller one with a good performance.

For these reasons it seems preferable to treat the size of countries in a continuous manner. A good example is given by the Asian Development Bank for the allocation of the resources of the Asian Development Fund, where in the PBA formula contains includes 0.6 as an exponent on the population size.

In fact, there are several possible ways to treat population in a non-linear way, so that *ceteris paribus* the allocation per capita increases when the population increases. This could be done by applying a positive fraction as an exponent on population size, taking the log of the population or the combination of both. This approach may possibly produce results close to the lump treatment applied by several MDBs, but it fully takes into account the heterogeneity of size among small countries.

A complementary approach: taking vulnerability into account

In this framework, a non-linear treatment of smallness could capture the vulnerability associated with smallness. But not all vulnerabilities are linked with population size. Other exogenous sources of vulnerability should be taken into account. The structural economic vulnerability, as measured by the EVI (see above) should be considered as a relevant criterion for aid allocation (see Guillaumont *et al.*, 2017a). The EVI scores are relatively high for small countries, not only due to the fact that the population size is one of the components of the EVI, albeit with a relatively low weighting, but also because the other components of the index generally have higher scores for small states (e.g. the remoteness from world markets, the concentration of exports, the instability of exports of goods and services or the instability of agricultural production).

However, the level of these components can differ among small countries. It should be recalled that the legitimacy of this criterion has been enhanced in December 2012 by a Resolution of the UN General Assembly on graduation of LDCs,[5] that invites development partners to use three LDC identification criteria, namely GNI per capita, the Human Asset Index (HAI) and the EVI.

Another vulnerability to take into account in this regard is that relating to climate change, which is on average high in small states (see Nurse *et al.*, 2014), but with strong differences between them. For this reason, it makes sense to use as a criterion for aid allocation an index of vulnerability to climate change such as the physical of vulnerability to climate change index

(PVCCI) developed by Ferdi. Because it is 'physical', in other words exogenous and independent of policy measures, it can be used as a criterion for aid allocation, particularly in connection with adaptation to climate change (Guillaumont, 2015a, 2015b).

5 Conclusion: tackling smallness

The level of aid received by SDS and SIDS is relatively high, considered either per capita or as a ratio to their GNI, even if its total amount is low (it does not exceed 5% of the total amount of ODA). The rationale proposed in this paper for this relatively high level of ODA is grounded in the relatively high economic and climate change vulnerability of the small developing countries. But these countries, either by their population size or by the level of the vulnerabilities they face, are heterogeneous.

So the preferential treatment small states deserve in aid allocation should be implemented on the basis of continuous criteria of population size as explained above, as well as on the basis of vulnerability indices, rather than on the basis of membership to a debatable category of small countries or through the allocation of a lump amount of funds.

Notes

1 SIDS is an acronym for Small Island Developing States.
2 Among the 37 independent countries considered as SIDS by the United Nations (https://sustainable development.un.org/topics/sids/list) five are not 'small', i.e. they have a population higher than 1.5 million. These are Cuba, Dominican Republic, Haiti, Papua New Guinea and Singapore, and among the 44 independent developing countries considered as SDS 10 are not islands (Bhutan, Botswana, Djibouti, Equatorial Guinea, Gabon, Gambia, Lesotho, Namibia, Qatar, Swaziland). Moreover, within each of the two groups, several countries no longer can be considered as 'developing' and are no longer on the OECD/DAC list of the countries eligible for ODA.
3 Details on the composition of EVI are given in United Nations Committee for Development Policy (2015) and Guillaumont (2015a).
4 For instance the population of Tuvalu compared to that of Mauritius or Trinidad and Tobago.
5 United Nations General Assembly (2012) General Assembly resolution A/C.2/67/L.51 on smooth transition for countries graduating from the list of least developed countries, New York.

References

Guillaumont, P. (2009). *Caught in a trap, Identifying the Least Developed Countries*. Paris: Economica.
Guillaumont, P. (2015a). Measuring Structural Vulnerability to Allocate Development Assistance and Adaptation Resources. *Ferdi Working Paper*, No. 68 (rev.).
Guillaumont, P. (2015b). Measuring vulnerability to climate change for allocating funds to adaptation. In Barrett, S., Carraro, C. and de Melo, J. (eds), *Towards a workable and effective climate regime*. London: CEPR Press: 515–533.
Guillaumont, P., Guillaumont, Jeanneney S., and Wagner, L. (2017a). 'How to Take into Account Vulnerability in Aid Allocation Criteria and Lack of Human Capital as Well: Improving the Performance Based Allocation'. *World Development*, Vol. 90: 27–40.
Guillaumont, P., Simonet, C., Closset, M. and Feindounou, S. (2017b). An Index of Physical Vulnerability to Climate Change. Who are the Most Vulnerable Countries? *Ferdi Working Paper* (forthcoming).
Guillaumont, P. and Wagner, L. (2015). Performance-based allocation (PBA), still alive? In Mak Arvin, B. and Lew, B. (eds) *Handbook on the Economics of Foreign Aid*. Cheltenham: Edward Elgar Publishing: 19–27.
Nurse, L. A., McLean, R. F., Agard, J., Briguglio, L. P., Duvat-Magnan, V., Pelesikoti, N., Tompkins, E. and Webb, A. (2014). Small islands. In *Climate Change 2014: Impacts, Adaptation, and Vulnerability (IPCC AR4 Report)*. Cambridge and New York: 1613–1654.
United Nations Committee for Development Policy (2015). *Handbook on the Least Developed Country Category: Inclusion, Graduation and Special Support Measures*. New York: United Nations.

13

Dutch disease and the Pacific island countries

T. K. Jayaraman and Evan Lau

1 Introduction

Since the 1980s, Pacific island countries (PICs)[1] have been amongst the top most recipients of foreign aid per capita. Known as official overseas development assistance (ODA), the annual capital inflows from bilateral sources and multinational institutions have been a great support to PICs for meeting their budgetary expenditures. Furthermore, they have been supplementing domestic savings and real resources of PICs. They also augmented PICs' limited foreign exchange earnings from the narrow range of commodity exports, which have remained stagnant for some time.

Another category of unrequited transfers of funds from overseas has also come to the rescue of the PICs' economies. These transfers known as remittances from islanders who migrated to Australia, New Zealand, United States and Europe, are sent to their families still residing in the migrants' country of origin, have exceeded the PICs' annual ODA inflows.

As expected, regular inflows of remittances and aid have raised concerns as to whether these inflows are hurting the export competitiveness of the island nations, a phenomenon known as '*Dutch disease*'.[2] These concerns have become more pronounced since the world economic down turn in 2009, when the world demand for commodities began to decline and the already stagnant export earnings of PICs commenced to plunge.

In this chapter, we attempt to examine the validity of the Dutch disease hypothesis in the PICs, through a panel data approach. Our investigation is confined only to five PICs, namely Fiji, Samoa, Solomon Islands, Tonga and Vanuatu. The study does not cover Papua New Guinea (PNG)[3], which is considered as an outlier on various grounds. The remaining eight PICs were not included in our analysis due to data inadequacies. To the best of our knowledge, no empirical investigation so far been carried out to investigate the validity of Dutch disease in the PICs.

Since all the five countries under study have fixed exchange rate regimes, domestic money supply gets augmented with addition of foreign exchange earnings consequent to receipts of foreign aid and remittances which are in foreign currency. When these receipts get deposited in banking system, reserves of the banks rise. As a result, bank lending rises. The nature of public sector investment expenditure funded by aid money and private sector expenditure financed by remittances as well as bank lending, in turn determine the kind of output. If government spends aid moneys and public borrowing, if any, on improving substantially and expand the domestic supplies of water, electricity and other non tradables, domestic price level would fall relatively to foreign price level causing REER to fall. Employing the panel data analysis, the study finds strong evidence of direct and significant link between foreign capital inflows in terms of aid and remittances and appreciation of domestic currency.

The chapter is organized on the following lines: the next section presents a brief summary of the literature on the Dutch disease; the third section reviews the trends in aid and remittance inflows received by PICs; the fourth section outlines the methodology adopted for the empirical investigation; the fifth section reports the results; and the last section presents conclusions with policy implications.

2 Brief review of literature on Dutch disease

The term Dutch disease originally referred to the unintended negative impact of a resource boom on a country's non-resource tradable sector, which includes agriculture and manufacturing. The usage of the term is traced to the 1960 description of an unexpected rise in the appreciation of the Dutch currency, following a surge in the foreign exchange inflows due to the discovery of the North Sea gas fields in the Netherlands economy. The highly welcome, favourable development of addition of real resources in terms of foreign exchange made the Dutch currency stronger, rendering the country's exports less attractive to foreigners (International Monetary Fund, 2003). As a result, the traditional export sector was negatively affected.

The Dutch experience indicates that the adverse impact of the reduction in the production of exportable or tradable goods generally leads to re-allocation of resources from the tradable goods to the non-tradable goods sector, leading to an eventual decrease in economic growth. In many cases, aggregate economic activity slows down over a period (Tuano-Amador et al., 2007). This decrease in growth over time due to getting rich with rising level of foreign exchange reserves is described as the Dutch disease, because manufacturing, which tends to be more competitive and innovative than other sectors and hence characterized by technological spillovers, gets less incentives to grow (Oomes and Kalcheva, 2007).

The phenomenon of Dutch disease was articulated in a highly acclaimed contribution by Corden and Neary (1982) along the following lines. A boom in one traded goods sector squeezes profitability in other traded goods sectors, both by directly bidding resources away from them and by placing upward pressure on the exchange rate.

One implication of this tendency us that rising earnings from any natural resource endowments sector, including the tourism sector, as a result of an attractive combination of surf, sun and sand, when spent by citizens within the economy would lead to a rise in the price of non-tradable goods including water, electricity, land and house rents and services. The eventual result would be an increase in real exchange rate[4] hurting the competitiveness of tradable goods, both exportable and importable.

Over time, the usage of the term Dutch disease has been extended to cover the impact of all unrequited capital transfers, including foreign aid and remittances on export competitiveness as well.

Focusing attention on the effect of capital inflows on domestic relative prices and output, Corden (1984) dubbed the small states as price takers since prices of all their traded goods are fixed on world markets. Therefore, specifically with reference to small island states, an increase in domestic expenditure would result only in the rise of the prices of goods that are not internationally traded. The resultant relative price change would lead to a change in the composition of output, with the traded goods sector contracting. The aggregate output falls, justifying the description of the relative price effect as 'Dutch disease' (Fielding, 2007).

There are two major channels of conveyance of the Dutch disease effect of aid and remittance (IMF, 2003, Ratha, 2013). As income transfers, inflows of aid and remittances are expected to result in a *spending effect* causing an increasing in the consumption of tradable and non-tradable goods. Since prices of tradable goods are determined outside the small economies, the relative prices of the domestic, non-tradable goods increase and contribute to boost the overall domestic price level. This leads to higher real exchange rate, fuelling and fuelled by a *resource movement effect*: Rising non-tradable prices shift resources away from production of tradables to production of non-tradables. These shifts exert upward pressures on wages and other production costs, and ultimately the overall price level. The resulting appreciation in real exchange rate would consequently hurt the export competitiveness (Acosta *et al.*, 2009).

Aside from spending effect consequent to rise in inward remittances, there is also the effect flowing out of consumption-leisure trade-off, relating to reduction in the overall supply of labour in the economy. When demand grows and consumption rises as a result of increased remittance inflows, reduction in labour supply would tend to exacerbate price increases, especially in the non-tradable sector. The overall rise in price level would push the domestic currency to appreciate even further.

There are a number of empirical studies testing the Dutch disease hypothesis. Due to data constraints mainly imposed by inadequate number of years covered by time series, most of the studies happen to be panel studies. One of the earlier studies, by Adenauer and Vagassky (1998), dealt with the countries of the West African Economic and Monetary Union, and found convincing evidence that capital inflows led to substantial real exchange rate appreciation.

Rajan and Subramanian (2005) conducted a larger cross-country study, covering Asian and Latin American countries and concluded that foreign aid inflows lead to the Dutch disease. A smaller panel data study focusing on 13 Latin American countries, by Amuedo-Dorantes and Pozo (2004), confirms that remittances lowered export competitiveness. Lopez *et al.*, (2008) reconfirmed this findings for a larger sample of countries, followed by Lartey *et al.*, (2012) who also segregated the resource movement and the spending effects and found remittances to shrink the tradable sector (relative to the non-tradable sector) – a finding consistent with the foregoing discussion.

There are also a few notable country studies. A study by White and Wignaraja (1992) on Sri Lanka established that aid inflows contributed to exchange rate appreciation. Similar finding was reached by Vargas-Silva (2009) for Mexico, Bayangos and Jansen (2010) for Philippines and Bourdet and Falck (2006) for Cape Verde. On the other hand, Andrade and Duarte (2011) concluded that the Portuguese economy suffered from the Dutch disease since the second half of the 1990s, and loss of external competitiveness resulting from stagnant output since 2002.

3 Aid and remittance inflows of PICs

Most of the PICs, which became politically independent in the second half of the last century, have been amongst the largest aid recipients since the 1980s. Recognizing the challenges faced by PICs, which included limited resource base, narrow range of exports and inadequate tax revenue to meet recurrent expenditure in the annual budgets, the former colonial rulers in their geopolitical interests continued their financial assistance for meeting annual recurrent and capital expenditures. Aid flows were a great support to their budgets until the early 1990s.

Following the fall of Berlin Wall signifying the end of the Cold War in the late 1980s, in the emerging uni-polar world attention came to be focused on rehabilitation of the Eastern

Table 13.1 PICs: aid (% of GDP), 1982–2014

Year	Fiji	Samoa	Solomon I.	Tonga	Vanuatu
1982–1989 ★	3.3	25.5	22.0	23.0	27.1
1990–1999 ★	2.9	27.5	14.4	16.6	20.2
2000–2004 ★	1.9	12.6	17.6	11.1	12.7
2005–2009 ★	1.9	10.2	47.0	9.8	13.3
2010	2.5	25.7	68.6	18.5	16.0
2011	2.2	15.5	50.5	20.6	11.8
2012	2.8	17.6	32.7	16.7	13.8
2013	2.2	15.5	27.4	18.3	11.4
2014	2.1	12.0	18.1	18.2	12.1

Source: World Development Indicators, World Bank (2014).* average

European states. As a result, donors scaled down the aid flows to PICs with a view to funding only capital expenditure part of PICs' budgets rather than operating part. Almost coinciding with this decision there was the release of a study by World Bank (1993) on PICs, which observed that PICs, despite high per capita aid, performed dismally in comparison to similarly placed island countries in the Caribbean and Indian Ocean regions. Poor growth in PICs marked by stagnation in per capita incomes in the midst of plentiful aid over two decades came to be looked upon as a 'Pacific Paradox' (World Bank 1993). Following the findings of the World Bank study, reform programmes were initiated in several PICs in the late 1990s.

Table 13.1 show that Solomon Islands, Tonga, Samoa and Vanuatu received relatively larger aid inflows as percentage of GDP. However, there have been wide fluctuations in aid flows.

Migration has become an outlet for many in PICs, as islanders have been seeking employment in metropolitan countries on a regular basis. PICs also happen to be amongst the world's highest recipients of remittances. Emigrants from PICs have been remitting funds on a regular basis to their families still living in the emigrants' country of origin. Regular monthly remittance inflows have proved a great support for families to keep up their consumption levels as well as meeting educational expenses for children and medical expenses for the elderly.

Among the PICs, Samoa and Tonga are the largest recipients of remittances as percent of GDP of which been shown in Table 13.2.

The next section deals with the empirical investigation of relationship between aid, remittances, domestic credit and real exchange rate.

4 Modelling, methodology and data

We now proceed to undertake the empirical investigation for testing the hypothesis that aid and remittances positively affect the real exchange rate. For the investigation purposes, we use the indices of the trade weighted real effective exchange rate (REER) (International Monetary Fund, 2014). Due to severe data constraints, we employ a minimum set of variables which have relatively longer time series and which are consistent and reliable.

We introduce a policy variable to capture the effect of government's fiscal and monetary stances on REER. This is represented by domestic credit as a ratio of GDP (DOMCRE). Expansionary fiscal and monetary policies, represented by rise in DOMCRE are likely to influence REER. We cannot say *a priori* whether REER and DOMCRE will move in the same direction or not. The

Table 13.2 PICs: remittances (% of GDP), 1982–2014

Year	Fiji	Samoa	Solomon I.	Tonga	Vanuatu
1982–1989★	1.7	25.1	0.2	23.1	6.6
1990–1999★	1.5	21.8	0.4	18.1	7.6
2000–2004★	4.9	16.6	1.3	31.3	7.5
2005–2009★	5.8	17.9	2.0	27.5	1.4
2010	5.5	21.1	2.1	20.9	1.7
2011	4.2	21.0	1.9	17.8	2.7
2012	4.8	22.1	2.0	25.7	2.8
2013	4.9	20.7	1.9	27.9	3.0
2014	4.6	17.6	1.4	26.3	3.5

Source: World Development Indicators, World Bank (2014).

sign of the coefficient may either be positive or negative. If policy measures would lead to rise in supply of non-tradable goods such as water and electricity, housing and other infrastructural facilities and other services, the resultant domestic inflation would be low and therefore there might be a fall in REER, given the world price level. On the other hand, if economic policies such as expansionary monetary and fiscal policies happened to be inflationary, REER would rise reducing the competitiveness of the economy's exports given the world price level.

The model

The empirical model for estimation purposes is written as follows:

$$REER_{i,t} = \beta_0 + \beta_1 AID_{i,t} + \beta_2 REM_{i,t} + \beta_3 DOMCRE_{i,t} + \varepsilon_{i,t} \tag{1}$$

where REER = real exchange rate in index number;

AID = aid as percent of GDP;

REM = remittance inflows as percent of GDP;

DCGDP = domestic credit as percent of GDP;

ε = white noise error term.

The subscript i refers to the observation in the ith country and the subscript t to the year of the observation.

With the growing interest of cross-country data over time especially in empirical macroeconomic, the focus of panel data econometrics has shifted towards the stationary and cointegration dimensions (Asteriou and Hall, 2016; Baltagi, 2013). To this end, this research adopts the non-stationary panel data analysis which considered a larger T (length of time series) compared to N (number of countries) rather than the usual panels with large N and small T[5]. Our study uses accordingly the more sophisticated panel cointegration tests along the lines of Pedroni (1999, 2001, 2004) and Kao (1999).

Method

Unit root and stationary tests

To estimate equation (1) we adopt the procedures of Maddala and Wu (1999), Hadri (2000), Levin *et al.*, (2002) and Im *et al.*, (2003) for conducting panel unit root and stationarity tests in order to unleash more conclusive evidence with regard to the order of integration of the series under investigation. The null hypothesis of these tests is that the panel series has a unit root (non-stationary) except for the Hadri test. The Hadri test is similar to the KPSS type unit root test, with a null hypothesis of stationarity in the panel.

Cointegration

For examining the existence of any long run equilibrium relationship between the variables under investigation, we resorted to Pedroni (1999, 2001, 2004) and Kao (1999) panel coin-tegration tests. Pedroni (1999, 2001, 2004) considers seven different statistics, four of which are based on pooling the residuals of the regression along the within-dimension (panel test) of panel and the other three are based on pooling the residuals of the regression along the between-dimension (group test) of the panel. The within-dimension tests take into account common time factors and allow for heterogeneity across countries. The between-dimension tests are the group-mean cointegration tests, which allow for heterogeneity of parameters across countries. Meanwhile, Kao (1999) proposed DF and ADF-type tests for $\varepsilon_{it}$where the null is specified as no cointegration. In this study, we only report the ADF-type test.

Fully modified OLS (FMOLS) estimates

To obtain the long run estimates of the cointegrating relationship, we adopted the panel group mean Fully Modified OLS (FMOLS) following the work by Pedroni (2000). The FMOLS procedure accommodates the heterogeneity that is typically present both in the transitional serial correlation dynamics and in the long run cointegrating relationships.

Granger Causality Tests

To specify the causal direction of these variables, we relied on the panel non-causality test developed by Dumitrescu and Hurlin (2012). This is a simple extension of the Granger (1969) relax the '*homogeneity*' of cross-section units assumption made by Holtz-Eakin *et al.* (1988, 1989) in the panel data setting.[6] By preserving the heterogeneity of cross-sectional units, it allows us to test the direction of causality between these macroeconomic variables without imposing the same dynamic model for all the countries of the sample. We consider the panel heterogeneous autoregressive model as follows:

$$y_{it} = \phi_i + \sum_{k=1}^{K} \gamma_i^{(k)} y_{i,t-k} + \sum_{k=1}^{K} \beta_i^{(k)} x'_{i,t-k} + \varepsilon_{i,t} \qquad (2)$$

where x and y are two stationary variables, observed on t periods for n countries. The panel is balanced, individual effects are assumed to be fixed and the lag-order k are identical for all cross-section units of the panel. $\gamma_i^{(k)}$ denote the autoregressive parameters, and $\beta_i^{(k)}$ are the regression coefficients' slopes; both parameters differing across countries. By definition, x cause y if and only if the past values of the variable x observed on the ith country improve the forecasts of the variable y for this country i only.

To test the causality relationship, the null hypothesis of homogeneous non-causality (HNC), i.e., there is no causal relationship from x to y for all the countries of the panel $(\beta_i = (\beta^{(i)}...\beta^{(k)})' = 0, \forall = 1...N)$ in Equation 2. Under the alternative hypothesis, there exists a causal relationship from x to y for at least one country of the sample[7]. The test statistic is given by the cross-sectional average of individual Wald statistics defined for the Granger non-causality hypothesis for each country (W_{HNC}), and converges to a chi-squared distribution with K degrees of freedom. They show that the standardized version of this statistic, appropriately weighted in unbalanced panels, follows a standard normal distribution and it is represented by (Z_{HNC}). For more details, the reader can refer to Dumitrescu and Hurlin (2012).

The data

The study uses annual data covering a 33-year period (1982–2014) relating to five PICs for the empirical analysis. Data for the empirical study are drawn from three sources: World Bank (2014) for AID and REM both as percentages of GDP. The REER data series for Fiji are drawn from IMF (2014), and for others are calculated by the authors[8] (Table 13.3). The data series on DOMCRE (Table 13.4) are sourced from Asian Development Bank (2014). Since the five PICs under study have a high degree of commonalities, we resort to the panel data

Table 13.3 PICs: REER index (base 2010= 100), 1982–2014

Year	Fiji	Samoa	Solomon I.	Tonga	Vanuatu
1982–1989 ★	67.0	109.5	86.9	168.6	107.6
1990–1999 ★	83.8	126.8	102.9	89.1	95.1
2000–2004 ★	91.5	126.9	99.5	84.8	104.1
2005–2009 ★	88.8	109.0	103.3	93.5	104.4
2010	100.0	100.0	100.0	100.0	100.0
2011	96.7	99.1	97.0	106.0	101.5
2012	93.8	97.1	88.7	106.7	102.4
2013	92.9	95.5	82.6	108.1	98.7
2014	93.8	95.5	78.0	103.8	94.6

Source: Asian Development Bank (2014).

Note: * average.

Table 13.4 PICs: domestic credit (as % of GDP), 1982–2014

Year	Fiji	Samoa	Solomon I.	Tonga	Vanuatu
1982–1989 ★	33.2	15.8	24.5	24.7	23.3
1990–1999 ★	41.8	5.6	24.4	31.5	32.8
2000–2004 ★	79.8	23.5	33.8	40.5	40.6
2005–2009 ★	124.3	50.98	34.0	47.7	47.8
2010	132.3	63.9	27.2	40.3	63.7
2011	115.6	62.7	14.1	29.9	67.7
2012	114.4	61.2	11.8	27.1	70.0
2013	111.9	67.2	21.0	28.6	68.7
2014	113.1	77.4	22.2	29.5	79.1

Source: Asian Development Bank (2014).

Note: * average.

techniques to estimate equation (1). The four variables included in the analysis are transformed into logarithmic form prior to estimation.

5 Empirical results

The long run estimates for the panel of PICs, presented in equation below show that AID and REM have positive signs and are found statistically significant. Additionally, we found that DOMCRE has a negative sign and also statistically significant.

$$REER = 0.169 \text{ AID} + 0.300 \text{ REM} - 0.499 \text{ DOMCRE}$$

$$(2.444) \qquad (4.233) \qquad (-10.778)$$

where the figures in parenthesis are t-statistics.

Since the variables are in log form, values of the estimated coefficients denote the elasticity magnitudes: one percent rise in AID gives rise to 0.169% increase in REER. The elasticity estimate of REER with respect to REM is 0.300, indicating one percent increase in REM leads to 0.3% rise in REER.

These results confirm the hypotheses that aid and remittances lead to appreciation of the real exchange rate. As regards economic policies of the government represented by DOMCRE, we note that the sign of the estimated coefficient is negative. As stated earlier, there could not be any *a priori* conclusion whether or not REER and DOMCRE will move in the same direction. The sign of the coefficient obtained being negative means that if government policy had led to rise in the supply of non-tradable goods such as water and electricity, domestic inflation would have fallen; a fall in would lead to a decrease in REER, given the world price level. Thus, the negative sign confirms that expansionary fiscal and monetary policies, which were apparently directed towards raising domestic output of non-tradables have indeed contributed to a downward scenario.

As to the reliability of the results, Appendix 1 shows that the variables REER, AID, REM and DOMCRE are of an *I(1)* process as the pooled data are stationary in their first differences, indicating that all the variables are integrated of the order 1 or I (1). Panel Cointegration and FMOLS test results are presented in Appendix 2. In Appendix 3, we report two statistics relating to causality tests namely the average Wald statistic (W_{HNC}) and the standardized statistic (Z_{HNC}) based on the asymptotic moments. In order to assess the sensitivity of our results to the choice of the common lag-order, we report these two statistics for one and for two lags.

The empirical investigation uses the available data of a limited period. In the absence of data for a fairly long period of annual observations, which are necessary for meaningful analysis for each country, the investigation takes up a panel approach. The reader is, accordingly, cautioned that the results have to be looked upon as a generalization for the region rather than results for a particular PIC.

6 Summary and conclusions

The objective of the empirical study presented in this chapter is to examine the validity of the Dutch disease hypothesis in five PICs, with data pertaining to 33 years (1982–2014). The dependent variable employed in the study is the real effective exchange rate index, the nominal exchange rate having been defined as units of US dollars for one unit of domestic currency, which is duly adjusted for the relative variation between foreign price and domestic price levels;

with three explanatory variables namely (i) aid expressed as a percentage of GDP (ii) remittances also expressed as a percentage of GDP; and (iii) a policy variable, namely domestic credit as percentage of GDP.

The results presented in this chapter establish the presence of the phenomenon of the Dutch disease in PICs, hurting the attractiveness of its exports. The policy implications are clear and straight forward. Since the ratio of domestic prices to world price level is a determinant of real exchange rate, the governments should control domestic inflationary pressures. The domestic price level in PICs is largely influenced by prices of imports of basic necessities such as food and fuel, for which no import substitution is possible.

Accordingly, governments are well advised to adopt policy measures with the aim of (i) encourage output of non-tradables so as to increase their share in domestic production; (ii) promote agricultural output given that PICs have large areas of unutilized land — this would eventually lessen domestic inflationary pressure and further improve the economic conditions for these PICs; and (iii) improve revenue collection by strengthening enforcement measures and by cutting down needless public expenditures including reducing numerous sinecure government positions and privatizing inefficient and loss-making public enterprises of commercial nature. Such measures should eventually contribute to lessening the PICs' dependency on aid.

Notes

1 The 14 Pacific island countries members are: Cook Islands, Fiji, Kiribati, the Marshall Islands, Federated States of Micronesia, Nauru, Niue, Papua New Guinea, Samoa, Solomon Islands, Tonga, Tuvalu and Vanuatu. Six of the 14 PICs, namely Fiji, Papua New Guinea, Samoa, Solomon Islands, Tonga and Vanuatu have their own national currencies, while the remaining eight have been using currencies of their former rulers as legal tender.
2 The term refers to the consequences of a natural resource discovery in the Netherlands (see Section 2 for details).
3 The economy of PNG is much larger than that any of the other five PICs in terms of population (7.3 million) and, land mass (area 462,840 sq. km). The PIC with the second highest population is Fiji with only around 850, 000. Further, PNG's substantial mineral resources including natural gas, gold and copper, and non-mineral resources, including tree crops have provided the country with a very well diversified export base. For these reasons, PNG is considered as an outlier and hence excluded from the study.
4 The nominal exchange rate for the purpose of the study is defined as units of foreign currency per unit of domestic currency. The real exchange rate is therefore the nominal exchange rate multiplied by the ratio of domestic price to world price.
5 Baltagi and Kao (2000) and Chiang and Kao (2001) provide excellent and comprehensive survey for studying nonstationary panel data.
6 Dumitrescu and Hurlin (2012) allow for two subgroups of cross-section units: the first one is characterized by causal relationships from x to y, but it does not necessarily rely on the same regression model, whereas there is no causal relationships from x to y in the case of the second subgroup. Further, they consider a heterogenous panel data model with fixed Coefficients (in time). The dynamics of the variables may be thus heterogeneous across the cross-section units, regardless of the existence (or not) of causal relationships.
7 For example, x= AID and y= REER following the empirical model of Equation 1. In this scenario, if the null of HNC is rejected then AID Granger causes REER at least in one country of the PICs.
8 The nominal exchange rate has been defined, for the purpose of the study, as units of foreign currency per unit of domestic currency. Therefore, the real exchange rate is obtained by multiplying the nominal exchange rate, with the ratio of domestic price to world price and the index numbers over the period were derived. The data on nominal exchange rate, domestic price and world price indices were sourced from IMF's International Financial Statistics.

Appendix 1

Table 13.A1 Panel unit root tests results

	Test statistics					
	LLC	*IPS*	*MW (ADF)*	*MW (PP)*	*HADRI*	*Conclusion*
A: Level						
Model specification: individual effects						
REER	−0.485	−1.194	12.614	13.676	4.569	−
	(0.313)	(0.116)	(0.246)	(0.188)	(0.000)	
AID	−0.545	−0.994	11.899	15.151	3.361	−
	(0.292)	(0.160)	(0.291)	(0.126)	(0.000)	
REM	0.133	−0.337	9.039	9.712	4.810	−
	(0.553)	(0.367)	(0.528)	(0.466)	(0.000)	
DOMCRE	1.959	1.916	9.640	4.896	5.677	−
	(0.974)	(0.972)	(0.472)	(0.898)	(0.000)	
Model specification: individual effects and individual linear trends						
REER	−1.236	−0.430	9.913	7.39107	6.91486	−
	(0.108)	(0.333)	(0.448)	(0.6881)	(0.000)	
AID	1.204	−0.226	9.012	14.136	2.244	−
	(0.885)	(0.410)	(0.530)	(0.166)	(0.012)	
REM	1.746	0.143	7.018	14.379	4.222	−
	(0.959)	(0.556)	(0.723)	(0.156)	(0.000)	
DOMCRE	1.038	0.976	12.609	6.746	4.251	−
	(0.850)	(0.835)	(0.246)	(0.749)	(0.000)	
B: First differences						
Model specification: individual effects						
ΔREER	−4.226	−6.521	59.0668	80.6469	−0.16864	I(1)
	(0.000)	(0.000)	(0.000)	(0.000)	(0.567)	
ΔAID	−11.463	−8.220	76.920	121.666	−0.895	I(1)
	(0.000)	(0.000)	(0.000)	(0.000)	(0.814)	
ΔREM	−10.870	−7.242	66.626	128.101	−1.179	I(1)
	(0.000)	(0.000)	(0.000)	(0.000)	(0.880)	
ΔDOMCRE	−7.239	−5.780	56.394	79.403	1.055	I(1)
	(0.000)	(0.000)	(0.000)	(0.000)	(0.145)	
Model specification: individual effects and individual linear trends						
ΔREER	−3.363	−6.489	55.4353	76.4891	−0.84446	I(1)
	(0.000)	(0.000)	(0.000)	(0.000)	(0.8008)	
ΔAID	−7.808	−7.145	61.481	369.459	0.634	I(1)
	(0.000)	(0.000)	(0.000)	(0.000)	(0.262)	
ΔREM	−9.467	−5.835	49.576	115.897	0.391	I(1)
	(0.000)	(0.000)	(0.000)	(0.000)	(0.347)	
ΔDOMCRE	−5.514	−4.728	42.748	74.419	1.162	I(1)
	(0.000)	(0.000)	(0.000)	(0.000)	(0.122)	

Notes: IPS, LLC and HADRI indicated the Im *et al.* (2003), Levin *et al.* (2002) and Hadri (2000) panel unit root and stationary tests. MW (Fisher-ADF) and MW (Fisher-PP) denotes Maddala and Wu (1999) Fisher-ADF and Fisher-PP panel unit root test. The IPS, LLC, MW (Fisher-ADF) and MW (Fisher-PP) examines the null hypothesis of non-stationary while HADRI tests the stationary null hypothesis. The four variables were grouped into one panel with sample N=33, T=5. The values in parenthesis are the probability of rejection. Probabilities for the MW (Fisher-ADF) and MW (Fisher-PP) tests are computed using an asymptotic χ^2 distribution, while the other tests follow the asymptotic normal distribution.

Appendix 2

There is evidence to reject the null hypothesis of no cointegration for four out of the seven statistics provided by Pedroni (1999, 2001, 2004). Similarly, the null hypothesis of no cointegration using the ADF-type statistics from Kao (1999) panel cointegration tests is rejected suggesting that the four-dimensional model of REER for the PICs is in fact cointegrated (see Panel B). Rejection of the null hypothesis of no cointegration between the I(1) series in the panel implies that the four variables do not drift apart and they continue to move in the same direction in the long run in the multi-country panel PICs setting.

Table 13.A2 Panel cointegration and regression results

A: Pedroni residual cointegration test	
Panel cointegration statistics (within-dimension)	
Panel v-statistic	−0.918 (0.820)
Panel PP type ρ-statistic	−0.929 (0.176)
Panel PP type *t*-statistic	−2.835 (0.002)**
Panel ADF type *t*-statistic	−2.828(0.002)**
Group mean panel cointegration statistics (between-dimension)	
Group PP type ρ -statistic	−0.891 (0.186)
Group PP type t − statistic	−3.355 (0.000)**
Group ADF type *t*- statistic	−3.403 (0.000)**
B: Kao residual cointegration test	
ADF	−2.057 (0.019)**
C: Fully modified OLS (FMOLS) estimates	
Variables	FMOLS
AID	0.169 (2.444)**
REM	0.300 (4.233)**
DOMCRE	−0.499 (−10.778)**

Notes: The number of lag truncations used in the calculation of the seven Pedroni statistics and Kao ADF is 1. The values in [] and () are probability and t-statistics respectively. Asterisks (**) and (*) shows significance at 5% and 10% level.

Appendix 3:

The results of the causality test can be summarized as follows:

- There is a significant causal relationship running from AID to REER.
- We observe that REM does Granger-cause AID.
- Bi-directional causality is detected, running from DOMCRE ↔ AID. The past values of the domestic credit and aid mutually have been reinforcing each other. This bidirectional causality shows that expansionary policies attract AID; and AID Granger causes DOMCRE.
- AID, which is influenced by DOMCRE and REM, ultimately Granger-causes REER.

Table 13.A3 Dumitrescu and Hurlin panel Granger-causality tests

Direction of causality	Lag	W^{HNC}	Z^{HNC}	Probability
REER → AID	1	1.94486	−0.21056	0.833
	2	1.58497	−0.55222	0.508
AID → REER	1	6.63796**	4.24473**	0.000
	2	6.21985**	3.84781**	0.000
REM → AID	1	5.35596**	3.02770**	0.002
	2	4.66768**	2.37429**	0.018
AID → REM	1	0.77850	0.08925	0.928
	2	0.94601	0.28632	0.775
DOMCRE → AID	1	6.88359**	3.21952**	0.001
	2	6.02831**	6.89134**	0.000
AID → DOMCRE	1	3.03718**	2.73067**	0.006
	2	4.14781**	4.27557**	0.000
REM → REER	1	1.44382	−0.68622	0.493
	2	1.00880	0.31942	0.749
REER → REM	1	5.33003**	5.92002**	0.764
	2	3.87347**	3.89395**	0.564
DOMCRE → REER	1	1.55172	0.66440	0.506
	2	1.79628	−0.35162	0.725
REER → DOMCRE	1	1.28903	0.29900	0.000
	2	0.66019	−0.57571	0.000
DOMCRE → REM	1	1.88818	−0.26438	0.791
	2	1.79628	−0.35162	0.725
REM → DOMCRE	1	1.59351	−0.54412	0.586
	2	1.44396	−0.68608	0.492

Notes: Null hypothesis is no causality. Estimations are based on the pooled data for 1982–2014 and 5 Pacific Island Countries (N=5, T=33). Asterisks (**) and (*) shows significance at 5% and 10% level.

References

Acosta, P. A., Lartey, E. K. and Mandelman, F. S. (2009). 'Remittances and the Dutch Disease'. *Journal of International Economics*, 79(1): 102–116.

Adenauer, I., Vagassky, L. (1998). 'Aid and the Real Exchange Rate: Dutch Disease Effects in African Countries'. *Intereconomics: Review of International Trade and Development*, 33(4): 177–185.

Amuedo-Dorantes, C. and Pozo, S. (2004). 'Workers' Remittances and the Real Exchange Rate: A Paradox of Gifts'. *World Development*, 32(8): 1407–1417.

Andrade, J. S., Duarte, A. (2011). 'The Fundamentals of the Portuguese Crisis'. *Panoeconomicus*, 58: 195–218.

Asian Development Bank (2014). *Key Indicators*. Manila: Asian Development Bank.

Asteriou, D. and Hall, S. G. (2016). *Applied Econometrics*. London: Palgrave.

Baltagi, B. H. (2013). *Econometric Analysis of Panel Data*. London: John Wiley & Sons Ltd.

Baltagi, B. H. and Kao, C. (2000). Nonstationary Panels, Cointegration in Panels and Dynamic Panels: A Survey. In Baltagi, B. H., Fomby, T. B. and Hill, R. C. (eds) *Advances in Econometrics Volume 15: Nonstationary Panels, Cointegration in Panels and Dynamic Panels*: 7–51. Greenwich, CT: JAI Press.

Bayangos, V. and Jansen, K. (2010). *Remittances and Competitiveness: The Case of the Philippines*. The Hague: Institute of Social Studies Working Paper No. 492.

Bourdet, Y. and Falck, H. (2006). 'Emigrants' Remittances and Dutch Disease in Cape Verde'. *International Economic Journal*, 20(3): 267–284.

Chiang, M. H. and Kao, C. (2001). *Nonstationary panel time series using NPT 1.2 – A user guide*. Center for Policy Research, Syracuse University.

Corden, W. M. (1984). 'Booming Sector and Dutch Disease Economics: Survey and Consolidation'. *Oxford Economic Papers*, 36(3): 359–380.

Corden, W. M. and Neary, J. P. (1982). 'Booming Sector and De-industrialization in a Small Open'. *Economic Journal*, 92(4): 359–380.

Dumitrescu, E-I. and Hurlin, C. (2012). 'Testing for Granger non-causality in heterogeneous panels' *Economic Modelling*, 29(4): 1450–1460.

Fielding, D. (2007). Aid and Dutch Disease in the South Pacific. *World Institute for Development Economic Research Paper* No. 2007/50. United Nations University.

Granger, C. W. J. (1969). 'Investigating causal relations by econometric models and crossspectral methods'. *Econometrica*, 37(3): 424–438.

Hadri, K. (2000). 'Testing for stationarity in heterogeneous panel data'. *Econometrics Journal*, 3(2): 148–161.

Holtz-Eakin, D., Newey, W. and Rosen, H. S. (1988). 'Estimating vector autoregressions with panel data'. *Econometrica*, 56(6): 1371–1395.

Holtz-Eakin, D., Newey, W. and Rosen, H. S. (1989). 'The revenues-expenditure nexus: evidence from local government data'. *International Economic Review*, 30(2): 415–429.

Im, K. S., Pesaran, M. H. and Shin, Y. (2003). 'Testing for unit roots in heterogeneous panels'. *Journal of Econometrics*, 115(1): 53–74.

International Monetary Fund (IMF) (2014). *International Financial Statistics, CD ROM 2014*. Washington, DC: IMF.

International Monetary Fund (IMF) (2003). 'Dutch Disease: Too Much Wealth Used Unwisely'. *Finance and Development*, 40(1).

Kao, C. (1999). 'Spurious regression and residual-based tests for cointegration in panel data'. *Journal of Econometrics*, 90(1): 1–44.

Lartey, K. K., Mandleman, F. S. and Acosta, P. A. (2012). 'Remittances, Exchange Rate Regimes and the Dutch Disease: A Panel Data Analysis'. *Review of International Economics*, 20(2): 377–395.

Levin, A., Levin, A., Lin, C.F. and Chu, J.C.S. (2002). 'Unit root tests in panel data: asymptotic and finite sample properties'. *Journal of Econometrics*, 108(1): 1–24.

Lopez, H., Molina, L. and Bussolo, M. (2008). Remittances and the Real Exchange rate. *World Bank Policy Research Working Paper* No. 4213.

Maddala, G. S. and Wu, S. (1999). 'A comparative study of unit root tests with panel data and a new simple test'. *Oxford Bulletin of Economics and Statistics*, 61: 631–652.

Oomes, N. and Kalcheva, K. (2007). Diagnosing Dutch Disease: Does Russia Have the Symptoms. *IMF Working Papers* WP/07/22. Washington, DC: International Monetary Fund.

Pedroni, P. (1999). 'Critical values for cointegration tests in heterogeneous panels with multiple regressors'. *Oxford Bulletin of Economics and Statistics*, 61(1): 653–670.

Pedroni, P. (2000). 'Fully modified OLS for heterogeneous cointegrated panels'. *Advances in Econometrics*, 15: 93–130.

Pedroni, P. (2001). 'Purchasing power parity tests in cointegrated panels'. *The Review of Economics and Statistics*, 83(4): 727–731.

Pedroni, P. (2004). 'Panel cointegration: asymptotic and finite sample properties of pooled time series tests with an application to the PPP hypothesis'. *Econometric Theory*, 20(3): 597–625.

Rajan, R. G. and Subramanian, A. (2005). *What Undermines Aid's Impact on Growth?*. NBER Working Paper No, 11657.

Ratha, A. (2013). Remittances and the Dutch Disease: Evidence from Cointegration and Error-Correction Modeling. *Working Paper* No. 26, Economics Faculty Working Papers, St. Cloud State University.

Tuano-Amador, M.C.N., Claveria, R. A., Co, F. S. and Delloro, V. K. (2007). 'Philippine Overseas Workers and Migrants' Remittances: The Dutch Disease Question and the Cyclicality Issue'. *Bangko Sentral Review*, January: 1–23. Manila: The Bangko Sentralng Pilipinas

Vargas-Silva, C. (2009). 'The Tale of Three Amigos: Remittances, Exchange Rates and Money Demand in Mexico'. *Review of Development Economics*, 13(1): 1–14.

White, H., Wignaraja, G. (1992). 'Exchange Rates, Trade Liberalization and Aid: The Sri Lankan Experience'. *World Development*, 20(10): 1471–1480.

World Bank (1993). *Pacific Island Economies: Toward Efficient and Sustainable Growth*. Washington, DC: World Bank.

World Bank (2014). *World Development Indicators*. Washington, DC: World Bank.

14

The determinants and growth effects of foreign direct investment in small economies[1]

Robert Read

1 Introduction

Inflows of foreign direct investment (FDI) have long been regarded as being a key factor in stimulating the economic growth of host-countries. These inflows represent an additional source of capital for investment and may also help to alleviate critical growth constraints arising from the scarcity of capital, particularly in developing countries. FDI also embodies investor-specific 'packages' of additional complementary growth factors, including: advanced and/or established proprietary production technologies; expertise in regional and global supply-sourcing logistics, distribution and market access; superior organizational and managerial know-how; and well-known brand names and other intellectual property. This inherent heterogeneity distinguishes FDI from loan and equity capital. Inflows of FDI therefore have the potential to accelerate the transfer, acquisition and absorption of advanced technologies and knowledge in host-countries, so enhancing domestic human capital and stimulating further growth and development.

The extensive empirical literature on the host country impacts of FDI focuses primarily on leading industrialized economies and some emerging and developing countries. The analysis of FDI inflows to small economies and their impact however, is a neglected area of research. Large-scale cross-country empirical investigations omit most small economies because of a lack of comprehensive data and the low value of the inflows. While inflows of FDI to small economies were only 9.2% of the global total 2011–2015 (UNCTAD, 2016), they represent a critical potential source of investment, technology, know-how and therefore growth. The analysis of the pattern of FDI and its growth effects in small economies is therefore worthy of more serious research.

This chapter attempts to redress the limited attention paid to FDI inflows and their growth effects in small economies. The following section provides a brief discussion of the principal determinants of growth in small economies with reference to their key characteristics, the determinants of FDI inflows and the principal types of FDI. The pattern of FDI in small economies is then analysed together with a review of available cross-country empirical studies of the determinants of FDI. Section 3. outlines the direct and indirect local linkage and spillover growth effects of FDI in host countries in the context of the principal findings of empirical studies of its impacts in small economies. The final section summarizes the key findings and identifies key policy issues relating to attracting FDI inflows to small economies and maximizing their beneficial domestic growth effects via linkages and spillovers.

2 Small economies and inflows of FDI

This section assesses the extent to which small economies are able to attract inflows of FDI given their salient characteristics. In so doing, it draws upon the insights of the substantial conceptual, theoretical and empirical literatures analysing the growth challenges facing small economies and the determinants and host country effects of FDI inflows.

The neglect of small economies by the mainstream FDI literature is, to some extent, unsurprising given the relatively low value of inflows. These averaged $138.6 billion annually 2011–2015 (9.2%) of global FDI (UNCTAD, 2016). Nevertheless, its contribution and consequent growth effects through the creation of local linkages and spillovers are of potentially critical importance to host countries. The magnitude and impact of these FDI inflows can be expected to be determined primarily by the distinctive structural characteristics of small economies.

Growth in small economies

A substantial cross-disciplinary conceptual, theoretical and empirical literature has emerged in the last two decades investigating the nature and implications of the growth challenges facing small economies – and small island economies in particular. This literature builds upon a number of significant earlier contributions, notably by Kohr (1957, 1961), Robinson (1960), Selwyn (1975), Jalan (1982), Dommen and Hein (1985) and Ashoff (1989). There remains however, no general consensus regarding the precise definition of a small economy. This study adopts a population size threshold of 5 million which is at variance with standard international institutional definitions (the Commonwealth, United Nations and World Bank) and many studies but facilitates the inclusion of the relatively abundant body of empirical research on the effects of FDI in Ireland.

The principal structural characteristics of small economies can be summarized as: a small domestic market in terms of population and/or aggregate GDP/GNP; a limited domestic resource base (natural resources and the supply of labour); a narrow structure of domestic output, exports and export markets; a high degree of structural openness to trade owing to specialization in output and diversified consumption; and additional trade costs of remoteness and/or being land-locked (reviewed in Armstrong and Read, 2003). These characteristics have critical implications for the growth and development strategies of small economies because they greatly constrain the scope and structure of domestic economic activity as well as policy autonomy (Armstrong et al., 1998).

The principal inference is that the structural characteristics of small economies render them unlikely to be particularly attractive locations for inflows of FDI. The importance of several key 'conditioning' variables identified in endogenous growth models however, suggests that such a conclusion might be overly hasty. The absolute value of FDI inflows to small economies is low simply because of their size but their relative value coupled with the magnitude of their growth impact may nevertheless be significant. These key conditioning growth variables are:

Openness to International Trade: Outward-oriented trade policies are positively associated with economic growth in many large-scale cross-country statistical models. This is because openness enhances domestic competitiveness according to comparative advantage as well providing access to imports embodying advanced technologies. Trade openness in small economies is size-induced, i.e. it is determined structurally, given their need for specialization in output and exports (Demas, 1965). This leads to significant asymmetries between domestic production and consumption that can only be resolved by imports (Kuznets, 1960). International trade therefore increases the extent of the market in small economies by alleviating the constraints of their size (Marcy, 1960), with large positive multiplier effects on growth (Ashoff, 1989). The critical importance of tradeable goods and services therefore necessitates the adoption of growth strategies based upon internationally competitive export-oriented activities, with limited scope for protectionist import-substituting policies (Marcy, 1960; Scitovsky, 1960). The extent of this reliance on international trade is reflected by the high trade to GDP ratios in small economies, which generally exceed 100%.

Human Capital: The domestic stock of human capital is positively associated with a country's labour productivity and therefore growth but is not subject to significant diminishing returns. Investment in education and training enhances human capital and is therefore expected to have a positive long-run impact on productivity and growth as well as improving domestic absorptive capacity. In small economies, the supply of labour is limited by their population size (and migratory flows) such that orthodox low-cost labour-intensive industrialization is generally infeasible. Instead, their comparative advantage lies primarily in human capital-intensive activities dependent upon their stock of human capital (Bhaduri *et al.*, 1982). The empirical relationship between sectoral specialization and growth in small economies highlights the importance of human capital-intensive activities, notably in financial services and natural resources (Armstrong and Read, 1995, 2000, 2001; Armstrong *et al.*, 1998; Read *et al.*, 2012). Tourism is also critically important to many small economies but its growth effects are limited by its reliance on low-skilled seasonal labour. Out-migration of skilled labour in small developing economies is also several orders of magnitude greater than for other countries – 43.2% compared with 7.4 and 3.5 respectively (Docquier and Schiff, 2008). In more prosperous small economies however, the direction of these migratory flows appears to be reversed (Armstrong and Read, 1995, 1998a).

Dynamic Regional Location: Insights from new economic geography, as well as endogenous growth theory, suggest that location within or close to relatively prosperous dynamic regions (e.g. North America, Western Europe and East Asia) contributes significantly to economic growth. Proximity along with trade interaction is strongly associated with the growth success of many small economies (Armstrong *et al.*, 1998; Armstrong and Read, 2001; Read *et al.*, 2012) while remoteness has an additional negative effect over and above regional location (Armstrong and Read, 2004, 2006).

Good Governance: This is viewed as a critical additional determinant of economic growth in the endogenous growth literature through its impact on the quality of decision-making and policy implementation. Many small economies have made very effective use of their limited policy autonomy and flexibility to formulate and implement successful niche growth strategies (see Kakazu, 1994; Armstrong and Read, 1998a, 2002; Baldacchino and Milne, 1999). Small economies also score consistently highly on the UNDP Human Development Indicators (Briguglio, 1995; Read, 2018) and for institutional quality (Congdon Fors, 2007, 2014; Read 2015, 2018). This lends strong support to the view that governance and institutional quality have been important growth factors for small economies.

All of these variables, individually and in combination, are attractive to foreign investors and can be expected to affect the magnitudes of FDI inflows to small economies as well as their growth impact in terms of linkage and spillover effects.

Determinants of FDI in small economies

The most enduring framework for analysing FDI is Dunning's 'OLI' theory. This identifies three preconditions for firms to engage in international production; ownership ('O'), location ('L') and internalization ('I') advantages (Dunning, 1973, 1977). Key location factors include: the local availability of low-cost inputs, labour skills, human capital, research and development (R&D), producer and supplier clusters, infrastructure, a large domestic market, government policies and a favourable 'business culture' (Dunning, 1973, 1977). These factors are elaborated upon and extended in Porter's 'diamond' (Porter, 1990). A useful general survey of the empirical determinants of FDI can be found in Blonigen (2005).

The principal location 'advantages' of small economies are broadly similar to those of larger economies, apart from their lack of a large domestic market and abundant low-cost labour. FDI inflows can be expected to be primarily export-oriented, particularly in the key sectors of financial services, tourism and, in some cases, natural resources. The propensity for specific motives for FDI inflows in small economies can be considered using Behrman's typology (Behrman, 1972).

Resource-Seeking FDI: Many small economies possess valuable renewable and non-renewable natural resources, in some cases including extensive marine resources through their sizeable Exclusive Economic Zones (EEZs). Further, tourism is usually based upon local natural resource endowments, supported by complementary inputs of low-skilled labour. This labour however, may be subject to a domestic supply constraint. The potential for FDI in downstream resource-based processing and related activities is not clear cut given the need for substantial economies of scale and internationally competitive labour skills.

Efficiency-Seeking FDI: This is generally reliant upon relatively labour-intensive manufacturing and assembly activities in accord with the international division of labour. This FDI is unlikely to be particularly prevalent in small economies given their labour supply constraint. Sectoral specialization in many high-income small economies however, reveals activities intensive in human capital that encounter less severe economies of scale constrains arising from small scale operations – niche manufacturing, financial services, data-processing and offshore call-centres.

Market-Seeking FDI: It is hard to make a convincing case for market-seeking FDI in small economies, regardless of per capita income, even in the case of extreme remoteness where trade costs may be prohibitive. Small economies tend to be supplied (if at all) by exports from low-cost regional supply sources unless located centrally within a larger global region (e.g. Luxembourg and Liechtenstein).

Strategic Asset-Seeking FDI: Small economies are unlikely to be an arena for regional or global strategic interaction between major firms in spite of limited domestic competition and potential monopoly profits. Apart from deposits of strategically important natural resources, small economies are unlikely to attract significant inflows of this type of FDI.

This discussion highlights the limited attractiveness of small economies to most of the principal types of FDI. Resource-seeking and, possibly, efficiency-seeking motives are the most likely to drive these inflows but even these may be hard to attract to poor and remote small developing economies. Nevertheless, inflows of FDI of any type have the potential to generate significant domestic growth effects.

The pattern of FDI inflows to small economies

The pattern of global FDI inflows to 69 small economies with populations below five million for which data is available is shown in Table 14.1. The five-year average 2011 to

Table 14.1 FDI inflows to small economies[1] by region, 2011–2015 ($ million)[2]

Region	Total FDI inflows	Share of world (%)	FDI to small economies	Small economies share by region (%)	Small economies share/world (%)	Share small economies (%)
Europe	418,836	27.8	104,660	25.0	6.9	75.52
Africa	53,495	3.6	5,892	11.0	0.4	4.25
Asia	455,265	30.2	10,632	2.3	0.7	7.67
Caribbean	5,095	0.3	4,557	89.4	0.3	3.29
Latin America	188,220	12.5	9,457	5.0	0.6	6.82
Oceania	2,600	0.2	483	18.6	0.0	0.35
Transition	64,002	4.2	2,910	4.5	0.2	2.10
World	**1,508,818**	**100**	**138,591**		**9.2**	**100**

Source: Calculated from Annex Table 1, UNCTAD (2016).

Notes: [1] Small economies taken as having populations of less than 5 million in 2013; [2] FDI inflows are calculated as the 5-year average for 2011–15.

2015 is used to smooth year-on-year fluctuations. These 69 economies were the recipients of an annual average of $138.6 billion or 9.2% of global FDI inflows, a figure greater than total FDI inflows to Africa and three quarters of inflows to Latin America in the same period. Western Europe dominates the regional distribution with $104.7 billion of total inflows to small economies (75%) and comprising 25% of the regional total. Inflows of FDI to small economies elsewhere were close to $10 billion only in Asia and Latin America.

A lack of data availability means that it is not possible to analyse the sectoral pattern of FDI inflows to small economies. Global FDI data however, shows that manufacturing received a 27% share in 2014 compared with 49% in 1990, services 64% compared with 41% and the primary sector was unchanged with 7% (UNCTAD, 2016). The significant increase in the share of services occurred simultaneously with a substantial increase in the real value of global FDI, in spite of the effects of the 2007 global financial crisis.

The strong inference from the discussion of growth and specialization in small economies is that services FDI must take a disproportionate share of their total inflows. The findings regarding the sectoral determinants of FDI however, are mixed. Read and Soopramanien (2003) find that FDI inflows accord with the sectoral determinants of growth in small economies; natural resources are positive and significant, agriculture is negative and manufacturing inconclusive. Read (2008) however, finds that the sectoral pattern of FDI inflows to 37 small island developing states (SIDS) is insignificant.

Data for the 49 small economies in Table 14.1 that are in receipt of annual average FDI inflows of at least $100 million 2011–2015 are shown in Table 14.2. Inflows are dominated by Ireland, Luxembourg and Malta, which received a combined inflow of $103.8 billion – 74.9% of total FDI in small economies. Only 12 other countries received inflows greater than one billion dollars while some $4.4 billion was divested (negative FDI) from Cyprus. Some of these inflows reflect, at least in part, the presence of large financial services sectors; notably, in The Bahamas, Bahrain, Cyprus, Lebanon, Liberia, Luxembourg and Panama.

Table 14.2 FDI inflows to small economies[1], 2011–2015 ($ million, 5-year average)[2, 3]

	FDI inflows	Share of region (%)[4]	Share of world (%)	FDI in GFC (%)
Europe	**418,836**	**100**	**27.8**	**–**
Croatia	1,592	0.4	0.1	14.7
Cyprus	−4,362	−1	−0.3	−120.9
Estonia	766	0.2	0.1	11.9
Iceland	580	0.1	0.0	22.1
Ireland	49,076	11.7	3.3	98.4
Latvia	941	0.2	0.1	13.5
Lithuania	664	0.2	0.0	7.5
Luxembourg	40,777	9.7	2.7	346
Malta	13,960	3.3	0.9	716.1
Slovenia	666	0.2	0.0	7
Total small economies	104,660	24.9	6.9	–
Africa	**53,495**	**100**	**3.5**	**–**
Botswana	633	1.2	0.0	12.3
Cabo Verde	116	0.2	0.0	16.4
Djibouti	150	0.3	0.0	n/a
Equatorial Guinea	865	1.6	0.1	13.7
Gabon	787	1.5	0.1	15.6
Lesotho	148	0.3	0.0	n/a
Liberia	724	1.4	0.0	199
Mauritania	820	1.5	0.1	28.3
Mauritius	388	0.7	0.0	15
Namibia	913	1.7	0.1	25.9
Seychelles	213	0.4	0.0	45.3
Small economies	5,892	11	0.4	–
Asia	**455,265**	**100**	**30.2**	**–**
Bahrain	1,086	0.2	0.1	19.7
Brunei	615	0.1	0.0	11.2
Kuwait	1,762	0.4	0.1	7.2
Lebanon	2,857	0.6	0.2	22.3
Maldives	334	0.1	0.0	n/a
Mongolia	2,377	0.5	0.2	43.9
Oman	1,008	0.2	0.1	4.9
Qatar	521	0.1	0.0	0.9
Small economies	10,632	2.3	0.7	–
Caribbean	**5,095**	**100**	**0.3**	**–**
Antigua & Barbuda	123	2.4	0.0	44.9
Bahamas	1,140	22.4	0.1	47.3
Barbados	276	5.4	0.0	46.5
Jamaica	522	10.3	0.0	17.2
St Kitts & Nevis	112	2.2	0.0	38.2

	FDI inflows	Share of region (%)[4]	Share of world (%)	FDI in GFC (%)
St Vincent & Grenadines	118	2.3	0.0	64.7
Trinidad & Tobago	2,077	40.8	0.1	60.8
Small economies	4,557	89.4	0.3	–
Latin America	**188,220**	**100**	**12.5**	**–**
Belize	119	0.1	0.0	42.8
Costa Rica	2,625	1.4	0.2	n/a
Guyana	226	0.1	0.0	33.6
Panama	3,931	2.1	0.3	20.6
Suriname	174	0.1	0.0	5.6
Uruguay	2,381	1.3	0.2	20.7
Small economies	9,457	5	0.6	–
Oceania	**2,600**	**100**	**0.2**	**–**
Fiji	343	13.2	0.0	39.6
Small economies	483	18.6	0.0	–
Transition	**64,002**	**100**	**4.2**	**–**
Albania	1,022	1.6	0.1	29.1
Armenia	423	0.7	0.0	16.9
Bosnia & Herzegovina	389	0.6	0.0	11.7
FYR Macedonia	281	0.4	0.0	9.1
Moldova	231	0.4	0.0	12.9
Montenegro	564	0.9	0.0	65
Small economies	2,910	4.6	0.2	–
World	**1,508,818**	**–**	**100.0**	**–**
Total small economies	138,591	–	9.2	–

Source: Calculated from Annex Table 1, UNCTAD (2016); and World Bank online data base (accessed April 2017). GFC – gross fixed capital, five-year average 2011–15, where available.

Cross-country determinants of FDI in small economies

This section provides a summary survey of the principal findings of the limited number of cross-country empirical studies analysing the determinants of inflows of FDI to small economies. The first large-scale cross-country study finds that they attract disproportionately large volumes of FDI, contrary to *a priori* expectations (Read and Soopramanien, 2003).

The most substantive contribution to the empirical literature investigates the determinants of FDI in 37 SIDS (Read, 2008). The study finds that country size (population) is insignificant in FDI inflows as is SIDS status but there is a negative and significant effect for High and Low income countries while for upper- and lower-middle income countries they are insignificant. Openness to trade is positive and significant and identified as being the principal determinant of FDI, lending support to Bhagwati's hypothesis of the complementarity between trade and FDI. Location in Western Europe has a positive and significant effect on FDI inflows while the Middle East & North Africa and South Asia have a negative and significant effect. This suggests that small economies in the Caribbean, in close proximity to North America, and those in the

Pacific, remote from most major markets, are neither unduly advantaged or disadvantaged in attracting FDI. None of the sectoral variables however, are found to be significant.

Kolstad and Villanger (2004a, 2004b, 2008) find no systematic variation in FDI and domestic investment between countries by population for a panel of 135 countries 1980–2002. Small economies in the Caribbean however, are found to attract greater FDI inflows, primarily in tourism, than those in other regions. Domestic investment is also found to be greater in larger, more stable, open wealthier countries, implying that small economies are at a disadvantage, hence their greater reliance on inflows of FDI. The study concludes that foreign and domestic investment are both higher in those countries that are: more open to trade; larger, with wealthier domestic markets; and have greater economic and political stability.

Singh *et al.* (2008) investigate the determinants of FDI inflows for 29 small developing states. Market size, measured by population, is found to be positive and significant at the 10% level; openness to trade at the 5% level; and growth and the existence of a tourism sector at the 1% level. In spite of some specification issues and small sample size, these findings are broadly in line with earlier studies. Interestingly, bidirectional causality between openness to trade and FDI inflows is identified but not discussed further.

In a study of FDI in seven Pacific island economies, Feeny *et al.* (2014) also find that smaller economies generally enjoy greater *pro rata* inflows of FDI. For these particular Pacific economies however, they find a small but significant negative effect on growth, principally because domestic investment is crowded out by FDI.

Hunya (2004) argues that the key factors determining FDI in Estonia, Latvia and Lithuania have been favourable market reforms and privatization. These have led to substantial inflows to the energy, telecommunications, transport and finance sectors. There has been very little market-seeking or export-oriented FDI in manufacturing however, owing to their lack of competitiveness relative to other Eastern EU member states.

There is a degree of consensus in the findings of these studies regarding the principal determinants of FDI. Small economies have been unexpectedly successful in attracting relatively high inflows of FDI, which appears to owe much to strong complementarities with openness to trade, so facilitating export-oriented investments. These inflows assume even greater importance given that small economies generate lower rates of domestic private investment (Kolstad and Villanger, 2004a, 2008), some of which may also be 'crowded-out' (Feeny *et al.*, 2014).

3 Evidence of the growth effects of FDI in small economies

FDI was originally viewed solely as a mechanism for transferring capital between countries; i.e. a substitute for domestic investment financed by foreign savings. Hymer (1960) and Dunning (1973, 1977) however, emphasize the critical importance of FDI as heterogeneous capital embodying distinct 'packages' of firm-specific technology and know-how. Its contribution to economic growth in host countries is therefore potentially much greater than just an alternative source of investment. Inflows of FDI are a means to alleviate critical shortages of indigenous R&D, technology, advanced skills and know-how, particularly in developing countries. In addition, it can accelerate the local acquisition and absorption of new technologies, improve the stock of domestic human capital and enhance domestic competitiveness through the creation of linkages and spillovers. For these reasons, FDI is often incorporated as an additional 'conditioning' variable in 'new' growth theory.

The extensive theoretical and empirical literature on the host country growth impacts of FDI distinguishes between its direct and indirect linkage and spillover effects. Direct effects include job creation and technology transfer leading to improved productivity, higher wages, local upstream and downstream linkages and international trade effects. Indirect effects include technology and knowledge spillovers, agglomeration economies and increased competitive intensity, all of which enhance domestic labour skills and productive efficiency and so contribute to long-run growth. For detailed surveys of these effects, see Blomström and Kokko (1998), Lipsey (2002) and Görg and Greenaway (2004).

Evidence on the creation of local linkages and spillovers in small economies is scarce. The great bulk of economic activity and FDI inflows generally occur in the services and natural resource sectors. Linkage effects in resource extraction are generally confined to employment with few spillovers. In spite of their critical importance, few studies attempt to address the growth impacts of FDI in the financial services and tourism sectors in small economies. The discussion of linkages and spillovers in financial services in particular relies upon inferences derived from several more broad-based empirical studies.

There is an extensive body of empirical literature analysing the growth effects of manufacturing FDI in Ireland, hence the choice of a five million population size threshold here. Ireland is included in this review in spite of several caveats – its size (4.7 million population in 2016); industrialized status; favourable tax regime for foreign investors; and location in Western Europe. Inflows of FDI to Ireland alone averaged $49.1 billion 2011–2015, some 3.3% of global FDI, making it the leading European destination with a share of 11.7% (Table 14.2). It was also the leading recipient among small economies with a share of 35.4% (Table 14.2).

Employment, technology, productivity and wage effects of FDI

These effects of FDI are inter-related such that they are usually dealt with together. The host-country direct employment effects of FDI inflows are generally overwhelmingly positive, being highly visible and therefore most easily measured, although their magnitude is likely to vary between sectors. In small developing economies in particular however, FDI inflows may affect the structure of domestic output as workers switch from traditional activities (e.g. agriculture and fisheries) into more modern ones, particularly labour-intensive activities such as tourism (Meyer, 2007).

Inflows of advanced technology can be expected to raise domestic labour productivity and therefore wages. Its growth effects however, depend upon its assimilation, determined by the absorptive capacity of local human capital and the technology 'gap' between home and host countries (Glass and Saggi, 1998). Technology transfer may also exacerbate inequality by widening wage disparities between skilled and unskilled labour in foreign and local firms.

Foreign affiliates often pay a wage premium to their employees because their prestige enables them to recruit the best workers. These employees tend to be more productive because they have access to superior technology and knowledge capital and are therefore better paid (see Driffield, 1996; Barrell and Pain, 1997). Higher wages may also reduce labour turnover and so limit spillovers of proprietary and tacit knowledge to competitors (Javorcik, 2004; Kugler, 2006; Blalock and Gertler, 2008). Many developing countries lack sufficient absorptive capacity to benefit fully from technology transfer owing to the scarcity of human capital. This may result in labour market crowding-out as foreign affiliates deprive local firms of scarce skills (see Driffield and Taylor, 2000; Lipsey, 2002; Lipsey and Sjöholm, 2004).

Inflows of FDI to Ireland have been mainly in 'non-traditional' export-oriented high technology manufacturing sectors (electronics, information technology and pharmaceuticals). Higher labour productivity in foreign affiliates, reflected in a wage premium of 25%, is partly a result of increasing returns to scale and the employment of substantially greater proportions of skilled labour than domestic firms (Barry and Bradley, 1997). This study also finds that higher wages in foreign affiliates raise wages in the domestic sector, suggesting possible crowding-out in the labour market. This has led to wage rises and lower productivity and profitability in domestic firms as they have had to increase their reliance upon the employment of lower skilled labour (Barry et al., 2005).

The technology and productivity effects of FDI inflows in natural resources and manufacturing in Fiji and Samoa are severely constrained by an acute shortage of specialist skills, particularly in Fiji because of its greater relative level of technical sophistication (Driffield and Read, 2004). This has occurred in spite of government efforts to improve formal technical and vocational education and training over and above in-house training by foreign investors. The shortage of skilled labour in the Pacific islands is primarily the result of out-migration because of better opportunities elsewhere. Instead, foreign affiliates have turned to employing more costly expatriates and substituting capital for labour (i.e. de-skilling), both of which reduce the direct domestic employment effects of FDI. The strongest direct employment effects of FDI in Fiji and Samoa are found for unskilled labour and suggest the emergence of increasingly dualistic local labour markets (Driffield and Read, 2004).

Tourism is based upon local natural resource endowments and supported by low-skilled labour. The evidence from the tourism sector in small economies suggests that inflows of FDI have a greater employment impact than local investment because it is focused on up-market hotels with higher worker/guest ratios (Davidson and Sahli, 2015). Tourism FDI generally embodies low levels of technology and know-how, hence its reliance on low skilled labour. Nevertheless, its employment effects are positive in developing host economies because productivity and wages tend to be greater than in alternative traditional activities (Oxford Economics, 2011; Ali and Ngude, 2014).

Financial services sectors in small economies are export-oriented, contrary to the non-tradeability assumption of the literature on FDI in services (e.g. Kolstad and Villanger, 2004). Several possible broader host country effects of an increased foreign presence in financial services are outlined by Goldberg (2004). Inflows of FDI in financial services need to be internationally competitive and supported by an appropriate infrastructure together with human capital, the quality of which is more important than its cost (Ramasamy and Yeung, 2010). This FDI can therefore be expected to generate greater positive productivity and wage effects per local worker employed than tourism.

There is evidence of positive employment, productivity and wage effects of FDI in small economies across all sectors. The strongest growth effects however, are likely to be determined by the extent to which FDI inflows combine with local skilled labour. Manufacturing has been a key sector in Ireland's recent growth but its potential contribution to small economies generally appears to be limited relative to financial services and tourism (Section 2.). The availability of skilled labour remains a critical constraint for small economies, even in larger relatively well-developed host countries such as Ireland. Its high growth 'Celtic Tiger' phase 1993–2007 was driven by inflows of FDI, with domestic skill shortages being partly relieved by returning migrants (O'Leary, 2015). In contrast, there is little evidence to date of return migration in the Pacific islands, so limiting the domestic employment, technology transfer, productivity and wage growth effects of FDI.

Vertical local linkage effects of FDI in small economies

FDI is expected to generate positive local vertical linkage effects, both upstream (backward) with input suppliers and downstream (forward) with users of intermediate and final goods and services. These linkages are generated through volume, quality and price effects, hence the use of local content requirements by many developing host countries. Upstream supply linkages, in particular, are a critical means of generating beneficial spillover effects for local firms (Javorcik, 2004), in that they provide channels for the greatest interaction between buyers and sellers (Lall, 1996). Further, the creation of local linkages by foreign affiliates indicates a sunk commitment to a host-country, implying that they are less likely to be 'footloose' (Driffield and Mohd Noor, 2000). Vertical linkages may also generate indirect local spillover effects (discussed below). The analysis of linkage effects in small economies focuses principally on the creation of backward linkages with local suppliers, primarily because most FDI inflows are export-oriented and create few forward linkages.

There is evidence of strong linkage creation in manufacturing in European small economies. Some 24% of inputs in the Irish electronics sector are sourced locally and this share is increasing over time (Görg and Ruane, 1998, 2000, 2001). Larger foreign affiliates and those with higher export ratios also have lower local linkages, possibly indicating local supply constraints. This confirms the findings of previous studies (McAleese and McDonald, 1978; O'Malley, 1992, 1995). The domestic employment impact of these linkages is substantial; for every one hundred jobs created by foreign affiliates, a further 21 are created upstream, excluding inter-sectoral effects (Görg and Ruane, 1998, 2000, 2001). FDI downstream is also positively related to upstream entry by domestic firms (Görg and Strobl, 2002). There is also evidence of backward linkage creation in 17 European transition economies, six of which have populations below five million – Albania, Croatia, Estonia, Latvia, Lithuania and Slovenia (Gorodnichenko et al., 2007).

The evidence from small developing economies however, is less encouraging. There are limited backward linkages in apparel and footwear in Fiji, although the effects are greater in the former (Driffield and Read, 2004). This is primarily because these FDI inflows depend mainly upon imported inputs. Few backward linkages are found in tuna fishing in Fiji and Samoa, their principal economic contribution being the payment of licence fees. Substantial backward linkages are evident in coconut processing in Samoa, for which some 90% of inputs by value (mainly coconuts) are sourced locally. There is little evidence of forward linkages being created in any of these activities (Driffield and Read, 2004).

The extent to which tourism stimulates backward linkages in host countries is the subject of debate (e.g. Archer and Fletcher, 1996; Cai et al., 2006; Honek, 2012). The extent of linkage creation is determined by; the type of tourism, the level of host country development and host country size. Traditional tourism is more likely to generate greater local linkages than enclave and/or all-inclusive resorts, particularly in larger more developed host countries (Meyer, 2007; Mitchell and Ashley, 2010). More open trade policies and greater domestic stocks of human capital are also factors (Lejàrraga and Walkenhorst, 2010). Tourism may also offer greater potential for linkage creation in developing countries than agriculture and manufacturing (Honek, 2012). Tourist expenditure data from The Gambia provides cautious grounds for optimism regarding local backward linkage creation in small host countries, notably in food and transportation (Mitchell and Faal, 2008). Significant supply constraints on sourcing of food and drink locally in Cabo Verde (Mitchell, 2008) however, are probably more typical of the challenges facing small (island) economies in creating linkages and retaining greater value added from tourism.

Two key host country effects of FDI in financial services are identified in the literature; the creation of direct and indirect downstream linkages; and its complementarity with manufacturing FDI. In the context of small economies however, neither effect is particularly relevant given its export-orientation and limited domestic manufacturing activity. Any linkage effects may therefore be insignificant. There is little or no empirical evidence available on linkage creation in export-oriented financial services (Fernandes and Paunov, 2011).

The major challenge for small economies in creating local linkages is the narrowness and shallowness of their domestic activity, rendering the local sourcing of inputs costly or virtually impossible. The available evidence suggests that Ireland and European transition economies may be sufficiently industrialized to sustain deeper and broader ranges of productive manufacturing and service activities in support of FDI. In small developing economies, the evidence is generally less positive, with the exception of natural resources. For example, Fiji and Samoa lack the capacity to support backward linkages in manufacturing and this also holds true for tourism in Cabo Verde but less so in The Gambia. Few, if any, significant linkage effects are anticipated to occur in financial services.

International trade effects of FDI in small economies

The impact of FDI inflows on trade is likely to be, at least, partly policy-determined as well as being closely related to the objectives and modes of entry and market servicing of foreign affiliates. FDI can generally be expected to improve the overall trade position of host countries, given improvements in domestic productivity and competitiveness through technology transfer. Large-scale cross-country empirical studies however, find only limited support for Bhagwati's propositions regarding the inter-relationships between host-country trade policy regimes, inflows of FDI and growth (Balasubramanyam and Salisu, 1991; Balasubramanyam et al., 1996; Borensztein et al., 1998; De Mello, 1999; and Makki and Somwaru, 2004). Borensztein et al. include the caveat that developing countries may need to accumulate a critical minimum threshold stock of human capital before positive growth effects can occur.

The trade effects are also likely to differ according to whether FDI is horizontal or vertical. Horizontal replicates specific production processes in host countries as a result of the trade-off between the costs of exporting versus FDI, determined by cost structures, market size and trade costs. Horizontal FDI and trade are therefore substitutes; high trade costs might encourage horizontal FDI even in small markets. Vertical FDI is generally associated with resource- and efficiency-seeking and is therefore complementary with trade, with outputs playing an integral role in global value chains.

Foreign manufacturing affiliates in Ireland are larger, more productive and more profitable than domestic firms and almost entirely export-oriented (Barry and Bradley, 1997), while local input sourcing varies positively with age and inversely with size (Görg and Ruane, 1998, 2000, 2001). The net trade balance is therefore strongly positive. Similarly, foreign-owned tuna fishing and manufacturing affiliates in Fiji and Samoa are also highly export-oriented (Driffield and Read, 2004), with few inputs apart from natural resources (tuna and coconuts) being sourced locally. Export-oriented FDI in manufacturing in the Pacific islands appears to be particularly precarious because trade costs on imported inputs are duplicated.

The trade effects of FDI in tourism depend upon the extent to which the sector is reliant upon imported rather than domestic inputs. The 'leakage' of tourism revenues in the Caribbean economies has been estimated to average 70% and 80% to 90% in some islands (Patullo, 1996) although there is some scepticism regarding these claims (e.g. Mitchell and Ashley, 2010). Leakages in The Gambia are estimated to be less than 50% (Mitchell and Faal, 2008) but rather higher in Cabo Verde (Mitchell, 2008). The net trade impact, as with linkages, is likely to vary according to the type of tourism and the size and development level of the host economy (Meyer, 2007). There is a growing policy literature on improving the net contribution of tourism to host countries (e.g. Lejàrraga and Walkenhorst, 2007, 2010; UNCTAD, 2007; Markandya *et al.*, 2011).

In financial services, the net trade impact of FDI is expected to be positive given its export-orientation and limited need for imported inputs. The magnitude of domestic value added however, is dependent upon the quantity and quality of the local human capital employed (i.e. call centres versus more sophisticated financial and insurance activities).

Evidence of the trade effects of FDI inflows to small economies is broadly positive. The primary objectives are export-oriented efficiency-seeking manufacturing and services as well as resource-seeking, including tourism. The net impact on the host country trade balance however, is dependent on the extent to which foreign affiliates rely upon imported as opposed to local inputs.

Technology spillover effects of FDI in small economies

The transfer of technology may generate spillover effects through diffusion to domestic firms. The transmission mechanisms include: upstream and downstream linkages; local sub-contracting; local licensing; and training. The potential for technology spillovers is determined by the technology gap between foreign and domestic firms, the absorptive capacity of local human capital and the extent to which local linkages are created by foreign affiliates (Glass and Saggi, 1998). Upstream supply linkages with local sub-contractors and licensees in particular, may involve formal and informal technology transfer, including improved technical specifications and production know-how. Additional spillovers may arise as a result of the availability of new intermediate goods and services that improve the efficiency and/or quality of downstream activities or create completely new ones.

No evidence of productivity spillovers is found for a sample of 289 Uruguayan manufacturing firms in industries with a foreign presence (Kokko *et al.*, 1996). When this sample is split according to the size of the technology gap however, significant spillovers are found where this gap is small but none where it is large. Further, these spillovers are found to be firm- rather than industry-specific. Manufacturing productivity in indigenous plants in Ireland is found to be greater in those sectors in which foreign affiliates have the greatest share of employment (Kearns, 2000; Ruane and Ugur, 2002). Using firm survival as a proxy for technology spillovers for 17,000 Irish firms, 1973–96, Görg and Strobl (2003, 2004) find evidence of technology spillovers among indigenous firms in high technology sectors with greater absorptive capacity but not those in lower technology sectors. It is difficult however, to disentangle positive productivity spillovers from larger negative labour market crowding-out effects (Barry *et al.*, 2005). There is little evidence of technology spillovers in resources and manufacturing in Fiji and Samoa, primarily because of the low technological capacity of local firms, where they exist (Driffield and Read, 2004).

FDI in tourism has low levels of technological sophistication, as opposed to know-how, and embodies little in the way of new or proprietary technologies. A similar argument can perhaps be made for the financial services sector. This relies upon good quality infrastructure, human capital and know-how rather than proprietary technologies *per se*.

The limited evidence on technology spillovers is broadly positive although it appears to be confined to manufacturing in more developed host countries. The technology gap however has opposite effects in Ireland and Uruguay, which might be explained by their relative levels of development and absorptive capacity of local skilled labour. More generally, the potential for technology spillovers in many small economies presupposes the existence of local firms producing similar goods and services, which may not be the case.

Knowledge spillover effects of FDI in small economies

FDI may also generate important knowledge spillovers which improve the absorptive capacity of host country labour and therefore its productivity through formal training, 'learning-by-doing' and the acquisition of tacit knowledge. These spillovers arise from the transfer of production, exporting and logistics know-how, organizational and management techniques. They may also occur through demonstration effects via agglomeration and competition – depending upon the absorptive capacity of local labour – and flows of skilled labour and managers from foreign affiliates to local firms (Görg and Strobl, 2005).

Manufacturing FDI in Ireland generates local knowledge spillovers in R&D, training and exporting that increase the productivity of indigenous exporters (Cassidy *et al.*, 2005). These effects are also enhanced by managers and skilled labour moving from domestic exporting firms to non-exporters. Spillovers in manufacturing firms in European transition economies however, appear to be independent of the absorptive capacity of their labour, in spite of productivity differences, but vary by sector and firm type (Gorodnichenko *et al.*, 2007).

Knowledge spillovers in manufacturing in Fiji and Samoa are highly constrained by the low technological capacity of local firms (if they exist) as well as the low turnover of skilled workers because of the foreign affiliate wage premium coupled with limited alternative employment opportunities (Driffield and Read, 2004). Some spillovers may have occurred in the apparel sector via local sub-contracting in the form of quality control, organization and management.

Firm-specific know-how is the principal source of competitive advantage in tourism, notably international hotel management styles and brand identities. Knowledge spillovers in the sector depend upon both the transfer of know-how to local employees through learning-by-doing as well as training – particularly at the managerial level – and its subsequent transfer to domestic firms. In The Gambia, indigenous managers employed in foreign-owned hotel chains receive more training, hold more skilled positions and potentially have greater (in-house) mobility than those in locally-owned hotels (Davidson and Sahli, 2015). Many international hotel chains employ at least some expatriates in senior positions but they also undertake extensive training of local employees in many developing countries and there is evidence of high mobility of indigenous managers between foreign-owned and domestic hotels (UNCTAD, 2007, Chapter III). Evidence from elsewhere in Africa however, suggest that hotels prefer to recruit skilled hotel workers rather than engage in training (Fortanier and Van Wijk, 2010). Some countries, such as Mauritius have established their own colleges of hotel management. The evidence from tourism offers mixed support for the prevalent view in the literature that foreign firms limit the extent of such horizontal knowledge spillovers to prevent the leakage of elements of their competitive advantage.

FDI in financial services embodies a high degree of know-how and expertise in the provision of specific services, supported by international goodwill and branding (Dunning and Norman, 1987). The lack of empirical evidence on FDI-related knowledge spillovers in the sector however, necessitates the drawing of inferences. International financial institutions target host countries with good stocks of human capital, often aided by favourable tax regimes, as locations for their export-oriented offshore activities. These firms can be expected to undertake significant training of their local employees. Beneficial spillovers however, arise from the transfer and utilization of this knowledge by domestic firms which, in many cases, do not exist in this sector in small economies.

The empirical evidence suggests that knowledge spillovers in small economies are broadly positive in manufacturing – although more limited in less developed host countries – but less so in tourism and financial services. It is clear that there is greater potential scope for knowledge as opposed to technology spillovers in small economies because they are more likely to occur between sectors. The critical issue for small economies however, is that much of their productive activity is in financial services and tourism rather than manufacturing such that the potential for these spillovers may therefore be very limited.

Agglomeration effects of FDI in small economies

The presence of technologically-advanced foreign affiliates in a host-country may encourage the agglomeration (i.e. clusters) of similar local enterprises (Cantwell, 1989). This may generate additional spillover effects through formal technology transfer and/or informal assimilation and upgrading of local technological capabilities (Caves, 1996) as well as promoting local sub-contracting and creating a localized pool of specialized skilled labour.

There is some evidence of agglomeration in manufacturing in Ireland as a consequence of FDI, chiefly among key international players, although it is unclear whether this also includes domestic sub-contractors (Barry and Bradley, 1997). Limited agglomeration by foreign affiliates and local sub-contractors is also observed in the apparel sector in Fiji. Agglomeration has not occurred in footwear however, owing to local firms being unwilling to co-operate in joint purchasing and sub-contracting (Driffield and Read, 2004). Agglomeration is a key location determinant for both FDI in tourism and financial services in small economies because of the importance of natural resources in the former and infrastructure for both. This is likely to promote the emergence of a pool of local labour with requisite skills in these sectors as well as supply linkages with domestic firms in tourism.

The extent to which FDI inflows may create beneficial agglomeration effects in small economies is unclear. These depend upon interactions between clusters of foreign and local firms, facilitated by supply linkages, technology and knowledge spillovers and competition. While some agglomeration economies may arise, they may not be particularly significant.

Competition spillover effects of FDI in small economies

FDI is viewed as stimulating improvements in the efficiency and therefore cost-competitiveness of domestic firms, although the empirical evidence suggests that this depends upon the size of the technology gap (Cantwell, 1989; Kokko, 1994). Competition issues however, are not unusual in small economies. Economies of scale mean that very few firms can be supported within a sector (Armstrong and Read, 1998b) such that more efficient foreign affiliates may crowd-out local firms (Aitken and Harrison, 1999).

Much of the surge of manufacturing FDI inflows to Ireland has occurred in new activities, notably electronics, information technology and pharmaceuticals, such that there has been limited potential for competition spillovers of any kind. Evidence of the extent to which backward supply linkages have enhanced the competitiveness of domestic sub-contractors however, are mixed; Ruane and Ugur (2002) and Görg and Strobl (2003, 2004) find positive efficiency effects while Barry and Bradley (1997) and Görg and Strobl (2002) find none. Productivity spillovers from foreign to domestic manufacturing firms are observed in Uruguay where the technological gap between them is relatively small (Kokko et al., 1996).

The scope for positive competition spillovers in small developing economies appears to be more limited. Some indications of negative spillovers in tuna fishing and coconut processing are found in Samoa (Driffield and Read, 2004). One foreign affiliate's investment in large scale on-shore fishing support facilities created a benign natural monopoly which has facilitated new entry by local firms. FDI in coconut processing increased upstream demand for locally-grown coconuts. This might normally be considered to be beneficial but, in this case, the domestic supply response was highly inelastic leading to higher prices and costs for firms across the sector.

In tourism, the presence of foreign-owned hotels is reported to have been a welcome stimulus for greater efficiency by some indigenous hoteliers UNCTAD (2007). In Mauritius however, there is evidence of FDI crowding out domestic private capital (Seetanah and Khadaroo, 2009), with adverse implications for local participation in the sector. The domination of foreign affiliates in the offshore financial services sector in small economies suggests that there are likely to be few potential host country competition spillover effects of any kind.

The evidence suggests that FDI may generate positive competition spillovers in export-oriented activities but may otherwise 'crowd-out' local firms (Driffield and Read, 2004). A small domestic market means that the presence of foreign affiliates may disturb a delicate equilibrium with unforeseen competitive effects, such as in the case of Samoa.

Linkage and spillover effects of FDI in small economies

The general conclusions regarding linkage and spillover effects of FDI across sectors are presented in Table 14.3. These growth effects seem to be weaker in small economies because of their structural characteristics, particularly with regard to spillovers, than might generally be anticipated in larger industrialized economies. The dearth of studies of FDI in financial services means that most of these spillover entries remain blank.

Small economies are surprisingly successful in attracting inflows of FDI but face critical constraints in creating local linkage and spillover growth effects. Host country level of development appears to be an important determinant of the types of FDI attracted (resource- and efficiency-seeking) as well as the linkages that can be supported. The size of the technology gap and the absorptive capacity of local labour are key factors. Linkage and spillover effects can be expected to be greater in more industrialized economies and this is borne out by the evidence for Ireland, European transition economies and Uruguay. Narrow and shallow production structures in

Table 14.3 Summary of FDI linkage and spillover effects in small economies

	Resources	Manufacturing	Tourism	Financial
Linkage effects				
Employment	MP	SP	SP	SP
Technology	WP	SP	NO	MP
Wages	MP	SP	MP	SP
Vertical linkages	MP	MP	WP	n/a
International trade	SP	SP	MP	SP
Spillover effects				
Technology	WP	MP	NO	n/a
Knowledge	WP	MP	WP	n/a
Agglomeration	WP	MP	MP	MP
Competition	NE	NE	NE	n/a

Notes: SP: strongly positive effect; MP: moderately positive effect; WP: weak positive effect; NE: negative effect; NO: no effect; n/a, no evidence available.

small developing economies are exacerbated by high levels of out-migration (e.g. in Fiji and Samoa) and limit their potential to create beneficial linkages and spillovers. Domestic shortages of skilled labour limit technology transfer along with technology and knowledge spillovers, regardless of the level of host country development. In Ireland, this constraint was relieved by return migration of skilled labour during the 1990s whereas in Fiji and Samoa foreign affiliates have had to have recourse to expatriates.

FDI in natural resource extraction, including agriculture and fisheries, may possibly be complemented by processing prior to exportation. The direct effects of FDI therefore tend to be dominated by the payment of resource rents, with few linkages and spillovers, such as in tuna and coconut-processing in Fiji and Samoa.

Much of the evidence of the effects in manufacturing relates to efficiency-seeking FDI in export-oriented labour-intensive assembly operations in Ireland, which might be regarded as an 'outlier' given its size, location, membership of the EU and tax incentives. Nevertheless, it was the leading European recipient of FDI inflows 2011–2015 and it was responsible for 35.4% of total inflows to small economies during this period. The evidence for Ireland, European transition economies and Uruguay, demonstrates that beneficial linkages and spillover effects, over and above employment, are more likely to be created in industrialized small economies; e.g. the entry of domestic firms in upstream supply activities in Ireland. Evidence from smaller scale manufacturing in Fiji and Samoa however, is less encouraging; their remoteness limits their attractiveness to both efficiency- and resource-seeking FDI because of high trade costs while they generate fewer local linkage and spillover effects because of their size and development level.

Tourism and financial services are two of the most important sectors in many small economies, with growth being driven by substantial inflows of FDI. The empirical evidence suggests, on balance, that inflows of FDI in tourism have a generally positive impact, even in small economies. Some caveats remain however, with respect to the impact on domestic agricultural employment and output and the extent to which local linkages replace imports without distorting the local market. The lack of empirical studies of FDI in financial services precludes the drawing of clear conclusions.

A final comment is necessary regarding competition and crowding-out effects of FDI in small economies. The mainstream literature argues that the presence of foreign affiliates increases competitive intensity and therefore has positive domestic spillover effects. The empirical studies surveyed here find evidence of adverse competitive effects in some form or another across all sectors with the exception of financial services for which there is no data.

4 FDI in small economies: conclusions and policy issues

The potential of FDI inflows to contribute to the growth and development of host country economies is now generally acknowledged both in the research literature and more widely among policy-makers. FDI augments domestic investment as well as providing advanced technology and know-how that further enhances the economic growth process. The analysis of FDI inflows to small economies however, is a neglected field of investigation, reflecting their marginality in the mainstream literature as well as the low absolute value of these investment flows and the limited availability of robust data. Nevertheless, inflows of FDI offer additional opportunities for growth in small economies, particularly developing ones, where domestic sources of capital, technology and know-how may be very limited. This chapter attempts addresses this neglect by reviewing the magnitudes, determinants and impacts of FDI inflows to small economies in the context of the relevant conceptual, theoretical and empirical literature.

Principal conclusions

Small economies attract greater inflows of FDI than expected, given their limited market size and difficulty in sustaining large-scale economic activities that attract market- and efficiency seeking FDI. These flows can be partly explained by their size-induced structural openness to international trade combined with its complementary growth relationship with FDI (Bhagwati, 1978). FDI inflows to small economies are primarily motivated by resource- and export plat-form efficiency-seeking, broadly in accord with empirical findings on the sectoral determinants of their growth. Export-oriented manufacturing FDI in Ireland also fits this pattern in spite of the sector being an insignificant factor in the growth of small economies more generally.

The creation of linkages and spillovers are important by-product host country growth effects of FDI. Foreign affiliates with extensive local linkages also tend to have a greater long-run commitment to a host country than more footloose investments dependent upon tax breaks. The review of the empirical evidence suggests that small economies are often unable to reap the full growth effects of FDI because of the narrowness and shallowness of their domestic activity and crowding-out in various forms. The evidence for Ireland however, highlights several positive impacts of FDI over and above standard employment, technology transfer, productivity and trade effects; notably the creation of local linkages that have encouraged entry by domestic upstream sub-contractors. A worrying feature across many small economies is crowding-out, with foreign affiliates out-competing local firms for limited investment opportunities, domestic skilled labour and local inputs. Ireland has been a victim of its own success; FDI has absorbed the available local skilled labour but has also encouraged return migration by the Irish diaspora. Fiji and Samoa also have long-standing high levels of out-migration but persistent shortages of skilled labour have been relieved by expatriate employment that have reduced the growth effects of FDI by limiting the development of local linkages and spillovers. There have been some positive competition spillovers in Ireland with respect to new firm entry and the increasing efficiency of local sub-contracting because most FDI inflows have occurred in non-traditional sectors. In contrast, the evidence of adverse competition spillovers in Mauritius and Samoa give reason for concern.

FDI in small economies: policy issues

Several important policy issues emerge from this review of the impacts of FDI in small economies. The first is targeting 'appropriate' inflows of FDI; a major challenge for many developing economies is that they have broadly similar factor endowments and patterns of activity which mean that they are competing with each other for FDI; i.e. 'fallacy of composition'. This is particularly pertinent for small economies because their narrow and shallow economic structures constrain the creation of local linkages and spillovers. Resource-based FDI in Fiji and Samoa generates few growth effects over and above direct employment and natural resource rents. Ireland's success in attracting FDI owes much to its skilled labour coupled with proximity to the EU market. The proximity of Fiji and Samoa to high wage Australia and New Zealand suggests the potential for greater efficiency-seeking manufacturing FDI, which appears more likely to generate growth-enhancing linkage and spillover effects. The magnitude of the growth effects of FDI in tourism depends greatly upon linkage creation to reduce the sector's import-dependence as well as knowledge transfers to local employees through formal and informal training. Little is known about the impacts of FDI in financial services over and above an increase in employment although domestic value added created is likely to be substantially greater than in tourism because of the human capital content of the local labour employed.

Policies towards attracting inflows of FDI should not be separated from consideration of the growth effects of beneficial local linkage and spillover creation. Many host countries – and developing ones in particular – expend considerable resources on attracting inflows of FDI yet remain passive with regard to local employment, supply sourcing and training decisions made by foreign affiliates. Greater importance therefore needs to be attached to 'aftercare' in support of local linkage and spillover creation so as to maximize the domestic growth effects of FDI inflows, particularly where distortions and market failures are present. A critical challenge for many small developing economies (e.g. Fiji and Samoa) is to break the cycle of high skilled out-migration (i.e. 'brain drain'), a lack of skilled domestic employment and low investment. This requires governments to target shortages of key skills through increased funding for technical and vocational training and skills acquisition as well as matching available skills to FDI inflows. Relying upon the growth of the tourism sector is unlikely to remedy the leakage of valuable skills overseas, regardless of whether it is financed by FDI or domestic capital. The financial services sector might offer better opportunities for highly skilled local labour in small economies to increase its productivity and therefore wages although it faces several important challenges to its own long-term survival. These include securing a competitive operating niche within the sector – there is already evidence of 'congestion' in some regions (e.g. the Caribbean). There are also issues of financial supervision, banking secrecy and international legislation on tax havens.

This survey highlights the dearth of studies of the determinants of FDI inflows to small economies. There are even fewer analyses of the growth effects of FDI via the creation of local linkages and spillovers. Further and more substantive research is therefore needed on its con-tribution to key growth sectors in small economies – and developing ones in particular. Table 14.3 effectively constitutes an agenda for future research. There is an evident need for a fuller understanding of the impacts of FDI in the financial services sector in particular and this should be complemented by further analyses of other key sectors in small economies, notably natural resources and tourism. This would improve the limited body of current knowledge regarding the growth effects of linkages and spillovers in small economies and enhance the quality of policy-making with respect to FDI inflows.

Note

1 This research is part of an ongoing investigation of inflows of FDI to small economies and their growth effects. The paper has its genesis in research undertaken for the Foreign Investment Advisory Service (FIAS) of the World Bank's International Finance Corporation (Sydney) on behalf of the Pacific Islands Forum Secretariat in 2003 and a UNU WIDER project on Fragility & Development in 2006. Useful feedback and comments on an earlier draft of the paper by Dr Hilary Ingham (University of Lancaster) and Professor Nick Perdikis (Aberystwyth University) is greatly appreciated. Nevertheless, all errors of interpretation and fact remain the sole responsibility of the author.

References

Aitken, B. and Harrison, A. E. (1999). 'Do domestic firms benefit from direct foreign investment? Evidence from Venezuela'. *American Economic Review*, 89(3): 605–618.

Ali, J. S. and Ngude, Z. (2014). Assessing the contribution of inflow of foreign direct investment (FDI) in the creation of employment opportunities to the people of Zanzibar: A case of tourism sector. Dar es Salaam: Centre for Foreign Relations. https://papers.ssrn.com/sol3/papers.cfm?abstract_id=2548122, accessed July 2017.

Archer, B. and Fletcher, J. (1996). 'The economic impact of tourism in The Seychelles'. *Annals of Tourism Research*, 23(1): 32–47.

Armstrong, H. W., de Kervenoael, R. J., Li, X. and Read, R. (1998). 'A comparison of the economic performance of different micro-states and between micro-states and larger countries'. *World Development*, 26(4): 639–656.

Armstrong, H. W. and Read, R. (1995). 'Western European micro-states and EU autonomous regions: the advantages of size and sovereignty'. *World Development*, 23(8): 1229–1245.

Armstrong, H. W. and Read, R. (1998a). 'Trade and growth in small states: The impact of global trade liberalisation'. *The World Economy*, 21(4): 563–585.

Armstrong, H. W. and Read, R. (1998b). 'Trade, competition and market structure in small states: The role of contestability'. *Bank of Valletta Review*, 18: 1–18.

Armstrong, H. W. and Read, R. (2000). 'Comparing the economic performance of dependent territories and sovereign micro-states'. *Economic Development & Cultural Change*, 48(2): 285–306.

Armstrong, H. W. and Read, R. (2001). Explaining differences in the economic performance of micro-states in Africa and Asia. In Lawrence, P. and Thirtle, C. (eds) *Africa & Asia in Comparative Development*: 128–157. Basingstoke: Palgrave.

Armstrong, H. W. and Read, R. (2002). The importance of being unimportant: The political economy of trade and growth in small states. In Murshed, S. M. (ed.) *Issues in Positive Political Economy*: 71–88. London: Routledge.

Armstrong, H. W. and Read, R. (2003). The determinants of economic growth in small states. *The Round Table*, XCII (368): 99–124.

Armstrong, H. W. and Read, R. (2004). Small states and small island states: Implications of size, location and isolation for prosperity. In Poot, J. (ed.) *On the Edge of the Global Economy: Implications of Economic Geography for Small & Medium-Sized Economies at Peripheral Locations*: 191–223. Cheltenham: Edward Elgar.

Armstrong, H. W. and Read, R. (2006). 'Insularity, remoteness, mountains and archipelagos: A Pacific perspective on the problems facing small states'. *Asia Pacific Viewpoint*, 47(1): 77–90.

Ashoff, G. (1989). *Economic & Industrial Development Options for Small Third World Countries*. Occasional Paper No. 91. Berlin: German Development Institute.

Balasubramanyam, V. N. and Salisu, M. A. (1991). EP, IS and foreign direct investment in LDCs. In Koekkoek, A. and Mennes, L. B. (eds) *International Trade & Global Development*: 224–248. London: Routledge.

Balasubramanyam, V. N., Salisu, M. A. and Sapsford, D. R. (1996). 'Foreign direct investment and growth in EP and IS countries'. *The Economic Journal* 106(434): 92–105.

Baldacchino, G. and Milne, D. (eds) (1999). *A Political Economy for Small Islands: The Resourcefulness of Jurisdiction*. Basingstoke: Macmillan.

Barrell, R. and Pain, N. (1997). 'Foreign direct investment, technological change and economic growth within Europe'. *The Economic Journal*, 107(445): 1770–1786.

Barry, F. and Bradley, J. (1997). 'FDI and trade: The Irish host-country experience'. *The Economic Journal*, 107(445): 1798–1811.

Barry, F., Görg, H. and Strobl, E. (2005). 'Foreign direct investment and wages in domestic firms in Ireland: Productivity spillovers versus labour market crowding out'. *International Journal of the Economics of Business*, 12(1): 67–84.

Behrman, J. N. (1972). *The Role of International Companies in Latin America: Autos & Petrochemicals*. Lexington, MA: Lexington Books.

Bhaduri, A., Mukherji, A. and Sengupta, R. (1982). Problems of long-term growth in small economies: A theoretical analysis. In Jalan, B. (ed.) *Problems & Policies in Small Economies*: 49–68. Beckenham: Croom Helm for the Commonwealth Secretariat.

Bhagwati, J. N. (1978). *Anatomy & Consequences of Exchange Control Regimes, Vol. 1*, Studies in International Economic Relations, No. 10. New York: National Bureau of Economic Research.

Blalock, G. and Gertler, P. (2008). 'Welfare gains from foreign direct investment through technology transfer to local suppliers'. *Journal of International Economics*, 74(2): 402–421.

Blomström, M. and Kokko, A. (1998). 'Multinational corporations and spillovers'. *Journal of Economic Surveys*, 12(3): 247–277.

Blonigen, B. A. (2005). 'A review of the empirical literature on FDI determinants'. *Atlantic Economic Journal*, 33: 383–403.

Borensztein, E., De Gregorio, J. and Lee, J.-W. (1998). 'How does foreign direct investment affect economic growth?'. *Journal of International Economics*, 45(2): 115–135.

Briguglio, L. (1995). 'Small island developing states and their economic vulnerabilities'. *World Development*, 23(10): 1615–1632.

Cai, J., Leung, P.-S. and Mak, J. (2006). 'Tourism's forward and backward linkages'. *Journal of Travel Research*, 45(1): 36–52.

Cantwell, J. A. (1989). *Technological Innovation & Multinational Corporations*. Oxford: Basil Blackwell.

Cassidy, M., Görg, H. and Strobl, E. (2005). 'Knowledge accumulation and productivity: Evidence from plant level data for Ireland'. *Scottish Journal of Political Economy*, 52(3): 344–358.

Caves, R. E. (1996). *The Multinational Enterprise & Economic Analysis*. Cambridge: Cambridge University Press.

Congdon Fors, H. (2007). Island status, country size and institutional quality of former colonies. *Working Papers in Economics*, No. 257. Handelshogskolan: Göteborg University.

Congdon Fors, H. (2014). 'Do island states have better institutions?'. *Journal of Comparative Economics*, 42(1): 34–60.

Davidson, L. and Sahli, M. (2015). 'Foreign direct investment in tourism, poverty alleviation and sustainable development: A review of the Gambian hotel sector'. *Journal of Sustainable Tourism*, 23(2): 167–187.

Demas, W. G. (1965). *The Economics of Development in Small Countries: With Special Reference to the Caribbean*. Montreal: McGill University Press.

De Mello, L. R. (1999). 'Foreign direct investment-led growth: Evidence from time series and panel data'. *Oxford Economic Papers*, 51(2): 133–151.

Docquier, F. and Schiff, M. (2008). Measuring skilled emigration rates: The case of small states. *IZA Discussion Paper* No. 3388. Berlin.

Dommen, E. C. and Hein, P. L. (eds) (1985). *States, Microstates & Islands*. London: Croom Helm.

Driffield, N. (1996). *Global Competition & the Labour Market*. Reading: Harwood.

Driffield, N. and Mohd Noor, A. H. (2000). 'Foreign direct investment and local input linkages in Malaysia'. *Transnational Corporations*, 8(1): 1–23.

Driffield, N. and Read, R. (2004). *Linkages & Flow-On Impacts of Foreign Investment in Pacific Island Economies, Final Report*. Sydney: FIAS/Pacific Islands Forum.

Driffield, N. and Taylor, K. (2000). 'FDI and the labour market: A review of evidence and policy implications'. *Oxford Review of Economic Policy*, 16(3): 90–103.

Dunning, J. H. (1973). 'The determinants of international production'. *Oxford Economic Papers*, 25(3): 289–336.

Dunning, J. H. (1977). Trade, location of economic activity and the MNE: A search for an eclectic approach. In Ohlin, B., Hesselborn, P. O. and Wijkman, P. M. (eds) *The International Allocation of Economic Activity, Proceedings of a Nobel Symposium held at Stockholm*: 395–418. London: Macmillan.

Dunning, J. H. and Norman, G. (1987). 'The location of offices of international companies'. *Environment & Planning A*, 19(5): 613–631.

Feeny, S., Iamsiraroj, S. and McGillivray, M. (2014). 'Growth and foreign direct investment in the Pacific Island countries'. *Economic Modelling*, 37(3): 332–339.

Fernandes, A. M. and Paunov, C. (2011). 'Foreign direct investment in services and manufacturing productivity'. *Journal of Development Economics*, 97(2): 305–321.

Fortanier, F. and Van Wijk, J. (2010). 'Sustainable tourism industry development in Sub-Saharan Africa: Consequences of foreign hotels for local employment'. *International Business Review*, 19(2): 191–205.

Glass, A. and Saggi, K. (1998). 'International technology transfer and the technology gap'. *Journal of Development Economics*, 55(2): 369–398.

Goldberg, L. (2004). *Financial-sector FDI and host countries: New and old lessons*, No. w10441. National Bureau of Economic Research.

Görg, H. and Greenaway, D. (2004). 'Much ado about nothing? Do domestic firms really benefit from foreign direct investment?' *The World Bank Research Observer*, 19(2): 171–197.

Görg, H. and Ruane, F. P. (1998). Linkages between multinationals and indigenous firms: Evidence for the electronics sector in Ireland. *Trinity Economic Papers Series, Technical Paper*, No. 13. Dublin: Trinity College.

Görg, H. and Ruane, F. P. (2000). 'An analysis of backward linkages in the Irish electronics sector'. *The Economic & Social Science Review*, 31(3): 215–235.

Görg, H. and Ruane, F. P. (2001). 'Multinational companies and linkages: Panel data evidence for the Irish electronics sector'. *International Journal of the Economics of Business*, 8(1): 1–18.

Görg, H. and Strobl, E. (2002). 'Multinational companies and indigenous development: An empirical analysis'. *European Economic Review*, 46(7): 1305–1322.

Görg, H. and Strobl, E. (2003). 'Multinational companies, technology spillovers and plant survival'. *The Scandinavian Journal of Economics*, 105(4): 581–595.

Görg, H. and Strobl, E. (2004). Foreign direct investment and local economic development: Beyond productivity spillovers. *Research Papers*, No. 2004/11. University of Nottingham, Leverhume Centre for Research On Globalisation and Economic Policy.

Görg, H. and Strobl, E. (2005). 'Spillovers from foreign firms through worker mobility: An empirical investigation'. *The Scandinavian Journal of Economics*, 107(4): 693–709.

Gorodnichenko, Y., Svejnar, J. and Terrell, K. (2007). Why does FDI have positive spillovers? Evidence from 17 emerging market economies. *IZA Discussion Paper* No. 379. Berlin: IZA.

Honek, D. (2012). LDC export diversification, employment generation and the green economy: What roles for tourism linkages?. *WTO Staff Working Paper*, No. ERSD-2012–24. Geneva: WTO.

Hunya, G. (2004). FDI in small countries: The Baltic States. *WIIW Research Reports*, No. 307. Vienna: Wiener Institut für Internationale Wirtschaftsvergleiche.

Hymer, S. (1960). *The international operations of national firms: A study of direct foreign investment*. PhD Thesis. Boston: MIT.

Jalan, B. (ed.) (1982). *Problems & Policies in Small Economies*. Beckenham: Croom Helm for the Commonwealth Secretariat.

Javorcik, B. S. (2004). 'Does foreign investment increase the productivity of domestic firms? In search of spillovers through backward linkages'. *American Economic Review*, 94(3): 603–627.

Kakazu, H. (1994). *Sustainable Development in Small Island Economies*. New York: Westview Press.

Kearns, A. (2000). *Essays on the consequences of research and development for manufacturing firms in Ireland*. PhD thesis. Dublin: Trinity College.

Kohr, L. (1957). *The Breakdown of Nations*. London: Routledge & Kegan Paul.

Kohr, L. (1961). 'The economic consequences of the size of nations'. *Midwest Journal of Political Science*, 5 (1): 78–81.

Kokko, A. (1994). 'Technology market characteristics and spillovers'. *Journal of Development Economics*, 43 (2): 279–293.

Kokko, A., Tansini, R. and Zejan, M. C. (1996). 'Local technological capability and productivity spillovers from FDI in the Uruguayan manufacturing industry'. *Journal of Development Studies*, 32(4): 602–611.

KolstadI. and Villanger, E. (2004a). Promoting investment in small Caribbean states. *CMI Report*, 2004:9. Bergen: Chr. Michelsen Institute.

Kolstad, I. and Villanger, E. (2004b). Determinants of foreign direct investment in services. *Working Paper*, 2004:2. Bergen: Chr. Michelsen Institute.

Kolstad, I. and Villanger, E. (2008). 'Foreign direct investment in the Caribbean'. *Development Policy Review*, 26(1): 79–89.

Kugler, M. (2006). 'Spillovers from foreign direct investment: within or between industries?'. *Journal of Development Economics*, 80(2): 444–477.

Kuznets, S. (1960). The economic growth of small nations. In Robinson, E. A. G. (ed.) *The Economic Consequences of the Size of Nations*: 14–32. London: Macmillan.

Lall, S. (1996). *Learning from the Asian Tigers*. Basingstoke: Macmillan.

Lejàrraga, I. and Walkenhorst, P. (2007). *Diversification by deepening linkages with tourism*. Washington, DC: World Bank.

Lejàrraga, I. and Walkenhorst, P. (2010). 'On linkages and leakages: Measuring the secondary effects of tourism'. *Applied Economic Letters*, 17(5): 417–421.

Lipsey, R. E., (2002). *Home- and host-country effects of foreign direct investment*. NBER Working Paper, No. 9293. Reprinted in Baldwin, R. E. and Winters, L. A. (eds) (2004) *Challenges to Globalization: Analyzing the Economics*: 333–382. Chicago, IL: University of Chicago Press.

Lipsey, R. E. and Sjöholm, F. (2004). *Host-country impacts of inward FDI on host-countries: Why such different answers?*. Stockholm School of Economics, Working Paper No. 192. Reprinted as Impact of inward investment on host-countries: Why such different answers?. In Moran, T. H., Graham, E. M. and Blomström, M. (eds) (2005) *Does Foreign Direct Investment Promote Development?*: 23–43. Washington, DC: Institute of International Economics.

McAleese, D. and McDonald, D. (1978). 'Employment growth and the development of linkages in foreign-owned and domestic manufacturing enterprises'. *Oxford Bulletin of Economics & Statistics*, 40(4): 321–339.

Makki, S. S. and Somwaru, A. (2004). 'Impact of foreign direct investment and trade on economic growth: Evidence from developing countries'. *American Journal of Agricultural Economics*, 86(3): 795–801.

Marcy, G. (1960). How far can foreign trade and customs agreements confer upon small nations the advantages of larger nations? In Robinson, E. A. G. (ed.) *The Economic Consequences of the Size of Nations*: 265–281. London: Macmillan.

Markandya, A., Taylor, T. and Pedroso, S. (2011). Tourism and sustainable development: Lessons from recent World Bank experience. www.researchgate.net/publication/228633965, accessed July 2017.

Meyer, D. (2007). 'Pro-poor tourism: from leakages to linkages: A conceptual framework for creating linkages between the accommodation sector and poor. neighbouring communities'. *Current Issues in Tourism*, 10(6): 558–583.

Mitchell, J. (2008). *Tourist Development in Cape Verde: The Policy Challenge of Coping with Success*. London: ODI.

Mitchell, J. and Ashley, C. (2010). *Tourism & Poverty Reduction: Pathways to Prosperity*. London: ODI and Earthscan.

Mitchell, J. and Faal, J. (2008). The Gambian tourist value chain and prospects for pro-poor tourism. *ODI Working Paper*, No. 289. London.

O'Leary, E. (2015). *Irish Economic Development: High-Performing EU State or Serial Under-Achiever?* Abingdon: Routledge.

O'Malley, E. (1992). 'Industrial structure and economies of scale in the context of 1992', in *The Role of Structural Funds: Analysis of Consequence for Ireland in the Context of 1992*. Policy Research Series Paper, No. 13. Dublin: The Economic and Social Research Institute.

O'Malley, E., (1995). An analysis of secondary employment associated with manufacturing industry. *General Research Series paper*, No. 6. Dublin: The Economic and Social Research Institute.

Oxford Economics (2011). *Methodology for Producing the 2011 WTTC/OE Travel & Tourism Economic Impact Research*. London: Oxford Economics.

Patullo, P. (1996). *Last Resorts: The Cost of Tourism in the Caribbean*. London: Cassell.

Porter, M. E. (1990). *The Competitive Advantages of Nations*. New York: Free Press.

Ramasamy, B. and Yeung, M. (2010). 'The determinants of foreign direct investment in services'. *The World Economy*, 33(4): 573–596.

Read, R. (2008). 'Foreign direct investment in small island developing states'. *Journal of International Development*, 20(5): 502–525.

Read, R. (2015). *Governance and economic growth in small economies*. Unpublished ms.

Read, R. (2018). Small is beautiful: Country size and national wellbeing in small economies. In Briguglio, L. (ed.) *Handbook of Small States: 386–402*. London: Routledge.

Read, R., Armstrong, H. W. and Picarelli, N. (2012). Binding Growth Constraints in Small Island Economies: Evidence Focusing On the Organisation of Eastern Caribbean States. *Report for the Latin American & Caribbean Section of the World Bank*.

Read, R. and Soopramanien, D. (2003). FDI in small states: an exploratory investigation. Paper presented at the 28th IESG Annual Conference, International Factor Mobility, Trade & Growth, University of Birmingham, 9–10 September. Mimeo.

Robinson, E. A. G. (ed.) (1960). *The Economic Consequences of the Size of Nations*. London: Macmillan.

Ruane, F. and Ugur, A. (2002). Foreign direct investment and productivity spillovers in Irish manufacturing industry: Evidence from firm-level panel data. *Trinity Economics Papers* 02/06. Dublin: Trinity College.

Scitovsky, T. (1960). International trade and economic integration as a means of overcoming the disadvantages of a small nation. In Robinson, E. A. G. (ed.) *The Economic Consequences of the Size of Nations*: 282–290. London: Macmillan.

Seetanah, B. and Khadaroo, J. (2009). 'An analysis of the relationship between transport capital and tourism development in a dynamic framework'. *Tourism Economics*, 15(4): 785–802.

Selwyn, P. (ed.) (1975). *Development Policy in Small Countries*. Beckenham: Croom Helm.

Singh, D. R., McDavid, H., Birch, A. and Wright, A. (2008). 'The determinants of FDI in small developing nation states: An exploratory study'. *Social & Economic Studies*, 57(3–4): 79–104.

UNCTAD (2007). *FDI in Tourism: The Development Dimension*. Geneva: UNCTAD.

UNCTAD (2016). *World Investment Report, 2016*. Geneva: UNCTAD.

Part IV
Regulatory issues

15

When international 'best practice' is not: power sector reform in small island states

Matthew Dornan

1 Introduction

Small island states have led the world in establishing ambitious renewable energy targets over the last decade. This has made the electricity sector a dynamic sector in small island economies, with considerable investment in new generation capacity, much of it donor-funded. Achievement of renewable energy targets has been one objective on which reform of the power sector has been advocated in recent years. These reforms draw on what is considered international 'best practice' and follow on from an earlier and quite different set of reforms that aimed at liberalizing the sector.

This chapter discusses the impact of these reforms and explores the strengths and weaknesses of different ownership and regulatory arrangements in the electricity sectors of small island states.

Two waves or generations of regulatory reform can be identified, each with its own conceptualization of 'best practice'. In the earlier wave that commenced in the 1980s, the introduction of competition and private sector involvement, in what was traditionally a sector dominated by the state, was advocated on efficiency and performance grounds, and in light of the poor performance and reach of state-owned utilities. Best practice in this first generation of reforms involved competition between companies at multiple levels: when generating electricity (the wholesale market) and when selling it to consumers (the retail market). Transmission and distribution functions remained fully regulated under all regulatory models, given their intrinsic monopoly characteristics. This liberalization agenda led to significant changes the electricity sectors of many developed economies and in the economies of developing countries in Latin America. However, its impact was more limited in small island states, with some notable exceptions.

More recently, a second wave of reform has taken place, focused on establishing regulatory oversight that is independent from elected officials in the sector. These second generation reforms are aimed at encouraging new investment and ensuring appropriate pricing in the sector. Best practice is framed around independent price regulation – both in the case of retail and feed-in tariffs. In practice, this often involves a dominant power utility that generates most of the electricity in the grid, but which purchases some electricity from independent power producers. This second wave of reform has had a greater (if still limited) impact in small island states. Its advocacy should be placed in context, with small island states establishing ambitious renewable energy targets which, if met, would see most move toward an electricity network dominated by renewable energy technologies.

In discussing the strengths and weaknesses of different regulatory arrangements, a central argument of this chapter is that international 'best practice' is often not appropriate in small island states. The chapter identifies a number of factors that influence what is an appropriate regulatory structure. It also explores novel solutions suggested for small island states as a means of overcoming constraints associated with small size – solutions such as regional regulation. It is evident from this discussion that no one model is appropriate across the diverse range of small island states.

The chapter proceeds as follows: Section 2. discusses the international context for power sector regulation. Section 3. briefly highlights the features that make the electricity sectors of small island states unique while Section 4. overviews the experience of small island states with power sector reform. Section 5. provides an analysis and discusses some of the strengths and weaknesses of different models. Section 6. concludes the chapter.

2 How is the power sector regulated internationally?

International thinking and practice on power sector reform has undergone significant change in recent decades. The first electricity networks were fragmented, having largely been developed by private firms, cooperatives, and city councils. Subsequent consolidation saw a (often) state-owned utility become responsible for the generation, distribution and retailing of electricity across countries or large areas. These vertically integrated state-owned monopolies were considered necessary for achieving the economies of scale required in electricity generation, with government ownership crucial for energy security, safeguarding consumers against abuse of market power, and ensuring that utilities pursued non-commercial objectives that had important social benefits, such as rural electrification.

Consensus around this model began to break down in the 1980s. There was a push – part of a broader move toward deregulation and liberalization – to dismantle vertically integrated monopolies in the electricity sector, introduce competition, and in some cases, to privatize state-owned electricity utilities. The rationale for these first generation reforms was that the introduction of competition and private sector participation to the sector could increase efficiency and lower generation costs.

Initial moves to liberalize the electricity sector primarily occurred in developed countries, although there were some early developing country reformers, such as Chile. Liberalization was subsequently pursued in many developing countries, especially in Latin America, often with the-support of international financial institutions (and sometimes as a condition of structural adjustment loans). In developing countries, reform objectives generally went beyond efficiency and lower generation costs. Proponents of reform argued that in developing countries liberalization could improve performance in the power sector, which in many cases was plagued by poor management and inadequate retail prices – undermining the ability of power utilities to manage electricity infrastructure – and poor management. It was also often argued that liberalization was the key to widening access to electricity through private sector financing of grid expansion and investment in generation capacity (Choynowski, 2004; Gratwick and Eberhard, 2008; Rosenzweig et al., 2004).

Table 15.1 Ownership and regulatory structures in the power sector

Operational model	Ownership and regulatory structure
Vertically integrated monopoly	One vertically integrated (generally state-owned) monopoly utility is responsible for generation, transmission, distribution, and retail components of power supply. Prices are set by government or an independent regulator.
Monopsony	One vertically integrated (generally state-owned) monopoly utility is responsible for most generation and for all transmission, distribution, and retail components of power supply. Independent Power Producers sell power to the utility. Retail and feed-in prices are regulated by an independent regulator.
Wholesale competition	Numerous companies generate electricity, selling it to distribution companies in a (largely) unregulated wholesale market. Transmission and distribution fees are set by an independent regulator. Retail prices are regulated by an independent regulator.
Full customer choice	Numerous companies generate electricity, selling it to distribution companies in a (largely) unregulated wholesale market. There is also competition in the retail market, with retail prices (largely) unregulated. Transmission and distribution fees are set by an independent regulator.

Source: Adapted from Choynowski (2004).

Power sector reform can be understood with reference to four models of ownership and regulation identified in the literature – shown in Table 15.1 (Choynowski, 2004). State-owned vertically integrated monopolies remain the most common model, despite the reforms highlighted above.

The second most common structure is the monopsony model, where limited competition is introduced in electricity generation through the sale of power to the dominant utility by independent power producers (IPPs). As noted below, the monopsony model has increased in popularity and can be considered the best practice model for second generation reformers where independent price regulation is in place.

The third and fourth models are more complex, involve more competition, and require the 'unbundling' of the dominant power utility's control over generation, distribution and retailing. The 'wholesale competition model' involves full competition at the generation level, with distribution companies bidding for electricity from generation companies in a wholesale market. The 'full customer choice' model, considered best practice by many first generation reformers, involves competition at every level of the power sector with the exception of the transmission and distribution network.

The four models of power sector regulation are commonly represented as a continuum involving different levels of competition. This continuum was used in the past to demonstrate progress in power sector reform, with countries expected over time to move from a vertically integrated monopoly (the least desirable structure) to a full customer choice model (the most desirable, or best practice model) (Gratwick and Eberhard, 2008; Stern, 2000).

The full suite of reforms was never implemented in most countries, despite advocacy for reform. Besant-Jones' (2006) survey of reform around the world found that only 19 countries had introduced extensive competition in both retailing and generation, and that this had occurred primarily in Europe and Latin America. Vertically integrated monopolies remained in place in 79 countries; while in 52 countries, IPPs sold electricity to a single buyer. Gratwick and Eberhard (2008) conclude that the 'standard model' of (first generation) power sector reform is inaccurate, especially in developing countries, and that instead:

> What we find in the power sector of most developing countries is a confused and contested policy and institutional space that arises from the fact that the incumbent state-owned utility remains intact and dominant, but where IPPs are also invited into the market, often with less than enthusiastic support from the incumbent.

The failure to implement the full suite of 'best practice' reforms has numerous explanations. In developed countries liberalization has been politically contentious, limiting the extent to which governments are willing implement reform, even when supportive in theory. Political opposition has also been strong in developing countries, in part owing to the fact that many governments in developing countries previously subsidized electricity, meaning that liberalization would increase electricity tariffs (Besant-Jones, 2006; Choynowski, 2004).

But efficiency and lower generation costs were always only part of the reason reforms were implemented in developing countries (Newbery, 2001). Instead, reforms were commonly driven by crises in the electricity sector where supply had not kept pace with rising demand for power (Gratwick and Eberhard, 2008). It was hoped that reform would lead to investment in electricity sector infrastructure by the private sector; where this investment did not materialize, reforms were often abandoned (Newbery, 2001).

Support for first generation reforms or full liberalization has wavered in the last decade as a result of mixed experiences (Besant-Jones, 2006). Possibly the most famous example of problematic reform is the power crisis that affected California in 2001, which was caused by manipulation of the wholesale market by sellers who enjoyed monopoly power. But there are other, less extreme, examples. In both the United Kingdom and Chile, two countries commonly cited as examples of successful power sector reform, prices for consumers have not fallen despite lower generation costs resulting from efficiency gains. This was due to the monopoly power enjoyed by private sector utilities and the use of price cap regulation, both of which ensured efficiency gains boosted profits rather than reduced retail prices (Choynowski, 2004; Gratwick and Eberhard, 2008).

There is also increased recognition of the importance of regulation (Stern, 2000), and of the difficulties and risks entailed in liberalizing the electricity sector: an industry where supply and demand are highly inelastic (or less responsive to price signals) (Borenstein, 2002, Besant-Jones, 2006, Rosenzweig et al., 2004). This is especially so in developing countries, where weak institutions make regulation especially challenging. In countries where reforms have been successful, they have involved careful sequencing and have been supported by effective institutions. Most examples of successful reform have occurred in developed countries (Besant-Jones, 2006; Choynowski, 2004; Gratwick and Eberhard, 2008; Kessler and Alexander, 2005).

Advocacy for power sector reform has not disappeared. But it has changed focus, and become more modest in its objectives. First generation reforms in the 1980s and 1990s were focused primarily on the dismantling of vertically integrated state-owned monopolies, introduction of competition, and in some cases, privatization. Nowadays, the World Bank and Asian Development Bank (ADB), strong advocates of power sector liberalization in the past, support such extensive reforms only on a case by case basis. Both are instead more likely to push for independent regulation of the sector in what can be considered a second wave of reform (ADB, 1995, 2009). Second generation reform typically has a number of objectives. One is to ensure that retail electricity prices reflect costs of supply, thereby avoiding regressive subsidies and improving the financial health of power utilities (leading to better management in the sector). The second it ensuring that feed-in tariffs are sufficiently high so as to incentivize independent power producers to invest in generation capacity and sell power to the electricity grid – a reform that can be understood as moving countries with the monopoly model of regulation toward the monopsony model. A third objective, pursued only in some cases, is the use of regulatory mechanisms to incentivize private sector investment that helps widen access to electricity.

Independent regulation has thereby become the new 'best practice' regulatory model, reflecting the limited implementation and success with a first wave of more ambitious reform in the sector. In practice, independent regulation has commonly occurred under a monopsony ownership structure. Advocacy of reform has differed across small island states, but in many cases it has been linked to foreign aid or concessional finance – often for renewable energy development. The World Bank and ADB have been the strongest advocates of reform in small island states of the Pacific. In the Caribbean, USAID has actively advocated and supported such reform. The suitability in small island states of what is considered international 'best practice', both in the first and second waves of reform, is discussed in the next section.

3 The electricity sector in small island states

The two defining features of small island states are size and the absence of land borders with neighbouring states. Both have important ramifications for the electricity sector. Almost all electricity networks in small island states are isolated networks, meaning that they are not connected to other networks, including those of other countries (in some small island states undersea cables provide a link, but these are costly and are very much the exception). Energy security, an important consideration for all electricity networks, is far more challenging for isolated networks. Such networks must be self-sufficient in the production of electricity – electricity is not imported from neighbouring networks, such as occurs in other small states (e.g. Luxembourg). This means backup generation (or storage) is required, which increases the economic cost of supply. The lack of a connection with other networks also makes the integration of renewable energy technologies that produce electricity intermittently more complicated and costly, especially at high levels of penetration.

Size of the network

The small scale of networks in small island states presents other economic challenges. Limited demand for electricity constrains the ability of power utilities to achieve economies of scale in generation. Unit costs are higher as a result. Although this situation has changed considerably in the last decade due to technological advances that have lowered the cost of renewable energy technologies (especially solar-power), the absence of economies of scale is still important in

Table 15.2 Fossil-fuel-based electricity production in small island states (% of total production)

Pacific		Caribbean		Other	
Cook Islands	100	Antigua and Barbuda	100	Bahrain	100
Fiji	53	Bahamas	100	Cape Verde	71
Kiribati	100	Barbados	100	Comoros	95
Marshall Islands	100	Belize	4	Maldives	100
Micronesia Fed. States	100	Dominica	69	Malta	96
Nauru	100	Grenada	100	Mauritius	79
Niue	100	Guyana	100	Sao Tome/ Principe	86
Palau	87.67	Jamaica	90	Seychelles	100
Samoa	67	St Kitts and Nevis	100		
Solomon Islands	100	St Lucia	100		
Timor Leste	100	St Vincent /Grenadines	83		
Tonga	94	Trinidad and Tobago	100		
Tuvalu	99				
Vanuatu	86				

Source: Data is taken from Energy Information Association (EIA) (2017) and is for 2014 (the latest year for which data was available across most countries). In the case of Tonga, Tuvalu and Vanuatu, EIA data incorrectly reports fossil-fuel production as 100% of total production in 2014. These figures have been corrected using data from PPA (2016) and Tonga Power Limited's 2014 annual report. EIA did not have data for FSM, so the table uses Pacific Power Association (PPA) data instead (utilities in all four states reported 100% fossil-fuel based generation in 2014).

explaining why electricity supply costs are higher in small island states than in larger countries (Dornan and Jotzo, 2015). Electricity in small island states is instead commonly generated using oil-fired generators (Table 15.2), although renewable energy investments are leading to greater diversity of generation sources over time.

Compounding these challenges are the geography and population distribution of some small island states. Where small populations are spread across island archipelagos, or where networks are fragmented and limited to urban centres, the 'national market' is segmented into smaller sub-national markets. This makes it harder still to achieve economies of scale. It also means that utilities must install expensive back-up or latent generation capacity (or storage), in order to safeguard the security of electricity supply (Dornan 2014a).

Differences between small island states

It is important to also acknowledge differences across the electricity sectors of small island states. The most important is size of the network. While all electricity networks in small island states are small by global standards, they do vary immensely with one another. Cuba, for instance, consumes more than 20,288 GWh of electricity each year. In the independent state of Tuvalu, with just 10,000 people, the figure is less than 6 GWh.

Another difference is access to electricity, which is closely linked to income. Many small island states enjoy high levels of access to electricity, but this is not universal. Access rates are especially low in the Melanesian states of the West Pacific, where countries like Papua New Guinea, Solomon Islands, and Vanuatu have rates of electricity access comparable to those Sub-Saharan Africa.

A third difference is the renewable energy resources that are available across small island states. These vary enormously between countries, with smaller atoll island nations especially constrained in the options available to them.

Such attributes influence the priorities for development of the electricity sector, with ramifications for regulation. Regulatory incentives for expanding access to electricity are generally non-existent, and indeed often hinder electrification through the granting of a monopoly to the incumbent utility. This is of particular concern in states with low electrification rates. Regulatory mechanisms for the promotion of renewable energy development and (especially) demand side management are often lacking in small island states, despite the high level renewable energy ambitions of their governments.

4 Regulation and reform in small Island states

The power sectors of most small island states were developed as vertically integrated monopolies, as occurred across most of the world. In a majority of small island states, the state either controlled or had a share in this monopoly – in many cases after purchasing private companies that had initially developed small networks. State control or investment in the monopoly utility was often used as a means to achieve government objectives without the need for regulatory oversight. Regulatory oversight, where it did exist, was more commonly put into place where vertically integrated monopoly utilities were controlled by the private sector, although there were some cases where private sector utilities enjoyed unregulated monopolies, such as Vanuatu (until recently), Grenada, and Aruba and Curacao (Shirley and Kammen, 2013, Dornan, 2015b). Legislation in the electricity sector was generally dated and modelled on legislation in metropolitan countries.

The monopoly model worked reasonably well in small island states where governments are effective and corruption is limited, especially where governments had a stake in ownership. It worked less well where these conditions were not met. Many power utilities in the Pacific, for example, were obliged by political leaders to price electricity below its full cost, with the result that power utilities were placed under financial pressure and were unable to adequately maintain generation equipment and the network (Dornan, 2014a). By design, the monopoly model of regulation did not attract investment from other parties. This has acted as a barrier to the expansion of access, and to renewable energy development, especially where combined with a tariff setting regime that is politicized and a regulatory regime that has not prioritized renewable energy development (Dornan, 2014a, Timilsina and Shah, 2016).

The impact of first generation reforms aimed at liberalizing the electricity sector has been limited in small island states – more limited than in other developing countries. Size is clearly important in determining whether liberalization is appropriate: no country with less than 1,000 MW of installed capacity had established a wholesale market that features competition (Dornan, 2014b). Most small island states have instead retained a monopoly structure, or have moved toward the monopsony model (often only in recent years). However, there are exceptions.

In Fiji, the vertically integrated state-owned monopoly that supplied electricity was in 1998 broken up into three companies responsible for generation, distribution and retailing, with technical assistance provided by the Asian Development Bank. This structure was short-lived: a change of government the following year saw the 'unbundling' reversed (Dornan, 2014b). In Aruba, generation and distribution were also unbundled, but no competition was introduced. The state subsequently took control of both functions (Shirley and Kammen, 2013). Singapore has recently announced it will fully liberalize its electricity sector in 2018.

Reform of the electricity sector in small island states has been more pronounced in recent years, although it has involved second generation reforms, aimed at establishing an appropriate pricing structure and in some cases, at introducing independent power producers (the monopsony model), rather than the introduction of competition. Efforts to expand renewable energy supply – often with reference to a response to climate change – have been used to justify many of these reforms.

Small island states have established renewable energy targets that are among the most ambitious in the world (Dornan and Shah, 2016, Timilsina and Shah, 2016). Whereas most countries have established renewable energy targets below 40% of total generation, most small island states have established targets above this number (see Table 15.3). The scale of investment needed for these developments is beyond what is possible for existing monopoly utilities. New sources of funding are needed, including climate change funding, development assistance, and private sector investment (Betzold, 2016). Removing the legislated monopoly over generation that is enjoyed by existing utilities, and thereby enabling independent power producers to invest in new generation capacity, is one way that some small island states have attempted to address this issue (Timilsina and Shah, 2016). Strengthening the financial position of state-owned utilities through appropriate pricing, thus better enabling them to develop renewable energy resources, is another. Regulatory oversight that ensures adequate retail and feed-in tariffs has been important in both cases.

In summary, while the ambitious liberalization agenda of the 1980s and 1990s had limited impact in small island states, a second wave of reforms aimed at facilitating investment by independent power producers has had a greater effect, even if only in some countries. This second wave of reform has been driven in large part by an ambitious agenda to develop renewable energy resources, often as a result of advocacy and support by external actors like the multilateral development banks and USAID that are also assisting to develop renewable energy sources.

Failure to implement the earlier, first wave of more ambitious liberalization reforms likely reflected a recognition that competition would always be limited in small island states where electricity networks are limited in size – a point emphasized by Stern (2000). It is hard to imagine that in very small states the cost reductions driven by competition would ever outweigh the overheads associated with different generation, distribution and retailing companies, as well as regulatory oversight (which would include a centralized dispatch function). The same limitations do not all apply to 'best practice' in the second wave of reform, which commonly involves a monopsony model where independent power producers supply a dominant power utility that is responsible for some generation and for all distribution and retail sales. However, even this second model presents challenges, such as the need for regulatory oversight. Its feasibility in small island states is discussed next.

5 Discussion

Consensus around what constitutes 'best practice' regulation in the electricity sector has changed over time and in response to the mixed results of early liberalization. It is clear that the initial liberalization agenda, which focused primarily on the introduction of competition, was not well suited to small island states. The importance of economies of scale in generation, fixed costs associated with administration, and the cost of regulation all serve to make competition

Table 15.3 Renewable energy targets in the electricity sector in small island states

Country	Target
Pacific	
Cook Islands	100% by 2020
Fiji	100% by 2030
Marshall Islands	20% by 2020
Niue	100% by 2020
Palau	45% by 2025
Samoa	100% by 2017
Solomon Islands	50% by 2015
Timor Leste	50% by 2020
Tonga	100% by 2030
Tuvalu	100% by 2020
Vanuatu	65% by 2020
Caribbean	
CARICOM★	47% by 2027
Antigua and Barbuda	15% by 2030
Bahamas	30% by 2030
Barbados	29% by 2029
Belize	100% (no date)
Dominica	100% (no date)
Jamaica	30% by 2020
St Kitts and Nevis	20% by 2015
St Lucia	35% by 2020
Trinidad and Tobago	60MW by 2030
Other	
Bahrain	5% by 2030
Cape Verde	50% by 2020
Maldives	16% by 2017
Mauritius	35% by 2025
Seychelles	15% by 2030

Source: Compiled using Ren21 (2015), IRENA (2015), UN Intended Nationally Determined Contributions, and country planning documents.

Note: ★ Target is for electricity generation across the entire Caribbean Community. This regional target was agreed by national leaders from these countries.

uneconomic in small electricity networks. As a result, full liberalization was not implemented in small island states, although a number of countries made moves in that direction (some of which were subsequently reversed).

A second generation of power reform advocated nowadays in small island states is more concerned with regulatory oversight. One objective behind price regulation that is at arm's length from government (and the political incentives of leaders) is that it can facilitate the establishment of conditions for investment by independent power producers. In small island states, this is both an acknowledgement that ambitious renewable energy targets cannot be financed using the traditional state-owned monopoly utility model, and the result of advocacy and support from external providers of foreign aid and development finance. Independent price regulation is also aimed at shoring up the financial position of dominant utilities already operating in the sector, in recognition that politicized tariff setting by government has in the past contributed to poor performance and, in some countries, to the failure to widen access to electricity (Dornan, 2015a).

This second wave of power reform is less problematic for small island states than the first. Economies of scale constraints to competition are less relevant in the monopsony model, central to which is a dominant power utility. However, the monopsony model is not without its challenges. In order to function well, such a model requires independent regulation, to ensure that an adequate feed-in tariff is paid to independent power producers, that electricity prices charged to consumers reflect costs, and to provide a means of preventing the abuse of market power by the dominant utility (especially important where the utility is no longer controlled by government). Independent regulation has fixed costs, which potentially overwhelm the benefits of reform for the smallest networks – an issue of particular importance in microstates, or the smallest of the small island states (e.g. Nauru or Tuvalu, with 10,000 people each). A related challenge are the human resources necessary for regulation. As Stern (2000) notes:

> … to provide effective regulation in electricity requires not just substantial numbers of staff, it requires substantial numbers of staff with particular and scare specialist skills e.g. economists, lawyers, accountants, financial analysts as well as engineers. These services are also needed in the regulated companies. It remains a very open question as to whether poorer and particularly small countries are able to find the necessary numbers of people with these scarce skills available to staff regulatory institutions and to run the new companies and to provide for a policy capacity in the relevant Ministries.

Effective independent regulation in small island states also faces challenges unrelated to resources. Regulatory capture, whereby an independent regulatory agency is too heavily influenced by the regulated entity, is a risk in any country. But it is especially likely to happen in a small state where expertise in the sector is limited to a small number of people. In this context, personal relationships between experts are of increased importance, making confrontation between the regulator and regulated entity unlikely – no matter how warranted. This undermines effective regulation. Stern's paper on regulation in small states again summarizes the problem succinctly:

> For very small countries (e.g. under 3 million people), there is the problem that the political, economic and social elite is typically sufficiently small and regularly interactive that any genuine separation of powers can become virtually impossible. Since regulation (and, in particular, the separation of regulation from policy) depends on the separation of powers, this can make the establishment of separate regulatory agencies a notional rather than a genuine exercise.

6 Addressing challenges associated with independent regulation

The challenges associated with independent regulation in small states have been acknowledged previously (Stern, 2000, Dornan *et al.*, 2013). This paper goes further in discussing the evolution of regulatory reform internationally and its implications for small island states. A number of approaches to addressing challenges associated with independent regulation in small island states have been proposed. Two of the most popular are discussed below.

The first is regional regulation, or the pooling of resources for regulation. Most commonly what is proposed is a number of small island states pooling their resources in order to establish a regional regulatory agency. This approach has the potential to make regulation more economically feasible for small states. It also addresses the challenge of establishing a truly independent regulatory body in small states. However, experience suggests that establishing such an agency is challenging. The best example of an organization responsible for regulating the electricity sector across multiple small island states is the Eastern Caribbean Regulatory Authority (ECERA), which has taken years to develop and is not yet fully established. A number of similar organizations have been established in other sectors of small island states – see Dornan and Newton Cain (2014) and Warner and Anatol (2015) for a summary of developments in the Pacific and the Caribbean. A common problem has been the perceived lack of legitimacy of these organizations. The public attention electricity prices receive makes this deeply problematic. A related approach involving use of regulatory capacity in metropolitan states is subject to the same issue (Dornan and Newton Cain, 2014, Stern, 2000).

A second approach for addressing challenges associated with independent regulation in small island states is the establishment of a regulatory body responsible for regulation across multiple sectors. This model has clear advantages in terms of reducing the cost of regulation. It is increasingly used in the Pacific islands. In the case of electricity supply, multi-sector regulators have been given the power to regulate prices in Fiji (in 2002), Papua New Guinea (2002), Vanuatu (2007), and Samoa (2009). Multi-sector regulators also control electricity prices in a number of Caribbean states, including Jamaica and in Trinidad & Tobago.

There are a range of models for multi-sector regulation. A multi-sector regulator could be large, as in the case of the Australian Competition and Consumer Commission, which incorporates the Australian Energy Regulator. But it could also be small, drawing on external expertise as required. In an extreme form, a multi-sector regulator could operate only as a secretariat for external commissioners, a model which would have the added value of reducing the risk of regulatory capture. Such an approach might seem suited to small island states, but it too is not without flaws. External expertise is costly, and establishing sound contracts requires another set of specialized skills (Stern, 2000). The model may still be too costly for microstates, although in poorer states, an arrangement subsidized by development partners is an option (as occurs in Vanuatu).

Neither alternative comprehensively addresses the challenges of independent regulation for microstates. Where does that leave those countries? The traditional monopoly model, despite its weaknesses, minimizes the need for specialist regulatory expertise. It has also worked well in some contexts, although this is very much dependent on political leadership. In part, the push for independent regulation in small island states recently has come about due to a desire to attract private sector investment. On this point, it is important to note that such investment can occur without independent regulation, through regulation by contract. The key advantage of such an arrangement is its low cost. But to be workable, a strong judicial system is crucial. This condition is often not met in poorer microstates. Contract by regulation also involves greater risk for potential investors. As Stern notes: 'There are clear advantages in relying on defined regulatory processes by which contractual issues can be re-opened at regular intervals or triggered by certain events or by major concerns of the parties rather than on regulatory contracts.'

7 Conclusion

This chapter has investigated the appropriateness of different ownership and regulatory structures in the electricity sectors of small island states. It is clear from the discussion that the size of the electricity sector is an important determinant of the appropriateness of regulatory models. It is also clear that models considered 'best practice' internationally are often not suited to small island states.

This disconnect between international best practice and what is appropriate in small island states is most evident in the first wave or generation of power sector reforms advocated in the 1980s and 1990s. Liberalization aimed at introducing competition was never appropriate for small electricity networks, given the importance of economies of scale in generation and the overhead costs associated with regulation. Few small island states implemented such reforms. A second wave or generation of reforms, aimed at establishing independent regulatory oversight (with a view to encouraging investment in the sector – both public and private) has also been somewhat problematic for small networks owing to its fixed costs.

A number of responses have been proposed, including regulation by a regional body, and national regulatory agencies responsible for various economic sectors. Neither approach is without its problems. The legitimacy of a regional approach is subject to question, especially given that price setting in the electricity sector is so politically charged. The multi-sector model is likely to be too costly for microstates (the smallest of the small island states).

Other factors are also important in determining which ownership and regulatory model is most appropriate in a given context. Governance is especially important. Where political leadership has not intervened in technical issues or insisted on electricity prices that are below cost, there is less of a motive for establishing independent regulation. Similarly, where a good judicial system is in place, contract by regulation may be sufficient to attract private sector investment – assuming it is needed in the first place. The implication is that traditional monopoly models of regulation may be appropriate in some small island states after all. However, this will depend on the context. What is clear is that one standard model of regulation is inappropriate across small island states. Solutions need to be tailored.

The subject of regulation in the electricity sector is of considerable importance in small island states given their renewable energy ambitions. A range of regulatory reforms and initiatives are needed in most small island states if ambitious renewable energy targets are to be met. This chapter has stressed that there is no one regulatory structure that is best suited to enabling small island states achieve their ambitions. What is also clear is that regulatory models advocated internationally are often not appropriate for small island states.

References

ADB (1995). *The Bank's Policy Initiatives for the Energy Sector*. Manila: Asian Development Bank.

ADB (2009). *Energy Policy*. Manila: Asian Development Bank.

Besant-Jones, J. E. (2006). Reforming power sector markets in developing countries: what have we learned. *Energy and Mining Sector Board Discussion Paper*. Washington, DC: the World Bank Group.

Betzold, C. (2016). 'Fuelling the Pacific: Aid for renewable energy across Pacific Island countries'. *Renewable and Sustainable Energy Reviews*, 58: 311–318.

Borenstein, S. (2002). 'The Trouble with Electricity Markets: Understanding California's Restructuring Disaster'. *Journal of Economic Perspectives*, 16: 191–211.

Choynowski, P. (2004). Restructuring and Regulatory Reform in the Power Sector: Review of Experience and Issues. *ERD Working Paper Series*. Manila: Asian Development Bank.

Dornan, M. and Jotzo, F. (2015). 'Renewable Technologies and Risk Mitigation in Small Island Developing States: Fiji's Electricity Sector'. *Renewable and Sustainable Energy Reviews*, 48: 35–48.

Dornan, M. and Newton Cain, T. (2014). 'Regional Service Delivery among Small Island Developing States of the Pacific: An Assessment'. *Asia and the Pacific Policy Studies*, 1: 541–560.

Dornan, M. and Shah, K. U. (2016). 'Energy policy, aid, and the development of renewable energy resources in Small Island Developing States'. *Energy Policy*, 98: 759–767.

Dornan, M. (2014a). 'Access to electricity in Small Island Developing States of the Pacific: Issues and challenges'. *Renewable and Sustainable Energy Reviews*, 31: 726–735.

Dornan, M. (2014b). 'Reform despite politics? The political economy of power sector reform in Fiji,1996–2013'. *Energy Policy*, 67: 703–712.

Dornan, M. (2015a). 'Reforms for the expansion of electricity access and rural electrification in small island developing states'. *AIMS Energy*, 3: 463–479.

Dornan, M. (2015b). 'Renewable Energy Development in Small Island Developing States of the Pacific'. *Resources*, 4: 490–506.

Dornan, M., Mcgovern, K., Alejandrino-Yap, C. and Austin, J. (2013). *Infrastructure Maintenance in the Pacific: Challenging the build, neglect, rebuild paradigm*. Sydney: Pacific Regional Infrastructure Advisory Center.

Energy Information Administration (EIA) (2017). *International Energy Statistics*. US Department of Energy.

Gratwick, K. N. and Eberhard, A. (2008). 'Demise of the standard model for power sector reform and the emergence of hybrid power markets'. *Energy Policy*, 36: 3948–3960.

IRENA (2015). *Renewable Energy Target Setting*. Abu Dhabi: International Renewable Energy Agency.

Kessler, T. and Alexander, N. (2005). Financing and Provision of Basic Infrastructure: synthesis, commentary and policy implications of water and electricity service case studies. *Making it Flow: Learning from Commonwealth Experience in Water and Electricity Provision*. London: Commonwealth Foundation.

Newbery, D. M. (2001). *Privatization, Restructuring, and Regulation of Network Utilities*. Cambridge, MA: MIT Press.

Pacific Power Association (PPA). (2016). *Pacific Power Utilities Benchmarking Report 2013 and 2014 Fiscal Years*. Republic of Palau: Pacific Power Association.

Ren21Renewables (2015). *Global Status Report*. Paris: REN21 Renewable Energy Policy Network.

Rosenzweig, M. B., Voll, S. P. and Pabon-Agudelo, C. (2004). 'Power Sector Reform: Experiences from the Road'. *The Electricity Journal*, 9: 16–28.

Shirley, R. and Kammen, D. (2013). 'Renewable energy sector development in the Caribbean: Current trends and lessons from history'. *Energy Policy*, 57: 244–252.

Stern, J. (2000). 'Electricity and telecommunications regulatory institutions in small and developing countries'. *Utilities Policy*, 9: 131–157.

Timilsina, G. R. and Shah, K. U. (2016). 'Filling the gaps: Policy supports and interventions for scaling up renewable energy development in Small Island Developing States'. *Energy Policy*, 98: 653–662.

Warner, R. and Anatol, M. (2015). 'Caribbean Integration – Lessons for the Pacific?' *Asia and the Pacific Policy Studies*, 2: 183–196.

16

Regulatory frameworks in small states – with special reference to telecommunications

Omar Dhaher

1 Introduction

Following the liberalization of the telecommunications sector in the United States and Europe, other countries, including many small states, followed suit and opened up their telecommunications' sector to competition. This chapter analyses the viability of competition in small states given their economic and social characteristics and the impact of these characteristics in adopting regulatory frameworks.

The issue of country size is important when discussing regulatory frameworks. If the domestic market size is small and commercial activities are limited, competition may not be beneficial or viable, and independent national regulatory authorities may have to be structured in such a way as to take account of the special constraints faced by small states.

This chapter discusses the above issues. Section 2. discusses the definition of small country size with regard to network industries, more precisely telecommunications while Section 3. deals with the special regulatory constraints of small states with reference to market entry, economic and social realities and the institutional setup of regulators. Section 4. presents a brief conclusion.

2 Small country size and telecommunications regulations

Regulation of public utilities

The OECD defines regulation as an 'imposition of rules by government, backed by the use of penalties that are intended specifically to modify the economic behaviour of individuals and firms in the private sector'.[1] Government intervenes through economic and/or non-economic policy measures to alter market outcomes. In a free market economy, sellers and buyers negotiate price and quantity, free from any kind of intervention, where entry to and exit from the market is free and where the most efficient players survive in the market. If any inefficiency occurs then it is corrected through Adam Smith's 'invisible hand'. Hence, according to this argument, there should be no place for government intervention in free market economy.

However, it is well known that the invisible hand does not always do its job. Sometimes market forces fail to eliminate inefficiencies and distortions. The Global Financial Crisis in 2007 is a prime example of such failure. Advocates of government intervention in the market for a good or a service have developed several theories to support their arguments, including the public interest theory, capture theory, and economic theory of regulation (Posner, 1974). The central argument of all these theories are summed up by Kahn (1971: 18/I) as the need for 'the visible hand of regulation to replace the invisible hand of competition'.

The rationale for regulation can be based on normative analysis and on positive theory. The normative approach relates to intrinsic characteristics of the market or industry (which in our case is telecommunications), which lead to market failure and renders competition either impossible or undesirable. Market failure occurs when competition simply does not work and the market needs to be regulated[2] a situation often associated with natural monopolies, capacity constraints and network effects. The positive theory rationale for regulation is not based on the structure of the market, but relates to regulatory arrangements intended to satisfy the interests of particular groups (Viscusi et al., 2005: 380).

The rational for regulation applies to all states including small ones. But small states face special constraints mostly because these are often unable to support a sufficiently large number of players, particularly in industries where economies of scale and scope and sunk costs are present.

Small country size and telecommunications

Although there is no single widely accepted definition of small states, the following four indicators are mostly used[3]:

Population: Various population thresholds are used to define a small state. The Commonwealth Secretariat and the Word Bank use an arbitrary population cut-off point of 1.5 million.[4]

GDP/GNP: Gross domestic/national product measures are used to indicate the magnitude of economic activities by a state, which can be used to estimate market size and the potential of scale economies.

Geographical area: Is used to determine availability of land and proxy for natural resources endowment.

Share of international trade: Such an indicator is used by the World Trade Organization for defining small vulnerable economies, and relates to countries' influence in international markets.

The International Telecommunication Union (ITU) describes Small Island Developing States (SIDS) as 'a special group of developing countries which face social, economic and environmental vulnerabilities. Most common challenges faced by SIDS are high costs for telecommunication infrastructure, energy and transportation, apart from minimum resilience to natural disasters.'[5]

In the case of telecommunications regulation, it can be argued that a state is small if (a) its market size is small and it is difficult for operators to produce at an efficient scale of production; (b) its location is remote and isolated with significant transportation and procurement costs; and (c) it has natural or artificial restrictions on trade with its neighbouring countries.

Market size

Small populations and limited resource bases determine how many operators can participate in the market and achieve productive efficiency. Productive efficiency is linked with the minimum efficient scale of production (MES), which is defined by Mankiw (2008: 278) as 'the quantity of output that minimizes average total cost'. This implies that due to its domestic

Table 16.1 Economies of scale in fixed and mobile telecommunications markets

	Fixed	*Mobile*
Core network	Major economies of scale	Substantial economies of scale
Access network	No substantial economies of scale	Substantial economies of scale
Retail activities	Diseconomies of scale	Few economies of scale

market, a small state would be better off having one or just a few operators, who would produce the highest quantity possible to achieve economies of scale and scope

Competition may be feasible in the mobile telephony market, where many players could produce under the minimum efficient scale (see Table 16.1), whereas the fixed telephony market is likely better off having one operator serving the small market. However, competition may also be feasible in the fixed market if the market density is large enough to support many players, if the adoption of new technology reduces costs and introduces new products as close substitutes to existing ones and if there is the possibility of market integration with neighbouring countries.

Isolation and remoteness

For some small states, isolation and remoteness result in high transportation and communication costs, adding to the economic disadvantages faced by these states. Armstrong and Read (2000: 288) note that isolated and remotely located small states 'face particularly high transport costs, transport monopoly difficulties, transport reliability issues, and diseconomies in loads, routing, and return shipments.'

The problem of high costs can be mitigated by regional cooperation and agreements to have a shared backbone infrastructure that would reduce average cost and allow all remote islands achieve a degree of scale economies.

Natural or artificial restrictions on trade with neighbouring countries

In network industries, including, telecommunications, this factor is of major importance. For example, Hong Kong SAR[6] is considered a small economy by area (1,108 km^2), but not so small in terms of population (7.16 million in 2016) and GDP ($316 billion in 2016). Hong Kong could be considered as small for some industries, such as agriculture, and not so small for other industries, given its interconnections with its neighbouring countries. Samoa is an example of natural restrictions on trade. Remote states like Samoa have a natural structural disadvantage when it comes to trade as remoteness decreases the state's ability to integrate with neighbouring markets.

Gal (2001) examines smallness from state's ability to support competition in the domestic market and looks at barriers to entry in the market as well as problems of integration. She considers that remoteness and isolation of New Zealand and Australia constitute a natural entry to barrier that affects their ability to benefit from trade with other countries. Because of that, Gal classifies New Zealand and Australia as small states.

Conversely, applying Gal's definition of small states to Luxembourg,[7] this country would not be considered a small state, given that, as an EU member, it does not have barriers within the internal European market and therefore its domestic market for some industries is integrated with its neighbouring countries.

With regard to artificial restrictions, the Israeli–Palestinian conflict is a prime example. Although Israel has signed peace agreements with Egypt, Jordan, and the Palestinian Authority, restrictions on trade still apply formally either through tariffs and taxation or informally through popular boycott movements. In June 2014, the CEO of the partly state-owned French telecommunications operator Orange announced his company's intention to cut ties with its Israeli partner (Partner[8]) which carries its brand.[9] This announcement came as a boycott campaign against Mobinil, the Egyptian partner of Orange which accused Mobinil and Orange of aiding Partner building antenna in confiscated Palestinian land and serving illegal Israeli settlements in the West Bank.

On the other hand, Israeli control of spectrum in the West Bank and Gaza saw a very slow process of licensing a mobile network by the Palestinian Authority. Jawwal, the incumbent operator had to wait 2 years until 2G spectrum for the West Bank and Gaza was released, while Wataniya-Palestine had to wait 3 years until it got its 2G spectrum in the West Bank, only after diplomatic pressure from the envoy of the Quartet, Tony Blair. After years of negotiations, political pressure, and lobbying, Israel is set to release 3G spectrum to the two operators. Interconnection and roaming charges between Israeli and Palestinian mobile operators are high.

3 Transposition of regulatory frameworks in small states

After the wave of deregulation of the telecommunications sector that started in 1980s with the breakup of AT&T in the United States, a process followed by Europe in the 1990s, developing countries, including many small states, followed suit and liberalized their telecommunications market. Many small states, adopted telecommunications regulatory frameworks from universally accepted practices, often without due consideration of economic, social, cultural and political implications associated with small country size. While arguing in favour of the creation of telecommunications regulatory frameworks, Mollel (2008: 2) states 'there is no 'one size fits all' solution and transplanting legal models to developing countries' environments does not work.' He argues further that legal and telecommunications regulatory frameworks should be shaped by the country's local culture, economic and political environment.[10] In the case of small states this argument applies *a fortiori*.

There were different reasons behind the deregulatory movement, including the normative and positive rationales described above. Saleh (2010) argues that deregulation of the telecom sector was necessary for globalization as multinational companies needed to communicate regularly with all its branches and plants across the globe. The classic PTT regulatory model (in the form of a monopolized telecommunications undertaking owned, operated and regulated by the government or its agency) was not compatible with the interests of such large companies.

In small states there is often a close relationship between business and the political class. This may have its benefits in that it may ensure a fast response to policy reforms. However, deregulatory changes adopted by small states sometimes tended to be somewhat arbitrary and depended on the mood of the policy makers rather than substantive economic analysis. For example, Favaro *et al.* (2004) refer to the mistakes the government of Samoa made during the liberalization process, mainly due to the lack of experience. As a result the government of that island state had to approach the World Bank and ask for their help to broker a better deal with operators and achieve better competitive results and quality of service. Stirton and Lodge (2002) found that Jamaica had to wait until its institutions evolved in order to reap the benefits of market liberalization.

In many cases, the government monopoly was replaced by private monopolies or oligopolies, often including the incumbent operators, due to the fact that the small size of the domestic market did not permit participation by many players.

According to the implementation report of the European Commission (2015), the operators that enjoyed monopoly power before the liberalization of telecommunications (incumbent operators) in Cyprus, Luxemburg and Malta enjoy high market shares in all markets (fixed, mobile, and data) and were able to strengthen their dominance through bundling offers that alternative operators could not competitively match. For example, in Luxembourg, the incumbent operator enjoys further dominance as it has about 61% of the fixed market share and the ability to offer free on-net calls as part of bundled offers. Alternative operators cannot replicate such offering due to high interconnection fees they have to the incumbent. In addition, interconnection charges for terminating local and single transit are higher than the EU average. In broadband markets, a study by Van Dijk (2015) for the European Commission found that the cheapest offers in Luxembourg are up to 70% more expensive than the EU average.

In Malta, almost all forms of competition are between the two incumbents of telecom and cable networks. However, within the same network, competition and number of alternative operators are limited. This is especially present in the broadband sector, where number of ISPs is decreasing, and alternative wireless broadband solutions did not pick up (3% of market share) (European Commission, 2015).

In Cyprus, the potential of liberalization is not fully realized as the 100% state owned incumbent has a strong position in fixed, mobile, and data markets. In addition, willingness of alternative operators to invest in the market is met by delays in decision making with regard to allocating frequency for wireless fixed access and mobile (ibid.).

4 The Special Regulatory Constraints of Small States

Small states face an array of special regulatory constraints. These states may be grouped under four headings, namely (a) entry into the market; (b) economic factors; (c) social and cultural matters; and (d) institutional design. This section deals with these constrains in turn.

Entry into the market

If the market structure cannot support a large number of players, regulatory authorities in small states face a trade-off between allocative and productive efficiencies. On the one hand, a market structure based on one or a small number of operators, brings with it the risk of market power and higher prices, especially since the probability of collusion is higher in small states than in larger states, due to, among other things, easier ties of business with the political elite. On the other hand, more firms than the market can support would lead to inefficient level of production and, again, this could lead to the risk of higher prices. Allocative efficiency favours many competing players (open entry); while productive efficiency favours few players that can achieve the minimum scale of production (controlled entry).

According to Cadman and Twomey (2006: 21), open entry supporters argue that market forces should decide as to which firms are efficient enough to stay in the market, in which case potential entrants would decide after a complete assessment of the market, the state of competition, and potential streams of revenues to enter such market or not. In addition, controlling entry to the market means a higher risk of collusion and anti-competitive practices. Controlled entry supporters draw attention to two potential problems associated with open entry. The first problem is related to the possibility of high number of firms chasing a limited number of revenue streams that might lead to the destructive competition problems and compromise quality of service. Secondly, and most importantly, significant parts of investments in telecommunications are sunk, and exiting firms will not be able to recover such costs. Such loss of investment does not only affect exiting firms, but also the economy as a whole, since such costs represent a larger share in small state's economy.

The experience of some countries (in the Caribbean, in particular) shed light on the two approaches. Jamaica opted for an open entry, which resulted in large number of new entrants. However, few were able to survive, only 7 out of 72 Internet Service Providers and 3 out of 17 firms that offered international voice providers, most probably because of insufficient investment (Cadman and Twomey, 2006: 19).

Within the EU, where general authorization (open entry) is implemented, the number of operators remained just a few in Cyprus, Luxemburg, and Malta (see Table 16.2)

Cadman and Twomey (2006) argue that concentration should not be an issue that regulators would be overly concerned about, rather it is something to be expected in small domestic markets.

Another issue arises when telecommunications undertakings in larger states decide to enter a small state's telecommunications market. The firms from the larger states can take advantage of the economies of scale in the large market in their country and use it as leverage in the small market. Ovum and Indepen (2005: 30) argued that there should not be major differences in market power between the small state incumbent and a new entrant from a large state in the market. However, in that case, the regulatory authorities will need to find the right balance if they impose different regulatory requirements on the small-state incumbent.

Economic considerations associated with regulation

Because of efficiency implications, and the small size of domestic markets, market structures tend to be different in small states, compared to larger states. Therefore, one often sees in small states oligopolistic, and even monopolistic, market structures. Briguglio (2017) and Gal (2003) argue that the behaviour of dominant firms, which otherwise might be considered as abusive, could be driven by economic considerations. For example, in an oligopolistic market, a common occurrence in small states, price discrimination, often considered as an abuse of dominance, might result in lower prices for consumers and may lead firms to improve the quality of their product.

With regard to excessive pricing, another practice often considered as an abuse of dominance, it can be argued that this is due to the weak procurement power of operators in small states,

Table 16.2 Number of operators in Cyprus, Estonia, Luxembourg, Malta, and Slovenia by market

Country	Fixed market	Mobile market	Broadband market
Cyprus	2[11]	3	N/A[12]
Estonia	2	3	Several
Luxembourg	Several[13]	3[14]	Several[15]
Malta	2[16]	3	2[17]
Slovenia	4	4	Several

Source: European Commission (2016), available at: https://ec.europa.eu/digital-single-market/en/news/edpr-country-profiles-telecom-annex/.

resulting in higher equipment costs. A relatively high price would also be expected due to higher transportation cost in the case of island states. The regulatory and competition authorities might treat relatively high prices as excessive when they, erroneously, benchmark domestic prices against those prevailing in a large state.

With regard to foreclosure of the market, yet another practice often considered as an abuse of dominance, the impact of new entrants capitalizing on the market for a short period before making an exit has far more adverse effects on small economies as it could leave customers and other stakeholders at a disadvantage and destabilize the market to a greater degree. For example, in Malta, the shock exit of a supermarket chain left its business creditors at a disadvantage, and severely destabilized the market (Briguglio and Buttigieg, 2004: 8). These authors argue that this does not mean that barriers to entry should be encouraged, but that (a) the limited number of players that can be accommodated in a small market constrains competition possibilities; and (b) the high degree of instability that arises by the entry and exit of a relatively large firm should be given due importance when assessing consumer welfare in the context of competition law.

With regard to refusal to grant access to essential facilities, Briguglio and Buttigieg refer to the constraints of replicating infrastructural facilities, in which case there could be more scope for the application of the essential facilities doctrine in small jurisdictions. This of course leads to the argument that refusal to grant third party access to essential facilities owned and controlled by a dominant firm should be more readily checked in a small market. What to a regulatory agency in a large market would not appear to be an essential facility as it could be replicated by a potential entrant who is just as efficient as the incumbent, in a small jurisdiction the first entrant would be able to monopolize the sector where there are heavy sunk costs. Thus, in a small state context refusal to grant access or to grant access on equal terms could be deemed an abuse of a dominant position, whereas in larger states it might not.

In addition to the above market practices, often associated with market dominance, there is also the issue of cost of regulation. The cost of regulation is subject to economies of scale, with Cadman and Twomey (2006: 22) stating that the costs of administration per head of population decreases as the size of economy increases. Ovum and Indepen (2005: 34) show that regulatory authorities' costs (as percentage of telecommunications revenues) in small states are eight times higher than costs in large states. The high cost of regulation, due to a large extent to overhead costs indivisibility, renders some regulatory practices too costly compared to the benefits that could arise from such practices.

Infrastructure competition, which is encouraged by regulators, also encounters constraints in small states. This is because in the short term, the large investments that new entrants need to make will not be feasible for a small market share. In the EU, regulatory authorities follow the Cave and Vogelsang (2003) Ladder of Investment (LOI) to encourage new entrants migrating from the incumbent operator's network to their own network. However, Bourreau et al. (2010) argue that in order for the LOI to work, new entrants must build a large enough customer base, which might not be possible in small states, where the population and market size are small.

Social and cultural considerations

In a small state, given the small number of companies, Universal service obligation of providing reasonable access to all people in the country on an equitable basis may be constrained. Symeou and Pollit (2007) and Sutherland (2010) argue that liberalization negatively affects affordability of the incumbent undertaking to provide such universal service because it prohibits or minimizes cross subsidization that monopoly structure can use to cover cost of universal service. On the other hand, competition from mobile technology in most populated and profitable areas provide the incumbent with an incentive to expand its fixed network to un-served and less profitable areas. However, the incumbent will be able to do so, only if it can take advantage of economies of scale and achieve the minimum efficient scale of production.

Symeou and Pollit (2007) argue that incumbent in a small state may be able to exploit economies of scale and achieve the minimum scale of production if there is some form of regional cooperation[18] or if the scope of universal service is re-defined. Through regional cooperation, a set of operators in adjacent states act as universal service providers for the region. This is in line with the EU policy of a single digital market as economic integration benefits the small states of the EU in terms of reducing costs and access to larger markets (European Commission, 2012). The scope of Universal Service Obligation can be redefined from fixed telephony to voice telephony to allow other operators or service providers that use cellular or wireless technologies to provide such universal service. This approach is consistent with the concept of technological neutrality, proposed by the 2002 EU telecommunications regulatory framework and is reflected in the Universal Service Directive (2002/22/EC),[19] which states that 'member states shall ensure that all reasonable requests for connection at a fixed location to a public communications network are met by at least one undertaking'.

An important factor that may negatively affect the operation of the regulatory authorities is the close relationship between politicians and business that often exist in small states, particularly where the culture of competition is not ingrained in society, where the rule of law slack and where control of corruption is weak. Regulatory authorities will find it difficult to maintain their independence and gain adequate support from other institutions such as the judicial system. (Smith and Wellenius, 1999: 3). To tackle the negative effects of political elite-business relationship, the long-term solution would be to strengthen the rule of law. Such a solution requires the development of proper checks and balances that separate the regulator from the government– an important requisite to eliminate or minimize the influence of the political elite, as Cadman and Twomey (2006: 24) argue – but this takes time. In the short-term the regulatory authorities' structure and mandate should be re-designed so as to safeguard regulatory authorities from political capture. One way to do this is to put in place specific set of rules applicable to a particular regulatory arrangement, instead of waiting for the development of a broad rule of law culture (Smith, 1997).

Institutional design of the regulatory authority

The global wave of telecommunications liberalization has pressurized many small states to reform their regulatory policies. In telecommunications, liberalization requires the separation of regulation and operation, with an independent regulatory authority established to oversee the implementation of the sector's `regulatory policy. Again here, the indivisibilities of overhead costs and limitations in reaping the benefits of economies of scale pose serious constraints on small states. In addition, there is the problem of lack of qualified and experienced staff and limited resources. In this regard one has also to keep in mind the fierce competition on recruitment from the private sector, which attracts the best qualified and experienced personnel as a result of better compensation package.

With regard to staff and resources of regulatory authorities, economies of scale also prevail in the institutional design, where the cost of public administration per head of population decreases as the market size increases. Smith and Wellenius (1999: 4) argue that an effective regulator requires substantial professional cadres able to handle complex regulatory concepts and processes. They also contend that when the number of staff is small, prioritizing regulatory issues becomes inevitable. Adjustments to regulatory authorities' structure and functions would need to be made to ensure that regulatory authorities fulfil their mandate.

Among cheaper alternative regulatory methods, benchmarking could be a possible solution as Cadman and Twomey (2006) suggest. However, regulatory authorities need to be careful so as not to benchmark against large states, which would prove to be inappropriate since the characteristics of small states are different, as already argued. In general, benchmarking could be successful if the states that are used for such an exercise have a set of similar characteristics to the one being benchmarked. Article 13(2) of the Access Directive (2002/19/EC) and Article 17(2) of the Universal Service Directive (2002/22/EC) allows regulatory authorities to use international benchmarking to compare and set price controls, cost accounting methods, and tariffs, provided they use comparable state(s) in to accurately address the issue at hand (Queck *et al.*, 2010).

Another possible solution for regulatory authorities to lower the cost of regulatory intervention is by putting more emphasis of negotiation between operators. The rule of thumb should be that regulatory authorities would not intervene unless involved parties fail to agree. This is used in interconnection agreements where regulatory authorities wait for interested operators and service providers to reach an interconnection price.

Another possible solution to overcome problems related to cost of regulation and limitations of personnel is to simplify regulatory practices. The European Commission (2010, para 12) in its recommendation on fixed and mobile termination rates recognized that implementing long-run incremental cost costing method (LRIC) can be challenging for regulatory authorities that have limited resources. It allows such authorities to apply different costing methodologies so long as outcomes of such methodologies are consistent with the recommendation and generates efficient outcomes that are consistent of competitive markets outcomes. Moreover, the recommendation allowed states with limited resources to extend the deadline for having a LRIC costing model available to 1 July 2014 instead of 31 December 2012.

Regulatory authorities have additional choices to reduce costs namely merger of authorities, or regional cooperation (known as cross-border regulatory authorities).

The first option involves a structural change, where a telecommunications regulatory authority becomes part of a larger organization. The purpose is to cut the cost of establishing and maintaining several institutions that can carry out their activities under the administration of one institution and to have a larger pool of expertise at disposal. A telecommunications regulatory authority can merge with other network industries regulatory authorities, such as electricity, gas, and railroads, where the fundamental features of such industries are similar or with the competition authority, since there is a relationship between sector-specific regulation and competition law. The 'Institut Luxembourgeois de Regulation' is an example of a merge with other network industries as it regulates Telecommunications, Electric, and Gas sectors under one authority,[20] while New Zealand combines both regulatory authority and competition authority under one authority. The merger of regulatory authorities approach is also followed in Hungary, Jamaica, Latvia, Malawi, Netherlands and Slovenia.

With regard to cross-border regulatory authorities, in such a scheme each regulatory authority keeps its structure, but the regulatory authorities concerned set up a larger regulatory body that oversees regulatory issues in participating states. This option can be employed to minimize the cost of regulation even further and to share the limited resources. One of the benefits of sharing expertise is that every individual state bypasses the need of duplicating the level of technical expertise in each state (Favaro and Winter, 2004: 136). A similar culture or a common language helps in setting up this kind of institution. There are many examples of such bodies. In the EU, Body of the European Regulators for Electronic Communications (BEREC) advices on regulatory issues across EU member states. While each member state gets to keep its national regulatory authority, national regulatory authorities can seek advice or involvement of

BEREC. Small states of the EU in particular are encouraged to seek BEREC's help and expertise. Another example is the Eastern Caribbean Telecommunications Authority (ECTEL).

The Eastern Caribbean countries' experience provides another example. C&W was the incumbent operator in each country in the Eastern Caribbean. It had strong ties with the political elite in every state. Lack of experienced civil servants helped C&W in exploiting each individual market and the drafting of regulations that suited its interests. Having the experience of past cooperation among institutions (such as central banks) and being able to capitalize on the social cohesion, the Eastern Caribbean countries decided to form the Eastern Caribbean Telecommunications Authority (ECTEL) to utilize existing and fragmented expertise, and save costs by not replicating the same job function in each country. ECTEL was able to introduce liberalization and competition to the telecommunications market, and restrict C&W powers (Favaro and Winter, 2004). In the Persian Gulf, telecommunications regulators of small states such as Bahrain and Qatar benefit from being part of the Gulf Cooperation Council, as regulatory issues such as mobile roaming are tackled collectively, which helps in reducing the problem of staff scarcity.

5 Conclusion

This chapter argued that the classic definition of smallness (usually the size of the population) cannot be fully useful when it comes to discussing network industries, especially telecommunications. Technological advancement, economies of density, and integration with neighbouring countries should also be taken into consideration in the definition of small country size. Defining small states in terms of these attributes may explain why competition in mobile telephony, data markets, and, in some cases even in fixed telephony, was beneficial in some small states and no so in others.

Many small states followed larger states in liberalizing their telecommunications market. Regardless of the reason behind this decision, the transposition of a set of regulatory measures from larger to smaller states has yielded mixed results. The small states where the economics of density existed or where trade integration with neighbouring countries was strong, were able to benefit from a regulatory framework that was essentially designed for larger states.

Remote and isolated small states face particular challenges with regard to implementing regulatory frameworks that promote competition. From an economic point of view, most of these states lack the capability to support many companies within their small domestic market. Oligopoly or even a monopoly structures prevail where the domestic market is small. However, technological advances are making it possible for some segments of the market to become competitive. Mobile markets are likely to support competition, while new technologies and new platforms of communications technologies are making it feasible for new companies to enter the market and challenge the incumbent operators.

The chapter has also argued that the domestic market of small states is likely to create problems relating to entry of new players and in putting in place effective regulatory frameworks due to scale economies and difficulties in finding trained and experienced personnel. A number of remedies, mostly derived from the literature, were proposed as possibly enabling regulatory authorities in small states to reduce constraints associated with the small market size and lack of capacity.

Another problem identified in this chapter with regard to regulatory arrangements in small states relates to impartiality, given that in small states members of the government and private business tend to be close to each other, a problem that is especially severe where the rule of law is slack and control of corruption is weak.

Finally the chapter argued that many of these regulatory problems can be mitigated by regional cooperation or by pooling regulatory arrangements of different similar services.

Notes

1 https://stats.oecd.org/glossary/detail.asp?ID=3295/.
2 There is vast literature explaining why competition would not be desirable and presenting reasons for regulation. Kaysen and Turner (1959), argues that competition is not desirable in (a) situations in which competition, as a practical matter, cannot exist or survive for long, and in which, therefore, an unregulated market will not produce competitive results; (b) situations in which active competition exists, but where, because of imperfections in the market, competition does not produce one or more competitive results; (c) situations in which competition exists, or could exist, and has produced or may be expected to produce competitive results, but where in the light of other policy considerations, competitive results are unsatisfactory in one or more respects. Kahn (1971: 11/I), provides a rationale to regulate network industries (electricity, telecommunications, water gas, and rail) due to (a) the importance of such industries as essential inputs to other industries or infrastructure prerequisite to economic development; (b) public utilities are natural monopolies; and (c) competition simply does not work well. Baldwin et al. (2012) provide an exhaustive list of reasons for regulation; among them: natural monopolies, windfall profits, externalities, information inadequacies, continuity and availability of service, and anti-competitive behaviour and predatory pricing. Viscusi et al. (2005: 376) list natural monopolies and externalities as reasons behind regulation. Decker (2015: 14) lists efficiency, control of monopoly power, and externalities as a normative rationale for public utility regulation:
3 For more on the subject of small states' definition, see Armstrong and Read (2000), Read (2001), Crowards (2002), Cadman and Twomey (2006) and Symeou and Pollit (2007).
4 www.cpahq.org/cpahq/cpadocs/meetingchallengeinglobaleconomyl.pdf/.
5 www.itu.int/en/ITU-D/Conferences/WTDC/WTDC14/Pages/ConnectingSIDS.aspx/.
6 www.cia.gov/library/publications/the-world-factbook/geos/hk.html/.
7 Luxembourg would be classified as a small state under Read (2001) or Crowards (2002) definition. It is, as a sovereign political country with a small population ($\approx$ 503 thousands), small land area ($\approx$2600km^2), with a weak position in international trade.
8 http://partner.co.il/en/.
9 http://america.aljazeera.com/articles/2015/6/4/frances-orange-plans-to-pull-out-of-israel.html/.www.theguardian.com/world/2015/jun/04/orange-says-it-plans-to-terminate-contract-with-brand-partner-in-israel/.
10 For further debate on transposition of regulations see: Edwards (2007), Kingsley (2004), Legrand (1997), Peerenboom (2013), Salim (2009), and Watson (1974).
11 Incumbent operator is 100% state owned and has a market share around 90%.
12 The incumbent could have had about 70% of the market share in 2012.
13 Incumbent operator had 79% of market share in December 2010.
14 Incumbent mobile operators had 53% market share in 2011.
15 Incumbent operator had 72% of the market share in 2012.
16 Previously five operators used four networks, 1 fixed (copper-based), 1 cable, and two wireless networks. Currently, all operators except the incumbent operators of the fixed and cable networks left the market. The fixed incumbent operator had 50.9% of the market share, while the cable incumbent operator had 49.1% market share in 2012.
17 The European Commission (2010: 291) notes that in 2009, the number of ISP providers was decreasing, with the largest independent ISP existing the market, while the 2nd largest independent ISP has informed the regulator that it will stop taking new customers and offering new services. The Commission also notes that number of subscribers connecting with third party retail providers was decreasing, and the market was heading towards a duopoly. This is confirmed in the Commission's (2012) report, as the remaining players in the broadband market were the fixed network and cable network incumbents.
18 According to Schiff (2002: 11), coordination of small states on public good such as water basin, infrastructure industries, the environment, and other energy sources can generate large benefits.

19 Directive on universal service and users' rights relating to electronic communications networks and services (Universal Service Directive). OJ L 108, 24.4.2002, amended by Directive 2009/136/EC of the European Parliament and of the Council of 25 November 2009 L 337 11 18.12.2009.

20 This is referred by the ITU (2017) as the fifth generation of regulation (G5) or collaborative regulation, where the telecommunications regulator "defines the foundation, platforms and mechanisms for working with other sector regulators to help achieve the Sustainable Development Goals."

References

Armstrong, H. and Read, R. (2000). 'Comparing the Economic Performance of Dependent Territories and Sovereign Microstates'. *Economic Development and Cultural Change, University of Chicago Press*, 48(2): 285–306.

Baldwin, R., Cave, M. and Lodge, M. (2012). *Understanding Regulation*. Oxford: Oxford University Press.

Bourreau, M., Dogan, P. and Manant, M. (2010). 'A Critical Review of the 'Ladder Investment' Approach'. *Telecommunications Policy*, 34(11): 683–696.

Briguglio, L. (2017). Competition Law and Policy in Small States. In *Small States in a Legal World*. Springer International Publishing: 23–34.

Briguglio, L. and Buttigieg, E. (2004). 'Competition Constraints in Small Jurisdictions'. *Bank of Valletta Review*, 30.

Cadman, R. and Twomey, P. (2006). *The Regulation of Telecommunications Industries in Small Economies*. SPC Network Ltd.

Cave, M. and Vogelsang, I. (2003). 'How Access Pricing and Entry Interact'. *Telecommunications Policy'*, 27: 717–727.

Crowards, T. (2002). 'Defining the category of 'Small' States'. *Journal of International Development*, 14(2): 143–179.

Decker, C. (2015). *Modern Economic Regulation: An Introduction to Theory and Practice*. Cambridge: Cambridge University Press.

Edwards, G. (2007). *Legal transplants and economics: the World Bank and Third World economies in the 1980s – A case study of Jamaica, the Republic of Kenya and the Philippines*. Master's thesis, Institute of Advanced Legal Studies.

European Commission (2010). *Progress Report on the Single European Electronic Communications Market 2009*. Brussels: Commission of the European Communities.

European Commission (2012). *Digital Agenda for Europe Scoreboard 2012*. Commission of the European Communities. doi:10.2759/83934.

European Commission (2015). *Implementation of the EU regulatory framework for electronic communication – 2015, SWD(2015)*. Brussels: Commission of the European Communities.

Favaro, E. and Winter, B. (2004). Telecommunications Regulation in the Eastern Caribbean. In Favaro, E. (ed.). *Small States, Smart Solutions: Improving Connectivity and Increasing the Effectiveness of Public Services*. Washington, DC: World Bank.

Favaro, E., Halewood, N. and Rossoto, C. M. (2004). From Monopoly to Competition: Reform of Samoa's Telecommunications Sector. In Favaro, E. (ed.). *Small States, Smart Solutions: Improving Connectivity and Increasing the Effectiveness of Public Services*. Washington, DC: World Bank.

Gal, M. (2001). 'Size Does Matter: The Effects of Market Size on Optimal Competition Policy'. *University of Southern California Law Review*. 1437–1478.

Gal, M. (2003). *Competition Policy for Small Market Economies*. Harvard, MA: Harvard University Press.

ITU (2004). *ICTs in the Eastern Caribbean: St Lucia Case Study*. Switzerland: International Telecommunication Union.

ITU (2017). *ICT Trends and Developments in Asia and the Pacific*. Regional Preparatory Meeting for WTDC-17 for Asia and the Pacific (RPM-ASP), Bali, Indonesia, 21–23 March.

Kahn, A. (1971). *The Economics of Regulation: Principles and Institutions*. Harvard, MA: MIT Press.

Kaysen, C. and Turner, D. (1959). *Antitrust Policy: An Economic and Legal Analysis*. Cambridge, MA: Harvard University Press.

Kingsley, J. (2004). 'Legal Transplantation: Is This What The Doctor Ordered and Are the Blood Types Compatible? The Application of Interdisciplinary Research to Law Reform in the Developing World – A Case Study of Corporate Governance in Indonesia'. *Arizona Journal of International & Comparative Law*, 21(2): 493–534.

Legrand, P. (1997). 'The Impossibility of Legal Transplants'. *Maastricht Journal of European and Comparative Law*, 4: 111–124.

Mankiw, G. (2008). *Principles of Economics*. South-Western Cengage Learning.

Maxwell, W. (2002). *Electronic Communications: The New EU Framework*. New York: Oceana Publications, Inc.

Mollel, A. (2008). The legal and regulatory framework for ICT in developing countries: Case study of ICT and the law of evidence in Tanzania. ICT4D PG symposium.

Ovum and Indepen (2005) Applying the EU Regulatory Framework in microstates. Report to the CYTA, EPT and Maltacom.

Peerenboom, R. (2013). 'Toward a methodology of successful legal transplants'. *The Chinese Journal of Comparative Law* 1(1): 4–20.

Posner, R. (1974). Theories of Economic Regulation. *NBER working paper series, Working Paper* No. 41.

Queck, R., de Streel, A., Hou, L., Jost, J. and Kosta, E. (2010). The EU Regulatory Framework Applicable to Electronic Communications. In Garzaniti, L. and O'Regan, M. (eds) *Telecommunications, Broadcasting, and the Internet*, third edition. New York: Thomson Reuters.

Read, R. (2001). Growth, Economic Development and Structural Transition in Small Vulnerable States. *World Institute for Development Economics Research, United Nations University, discussion paper* No. 2001/59.

Saleh, N. (2010). *Third World Citizen and the Information Technology Revolution*. New York: Palgrave Macmillan.

Salim, M. (2009). 'Are Legal Transplants Impossible?'. *Journal of Comparative Law*, 4(1): 182–195.

Schiff, M. (2002). Regional Integration and Development in Small States. *The World Bank, Working Paper* No. 2797.

Smith, P. and Wellenius, B. (1999). *Strategies for Successful Telecommunications Regulation in Weak Governance Environment*. Washington, DC: The World Bank.

Smith, W. (1997). Utility Regulators-The Independence Debate. *The World Bank Group, Note* No. 127.

Stirton, L. and Lodge, M. (2002). *Levy and Spiller's 'Institutional Endowment' Hypothesis after Fifteen Years of Regulatory Reform in Jamaica: Misguided theory. prophets of doom, or an explanation of institutional change?*. Manchester, UK: CRC International Workshop, Centre on Regulation and Competition.

Sutherland, E. (2010). 'International mobile roaming in the Arab states'. *Info*, 13(2): 35–52.

Symeou, P. C. and Pollit, M. G. (2007). Telecommunications in small economies: the impact of liberalization and alternative technologies on universal service. *Working Paper*. Judge Business School, Cambridge University.

Van Dijk (2015). *Broadband Internet Access Cost (BIAC) Autumn 2015*. Brussels: Van Dijk Management Consultants.

Viscusi, W., Harrington, J. and Vernon, J. (2005). *Economics of Regulation and Antitrust*. Harvard, MA: MIT Press.

Watson, A. (1974). *Legal Transplants: An Approach to Comparative Law*. Athens: University of Georgia Press.

17

Small states and regional competition and consumer law agreements: some key features, lessons and experiences

George R. Barker

1 Introduction and outline

Small states may choose to enter regional cooperation agreements on competition and consumer law because they derive various benefits from such arrangements including to exploit scale economies, and overcome inter-jurisdictional externalities, while retaining independence or sovereignty.

These states face critical decisions both on what substantive legal rules to adopt on competition and consumer law, and what procedural arrangements to adopt for enforcement. This chapter reviews and collates key features of seven regional competition and consumer law agreements (RCCLA) in which small states participate.

The chapter is organized in eleven sections. Section 2, which follows this brief introduction, identifies the small states that will form the subject of discussion, while Section 3 discusses the rationale for small states to join regional competition and consumer law agreement. Sections 4.10 then presents overviews of seven regional competition and consumer law arrangements in the Caribbean region, Pacific region, Africa and Asia, and goes into some detail to describe such arrangements. Section 11 concludes the chapter with an assessment of the extent to which regional competition and consumer law agreements that small states may draw on have been successfully operationalized.

Our review suggests that CARICOM in the Caribbean has developed the most successful RCCLA covering 13 small member states. Generally, however, this review suggests that despite potential benefits from RCCLA, and frequent mention of the potential of RCCLA in the academic literature, for most of the 40 small independent states we examine in the World Bank's small state database, generally the regional associations they belong to have either failed to successfully develop operational RCCLA arrangements, or have not even begun to develop one.

2 Defining small states

The World Bank maintains the World Development Indicators (WDI) database[1] which includes demographic and economic data on 216 states. This data can be used to analyse the size

Table 17.1 World Bank Small State Database

Category	Number
World Bank WDI database: Population less than 1.5 million	66
Less 20 dependencies	20
Less 4 very wealthy states =Andorra, Liechtenstein, Luxembourg and Monaco	4
Plus 8 states with populations greater than 1.5 million*	8
World Bank Small State Database (WSSDB)	50

Note: *Botswana, Gabon, Gambia, Guinea Bissau, Jamaica, Lesotho, Namibia and Qatar.

distribution of states, and identify small states in connection with the issue of regional agreements. We then considered the World Bank definition of small states as those with populations less than 1.5 million.[2] It turns out that this corresponds to the smallest 30% (smallest three 'deciles') in our ranked distribution of states, including 66 of the 216 countries in the World Bank database.

The World Bank Small State Database (WBSSD) by comparison consists of 50 countries.[3] Table 17.1 explains how these two numbers are reconciled.

As shown in the third row the World Bank excludes 20 of the 66 countries with populations less than 1.5 million in its World Bank WDI database that are in effect dependencies, being so closely related to, or part of, another larger country (such as the US,[4] the UK, France, the Netherlands, Denmark and China) that they are not considered member states of the UN in their own right. It is also noteworthy that many of these 20 excluded dependent countries possessed very high GDP per capita. We will not consider these countries in our further analysis of small states' involvement in RCCLA.

Constraints faced by small states

Small states with populations less than 1.5 million are likely to face particular problems, including lack of scale economies in government functions, and inter-jurisdictional externalities, which they may reasonably seek to address through the development of regional cooperation agreements with other neighbouring states. The relatively small size of the very small states with which we are concerned implies that they are likely to have a limited tax base and regulatory capacity to effectively resource enforcement of appropriate competition and consumer regulation.

The fact that domestic markets may be dominated by a small number of firms with significant market shares does not however necessarily indicate a problem. Indeed, given the small scale of many markets in small states, it will generally be efficient to have fewer firms supplying any particular market, compared to what one may observe in larger markets. However, to efficiently limit the scope for collusive, oligopolistic and/or monopolistic behaviours that adversely impact social welfare requires the attention of policy makers to ensure that there are low barriers to trade, investment and market entry; and well-targeted and efficiently designed competition and consumer policy.

Regional classification of small developing states

Regional agreements may hold appeal to small states enabling them to secure economies of scale while retaining significant independence or sovereignty, and avoiding fully merging to form a larger unified or more federated state.

Table 17.2 World Bank small state categories

Regional grouping	Number of countries	Total population	GDP per capita (2015 US$)	Total GDP (estimated)
Caribbean	13	7,116,360	9,406	66,935,278,418
Pacific island	11	2,353,344	3,641	8,568,338,903
'Other small states'	26	28,593,188	13,145	375,866,314,426
Total	**50**	**38,062,892**	**11,859**	**451,369,931,748**

Source: Word Bank. http://data.worldbank.org/region/SST/.

Table 17.3 Regional arrangements of the 'other small states' category

Regional arrangements	Number of small states	Total population	GDP per capita (2015 US$)	Total GDP(est.)
COMESA	5	4,229,205	4,290.09	18,143,649,358
SADC	3	6,856,337	4,107.04	28,159,262,462
ECOWAS/ WAEMU	3	4,355,751	826.22	3,598,810,836
ECCAS	3	2,760,696	9,701.20	26,782,052,334
SAARC	2	1,183,993	4,639.55	5,493,192,280
Total	**16**	**19,385,982**	**4,238.99**	**82,176,967,271**

Source: Word Bank. http://data.worldbank.org/region/SST/.

The World Bank classifies the 50 small states in its small-state database into three sub-categories, namely Pacific Island,[5] Caribbean[6] and 'other small states'[7] as shown in Table 17.2 by row. The remaining four columns in Table 17.3 identify the number of countries, total population, GDP per capita (weighted average), and total GDP in each of these sub-categories.

Sections 4. to 10. of this chapter review seven different regional approaches to economic regulation within the above small states groupings and collate key features of relevant policy and legislative frameworks. In this regard, the associations covering the first two small-state regions shown in Table 17.3 will include the Caribbean Community and Common Market (CAR-ICOM) and the Pacific Island Forum (PIF). The Caribbean Community and Common Market and the Pacific Island Forum consist mostly of small states, as we shall explain in Sections 4. and 5. Together they include 24 out of the 50 small states covered in this chapter.

Turning to the remaining 26 'other small states' in Table 17.2, 16 are members of five associations shown in Table 17.3 which are described more fully below.

- The *Common Market for Eastern and Southern Africa (COMESA)*. Five small states in the WBSSD belong to COMESA, namely Comoros, Djibouti, Mauritius, Seychelles and Swaziland.
- The *Southern African Development Community (SADC)*. Three states in the WBSSD belong to SADC, namely Botswana, Namibia and Lesotho. These are not strictly speaking small states with populations above the 1.5 million threshold. Three other SADC states, that are smaller than 1.5 million (namely Seychelles, Swaziland, and Mauritius) have already been counted as members of COMESA.

- The *Economic Community of West African States (ECOWAS)*. Three small states in the WBSSD belong to ECOWAS, namely Cabo Verde, the Gambia, and Guinea-Bissau, the last two countries with populations not much higher than 1.5 million. There is a significant overlap in the members of ECOWAS and the West African Economic and Monetary Union (WAEMU) – so we will consider these two arrangements together in what follows
- The *Economic Community of Central African States (ECCAS)*. Three small states in the WBSSD belong to ECCAS, namely Gabon, Equatorial Guinea, and São Tomé and Príncipe. Again, Gabon's population is more than 1.5 million, and so does not strictly meet the World Bank definition of a small state.
- The *South Asian Association for Regional Cooperation (SAARC)*. Two small states from the WBSSD belong to SAARC, namely Maldives and Bhutan.

Of the ten remaining small states in the WBSSD, six[8] are quite wealthy and are in some way either directly or indirectly associated with the European Union (EU) or the European Free Trade Association (EFTA). They will not be considered further here. This is consistent with the World Bank itself excluding four other wealthy European states from the WBSSD. Three other countries in the top quartile of countries by GDP per capita will be excluded from further consideration namely: Qatar and Bahrain, that belong to the Gulf Cooperation Council (GCC); and Brunei Darussalam that belongs to the Association of South East Asian Nations (ASEAN). All of these nine excluded small states then are relatively wealthy, and for that reason shall not be considered further here. The remaining 10th state in the WBSSD that will not be considered is East Timor as it is not a member of any regional co-operation agreement, although it has been trying to be a member of ASEAN since gaining independence in 2002.

3 Rationale for regional cooperation

There are two main rationales for small states seeking to join regional arrangements on competition and consumer regulation (in either a federal or cooperative arrangement). The first relates to the cross-border effects and regulatory externalities rationale – where the conduct of parties in one market affects parties in another. This, in turn, implies that regulation of conduct has similar cross-border effects. It may provide incentives to have a matter regulated from a regional level or perspective to ensure it is optimally deterred. For example, a cartel operating a collusive agreement or practise across several jurisdictions, or an abuse of market-power or merger in one market/jurisdiction may have adverse competitive effects in multiple jurisdictions.

The second rationale relates to economies of scale in resourcing or capacity– if there are significant fixed costs to establishing a regulatory agency, then 'case' or 'unit' costs for a regulatory agency will fall as it decides more cases. Thus, the more regulatory activity a regulatory agency supports, the lower its likely unit costs, as it will be able to spread its fixed costs. This rationale entails an incentive to share in a regional regulatory resource so as to share the direct costs of regulating – even though the matters regulated may be purely local issues. A regional regulator may have 'greater capability', or be able to achieve higher output, higher quality and greater speed in its decisions at lower unit costs.

We shall focus here on the second rationale, which is more relevant to very small states in the WBSSD as the cross-border effects and regulatory externalities rationale may not be strong for very small states for two reasons. First small states are unlikely to generate significant cross-border externalities requiring regional solutions. Second small states as minority members of a regional arrangement are not likely to be able to yield much influence to limit cross-border externalities generated by other members. Very small states must however look for economic ways to deliver legal services domestically. Therefore, the option of sharing the cost of a regional regulator may become attractive.

4 The Caribbean Community and Common Market (CARICOM)

Table 17.4 in the first 13 rows, summarizes data for the 13 small states in the Caribbean sub-category of the World Bank's Small States Database (WBSSD),[9] ranked in alphabetical order. All of these 13 states are members of the Caribbean Community and Common Market (CARICOM). Jamaica is included in the WBSSD although its population exceeds 1.5 million. Table 17.4 in the bottom two rows identifies Montserrat and Haiti, who are also members of CARICOM, but excluded from the WBSSD, because Montserrat is a British Overseas Territory and Haiti's population is over 10 million. Thirteen of the 15 members of CARICOM are thus very small (excluding Jamaica and Haiti), and together account for 87% of CARICOM's membership and 24% of CARICOM's population.

CARICOM evolved out of the Caribbean Free Trade Association (CARIFTA), which first came into effect on May 1, 1968, with the participation of four Caribbean countries (Antigua,

Table 17.4 CARICOM members' economic and demographic data

	Small states	(1) GDP per cap.	(2) Population	GDP est. (1)*(2)	Join date
1	Antigua and Barbuda	13,715	91,818	1,259,259,259	4 July 1974
2	Bahamas, The	22,817	388,019	8,853,519,100	4 July 1983
3	Barbados	15,429	284,215	4,385,250,000	26 July 1974
4	Belize	4,879	359,287	1,752,861,128	1 May 1974
5	Dominica	7,116	72,680	517,218,963	1 May 1974
6	Grenada	9,212	106,825	984,074,074	1 May 1974
7	Guyana	4,127	767,085	3,166,029,056	1 August 1973
8	Jamaica	5,106	2,793,335	14,262,190,323	1 August 1973
9	St. Kitts and Nevis	15,772	55,572	876,478,556	1 August 1973
10	St. Lucia	7,736	184,999	1,431,135,704	1 May 1974
11	St. Vincent and the Grenadines	6,739	109,462	737,683,556	1 May 1974
12	Suriname	9,485	542,975	5,150,291,217	4 July 1995
13	Trinidad and Tobago	17,322	1,360,088	23,559,287,484	1 August 1973
14	Haiti	818	10,711,067	8,765,329,890	2 July 2002
15	Montserrat	12,384	4,932*	61,078,874*	1 May 1974

Source: http://data.worldbank.org/region/caribbean-small-states?view=chart with population and GDP per capita data from 2015, unless otherwise noted.

Note: * Data for Montserrant is obtained from http://data.un.org/CountryProfile.aspx?crName=Montserrat and http://caricom.org/about-caricom/who-we-are/our-governance/heads-of-government/montserrat/.

Barbados, Trinidad and Tobago, and Guyana). Five others joined CARIFTA in July (Dominica, Grenada, St Kitts/Nevis/Anguilla, Saint Lucia and St Vincent) with a further two (Jamaica and Montserrat) joining on August 1, 1968, bringing the total to 11. British Honduras (Belize) became the twelfth member in May 1971.

Despite being a free-trade area, CARIFTA did not provide for the free movement of labour and capital, nor the coordination of agricultural, industrial and foreign policies. In 1972, Commonwealth Caribbean leaders decided to transform CARIFTA into a common market and establish the Caribbean Community, of which the common market would be an integral part.

The Caribbean Community and Common Market (CARICOM) was thus established by the Treaty of Chaguaramas, which was signed by 4 countries, including Barbados, Jamaica, Guyana, and Trinidad and Tobago on July 4, 1973, and came into effect on August 1, 1973. The treaty created the Caribbean Community as a separate legal entity from the common market, which had its own discrete legal personality. This arrangement facilitated states joining the community without being party to the common-market regime.[10] By the end of 1974 another seven states had joined CARICOM, together with Montserrat, a British Overseas Territory. The Bahamas became the thirteenth member state of the community on July 4, 1983, but not a member of the common market. Suriname became the fourteenth member state of the Caribbean Community on July 4, 1995. Haiti secured provisional membership on July 4, 1998 and became the first French-speaking Caribbean state to gain full membership of CARICOM on July 3, 2002. Haiti's membership was temporarily suspended as a result of political unrest from February 2004. This lasted until June 2006, when the country was reinstated.

Revised Treaty of Chaguaramas (RTC) published in 2001[11] established the CARICOM Single Market and Economy (CSME), a move that was intended to deepen economic integration of members. The RTC applies to all CARICOM member states, except the Bahamas and Montserrat. The Bahamas retained its membership of the community through a Special Membership Agreement signed in February 2006, which maintains its membership and participation in the community as it existed immediately prior to the entry into force of the RTC.[12]

CARICOM has perhaps the most developed regional competition and consumer law agreement among the regional arrangements discussed in this chapter. Chapter Eight of the RTC Part one covers competition policy, and part two consumer protection. Chapter Eight of the RTC thus provides the community shall establish appropriate norms and institutional arrangements to prohibit and penalize anti-competitive conduct (but excluding mergers), while member states shall adopt competition legislation, establish institutions and procedures for enforcement, and ensure access to enforcement authorities by nationals of other member states.

A critical institution in the development of CARICOM law (and in any such regional arrangement) is the regional judicial tribunal, which was established in 2001.[13] The Caribbean Court of Justice (CCJ) had a long gestation period commencing in 1970 when the Jamaican delegation at the Sixth Heads of Government Conference (which convened in Jamaica) proposed the establishment of a Caribbean Court of Appeal as a substitute for the Judicial Committee of the Privy Council. Member states that opted to sign the agreement establishing the CCJ agreed to enforce its decisions in their respective jurisdictions, as they would the decisions of their own superior courts. The CCJ has been designed to be more than a court of last resort for member states of the Caribbean Community; in addition to replacing the Judicial Committee of the Privy Council, the CCJ is vested with an original jurisdiction in respect of the interpretation and application of the Treaty Establishing the Caribbean Community.

By interpreting and applying the RTC by which CSME was established, the CCJ plays a critical role in determining how the CSME functions. In effect, the CCJ exercises both an appellate and an original jurisdiction. In the exercise of its appellate jurisdiction, the CCJ considers and determines appeals in both civil and criminal matters from common-law courts within the jurisdictions of member states of the community and which are parties to the agreement establishing the CCJ. In the discharge of its appellate jurisdiction, the CCJ is the highest municipal court in the region. In the exercise of its original jurisdiction, the CCJ will be discharging the functions of an international tribunal applying rules of international law in respect of the interpretation and application of the treaty. On the issue of the original jurisdiction of the court, it should also be mentioned that adjudication by the CCJ is only one of six modes of dispute-settlement provided for under the RTC. The five other modes are: offices, mediation, consultations, conciliation and arbitration.

Provision was made in Chapter Eight of the RTC for the establishment of a Competition Commission at regional level to apply competition rules in respect of anti-competitive cross-border business conduct. The Commission's other aims were to promote competition and consumer protection law in the community, and to coordinate the implementation of the community competition and consumer protection policy.

The CARICOM Competition Commission (the Commission) was finally inaugurated on January 18, 2008. The Commission has powers in respect of cross-border transactions, or transactions with cross-border effects, to monitor, investigate, detect, make determinations or take action to inhibit and penalize enterprises whose business conduct prejudices trade or prevents, restricts or distorts competition within the CSME.

Article 174 (4) of the RTC ascribes remedial and penalization powers to the Commission in respect of anti-competitive business practices. In and of itself, these powers do not oust the jurisdiction of the CCJ. So, **Article 175 (11)** and **(12)** of the RTC provides that the Commission may request the CCJ's assistance in enforcing compliance of any decision made by the Commission. Further, **Article 176 (6)** provides that Chapter Eight of the RTC (competition law framework) is without prejudice to the right of a member state to initiate proceedings before the court at any time. In this regard, the CCJ's Original Jurisdiction (OJ) Rules speak to procedural matters that specifically concern the Competition Commission (see Part 11 of the CCJ OJ Rules 2017), including provision for service of documents on persons and organs within the community, as well as any members of the Council for Trade and Economic Development (COTED)[14] which may have been affected or involved. The relationship between the CCJ and the Competition Commission is discussed in more detail in Trinidad Cement Ltd v the Competition Commission [2012] CCJ 4 (OJ),[15] where it is stated that the Commission enjoys full juridical personality and that no power exercised by an institution created under the RTC can escape the judicial scrutiny of the CCJ, due to the compulsory and exclusive Original Jurisdiction.

Although CARICOM is more advanced than any other regional approach to economic regulation employed by the small states discussed in this chapter, it is noteworthy that, as with other regional arrangements, progress has taken time and remains incomplete at a national level, in that only three member states have functioning competition commissions (Jamaica, Barbados and Guyana). A handful of other states including Guyana, Trinidad and Tobago, have competition laws, but no national authority.[16]

As with all characterizations of 'success', opinions differ on whether CARICOM may be described as an example of a region that has successfully implemented regional approaches to economic regulation. As with many regional initiatives, matters relating to administration and cooperation between member states can be improved. Nonetheless, our broader study of the CARICOM economic regulatory structure confirms it may offer a model for others – such as member states of the Pacific Island Forum Island Countries as outlined below.

5 Pacific Islands Forum

Table 17.5 summarizes population and GDP per capita data for the eleven Pacific Island countries in the World Bank small states database.

All of these states are members of the Pacific Islands Forum. The Pacific Islands Forum was founded in 1971. In its earliest incarnation, it was named the South Pacific Forum, as its seven founding members were all located in the South Pacific: Australia, the Cook Islands, Fiji, Nauru, New Zealand, Tonga and Samoa. In 2000, the name was changed to the Pacific Islands Forum (PIF) to better reflect the geographic location of its members in the North and South Pacific.

The Pacific Islands Forum is now a political grouping of 18 members, as indicated above: Australia, Cook Islands, Federated States of Micronesia, Fiji,[17] French Polynesia, Kiribati, Nauru, New Caledonia, New Zealand, Niue, Palau, Papua New Guinea, the Republic of Marshall Islands, Samoa, the Solomon Islands, Tonga, Tuvalu and Vanuatu.[18] Tokelau was granted Associate Member status in 2014, having previously been a Forum Observer from 2005 up until this time.[19]Table 17.6 identifies population and GDP per capita data for the seven PIF countries not included in the WBSSD.

Australia and New Zealand (NZ) are generally wealthier than the other members of PIF. It appears that the term Forum Island Countries (FIC) is often used to describe independent PIF countries excluding Australia and NZ. The next four countries in the table are in a close, if not dependency relationship with a larger state: with Cook Islands, and Niue[20] in free association with New Zealand; and French Polynesia, and New Caledonia, both French overseas 'Collectivities'. This leaves Papua New Guinea (PNG) as the only remaining independent state that is part of PIF, but it is not technically a small state using the World Bank threshold of 1.5 million.

According to the World Bank population threshold criteria then 83% of the PIF members are small states (slightly less than CARICOM which was at 87%) incorporating 6% of the total population of PIF (again less than CARICOM at 24%).

Table 17.5 Small-state members of the Pacific Islands Forum

Small states	Population (1)	GDP per capita (2)	GDP Estimate (1)*(2)
Fiji	892,145	4,961	4,425,503,075
Kiribati	112,423	1,424	160,121,929
Marshall Islands	52,993	3,386	179,432,574
Micronesia, Fed. Sts.	104,460	3,015	314,971,100
Nauru	12,475	8,053	100,459,773
Palau	21,291	13,499	287,400,000
Samoa	193,228	3,939	761,037,916
Solomon Islands	583,591	1,935	1,129,164,719
Tonga	106,170	4,099	435,142,409
Tuvalu	9,916	3,295	32,673,278
Vanuatu	264,652	2,805	742,432,131
Total	**2,353,344**	**3,641**	**8,568,338,903**

Source: http://data.worldbank.org/region/pacific-island-small-states data is from 2015/.

Table 17.6 Other Pacific Island forum members

	Population (1)	GDP per capita (2)	GDP estimate(1) ★ (2)
Australia	23,789,752	56,291	1,339,140,527,498
New Zealand	4,595,700	37,808	173,754,075,211
Cook Islands[a]	17,459	6,157	107,500,000
Niue[b]	1,611	15,767	25,400,000
French Polynesia[c]	282,764	14,531	4,108,780,685
New Caledonia[d]	273,000	12,580	3,434,229,464
Papua New Guinea	7,619,321	2,268	17,281,934,661

Source: World Bank World Development Indicators: https://data.worldbank.org/country, data 2015 unless noted otherwise.

Notes: a Data obtained from Ministry of Finance and Economic Management Government of Cook Islands. GDP is in NZ dollars, see http://www.mfem.gov.ck/statistics/economic-statistics/national-accounts Population is 2016 Census estimate, preliminary result (includes Tourists) see http://www.mfem.gov.ck/census.
b Population 2011, GDP in NZ dollars. Data obtained from Statistics Niue http://niue.prism.spc.int
c http://data.worldbank.org/country/french-polynesia
d http://data.worldbank.org/country/new-caledonia?view=chart/.

Consistent with our analysis of CARICOM, it has taken time for Pacific Island states to develop the kind of trade and competition law arrangements that promote social welfare. Indeed, the PIF has made slower progress than CARICOM, despite comprising similar small island state memberships. Whereas the Caribbean Free Trade Association (CAR-IFTA) came into effect on May 1, 1968, the South Pacific Forum (SPF) was not established till 1971. The forum's secretariat was only established as a trade bureau in 1972, and later became the South Pacific Bureau for Economic Cooperation (SPEC). In 2000, when the name of the forum itself changed, the SPEC became the Pacific Islands Forum Secretariat (PIFS).[21] The Pacific Agreement on Closer Economic Relations (PACER) followed soon after the new millennium. Signed at Nauru on August 18, 2001, PACER came into force on October 3, 2002. An umbrella agreement between members of the Pacific Islands Forum, PACER provides a framework for the future development of trade cooperation.

Negotiations on a PACER Plus agreement between Australia, New Zealand and 12 smaller forum countries (Cook Islands, Federated States of Micronesia, Kiribati, Nauru, Niue, Palau, Republic of Marshall Islands, Samoa, Solomon Islands, Tonga, Tuvalu, and Vanuatu) started in August 2009. The office of Chief Trade Adviser was established on March 29, 2010 to provide independent advice and support to the Pacific Forum Island Countries (FIC) in the PACER Plus trade negotiations with Australia and New Zealand. The PACER Plus Agreement was finally concluded on April 20, 2017. The agreement now needs to be signed and ratified before it can come into force some countries have already signed.

In parallel with the developments in free-trade arrangements outlined above over the past ten years, there have also been efforts to develop a regional competition and consumer law agreement.[22] In 2007 the Pacific Island Forum Economic Minister Meeting (FEMM) noted the potential to establish a policy framework and common regulatory laws amongst FIC.[23] Further, the 2008 FEMM endorsed a Regional Regulatory Stepladder, which included specific activities and actions to be taken at national and regional levels to improve regulation through regional cooperation. The FEMM even directed the Secretariat in coordination with relevant development partners, to develop a model regulatory and policy framework, and seek support for its implementation. Whilst allowing enough flexibility for application at national level, this proposed model law was intended to allow for greater FIC collaboration, as well as providing a legislative basis from which the proposed regional arrangements could be brought into force. At the 2008 FEMM, ministers also considered the possibility of setting up a regional regulator for one priority sector identified by the workshop participants. Over the medium term, based on lessons from the proposed regional arrangements, this service provision could then be extended to other priority sectors.

In response to the 2008 FEMM mandate, the Secretariat commissioned a report on model regulatory and policy framework for FICs. It was duly presented at the 2010 FEMM meeting.[24] The draft report was widely circulated among member countries and relevant stakeholders for comment, and peer-reviewed by the World Bank and the Asian Development Bank, before it was finalized. The report included a Draft Model Competition and Consumer Protection Law that could be adapted and introduced in national legislature. The implementation roadmap proposed by the report had the following key phases of activity:

Phase 1: decision phase in which decisions are taken at regional and national level relating to the uptake of competition and consumer regulation. Key decisions required to endorse the draft model law, with a view to adapting appropriate provisions, and identifying necessary legal and policy reforms at national levels.
Phase 2: adoption/adaptation phase in which activity is undertaken to implement the model regulatory and legislative framework within each FIC.
Phase 3: in which competition and consumer regulation is administered in those FICs that adopt the model regulatory and legislative framework.

Up to now, there has been little progress on any of these steps. There would seem to be scope for lessons to be learned by PIF nations from CARICOM experience, given the degree of comparability between the current CARICOM member states and the Pacific Island Forum countries, (being typically relatively small island economies, all of which tend to have common-law traditions, with relatively low per capita incomes). The more advanced nature of the CARICOM regional trade, and competition and consumer-protection law arrangements may be significant factors in helping the CARICOM region enjoy higher economic growth than its PIF counterparts. Having said that the CARICOM region's geographical proximity to large markets such as US may also be a factor. The Pacific region as a whole is also culturally diverse, and significantly bigger geographically than CARICOM. For the latter reasons it may be easier to achieve progress in regional arrangements in the Pacific at the sub-regional level, e.g. Micronesia, Polynesia and Melanesia.[25]

6 The Common Market of East and Southern Africa (COMESA)[26]

There are five states in the World Bank's Small State Database (WBSSD) that are members of the Common Market of East and Southern Africa (COMESA) – namely the Seychelles, Swaziland, Djibouti, Comoros, and Mauritius. COMESA however tends not to be dominated by small states and on this basis alone is very different from CARICOM and PIF. Table 17.7 summarizes available population and GDP per capita data taken from the World Bank World Development Indicators, for the small states members of COMESA, ranked by population size from smallest to largest, with dates of joining in brackets.

Table 17.7 The small-state members of COMESA

Small state	Population	GDP per capita(US$, 2015)
Comoros (Dec 21, 1981)	788,474	717
Djibouti (Dec 21, 1981)	887,861	1,945
Mauritius (Dec 21, 1981)	1,262,605	9,252
Seychelles (2001)	93,419	15,390
Swaziland (Dec 21, 1981)	1,286,970	3,200

Source: World Development Indicators https://data.worldbank.org/country, 2015.

There are major differences between COMESA and CARICOM and PIF. Based on the available data for example the five small member states of COMESA constitute only 26% of COMESA's total 19 members. This is obviously much lower than the 87% for CARICOM and 83% for PIF. The five small states further constitute a tiny share of the total population of COMESA at 0.85%, which compares to 24% for CARICOM and 6% for PIF.

Three of COMESA's member states (DRC, Egypt and Ethiopia) are large, all being above 65 million, and in total constitute 53% of the population of COMESA, and 82.5% of the total GDP of COMESA. A further nine COMESA states (47%) are medium-sized being above 10 million and less than 65 million. Thus the 12 states larger than 10 million in COMESA constitute 97% of the total population, and 93% of the total GDP of COMESA far outweighing the small states.

Based on population size alone COMESA potential market size is thus considerably larger in total than CARICOM and the PIF countries combined. The 19 member states of COMESA have a total population over 500 million compared to CARICOM and PIF combined total of around 57 million. On trade COMESA's annual import bill was around US$152 billion and its export bill over US$157 billion (all Figures 2008) – COMESA forms a major market place for both internal and external trading. COMESA's territory on the map of the African continent covers a geographical area of 12 million square kilometres. All the same, nearly all COMESA states are poorer than the poorest state in CARICOM, with GDP per capita of less than US $3,600. The only two exceptions are the Seychelles and Mauritius which are both small island states more comparable to CARICOM's membership.

The history of COMESA began in December 1994, when it was formed to replace the Preferential Trade Area (PTA) which had existed since the earlier days of 1981. COMESA (as defined by its treaty) was established 'as an organisation of free independent sovereign states which have agreed to cooperate in developing their natural and human resources for the good of all their people'. As such it has a wide-ranging series of objectives and priorities, which necessarily include the promotion of peace and security within the region.

A free trade agreement (FTA) was achieved on October 31, 2000 when nine of the member states – namely Djibouti, Egypt, Kenya, Madagascar, Malawi, Mauritius, Sudan, Zambia and Zimbabwe – eliminated their tariffs on COMESA-originating products, in accordance with the tariff-reduction schedule adopted in 1992. This followed a trade liberalization programme that commenced in 1984 on reduction and eventual elimination of tariff and non-tariff barriers to intra-regional trade. Burundi and Rwanda joined the FTA on January 1, 2004. These eleven FTA members have not only eliminated customs tariffs but are working on the eventual elimination of quantitative restrictions and other non-tariff barriers.

As with CARICOM, the establishment of the Court of Justice (Court) of the Common Market for Eastern and Southern Africa (COMESA) was a major event in the history of

COMESA as an organization – and in the development of COMESA community law and jurisprudence. The Court was established in 1994 under Article 7 of the COMESA Treaty as one of the organs of COMESA. The authority which is the supreme policy organ of COMESA appointed the judges of the court during its third summit on June 30, 1998 at Kinshasa in the Democratic Republic of Congo. The registrar of the court was also appointed by the COMESA Council of Ministers (the Council), during its meeting in June 1998 at Kinshasa in the Democratic Republic of Congo. To ensure the independence of the Court, Article 9 (2) (c) of the COMESA Treaty provides that the Council shall give directions to all other subordinate organs of COMESA other than the Court in the exercise of its jurisdiction. The seat of the Court was temporarily hosted within the COMESA Secretariat from 1998, but in March 2003, the COMESA Authority decided that the seat of the Court should be in Khartoum, in the Republic of Sudan.

Further, COMESA developed a detailed framework for a regional approach to cross-border issues and international cooperation in competition matters through its formulation and adoption of a regional competition policy and law in 2004. The COMESA Competition Regulations were formulated and adopted in accordance with the provisions of Article 55 of the COMESA Treaty, which prohibits any practice which negates the objective of free and liberalized trade, including 'any agreement between undertakings or concerted practice which has as its objective or effect the prevention, restriction or distortion of competition within the Common Market' and provides for the adoption of regulations aimed at promoting competition within the member states.

The COMESA Competition Regulations of December 2004 consist of a preamble and five parts. Part 1 covers certain preliminary matters, including exemptions and obligations of member states. Part 2 covers institutions, including the creation of a regional competition commission. Part 3 covers anti-competitive business practices and conduct; part 4, mergers and acquisitions; and Part 5, consumer protection.

The preamble to the COMESA competition regulations clearly spells out the broad objectives and aims of regional competition law in addressing competition concerns of a cross-border nature. The stated main purpose of the regulations is 'to promote and encourage competition by preventing restrictive business practices and other restrictions that deter the efficient operation of markets, thereby enhancing the welfare of the consumers in the Common Market, and to protect consumers against offensive conduct by market actors'.

Also indicated are various forms of cooperation in areas such as the elimination of restrictive business practices that affect trade between member states, consultations and conciliation on matters related to anti-competitive practices affecting regional and international trade, and notification, exchange of information, co-ordination of actions and consultation among member states in the enforcement of competition law. In addition, there are provisions relating to relationships between national competition authorities and the regional authority.

Under the regulations the COMESA Competition Commission is vested with international legal personality, as well as the legal capacity required for the performance of its functions under the Treaty in the territory of each member state, and the power to acquire or dispose of movable and immovable property in accordance with the laws and regulations in force in each member state. The functions of the Commission under Article 7 are to apply the provisions of the regulations with regard to trade between member states and be responsible for promoting competition within the Common Market. Thus, for example the Commission must be notified of all cross-border transactions requiring approval of the Commission.

COMESA however lags slightly behind CARICOM to the extent that it appears COMESA's competition law rules were not formulated until 2004 (whereas CARICOM's were established in 2001) and COMESA's competition commission to implement COMESA competition policy and law was not fully established until during 2009, and did not become operational until 2013 (whereas CARICOM's was inaugurated in 2008). Although COMESA's regulations and it's Commission are now operational, COMESA does not yet however really provide much evidence as to the likely operational success or otherwise of its RCCLA.

7 The Southern African Development Community (SADC)[27]

There are six states in the World Bank's Small State Database (WBSSD) that are members of the Southern African Development Community (SADC) – namely the Seychelles, Mauritius Swaziland, Lesotho, Botswana, and Namibia. Table 17.8 further summarizes population and GDP per capita in 2015 for each of the small state member countries of SADC, using data taken from the World Bank's World Development Indicators.

Only three members of SADC qualify as small states under the World Bank cut-off of 1.5 million in population – namely the Seychelles, Mauritius and Swaziland, accounting for just 20% of the SADC membership. This is much lower than CARICOM (87%), and PIF83%, and slightly lower than COMESA (26%), which not only has Seychelles, Mauritius and Swaziland as members – like SADC – but also Comoros and Djibouti. The three small SADC states further constitute a tiny share of the total population of SADC at 0.82%, which is comparable to COMESA (0.85%), but less than CARICOM (24%), and PIF (6%).

SADC has been in existence since 1980, when it was formed as a loose alliance of nine majority-ruled states in Southern Africa known as the Southern African Development Coordination Conference (SADCC). The main aim of this alliance was to coordinate development projects, in order to lessen the states' economic dependence on the then apartheid South Africa. The nine founding member states were: Angola, Botswana, Lesotho, Malawi, Mozambique, Swaziland, United Republic of Tanzania, Zambia and Zimbabwe.

The transformation of the organization from a coordinating conference into a development community (SADC) took place on August 17, 1992 in Windhoek, Namibia when the SADC Declaration and Treaty (SADC Treaty) was signed at the Summit of Heads of State and Government, thereby giving the organization a legal character. SADC was established under Article 2 of the SADC treaty by SADC member states, represented by their respective heads of state and government, or duly authorized representatives to spearhead economic integration of Southern Africa.

Under the SADC Treaty of 1992, a Trade Protocol was developed as a framework agreement to establish a free-trade area (FTA) under which a tariff phase-down programme was

Table 17.8 Small-state members of SADC

Small state	Population 2015	GDP per capita (US$, 2015)	GDP
Botswana	2,262,485	6,360	14,389,404,600
Lesotho	2,135,022	1,067	2,278,068,474
Mauritius	1,262,605	9,252	11,681,621,460
Namibia	2,458,830	4,674	11,492,571,420
Seychelles	93,419	15,390	1,437,718,410
Swaziland	1,286,970	3,200	4,118,304,000

Source: World Development Indicators, https://data.worldbank.org/country 2015/.

negotiated and agreed upon. There have been a number of amendments to the SADC Treaty over time.

In terms of the judicial and administration arrangements relevant to the development of RCCLA in SADC, the Tribunal, established by Article 9 of the SADC Treaty Amendment of 2001, is entrusted with the responsibility to ensure adherence to, and proper interpretation of, the provisions of the SADC Treaty and subsidiary instruments, and to adjudicate upon disputes referred to it. The protocol on the Tribunal was signed in Windhoek, Namibia during the 2000 Ordinary Summit.

The Treaty also lays out the functions of the Secretariat, as the principal executive institution of SADC responsible for, amongst other functions, the strategic planning and management of SADC programmes, implementation of decisions of SADC policy organs and institutions, that might include any RCCLA.

SADC formulated a Regional Indicative Strategic Development Plan (RISDP) in March 2001 that was adopted and approved by the SADC Summit in August 2003. The RISDP outlined a series of milestones relating to the setting up of a free trade (achieved in 2008), a customs union by 2010 (not yet attained), a common market 2015 (delayed), a monetary union 2016 (delayed) and a single currency by 2018 (also been delayed).

In general SADC has lagged behind CARICOM in the development of a regional approach to competition. In 2008 the 14 SADC member states agreed that 'the SADC Secretariat shall establish a standing competition and consumer policy and law committee (CCOPOLC) to implement the system of cooperation' between national regimes that can harness the collective efforts of relevant national authorities and add value to national enforcement efforts in the face of problems affecting more than one country. The SADC Declaration on Competition and Consumer Policies (2009) was then signed in 2009[28] under which the SADC Secretariat was directed to establish a standing Competition and Consumer Policy and Law Committee (CCOPOLC) to implement the system of cooperation in the application of Member States respective competition and consumer protection laws.

CCOPOLC has become a forum that fosters cooperation and dialogue among competition authorities aimed at encouraging convergence of laws, analysis and common understanding. In undertaking this role CCOPOLC has regard to the United Nations' Set of Principles and Rules on competition as a basis for consensus-building in international cooperation in competition policy, while taking into account the development needs and existing commitments on competition policy of member States.

At the time of the CCOPOLC announcement, SADC countries recorded as having adopted competition laws included: Zimbabwe, Malawi, Namibia, Mauritius, South Africa, Tanzania and Zambia. However, only Malawi, South Africa, Tanzania, Zambia and Zimbabwe had operational competition authorities at that time. The SADC Secretariat strives to facilitate the establishment of competition authorities in those Member States that have no such institutions, and competition and consumer protection advocacy programmes.

However, like COMESA, SADC has lagged behind CARICOM in developing RCCLA.

8 ECOWAS[29] and WAEMU[30]

ECOWAS is a regional group of 15 West African countries, founded on May 28, 1975, with the signing of the Treaty of Lagos. The 15 members of ECOWAS are: Benin, Burkina Faso, Cape Verde, Côte d'Ivoire, Gambia, Ghana, Guinea, Guinea-Bissau, Liberia, Mali, Niger, Nigeria, Senegal, Sierra Leone, and Togo.[31]

Table 17.9 Small-state members of ECOWAS

Small state	Population	GDP per capita (US$ 2015)	GDP
Cape Verde	520,502	3,080	1,603,239,233
Gambia, the	1,990,924	472	938,794,719
Guinea-Bissau	1,844,325	573	1,056,776,883

Source: World Development Indicators: https://data.worldbank.org/country/, 2015.

Table 17.9 summarizes population and GDP per capita in 2015 for the three current member countries of ECOWAS that are part of the World Bank's Small State database. Cape Verde is the only small member state of ECOWAS with a population of less than 1.5 million. Cape Verde constitutes only 7% of ECOWAS's total 15 members. This is much lower than for CARICOM (87%) and PIF (83%), and also lower than COMESA (26%) and SADC (20%). Cape Verde's share of ECOWAS' total population at 0.15% is considerable less than small state's share in CARICOM (24%), PIF (6%), SADC (0.82%), and COMESA (0.85%).

Although only one of ECOWAS's member states is large, Nigeria being above 65 million, it nevertheless constitutes 52% of the total population of COMESA, and 77% of the total GDP of ECOWAS. Cape Verde is only 0.25% of the total GDP of ECOWAS. A further 8 ECOWAS states (53%) are medium-sized being above 10 million and less than 65 million.

ECOWAS's mission is to promote economic integration and to achieve 'collective self-sufficiency' for the member states by means of economic and monetary union, and the creation of a single large trading bloc. Very slow progress towards this aim meant that the treaty was revised in Cotonou on July 24, 1993, towards a looser collaboration. One of the promising developments with the Revised Treaty however was the decision to replace the non-existent Tribunal originally envisioned to enforce Treaty rights, with a Court of Justice.[32] The judges of the Community Court of Justice were however not appointed until January 30, 2001.

The Court has a twofold role: to settle, in accordance with international law, legal disputes submitted to it by States (Contentious cases) and to give advisory opinions on legal questions referred to it by the member states and any institution of the Community. This creates a foundation for judicial supervision of an RCCLA. There has however been little or no progress on establishing an RCCLA for it to perform such a role. The effect of limits on standing in the Court moreover was that until 2003, the Court was generally idle. It only decided its first case in 2004, then, with relaxation of standing, more cases ensued, although by 2016 it had decided only 115 cases in 13 years, but none relate to competition law.[33]

This slow progress may be due to the imbalance in population size, with Nigeria contributing greater mass. Given the predominance of larger states and the region's slow progress in developing RCCLA, we will not spend further time on ECOWAS.

The West African Economic and Monetary Union (WAEMU)[34] is an organization formed out of a subset of the membership of ECOWAS listed above, established to promote economic integration among countries that share a common currency: the CFA franc. The members of WAEMU are Guinea-Bissau, Togo, Benin, Senegal, Mali, Niger, Burkina Faso, and Cote d'Ivoire. Cape-Verde's absence as a very small state member of ECOWAS is notable.

WAEMU is a customs union and monetary union created by a treaty signed at Dakar, Senegal, on January 10, 1994 by the heads of state and government of Benin, Burkina Faso, Côte d'Ivoire, Mali, Niger, Senegal, and Togo. On May 2, 1997, Guinea-Bissau, a former Portuguese colony, became its eighth (and only non-Francophone) member state.

WAEMU however exhibits greater balance in population size than ECOWAS, with no very large states, and most members being medium-sized states and could potentially be a more relevant regional cooperation agreement between the states in West Africa. In terms of its achievements to date, WAEMU members have implemented macroeconomic convergence criteria and an effective surveillance mechanism; have adopted a customs union and common external tariff (early 2000); have harmonized indirect taxation regulations; and have initiated regional structural and sectoral policies. ECOWAS and WAEMU have developed a common programme of action on trade liberalization and macroeconomic policy convergence, and agreed on common rules of origin to enhance trade, while ECOWAS has agreed to adopt WAEMU's customs declaration forms and compensation mechanisms.

WAEMU appears to be quite advanced in the implementation of competition law in its region – as we can see from the following brief review of some of its main provisions. For example, under Article 88 paragraphs (a) and (b), and Article 89 paragraph 3 of the WAEMU Treaty of 2001, WAEMU established competition-law rules and procedures by regulation which are applicable to anti-competitive business practices,[35] abuse of dominance, anti-competitive agreements, and cartels.[36]

Under Article 6 of the regulation pursuant to articles 4 (a), 7 and 76 (c) of the WAEMU Treaty, member states are to refrain from any measures liable to hinder the implementation of this competition regulation. Members shall refrain, in particular, from enacting or maintaining, in regard to public undertakings and undertakings to which they grant special or exclusive rights, any action contrary to the rules and principles laid down in Article 88 paragraphs (a) and (b) of the Treaty of Union. Also, member states will not enact measures enabling private companies to evade the constraints imposed by Article 88 paragraphs (a) and (b) of the WAEMU Treaty. Further, under Article 6.2, undertakings entrusted with the operation of services of general economic interest, or having the character of a revenue-producing mono-poly, are subject to treaty rules on competition. Further, there is a Commission established under WAEMU, which enforces the provisions of these regulations. If the member state con-cerned does not comply with a decision, the Commission may refer the matter to the WAEMU Court of Justice, in accordance with articles 5 and 6 of Additional Protocol, No. 1 of the Treaty.

We do not present further detail on the operation of WAEMU given it does not include any small states according to the World Bank's cut-off of 1.5 million. However, it does appear to be quite advanced in the implementation of competition law.

9 The Economic Community of Central African States (ECCAS)[37]

There are the three small-states from the World Bank Small State Database that are members of the Economic Community of Central African States (ECCAS), identified in Table 17.10 together with available population and GDP per capita data.

Table 17.10 Small-state members of ECCAS

Small state	Population	GDP per capita
Equatorial Guinea	845,060	14,440
Gabon	1,725,292	8,266
Sao Tome and Principe	190,344	1,669

Source: World Development Indicators, https://data.worldbank.org/country, 2015.

Only two of these states have populations below 1.5 million namely Sao Tome and Principe, and Equatorial Guinea, amounting to 11% of the membership and 0.59% of the total population of ECCAS. These are greater shares than for ECOWAS (7% share of membership and 0.15% of population), but less than COMESA (26% and 0.85%), and SADC (20% and 0.82%) and much less than for CARICOM (87% and 24%) and PIF (83% and 6%).

The Economic Community of Central African States (ECCAS) originated in December 1981, when the leaders of the Customs and Economic Union of Central African States (UDEAC)[38] agreed to form a wider economic community of Central African States. ECCAS was thus established on October 1983 by members of UDEAC, Sao Tome and Principe and members of the Economic Community of the Great Lakes Countries, Zaire, Burundi and Rwanda. ECCAS has trade and market integration is its core objective. ECCAS was however inactive for several years due to financial constraints, conflicts in the Great Lakes area as well as the war in Democratic Republic of Congo where member States (Rwanda and Angola) were fighting on different sides.

The organizational structure of ECCAS consists of various institutions including the Conference of Heads of State and Government, which is the supreme body of ECCAS, the Council of Ministers, the Court of Justice and the General Secretariat, which is the executive organ of the Community.

Article 6 of the Treaty Establishing ECCAS indicates the creation of a free trade area and a customs union in twenty-years. In July 2004, ECCAS launched its free trade area with the aim of establishing a customs union of common external tariff by 2008. The timetable for establishing the free trade area was however postponed due to the weak domestication of agreed procedures by member States. On average, member States reduced only 34 percent of tariff lines on intra-ECCAS tariffs to zero, making ECCAS the region to have the lowest share of intra-regional trade in terms of gross domestic product compared to Africa's five sub-regions. To meet the integration challenges, ECCAS Member States adopted in 2007 a strategic integration plan and a vision called the ECCAS Strategic Vision at the Horizon 2025 that aims at building a competitive regional environment to attract private investments in growth areas. ECCAS is implementing trade facilitation programmes, including the construction of one-stop border posts that are becoming more frequent in the region.

ECCAS has undertaken studies on competition policy, however it seems little progress has been made operationalizing a regional competition policy. Given the extensive delays in making policy operational by ECCAS and its failure to operationalize a Regional Competition and Consumer Law Agreement we shall not consider ECCAS further.

10 South Asian Association for Regional Co-operation (SAARC)[39]

Two states that qualify as small states using the World Bank cut-off of 1.5 million in population size (Maldives and Bhutan) are members of the South Asian Association for Regional Co-operation (SAARC). Table 17.11 summarizes available population and GDP per capita data on these states taken from the World Bank World Development Indicators.

Table 17.11 Small-state members of SAARC

Small state	Population	GDP per capita
Bhutan	774,830	2,656
Maldives	409,163	8,396

Source: World Development Indicators: https://data.worldbank.org/country, 2015.

These two member states account for 25% of the 8 members of SAARC but only a tiny share (or 0.07%) of the total population of SAARC. This is much less in terms of membership and population shares than for CARICOM (87% and 24%) and PIF (83% and 6%,) and also less than for COMESA (26% and 0.85%). The small states in SAARC however have a greater share of membership, although much lower shares of total populations than ECCAS (11% share of the membership and 0.59% of population) ECOWAS (7% share of membership and 0.15% of population) and SADC (20% and 0.82%). The small states in SAARC are also only 0.18% of the total GDP of SAARC.

SAARC thus tends to be dominated by large states. Three of SAARC's member states (India, Pakistan and Bangladesh) are very large, all being well above 65 million, and although only 27% of the total membership they constitute 96% of the population of SAARC, and 82.5% of the total GDP in the region. A further two states (18%) are medium-sized being above 10 million. Thus the five states larger than 10 million in SAARC constitute 99.4% of SAARC's total population and 84% of the total GDP of SAARC. The largest member of course is India whose population is over three times that of all other members combined, while India's GDP is twice that of the others combined. It has been claimed that it is difficult for 'countries to establish balanced relations when one has a significant advantage in power over the other states'. (Thornton, 1991: 135). Moreover, divisions among South Asian countries may have made regional cooperation on economic matters difficult.

SAARC was established on 8 December 1985, and consists of eight Member States: Afghanistan, Bangladesh, Bhutan, India, Maldives, Nepal, Pakistan and Sri Lanka. The Secretariat of the Association was set up in Kathmandu on 17 January 1987. The primary objectives of the Association as outlined in the SAARC Charter include: to promote the welfare of the peoples of South Asia and to improve their quality of life; to accelerate economic growth, social progress and cultural development in the region and to provide all individuals the opportunity to live in dignity and to realize their full potential.

At their Eighteenth SAARC Summit held in Kathmandu on 26–27 November 2014, the Heads of State or Government renewed their commitment to achieve South Asian Economic Union (SAEU) in a phased and planned manner through a Free Trade Area, a Customs Union, a Common Market, and a Common Economic and Monetary Union.

SAARC however has only made slow progress towards freer cross border trade. The SAARC Preferential Trading Agreement (SAPTA) was not adopted until 1993, eight years after the founding of SAARC. This was replaced by SAARC Free Trade Agreement (SAFTA) signed on 6th January 2004 in Islamabad. It became effective on 1 July 2006. SAARC Agreement on Trade in Services (SATIS) was signed in 2010 based on a 'positive list' approach and 'GATS-plus'. There are, however, overlapping trade agreements and unilateral policy announcements among member countries that are seen to undermine the regional agreements. Bilateral FTAs thus also exist between, India- Bangladesh, India-Sri Lanka; Pakistan – Sri Lanka; and India-Sri Lanka – Pakistan. Nevertheless, intra-SAARC trade appears to be limited despite the fact that all are located within close proximity of one another and all are part of the World Trade Organization (WTO). Thus intra-SAARC trade appears to be only about 5% of the region's global trade, which compares poorly to: intra-EU trade of 55%; intra-NAFTA of 52%; and intra-ASEAN of 20%.

A significant number of SAARC members already have national competition laws including Bangladesh, India, Pakistan, Sri Lanka, and Nepal. Bhutan and Maldives, the two small states members of SAARC are without competition laws.

It does not seem likely that SAARC will develop a detailed RCCLA in the short run at least. Instead the cooperation arrangement identifies a number areas of co-operation including human resource development, transport, health/population, telecommunications, science/meteorology technology, agriculture/rural development migration; cooperatives and the blue economy. An RCCLA is not mentioned under any of these headings, and appears unlikely in the short run at least.

11 Conclusion

In this chapter we have reviewed a number of regional co-operation agreements in which small states participate. The chapter assesses the extent to which these regional arrangements have developed operational regional competition and consumer law agreements.

Our review suggests it is important to distinguish between at least two different (but complementary) rationales for regional cooperation (either in a federal or cooperative arrangement) for small states, as they imply different governance or administrative structures. These two rationales are:

1   First the cross-border effects and regulatory externalities rationale – where the conduct of parties in one market affects parties in another, this in turn implies that regulation of the conduct has similar cross-border effects. This rationale may provide incentives to have a matter regulated from a regional level or perspective to ensure it is optimally deterred.

2   The second rationale relates to economies of scale in resourcing or capacity– if there are significant fixed costs to establishing a regulatory agency, then 'case' or 'unit' costs for a regulatory agency will fall as it decides more cases. This rationale entails an incentive to share in a regional regulatory resource so as to share the direct costs of regulating – even though the matters regulated may be purely local issues.

Our review however suggests that despite these potential rationales, and frequent mention of the potential of RCCLA in the literature, there has largely been a fundamental failure to see RCCLA evolve successfully to become operational arrangements for the 40 small independent states found we examined in the World Bank small state database.

CARICOM's regional competition and consumer law agreement covers 13 small states, and is the most advanced reviewed here. It is also most relevant to small states mainly because such states make up a large majority (87%) of its membership, and 24% of total CARICOM population. PIF has 11 small states, constituting 83% of its members, and 6%, of total PIF population. But PIF has only recently begun work towards a regional competition and consumer law arrangement and is lagging well behind CARICOM in this regard.

Turning to Africa, COMESA has five small states that constitute 26% of COMESA's member states and 0.85% of total COMESA population. It has established a framework for cross-border and international cooperation in competition matters, however, COMESA seems to lag well behind CARICOM in terms of the implementation of a regional approach to competition and consumer protection law. Likewise, the South African Development Community (SADC), which includes three small states (20% of membership and 0.82% of total SADC), lags well behind CARICOM in the implementation of a regional approach to competition and consumer protection law.

Other attempts at RCCLA in regional associations involving small states that we discussed (ECOWAS/WAEMU three small states, ECCAS three small states, and SAARC two small states) have either not succeeded so far to develop an RCCLA, or have not even begun to develop one.

Notes

1 Data source: World Development Indicators (WDI) http://data.worldbank.org/indicator/SP.POP. TOTL, as updated on 26/05/17.

2 Available at: www.worldbank.org/en/country/smallstates/overview#3. The World Bank's definition of small states as those with populations less than 1.5 million might be better understood to define 'very small' states, as even though such states constitute 30% of states in the World Bank's wider data set, if one adds the populations of all these countries together, they constitute only 0.31% of the world population. We use the World Bank's Small State Database (WBSSD) as the focus of our analysis however mainly because the very small states in it might be expected to benefit most from RCCLA due to the economies of scale rationale discussed in Section 3.

3 See http://data.worldbank.org/region/SST. The 50 countries include: Antigua and Barbuda, The Bahamas, Bahrain, Barbados, Belize, Bhutan, Botswana, Brunei Darussalam, Cabo Verde, Comoros, Cyprus, Djibouti, Dominica, Equatorial Guinea, Estonia, Fiji, Gabon, The Gambia, Grenada, Guinea-Bissau, Guyana, Iceland, Jamaica, Kiribati, Lesotho, Maldives, Malta, the Marshall Islands, Mauritius, Federated States of Micronesia, Montenegro, Namibia, Nauru, Palau, Qatar, Samoa, San Marino, Sao Tome and Principe, Seychelles, Solomon Islands, St Kitts and Nevis, St Lucia, St Vincent and the Grenadines, Suriname, Swaziland, Timor-Leste, Tonga, Trinidad and Tobago, Tuvalu, and Vanuatu.

4 The three excluded US related territories are American Samoa, Guam, the Northern Mariana Islands and Virgin Islands (U.S.)

5 http://data.worldbank.org/region/pacific-island-small-states?view=chart/.

6 http://data.worldbank.org/region/caribbean-small-states?view=chart/.

7 http://data.worldbank.org/region/other-small-states?view=chart/.

8 There are three small states in the World Bank's 'other' category that are full members of the EU (Cyprus, Estonia and Malta), and one that is a member of EFTA (Iceland). A fifth (San Marino) has a special relationship with Italy – a member of the EU – while the sixth, Montenegro, is an EU candidate. These countries are all relatively wealthy, with five being in the top quartile (25%) of countries by GDP per capita, and the other, Montenegro, being in the top half.

9 http://data.worldbank.org/region/caribbean-small-states?view=chart/.

10 See CARICOM website for discussion of the original Treaty of Chaguaramas: http://caricom.org/about-caricom/who-we-are/our-governance/the-original-treaty/.

11 Article 2 of the revised treaty establishes the Caribbean Community, including the CSME, as successor to the Caribbean Community and Common Market.

12 The CARICOM has five current associate members, which are not however bound by provisions of the CSME in Chapter Eight on consumer and competition law outlined below, namely Bermuda, Cayman, Turks & Caicos, British Virgin Islands and Anguilla.

13 www.caribbeancourtofjustice.org/about-the-ccj/ccj-concept-to-reality/.

14 The Council for Trade and Economic Development (COTED) promotes trade and economic development of the Caribbean Community (CARICOM) and oversees the operations of the Single Market and Economy. See www.caricom.org/about-caricom/who-we-are/our-governance/organs-and-bodies-of-the-community/council-for-trade-and-economic-development-coted/.

15 A copy of the judgment is available on the CCJ website: www.caribbeancourtofjustice.org/.

16 See www.oecd.org/competition/latinamerica/SII-CCC.pdf. See also (Lee, 2009).

17 In 2009 Fiji was suspended from the Pacific Islands Forum, but following the general election of 17 September 2014, the Forum lifted the suspension in October 2014. Fiji's Prime Minister Frank Bainimarama has recently called for the 'undue influence' of Australia and New Zealand to be addressed.

18 See Pacific Islands Forum Secretariat website www.forumsec.org/pages.cfm/about-us/?printerfriendly=true/.

19 Current Forum Observers include: American Samoa (2011), Guam (2011), the Northern Marianas (2011), Timor-Leste (2002), Wallis and Futuna (2006), the Commonwealth (2006), the United Nations (2006) the Asian Development Bank (2006), Western and Central Pacific Fisheries Commission (2007), the World Bank (2010), the ACP Group (2011), and the International Organization for Migration (2014).

20 Niue is part of Cook Islands, but because of remoteness is administered separately, see http://data.un.org/CountryProfile.aspx?crName=Cook%20Islands/.

21 www.forumsec.org/.

22 *The Pacific Plan* was endorsed by Leaders at the Pacific Islands Forum meeting in October 2005, designed in part to strengthen regional cooperation and integration in areas where the region could gain the most. The Pacific Plan is based on the concept of regionalism: that is, countries working together for their joint and individual benefit. Regionalism under the Pacific Plan does not imply any limitation on national sovereignty (http://www.forumsec.org/resources/uploads/attachments/documents/Pacific_Plan_Nov_2007_version1.pdf). The *Framework for Pacific Regionalism* was endorsed by Pacific Islands Forum Leaders in July 2014 following a Forum Leaders' Special Retreat on the Pacific Plan Review, Cook Islands, May 2014. Rather than providing a list of regional priorities, it sets out a robust process through which regional priorities will be identified and implemented. (http://www.forumsec.org/resources/uploads/embeds/file/Framework%20for%20Pacific%20Regionalism_booklet.pdf) The Forum Secretariat conducts an annual process of Pacific wide consultations with stakeholders to inform regional policy development. Thus in 2017 the Secretariat is engaged in policy consultations with submissions due in 28th February 2018. Once developed, a report on regional policy priorities will be circulated to Forum Members for comment, and it will be tabled at key regional meetings, FEMM, FFMM, FOC, CRGA for additional commentary before it is forwarded to Forum Leaders for final consideration and endorsement at the meeting in Nauru, September 2018. http://www.forumsec.org/pages.cfm/strategic-partnerships-coordination/framework-for-pacific-regionalism/?printerfriendly=true.

23 PIFS(07)FEMP.04. 'Regulation and Regional Economic Integration: Regional Options for Economic Regulation'.

24 Available at www.forumsec.org/resources/uploads/attachments/documents/FEMN.08_Update_on_the_Regional_Regulatory_Stepladder.pdf/.

25 For example there has been some success in Melanesia through the Melanesian Spearhead Group, that consists of Fiji, Papua New Guinea, Vanuatu, Solomon Islands and the Front de Liberation Nationale Kanak et Socialiste (FLNKS) from French Territory of New Caledonia and which has a trade agreement already in operation (http://www.msgsec.info/).

26 See homepage at http://about.comesa.int/lang-en/home/.

27 See homepage at www.sadc.int/.

28 www.sadc.int/files/4813/5292/8377/SADC_Declaration_on_Competition_and_Consumer_Policies.pdf/.

29 www.ecowas.int/about-ecowas/basic-information/.

30 www.uemoa.int/.

31 Two members have been suspended: Guinea (after a 2008 coup d'état) and Niger (after a 2009 auto-coup). Mauritania withdrew having announced its intention to do so in December 1999.

32 www.courtecowas.org/site2012/index.php?option=com_content&view=article&id=10&Itemid=10/.

33 www.courtecowas.org/site2012/index.php?option=com_content&view=article&id=157&Itemid=27/.

34 Or UEMOA from its name in French, Union économique et monétaire ouest-africaine, see https://ustr.gov/countries-regions/africa/regional-economic-communities-rec/west-african-economic-and-monetary-union-uemoa/.

35 See www.uemoa.int/actes/2002/reglement_2_2002_CM_UEMOA.htm/.

36 See www.uemoa.int/actes/2002/reglement_3_2002_CM_UEMOA.htm/.

37 www.ceeac-eccas.org/index.php/fr/.

387 UDEAC was created in 1964 by five current members of ECCAS including: Cameroon, the Central African Republic, Chad, the Republic of Congo (Brazzaville), and Gabon and became operational in 1966. Despite the member states traditional bonds, and shared heritage from being former French Central African colonies, plus a common monetary policy based on the Franc CFA, UDEAC's operational capabilities were poor, and the members' interest in regional policies and activities waned. Ultimately in March 1994, UDEAC was replaced by CEMAC, which is a customs and monetary union between the same six member states. While the monetary union is operating, the operationalization of the customs union under CEMAC has not yet been realized.

39 http://saarc-sec.org/about-saarc.

References

Lee, Barbara (2009). CARICOM Competition Commission: Enhancing Competition Enforcement in the Caribbean Community. Paper presented to ICN 8th Annual Conference, Zurich, Switzerland, June 3–4.

Thornton, T. P. (1991). Regional Organizations in Conflict Management. *Annals of the American Academy of Political and Social Science*, Vol. 518 (Nov.).

Part V
Social issues

18

Behavioural economics and small states: a focus on social preferences

Marie Briguglio and Jonathan Spiteri

1 Introduction

Behavioural economics has emerged as one of the most exciting and vibrant areas of research within modern economic thought over the last few decades. Its meteoric rise may at first glance seem anomalous given that it is largely premised on the perceived fallacies of the dominant neo-classical paradigm in economic theory. Nonetheless, behavioural economics is now firmly ensconced in mainstream academic research with a burgeoning literature (Cartwright, 2014). It also forms an increasingly popular component of undergraduate and graduate economics programmes around the world (Angner, 2016).

Although studies that relate behavioural economic principles to various contexts have increased rapidly, the application of behavioural economics to the myriad of issues faced by small states has, by contrast, received scant attention in the literature. This paucity can in part be explained by the fact that there is considerable heterogeneity among small states in terms of their socio-political and cultural characteristics, which in turn may hinder the generalization of behavioural economic insights across these countries. Nonetheless, the literature on small country issues has identified a sufficiently-large number of peculiarities that are common to many small economies around the world, which shape the socio-economic landscape of these countries. Recent years have witnessed a growing appreciation for the somewhat idiosyncratic economic situation of small states worldwide (International Monetary Fund, 2015), along with a thriving research agenda that has helped to identify some of the tendencies shared by these nations, including insularity, limited domestic markets characterized by significant imperfections, and volatility due to external economic shocks (e.g. Briguglio, 1995; Briguglio *et al.*, 2009).

In the light of this, the aim of this study is to analyze some of the key findings from the behavioural economics literature and to discuss their implications for small states. In particular, this paper will focus on how social preferences like trust, inequality aversion, altruism and reciprocity influence economic outcomes in small states. Standard economic theory has typically ignored such factors, instead opting to treat individuals as fully rational, narrowly self-interested decision-makers. Nonetheless, pioneering work by the likes of Fehr and Schmidt (1999) has shown both the importance of such social preferences in people's daily economic interactions, and in turn how they can lead to outcomes that are systematically different to those predicted by rational choice theory. Social preferences now constitute one of the strongest elements of contemporary research within behavioural economics, and it is to be expected that such preferences should have a role to play in the economics of small countries too.

The paper proceeds as follows: In the next section we briefly synthesize the expansive behavioural economics literature on social preferences, focusing on the concepts of trust, inequality aversion, altruism and reciprocity. The section then proceeds to review the economics literature on small states focusing on both the definition of 'small' as well as key characteristics which pertain to such states, drawing particular attention to those which may be ripe for juxtaposition with the social preferences literature. In Section 3 we briefly outline the method which we employ in the paper. We present the findings in Section 4; Section 5 concludes the paper.

2 Literature review

Social preferences in behavioural economics

The basic underlying postulate of behavioural economics is that people's decision-making processes differ systematically from rational choice theory that forms the basis of the majority of economic models (Thaler, 1980). The idea of human beings as fully rational self-interested thinkers, or *homo economicus*, posits that people consider all available information before taking optimal decisions that are individually-consistent and nominally self-interested. This assumption, which gained significant traction following efforts by Frisch (1926) and von Neumann and Morgenstern (1944) to model preferences mathematically, has been subject to intense scrutiny due to its perceived detachment from reality (e.g. Allais, 1953; Simon, 1957; Scitovsky, 1976).

It is within this context that key concepts underpinning modern-day behavioural economics emerged, advocating that standard economic models should incorporate insights from cognitive psychology and neurobiology in order to more fully explain human decision-making processes (Ariely, 2008). Behavioural concepts, in fact, emphasize the idea that when making choices in their daily lives, people often stray from the predictions based on full rationality. Tversky and Kahneman (1974; 1979), widely considered to be the forefathers of the field, showed that decisions are usually based on a series of heuristics or shortcuts as opposed to the slow, informed deliberation of *homo economicus*.

Perhaps the most oft-discussed feature underpinning neoclassical economic thought is the characterization of people as self-interested agents with little regard for other people's wellbeing. Social preferences, instead, refer to individual preferences that do not solely depend on one's own outcomes but also on the outcomes of others (Levitt and List, 2007). These preferences, which include trust, inequality aversion, altruism and reciprocity, represent an important departure point for mainstream economic thought given the long-standing belief that people are primarily driven by self-interest (Rabin, 1993; Fehr and Schmidt, 1999). Research on social preferences has uncovered various ways in which these factors can systematically alter the standard decision-making predictions of rational choice theory.

The standard economic model can, in fact, easily incorporate other-regarding preferences – a case in point being the extensive literature on the 'warm-glow' effect elicited by charitable giving (e.g. Andreoni, 1989, 1990; Cornes and Sandler, 1984; Steinberg, 1987). Given the lack of clarity on the processes underpinning this warm glow effect (Andreoni and Payne, 2013), and in view of overwhelming evidence rejecting the notion of purely self-interested preferences (Roth *et al.*, 1991; Fehr and Gächter, 2000; Camerer, 2001), a concerted effort has been made to overhaul the mainstream economic model in order to adequately reflect people's behavioural tendencies. As a result, the study of social preferences and their role in individual decision-making has flourished in recent years, both from a theoretical and experimental standpoint.

Although many categorizations have been used in the literature, we can focus on two main types of social preferences (Kamas and Preston, 2012), namely **distributive** preferences and **reciprocal** preferences. *Distributive preferences* are primarily concerned with the final distribution of outcomes across economic agents, and incorporate preferences like inequality or inequity aversion (Fehr and Schmidt, 1999) and altruism (Cooper and Kagel, 2009). *Reciprocal preferences* focus on how people reward or punish others in response to their behaviour (Falk and Fischbacher, 2006), and are intimately-related to the notions of trust and reciprocity (Berg *et al.*, 1995).

There exist plenty of examples in the literature of the role that social preferences can play in the determination of a community's economic fortunes. For example, Burchardi and Hassan (2013) find that households with interpersonal ties across the East-West divide in Berlin recorded higher personal incomes after the fall of the Berlin Wall in 1989, with these linkages also encouraging higher investment and regional development. Moreover, the extensive literature on social capital also suggests that reciprocal social preferences like trust and reciprocity can lead to improved economic outcomes through several channels, like the reduction of information frictions (e.g. Coleman, 1988), peer monitoring (Stiglitz, 1990) and the effective provision of public goods (Sugden, 1984). In addition, work on distributive social preferences like inequality aversion has also shown how these preferences may have important socio-economic consequences, from political support for the welfare state (Fong, Bowles and Gintis, 2006) to the extent of tax evasion in a country (Alm, Sanchez and de Juan, 1995). Furthermore, Fehr and Fischbacher (2002) relate how other-regarding motives can encourage cooperation, even in competitive environments.

Interestingly, social preferences may also act as a hindrance to economic prosperity. For example, Krueger and Mas (2004) report how concerns regarding unfairness and wage inequalities among workers can lead to a significant drop in the quality of output produced. Similarly, Fehr and Schmidt (1999) find that the presence of even a small minority of selfish individuals can trigger negative reciprocity in a group, leading to the unravelling of cooperation and free-riding. Kahneman, Knetsch and Thaler (1986) also show how concerns for fairness can act as a restriction on profit-maximising behaviour.

The economics of small states

The study of small economies as entities that require a specialized and tailored focus has garnered significant interest over the years (Kuznets, 1960; Lloyd and Sundrum, 1982). This has resulted in a diverse literature dealing with a variety of issues, from optimal monetary and exchange rate policies (Cardia, 1991; Sjaastad, 1989) to matters related to development aid and efforts to reduce poverty (Collier and Dollar, 1998). Various measurements have been put forward in the literature in order to define what is meant by a 'small country', including population size (Armstrong *et al.*, 1996), geographical area (Jalan, 1982), trade flows (Davenport, 2001) and composite indices of economic and geographical characteristics (Downes, 1988). The most commonly-used definition is the one provided by the Commonwealth Secretariat[1], which states that countries with a population size below 1.5 million people should be considered as 'small'.

But the idea of distinguishing between countries on the basis of size for analytical purposes is not without controversy. Indeed, authors like Rose (2006) and Easterly and Kraay (2000) report no statistically-significant relationship between country size and various economic indicators, including GDP growth rates, competitiveness and educational outcomes. However, the authors also find that small countries have a higher openness to international trade and, crucially, greater volatility in per capita growth rates, mainly as a result of this openness.

This latter finding goes to the heart of why so much effort has been expended to identify the unifying characteristics of small countries. It is an idea succinctly encapsulated by Briguglio (1995), who argues that small countries face unique challenges to their economic wellbeing due to their physical and economic constraints, which render them more vulnerable to external shocks. Consequently, although there is significant variation across small countries, an appreciation of these common peculiarities is essential in order to develop policies that improve the economic resilience of the most vulnerable economies (Briguglio *et al.*, 2006; Turvey, 2007). The continued efforts by international institutions like the Commonwealth Secretariat World Bank (Commonwealth Advisory Group, 1997), the World Bank (Commonwealth Secretariat and World Bank, 2000) and the United Nations (2015) to recognize the situation of small economies and their vulnerabilities has helped to vindicate this approach and formalize the analysis.

An extensive number of vulnerabilities have been identified in relation to small countries. These include the small size of domestic markets, both in terms of goods/services as well as labour supply, significant market imperfections caused by limited competition, and impairments on the ability to reap economies of scale. From a governance perspective, small countries face public administration problems due to indivisibilities and nepotism, resulting in large, pervasive governments. And finally, small states tend also to contend with significant environmental issues like limited natural resources and susceptibility to trans-boundary pollution like sulphur dioxide (for a more complete and exhaustive treatment of the main characteristics of small countries, please refer to Briguglio, 1995, and Liou and Ding, 2002).

What are the small state peculiarities that may have analytical relevance from a behavioural economics/social preferences perspective? One which merits consideration is the size of domestic markets. The standard implications of economic smallness have been well-documented, and lead to an over-reliance on international trade flows, both in terms of imports and exports, limitations in diversification in economic activity (Armstrong and Read, 1998), and vulnerability to external economic shocks (Briguglio, 2016). Size also limits the private sector's ability to benefit from economies of scale (Romer, 1986), which in turn further dissuades domestic entrepreneurship, reduces competition and constrains external competitiveness. Linked to this is the fact that small economies also tend to be characterized by various market imperfections due to the lack of competition, with a few domestic operators dominating the market and setting prices (Briguglio, 1995).

From a behavioural economics perspective, one direct consequence of limited market size is that interactions between buyers and sellers are necessarily more frequent under such conditions (*ceteris paribus*). Market operators must increasingly rely on one another due to their relative importance for the industry as a whole (Eskelinen *et al.*, 2002). These conditions may encourage the propagation of various social preferences like trust and fairness, which can have an important impact on economic outcomes by fostering cooperation and mutual solidarity.

3 Method

In what follows, we apply the insights gleaned from the Behavioural Economics literature in order to assess its possible relevance to small states. We ask first whether there are theoretical expectations for social preferences to be more prevalent in small states, effectively juxtaposing the behavioural literature with that on 'smallness'. Given that the literature on social preferences has contributed to a more complete understanding of an economy's underlying machinations, it is perhaps self-evident that social preferences should have a role to play in shaping the economic interactions of people in small countries (Baldacchino, 2005). Indeed, the communitarian view of social capital as espoused in the public policy literature (Woolcock and Narayan, 2000) describes small countries as fertile breeding grounds for social preferences due to their size as well as the formation of integrated communities and social networks.[2] Social preferences have also received some attention in describing daily life in small countries (Baldacchino, 2005).

We then proceed to examine some empirical evidence that tests our expectations. To do this we use data from various secondary sources in order to capture the various social preferences that are most relevant to our analysis. More specifically, we look at trust, inequality aversion, altruism and reciprocity across different countries, using constructs that are typically used in the literature to represent each preference. A summary of the key constructs used, including data sources, is provided in Table 18.1.

We relate each variable to population size in order to obtain a baseline understanding of how each social preference correlates with country size. This enables us to assess whether there is any evidence that trust, inequality aversion, altruism and reciprocity are more prevalent in small states, and thus derive generalized stylized facts regarding the importance of these social preferences for economic activity in these countries.

4 Analysis

Trust

We begin with trust, which Fukuyama (1995) defines as the belief, within a group of people, that others within the group will behave in a cooperative, upstanding and consistent manner. Trust is perhaps the most readily-considered preference when discussing small countries. Maskell (1998) states that small economies tend to benefit from increased levels of trust within their respective societies. The reasons for this shared trust are numerous and have been explored by several authors. Firstly, the pressure to conform to social norms in small countries is considerably higher (Dahl and Tufte, 1973; Baldacchino, 2012), thus encouraging compliance and deterring deviance (Perry, 2001). Secondly, social linkages are easier to foster among small, homogeneous groups with shared backgrounds and close physical proximity (Morduch, 2003; Alesina and La Ferrara, 2005), since they increase the likelihood that people will participate in a wide variety of joint activities which help to foster trust and cooperation. Furthermore, the evolution of shared trust is also, in some cases, a matter of necessity in small economies due to the size of local industries characterized by the presence of a handful of key players, whose actions are strategically entwined and could have serious repercussions for the entire sector (Maskell, 1998). Experimental evidence supports this assertion, with participants in small groups typically exhibiting greater levels of trust relative to larger groups in social dilemma settings where strategic behaviour can affect others (Sato, 1988).

Figure 18.1 shows the proportion of people in a sample of 92 countries (listed in the Data Appendix) who express high levels of trust in others (taken from the World Values Survey, 2010–2014), plotted against the log of population size. Overall, we observe a somewhat negative correlation between the two variables, which suggests that trust levels are higher in smaller economies, although the correlation is weak.

One potential pitfall with the above analysis is that small states (defined earlier as having a population size below 1.5 million) are somewhat under-represented in our dataset due to a lack of data on trust levels in these countries. This may raise concerns that our results are skewed towards

Table 18.1 Summary of key data and sources

Variable of interest	Data construct	Source
Trust	Survey question: 'Generally speaking would you say that most people can be trusted or that you need to be very careful in dealing with people?' (binary response).	Source: World Values Survey (2010–2014). www.worldvaluessurvey.org/WVSDocumentationWV6.jsp/.
Index of peaceful collective decision making	Aggregate indicator incorporating: the extent of people's involvement in selecting their government, freedom of expression; freedom of association and a free media (the 'voice and accountability' index); and political stability within a country.	World Bank Group (2013). World Governance Indicators (2013). (http://info.worldbank.org/governance/wgi/#home).
Inequality aversion	Gini coefficient	World Bank Group (2012). Gini Coefficient: World Development Indicators (2012). http://data.worldbank.org/indicator/SI.POV.GINI/.
Altruism	World giving index (proportion of people who had either helped a stranger, donated money or volunteered time for a good cause in the last month)	World Giving Index, 2011.Charities Aid Foundation (2011).www.cafonline.org/about-us/publications/2011-publications/world-giving-index-2011/.
Reciprocity	Tax morale – average of people's perception regarding the acceptability of tax avoidance or evasion. Likert scale ranging from 1 to 10, with 1 denoting 'Never justifiable' and 10 denoting 'Always justifiable'.	World Values Survey, Wave 6, (2010–2014). www.worldvaluessurvey.org/WVSDocumentationWV6.jsp/.
Importance of democracy in society	Survey question: 'How important is it for you to live in a country that is governed democratically? On this scale where 1 means it is "not at all important" and 10 means "absolutely important" what position would you choose?'	World Values Survey, Wave 6, (2010–2014). www.worldvaluessurvey.org/WVSDocumentationWV6.jsp/.
Population size	Population	World Bank Group (2015). Population Estimates and Projections: Population Statistics. http://data.worldbank.org/data-catalog/population-projection-tables/.

larger or mid-sized countries, which would limit our ability to extrapolate the findings to other smaller states.

We can address such concerns by using another proxy for trust as proposed in the World Bank's World Development Report (2013), namely the index of peaceful collective decision-making. This index, which is used to measure social cohesion, is an aggregate indicator that incorporates the extent of people's involvement in selecting their government, freedom of expression, freedom of association and a free media (the 'voice and accountability' index) as well as political stability within a country. These data form part of the World Governance

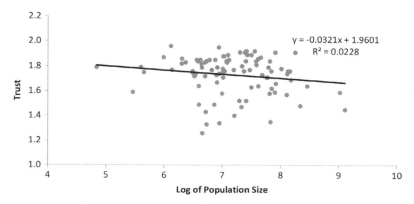

Figure 18.1 Share of people (%) expressing high levels of trust in others and population size (2011)

Indicators and cover almost 200 countries, including many small states. We therefore use this index as a proxy for trust, and plot it against the log of population size for a sample of 190 countries (listed in the Data Appendix). The results are shown in Figure 18.2, where once again we obtain a negative correlation between our two variables, in line with our original findings. Therefore, the data provides some evidence that small states may benefit from greater levels of trust among its people.

Several authors have alluded to this phenomenon as a key determinant in explaining the continued economic success of small states (Alesina and La Ferrara, 2005), particularly in terms of their well-documented resilience and their adaptability to exogenous changes in their economic circumstances (Katzenstein, 1985; Briguglio, 2016). In addition, trust is a key component in helping to overcome problems in credit market institutions caused by weak monetary transmission in small developing countries, by encouraging greater use of informal financing arrangements like microcredit and microfinance to promote entrepreneurship and development (Epstein and Yuthas, 2011).

Inequality aversion

Another key social preference is inequity/inequality aversion, or people's distaste for unequal outcomes. As pointed out in the seminal work by Fehr and Schmidt (1999), people typically

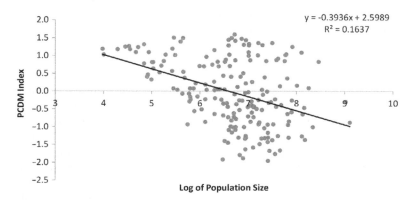

Figure 18.2 Index of peaceful collective decision-making (PCDM) and population size (2011)

dislike any form of inequitable outcome, encompassing situations where the individual receives more than others (advantageous inequality aversion) as well as situations where the individual receives less than others (disadvantageous inequality aversion). Inequality aversion is related to the basic sense of fairness, although studies have shown that whereas disadvantageous inequality can be observed across various societies by middle childhood, advantageous inequality only emerges later on in childhood and varies considerably by cultural background, with the greatest incidence among children from Western societies (Blake *et al.*, 2015).

In contrast to the literature on trust, comparatively scant attention has been afforded to the prevalence or otherwise of inequality aversion in small countries. Nonetheless, we can look at the main factors and processes which have been identified that perpetuate inequality aversion and its impact on cooperation. More specifically, recent work by Nishi *et al.* (2015) focuses on wealth visibility and its role in determining the extent of inequality aversion and cooperation. This idea is related to various studies (e.g. Tricomi *et al.*, 2010; Dawes *et al.*, 2012) which show that knowing your neighbour's wealth can trigger a variety of psychological processes which lead to interpersonal comparisons across individuals.

When such comparisons take place in the presence of visible wealth disparities, this may set off inequality averse preferences due to competitive instincts and concerns regarding social standing (Loughnan *et al.*, 2011; Kuziemko *et al.*, 2014). In turn, these preferences lead to lower levels of cooperation and lower overall wealth within a community, thereby heightening initial inequality (Nishi *et al.*, 2015). The issue is exacerbated further given that people's decision-making processes often rely on heuristics including that which accords disproportionate attention to factors which are salient (Malhotra, 1982). High wealth visibility, present in small states, may emphasize any income disparities across people. If geographical and social proximity enhance wealth visibility, then inequality aversion may be a particularly important consideration for small economies.

In addition, although wealth per adult[3] is on average higher in small economies, its distribution is considerably more equal in smaller countries, with 54% of total wealth held by the wealthiest 10% of the population relative to the 62% in large countries[4] (Natella and O'Sullivan, 2014). This may be evidence of higher inequality aversion in small countries, since this would create an environment where abnormally high levels of income are frowned upon and governments are compelled to allocate more resources towards redistributive policies. Nonetheless, it is also likely that small countries are inherently more prone to lower levels of income inequality. For example, Pryor (1973) argues that more populous countries are typically more heterogeneous in terms of its citizens, and thus more likely to have greater income inequality due to vastly differing skills and outcomes. Finally, lower inequality may simply be due to the disproportionate role of the state and of public employment in small states (as mentioned previously), which may reduce income differentials. Thus, the lower levels of income inequality observed in small states may be due to a multitude of factors, and merits its own empirical analysis to fully understand the data.

The available statistics regarding income distribution would seem to indicate that small countries tend to have less income inequality on average relative to larger nations. This is shown in Figure 18.3, where we can observe a positive correlation between income inequality (as measured by the Gini coefficient) and (log of) population size within a sample of 81 countries (listed in the Data Appendix). Again here the correlation coefficient is on the low side.

Regardless of what leads to lower inequality in small states, it is also important to understand its consequences and implications. Roth (2015) has shown that conspicuous consumption is less prevalent in societies with high levels of social interactions, consistent with Veblen's (1899) claim regarding the societal pressures and norms that prevent overt displays of wealth. This

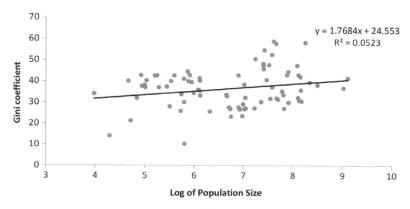

$$y = 1.7684x + 24.553$$
$$R^2 = 0.0523$$

Figure 18.3 Gini coefficient and population size (2011)

resonates with the small country experience given the high levels of social capital, coupled with the inherently-negative disposition of people towards inequality. Indeed, small communities have been described as being more likely to ostracize people who stand out (Baldacchino, 2008), which further dissuades such open vaunting of wealth. Therefore, although inequality aversion may be amplified in small countries due to the high visibility of any form of conspicuous consumption, the relatively lower levels of wealth inequality coupled with social norms dissuading such behaviour may help to reduce its incidence.

Altruism

A closely-related social preference to the ones described above is altruism, which is the selfless concern for others (Fields, 2004). The true nature of altruism has attracted significant debate across various academic fields, with the traditional idea of 'pure' altruism (actions that only benefit others) eschewed in recent years in favour of 'impure' altruism, whereby seemingly selfless actions also provide utility to the individual, in the form of a warm glow effect (Andreoni, 1989). Regardless of the underlying motivations, altruistic actions are an important foundation for several economic activities like charitable giving (List, 2011), while also facilitating social interactions and the development of trust.

Once again, the literature on altruism in small countries is somewhat limited, with authors like Hansson and Slade (1977) arguing that it is cultural differences and not size which are the main driving force behind the predominance or otherwise of altruistic tendencies. Nonetheless, some studies (Darley and Latané, 1968; Clark and Word, 1974) have suggested that people are more likely to intervene in emergency situations when alone rather than when they form part of a group. This is part of the social psychology literature on the *bystander effect*, where the probability of an individual assisting someone in need is inversely proportional to the number of bystanders.

One issue with bystander type studies is that they implicitly assume that the 'victim' only requires one helper, which exacerbates the free-rider motive, thereby rendering the link with altruism in small countries somewhat tenuous. However, recent experimental work by Luhan *et al.* (2009) and Panchanathan *et al.* (2013) show, using an N-person dictator game, that even when the recipient's utility increases with the number of helpers, altruism (as captured by the size of individual donations) falls as the group size increases. In a one-on-one situation, the level of advantageous inequality between the helper and recipient is large, leading to larger outlays.

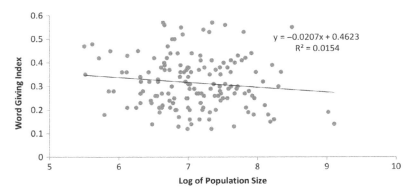

Figure 18.4 World Giving Index and population size (2011)

However, when the group size is large only a small donation by each is necessary in order to significantly reduce this inequality.

Another perspective which suggests increased altruism in small states is that provided by the work of Levine and Crowther (2008). The authors show that altruism is significantly correlated with the degree of similarity shared by the people involved. Evidence shows that homogeneity in terms of culture, ethnicity, language and religion is an important feature of small countries (Natella and O'Sullivan, 2014), which in turn is ideal for the proliferation of altruistic preferences within society since people from similar backgrounds are more likely to empathize with and assist one another.

These perspectives, together, suggest that altruism may indeed be more pronounced in small countries. We can assess the validity of this assertion by looking at data on global charitable giving and how it correlates with population size. This is provided in Figure 18.4, where we use the World Giving Index for 2011, published by Charities Aid Foundation (2011)[5], as our measure of altruistic behaviour, for 153 countries (listed in the Data Appendix). Altruistic behaviour as captured by the World Giving Index is negatively-correlated with the log of population size. The observed correlation is not particularly strong, perhaps due to underlying factors that are omitted from the analysis like GDP per capita levels, annual growth rates, governance, etc., coupled with the under-representation of small countries from the Caribbean and Pacific regions.

Nonetheless, if this correlation bears out in more rigorous analysis, it is potentially an important finding since several small developing island states tend to be prone to natural disasters due to their tropical location (Briguglio, 1995). In times of crisis any altruistic initiatives may prove to be of immense help for those worse hit by these disasters, further helping to build the country's overall resilience to such occurrences. Given also that supply of public goods by governments in small countries may be significantly hampered, both due to indivisibilities in the cost of provision as well as market inefficiencies, people in these countries may have to rely on community or group-based delivery of public goods.

Reciprocity

Finally, we take a brief look at reciprocity, which refers to people's response to another person's action with an action which is deemed to be equivalent. As pointed out by Fehr and Gächter (2000), this concept encompasses both positive responses to favourable actions as well as punishments /negative responses to perceived slights. The existence of both positive and negative reciprocity has been shown in various settings within the behavioural economics literature, from employee theft rates following a cut in wages (Giacalone and Greenberg, 1997) to the increased purchase of products from supermarkets following the distribution of free samples (Cialdini, 1993). Reciprocity is closely-linked to cooperative behaviour (Polanyi, 1945), and has important implications for various economic outcomes like the provision of public goods (Fehr and Gächter, 2002), the enforcement of incomplete contracts (Bewley, 1999) and the design of effective performance incentives (Gneezy and Rustichini, 2000).

Given the contrasting nature of the concept, it should come as no surprise that evidence regarding group size and reciprocal behaviour is somewhat mixed. Boyd and Richerson (1988) report that reciprocity is likely to vary in a group due to several factors, namely the frequency of interactions between people (tit-for-tat behaviour), the extent to which self-interested individuals can be prevented from receiving the benefits of long-term cooperation by other reciprocators, and the extent to which reciprocators can seek each other out and interact with one other (assortative matching). All of these factors are consistent with characteristics of small communities, particularly due to the size of domestic markets and proximity to other people, which lead to the formation and propagation of social ties (Granovetter, 1983). In fact, the canonical view of cooperative situations, particularly with regards to public goods, has been that larger group size negatively affects the probability of cooperation as well as contributions towards public goods due to free-rider issues (Olson, 1965).

However, a growing literature has emerged calling into question the negative correlation between group size and the extent of reciprocity. Elster (1989) states that large groups may be more efficient in collective-action situations like the provision of public goods, since the non-rivalrous nature of the good means that larger group sizes may reap higher individual prizes than smaller groups, which in turn may encourage *greater* reciprocity. Isaac *et al.* (1994) support this idea, with experimental results suggesting that higher efficiency in the provision of public goods arises as the marginal benefit of individual contributions towards the public good increases. Thus, the relationship between group size and reciprocity may not be as clear cut as previously thought. In fact, Gächter and Herrmann (2009) argue that free-rider concerns suggested by Olson (1965) may be counteracted by the *heterogeneity* of people in larger groups, which may contain more free-riders *but also* more reciprocators who are willing to cooperate if others also cooperate. A larger number of reciprocators can also deter free-riding due to the higher marginal cost of punishment (i.e. raising the threat of negative reciprocity). This said, Carpenter (2007) cautions that the efficiency of public goods provision in large groups depends crucially on the ability of people to effectively monitor each other. If this is hindered, then free-riding may become easier to conceal from others and avoid punishment.

Empirical evidence on reciprocity and country or group size is hard to come by. Nonetheless, a useful construct that can signal reciprocal behaviour is that on people's perceptions regarding tax avoidance/evasion (also known as tax morale). The idea behind using this data, as suggested in Herrmann *et al.* (2008), is that it is associated with free-riding and conditional cooperative behaviour in social settings, both of which are intimately-related to reciprocity preferences. We therefore use data on tax morale from the World Values Survey 2010–2014, and relate this to population size in Figure 18.5 for a sample of 55 countries (listed in the Data Appendix). Attitudes towards tax avoidance and evasion are slightly stronger in larger countries, although the magnitude of this positive correlation is very weak. Scatter plots using people's attitudes towards social benefits fraud and willingness to avoid public transport fares yield similarly insignificant results, suggesting that the extent of free-riding tendencies have little correlation with population size.

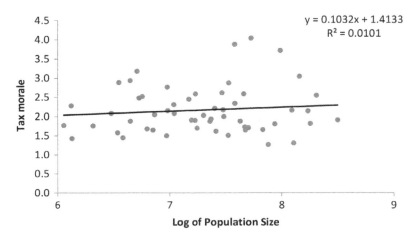

Figure 18.5 People's attitudes towards tax avoidance or evasion and population size, 2010–2014

This broadly confirms the ideas discussed earlier by the likes of Gächter and Herrmann (2009) who maintain that reciprocity is not related to group or population size. Instead, the authors argue that it is culture which has an important role to play in shaping patterns of both positive and negative reciprocity, both in terms of how people learn to reward and punish behaviour as well as determining the appropriate reactions to benefits or losses inflicted by others. This tallies with other results in Herrmann *et al.* (2008) who focus on the importance of *antisocial punishment*, or the threat of punishment in response to pro-social or *cooperative* behaviour. The authors report that antisocial punishment, which deters reciprocity, is more likely to emerge in societies with weak democratic values and/or weak legal institutions. Democratic values are associated with civic cooperation among people, which would view free-riding as socially unacceptable and thus punishable, whilst cooperative behaviour would be the norm. Conversely, the absence of such values may lead cooperative behaviour to be considered as anti-social or deviant, and thus punishable by others within the community. The data seem to lend some evidence to this possibility.

Figure 18.6 plots the aforementioned tax morale against people's perception of the importance of democracy in society (again from the World Values Survey, 2010–2014, using

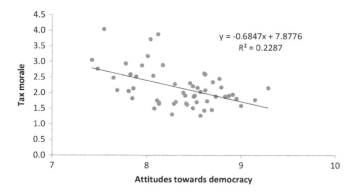

Figure 18.6 Tax morale and attitudes towards democracy

the same countries as in Figure 18.5). The results show a negative correlation between the two variables, which suggests that reciprocity is more likely to emerge as a social norm in countries with stronger democratic or civic cooperation values.[6] Clearly this is a question that merits further investigation. Reciprocity is crucial for the provision of community-based public goods like private saving and insurance mechanisms (Conning and Kevane, 2002) and the protection of natural resources like estuaries and forests (Shackleton *et al.*, 2002).

In small developing countries such private initiatives may be even more salient since indivisibilities and an inability to benefit from organizational economies of scale may result in their under-provision by government agencies. In addition, seminal work by Fehr and Falk (1999) shows that the fear of negative reciprocity contributes towards downward wage rigidity due to employer concerns regarding retaliatory action by workers in response to lower wages. Labour market imperfections are one of the key characteristics of small economies (Kilponen *et al.*, 2006), and understanding the role played by social preferences like reciprocity may help mitigate against these issues, especially since they hamper economic adjustment and dampen external competitiveness which, in turn, is one of the cornerstones of small states' economic success.

Synthesis

Based on our analysis, we can report a number of stylized facts about social preferences in small economies.

1 **Trust** appears to be more prevalent in small countries, possibly due to the frequency of social interactions as well as the homogeneity and interdependency of economic agents, and could be a crucial part of these nations' continued economic success and resilience.
2 Small country size and proximity of people significantly increase the likelihood of triggering **inequality aversion**, since public displays of affluence or conspicuous consumption would be extremely visible in these communities. This fact may help to explain why income inequality (as measured by the Gini Coefficient) is lower in small countries, with social norms favouring a more equitable distribution of income across society.
3 **Altruism** is more likely to emerge in smaller countries due to cultural as well as economic similarities and familiarity among people, with data suggesting that charitable giving per capita is negatively-correlated with population size.
4 The relationship between group size and **reciprocity** is not clear cut, possibly because the frequency of interactions between people in small communities is counteracted by greater efficiency in reciprocating transactions (like the provision of public goods) in larger countries. Cultural background may be a better determinant of reciprocity in a country, particularly people's attitudes towards democracy and the strength of its legal institutions.

5 Discussion and conclusion

The aim of this chapter was to analyze the importance of social preferences for economic outcomes in small country contexts. We examined four key constructs, namely: trust, inequality aversion, altruism and reciprocity, and sought to link them to small population size and other characteristics of small countries, such as visibility and homogeneity. We also discussed how the presence of such social preferences in small states may impact on the economic outcomes within such countries, relying on the various findings derived from the extensive behavioural economics literature that has emerged in recent years.

The findings merit some caution in interpretation. For a start, we have only looked at simple correlations between proxies for social preferences and population size, and that there may be various uncontrolled factors that contribute to the correlations examined. Correlation is an insufficient condition for causality, although it certainly serves its purpose in flagging the potential for further investigation. Future research can attempt more sophisticated analysis, considering the other drivers of social preferences, and attempting to identify the mechanisms at play in small countries that may be responsible for stronger social preferences.

Another consideration is the lack of data on proxies that capture social preferences, specifically trust and reciprocity in small countries, particularly microstates. This is a common issue for small states studies, although when it comes to social preferences the problem is perhaps even more acute due to the nascent nature of this field within the context of small countries. We have tried, wherever possible, to use alternative variables with greater global coverage to confirm our results (e.g. the index of peaceful collective decision making as a proxy for trust), but clearly this is far from a definitive solution. Indivisibilities in the data collection process, both in terms of costs and labour, severely hamper the ability of small states to gather and maintain large volumes of high quality datasets, which in turn undermines policymaking.

Even with these caveats in mind, the evidence from the behavioural economics literature, coupled with the analysis conducted in this chapter, demonstrate that social preferences may indeed have a key role to play in shaping the economic fortunes of small countries. The immediate implication of these findings is that governments and authorities in these countries should take into account the presence and impact of social preferences in the design of more effective public policies. A more ambitious policy recommendation is that governments should nurture such social preferences given that they complement several economic goals, and in several cases may offset certain vulnerabilities. Concurrently, it is also important to understand the role of public institutions in shaping social preferences within a country or community (Kim et al., 2016). The ultimate success or otherwise of policy may rest on the extent to which such preferences are embedded within the fabric of society.

Data appendix

Table 18.A1

Country	TI	PCDMI	GC	WGI	TM	AD
Afghanistan		-1.68		0.38		
Albania	1.76	-0.35		0.24		
Algeria	1.89	-1.38		0.25	3.88	8.12
Andorra	1.79	1.32	31.88			
Angola		-1.32		0.41		
Antigua & Barbuda		0.41				
Argentina	1.84	-0.44	52.52	0.3	1.88	8.5
Armenia	1.75	-0.68		0.23	2.08	8.62
Australia	1.52	1.3	30.11	0.57	1.88	8.83
Austria	1.67	1.31	26.53	0.52		
Azerbaijan	1.79	-1.01		0.32	1.5	8.08
Bahamas		1.02				
Bahrain		-0.23	10.24	0.36		
Bangladesh	1.76	-0.65	30.72	0.15		
Barbados		1.2				
Belarus	1.58	-0.71		0.25	2.77	7.48
Belgium	1.71	1.29	27.1	0.36		

Country	TI	PCDMI	GC	WGI	TM	AD
France	1.79	1.04	27	0.27		
Gabon		-0.23	41.45			
Gambia		0.04				
Georgia	1.82	-0.99		0.19		
Germany	1.66	1.25	29.81	0.44	1.45	8.69
Ghana	1.91	-0.1		0.37	1.62	8.43
Greece	1.76	0.87	32.08	0.14		
Grenada		0.82	37	0.23		
Guatemala	1.84	-0.6		0.43		
Guinea		-1.34		0.44		
Guinea-Bissau		-0.86	35.52			
Guyana		0.08	44.54	0.45		
Haiti		-1.31		0.38		
Honduras		-0.26		0.34		
Hong Kong				0.44		
Hungary	1.78	1.1	29.07	0.21	2.77	7.48
Iceland	1.59	1.51	26.94	0.47		

Table 18.A1 (continued)

Country	TI	PCDMI	GC	WGI	TM	AD
Belize		0.57		0.35		
Benin		0.41		0.25		
Bhutan		-0.29				
Bolivia		-0.05		0.31		
Bosnia & Herzego-vina	1.84	-0.44		0.21		
Botswana		0.75		0.32		
Brazil	1.91	0.09	58.23	0.3	2.55	8.07
Brunei		0.04	40			
Bulgaria	1.73	0.51		0.17		
Burkina Faso	1.85	-0.43		0.2		
Burundi		-1.8		0.12		
Cambodia		-0.73		0.16		
Cameroon		-0.93		0.29		
Canada	1.63	1.36	31.69	0.56		
Cape Verde		0.55				
Central African Rep.		-1.45		0.4		

Country	TI	PCDMI	GC	WGI	TM	AD
India	1.59	-0.3	36.8	0.19		
Indonesia	1.48	-1.01	39.41	0.36		
Iran	1.35	-0.95		0.28		
Iraq	1.52	-1.96		0.25	2.88	7.95
Ireland	1.64	1.29	32.84	0.56		
Israel	1.77	-0.53	42.8	0.39		
Italy	1.71	0.85	35.19	0.41		
Jamaica		0.06		0.36		
Japan	1.57	1.09	32.05	0.22	1.31	8.27
Jordan	1.72	-0.62		0.2	1.65	8.29
Kazakhstan		-0.5		0.21	2.59	8.62
Kenya		-0.93	47.68	0.41		
Kiribati		1.1	37.61			
Korea			31.24	0.29	1.71	8.31
Kosovo				0.21	2.94	7.78
Kuwait		-0.2		0.42	2.89	8.17

Table 18.A1 (continued)

Country	TI	PCDMI	GC	WGI	TM	AD
Chad		-1.26		0.29		
Chile	1.77	1.01	50.5	0.38	1.7	8.53
China	1.45	-0.88	41.53	0.14		
Colombia	1.86	-1.26	58.83	0.36	1.65	8.13
Comoros		-0.07		0.28		
Congo		-1.4		0.27		
Congo, Dem Rep.				0.21	2.05	7.81
Costa Rica		1.03		0.39		
Cote d'Ivoire	1.79	-1.49		0.19		
Croatia		0.41		0.22		
Cuba	1.87	-0.86				
Cyprus	1.75	0.71	34.31	0.36	1.77	9.15
Czech Rep.	1.75	1	26.8	0.29		
Denmark	1.33	1.42	23.24	0.44		
Djibouti		-0.56	39.96	0.28		
Dominica		0.78				
Dominican Rep.	1.74	0.22		0.34		

Country	TI	PCDMI	GC	WGI	TM	AD
Kyrgyzstan	1.83	-1.02		0.21	2.52	7.89
Laos		-1.01		0.5		
Latvia	1.83	0.83		0.23		
Lebanon		-0.73		0.37	3.18	8.01
Lesotho		0.03				
Liberia		-1.92		0.38		
Libya		-1.09			1.68	8.13
Liechtenstein		1.27		0.14		
Lithuania	1.74	0.89				
Luxembourg	1.75	1.5	25.8	0.42		
Macedonia	1.86	-0.64		0.27		
Madagascar		-0.25		0.12		
Malawi		-0.4		0.41		
Malaysia	1.91	-0.01		0.3		
Maldives		0.08	37.37	0.27	2.62	8.61
Mali	1.83	0.26				
Malta	1.79	1.4	42.7	0.48		

Table 18.A1 (continued)

Country	TI	PCDMI	GC	WGI	TM	AD	Country	TI	PCDMI	GC	WGI	TM	AD
Ecuador		-0.45		0.23	1.91	8.51	Marshall Islands		1.24	21.28			
Egypt	1.62	-0.85		0.26	1.81	8.95	Mauritania		-0.24		0.32		
El Salvador	1.85	0.12		0.23			Mauritius		0.7	35.9			
Equatorial Guinea		-0.93	33.73				Mexico	1.78	0.16	47.36	0.32	2.16	8.54
Eritrea		-1.09					Micronesia		0.82				
Estonia	1.77	0.97	33.2	0.21	2.28	8.3	Moldova	1.85	-0.34		0.26		
Ethiopia	1.76	-1.31		0.25			Monaco		1.18				
Fiji		0.23	42.8				Mongolia		0.7		0.32		
Finland	1.43	1.6	26.91	0.37			Montenegro		-0.16	29.99	0.18		

Notes

1 http://thecommonwealth.org/small-states/.
2 Such tightly-knit communities may also lead to isolationism and discrimination, which can have a negative effect on economic outcomes. This is also known as perverse social capital (Rubio, 1997).
3 Where wealth is measured as financial wealth plus net non-financial wealth (i.e. property value less debt).
4 The authors classify 'small countries' as having a population below 10 million, while 'large' countries as having a population over 25 million.
5 The World Giving Index uses survey data from 195,000 people across 153 countries, and is a composite of three separate measures of charitable giving, namely the proportion of people who give money to charities, the proportion who undertook volunteer work in the last month, and the proportion who helped out a stranger in the last month.
6 Similar results are also obtained when plotting attitudes towards democracy against both social benefits fraud and willingness to avoid paying public transport fares.

References

Alesina, A. and La Ferrara, E. (2005). 'Ethnic diversity and economic performance'. *Journal of Economic Literature*, 43(3): 762–800.
Allais, M. (1953). 'L'extension des théories de l'équilibre économique général et du rendement social au cas du risque'. *Econometrica*: 269–290.
Alm, J., Sanchez, I. and De Juan, A. (1995). 'Economic and noneconomic factors in tax compliance'. *Kyklos*, 48(1): 1–18.
Andreoni, J. (1989). 'Giving with impure altruism: Applications to charity and Ricardian equivalence'. *The Journal of Political Economy*, 97(6): 1447–1458.
Andreoni, J. (1990). 'Impure altruism and donations to public goods: A theory of warm-glow giving'. *The Economic Journal*, 100(401): 464–477.
Andreoni, J. and Payne, A. A. (2013). Charitable giving. *Handbook of Public Economics*, 5: 1–50.
Angner, E. (2016). *A Course in Behavioral Economics 2e*. London: Palgrave Macmillan.
Ariely, D. (2008). *Predictably irrational: the hidden forces that shape our decisions*. New York: HarperCollins Publishers.
Armstrong, H. W., Jouan de Kervenoael, R., Li, X. and Read, R. (1996). *The Economic Performance of Micro-States*. Report to UK ODA.
Armstrong, H. W. and Read, R. (1998). 'Trade and growth in small states: the impact of global trade liberalisation'. *The World Economy*, 21(4): 563–585.
Baldacchino, G. (2005). 'The contribution of 'social capital' to economic growth: lessons from island jurisdictions'. *The Round Table*, 94(378): 31–46.
Baldacchino, G. (2008). 'Studying islands: on whose terms? Some epistemological and methodological challenges to the pursuit of island studies'. *Island Studies Journal*, 3(1): 37–56.
Baldacchino, G. (2012). 'Islands and despots'. *Commonwealth and Comparative Politics*, 50(1): 103–120.
Berg, J., Dickhaut, J. and McCabe, K. (1995). 'Trust, reciprocity, and social history'. *Games and Economic Behavior*, 10(1): 122–142.
Bewley, T. F. (1999). *Why wages don't fall during a recession*. Harvard, MA: Harvard University Press.
Blake, P. R., McAuliffe, K., Corbit, J., Callaghan, T. C., Barry, O., Bowie, A., Kleutsch, L. *et al.* (2015). 'The ontogeny of fairness in seven societies'. *Nature*, 528: 258–262.
Boyd, R. and Richerson, P. J. (1988). 'The evolution of reciprocity in sizable groups'. *Journal of Theoretical Biology*, 132(3): 337–356.
Brickman, P., Coates, D. and Janoff-Bulman, R. (1978). 'Lottery winners and accident victims: Is happiness relative?'. *Journal of Personality and Social Psychology*, 36(8): 917.
Briguglio, L. (1995). 'Small island developing states and their economic vulnerabilities'. *World Development*, 23(9): 1615–1632.
Briguglio, L. (2016). 'Exposure to external shocks and economic resilience of countries: evidence from global indicators'. *Journal of Economic Studies*, 43(6): 1057–1078.
Briguglio, L., Cordina, G. and Kisanga, E. J. (eds) (2006). *Building the economic resilience of small states*. London: Formatek Publishing for the Islands and Small States Institute of the University of Malta and the Commonwealth Secretariat.

Briguglio, L., Cordina, G., Farrugia, N. and Vella, S. (2009). 'Economic vulnerability and resilience: concepts and measurements'. *Oxford Development Studies*, 37(3): 229–247.

Burchardi, K. B. and Hassan, T. A. (2013). 'The economic impact of social ties: Evidence from German reunification'. *The Quarterly Journal of Economics*, 128(3): 1219–1271.

Camerer, C. F. (2001). *Behavioral Economics*. Princeton, NJ: Princeton University Press.

Cardia, E. (1991). 'Dynamics of a Small Open Economy in Response to Monetary, Fiscal, and Productivity Shocks'. *Journal of Monetary Economics*, 28: 411–434.

Carpenter, J. P. (2007). 'Punishing free-riders: How group size affects mutual monitoring and the provision of public goods'. *Games and Economic Behavior*, 60(1): 31–51.

Cartwright, E. (2014). *Behavioral economics*, Vol. 22. New York: Routledge.

Charities Aid Foundation (2011). *2011 World Giving Index*.

Cialdini, R. B. (1993). *Influence: The psychology of persuasion*. New York: Morrow.

Clark, R. D. and Word, L. E. (1974). 'Where is the apathetic bystander? Situational characteristics of the emergency'. *Journal of Personality and Social Psychology* 29(3): 279.

Coleman, J. S. (1988). 'Social capital in the creation of human capital'. *American Journal of Sociology*: S95–S120.

Collier, P. and Dollar, D. (1998). Aid Allocation and Poverty Reduction. *Policy Research Working Paper*, No. 2041. Washington, DC: The World Bank.

Commonwealth Advisory Group (1997). *A Future for Small States: Overcoming Vulnerability*. London: Commonwealth Secretariat.

Commonwealth Secretariat and World Bank (2000). *Small States: Meeting Challenges in the Global Economy, Report of the Commonwealth Secretariat-World Bank Joint Task Force on Small States*. London: Commonwealth Secretariat; Washington, DC: the World Bank.

Conning, J. and Kevane, M. (2002). 'Community-based targeting mechanisms for social safety nets: A critical review'. *World Development* 30(3): 375–394.

Cooper, D. and Kagel, J. H. (2009). Other Regarding Preferences: A Selective Survey of Experimental Results. In Kagel, J. and Roth, A. (eds) *The Handbook of Experimental Economics*, Vol. 2. Oxford: Princeton University Press.

Cornes, R. and Sandler, T. (1984). 'The theory of public goods: non-Nash behaviour'. *Journal of Public Economics*, 23(3): 367–379.

Dahl, R. A. and Tufte, E. R. (1973). *Size and democracy*. Stanford, CA: Stanford University Press.

Darley, J. M. and Latané, B. (1968). 'Bystander intervention in emergencies: diffusion of responsibility'. *Journal of Personality and Social Psychology*, 8(4): 377.

Davenport, M. (2001). *A Study of Alternative Special and Differential Arrangements for Small Economies*. Interim Report, Commonwealth Secretariat.

Dawes, C. T., Loewen, P. J., Schreiber, D., Simmons, A. N., Flagan, T., McElreath, R., Bokemper, S. E., Fowler, J. H. and Paulus, M. P. (2012). 'Neural basis of egalitarian behavior'. *Proceedings of the National Academy of Sciences*, 109(17): 6479–6483.

Downes, A.S. (1988). 'On the statistical measurement of smallness: a principal component measure of country size'. *Social and Economic Studies*: 75–96.

Easterly, W. and Kraay, A. (2000). 'Small states, small problems? Income, growth, and volatility in small states'. *World Development*, 28(11): 2013–2027.

Elster, J. (1989). *The cement of society: A survey of social order*. Cambridge: Cambridge University Press.

Epstein, M. J. and Yuthas, K. (2011). 'The critical role of trust in microfinance success: Identifying problems and solutions'. *Journal of Developmental Entrepreneurship*, 16(4): 477–497.

Eskelinen, H., Hannibalsson, I., Malmberg, A., Maskell, P. and Vatne, E. (2002). *Competitiveness, localised learning and regional development: specialization and prosperity in small open economies*, Vol. 14. London: Routledge.

Falk, A. and Fischbacher, U. (2006). 'A theory of reciprocity'. *Games and Economic Behavior*, 54(2): 293–315.

Fehr, E. and Falk, A. (1999). 'Wage rigidity in a competitive incomplete contract market'. *Journal of Political Economy*, 107(1): 106–134.

Fehr, E. and Gächter, S. (2000). 'Fairness and Retaliation: The Economics of Reciprocity'. *Journal of Economic Perspectives*, 14(3): 159–181.

Fehr, E. and Schmidt, K. M. (1999). 'A theory of fairness, competition, and cooperation'. *Quarterly Journal of Economics*, 114(3): 817–868.

Fehr, E. and Fischbacher, U. (2002). 'Why social preferences matter–the impact of non-selfish motives on competition, cooperation and incentives'. *The Economic Journal*, 112(478): C1–C33.

Fehr, E. and Gächter, S. (2002). 'Altruistic punishment in humans'. *Nature*, 415(6868): 137–140.

Fields, R. M. (2004). The psychology and sociology of martyrdom. In Fields, R. M., *Martyrdom: The psychology, theology, and politics of self-sacrifice*: 23–81.

Fong, C. M., Bowles, S. and Gintis, H. (2006). 'Strong reciprocity and the welfare state'. *Handbook of the Economics of Giving, Altruism and Reciprocity*, 2: 1439–1464.

Frisch, R. (1957). 'Sur un problème d'économie pure'. *Metroeconomica*, 9(2): 79–111.

Fukuyama, F. (1995). *Trust: The social virtues and the creation of prosperity*. New York: Free Press.

Gächter, S. and Herrmann, B. (2009). 'Reciprocity, culture and human cooperation: previous insights and a new cross-cultural experiment'. *Philosophical Transactions of the Royal Society of London B: Biological Sciences*, 364(1518): 791–806.

Giacalone, R. and Greenberg, J. (1997). *Antisocial Behaviour in Organizations*. Thousand Oaks, CA: Sage Publications.

Gneezy, U. and Rustichini, A. (2000). 'Pay enough or don't pay at all'. *Quarterly Journal of Economics*, 115 (3): 791–810.

Granovetter, M. (1983). 'The strength of weak ties: A network theory revisited'. *Sociological Theory*, 1: 201–233.

Hansson, R. O. and Slade, K. M. (1977). 'Altruism toward a deviant in city and small town'. *Journal of Applied Social Psychology*, 7(3): 272–279.

Herrmann, B., Thöni, C. and Gächter, S. (2008). 'Antisocial punishment across societies'. *Science*, 319 (5868): 1362–1367.

International Monetary Fund (2015). *Macroeconomic issues in small states and implications for fund engagement*. Washington, DC: IMF.

Isaac, R. M., Walker, J. M. and Williams, A. W. (1994). 'Group size and the voluntary provision of public goods: Experimental evidence utilizing large groups'. *Journal of Public Economics*, 54(1): 1–36.

Jalan, B. (1982). Classification of economies by size. *Problems and Policies in Small Economies*. London: Croom Helm: 39–48.

Kahneman, D., Knetsch, J. L. and Thaler, R. (1986). 'Fairness as a constraint on profit seeking: Entitlements in the market'. *The American Economic Review*: 728–741.

Kamas, L. and Preston, A. (2012). 'Distributive and reciprocal fairness: What can we learn from the heterogeneity of social preferences?'. *Journal of Economic Psychology*, 33(3): 538–553.

Katzenstein, P. J. (1985) *Small states in world markets: Industrial policy in Europe*. Ithaca, NY: Cornell University Press.

Kilponen, J., Kinnunen, H. and Ripatti, A. (2006). *Demographic uncertainty and labour market imperfections in small open economy*, No. 227. Society for Computational Economics.

Kim, B. Y., Choi, S., Lee, J., Lee, S. and Choi, K. (2016). 'Do institutions affect social preferences?. Evidence from divided Korea'. *Journal of Comparative Economics*.

Krueger, A. B. and Mas, A. (2004). 'Strikes, scabs and tread separations: Labor strife and the production of defective Bridgestone/Firestone tires'. *The Journal of Political Economy*, 112(2): 253–289.

Kruger, J., Wirtz, D., Van Boven, L. and Altermatt, T. W. (2004). 'The effort heuristic'. *Journal of Experimental Social Psychology*, 40(1): 91–98.

Kuziemko, I., Buell, R. W., Reich, T. and Norton, M. I. (2014). 'Last-place aversion: Evidence and redistributive implications'. *The Quarterly Journal of Economics*, 129(1): 105–149.

Kuznets, S. (1960). Economic Growth of Small Nations. In E. A. G. Robinson (ed.) *The Economic Consequences of the Size of Nations: Proceedings of a Conference Held by the International Economic Association*. Toronto: MacMillan.

Levine, M. and Crowther, S. (2008). 'The responsive bystander: how social group membership and group size can encourage as well as inhibit bystander intervention'. *Journal of Personality and Social Psychology*, 95 (6): 1429.

Levitt, S. D. and List, J. A. (2007). 'What do laboratory experiments measuring social preferences reveal about the real world?' *The Journal of Economic Perspectives*, 21(2): 153–174.

Liou, F. M. and Ding, Chemg G. (2002). 'Subgrouping small states based on socioeconomic characteristics'. *World Development*, 30(7): 1289–1306.

List, J. A. (2011). 'The market for charitable giving'. *The Journal of Economic Perspectives*, 25(2): 157–180.

Lloyd, P. J. and Sundrum, R. M. (1982). Characteristics of Small Economies. In B. Jalan (ed.), *Problems and Policies in Small Economies*. London: Croom Helm Ltd.

Loughnan, S., Kuppens, P., Allik, J., Balazs, K., De Lemus, S., Dumont, K., Gargurevich, R.*et al.* (2011). 'Economic inequality is linked to biased self-perception'. *Psychological Science*, 22(10): 1254–1258.

Luhan, W. J., Kocher, M. G. and Sutter, M. (2009). 'Group polarization in the team dictator game reconsidered'. *Experimental Economics*, 12(1): 26–41.

Malhotra, N. K. (1982). 'Information load and consumer decision making'. *Journal of Consumer Research*, 8 (4): 419–430.

Maskell, P. (1998). 'Low-tech competitive advantages and the role of proximity: the Danish wooden furniture industry'. *European Urban and Regional Studies*, 5(2): 99–118.

Morduch, J. (2003). Consumption Smoothing Across Space: Tests for Village-Level Responses to Risk. In Stefan Dercon (eds), *Insurance against Poverty*. Oxford: Oxford University Press.

Natella, S. and O'Sullivan, M. (2014). *The success of small countries.* Credit Suisse Research Institute.

Nishi, A., Shirado, H., Rand, D. G. and Christakis, N. A. (2015). 'Inequality and visibility of wealth in experimental social networks'. *Nature*, 526(7573): 426–429.

Olson, M. (1965). *The logic of collective action*, Vol. 124. Harvard, MA: Harvard University Press.

Panchanathan, K., Frankenhuis, W. E. and Silk, J. B. (2013). 'The bystander effect in an N-person dictator game'. *Organizational Behavior and Human Decision Processes*, 120(2): 285–297.

Perry, M. (2001). 'Shared trust in small countries: The limits to borrowing models'. *New Economy*, 8(3): 175–177.

Polanyi, K. (1945). *Origins of our time: The great transformation.* London: Gollancz.

Pryor, F. L. (1973). 'Simulation of the impact of social and economic institutions on the size distribution of income and wealth'. *American Economic Review*, 63(1): 50–72.

Rabin, M. (1993). 'Incorporating fairness into game theory and economics'. *American Economic Review.* 1281–1302.

Romer, P. M. (1986). 'Increasing returns and long-run growth'. *The Journal of Political Economy*, 94(5): 1002–1037.

Rose, A. K. (2006). 'Size really doesn't matter: In search of a national scale effect'. *Journal of the Japanese and international Economies*, 20(4): 482–507.

Roth, A. E., Prasnikar, V., Okuno-Fujiwara, M. and Zamir, S. (1991). 'Bargaining and Market Behavior in Jerusalem, Ljubljana, Pittsburgh, and Tokyo: An Experimental Study'. *American Economic Review* 81 (5): 1068–1095.

Roth, C. (2015). *Conspicuous Consumption and Peer Effects: Evidence from a Randomized Field Experiment.* Available at SSRN 2586716.

Rubio, M. (1997). 'Perverse social capital – some evidence from Colombia'. *Journal of Economic Issues*, 31 (3): 805–816.

Sato, K. (1988). 'Trust and group size in a social dilemma'. *Japanese Psychological Research*, 30(2): 88–93.

Scitovsky, T. (1976). *The joyless economy: An inquiry into human satisfaction and consumer dissatisfaction.* New York: Oxford University Press.

Shackleton, S., Campbell, B., Wollenberg, E. and Edmunds, D. (2002). 'Devolution and community-based natural resource management: Creating space for local people to participate and benefit'. *Natural Resource Perspectives*, 76: 1–6.

Simon, H. (1957). A Behavioral Model of Rational Choice. In *Models of Man, Social and Rational: Mathematical Essays on Rational Human Behavior in a Social Setting.* New York: Wiley.

Sjaastad, L. A. (1989). Exchange Rate Rules for Small Countries. University of Western Australia, Department of Economics Discussion Paper 89(05).

Steinberg, R. (1987). 'Voluntary donations and public expenditures in a federal system'. *American Economic Review*, 77(1): 24–36.

Stiglitz, J. E. (1990). 'Peer monitoring and credit markets'. *The World Bank Economic Review*, 4(3): 351–366.

Sugden, R. (1984). 'Reciprocity: the supply of public goods through voluntary contributions'. *The Economic Journal*, 94(376): 772–787.

Thaler, R. (1980). 'Toward a positive theory of consumer choice'. *Journal of Economic Behavior and Organization*, 1(1): 39–60.

Tricomi, E., Rangel, A., Camerer, C. F. and O'Doherty, J. P. (2010). 'Neural evidence for inequality-averse social preferences'. *Nature*, 463(7284): 1089–1091.

Turvey, R. (2007). 'Vulnerability assessment of developing countries: the case of small-island developing states'. *Development Policy Review*, 25(2): 243–264.

Tversky, A. and Kahneman, D. (1974). 'Judgment under Uncertainty: Heuristics and Biases'. *Science*, 185: 1124–1131.

Tversky, A. and Kahneman, D. (1979). 'Prospect theory: An analysis of decision under risk'. *Econometrica*: 263–291.

United Nations (2015). *Vulnerability-Resilience Country Profile (VRCP): A country-owned analytical framework for assessment of sustainable development in Small Island Developing States*. New York: Department of Economic and Social Affairs, United Nations.

Veblen, T. (1994). The theory of the leisure class, in *The Collected Works of Thorstein Veblen*, Vol. 1 1899. Reprint. London: Routledge.

von Neumann, J. and Morgenstern, O. (1947). *Theory of Games and Economic Behavior*. Princeton, NJ: Princeton University Press.

Woolcock, M. and Narayan, D. (2000). 'Social capital: Implications for development theory, research, and policy'. *The World Bank Research Observer*, 15(2): 225–249.

19

Small is beautiful: country size and national wellbeing in small economies[1]

Robert Read

1 Introduction

Wellbeing is an elusive multi-dimensional concept that has attracted increasing attention from policy-makers and academic researchers in recent years. The conceptualization of wellbeing now extends far beyond simplistic utilitarian measures of material affluence, notably per capita income, to incorporate an increasing range of additional qualitative non-economic variables, all of which contribute to perceptions of 'happiness'. The broad consensus is that improved wellbeing is a 'good' thing for both individuals and societies and that it is, at least partly, shaped and influenced by national economic and social policies. Wellbeing in turn, is also believed to influence these policies and therefore affect growth.

This chapter addresses several goals of happiness and wellbeing in the context of their relationship with the size of countries, measured by population. It focuses on the well-established goals of per capita incomes, health, education and 'life satisfaction' as well as extending the analysis to a consideration of good governance and institutional quality. A strong case can be made for the inclusion of governance and institutional quality since they are highly influential in shaping policy choices and policy outcomes and therefore critical determinants of the extent to which other goals of wellbeing are achieved. The primary concern is with the differential effects of country size on happiness and wellbeing drawing upon inferences derived from the literature on small economies.

The rest of the chapter is organized as follows. Section 2 presents a brief summary of the literature on wellbeing. This is followed in Section 3 by a summary discussion of the size distribution of sovereign states in the world economy and their stratification into quartiles according to population. Section 4 analyses the size distribution of states across World Bank income categories according to 2013 World Bank GNI per capita income data. Similar analyses are then undertaken for UNDP non-income Human Development Indicator data, World Bank Worldwide Governance Indicators and UNDP Overall Life Satisfaction scores. The final section draws some conclusions regarding the relationship between country size and these different indicators of wellbeing.

2 The concept of wellbeing: a brief survey

There is considerable debate regarding the extent to which material 'progress' has actually improved human wellbeing, particularly since the onset of the Industrial Revolution (discussed in some depth by Harari, 2015). The 'Whig' view is that there has been a continuous and progressive enhancement of the human condition over time; 'all is for the best in the best of all possible worlds' (Leibniz, 1710) – a view ruthlessly parodied by Voltaire in the character of Dr. Pangloss in *Candide* (1759). Romantics on the other hand, regret the loss of innocence associated with the decline of hunter-gatherer and pastoral societies which have been superseded by the growth of anthropomorphic environmental destruction, justified by the supposed innate superiority of humans over other species. Any middle way between these opposing philosophies must retain fundamental elements of both, including environmental quality and many of the undoubted universal benefits of progress, such as improvements in health, living standards and communications.

From the perspective of evolutionary physiology, human biology has no explicit concern with either happiness or wellbeing (Harari, 2015). Instead, people are viewed as being inherently dissatisfied because they are trapped on a hedonic treadmill seeking permanent and limitless gratification. Psychological approaches however, focus on subjective wellbeing and factors determining individual happiness, chief among which are personality and disposition, including optimism (Diener, 1984; Diener *et al.*, 1999). Wilson (1967) states that individuals assess their own wellbeing according to a number of key 'goals'; notably, income, health, education, gender, age and job satisfaction. Michalos (1985) however, argues that individuals assess their own wellbeing according to a range of different standards or norms, including social comparison with others (Wood, 1996). In an attempt to explain the psychological response mechanism which balances and defends individuals' mood states against severe disturbance, Cummins (2010, 2012) proposes the concept of homeostatic protection. Homeostasis can then be tested by establishing norms of subjective wellbeing drawn from extensive survey data and investigating the determinants of significant variations around these norms.

Initial research into the economic relationship between material income – both personal and national – and happiness and wellbeing found only a small positive correlation (Easterlin, 1974); a result that has been replicated in many later studies (e.g. Di Tella *et al.*, 2003; Easterlin, 1995; Oswald, 1997). Many subsequent studies also investigate some of the measurable wellbeing 'goals' identified by Wilson (1967). Oswald finds that unhappiness and suicide rates are more strongly linked with lower job satisfaction and unemployment (Oswald, 1997). Di Tella *et al.* (2003) find support for these relationships and argue that recessions generate 'psychic losses' through job uncertainty and unemployment, which are partly alleviated by effective welfare safety nets.

It is important however, to recognize that social comparison remains an important element in determining happiness and wellbeing (Wood, 1996). Easterlin argues that a rise in the subjective wellbeing of everyone does not increase happiness since material norms remain constant; i.e., individuals are neither better nor worse off relative to their social comparators (Easterlin, 1995). This suggests that both inequality and changes in relative equality may also influence happiness and wellbeing.

3 The size distribution of countries in the global economy

The world's population currently stands at just over 7 billion people, most of whom inhabit 206 internationally-recognized sovereign states, of which 193 are full members of the United Nations. Table 19.1 presents summary population data for 196 sovereign states for 2013, ranked according to quartiles, quintiles and deciles.

Table 19.1 The size distribution of sovereign countries, 2013

Distribution	Country[1]	Population ('000)
Top (rank 1)	China	1,357,380
1st decile (rank 20)	Thailand	67,011
1st quintile (rank 39)	Morocco	33,008
1st quartile (rank 49)	Korea, DR	24,895
3rd decile (rank 59)	Romania	19,964
2nd quintile (rank 78)	Belgium	11,195
Median (rank 98)	Israel	8,059
Median (rank 99)	Papua New Guinea	7,321
3rd quintile (rank 118)	Costa Rica	4,872
7th decile (rank 137)	Mongolia	2,839
3rd quartile (rank 147)	The Gambia	1,849
4th quintile (rank 157)	Cyprus	1,141
9th decile (rank 176)	Vanuatu	253
Bottom (rank 196)	Nauru	9

Source: World Bank Development Indicators, available at http://databank.worldbank.org/data/; *CIA Factbook,* available at www.cia.goiv/library/publications/the-world-factbook/.

Note: [1] Column 2 of the table refers to the country ranked in the position cited in Column 1.

Column 2 of the table refers to the country ranked in that position in Column 1 and its population in 2013 (Column 3). The mean country size is just over 36 million but, owing to the heavy skewness of the population distribution at both its upper and lower ends, the median lies between 7.3 million (Papua New Guinea, ranked 99th) and Israel (8.06 million, ranked 98th).

Almost 37% of the world's population live in PR China and India alone, while the 31 most populous countries account for 90% of the global total. The aggregate population of the 98 countries lying below the median is 244.9 million, just 3.4% of the total, while that of the 49 countries in the lowest quartile is only 26.1 million (0.37%). This disparity reflects the existence of a plethora of very small nation states, 39 of which have populations below one million and 12 below 100,000. Relatively smaller countries, irrespective of the definition of size, therefore have an almost insignificant share of the global population. As such, they tend to be consistently excluded from large-scale cross-country analyses of economic growth. This tendency is somewhat unfortunate since the distinct characteristics of smaller economies combined with their evident growth success in recent decades suggests that the role of governance and institutions in their domestic policy-making are worthy of serious investigation.

The unit of analysis used in this chapter is population size, since the primary concern is with the performance of individual nation states rather than simply cross-country comparisons. Small size gives rise to significant challenges which have important implications for national economic structures and policies and therefore performance in terms of economic growth, per capita incomes, human development, governance and wellbeing (see, for example, Armstrong and Read, 2003; Briguglio, 1995). The focus on sovereign nation states therefore permits a deeper investigation of the effects of size on cross-country variations in several dimensions of wellbeing.

There is no general consensus regarding the definition of country size, even among the major international institutions. Many academic disciplines make use of a 'small' nation archetype to analyse the implications of variations in country size. These are often based upon 'smaller' Western European industrialized nations whose populations are considerably *greater* than the global median; e.g. The Netherlands (population 16.8 million); Belgium (11.2 million) and Switzerland (8.1 million). This suggests that there exists some degree of disconnect between abstract conceptualization, theory and reality across academic disciplines.

This methodological bifurcation in the academic literature may have arisen for several reasons. Until recently, many social sciences appeared to prioritize the focus on large size to the exclusion of any serious consideration of smaller countries, albeit with some notable exceptions (see Kohr, 1957). This predominantly Euro-centric concern is often reinforced by viewing 'smaller' (developing and emerging) economies − e.g. Singapore (population 5.4 million, rank 115) − as special or unique cases and therefore of little theoretical or conceptual interest. Many new sovereign nation states have emerged as a consequence of the post-1945 decolonization process as well as the more recent dissolution of some larger states (e.g. the Soviet Union, Yugoslavia, Indonesia/Timor-Leste, Sudan/South Sudan), leading to a corresponding decline in median country size. Finally, many of the countries in the lowest size quartile are systematically excluded from global cross-country statistical growth analyses because key international datasets are often severely truncated, so giving rise to possible upwards size biases in cross-country research findings. For example, the World Bank produces only broad Income Group classificatory data for many of the smallest economies.

4 Country size, growth, per capita incomes and wellbeing

In its most material sense, wellbeing is often conceptualized as being a simple positive function of per capita income − i.e. underlying the foundations of the 'consumer society'. As incomes rise, individuals are better able to satisfy their wants through consumption (and saving) and so enjoy greater wellbeing. The analysis therefore starts by investigating the relationship between country size and wellbeing based upon per capita incomes.

At first glance, there is no reason to expect any systematic relationship between country size, incomes and other measures of wellbeing, such that this distribution is essentially random. The impact of economies of scale on the unit costs of production and provision of a wide range of public goods (e.g. education and health services) however, suggests the possibility of a mildly negative relationship with income, at least for smaller economies (Alesina and Spolaore, 2003). The primary focus of the analysis here is variation in country performance by size according to various indicators of wellbeing. As such, scatter diagrams and standard regression techniques do not provide sufficient detail of variations according to country size. In order to avoid some of the difficulties associated with using arbitrarily-determined size thresholds for what is essentially a continuous distribution of countries, the set of 196 countries is instead stratified into four size quartiles, each of which contains 49 nations. These quartiles are termed: Large; Upper-Medium; Lower-Medium; and Small-sized countries.

The distribution of countries by size quartile for per capita GNI at purchasing power parity (PPP) in 2013 for the World Bank's four income categories is shown in Table 19.2. Each pair of columns gives the number and share of countries in the total and then by size quartile (High, Upper-Middle, Lower-Middle and Low, respectively) featuring in each World Bank Income category. The final row gives the total number of countries (195 for the World Bank GNI per capita dataset) and the number in each size quartile (maximum 49). Note that the

Table 19.2 Classification of countries by GNI per capita at PPP, 2013 ($US)[1]

World Bank Income group[1]	Total		Large[2]		Upper-Medium		Lower-Medium		Small	
	No.	(%)	No.	(%)	No.	(%)	No.	(%)	No.	(%)
Low	7	3.6	**1**	**2**	**4**[3]	**8.2**	2	4.1	**0**	**0**
Lower-Middle	46	23.6	12	26.1	**18**	**39.1**	**8**	**17.4**	**8**	**17.4**
Upper-Middle	57	29.2	14	24.6	**8**	**14**	**18**	**31.6**	17	29.8
High	85	43.6	22	25.9	19	22.4	21	24.7	23	27.1
Total	195	100	49	25.1	49	25.1	49	25.1	48	24.6

Source: World Bank, Development Indicators, available at: http://info.worldbank.org/data/.

Notes: 1. Low Income < $1,036; Lower-Middle Income $1,036 – $4,085; Upper Middle Income $4,086 – $12,615; High Income > $12,615
2. Large – top size quartile; Upper-Medium – second size quartile; Lower-Medium – third size quartile; Small – bottom size quartile.
3. Figures in bold indicate group shares that deviate by more than 25% from the expected value. Critical ranges for World Bank Income Groups: High Income, 16 – 27; Upper-Middle Income, 10 – 17; Lower-Middle Income, 9 – 14; Low Income, =2.

World Bank Income categories are not stratified, such that the distribution of countries between the categories is highly skewed; for example, there are seven Low- and 85 High-Income countries.

As stated above, if the size distribution of countries in the table is random and there is no systematic relationship between country size and per capita income (and therefore, implicitly, growth), then countries within the same income category should be distributed evenly across the four size quartiles. For the purposes of this analysis, the expected value for any cell is simply defined as lying within the range of 25% greater or less than its mean. Deviations of the observed values by more than plus or minus 25% of the mean are treated as notable and indicated in bold. Given that the number of countries in each World Bank Income category differs, the range of expected values varies between the categories accordingly (Table 19.2, note 3). For example, the expected number of countries featuring in the High-Income category in any size quartile is 21.25 (85 over four) so that the plus or minus 25% range lies between 16 and 27. The number of Large-sized countries in this category in the table (22) therefore lies close to the middle of the expected range.

The data presented in Table 19.2 reveal no systematic size effect among countries in the High Income category. There is however, evidence of major variations across the remaining three Income categories. Large countries are notably *under-represented* in the Low Income category. Upper-Medium-sized countries are notably *under-represented* in the Upper-Middle Income category and notably *over-represented* in the Lower-Middle and Low Income ones. Lower-Medium-sized countries are notably *over-represented* in the Upper-Middle Income category and notably *under-represented* in the Lower-Middle one. Small countries are notably *under-represented* in the Low and Lower-Middle Income categories and also lie just inside the upper bound of the Upper-Middle Income category. It is also worthy of remark that, although a substantial majority of all countries (irrespective of size) feature in the top two World Bank income categories, the proportions of Small- and Lower-Medium-sized countries (83.3% and 79.6%, respectively) are markedly greater than those of Upper-Medium- and Large-sized countries (55.1% and 73.5%, respectively).

These findings for per capita incomes are rather different to similar exercises undertaken prior to the 2008 global economic crisis (e.g. Armstrong *et al.*, 1998; Armstrong and Read, 2004) in which small economies with populations below 3 million were markedly over-represented in the High-Income category. There are two complementary explanations for this deterioration in their income performance. First, the stratification of the country data may have removed an implicit selection bias in the choice of the exogenous size threshold. Second, growth and per capita incomes in many small economies were severely affected by the crisis through its adverse impacts on two key sectors of their activity, financial services and tourism. This has meant that their position relative to larger economies has deteriorated significantly. In spite of the enduring impact of the global crisis however, variations in per capita income stratified by country size suggest that both Small- and Lower-Medium-sized countries still tend to outperform larger ones. The generally weakly positive relationship between incomes and wellbeing identified in the empirical literature suggests that Small- and Lower-Medium-size countries are therefore also likely to enjoy greater wellbeing.

The findings here for income per capita need to be considered in the context of the conceptual and empirical literature on small economies. The general consensus is that they face unique growth challenges that arise as a direct consequence of their small size. Many of these challenges result from the smaller scale and consequently higher unit costs of domestic activities compared with larger economies. These higher unit costs impose critical constraints on the structure and composition of domestic output in small economies, the provision of key services and the composition and pattern of their international trade; all of which have important implications for their growth potential and policy-making autonomy. Much of the conceptual literature therefore presumes that small economies will tend to *under-perform* relative to larger economies in terms of both their growth performance and per capita incomes.

In spite of small economies facing undoubted challenges however, empirical analyses find little or no evidence to support the view that their size has a systematically negative effect on growth and incomes (see, Armstrong *et al.*, 1998; Armstrong and Read, 2000, 2001, 2004; Easterly and Kraay, 2000; Milner and Westaway, 1993; Read *et al.*, 2012; Rose, 2006). Several factors are proposed in the literature in response to this lack of supporting evidence and to explain the counter-intuitive strong growth performance and high per capita incomes of many small economies (see, for example, Armstrong and Read, 1998, 2003; Briguglio, 1995; Read *et al.*, 2012; Robinson 1960). Notable among these are the adeptness of small economies at identifying growth opportunities and their design and implementation of highly effective growth-promoting strategies (see Armstrong and Read, 2002; Baldacchino and Milne, 1999; Kakazu, 1994; Marcy, 1960; Scitovsky, 1960). Further, the quality of institutions and optimal policy design are identified in new growth theory as playing a critical role in promoting good governance and facilitating growth (e.g. Acemoglou *et al.*, 2001, 2005; Sachs and Warner, 1995, 1997;). Most small economies certainly appear to have avoided the significant policy errors and policy inertia that have plagued the growth paths of many larger economies.

5 Country Size, Human Development and Wellbeing

Simple monetary measures of income are not necessarily a good indicator of actual wellbeing. Health and education, for example, are among the key wellbeing goals highlighted by Wilson (1967). The non-income UNDP Human Development Index (HDI) incorporates measures of life expectancy and educational attainment (mean years of schooling etc.) although wellbeing can be argued to be more specifically concerned with the realization of outcomes of health and education expenditure, notably quality of life and educational opportunities. Nevertheless, non-income HDI is a superior measure to simple income data and the scores can be regarded as a proxy to evaluate these dimensions of wellbeing and the extent of their variation between countries. This section therefore investigates the relationship between country size and well-being, based upon UNDP HDI scores.

HDI scores are calculated annually as weighted indices of economic and non-economic human development indicators, comprising; life expectancy, mean school years of education, expected years of education and GNI per capita. These are combined to produce a continuous index score ranging from zero to one. Countries are then grouped according to their index score into four categories – Very High, High, Medium and Low. The index also has two other forms: non-income HDI, which excludes GNI per capita and covers 186 countries but is only available for 2012; and inequality-adjusted HDI, available for 2013, which covers 132 countries, but omits many small economies. The analysis here uses non-income HDI because it includes education and health but excludes per capita incomes which have already been addressed separately in the previous section. Non-income HDI scores are based upon WHO and UNESCO data and, while not directly reflecting national expenditure on these sectors, the outcomes can be expected to be positively correlated with income. Variations between countries at similar income levels however, are likely to reflect differing blends of national political and social objectives.

The official categories are not used here because they have different ranges of magnitude and there are large variations in the number of countries in each category. Instead, the non-income HDI quartile ranges are stratified here so that each category contains the same number of countries; although the index ranges still differ (the ranges are given in Table 19.3, Note 2). The actual non-income HDI scores range from 0.313 (Niger) to 0.978 (Australia), with an overall mean score of 0.694 (120 states above and 67 below) and a median of 0.751 (Colombia) (UNDP, 2014). The results of the analysis of the non-income HDI by country size quartile are shown in Table 19.3, using the same methodology as in Table 19.2.

It can be seen from Table 19.3 that the pattern of non-income HDI scores broadly resembles those for per capita incomes (Table 19.2). The values for Large-sized countries all lie within the

Table 19.3 Classification of countries by (non-income) HDI, 2012

UNDP *HDI group*	*Total* *No.*	*(%)*	*Large*[1] *No.*	*(%)*	*Upper-Medium* *No.*	*(%)*	*Lower-Medium* *No.*	*(%)*	*Small* *No.*	*(%)*
Lowest quartile[2]	46	24.7	12	26.1	**173**	**37**	10	21.7	**7**	**15.2**
Third quartile	47	25	14	29.8	9	19.1	12	25.5	12	25.5
Second quartile	47	25	11	23.4	**6**	**12.8**	**15**	**31.9**	**15**	**31.9**
Top quartile	46	24.7	11	23.9	14	30.4	12	26.1	9	19.6
Total	*186*	*100*	*48*	*25.8*	*46*	*24.7*	*49*	*26.3*	*43*	*23.1*

Source: UNDP Human Development Indicators, available at https://data.undp.org/dataset/.

Notes: 1. Large: top size quartile; Upper-Medium: second size quartile; Lower-Medium: third size quartile; Small: bottom size quartile.
2. Non-income Human Development Index scores: Lowest quartile < 0.569; Third quartile 0.572 – 0.747; Second quartile 0.751 – 0.835; and Top quartile 0.836 –0.978.
3. Figures in bold indicate group shares that deviate by more than 25% from the expected value; critical ranges for all HDI quartiles: 9–14.

expected range, although the third HDI quartile value lies at the top of its upper bound. Upper-Medium-sized countries however, are notably *under-represented* in the second quartile and notably *over-represented* in the lowest quartile while the third quartile value lies just inside the lower 25% bound. Note that data is not available for three countries in this size quartile; two (South Sudan and Somalia) might be expected to appear in the lowest HDI quartile while Taiwan would be expected to be in the top quartile and would thus render the value of importance. Lower-Medium and Small-sized countries are both notably *over-represented* in the second quartile while the latter are also *under-represented* in the lowest quartile. Small-sized countries also lie just within the lower bound of the top quartile; this is likely to be the result of the omission of Monaco and San Marino, both of which would be expected to feature in this quartile. It is however, rather more difficult to predict the quartile distribution of the other omitted countries in this size category (the Marshall Islands, Nauru and Tuvalu) with any degree of confidence.

These findings suggest that there is a slightly stronger, although still relatively weak, inverse relationship between size and non-income HDI scores than in the case of per capita income. The scores for Small-sized (and, possibly, Lower-Medium-sized) countries however, are particularly marked in the context of health and education. Investment in these public goods is generally regarded as being 'lumpy'; i.e. there are significant unit cost savings from larger scale in these activities. High sunk and fixed costs in education, health and other social services in small economies have important implications for both the magnitude and efficiency of public expenditure – and therefore taxation – since they require a disproportionate share of government expenditure in domestic consumption (see, Alesina and Spolaore, 2003, 2005; Kuznets, 1960). This challenge is compounded by the critical role of education in providing a foundation for comparative advantage and growth in small economies (Armstrong *et al.*, 1998; Bhaduri *et al.*, 1982; Briguglio, 1995).

In this light, the non-income HDI findings are therefore more interesting than they might initially appear. Small- and Lower-Medium-sized countries appear to perform as well as, if not better than, larger countries that are less likely to incur disproportionate sunk and fixed costs in the provision of social goods. On this basis, it is possible to infer that there is a mild inverse relationship between country size and national wellbeing in terms of health and education over and above the effect of income.

The 2013 *Human Development Report* also reports the existence of a strong positive correlation between non-HDI scores and previous government expenditure (UNDP, 2014, Figure 3.2, p. 71). The empirical evidence therefore suggests that smaller economies have not been as heavily constrained by limitations in the scale of their social expenditure as is anticipated in some of the academic literature. Instead, the evidence suggests that these countries have prioritized health and education expenditures relative to their larger counterparts; perhaps unsurprisingly given the importance of human capital in their comparative advantage.

6 Country size, governance and wellbeing

The literature on small economies highlights the role of good quality policy-making institutions and governance as critical determinants of their growth performance, see Section 4. These policies are likely to have their origins in high levels of domestic social capital which, in turn, can be expected to result in greater national happiness and wellbeing, hence their inclusion here as an additional dimension. This section therefore incorporates the governance dimension as an additional goal in wellbeing and happiness, based upon recent data drawn from the World Bank's Worldwide Governance Indicators.

The World Bank's Worldwide Governance Indicators are arguably the most comprehensive statistical measures of governance in terms of the variety of component indicators. Further, this data is transformed across almost the full range from zero to 100 to highlight inter-country differences. All such institutional quality and governance data however, regardless of source, comes with a 'health warning'. The data may encourage spurious accuracy in analysis and conclusions owing to the fact that it is discrete rather than continuous. It should also be borne in mind that virtually all of this data are the outcome of subjective judgements made by expert assessors and may therefore exhibit systematic endogenous bias. Nevertheless, in spite of these caveats, the governance and institutional quality data may still reveal important underlying trends and patterns both across countries and over time.

Social capital is formed by the development of networks of trust and norms of reciprocity that nurture greater communal interaction (Coleman, 1990; Putnam et al., 1993). Small societies are argued to generate greater social cohesion than larger ones and this, in turn, encourages the growth of greater social capital. Societies with greater cohesion and social capital are viewed as having better quality institutions and therefore superior policy design, so engendering higher economic growth. This suggests that there is a positive causal link between social cohesion, good governance and increased national wellbeing in terms of both material income and the participation of individuals in decision-making. Studies of social capital also emphasize the existence of a causal link between social trust and societal happiness and wellbeing (e.g. Delhey and Newton, 2003; Inglehart, 1999; Putnam, 2000). Anthropologists, human geographers and sociologists however, would dispute the existence of such a link given that social preferences are argued to differ spatially according to local economic, environmental, social and cultural contexts. The testing of specific axioms of social values and behaviour in the emergent experimental economics literature provides a counter to this view of spatial variation in social preferences, arguing that ethnography and historical methods do not provide robust evidence of motive as opposed to context (see, for example, Heinrich et al., 2004, 2005).

A case can be made for social capital, governance and institutional quality – and therefore happiness and wellbeing – to be greater in smaller societies. The 'distance' between policy-makers and their constituents tends to be much shorter in terms of their proximity within local social networks. Building upon Hayek's arguments about the limits to social justice within larger societies, this therefore offers greater scope for the exercise of social peer pressure and the creation of reciprocal obligations as well as the promotion of greater communal involvement and consensus in decision-making (Hayek, 1978). House and Wolf (1978) find that trust is likely to be higher in smaller urban units while Putnam notes that 'residents of small towns and rural areas are more altruistic, honest and trusting than other Americans... In fact, even among suburbs, smaller is better from the social capital point of view' (Putnam, 1995: 205).

Several studies analyse the role of institutional links in small economies. Congdon Fors (2007, 2014) finds a significantly positive relationship between small island populations and institutional quality – using the World Bank Rule of Law indicator and Freedom House Political Rights (PR) score. Her analytical focus however, is insularity rather than small country size per se. A number of studies investigate the institutional and growth legacies of former colonial powers, linking with the burgeoning growth literature on this topic (e.g. Acemoglou et al., 2001, 2005; Alesina et al., 2005; Dollar and Kraay, 2003; Rigobon and Rodrik, 2005; Rodrik et al., 2002). Armstrong and Read (2000) find that growth and per capita incomes in (small) non-sovereign territories are greater than in both small and large sovereign economies, even after normalising for metropolitan fiscal transfers. Further, many small economies appear to remain highly dependent upon traditional trade, capital, migration and institutional linkages with former metropolitan countries (Bertram, 2004; Gibson and Nero, 2007).

The World Bank's Worldwide Governance Indicators cover six dimensions of governance: Voice and Accountability; Political Stability and Absence of Violence; Government Effectiveness; Regulatory Quality; Rule of Law; and Control of Corruption (Kaufmann *et al.*, 2010). Each indicator is calculated for a maximum of 196 economies and presented as a percentile rank (0–100), with the first ranked country given a value of 100, the median a value of approximately 50 and the lowest close to zero, with the other quartile values close to 75 and 25, respectively. The six indicators are aggregated here to produce a single unweighted mean score for each country. These range from 98.4 for Finland to 0.3 for Somalia. Monaco and San Marino are also included using observations for just three of the component indicators in order to maximize the data set covered. The mean of the aggregate mean scores is 47.77, the median 46.50 and the standard deviation 26.46. The results are presented in Table 19.4, using the same methodology as in Tables 19.2 and 19.3.

The data in the table are particularly striking in that three quarters (12 out of 16) of the quartile values lie outside the critical expected range. Small-sized countries are notably *over-represented* in the upper two governance quartiles and notably *under-represented* in the lower two; in fact, 36 out of 49 of these countries (73.5%) feature in the upper two quartiles. The scores for Large-sized countries are almost the exact opposite; they are notably *under-represented* in the upper two quartiles and notably *over-represented* in the lower two; 33 out of 49 of these countries (67.3%) feature in the lower half of the distribution. Upper-Medium-sized economies are also notably *under-represented* in the second quartile, lie close to the lower bound in the top quartile, are notably *over-represented* in the lowest quartile and are close to the upper bound in the third quartile. Lower-Medium-sized countries are notably *over-represented* in the second quartile and notably *under-represented* in the third quartile. A majority of these countries (29 out of 49–59.2%) also feature in the upper two quartiles. This evidence therefore strongly suggests that levels of wellbeing, in terms of governance and institutional quality, are markedly greater in smaller countries and generally *inversely* related to country size. In spite of this measure being a single composite dimension of governance and institutional quality, there appears to be a strong underlying causal link with the other dimensions of wellbeing and happiness investigated here; notably incomes, health and education.

The governance scores reveal stark contrasts between countries according to their size. There appears to be a consistent and marked inverse relationship between population size and

Table 19.4 Classification of countries by mean aggregate governance, 2013

Worldwide Governance Indicators	Total		Large		Upper-Medium		Lower-Medium		Small	
	No.	(%)	No.	(%)	No.	(%)	No.	(%)	No.	(%)
Lowest quartile	49	25	**17**	**34.7**	**17**	**34.7**	11	22.4	**4**	**8.2**
Third quartile	49	25	**16**	**32.7**	15	30.6	**9**	**18.4**	9	18.4
Second quartile	49	25	7	**14.3**	7	**14.3**	**16**	**32.7**	**19**	**38.8**
Top quartile	49	25	9	**18.4**	10	20.4	13	26.5	**17**	**34.7**
Total	196	100	49	25.0	49	25.0	49	25.0	49	25.0

Source: World Bank, Worldwide Governance Indicators, available at http://info.worldbank.org/governance/.

Figures in bold indicate group shares that deviate by more than 25% from the expected value. The critical ranges for all Governance Indicator quartiles are 10–15.

governance that is substantially more pronounced than in the case of either per capita income or human development. The data suggest that Small- and, to some extent, Lower-Medium-sized countries enjoy systematically better quality governance and, by implication, wellbeing than do larger (i.e. Large- and Upper-Medium-sized) countries. These results provide further support for Rigobon and Rodrik (2005), who find a weak positive relationship between social capital and economic performance as well as a significant negative relationship between population size and democratic institutions. They also contrast with Knack and Keefer (1997), who find little evidence of a positive impact of social capital on economic performance, albeit for a very limited sample of only 29 mainly large countries (with the exception of Iceland and Ireland). The latter's results and conclusions might also reflect persistent income disparities that limit the benefits of growth. The results presented here also provide a counterweight to the generally prevailing ethnographic view that small countries are more prone to rent-seeking behaviour and clientelism.

The evidence here provides additional empirical support for the view that the quality of institutions and governance in small economies surpass those in larger ones by necessity. Small economies have considerably less scope for policy inertia than do larger ones, where divisive and/ or mis-specified economic and social policies may persist, to the detriment of their long-term growth performance. The greater exposure of these countries to global economic conditions, owing to their high structural openness to trade, necessitates greater policy flexibility. Good governance aided by high quality institutions therefore facilitates rapid responses to sudden changes in external economic conditions, since any adverse effects of policy errors on growth and income are likely to be felt very quickly. It is also possible to infer that institutional quality and good governance are additional countervailing factors that enable small economies to deal with some of the challenges associated with their size. These findings also chime well with Kohr's advocacy of the superiority of small societies and nations over larger ones (Kohr, 1957).

A further determinant of the quality of social capital, institutions, governance, economic growth and therefore wellbeing in small economies may be their lower levels of ethnic and linguistic fractionalization. This fractionalization is low in many, but by no means all, small economies although there is little evidence to suggest that more homogeneous societies necessarily have greater cohesion (Alesina et al., 2005; Armstrong and Read, 2003). Small economies may also be more prone to rent-seeking behaviour and clientelism owing to the closer personal and kinship links between policy-makers and constituents (see Anckar, 2002; Armstrong and Read, 1998; Veenendaal, 2013).

An additional insight to be derived from the current study is the apparent under-performance of larger economies (both Large- and Upper-Medium-sized) in terms of growth, per capita incomes, human development and wellbeing. This complementary reverse interpretation of the evidence on country size and growth performance is highlighted in several previous studies (Armstrong et al., 1998; Armstrong and Read, 2000, 2001). The key research question then becomes why larger economies perform so poorly. The answer with respect to social capital, governance and institutions may lie, at least partly, with the greater disconnect between policy-makers and constituents. This disconnect is also likely to be exacerbated by the more limited exposure of larger economies to the full rigours of global economic conditions because of their lower degree of openness to trade and consequently less need for policy flexibility and agility.

7 Country size, happiness and wellbeing

The discussion of institutional quality and governance raises the intriguing issue as to whether the greater flexibility and responsiveness of small economies means that they therefore have a greater predisposition to target and achieve additional wellbeing goals. If this is indeed the case, it might be inferred that small economies might also be expected to exhibit greater across-the-board levels of wellbeing and happiness than larger economies. This section therefore analyzes the relationship between happiness and country size using UNDP data.

The UNDP *Human Development Report* publishes several country-level Social Integration measures relevant to happiness and wellbeing (UNDP, 2014, Table 9). The dimension most relevant to the discussion here is 'Overall Life Satisfaction, 2007–11', part of Perceptions of Individual Wellbeing. These scores are drawn from Gallup survey data and range from zero to ten, with individuals' scores representing the worst and best possible lives for themselves (Gallup, 2012). Data are available for 149 countries, with some 36 out of the total of 47 countries omitted belonging to the Small-size category (76.6%). This very severe data truncation is not unusual in the analysis of small economies but means that the results here for Small-sized countries should be interpreted with considerable caution.

The findings for the relationship between Overall Life Satisfaction (OLS) scores and country size are shown in Table 19.5. The number of countries in each OLS quartile is relatively similar but the country size quartiles are highly skewed owing to data being available for only 13 out of 49 (26.5%) Small-sized countries. The critical ranges are therefore calculated vertically. The data reveal that the distribution of Large- and Lower-Medium-sized countries across the OLS quartiles is essentially random. Three of these values however, lie just within their respective critical bounds; Large-sized countries in the two lowest OLS quartiles and Lower–Medium-sized ones in the bottom OLS quartile. The results however, are markedly different with respect to Upper–Medium- and Small-sized countries. The former are notably *under-represented* in the second OLS quartile, notably *over-represented* in the bottom quartile and lie at the lower bound of the top quartile. All four values for Small-sized countries however, are markedly different; they are notably *over-represented* in the top two quartiles and notably *under-represented* in the bottom two. These findings suggest that, for Upper–Medium- and Small-sized countries at least, there exists some form of important inverse relationship between Overall Life Satisfaction and country size. Extreme care however, must be exercised in placing too much emphasis on the results for the Small-size category given the paucity of the relevant data.

The OLS data appear to provide an appropriate global cross-section of levels of happiness and wellbeing for the period 2007 to 2011. The data however, are somewhat inadequate for the

Table 19.5 Classification of countries by overall life satisfaction, 2007–11

OLS group	Total No.	(%)	Large No.	(%)	Upper-Medium No.	(%)	Lower-Medium No.	(%)	Small No.	Share (%)
Lowest quartile	39	26.2	9	23.1	**19**	**48.7**	9	23.1	**2**	**5.1**
Third quartile	37	24.8	14	37.8	10	27	12	32.4	**1**	**2.7**
Second quartile	35	23.5	12	34.3	**7**	**20**	11	31.4	**5**	**14.3**
Top quartile	38	25.5	12	31.6	9	23.7	12	31.6	**5**	**13.2**
Total	*149*	*100*	*47*	*31.5*	*45*	*30.2*	*44*	*29.5*	*13*	*8.7*

Source: UNDP. Human Development Indicators, Available at: https://data.undp.org/dataset/.

Figures in bold indicate group shares that deviate by more than 25% from the expected value; critical ranges for OLS quartiles: Large-sized quartile, 9–14; Upper Medium-sized quartile, 9–15; Lower Medium-sized quartile, 9–14; Small-sized quartile, 3–5.

purposes of this study given the severely truncated nature of the country coverage at the lower end of the size distribution. Nevertheless, several intriguing findings can be elicited from the available data regarding the relationship between country size and happiness and wellbeing. This relationship appears to be weaker than in the cases of both per capita income and non-income HDI, with the exception of Small-sized countries. Again, this fits somewhat with the general empirical findings in the literature that the relationship between per capita income and happiness and wellbeing is positive although weak (e.g. Oswald, 1997). There is however, a much more pronounced inverse relationship between country size and happiness and wellbeing in the case of Upper-Medium-sized countries which is very similar to the findings for governance. Upper-Medium-sized countries feature disproportionately in the lowest OLS quartile and are either notably under-represented or close to the lower bounds of the critical 25% threshold in all three remaining quartiles. One final proviso relates to the interpretation of the cross-country scores for Overall Life Satisfaction. These may be influenced by additional unincorporated exogenous factors that are not directly connected with happiness and wellbeing; possibly including the effects of conflict, natural disaster and domestic political upheaval.

Many researchers continue to exclude many very small countries from their cross-country analyses or lack sufficient confidence to work with limited data sets and so tend to ignore the critical issues arising from the use of severely truncated data. The evidence here provides a strong inference that levels of happiness and wellbeing in countries are inversely correlated with population size although further investigation requires more comprehensive cross-country data if robust conclusions are to be derived.

8 Summary and conclusions

This chapter investigates the relationship between country size and several dimensions of wellbeing, namely, incomes, health and education, governance and happiness. The goals of happiness and wellbeing are complementary to income, health, education and broader life satisfaction with respect to family, employment and socio-political environment. The dataset of 196 sovereign countries is stratified into four equal population quartiles, so endogenizing the determination of the size thresholds and avoiding pitfalls associated with imposing essentially arbitrary exogenous classifications on continuous data.

The analysis of happiness and wellbeing with respect to per capita incomes finds that many Small- and Lower-Medium-sized countries continue to feature in the top two World Bank Income groups in spite of their being particularly adversely affected by the 2008 crisis. There appears to be a generally positive but weak inverse relationship between size and wellbeing overall with respect to per capita incomes. Small-sized countries however, are notably under-represented in the two lower World Bank Income categories while Lower-Medium-sized countries are notably over-represented in the Upper-Middle income category and notably under-represented in the Lower-Middle one.

The non-income HDI scores reveal a stronger apparent inverse relationship between size and wellbeing in terms of health and education than in the case of GNI per capita. Both Small- and Lower-Medium-sized countries are notably over-represented in the second HDI quartile while the former are also notably under-represented in the lowest HDI quartile. These findings provide an important caveat to the view that the provision of public goods in smaller economies encounters critical cost limitations arising from small scale. In fact, the evidence here appears to suggest that small countries actually outperform larger ones with respect to the provision of high quality health and education services.

Good governance is incorporated and analysed here as an additional dimension of happiness and wellbeing using The World Bank's Worldwide Governance Indicators. Governance is regarded in growth theory as a critical factor in the determination of growth-promoting policy choices and outcomes that affect national wellbeing as well as being key contributor to the growth success of small economies. The findings reveal marked systematic differences in governance scores between countries according to their size. Small-sized countries are notably over-represented in the upper two governance quartiles and notably under-represented in the lower two while Lower-Medium-sized countries are notably over-represented in the second quartile and notably under-represented in the third. A substantial majority of countries in both the Small- and Lower-Medium-sized quartiles therefore feature in the upper half of the governance score distribution. The overarching inference that can be drawn therefore is that there exists a marked inverse relationship between country size and good governance. This relationship appears to be considerably stronger than in the case of the other dimensions of wellbeing that are addressed here.

The relationship between country size and happiness is investigated using UNDP Overall Life Satisfaction scores, although this dataset is severely truncated at the lower end of the distribution. While care therefore needs to be exercised in interpreting the findings, Small-sized countries are still notably over-represented in the two upper OLS quartiles and notably under-represented in the lower two. Lower-Medium-sized countries however, appear to be distributed more randomly. This provides tentative further support for the existence of an inverse relationship between national wellbeing and country size.

It is evident that there exists some degree of correlation between per capita incomes, health and education, happiness and wellbeing and institutional quality and good governance. The direction of causation however, is not immediately apparent and its analysis is beyond the scope of this study. Good governance and institutional quality certainly exercise a critical influence over national policy formulation and implementation, regardless of country size, and so play a key role in the attainment of many wellbeing goals. The determinants of good governance and institutional quality however, remain the subject of intense debate in the academic and policy literature. The inverse relationship found here between country size and various dimensions of wellbeing raises important new and intriguing questions regarding its determinants.

The evidence presented in this chapter provides further empirical support for the long-held view that small economies have better quality governance, institutions and social capital (e.g. Anckar, 2002; Armstrong and Read, 1998; Briguglio, 1995; Congdon Fors, 2007, 2014) and, by implication, greater wellbeing. Governance, institutions and social capital are all identified as being critical 'conditioning' variables in the economic growth literature such that their contribution to growth and wellbeing in small economies merits further investigation. The strong performance of small economies here with respect to these key variables can be seen to be the conscious outcome of the need for optimal policy formulation given the challenges imposed by their size rather than being purely fortuitous. Greater levels of happiness and wellbeing in small economies may therefore simply reflect the success of these growth policies.

A final comment relates to the limited availability of comprehensive comparable international data. This continues to be a major constraint on the rigorous analysis of a wide range of important issues for small economies.

Note

1 This research is part of an extensive research project on the growth of small economies and the role of governance and institutions being undertaken by the author. Earlier drafts of this paper were presented

at the Workshop on Development & Wellbeing, Richmond University, London, 6 June 2014 and the International Workshop On Island Challenges, Samos, 1–3 October 2014. The author is grateful to insightful and constructive comments from participants at both workshops and, in particular, Parviz Dabir and Sabine Spangenberg (Richmond), Sven Wagner (Sails for Science, Samos) and Dorothea Schell (Samos). The revised chapter has also greatly benefited from detailed comments by Beate Ratter (Universität Hamburg) and Anthony Buckley (Dublin Institute of Technology). All errors of interpretation and fact however, remain the sole responsibility of the author.

References

Acemoglou, D., Johnson, S. and Robinson, J. A. (2001). 'The colonial origins of comparative development: an empirical investigation'. *American Economic Review*, 91(5): 1369–1401.

Acemoglou, D., Johnson, S. and Robinson, J. A. (2005). Institutions as a fundamental cause of long-run growth. In Aghion, P. and Durlauf, S. N. (eds) *Handbook of Economic Growth*, Vol. 1, Part A: 385–472. Amsterdam: Elsevier.

Alesina, A. and Spolaore, E. (2003). *The Size of Nations*. Cambridge, MA: MIT Press.

Alesina, A. and Spolaore, E. (2005). 'War, peace and the size of countries'. *Journal of Public Economics*, 89(7): 1333–1354.

Alesina, A., Spolaore, E. and Wacziarg, R. (2005). Trade, growth and the size of countries. In Aghion, P. and Durlauf, S. N. (eds) *Handbook of International Growth*, Vol. 1, Part B: 1499–1542. Amsterdam: Elsevier.

Anckar, D. (2002). Why are small island states democracies? *The Round Table*, XCI(365): 375–390.

Armstrong, H. W., de Kervenoael, R. J., Li, X. and Read, R. (1998). 'A comparison of the economic performance of different micro-states and between micro-states and larger countries'. *World Development*, 26(4): 639–656.

Armstrong, H. W. and Read, R. (1998). 'Trade and growth in small states: the impact of global trade liberalisation'. *The World Economy*, 21(4): 563–585.

Armstrong, H. W. and Read, R. (2000). 'Comparing the economic performance of dependent territories and sovereign micro-states'. *Economic Development & Cultural Change*, 48(2): 285–306.

Armstrong, H. W. and Read, R. (2001). Explaining differences in the economic performance of micro-states in Africa and Asia. In Lawrence, P. and Thirtle, C. (eds) *Africa & Asia in Comparative Development*: 128–157. Basingstoke: Palgrave.

Armstrong, H. W. and Read, R. (2002). The importance of being unimportant: the political economy of trade and growth in small states. In Murshed, S. M. (ed.) *Issues in Positive Political Economy*: 71–88. London: Routledge.

Armstrong, H. W. and Read, R. (2003). The determinants of economic growth in small states. *The Round Table*, XCII (368): 99–124.

Armstrong, H. W. and Read, R. (2004). Small states and small island states: implications of size, location and isolation for prosperity. In Poot, J. (ed.), *On the Edge of the Global Economy: Implications of Economic Geography for Small & Medium-Sized Economies at Peripheral Locations*: 191–223. Cheltenham: Edward Elgar.

Baldacchino, G. and Milne, D. (eds) (1999). *A Political Economy for Small Islands: the Resourcefulness of Jurisdiction*. Basingstoke: Macmillan.

Bertram, G. (2004). 'On the convergence of small island economies with their metropolitan patrons'. *World Development*, 32(2): 343–364.

Bhaduri, A., Mukherji, A. and Sengupta, R. (1982). Problems of long-term growth in small economies: a theoretical analysis. In Jalan, B. (ed.). *Problems & Policies in Small Economies*: 49–68. Beckenham: Croom Helm, for the Commonwealth Secretariat.

Briguglio, L. (1995). 'Small island developing states and their economic vulnerabilities'. *World Development*, 23(10): 1615–1632.

Coleman, J. S. (1990). *Foundations of Social Theory*. London: Belknap Press.

Congdon Fors, H. (2007). Island status, country size and institutional quality of former colonies. *Working Papers in Economics*, No. 257. Handelshogskolan: Göteborg University.

Congdon Fors, H. (2014). 'Do island states have better institutions?'. *Journal of Comparative Economics*, 42(1): 34–60.

Cummins, R. A. (2010). 'Subjective wellbeing, homeostatically protected mood and depression: a synthesis'. *Journal of Happiness Studies*, 11(1): 1–17.

Cummins, R. A. (2012). 'The determinants of happiness'. *International Journal of Happiness & Development*, 1(1): 86–101.

Delhey, J. and Newton, K. (2003). 'Who trusts? The origins of social trust in seven societies'. *European Societies*, 5(2): 93–137.

Diener, E. (1984). 'Subjective well-being'. *Psychological Bulletin*, 95: 542–575.

Diener, E., Suh, E. M., Lucas, R. E. and Smith, H. L. (1999). 'Subjective well-being: Three decades of progress'. *Psychological Bulletin*, 125(2): 276–302.

Di Tella, R., MacCulloch, R. J. and Oswald, A. J. (2003). 'The macroeconomics of happiness'. *The Review of Economics & Statistics*, 85(4): 809–827.

Dollar, D. and Kraay, A. (2003). 'Institutions, trade and growth'. *Journal of Monetary Economics*, 50(1): 133–162.

Easterlin, R. (1974). Does economic growth improve the human lot? Some empirical evidence. In David, P. A. and Reder, M. W. (eds) *Nations & Households in Economic Growth: Essays in Honour of Moses Ambramowitz*. London: Academic Press.

Easterlin, R. (1995). 'Will raising the incomes of all increase the happiness of all?'. *Journal of Economic Behaviour & Organization*, 27(1): 35–47.

Easterly, W. and Kraay, A. (2000). 'Small states, small problems? Income growth and volatility in small states'. *World Development*, 28(11): 2013–2027.

Gallup (2012). *Gallup World Poll Database*. Available at https://worldview.gallup.com, accessed 15 June 2015.

Gibson, J. and Nero, K. L. (2007). *Are Pacific Island Economies Growth Failures? Geo-Political Assessments & Failures*. Report for The Pasifika Project. Victoria University of Wellington: Institute for Policy Studies.

Harari, Y. N. (2015). *Sapiens: A Brief History of Humankind*. London: Harvill Secker.

Hayek, F. A. (1978). The atavism of social justice. In *New Studies in Philosophy, Politics, Economics & the History of Ideas*: 57–68. Chicago, IL: University of Chicago Press. Originally delivered as the 9th R.C. Mills Memorial Lecture at the University of Sydney, 6 October 1976.

Heinrich, J., Boyd, R., Bowles, S., Camerer, C., Fehr, E. and Gintis, H. (eds). (2004). *Foundations of Human Sociality: Economic Experiments & Ethnographic Evidence from Fifteen Small-Scale Societies*. Oxford: Oxford University Press.

Heinrich, J., Boyd, R., Bowles, S., Camerer, C., Fehr, E., Gintis, H., McElreath, R., Alvard, M., Barr, A., Ensminger, J., Smith, N., Hill, K., Gil-White, F., Gurven, M., Marlowe, F. W., Patton, J. Q., and Tracer, D. F. (2005). '"Economic man" in cross-cultural perspective: behavioural experiments in 15 small-scale societies'. *Behavioural & Brain Sciences*, 28(6): 795–855.

House, J. S. and Wolf, S. (1978). 'Effects of urban residence on inter-personal trust and helping behaviour'. *Journal of Personality & Social Psychology*, 36: 1029–1043.

Inglehart, R. (1999). Trust, well-being and democracy. In Warren, M. E. (ed.) *Democracy & Trust*: 88–120. Cambridge: Cambridge University Press.,

Kakazu, H. (1994). *Sustainable Development in Small Island Economies*. New York: Westview Press.

Kaufmann, D., Kraay, A. and Mastruzzi, M. (2010). *The Worldwide Governance Indicators: Methodology & Analytical Issues*. Available at www.govindicators.org/.

Knack, S. and Keefer, P. (1997). 'Does social capital have an economic payoff? A cross-country investigation'. *Quarterly Journal of Economics*, 112(4): 1251–1288.

Kohr, L. (1957). *The Breakdown of Nations*. London: Routledge & Kegan Paul.

Kuznets, S. (1960). The economic growth of small states. In Robinson, E.A.G. (ed.), *The Economic Consequences of the Size of Nations*: 14–32. London: Macmillan.

Leibniz, G. (1710). *Essays On the Goodness of God, the Freedom of Man & the Origin of Evil*.

Marcy, G. (1960). How far can foreign trade and customs agreements confer upon small nations the advantages of larger nations?. In Robinson, E.A.G. (ed.), *The Economic Consequences of the Size of Nations*: 265–281. London: Macmillan.

Michalos, A. C. (1985). 'Multiple discrepancies theory (MDT)'. *Social Indicators Research*, 16(4): 347–413.

Milner, C. R. and Westaway, T. (1993). 'Country size and the medium-term growth process: some cross-country evidence'. *World Development*, 21(2): 203–212.

Oswald, A.J. (1997). 'Happiness and economic performance'. *The Economic Journal*, 107(455): 1815–1831.

Putnam, R. D. (1995). 'Bowling alone: America's declining social capital'. *Journal of Democracy*, 6(1): 65–78.

Putnam, R. D. (2000). *Bowling Alone: The Collapse & Revival of American Community*. New York: Simon & Schuster.

Putnam, R. D., with Leonardi, R. and Nanetti, R. Y. (1993). *Making Democracy Work: Civic Traditions in Modern Italy*. Princeton, NJ: Princeton University Press.

Read, R., with Armstrong, H. W. and Picarelli, N. (2012). *Binding Growth Constraints in Small Island Economies: Evidence Focusing On the Organisation of Eastern Caribbean States*. Report for the Latin American & Caribbean Section. Washington, DC: The World Bank.

Rigobon, R. and Rodrik, D. (2005). 'Rule of law, democracy, openness and income: Estimating the inter-relationships'. *Economics of Transition*, 13(3): 533–564.

Robinson, E.A.G. (1960). The size of nation and the cost of administration. In Robinson, E. A. G. (ed.), *The Economic Consequences of the Size of Nations*: 223–240. London: Macmillan.

Rodrik, D., Subramanian, A. and Trebbi, F. (2002). *Institutions rule: The primacy of institutions over geography and integration in economic development*. NBER Working Paper, No. 9305. Cambridge, MA. Revised version, *Journal of Economic Growth*, 9(2): 131–165.

Rose, A. K. (2006). 'Size doesn't really matter: in search of a national scale effect'. *Journal of the Japanese & International Economies*, 20(4): 482–507.

Sachs, J. D. and Warner, A. M. (1995). *Economic convergence and economic policies*. NBER Working Paper, 5039. Washington, DC: National Bureau for Economic Research.

Sachs, J. D. and Warner, A. M. (1997). 'Fundamental sources of long-run growth'. *American Economic Review*, 87(2): 184–188.

Scitovsky, T. (1960). International trade and economic integration as a means of overcoming the disadvantages of a small nation. In Robinson, E. A. G. (ed.), *The Economic Consequences of the Size of Nations*: 282–290. London: Macmillan.

UNDP (2014). *Human Development Report, 2013, The Rise of the South: Human Progress in a Diverse World*. New York: UNDP.

Veenendaal, W. P. (2013). 'Democracy in microstates: why smallness doesn't produce democratic systems'. *Democratization*, 22(1): 92–112.

Voltaire (1759). *Candide*. London: Penguin Classics.

Wilson, W. (1967). 'Correlations of avowed happiness'. *Psychological Bulletin*, 67(4): 294–306.

Wood, J. V. (1996). 'What is social comparison and how should we study it?' *Personality & Social Psychology Bulletin*, 22(5): 520–537.

20

The effects of skilled emigration on small island nations

Satish Chand

1 Introduction

David Thoules, Duncan Haldane, and Michael Kosterlitz, the joint recipients of the 2016 Nobel prize in topology are the 'products of 20th Century 'brain-drain' that saw British-born researchers head west to the larger salaries and better laboratories of America'.[1] Britain is an island nation that has witnessed emigration of talent to the much larger United States of America. The migration of talent from small to large nations and to centres of innovation illustrates the importance of economic geography in driving productivity. Economic geography is an issue that mainstream economics ignored until Fujita *et al.* (2001) analysed the impact of the interaction between increasing returns, transport costs, and the movement of capital and labour on the spatial distribution of productivity. Kerr *et al.* (2016: 86) note that 70% of all high skilled emigrants to the OECD move to four Anglo-Saxon nations, the United States, the United Kingdom, Canada, and Australia. As of 2013, foreign-born software engineers constituted 70% of the total in Silicon Valley alone (ibid.: 86). How does the emigration of talent from small nations affect the source community? Is this a loss and, if so, what can be done to mitigate the costs of skilled emigration? These are the questions I attempt to answer in this chapter.

Small island nations experience high rates of emigration (Kerr *et al.*, 2016: 637). Beine *et al.* (2008) report 'a clear decreasing relationship between emigration rates and country size, with average emigration rates being about 7 times higher for small countries (with population lower than 2.5 million) than for large countries'. Britain is an island nation but it is not small in terms of population or GDP. However, the emigration of talent to the larger United States of America is indicative of a more general phenomenon of skills agglomeration and the benefits to the talented individual from the move. Note that I treat talent as being synonymous with skills on the assumption that latent talent is refined and revealed through nurture. Did Great Britain lose from this particular incidence of 'brain drain'? I use the case of small nations experiencing high rates of emigration of their skilled and tertiary-trained to throw light on the implications for those left behind.

Emigration would be Pareto improving if it raises the welfare of the emigrant without adversely affecting the welfare of anyone else. In the case where the decision to emigrate is made voluntarily, and with full information, the migrant must benefit from the movement. Assessing the effects on the source and host communities however has proved to be a lot more difficult. Comparisons to trade in goods where there is consensus within the extant literature that it increases the size of global GDP and that of the participating nations is instructive. Borjas (2015), for example, estimates that migration raises global GDP but notes the unequal distribution of these benefits between source and destination nations. A world free of borders delivers some 40 trillion US dollars in global GDP but with the movement of some 95% of the population of the developing world (numbering 5.6 billion individuals) to the developed world. This movement, according to the estimates from the model, leads to a redistribution of wealth from the workers in the North to the migrants from the South and to the owners of capital.

The distributional effects of migration on host communities revolves around estimates of the effect of immigration on the wages of natives: Card (1990) estimates these effects to be small while Borjas (2006) argues otherwise. Borjas (2015: 970) has further argued that: 'the gains from unrestricted immigration depend largely on how the infrastructure in the receiving economies adjusts to the influx of perhaps billions of persons'. The focus of this chapter being skilled emigrants from small island nations who are likely to number in the thousands implies that the wage effects in host nations are likely to be small. I will therefore ignore the wage effects of emigration on host communities. However, the wage effects of emigration at source can be large when emigrants constitute a large proportion of the workforce. In the case of Samoa (and Tonga), for example, some 76% (75%) of the tertiary trained locals emigrate (World Bank, 2016: 45).

The effect of emigration on source communities is through the stock of human capital left behind. The question is whether skilled emigration leads to a depletion of human capital, that is 'brain drain', at source. This question was first raised by Grubel and Scott (1966), and remains to be resolved some 50 years on. While on the one hand skilled emigration can lead to loss of skills for the source nation, it also provides the incentives for investment into education, which has the opposite effect – meaning that the net effect depends on which of the above dominates. Note that the incentives to invest in education are large in low wage nations, particularly in the presence of opportunities to emigrate. This is because the opportunity cost of spending time in tertiary training is low whist the potential gains from skilled emigration are large. Funding education in poor nations could be a problem to which remittances from those departed can be a solution, leading to a virtuous cycle of remittance-fuelled skilled emigration.

Emigration is critical to incentivizing investment into the acquisition of skills in small economies. This is because the opportunities for employment of skilled workers in small economies are limited. The geographic concentration of industry, which is possible only in large nations, allows for the supply of specialized inputs, lends the opportunity for employment of talent, and provides the competitive conditions for innovation (Fujita and Thisse, 2013). Consequently, industrial clusters in large nations are able to employ and remunerate those with highly specialized skills. A gifted nuclear scientist, as an example, is unlikely to be able to use all of her skills if left behind in a distant small island nation. Employment options are further constrained in a small nation by a relatively large public sector that has a pervasive presence in the marketplace.

My focus in this chapter is on the economic effects of emigration on small island nations: 'small' being defined arbitrarily by various authors as having populations less than 1 million, 2 million, or 3 million. Regardless of the ceiling and source of analysis, however, the evidence is that small nations experience high rates of emigration compared to large nations. The potential gains to the small nation in the form of income, employment, and return of talent in contrast are large. I argue that skilled emigration creates special problems for small nations but it also offers the opportunity to raise income and welfare of the source community.

The rest of this chapter is structured as follows. Section 2. presents some of the basic facts on emigration, Section 3. provides the analytical framework, Section 4. presents the evidence, while policy implications and conclusion bring the chapter to a close.

2 Why do islanders emigrate?

Humans have moved throughout recorded history and islanders are not an exception to this rule. If anything, prehistoric humans who first reached the islands did so through the ingenuity of crossing vast expenses of oceans using rudimentary technology. It is highly unlikely that you, the reader, have remained within the village (or country) of your birth. It is therefore instructive to think of the reasons why you moved when exploring reasons why people in general move. The answer to this question is likely to be different for every individual, but common themes emerge when comparing across individuals. I will provide a very brief exposition of my own reasons for moving to give you an opportunity to contrast this with yours.

I was born in a small village in rural Fiji where my folks grew sugarcane – some one hundred tons annually, which provided them an income around the poverty line. I attended the village primary school and then the nearest high school, which was a daily commute of 10 kilometres. A national scholarship gave the opportunity to attend university in the capital, Suva. This was the first of the many moves I have made since. Graduation from university secured me a teaching position in a remote part of Fiji; this was the second episode of packing the bags for a new home while a subsequent scholarship brought me back to Suva for further studies and an academic career. By then I was married and had a child, and Fiji had suffered its first coup d'état. A third scholarship for doctoral studies soon afterwards meant that I had to leave with the family for Australia where I have remained since. Australia and Fiji are both home, and I continue to support family in both nations. There is little doubt in my mind that these move-ments have benefitted me and my (extended) family, but what for those others left behind in the village or in Fiji?

My decision to hop from one place to another was driven largely by considerations of edu-cation and employment. It was the three scholarships that provided the means to move from the village to Suva and subsequently to Canberra, while it was employment that drew and anchored me to the newly-found habitats. In sum, it was a combination of the pull of education and the anchor of employment, together with a nudge from the military coup d'états that has planted me in Australia – home for the past two and half decades. As a child, I had never dreamt of leaving the village or Fiji after having first graduated from university; neither did I pursue tertiary education for the sake of emigrating; and I remain hopeful of retiring in the village of my birth. The particulars with regards to the factors responsible for your movements across space would be different, but access to basic services (such as education, healthcare, and the like) and income are likely to have played a role universally. The above explains movement for all; but the propensity to emigrate for those from small island nations is higher than their counterparts from elsewhere.

Poor, small nations are particularly prone to the emigration of skilled and professional workers. Docquier and Marfouk (2005) report that nations located in the South (i.e. poor nations) with populations of 2.5 million or less (i.e. small nations by their definition) experience an average emigration rate of skilled and professional workers of 27% compared to the 13% for lower-middle income group of nations with populations between 2.5 million and 10 million (Docquier and Marfouk, 2005: 21). The smallest of these nations are the most vulnerable: the top 10 source nations by rates of skilled and professional emigration are Guyana (89% emigra-tion for a population of 0.76 million), Grenada (85.1% emigration for a population of 0.11

million), Jamaica (85.1% emigration for a population of 2.7 million), Saint Vincent and the Grenadines (84.5% emigration for a population of 0.11 million), Haiti (83.6% emigration for a population of 10.7 million), Trinidad and Tobago (79.3% emigration for a population of 1.4 million), Saint Kitts and Nevis (87.5% emigration for a population of 0.06 million), Samoa (76.4% emigration for a population of 0.19 million), Tonga (75.2% emigration for a population of 0.11 million), and Saint Lucia (71.1% emigration for a population of 0.19 million).[2]

Income, however, is not the sole (and possibly not even the primary) reason for the emigration of talent. Gibson and McKenzie (2011b) show that migration decisions of the highly skilled and talented individuals from New Zealand, Tonga, and Papua New Guinea are influenced more by non-monetary factors such as risk- preferences, patience, and the predilection towards studying science or a foreign language. The decision to return home, moreover, is influenced by lifestyle and family choices – such as having a parent alive in the home nation. They find no evidence to suggest that those with law or medical degrees or those likely to lose income are less likely to return home compared to the others, with the sole exception of those with a PhD and strong career prospects abroad (ibid.: 27). Rather, the authors report that migrants 'are giving up approximately US$1,000 per week to return to their home countries' (ibid.: 28).

Talented islanders emigrate in search of employment, better basic services, and to modern infrastructure in large rich nations. They do so to overcome the handicaps of size and isolation handed to them via a birth-draw. Access to infrastructure seems to be more important than income for the highly talented individuals while the decision to return is affected by family obligations. There is some preliminary evidence to suggest that emigration for employment delivers development dividends at source: Gibson and McKenzie (2014: 242), for example, present evidence in support of the proposition that temporary migration from Tonga and Vanuatu to New Zealand for seasonal work increased household income, improved social outcomes, and raised investment including improved child school attendance at source but it did not increase self-employment opportunities. The last is supportive of the proposition that the limited market size at home is a constraint on home productivity.

In the next section I build a stylized model to capture the mechanics driving skilled emigration from small nations.

3 The model

A simple model to rationalize the differences in wages due to differences in the size of markets in small vis-a-vis large countries is presented next. The model elucidates the benefits of agglomeration where one highly skilled worker raises the productivity of his/her co-workers, leading to concentration of talent. A parallel logic applies to the concentration of talent in the top sporting teams such as those in the English Premier League where players of nearly every nationality compete. A prediction from the model is that differential rates of productivity growth across space undergirded by skill-agglomeration leads to a one-way flow of talent: from the periphery to the centres of innovation.

Following Docquier and Rapoport (2012), I assume that the output of the small economy (e.g. Fiji's) is characterized by a constant return to scale Cobb-Douglas technology to produce output (Y) using physical capital (K) and human capital (H); that is:

$$Y_t = A_t K_t^\alpha H_t^{1-\alpha} \tag{1}$$

where 'A' denotes total factor productivity, 'H' is the product of the number of workers with the average level of human capital per worker in the economy (i.e. H = Lh), 't' indexes time, and $\alpha \in (0, 1)$ is that share of rental income in GDP. The per capita output from (1) is given as:

$$y_t = A_t k_t^\alpha h_t^{1-\alpha} \tag{1a}$$

with wage rate per efficiency unit of labour at home given as:

$$w_t = (1 - \alpha)\frac{y_t}{h_t} \tag{2}$$

Let there be a much larger foreign economy (e.g. Australia) open to skilled emigrants that has a similar production function to (1). Both nations draw on the global capital market, implying that rental rates are arbitraged across space. Assume for simplicity that physical capital (i.e., K) depreciates fully in a single period, that investment into physical capital in the domestic econ- omy entails a risk premium, and that the rate of return to investment in physical capital is set exogenously by the global market. This leads to the following arbitrage condition:

$$(1 + \emptyset_t)(1 + \bar{r}_t) = \alpha \frac{y_t}{h_t} \tag{3}$$

where $\phi \geq 0$ is equal to the risk premium to investing at home vis-a-vis abroad, and $\bar{r}$ is the risk-free world interest rate. Rearranging equation (3) and substituting it into equation (2) allows domestic wages to be expressed as a function of the risk premium; that is:

$$w_t = \frac{1 - \alpha}{\alpha}(1 + \bar{r}_t)\emptyset_t \tag{4}$$

Equations (1a) to (4) now enable the derivation of wages at home relative to that abroad. That is:

$$\frac{w_t}{w_t^*} = \frac{(1 + \emptyset_t)}{(1 + \emptyset_t^*)} = \frac{A_t}{A^*_t}\left(\frac{k_t}{k^*_t}\right)^\alpha \left(\frac{h_t}{h^*_t}\right)^{-\alpha} \overset{def}{=} \omega_t \tag{5}$$

where superscript '*' denotes foreign (Australian) counterparts for the domestic (Fijian) vari- ables. The first RHS after the first equal sign in equation (5) follows from substitution for domestic and foreign wages as depicted in equation (4); noting the fact that the technology parameters and the global interest rate are exogenous and identical for home and foreign nations. The RHS term after the second equal sign in equation (5) follows from substitution of 'y' for $(1+\phi)$ from equation (3), which then is substituted out using equation (1a).

Equation (5) shows that relative wage (ω) is equal to the ratio of the risk premiums ϕ, which in turn is a function of the ratios of productivity, and physical and human capital intensities between home and foreign countries. One can drop the ratio of physical capital once the arbitrage condition shown in equation (3) is reached; thus relative wages are deter- mined by the ratios of total factor productivity and human capital for home and foreign economies. This result is in sharp contrast with the results of Docquier and Rapoport (2012: 695, equation 5) but consistent with Lucas (1988) who assumes the primacy of human capital in determining the level of productivity. The parameter ϕ proves central to determining relative levels of human capital in the domestic and the foreign economy. It can be decom- posed into two components: the first incorporates the standard risk premium relating to the institutional quality at home; and the second, which captures the transactions costs of inter- national trade borne by those engaging with the rest of the world (ibid.; footnote 12). The latter component is particularly important for small island economies given their large exposure to international trade.

The evolution of relative wages can now be derived from differentiating (5); i.e.:

$$\widehat{\omega}_t = \left(\widehat{\frac{A}{A^*}}\right) + \alpha\left[\left(\widehat{\frac{k}{k^*}}\right) + \left(\widehat{\frac{h^*}{h}}\right)\right] > 0 \tag{6}$$

where a caret ($^$) over a variable denotes its growth rate and time subscripts have been dropped for simplicity. Equation (6) depicts that the evolution of relative wages is the sum of three separate components: the relative change in productivity between home and foreign countries; and, the relative changes in the rates of intensity of physical and human capital weighted by the share of human capital in GDP. This sum is strictly positive in the steady state where $\left(\widehat{\frac{k}{k^*}}\right) = 0$, meaning that relative wages diverge with time. The divergence in wages reflects the economics of agglomeration where highly skilled activities take place in spatially concentrated locations. An implication from equation (6) is that wages for skilled workers diverge over time, and that the rate of this divergence is monotonic in the skill-intensity of production; meaning that the centres of innovation will continue to attract the talented.

Wage disparities as depicted above drive emigration of talent from small economies; meaning that they export human capital for foreign production. This could explain three empirical regularities: (i) small island nations on average experience higher rates of emigration; (ii) small island nations experience particularly high rates of skilled emigration; and, (iii) remoteness and the absence of a large domestic market raises the costs of doing business, limiting the opportunities for employment of local talent (Winters and Martins, 2004). These together suggest that emigration of highly skilled workers is likely to be part of the reality for small island economies.

4 Welfare effects of emigration

The notion of drain

I next look at the notion of 'brain drain' and then proceed to consider the welfare effects of this change. 'Brain drain' is quantified as the emigration of tertiary-trained workers from developing to developed nations; an issue that has attracted considerable academic attention (Beine *et al.*, 2008). This debate has arisen from the empirical fact that a significant proportion of the tertiary-trained from small, poor nations leave to live and work in large, rich nations (Bhagwati and Hamada, 1974; and Scott, 1966). In the case where visas into rich OECD nations are allocated on the basis of skills, emigration can amount to the 'international transfer of resources in the form of human capital … from developing to developed countries' (Beine *et al.*, 2008: 631). Bundred and Levitt (2000: 245) assert that the 'mass emigration of physicians from less-developed countries puts great pressure on those who remain in these countries'. The Lancet magazine in its endeavour to find solutions for the health crisis in many poor nations demands that 'rich countries stop recruiting from poorer nations' and that they (i.e. rich nations) 'can no longer be allowed to exploit and plunder the future of resource-poor nations' (Lancet, 2008: 1576).

The debate on whether the flows of skilled emigrants from poor to rich nations leads to an increase (i.e. brain-gain) or a depletion (i.e. brain drain) of the stock of trained personal at source remains unresolved. This is because of a lack of data on cross-border flows of skills, and the inability to create counterfactuals to the observed movements (Gibson and McKenzie, 2011a). Some progress however has been made in collecting and collating data on the migration of tertiary-trained workers. Docquier and Marfouk (2005) show that the OECD accounts for some 90% of the educated immigrants or as of the year 2000 a total stock of 20.4 million adults (i.e. aged 25 years and above) who were born overseas with nearly half of these living in the

USA, 13.4% in Canada, 7.5% in Australia, 6.2% in the UK, 4.9% in Germany, and 3% in France (ibid.: 17). The statistics also reveal that the rate of skilled emigration increased in the decade to 2000: 29.8% of all migrants in 1990 were skilled compared to 34.6% in 2000.

Small nations in the Caribbean and the Pacific displayed the highest rates of skill-selection: more than 75% of the tertiary trained emigrate with figures for Guyana of 89%, Grenada (85%), Jamaica (85%), Saint Vincent and the Grenadines (85%), Haiti (84%), Trinidad and Tobago (79%), Saint Kitts and Nevis (79%), Samoa (76%) and Tonga (75%). The comparative figures for larger nations such as Egypt are 4.6%, India (4.3%), and China (3.8%) (ibid.: 23, Table 4).

In terms of the destination nations, the data for the year 2000 shows that some 59% of the immigrants to Canada were skilled, followed by USA (43%), Ireland (41%), New Zealand (39%), Australia (37%), and the United Kingdom (35%). In terms of the stock of tertiary-trained migrants, some 50% live in the USA with Canada and Australia together accounting for another 20%. Therefore, at face value the above is evidence in support of brain drain.

Welfare implications

What of the counterfactual? On the question of the impact of emigration on human capital at source, Beine *et al.* (2008) simulate the net effects of emigration on the stock of skilled labour residing in developing nations using data for 2000. Their simulations, the lone example that exists in the extant literature, reveals a gain of 3% (i.e. a stock of 116.5 million in the 127 developing countries against a counterfactual of 113.2 million). Small nations (defined by the authors as those with populations of less than one million) however lose 33% of their stock of skilled labour (ibid.: 644). The authors use these results to claim that brain drain has been extremely detrimental in the Caribbean and the Pacific regions, warning that: '[t]he situation of many small countries in Sub-Saharan Africa and Central America, in particular, is extremely worrisome' (ibid.: 648).

There are at least two problems with the conclusion that losses in the stock of local tertiary-trained workers is worrisome for small nations. Taking the simulations at face value to begin with does not necessarily imply a deterioration in welfare of those left behind at source. There is no evidence to suggest that the emigration of a physician leads to poor health outcomes for those left at source. Bhargava *et al.* (2011) note that small island nations such as Dominica, Grenada, Saint Lucia, Saint Kitts and Nevis, Ireland, Antigua and Barbuda, Liberia, Jamaica and Fiji, which have experienced emigration rates in excess of 50% of their medically-trained personnel are likely to be most severely affected in terms of access to medical services (ibid.: 175). Their analysis however fails to provide evidence of a deterioration in the quality of medical care provided at source from the nations experiencing the highest rates of emigration (ibid.: 180).

The second problem with the simulation is the assumption of a given stock of tertiary trained regardless of the options to emigrate. It is possible that some physicians invested in their education with the purpose of emigrating. I will use observed data from Dominica, a nation with a 2004 total population of 71,213 to make my case. Some 99% of the physicians (i.e. 3,711 doctors in all) trained in Dominica were practising in the United States of America as of 2004 (data from Bhargava *et al.*, 2011). Had each trained doctor remained at home, Dominica would have five doctors for every one hundred individuals; a figure that is ninefold that of Cuba, which currently has the highest number of physicians per thousand individuals of the 192 nations listed in the above-mentioned dataset. It is hard to imagine that all 3,750 doctors would be working in Dominica, or as many would have pursued a career in medicine without the explicit intention of emigrating to the USA.

Much of the literature on brain drain ignores the fact that individuals choose careers in anticipation of the benefits that they will reap from the investment. The option to emigrate after acquiring the requisite qualifications are factored into the decision-making of the individual. Consequently, the stock of people from poor nations residing in rich countries is the product of three separate effects.

First, the numbers reflect the choices made by past generations in moving abroad, noting the fact that the majority who have moved have done so of their own volition. This positive-selection of migrants at source is incentivized by the potential gains to the individual from economies of agglomeration of human capital in rich nations (see Section 3).

Second, and complementing the positive selection noted above, are the skill-selective immigration policies of several rich nations – Australia, Canada, New Zealand, and the United States being the prime examples in the use of their visa system to attract global talent, while many European nations are contemplating doing the same (Beine *et al.*, 2008; Docquier and Marfouk, 2005).[3]

Third, the two of the above enumerated reasons provide the incentives for investment into acquisition of skills for emigration from poor nations. Consequently, emigration may not necessarily lead to a depletion of the stock of skilled personnel at source. Kiribati and Tuvalu, for example, provide maritime training to their nationals so that they can secure employment on foreign ships while Fiji trains soldiers for foreign peacekeeping missions. Put simply, there would be no such training without the employment prospects abroad.

There are further reasons why emigration can be welfare enhancing for both the emigrants and those left behind. If the return to skills net of the costs of acquisition is greater abroad than at home, then emigration provides an incentive to invest in the accumulation of human capital that in turn raises both the level and rate of growth of income through increased productivity (see Section 3.). Feedback effects from emigration on source nations in the form of remittances and return migration flow back to the source community, thus benefitting those staying at 'home'. On this question, Easterly and Nyarko (2009) ask if brain drain is good for Africa. Their analysis using Ghana as a case study reaches the conclusion that the value of remittances exceeds the costs of educating the emigrant. Skilled migrants moreover send remittances to fund public goods such as schools and hospitals, what Bhagwati (2009: 9) calls 'social remittances', compared to unskilled migrants who send 'family remittances'. And some emigrants return, providing opportunities for circulation of talent: anything between 20 to 50% of immigrants leave either for home or another destination within five years of arriving (Kerr *et al.*, 2016).

5 Policy implications

Small economies lack market scale while the geography of being remote from major centres of economic activity makes them vulnerable to shocks from the international economic environment; but there is disagreement over whether these problems are peculiar to small economies or if policies can be used to ameliorate these concerns: Srinivasan (1986: 218), for example, argues that 'smallness is neither a necessary nor a sufficient condition for poor development performance'. This argument raises questions over whether small economies do indeed have special problems, and if so do they call for special attention? In this section I first focus on the special problems of small states, and then turn to the potential problems from skilled migration before considering policy interventions to ameliorate the costs whilst maximizing the gains from skilled emigration.

The special problems of small states

Amongst the special problems faced by small nations are the limited ability to reap the benefits of economies of scale in the production of goods and services; their dependence on a narrow range of natural endowments and exports limiting the potential for domestic diversification, which exposes the nation to external economic shocks; and the vulnerability of many small nations to natural disasters because of being located in geologically active areas of the planet. The first of the above-mentioned leads to high costs of trade and transport (Hummels, 2007). But small states depend on international trade to access the full complement of goods and services for consumption, which in turn are paid for using the proceeds of their exports and remittances. The global market provides the opportunity for small states to diversify their risks from domestic production and local income-generation. A devastating cyclone for example can destroy all local supplies and diminish opportunities for income generation, leaving the community reliant on goods and services sourced from abroad, and remitted funds to pay for them.

Economic interdependence of nations is a phenomenon that is likely to grow with time (Docquier and Rapoport, 2012; Kerr et al., 2016). Small states will have to live with the realities of increased skilled emigration, and learn to use it for maximizing the welfare of the resident population. This will mean maximizing the income of their skilled emigrants, encouraging remittance flows back to source, and facilitating circular migration and foreign investments into local ventures with export potential. Each of these possibilities is discussed in some detail next.

Potential problems from skilled migration

Maximizing the earnings of highly skilled migrants necessitates that academic and professional qualifications are considered to be on par with those in receiving nations. Small states can do this by aligning their education systems and professional qualifications so that qualifications are portable across national borders. Several Pacific Island nations are on track to achieving this goal through adoption of the professional qualifications of Australia and New Zealand. Migrant receiving nations could assist by making their qualifications frameworks available for adoption by small states: again Australia and New Zealand have both expressed their willingness to do so. This in itself provides an opportunity for small island states to export 'rich-world' education at 'poor world' prices to the rest of the world. But the options for such exports may be limited to professions and disciplines that do not depend on large economies of scale (and agglomeration) as depicted in Section 3.

Similarly, return and circular migration will be facilitated through pensions that are portable across jurisdictions. Host nations could work in partnership with source counterparts to ensure that impediments to the circular flow of migrants are removed. Small states in particular could provide the option for those born in the nation to hold citizenship for life and to reclaim it at any time should it have been relinquished. This would allow migrants to return 'home' should they wish to do so – to retire, to reinvest, or to reverse a bad decision to leave in the first place. The diaspora moreover can connect source and destination communities. Such connectedness will provide the business links and the opportunity for increased financial flows back to the source nation. Last and perhaps just as important is the creation of space to allow immigrants to assimilate into the host community. Linguistic, family, and cultural connections into the host community have been responsible for chain migration, a phenomenon that is likely to remain important for the foreseeable future.

Mitigating the risks of brain drain

Bhagwati (1976) proposed a 'tax on brains' (i.e. the 'Bhagwati tax') where skilled migrants are required to compensate source nations for the cost of their education and the negative externality arising from their departure. The tax is premised on the loss of skills, which is claimed to have an adverse effect on welfare at source. The evidence in support of these assertions is far from clear. And the evidence on the negative externality from the departure of talent is just as dubious. Regardless, the rationale for a 'brain-tax' rests on views regarding the moral imperatives of those having departed to their kin left behind. The morality of a 'brain tax' is absent if one believes that the brain belongs to the individual. Grubel and Scott (1966) take this view, pointing out that the emigrant departs with his/her own marginal product that in any case belongs to the individual. Humans have after all moved over millennia to improve on their wellbeing; so why should those born in small nations be constrained from such mobility now? Additionally, what obligations if any do the emigrants have to their home nation if they left to escape war, famine, coup d'états, etc.?

What about asking emigrants to pay for the costs of their education at source? At first glance the answer seems to be in the affirmative: it is after all the reimbursement of the costs of education to the source nation. Closer scrutiny regarding the inter-generational transfers arising from such a proposal makes the answer more complex. Let me use my own case to explain the complexity. My education was funded by my parents and their kin through a combination of taxes and direct transfers, plus a loan extended to me from the government. Both the taxes and direct transfers were made by the previous generation meaning that the 'debt' is owed to them. Migrants repay this debt to the generation of their parents through remittances and by returning home to assist elderly relatives when required. And the value of these remittances oftentimes exceeds the initial outlays on education with beneficial spill-overs onto the subsequent generation (Easterly and Nyarko, 2009). Docquier and Rapoport (2012:704) note that highly-skilled emigrants send remittances that overcome liquidity constraints, raise investments in education, and reduce poverty in the home nation.

What about repayments for loans extended for tertiary studies? These loans, regardless of the source (public or private), are financial contracts that are entered into voluntarily and have sanctions for any breaches. In my own case the personal loan that I received from the Fijian government came with an obligation to serve the nation: I repaid the loan and served the bond to the government. And mine is far from an isolated case as Gibson and McKenzie (2011b) report that the 'best and brightest' from New Zealand, Papua New Guinea, and Tonga return home to serve their bonds to the home country. In cases when the debtors do abscond, enforcement of contracts becomes a legal responsibility where international cooperation could prove valuable.

6 Conclusion and caveats

Humans have moved throughout recorded history with globalization accelerating the pace of migration of skilled workers. In the context of modern day skilled workers, those 'who get a good draw in their current location tend to stay, while those who get a bad draw tend to leave' (Kennan and Walker, 2011: 246) The evidence of high rates of emigration of skilled workers from small nations suggests that they were handed a bad 'birth draw' with skilled emigration lending a means to mitigating some of this 'bad luck'.

The lack of scale and the benefits of specialization provide strong incentives for skilled and highly talented workers from small island nations to emigrate to improve on their circumstances. The key drivers for migration of the highly skilled workers include the differences in productivity and wages between source and destination countries. The former reflects the importance of location, including the effects of agglomeration of workers of similar skills and levels of access to financial and physical capital (Clemens, 2013; Moretti, 2012). A further reason for the migration of talent to OECD nations is the opportunity to acquire formal education and access to infrastructure to capitalize on talent, leading to a strong positive selection of highly educated emigrants from small (island) nations: a fact supported by the data (Peri, 2016). The concentration of workers in a given location, be this across national borders or within a sovereign state, raises returns to (and thickens the market for) skills, while providing the incentives for further spatial clustering of talent. There is little debate that skilled emigration raises the income of the individual and global GDP but the effects on the source community is less clear.

The debate on the effects of skilled-emigration on source nation has revolved around the question of brain drain. The stock of skilled labour in developing countries is the net effect of training less those who emigrate. Economists have been divided on whether emigration of 'brains' is a drain or a boon to the source nation. Access to emigration provides an incentive for workers at source to acquire the requisite skills for emigration. It is therefore wrong to assume that those who emigrate after having gained the requisite qualifications would have acquired the training without having the opportunity to emigrate in the first place. The simple arithmetic of subtracting the number of trained emigrants from the stock of domestically trained to reach a measure of 'brain drain' is, put simply, wrong. Data is now being assembled to answer this question, even though creating the counterfactual to what has been observed remains a challenge. The evidence however is clear that small nations experience the highest rates of skilled emigration: those in the Caribbean and the Pacific for example have witnessed nearly half of their tertiary-trained workers leave for the neighbouring metropolis.

The effects of emigration on the welfare of residents in the source nation is due to the offsetting effects of 'brain drain' and that from the reverse flow of remittances. Even though the evidence on the adverse effects of skilled emigration on source communities is weak at best, caution suggests that small nations will have to learn to live with emigration of their talented workers and use remittances, diaspora investment, etc. to benefit those remaining at home. This is because the incentives for skilled emigration are likely to strengthen with time (as explained in Section 3) as rich nations continue to select the 'best and the brightest' from abroad. The positive skill selection of migrants from poor countries will expand with: (i) increases in the wage-premium paid to skilled workers compared to their unskilled counterparts; (ii) the use of skill-selective immigration policies by an increasing number of rich destinations nations; and, (iii) the high transactions costs of emigration, which means that those with the means and the information, that is the rich from poor nations, will emigrate. Furthermore, multi-member households will encourage those with the highest potential to earn income to emigrate since transactions costs of emigration such as those for transportation and regulatory approvals are fixed per individual – an empirical regularity described as 'shipping the good apples out' (Hummels and Skiba, 2004).

Small source nations can use skilled emigration to the benefit of those remaining at home. The policy responses include those targeted at maximizing the income of the emigrants, and encouragement of the circular flow of capital and talent between source and destination. Harmonization of qualifications with those at destination will increase employability and income of the emigrants. Closer connections with the emigrants and shared citizenships will offer the options for circular migration and FDI. The diaspora can be encouraged to act as the bridge between source and destination communities, helping immigrants assimilate and strengthening businesses networks across jurisdictions. Last, portable pensions provide the option for emigrants to return home to retire.

In sum, the economic arguments for emigration of skilled workers from small nations to large rich nations are strong: the mobility raises the incomes of the migrants; it raises global GDP;

and, the option to emigrate ameliorates the penalty of a 'bad birth draw' for a talented individual being born in a small, poor nation. Small nations must learn to live with the reality of skilled emigration and use it as an opportunity to benefit those unable to leave.

Notes

1 See article titled 'The 2016 Nobel science prizes: Seven tickets to Stockholm', *The Economist* of 8 October, 2016, p. 71.
2 Population data is for the year 2015 and sourced from the World Development Indicators (online) database.
3 Australia introduced a points system in 1984 that privileges skilled applicants for residency; New Zealand did the same in 1991; Canada followed soon afterwards; while the US increased its quotas of H1-B visas for highly skilled workers from 110,200 in 1992 to 355,600 in 2000 (ibid.: 4).

References

Beine, M., Docquier, F. and Rapoport, H. (2008). 'Brain drain and human capital formation in developing countries: winners and losers'. *The Economic Journal*, 118(528): 631–652.

Bhagwati, J. (2009). Overview of Issues. In J. Bhagwati and G. H. Hanson (eds), *Skilled immigration today: prospects, problems, and Policies*. Oxford: Oxford University Press.

Bhagwati, J. and Hamada, K. (1974). 'The brain drain, international integration of markets for professionals and unemployment: a theoretical analysis'. *Journal of Development Economics*, 1(1): 19–42.

Bhagwati, J. N. (1976). 'Taxing the brain drain'. *Challenge*, 19(3): 34–38.

Bhargava, A., Docquier, F. and Moullan, Y. (2011) 'Modeling the effects of physician emigration on human development'. *Economics and Human Biology*, 9(2): 172–183.

Borjas, G. J. (2006). 'Native internal migration and the labor market impact of immigration'. *Journal of Human Resources*, Vol. 41(2): 221–258.

Borjas, G. J. (2015). 'Immigration and globalization: A review essay'. *Journal of Economic Literature*, 53(4): 961–974.

Bundred, P. E. and Levitt, C. (2000). 'Medical migration: who are the real losers?'. *The Lancet*, 356(9225): 245–246.

Card, D. (1990). 'The Impact of the Mariel Boatlift on the Miami Labor-Market'. *Industrial and Labor Relations Review*, 43(2): 245–257.

Clemens, M. A. (2013). 'Why do programmers earn more in Houston than Hyderabad? Evidence from randomized processing of US visas'. *The American Economic Review*, 103(3): 198–202.

Docquier, F. and Marfouk, A. (2005). *International Migration by Educational Attainment (1990–2000)*. Release 1.1. database, 1990, 16.

Docquier, F. and Rapoport, H. (2012). 'Globalization, brain drain, and development'. *Journal of Economic Literature*, 50(3): 681–730.

Easterly, W. and Nyarko, Y. (2009). Is the brain drain good for Africa?. In J. Bhagwati and G. H. Hanson (eds), *Skilled Immigration Today*. Oxford: Oxford University Press: 316–360.

Fujita, M., Krugman, P. R. and Venables, A. (2001). *The spatial economy: Cities, regions, and international trade*. London: MIT Press.

Fujita, M. and Thisse, J.-F. (2013). *Economics of agglomeration: cities, industrial location, and globalization*. Cambridge: Cambridge University Press.

Gibson, J. and McKenzie, D. (2011a). 'Eight questions about brain drain'. *The Journal of Economic Perspectives*, 25(3): 107–128.

Gibson, J. and McKenzie, D. (2011b). 'The microeconomic determinants of emigration and return migration of the best and brightest: Evidence from the Pacific'. *Journal of Development Economics*, 95(1): 18–29.

Gibson, J. and McKenzie, D. (2014). 'The development impact of a best practice seasonal worker policy'. *Review of Economics and Statistics*, 96(2): 229–243.

Grubel, H. B. and Scott, A. D. (1966). 'The international flow of human capital'. *The American Economic Review*, 56(1/2): 268–274.

Hummels, D. (2007). 'Transportation costs and international trade in the second era of globalization'. *The Journal of Economic Perspectives*, 21(3): 131–154.

Hummels, D. and Skiba, A. (2004). 'Shipping the good apples out? An empirical confirmation of the Alchian-Allen conjecture'. *Journal of Political Economy*, 112(6): 1384–1402.

Kennan, J. and Walker, J. R. (2011). 'The effect of expected income on individual migration decisions'. *Econometrica*, 79(1): 211–251.

Kerr, S. P., Kerr, W., Özden, Ç. and Parsons, C. (2016). 'Global talent flows'. *Journal of Economic Perspectives*, 30(1): 83–106.

Lancet (2008) 'Finding solutions to the human resources for health crisis'. *The Lancet*, 371(9624): 623.

Lucas, R. E. (1988). 'On the mechanics of economic development'. *Journal of Monetary Economics*, 22(1): 3–42.

Moretti, E. (2012). *The new geography of jobs*. Boston, MA: Houghton Mifflin Harcourt.

Peri, G. (2016). 'Immigrants, Productivity, and Labour Markets'. *Journal of Economic Perspectives*, 30(4): 3–30.

Srinivasan, T. N. (1986). 'The costs and benefits of being a small, remote, island, landlocked, or ministate economy'. *The World Bank Research Observer*, 1(2): 205–218.

Winters, L. A. and Martins, P. (2004). 'When comparative advantage is not enough: business costs in small remote economies'. *World Trade Review*, 3(03): 347–383.

World Bank (2016). Systematic Country Diagnostic For Eight Small Pacific Island Countries: Priorities For Ending Poverty And Boosting Shared Prosperity. Washington, DC: World Bank.

21

The effect of brain drain on productivity growth in small states[1]

Maurice Schiff and Yanling Wang

1 Introduction

An important literature exists on the effects of countries' human capital on their productivity growth, with most studies conducted in a closed-economy context. This chapter focuses on the differential impact of human capital in facilitating trade-related North-South technology diffusion and then analyzes its implications on South-North brain drain in small and large states. Small states are more dependent on the rest of the world, in terms of openness to trade (trade/GDP), to skilled migration rate (skilled migrants/population) and to imports of ideas, including technological knowledge from the North. Given small states' larger brain drain (BD), education levels are likely to be lower, ceteris paribus, and thus education is likely to have a larger productivity impact in those countries. Moreover, the impact of the interaction of education and technology diffusion from the North is also likely to be larger for small states. These hypotheses are examined here. It provides an empirical analysis of the impact on total factor productivity (TFP) growth in the South: i) of trade-related technology diffusion, human capital, and country size, and ii) of the interaction between all pairs of these variables, and between the three variables. The use of trade-related technology diffusion as a determinant of productivity (TFP) growth in the South is based on the assumption that North-South trade provides a vehicle for the diffusion to the South of technology developed in the North. Second, the South's absorption capacity – as measured by countries' average level of human capital – is hypothesized to affect TFP growth as well as the impact of trade-related technology diffusion on TFP growth.

This study relates to a large literature estimating gains from trade. Until about three decades ago, while trade theory emphasized the importance of trade liberalization, empirical estimates of the gains from trade were found to be disappointingly small. The development of endogenous growth theory in the 1980s (Romer, 1986; Lucas, 1988) allowed policy reform to generate large gains by moving the economy to a higher growth path. Grossman and Helpman (1991) expanded the endogenous growth model by applying it to the open economy. Based on the idea that goods embody technological know-how, they showed that countries can acquire foreign knowledge through trade and increase their growth rate through trade liberalization.

Coe and Helpman (1995) provided an empirical implementation of the model in Grossman and Helpman (1991). They constructed an index of 'foreign R&D', defined as the trade-weighted sum of trading partners' R&D stocks, and found for OECD countries that both domestic and 'foreign R&D' have a large and significant impact on *TFP*, and that the latter increases with the economy's openness. Coe *et al.* (1997) also examined the impact of North-South trade-related technology diffusion on *TFP* in the South and obtained similar results. This led to a number of other studies, inter alia, Engelbrecht (1997), Falvey *et al.* (2002), and Lumenga-Neso *et al.* (2005), which have tended to confirm Coe and Helpman's (1995) findings. Other studies have extended the approach to the industry level, including Schiff and Wang (2006) who included South-South trade-related technology diffusion in their analysis and found it to have a positive impact on *TFP* in the South, though a smaller one than that obtained from North-South trade.

If the technology is to have an impact on *TFP* growth in developing countries, it is crucial that developing countries have certain capacity to absorb trade-related technology transfers from the North, to adapt them to the specific conditions prevailing in their own country and to make productive use of them. That capacity has been found to be closely linked to the labour force's educational attainment level, for instance, Wang (2007), and Correa *et al.* (2008). Given that brain drain has a negative impact on labour force's education level, brain drain is likely to have negative impact on a country's absorption and adaptation capacity and therefore also on the rate of growth of *TFP*.

This chapter focuses on the impact of education and whether it differs in small and in large states, and then analyzes the implications of brain drain on TFP growth. The emigration rate of skilled workers in small states is much higher than in large states (Table 21.2), thus the implications of brain drain on TFP growth is significantly different in small states than in large ones.

The contribution of this chapter to the open-economy endogenous growth literature is twofold. First, it offers an empirical analysis of the relationship between North-South trade-related technology diffusion, education, country size and productivity growth in the South. Second, it examines how the impact on productivity growth of changes in such variables as the level of education, trade-related technology diffusion, and of a change in both variables, is affected by country size.

The main findings are:

i   Trade-related technology diffusion has a positive impact on productivity growth that is several times larger for small than for large states. Thus, an increase in the degree of openness has a greater impact on productivity growth in small than in large states.

ii Similarly, education has a positive impact on productivity growth that is several times larger for small than for large states. Hence, brain drain's negative impact on productivity growth in small states is a multiple of that in large ones.

iii The impact of trade-related technology diffusion on productivity growth increases with the level of education, and this increase is also several times larger for small than for large states. Consequently, the brain drain reduces productivity growth both directly as well as through its interaction with trade-related technology diffusion, with a greater reduction for small than for large states.

iv The continuous growth of the North's R&D over time has a positive impact on the South's *long-term* productivity growth, an impact that is substantially greater for small than for large states.

The remainder of the chapter is organized as follows. Section 2. presents the empirical framework. Section 3. describes the data and Section 4. provides the empirical results. Section 5. concludes.

2 Empirical Framework

Coe and Helpman (1995) developed an empirical model to estimate the impact on *TFP* of North-North trade-related technology diffusion. The estimation equation is:

$$\log TFP_{ct} = \alpha + \lambda_c + \lambda_t + \beta^d \log RD_{ct}^d + \beta^f \log RD_{ct}^f + \varepsilon_{ct}, \tag{1}$$

Where $\lambda_c(\lambda_t)$ is country (time) fixed effects, RD_{ct}^d (RD_{ct}^f) is the domestic (foreign) R&D stocks, RD^f is an error term, and subscript c (t) denotes country (year).

Coe et al. (1997) use a similar model to explain North-South trade-related technology diffusion. However, due to lack of data for most developing countries, the equations they estimate do not include domestic R&D. They only use the foreign R&D stock RD^f, which is referred to in this chapter as 'North foreign R&D' and is denoted by '*NRD*' in our study. Abstracting from domestic R&D is unlikely to be a major problem because most of the world's R&D is performed in developed countries. For instance, in 1995, 95% of the world's R&D expenditures took place in industrial countries (calculated from the World Bank database). Moreover, recent empirical work has shown that much of the technical change in individual OECD countries is based on the international diffusion of technology among the various OECD countries. A case in point is Eaton and Kortum (1999) where they estimate that 87% of French growth is based on foreign R&D. Since developing countries invest much fewer resources in R&D than OECD countries, foreign R&D must be even more important for developing countries as a source of growth.

In our chapter, we divide the manufacturing sector into high- and low- R&D intensity industries, trying to tackle the industry heterogeneity issues related to different R&D intensity in their production process. Following Coe and Helpman (1995) and Coe et al. (1997), we define the variable 'North-foreign R&D' of developing country c for industry j at year t, NRD_{ct} as:

$$NRD_{cjt} = \sum_k \frac{M_{cjkt}}{GDP_{cjt}} RD_{jkt}, \tag{2}$$

where c indexes developing countries and k indexes OECD countries. For year t, GDP_{cj} is the value added of industry j in country c, M_{cjk} is the value of imports of industry j in country c from OECD country k, and RD_{jk} denotes the R&D stock in industry j in OECD country k. Equation (2) says that, for industry j in any country c, NRD is the sum, over all OECD countries k, of the R&D stock of industry j in country k, weighted by country c's imports from OECD country k for industry j divided by country cj's value-added.

We estimate *TFP* equations as a function of *NRD*, human capital *YE*, defined as the average years of education for the population aged 25 and above, and a dummy variable for small states, *S3*. The number of countries with a population of 1.5 million or less (on average over the period) in our sample of fifty developing countries is too small to be of much relevance. We use instead a population of 3 million or less as our definition of 'small state', with twelve countries or close to one fourth (24%) of the sample fitting the definition.[2]

In the empirical estimation, we also introduce several interaction terms. Two of them are interactions between each of the two explanatory variables and *S3*, i.e. *NRD*S3* and *YE*S3*. The other two are interactions between the two explanatory variables both for small and large states, i.e. *NRD*YE* and *NRD*YE*S3*. A positive sign for the first two interaction variables would imply that the productivity-growth impact of *NRD* and *YE* is larger for small states, and similarly, a positive sign for *NRD*YE*S3* would imply that the impact of *NRD*YE* is larger for small states.

Given that changes in openness, foreign R&D and education are unlikely to have an immediate impact on productivity growth, the estimation equation is specified in terms of five-year changes in the log of TFP ($\Delta\log TFP$), in the log of NRD ($\Delta\log NRD$) and in YE (ΔYE), i.e.:

$$\Delta\log TFP_{cjt} = \alpha + \beta_N\Delta\log NRD_{cjt} + \beta_Y\Delta YE_{ct} + \beta_S S3 + \beta_{NS}\Delta\log NRD_{cjt} * S3$$

$$+ \beta_{YS}\Delta YE * S3 + \beta_{NY}\Delta\log NRD_{cjt} * \Delta YE_{ct} + \beta_{NYS}\Delta\log NRD_{cjt} * \Delta YE_{ct} * S3$$

$$+ \gamma_{ind}Ind + \sum_{c=2}\gamma_c D_c + \sum_{t=2}\gamma_t D_t + \varepsilon_{ct} \tag{3}$$

where D_c (D_t) indicates country (year) dummies, capturing country- (year-) specific fixed effects, and Ind is industry dummy with $Ind=1$ for high R&D intensity industries, and 0 for R&D low intensity industries. The equations estimated in Section 4. include equation (3) and variants thereof.

3 Data description

The data cover 50 developing (and transition) countries and 15 industrialized OECD trading partners over the period 1976 to 2002. The 50 developing countries – with the 12 small states in italics – are: Bangladesh, Bolivia, Bulgaria, Cameroon, Chile, Colombia, *Cyprus*, Ecuador, Egypt, El Salvador, Ethiopia, Greece, Guatemala, Hong Kong (China), Hungary, India, Indonesia, Iran, I.R. of, Israel, *Jordan*, Kenya, Korea, *Kuwait, Latvia, Macao (China)*, Malawi, Malaysia, *Malta*, Mexico, Morocco, Myanmar (Burma), Nepal, Nigeria, *Oman*, Pakistan, *Panama*, Peru, Philippines, Poland, Romania, Senegal, *Singapore, Slovenia*, Sri Lanka, Tanzania, *Trinidad & Tobago*, Tunisia, Turkey, *Uruguay* and Venezuela. We aggregate industry level data into two composite industries with high- and low-R&D intensities. The industries fall in high- and low R&D intensities are adapted from Schiff and Wang (2006), with more documented in the appendix.

The log TFP index is calculated as the difference between the logs of value-added and primary factor use, with the inputs weighted by their income shares, i.e. $\ln TFP = \ln Y - \alpha\ln L -(1-\alpha)\ln K$, where α is the mean labour share over the available time period. The labour share is derived as the ratio of the wage bill over value added.[3] Fixed capital formation used to construct capital stocks, value added, labour and wages, is from the World Bank data set described in Nicita and Olarreaga (2007), all reported in current US dollars at the 3-digit ISIC codes (Revision 2). Value-added and fixed capital formation are deflated by the US GDP deflator (1991=100), and capital stocks are derived from the deflated fixed capital formation series using the perpetual inventory method with a 5% depreciation rate.[4]

R&D expenditure for the 15 OECD countries is taken from OECD ANBERD with ISIC Revision 2 (2002) covering data from 1973 to 1998, and ANBERD with ISIC Revision 3 (2006) covering data from 1987 on. Since ANBERD ISIC 2 and ISIC 3 have 12 years of overlapping data, we are able to match the different specifications. The R&D stock in each country is constructed from R&D expenditures using the perpetual inventory method with a 10% depreciation rate.

Bilateral trade data of the 50 developing countries with the 15 industrialized OECD countries at the 4-digit ISIC 2 level are taken from Nicita and Olarreaga (2007). We construct bilateral trade shares for each year and each composite industry and each of the 50 developing countries with respect to each of the 15 OECD countries, which are then used to construct NRD, defined in equation (2).

Average years of education for the population aged 25 and above are obtained by annualizing the five-year averages in Barro and Lee (2001), and extrapolated to year 2002, which is at the country level. There are several countries included in the sample that are not included in the Barro and Lee dataset. We matched each of these countries with the countries included in Barro and Lee, using indictors such as real GDP per capita and government expenditure on education as a share of GDP per capita.

Due to missing observations for production and trade data, our sample is unbalanced. Our sample has 100 panels (50 countries, each with a composite high and low R&D intensity industry). Taking five-year first difference will leave each panel with 4 data points. However, due to missing data on production and bilateral trade, some countries have only two five-year first difference data points.

4 Empirical findings

Some concerns for unit root and endogeneity

We proceed by first testing whether the data contain unit root and whether NRD is endogeneous in order to choose a proper econometric model for the estimation. For the unit root test, all the test techniques for panel data are developed in the context of balanced panels. Thus, if we were to test unit root for our data, we have to exclude those data points which are missing in some panels. Doing so leaves us with two data points for each of the remaining panels, which makes it impossible to employ any of the unit root techniques. Thus, essentially, our data can be treated as panel data (100 panels), with not long enough period to be considered as time series data (maximum 4).

However, we still might face endogeneity problem as more productive countries might import more goods from overseas. We tested for the possible endogeneity problem using the methodology proposed by Wooldridge (2002), and the test results suggest that the endogeneity hypothesis is rejected. In what follows, the results are estimated using panel data fixed effects.

The results

Table 21.1 reports the main regression results. It shows that the coefficient β_N on $\Delta logNRD$ is positive and significant in all nine regressions. Denote the coefficient β_N for small states – i.e. for $\Delta logNRD*S3$ – by β_{NS} (see equation (3)). The value of β_N ranges from 0.269 to 0.615 and falls to a range of 0.269 to 0.397 when the variable $\Delta logNRD*S3$ is included in the regression. For instance, in equation (1), $\beta_N = 0.490$ (significant at the 1% level) and falls to 0.269 (significant at the 10% level) in equation (2), with $\beta_{NS} = 0.964$ (significant at the 1% level). The impact Φ_{NS} of $\Delta logNRD$ on $\Delta logTFP$ in small states is $\Phi_{NS} \equiv \beta_N + \beta_{NS} = 1.233$. Thus, the impact of $\Delta logNRD$ in small states is well over four times the impact in large countries ($\varphi_{NS} > 4 \beta_N$). The same result obtains for equations (6) and (9), while $\Phi_{NS} > 3 \beta_N$ for equations (5) and (8).

The coefficient β_Y of the education variable ΔYE for the full sample ranges from 0.721 to 0.807, with significance of 1% or 5% in equations (1), (2), (3) and (5). It falls to between 0.194 and 0.310 and is no longer significant when the small states variable, $\Delta YE*S3$, is included in the regression. For instance, in equation (1), $\beta_Y = 0.766$ (significant at the 5% level) for the full sample. Adding $\Delta YE*S3$ in equation (4) results in a value $\beta_Y = 0.242$ (not significant), with the coefficient for small states $\beta_{YS} = 1.075$ (significant at the 10% level). The impact of ΔYE for small states is equal to $\Phi_{YS} \equiv \beta_Y + \beta_{YS} = 1.317$, or over five times the impact in large countries

Table 21.1 TFP growth and small states

	(1)	(2)	(3)	(4)	(5)	(6)	(7)	(8)	(9)
ΔlogNRD	0.49	0.269	0.595	0.509	0.375	0.291	0.615	0.397	0.337
	(3.71)***	(1.83)*	(4.18)***	(3.87)***	(2.42)**	(1.98)**	(4.33)***	(2.57)***	(2.14)**
ΔYE	0.766	0.807	0.721	0.242	0.761	0.31	0.194	0.261	0.296
	(2.47)**	(2.66)***	(2.33)**	(0.56)	(2.52)**	(0.73)	(0.45)	(0.62)	(0.71)
S3	-0.117	0.338	0.048	-0.559	0.519	-0.087	-0.396	0.092	0.206
	(-0.09)	(0.27)	(0.04)	(-0.44)	(0.42)	(-0.07)	(-0.31)	(0.07)	(0.16)
ΔlogNRD*S3		0.964			0.982	0.949		0.966	1.158
		(3.12)***			(3.21)***	(3.09)***		(3.17)***	(3.59)***
ΔlogNRD*ΔYE			1.618		1.694		1.627	1.701	0.726
			(1.89)*		(2.03)**		(1.91)*	(2.05)*	(0.73)
ΔYE*S3				1.075		1.019	1.082	1.025	0.97
				(1.74)*		(1.69)*	(1.77)*	(1.71)*	(1.63)*
ΔlogNRD*ΔYE*S3									2.966
									(1.75)*
Adj. R2	0.25	0.28	0.26	0.26	0.3	0.29	0.27	0.3	0.31
obs	230	230	230	230	230	230	230	230	230

Note: Figures in parentheses are robust t-statistics. ***(**) (*) indicates 1(5) (10) % significance level. The sample includes 50 developing countries covering the period of 1976 to 2000. NRD is trade-related North foreign R&D, defined in Section 2. YE is the average years of schooling of the population aged 25 and above. S3 is the dummy variable capturing small states.

($\Phi_{YS} > 5\ \beta_Y$). Similar results are obtained in equations (6) to (9), with $\Phi_{YS} > 6\ \beta_Y$ in equation (7), $\Phi_{YS} > 5\ \beta_Y$ in equation (8), $\Phi_{YS} > 4\ \beta_Y$ in equations (6) and (9).

The coefficient β_Y of the interaction effect $\Delta\log NRD \star \Delta YE$ for the full sample ranges from 1.618 to 1.701, with significance level of 5% or 10%, in regressions (3), (5), (7) and (8).

We introduce the variable $\Delta\log NRD \star \Delta YE \star S3$ in equation (9), in which case β_{NY} falls to 0.726 and is no longer significant. On the other hand, $\beta_{NYS} = 2.966$ (significant at the 10% level), with the impact of $\Delta\log NRD \star \Delta YE$ in small states equal to $\Phi_{NYS} \equiv \beta_{NY} + \beta_{NYS} = 3.792 > 5\ \beta_{NY}$. To sum up, we find that the impact of an increase in education on TFP growth ($\Delta YE \star S3 > 0$) is larger for small states (equation (4) and (6) to (9) in Table 21.1) and the impact of the interaction of an increase in education and an increase in technology diffusion ($\Delta\log NRD \star \Delta YE \star S3$) is also larger for small states (equation (9) in Table 21.1).

The results provided in Table 21.3 imply that the impact of $\Delta\log NRD$, ΔYE and $\Delta\log NRD \star \Delta YE$ on $\Delta\log TFP$ is systematically greater in small states than in large ones. Equation (9) – which includes all seven explanatory variables and is our preferred equation – shows that the impact of these three variables in small states is at least four times the impact in large ones, and the impact of ΔYE and of $\Delta\log NRD \star \Delta YE$ is more than five times greater.

By construction, the increase in *NRD* either comes from the increase in the trade share, or the increase in North's R&D, or both. Our regression results indicate that the continuous growth in North's R&D over time has a positive impact on the South's *long-term* productivity growth, an impact that is substantially greater for small than for large states.

Implications of brain drain

Emigration of skilled workers has long been a problem for developing, especially small developing countries. Table 21.2 (taken from Docquier and Schiff, 2008) presents skilled and overall emigration rates in 2000, as well as the ratio of the former to the latter (the schooling gap), for 46 small developing states – defined by the UN as states with population below 1.5 million – and for other categories of interest. Skilled workers are defined as those with university education. Row 1 of Table 21.2 shows that small developing states experience an extremely high level of brain drain (43.2%).[5] In other words, three out of every seven individuals with university education live outside their country of origin. This rate is 2.8 times as large as the 15.3% overall migration rate.

The table also shows a brain drain for small (all) high-income states of 23% (3.5%) or a ratio of 6.5 for small versus all states. The same ratio for developing countries is close to 6 (43.2% versus 7.4%). In other words, the impact of country size on the brain drain seems robust across a wide range of incomes. Moreover, the brain drain for all developing countries (7.4%) is over twice that of high-income countries (3.5%) and the schooling gap is close to four times as high (4.9% versus 1.3% or 3.8 times).

The region with the highest small-state brain drain (74.9%) is the Caribbean (in 'Latin America and the Caribbean'), and Table 21.3 shows that several states' brain drain is well above 80%. The East Asia and Pacific region (mainly the South Pacific islands) follows, with a brain drain of 50.8%, with several countries over 70% (Table 21.3). Sub-Saharan Africa is next with 41.7%, with several countries over 60% (Table 21.3).[6]

Thus, as far as small states are concerned, three out of four skilled Caribbean individuals live outside their country of origin, two out of four in East Asia and Pacific, and two out of five in Sub-Saharan Africa. Though Sub-Saharan Africa (SSA) has the lowest brain drain among these

Table 21.2 Emigration rates in 2000 by country group (%)

	N	(1) Skilled emigration rate	(2) Average emigration rate	(3) Schooling gap
Small states (pop<1.5million)	*46*	*43.2*	*15.3*	*2.81*
by population size				
population from 0 to 0.5 million	32	41.7	21	2
population from 0.5 to 1 million	8	47.2	15.7	3
population from 1 to 1.5 million	6	40.9	9.8	4.2
By region/income				
East Asia and Pacific	12	50.8	17	3
Latin America and Caribbean	10	74.9	35	2.1
Sub-Saharan Africa	10	41.7	6	6.9
High-income countries	12	23	10.7	2.1
Other groups of interest				
Small Islands Developing States	37	42.4	13.8	3.1
Population from 1.5 to 3 million	15	20.9	7.1	3
Population from 3 to 4 million	13	18.5	10	1.8
World average	192	5.3	1.8	3
Total high-income Countries	41	3.5	2.8	1.3
Total developing countries	151	7.4	1.5	4.9

Note: Skilled (average) emigration rates are defined as number of skilled (all) migrants divided by the sum of skilled (all) migrants. Schooling gap=Skilled emigration rate / average emigration rate. The table is from Docquier and Schiff (2008).

three regions, its schooling gap is more than double that in the other two developing regions. The main reason is the smaller share of skilled individuals in the population.

As shown in Table 21.2, the share of migrants who are skilled is two times the share among residents (Docquier and Schiff, 2008), implying that the brain drain reduces the average level of education YE and reduces the absorption capacity of developing source countries. The reduction is much larger for small than for large states. The interaction effect of ΔYE and $\Delta \log NRD$ is positive, so that brain drain reduces the impact that the diffusion of technology from the North has on productivity growth, and this reduction is greater for small than for large states.[7]

Small states also tend to suffer from significantly higher brain drain rates. The brain drain in 2000 was 43.2% for small states or well over five times the brain drain for all developing countries (7.4%), with the former equal to over five times the latter. Thus, the negative impact of the brain drain is greater in small states both because *TFP* growth is more sensitive to the brain drain and because the brain drain is substantially greater than in large countries.

The results are subject to an important caveat, though it may increase rather than reduce the difference between the small and the large states impact on TFP growth. A recent literature has argued that the loss in human capital is smaller than the brain drain because of a brain gain, a concept unrelated to return migration by some of the skilled migrants. Rather, this literature

Table 21.3 Highest brain drain (%) in a sample of small states in 2000 (by region)

Region / Country	Brain drain (%)
1. Sub-Saharan Africa	
Cape Verde	67.4
Gambia	63.2
Mauritius	56.1
Seychelles	55.8
2. Caribbean	
Guyana	89.0
Grenada	85.1
St Vincent and the Grenadines	84.5
St Kitts and Nevis	78.5
3. Central America	
Belize	65.5
4. South Pacific	
Samoa	76.4
Tonga	75.2
Fiji	62.2
Micronesia, Federated States	37.8
5. Mediterranean	
Malta	57.6
Cyprus	33.2

argues that a brain gain obtains because the positive probability of emigration and of earning a higher salary abroad raises the expected return to education and provides an incentive to acquire more of it. The change in the stock of human capital or net brain gain is the difference between the brain gain and the brain drain.

Several studies argue that under certain conditions, the net brain gain might actually be positive, with the incentive effect of the brain drain on human capital accumulation larger than the brain drain itself. For instance, a recent study by Beine *et al.* (2008) finds that the net brain gain is negative for most developing countries, particularly in the case of small states, though it tends to be positive in the very large countries where the brain drain is small such as Brazil, China, India, and others. Thus, the brain drain would be expected to result in a reduction in TFP growth in most developing countries. This is particularly true for small states, and for four reasons. First, as shown in Tables 21.2 and 21.3, the brain drain in small states is close to six times that in large ones. Second, the large states may experience a net brain gain rather than a brain drain, which is certainly not the case for small states (Beine *et al.*, 2008). Third, TFP growth is more sensitive to the brain drain in small than in large states;

and fourth, small states are more open to trade which implies, ceteris paribus, a higher level of technology diffusion.

Thus, the difference in the impact of the brain drain on TFP growth between small states and the larger states may be even *greater* than in the absence of a brain gain because the *net* brain gain remains highly negative for small states while that for large states tends to be positive (Beine *et al.*, 2008).

5 Conclusion

This chapter examined the impact of North-South trade-related technology diffusion on *TFP* growth in the South. It contributes to the open-economy endogenous growth literature by offering an empirical analysis of the impact of the brain drain, education and country size on *TFP* growth, and of a combination of these variables. The main findings are the following. First, *TFP* growth increases with growth in trade-related technology diffusion, and the increase is substantially larger for small states than for large ones. Second, education has a positive impact on TFP growth, and the increase is substantially larger for small states than for large ones. Third, the share of migrants who are skilled is larger than the share of residents who are skilled, implying that the brain drain has a negative impact on the stock of human capital and thus on *TFP* growth; and that the impact is larger (in absolute value) for small than for large states. Fourth, the impact of the interaction of trade-related technology diffusion and education on TFP growth is positive, and this impact is greater for small than for large states. Thus, TFP growth in small states is more sensitive to changes in the brain drain, to changes in North-South trade-related technology diffusion, and to the interaction between the two. Moreover, small states are more open to trade and thus have higher levels of North-South trade-related technology diffusion. This is another reason why TFP growth in small states would react more strongly to changes in trade-related technology diffusion. Brain Drain levels are also substantially larger in small than in large states, causing greater losses in TFP growth in the former than in the latter. Hence, there are two reasons for the greater negative impact of the brain drain in small than in large states: i) the former's TFP growth is more sensitive to the brain drain, and ii) their brain drain is substantially larger. Finally, the continuous growth of the North's R&D over time has a positive impact on the South's *long-term* productivity growth, an impact that is substantially greater for small than for large states.

One needs to be cautious regarding the implications on the impact of brain drain on TFP growth, as these implications are subject to a caveat, which is related to what has been referred to as the brain gain. The idea is that the brain drain might lead people to acquire more education because this would raise their probability of migrating and because the education premium is higher in the North than in the South. In other words, the increase in the (expected) return to education would provide an incentive to invest in education. Since only a small share of people acquiring more education will be able to migrate while the bulk will not, the brain drain would be expected to generate a brain gain. Hence, the loss of human capital associated with the brain drain would be expected to be smaller than the brain drain itself.

Notes

1 Acknowledgements: we would like to thank David Tarr and Edgardo Favaro for their insightful comments. This chapter builds upon an earlier paper published in the *International Economic Journal*, 27(3): 399–414, 2013.

2 We use the average size of the population over the first half of our sample period to determine which states are small. If the average population were taken over the entire period, the population in nine countries would be smaller than three million and would be slightly above three million in three countries: 3.11 million for Uruguay, 3.15 million for Singapore and 3.40 million for Jordan.

3 For labour income share, if self-employed workers fail to report their wages, and if the under-reporting causes is substantial, then the labour income share would be under-understated. The under-reporting problem might cause some concern at the micro-level studies, but for the industry-level data, the under-reporting problem is unlikely to be major, as the industry-level data have already passed the edit by each country's statistics bureau.

4 Given that the data reported in Nicita and Olarreaga (2007) are in current US dollars, we use the US GDP deflator. In the empirical analysis, country-specific as well as year dummies are used in order to control for some of the distortions possibly introduced by the conversion.

5 For the brain drain data, the primary data source is from Özden and Schiff (2007) and Docquier and Schiff (2008). Since it is hard to track all emigrants, there might be measurement problems on brain drain data. Regarding the potential measurement problems on the implications, there are small, mainly because we are not doing quantitative analysis, but some general discussions. Regardless of the magnitudes of the measurements errors on brain drain, it is a general consensus that brain drain problems in small states are much more severe than for large countries.

6 Table 21.3 also shows countries in Central America (Belize) and the Mediterranean (Malta) with brain drain above 50% and Cyprus with brain drain above 30%.

7 A hypothesis for the greater impact on *TFP* growth in small than in large states of DlogNRD, D*YE* and their interaction relates to economies of scale. These would hold in the case of education if subject to a threshold effect, with a minimum education level needed to absorb the North's new technologies and adapt them to the South's circumstances. They might also hold in the case of *NRD* if new technologies that firms obtain through trade were adopted by other firms through a logistic process, with adoption proceeding at an increasing rate once a threshold level had been reached, a pattern that was later found to hold for a wide range of phenomena. Small states are much more open to trade than large ones and have therefore a greater *NRD*. With increasing returns, the impact of ΔlogNRD, ΔYE and their interaction on *TFP* growth would be greater for small states than for large ones (as, for instance, $TFP = h^\alpha NRD^\beta$; α, $\beta > 1$). The empirical findings in Table 21.1 show that this condition is satisfied in the case of small states but not large ones.

Appendix

I: R&D-intensive industries

The industry-level data were aggregated in two industry groups: R&D-intensive aggregate industry and low R&D-intensity aggregate industry in order to examine whether there were significant differences between the two. The R&D-intensity measure used (R&D expenditures divided by sales) is based on the US, the technologically more advanced country. The regressions were estimated by adding a dummy variable for R&D-intensive industries for all countries. The results are shown in Table 21.A1 below for all the sample countries (with no differentiation between small and large states).

The preferred specification is equation (5) which includes all the variables. It shows that the differential impact of North-South trade-related technology diffusion (i.e. of ΔlogNRD*Dr) on *TFP* growth in R&D-intensive industries relative to non-intensive industries is small and not significant. Second, the differential impact of the interaction of ΔlogNRD and education *YE* (i.e. of ΔlogNRD*YE*Dr) on *TFP* growth in R&D-intensive industries relative to non-intensive industries is not significant either. The regressions were also estimated with small state dummies, with similar results: variables interacted with the dummy Dr were not significant. Consequently, we decided to estimate the model without differentiating the impacts according to their R&D intensity.

Table 21.A1 TFP growth and R&D intensity

	(1)	(2)	(3)	(4)	(5)
ΔlogNRD	0.348	0.289	0.366	0.373	0.295
	(7.05)***	(5.27)***	(7.38)***	(7.46)***	(5.54)***
ΔYE	0.292	0.289	0.319	0.318	0.328
	(5.99)***	(5.97)***	(6.45)***	(6.47)***	(6.82)***
ΔlogNRD*Dr		0.043			0.03
		(1.30)			(1.53)
ΔlogNRD*ΔYE			0.326	0.217	0.148
			(3.33)***	(2.45)**	(1.69)*
ΔlogNRD*ΔYE*Dr				0.068	0.049
				(1.60)	(1.50)
obs	230	230	230	230	230
Adj. R2	0.23	0.23	0.24	0.24	0.24

Note: *** (**) (*) indicates 1 (5) (10) percent significance level. Figures in parentheses are robust t-statistics. The sample includes 50 developing countries covering the period of 1976 to 2002. NRD is trade-related North foreign R&D, defined in Section 2. YE is the average number of years of schooling of the population aged 25 and above. Dr is the dummy for R&D-intensive industries, and S3 is a dummy variable capturing small states.

II Country size in term of GDP, trade-related technology diffusion and TFP growth

This subsection explores another direction in measuring the size of the states directly by their size of gross domestic product (GDP), rather than the one used in the main text with a small states dummy variable. Quite often, in the group of developing and transition economies covered in the study, a country's GDP is closely related to population size, as countries with small population usually have smaller size of GDP if GDP per capita in each country is about the same. The two measurements will differ if GDP per capita is significantly different among the countries included in the sample. Nonetheless, this subsection uses GDP as country size to study how country's GDP affects trade-related technology diffusion, and on TFP growth. Note that smaller GDP implies smaller country size in general, but not necessarily a smaller population, and thus a small state as outlined by the criteria of the United Nations.

Table 21.A2 provides the estimation results. The difference between Table 21.1 and Table 21.A2 is that Table 21.1 contains small states dummy (S3), while Table 21.2 replaces it with ΔlnGDP. Thus, the estimated results in Table 21.A2 here reflect the change of GDP on NRD and on YE and thus on their estimated effects on TFP, not necessarily a differentiation between large and small states, as estimated in Table 21.1. Summarizing the results lead to the following conclusions:

First, increases in trade-related technology diffusion generate substantial effects on TFP growth in the South. That is consistent with the findings in Table 21.1. Second, increase in a country's GDP directly affects its TFP growth. For developing countries, the larger the increase is in its economy size, the faster is its TFP growth rate. Third, the increase of the economic size of GDP in developing countries increases their TFP growth not only through its direct effects, but also through NRD, i.e. a larger increase in GDP leads to increased effects of trade-related

Table 21.A2 TFP growth and small states in term of GDP size

	(1)	(2)	(3)	(4)	(5)	(6)	(7)	(8)	(9)
ΔlogNRD	0.247	0.173	0.339	0.247	0.252	0.170	0.342	0.215	0.374
	(2.27)★★	(1.55)	(2.92)★★★	(2.27)★★	(1.99)★★	(1.51)	(2.93)★★★	(1.99)★★	(2.73)★★★
ΔYE	0.120	0.170	0.105	0.109	0.149	0.038	0.003	-0.022	-0.033
	(0.46)	(0.66)	(0.40)	(0.28)	(0.57)	(0.10)	(0.00)	(0.06)	(0.09)
ΔlogGDP	1.061	0.698	0.992	1.051	0.733	0.560	0.894	0.557	0.425
	(3.98)★★★	(2.28)★★	(3.72)★★★	(2.82)★★★	(2.39)★★	(1.33)	(2.38)★★	(1.33)	(1.01)
ΔlogNRD★ΔlogGDP		0.649			0.504	0.674		0.529	1.190
		(2.36)★★			(1.70)★	(2.40)★★		(1.77)★	(2.82)★★★
ΔlogNRD★ΔYE			1.423		0.963		1.465	1.007	1.236
			(2.09)★★		(1.32)		(2.12)★★	(1.37)	(1.69)★
ΔYE★ΔlogGDP				0.024		0.292	0.227	0.373	0.818
				(0.04)		(0.48)	(0.37)	(0.61)	(1.29)
ΔlogNRD★ΔYE★ΔlogGDP									-2.268
									(2.20)★★
Adj. R2	0.35	0.37	0.36	0.35	0.37	0.36	0.36	0.37	0.38
obs	218	218	218	218	218	218	218	218	218

Note: Figures in parentheses are robust t-statistics. ***(**) (*) indicates 1(5) (10) % significance level. The sample includes 50 developing countries covering the period of 1976 to 2000. NRD is trade-related North foreign R&D, defined in Section 2. YE is the average years of schooling of the population aged 25 and above. GDP is the gross domestic product, a measure for country size.

technology diffusion on TFP growth. Fourth, although educational attainment fails to obtain any direct significant effects on TFP growth in the presence of GDP, it enhances the effects of trade-related technology diffusion on TFP growth. That is, for developing countries, the higher is the educational level, the larger of the effects of trade-related technology diffusion on TFP growth. This finding is also consistent with those reported in Table 21.1.

References

Barro, R. J. and Lee, J. W. (2001). 'International data on educational attainment: updates and implications'. *Oxford Economic Papers*, 53(3): 541–563.

Beine, M., Docquier, F. and Rapoport, H. (2008). 'Brain Drain and Human Capital Formation in Developing Countries: Winners and Losers'. *Economic Journal*, 118: 631–652.

Coe, D. T. and Helpman, E. (1995). 'International R&D Spillovers'. *European Economic Review*, 39(5): 859–887.

Coe, D. T., Helpman, E. and Hoffmaister, A. W. (1997). 'North-South R&D Spillovers'. *Economic Journal*, 107: 134–149.

Correa, P., Fernandes, A. and Uregian, C. (2008). Technology Adoption and the Investment Climate: Firm-Level Evidence for Eastern Europe and Central Asia. *World Bank Policy Research Working Paper* 4707.

Docquier, F. and Schiff, M. (2008). *Measuring Skilled Emigration Rates: The Case of Small States*. Mimeo, World Bank DECRG.

Eaton, J. and Kortum, S. (1999). 'International Technology Diffusion: Theory and Measurement'. *International Economic Review*, 40: 537–570.

Engelbrecht, H.-J. (1997). 'International R&D Spillovers, Human Capital and Productivity in OECD Countries: an Empirical Investigation'. *European Economic Review*, 41(8):1479–1488.

Falvey, R., Foster, N. and Greenaway, D. (2002). North-South Trade, Knowledge Spillovers and Growth. *Research Paper* No. 2002/23. Leverhulme Centre for Research on Globalisation and Economic Policy, University of Nottingham.

Grossman, M. G. and Helpman, M. (1991) *Innovation and Growth in the Global Economy*. Cambridge, MA: MIT Press.

Lucas, R. E., Jr (1988). 'On the Mechanics of Economic Development'. *Journal of Monetary Economics*, 22: 3–42.

Lumenga-Neso, O., Olarreaga, M. and Schiff, M. (2005). 'On 'Indirect' Trade-related Research and Development Spillovers'. *European Economic Review*, 49: 1785–1798.

Nicita, A. and Olarreaga, M. (2007). 'Trade, Production and Protection 1976–2004'. *World Bank Economic Review*, 21(1): 165–171.

Özden, Ç. and Schiff, M. (2007). *International migration, economic development and policy*. Washington, DC: World Bank and Palgrave Macmillan.

Romer, P. M. (1986). 'Increasing Returns and Long-Run Growth'. *Journal of Political Economy*, 94(5): 1002–1037.

Schiff, M. and Wang, Y. (2006). 'North-South and South-South Trade-Related Technology Diffusion: An Industry-Level Analysis of Direct and Indirect Effects'. *Canadian Journal of Economics*, 39(3): 831–844.

Wang, Y. (2007). 'Trade, Human Capital and Technology Spillovers: An Industry Level Analysis'. *Review of International Economics*, 15(2): 269–283.

Wooldridge, J. M. (2002). *Econometric Analysis of Cross Section and Panel Data*. Cambridge, MA: MIT Press.

22

Smallness compared: on democracy and modernization

Dag Anckar

1 Introduction

The study of politics involves several preponderances and distortions. Some are methodological and obstruct attempts at an innovative interplay between schools of thought, some are political, the implication of which is that democracies are studied widely more than non-democracies, some are geographical, meaning that some territories and regions are studied more than others. One particular bias relates to case selection in the comparative politics genre. There are some 200 independent countries in the world, and about one-fifth of these states are microstates, i.e. states with populations of less than 1 million people. Their large number notwithstanding, these small states have aroused only a limited and abstracted interest among political scientists, who often dismiss the study of small states in a language that reveals a view of small states as being insignificant and negligible. Characteristic sayings in studies are that 'the smallest states' are excluded (Vanhanen, 1990: 5); that 'a handful of very tiny states' have been left out (Lane and Ersson, 1994: 43), or that 'very small states' are dismissed (Sartori, 1976).

This chapter departs from a very different notion and certainly takes on board the observation by Veenendaal and Corbett (2015) and others (e.g. Rich, 2014) that the political science discipline remains poorer for not utilizing small states to a larger extent as research objects. Veenendaal and Corbett show that contra to received wisdom, democratic development in poor societies is certainly possible and that the systematic absence from studies of democratization and democratic conduct of small-state regions like the Pacific and the Caribbean greatly distorts our understanding of democratic transition. The point is particularly well made in the comments the authors offer in regard to Samuel Huntington's seminal 1991 work on *The Third Wave*. In this important work Huntington identified a series of democratic transitions in the period 1974–1990 that resulted in a global increase in the number of democracies from about 25% to more than 45%, this increase constituting the famous third wave. Excluded from these calculations were, however, all countries with less than 1 million inhabitants, and Veenendaal and Corbett show that this exclusion distorts findings – had Huntington included all countries that turned democratic in the actual time span, the number of democracies had risen from 36 to an impressive 56. Smallness would indeed have made a difference.

Inspired by this and similar turnouts in defence of small state research, the study that is conducted in this chapter undertakes two tasks. It first investigates to what extent it is really the case that small states are predisposed to democracy and that a full observation of these states therefore adds significantly to our knowledge of the actual spread of democratic ideals and democratic conduct. Second, the research investigates to what extent the observation of small states is likely to change or modify prevailing views of democracy and democratization. In particular, the research aims at grading the validity of the so-called modernization theory, which is perhaps the leading body of assumptions about democracy's emergence. An oft-quoted thesis in the frame of the theory reads: 'the more well-to-do a nation, the greater the chances that it will sustain democracy' (Lipset, 1959: 75). Small states, it would seem, are less well equipped to satisfy economy demands for democratic strength and advancement; if, then, it really proves to be the case that they perform in terms of democracy, such a finding may well question the durability of the belief that modernization links to and in fact supports democracy. It is the purport of this study to illustrate and elucidate this complex of problems by means of empirically derived classifications and observations.

2 Democracy: a bird's eye view

Democracy is of course a much contested concept and definitions abound – indeed, to quote an apposite observation, 'there are almost as many theoretical definitions of democracy as there are scholars who study democratic politics' (Lipset and Lakin, 2004: 19). The solution here to the essential task of finding a worth-while point of departure for an analysis of democratic similarities and disparities is to apply the well-known annual surveys since 1972 of the countries of the world by the Freedom House organization. The Freedom House understanding of freedom encompasses two set of characteristics that relate to political rights and civil liberties. Based on extensive checklists rights and liberties are rated for each country separately on a seven-category scale and the scales are thereafter merged to produce a classification of the countries and territories of the world in three categories: entities are 'Free' (F), 'Partly Free' (PF) or 'Not Free' (NF).

In line with several other political science studies (e.g. Veenendaal and Corbett, 2015; Karvonen, 2008; Lipset and Lakin, 2004; Lijphart, 1999; Denk and Silander, 2012), this research regards 'Free' countries only as adherents to a democratic formula; while this manipulation simplifies matters, it does not entail, however, over-simplification. One specific feature of the Freedom House data merits attention. Large-N studies of political life are often criticized for using inadequate data based on constitutional principle rather than actual political practice (Foweraker and Krznaric, 2000: 765); avoiding this pitfall, Freedom House score countries not only on basis of governmental intention or constitution, but relies also on real world situations caused by a variety of governmental and non-governmental factors. Importantly, while most other global analyses of the conditions for democratization, including Polity IV[1] and others (Campbell, 2008) and a landmark study by Teorell (2010) excludes small and/or very small states, the Freedom House index is updated on an ongoing basis as well as includes all states, small and large.

Freedom House data is used here in three consecutive Tables that mirror different size-based comparisons. The first table (Table 22.1) lists microstates of the world in the year 2016, the size threshold being set at a population of at least 1 million. These states form the small state population in this research. The states are classified in the table in three size-determined groups, size being defined in terms of population figures for the year 2016[2] – the somewhat unclear

Table 22.1 The microstates of the world, 2016, classified by population size in thousands and Freedom
House ratings

Size intervals		
1,000–500	499–100	<100
Djibouti 899 NF	Brunei 428 NF	Seychelles 96 PF
Fiji 897 PF	Malta 419 F	Antigua-Barbuda 92 F
Equatorial Guinea 869 NF	Bahamas 392 F	Dominica 72 F
Comoros 807 PF	Maldives 369 PF	Andorra 70 F
Bhutan 784 PF	Belize 366 F	St Kitts-Nevis 56 F
Guyana 770 F	Iceland 331 F	Marshall Islands 53 F
Montenegro 626PF	Barbados 285 F	Liechtenstein 37 F
Solomon Islands 594 PF	Vanuatu 270 F	Monaco 37 F
Luxembourg 576 F	Samoa 194 F	San Marino 31 F
Suriname 547 F	Sao Tomé & Principe 194 F	Palau 21 F
Cape Verde 526 F	St Lucia 186 F	Nauru 10 F
	Kiribati 114 F	Tuvalu 10 F
	St Vincent 109 F	Vatican City 1 NF
	Grenada 107 F	
	Tonga 106 F	
	Micronesia 105 F	

Note: F – 'Free' country; PF – 'Partly Free' country; NF – 'Not Free' country.

case of Bhutan, for which population figures that exceed even 2 million are reported in some sources (e.g. Whitecross, 2007: 104), is included in the research.

In the first group are 11 states with populations that exceed a 500,000 threshold; in the second group are 16 states with populations of less than 500,000 and more than 100,000; finally, in the third group are 13 states with populations of less than 100,000. As evident from the table, closely to three-fourth of the countries (73%) are in the democracy category, this corresponding closely to findings from several similar and earlier calculations (e.g. D. Anckar, 2002a, 2002b, 2008; 2010a). The general impression is therefore, again, that small country size is conducive to democracy and that it is a significant feature of small jurisdictions that they possess an ability to maintain democratic systems (e.g. Diamond and Tsalik, 1999; Ott, 2000; Srebrnik, 2004). Interestingly, however, as has been demonstrated also in earlier research (e.g. C. Anckar, 2008: 440–441; Anckar, 2010a), the size divide is really between cases that are below and go beyond the 500,000 threshold – while the former group has an overwhelming democracy surplus, the second group in fact has a definite democracy deficiency. Of 29 states in Table 22.1 with populations of less than 500,000, no less than 25 are democracies; of 11 states with populations of more than 500,000, only four are democracies. And to make doubly sure, three of these four democratic countries only barely cross the 500,000 threshold. It would appear, therefore, that several undemocratic microstates are 'large' on a microstate scale and are therefore not to the same extent as 'smaller' microstates sensitive to the democracy-building capacities that are inherent in smallness. Democracy, then, appears to be a characteristic of 'small' microstates but not of 'larger' microstates.

Still, as evident also from Table 22.1, the generalization that small size links to democracy is certainly less than law-like. For a variety of reasons (Anckar, 2010b), several small states maintain political regimes that do not qualify as democracies. Some of these small non-democracies, like Comoros (Thibaut, 1999a: 243–246), have suffered from conflicts between clans and regions and over constitutional orders to an extent which has fuelled a notorious political instability. Other small non-democracies such as Djibouti (Thibaut, 1999b: 315–318) and Equatorial Guinea (Fleischhacker, 1999), have been governed by authoritarian regimes of long-standing – in such cases microstate non-democracy has a tradition which serves as a drag on development and conform to the future by slow degrees, if at all. Also, in assessing the magnitude of the present democracy predominance among microstates one needs to recognize that the democracy surplus is to some extent technical in nature and a consequence of population growth, as some large-sized microstates that have suffered democracy defections, most notably Gabon, Guinea-Bissau, Kuwait, Oman, Swaziland and the United Arab Emirates, have over time simply disappeared from the microstate group (Anckar, 2010a: 7).

The second table (Table 22.2) likewise is of introductory nature as it lists 80 countries that are larger than microstates and serve as comparison objects in the impending analysis of the small-large divide. To secure a satisfying distribution in terms of geography, culture, diffusion, and other background variables, the materials are selected to reflect differing contexts. This means that Freedom House ratings are registered for a group of 20 randomly selected African states, a group of 20 randomly selected American states, a group of 20 randomly selected Asian states, and a group of 20 randomly selected European states, randomness meaning that the selection has been unsystematic. The Freedom House ratings of all these states are included in the respective lists. Finally, Table 22.3 compares observations on small states with observations on larger states, the small state universe being compared to the large state universe as conceptualized in terms of total figures as well as region-wise figures.

As indicated in Table 22.3, a difference between small states and larger states is evident: almost three fourths of the small states are in the democracy category as against clearly less than

---

Table 22.2 Four regionally defined groups of selected states, with Freedom House ratings, 2016

Africa

Angola (NF), Botswana (F), Burundi (NF), Cameroon (NF), Congo Kinshasa (NF), Egypt (NF), Eritrea (NF), Guinea (PF), Morocco (PF), Mozambique (PF), Namibia (F), Nigeria (PF), Rwanda (NF), Senegal (F), South Africa (F), South Sudan (NF), Swaziland (NF), Togo (PF), Uganda (NF), Zambia (PF)

Americas

Argentina (F), Bolivia (PF), Brazil (F), Canada (F), Chile (F), Colombia (PF), Cuba (NF), Ecuador (PF), El Salvador (F), Guatemala (PF), Haiti (PF), Honduras (PF), Mexico (PF), Nicaragua (PF), Panama (F), Paraguay (PF), Trinidad and Tobago (F), United States (F), Uruguay (F), Venezuela (PF)

Asia

Afghanistan (NF), Bangladesh (PF), China (NF), India (F), Israel (F), Japan (F), Kazakhstan (NF), Korea North (NF), Korea South (F), Kyrgyzstan (PF), Laos (NF), Malaysia (PF), Mongolia (F), Myanmar (NF), Nepal (PF), Pakistan (PF), Philippines (PF), Sri Lanka (PF), Turkey (PF), Uzbekistan (NF)

Europe

Albania (PF), Belarus (NF), Belgium (F), Bosnia-Herzegovina (PF), Denmark (F), Finland (F), France (F), Germany (F), Greece (F), Hungary (F), Italy (F), Moldova (PF), Portugal (F), Russia (NF), Slovenia (F), Spain (F), Sweden (F), Switzerland (F), Ukraine (PF), United Kingdom (F)

Note: F – 'Free' country; PF – 'Partly Free' country; NF – 'Not Free' country.

Table 22.3 Democracy profiles, small states compared to groups of larger states

Freedom status	Free	Partly free	Not free
Small states, % (N=40)	73	18	9
Larger states, % (N=80)	40	35	25
Larger states, Africa (N=20)	4	6	10
Larger states, Americas (N=20)	9	10	1
Larger states, Asia (N=20)	5	8	7
Larger states, Europe (N=20)	14	4	2

Note: Small states are defined as those with a population of up to 1 million and larger states as those with a population exceeding 1 million.

half of the larger states. Furthermore, whereas very few of the small states, four out of forty, end up in the category of Not Free nations, the corresponding figure for larger states is twenty out of eighty. In other words, small states populate the political top category in rich numbers and are barely present in the bottom category; in contrast, larger states are present in the top category to a much lesser extent and in the bottom category to a clearly higher extent. As regards the regional clusters of large states, differences in democracy ratings are to be expected, as comparisons are between, on the one hand, a set of countries from a region that is commonly regarded a heartland for democracy (Europe), and, on the other hand, three sets of countries from regions which are to a lesser degree appreciated as democratic forerunners (Africa, Americas, Asia). As is evident from the Table, the ratings indeed verify these assumptions.

An overwhelming majority of European states, seven out of ten, are Free nations, and of twenty nations only two, namely Russia and Belarus, are classified as Not Free – of Belarus it has been said that 'democracy, the rule of law, and human rights have traditionally not existed in Belarus' (Hansen, 2007: 88). In contrast, of the nations in the Asian group, only a handful are Free, like India, Israel, Japan and South Korea, with the majority falling into the Partly Free or Not Free categories. The Americas take a place somewhere in the terrain between high-performing Europe and less successful Asia, as about half of the American countries, including Argentina, Canada, Chile, and Panama, are 'Free' countries. Only one member of the American group (Cuba), is banished to the league of 'Not Free'-nations. Ratings range from bad to worst in Africa where an overwhelming majority, eight out of ten, are Partly Free or Not Free-nations, with only four nations out of twenty, namely Botswana, Namibia, Senegal and South Africa, qualifying for the Free-list and all these nations receiving individual Freedom House ratings that with narrow margins only entitle the entry into the 'Free'-category (e.g. Melber, 2010; Nagar, 2015; Osei-Hwedie and Sebudubudu, 2005).

In sum, then, small states show a democracy profile almost identical to that of the larger European states and clearly superior to the profiles of the other groups of larger states. When all classifications are summarized, the result is indisputable: small size predestines to democracy, insofar as the democratic regime form is much more common among small states than among larger states. The reason why this is so remains under-researched as well as unclear. Most probably, several different factors interact and contribute to linking small size and democracy (Srebrnik, 2004: 338–339). Anyhow, small is democratic, and democracy research is well advised to take this challenge seriously and to include more than hitherto small states in future research settings.

3 Modernization: dimensions and patterns

In this section the focus turns from democracy to modernization. The point of departure, however, is modest and unpretentious, and it needs to be stressed that the following is not, and is not intended to be, a systematic test of the vast body of assumptions and counter-assumptions that make up what is called modernization theory (Lipset and Lakin, 2004: 139–148). Rather, what follows is an attempt to draw on some central modernization dimensions and distinctions for identifying the position of small states in this regard. To that end and in line with the ambition of the chapter to find out the extent to which an inclusion or exclusion of small states in research settings make a difference in terms of findings and interpretations, for each and every of the selected modernization dimensions, which all are indicators of social and economic performance, small is compared to large and subgroups of large. These subgroups are the same regionally defined groups that were presented above. Consequently, the above research question may be rephrased as one about the performance differences between small and large – if such differences do not exist, smallness becomes a negligible factor which does not leave imprints on the patterns that are studied; if differences exist, smallness emerges a non-negligible condition, suggesting that small states should feature prominently in research on democracy.

Modernization I: income

The question if and to what extent democracy is related to economic development may be approached from many angles and with different sets of data and information. The first path examined here is, quite simply, to presuppose a positive relation between the level of development of a country and the per capita income of that same country (Przeworski and Limongi, 1997). The measure that comes to use here is the gross national income per capita in the year 2015, as measured in thousands of US dollars – data are from listings by The World Bank.[3] Cutting points have been used here to establish three classes – countries that exceed a 25,000 dollar mark are regarded as 'high' economies, whereas countries that stay below the 10,000 dollar mark are 'low' economies, and countries in the range of 10,000–25,000 dollars are 'medium' economies. In all, 28 countries are ranked 'high', whereas 33 are ranked 'medium' and 59 are ranked 'low'. The distribution of cases on regions and categories is reported in Table 22.4.

It appears that the difference between small and big states is quite narrow and in fact negligible: in both groups close to one third have high economies, whereas about half of the states are in the low economy category. Between individual small states there are big gaps in terms of income, some countries performing very well and others separated by broad margins. What is

Table 22.4 Income differences between small and larger states and between groups of larger states (GNI per capita)

GNP per capita level	High	Medium	Low
Small states, % (N=40)	32	23	45
Larger states, % (N=80)	29	30	51
Larger states, Africa (N=20)	0	2	18
Larger states, Americas (N=20)	2	11	7
Larger states, Asia (N=20)	3	4	13
Larger states, Europe (N=20)	10	7	3

Note: See text for the meaning of High, Medium and Low.

worth noting, however, is that the differences do not seem to reflect systematically in the support for democratic regimes: democracy is held in esteem to roughly the same extent by rich and poor. Among the twelve richest small states, led by countries like Liechtenstein, Luxembourg and Monaco, are nine democracies and three non-democracies; among the twelve poorest small states, including countries like Comoros, Sao Tomé and Príncipe and Solomon Islands, the corresponding ratio is eight to four. This is much different from, say, the situation in the 20 big European countries, where the five richest countries all are democracies and the five poorest countries all are non-democracies.

Also, it is obvious that the internal differences between the big states are conspicuous and to a large extent region-defined. Half of the European states are in the high economy category, Switzerland, Sweden, Germany, Denmark and Belgium being at the top, and three countries only, namely Albania, Bosnia and Herzegovina, and Moldavia, are to be found in the low economy category. The configuration in regard to African countries is quite the opposite. Here, almost all countries are low economies, Botswana and South Africa being the only exceptions, and countries like Burundi, Eritrea, Guinea, South Sudan, and Togo occupying bottom positions. From the point of view of modernization assumptions, it is an interesting observation that precisely Botswana and South Africa are among the very few African democracies, and that precisely the relatively poor cases of Albania, Bosnia and Herzegovina, and Moldavia are among the four European non-democracies.

Modernization II: employment

An important indicator of a country's economic strength and growth and a valid indicator also of labour market health, the unemployment rate is the share of the labour force that is jobless and actively looking for a job, expressed as a percentage. As is well known, methods for calculating and presenting unemployment rates vary from country to country, and countries operate their national statistics with varying degrees of sophistication. It may perhaps even be the case that some countries create misleading statistics for strengthening people's confidence in the domestic economy. Such reservations notwithstanding, it is reasonable to assume that employment statistics shed light on the shape of the economy and provides relevant information about general economic conditions in a country. However, since methods of calculation of unemployment rates may vary considerably, comparisons need really to be based on harmonized values, and such values for the countries of the world are published, among others, by the International Labour Organization.[4] The date of information varies somewhat, but is in most cases in the time interval 2014–2016, and the unemployment figures from this source have been classified here into three categories. Countries with unemployment rates at 7% or less have been placed in a 'high' employment category, whereas countries with unemployment rates of 20% or more are placed in a 'low' employment category, and countries with unemployment rates that fall between the two above figures are placed in a 'medium' employment category. The resulting distributions are given in Table 22.5.

Concerning small states, data is missing in the cases of Samoa, Solomon Islands, and Vatican City. Otherwise no specific small state profile appears, as there are among the small states cases with excellent as well as quite bad ratings, which do not correlate systematically with democracy achievements. For instance, several democratic Pacific small states, like Kiribati (38.2%), the Marshall Islands (36.0%), Micronesia (22.0%) and Nauru (23.0%) have less than impressive employment marks; in contrast, other democratic small Pacific islands like Palau (4.2%), Tonga (6.5%) and Tuvalu (6.5%) report good ratings. Several European small democracies, like Andorra (2.9%), Iceland (3.0%), Liechtenstein (2.3%) and Malta (5.2%) have good employment

Table 22.5 Employment level differences between small and larger states and between groups of larger states

Employment level	High	Medium	Low
Small states, % (N=40)	41	32	27
Larger states, % (N=80)	54	35	11
Larger states, Africa (N=20)	5	10	5
Larger states, Americas (N=20)	14	6	0
Larger states, Asia (N=20)	15	3	2
Larger states, Europe (N=20)	9	9	2

Note: See text for the meaning of High, Medium and Low.

performances, whereas, in contrast, several small and democratic Caribbean states, like Dominica (23.0%) and Grenada (24.5%), face employment difficulties. The fact that small states are scattered over the classification categories of course undermines to some extent any belief that small size in itself makes a notable difference. It is worth noting, though, that the small states are on average less successful than the bigger states, and that a systematic neglect of the small states category therefore is likely to convey a somewhat over-optimistic view of overall employment situations.

Interestingly, the rather clear-cut differences between regionally defined groups of larger states that came into sight in regards to income are not reflected in the employment figures. Rather, as Europe does not now maintain a dominating position, as America and Asia move into a lead with similar positions, and as the straggler position of Africa, while still noticeable, is far less conspicuous, the differences are smoothed out. While perhaps somewhat unexpected, the rather disappointing labour market performance of European countries is in fact a manifestation of a trend. For instance, while the talk some decades ago was of the 'European unemployment miracle', the miracle ended already in the 1970s and has not reappeared (Blanchard, 2004). Findings from the early 2000s were that the unemployment rate remained very high in four large continental countries, France, Germany, Spain and Italy (Blanchard, 2004), and the findings from this research largely confirm this pattern, France (10.0%), Italy (11.0%) and Spain (18.6%) still having high rates.

Modernization III: life expectancy

The third modernization component is life expectancy, which is a statistical measure of the average time people are expected to live. The most commonly used measure of life expectancy is at birth. Data supply is again plentiful, as life expectancy figures and lists of countries are reported by various statistical national agencies and international organizations. Again, caveats apply, as life expectancy figures are affected by other factors than modernization alone, such as wars, epidemics, and plagues; some of the sources used by some of the data providers for compiling statistics perhaps operate with questionable accuracy. On the whole, however, it is a reasonable assumption that differences in life expectancy figures between countries and different parts of the world reflect with some accuracy differences in ventures for public health and medical care.

The list of countries and respective life expectancies used here is provided by the World Bank and derives from sources as the United Nations Population Division and Census Reports

Table 22.6 Life expectancy differences between small and larger states and between groups of larger states

Life expectancy level	High	Medium	Low
Small states, % (N=40)	40	50	10
Larger states, % (N=80)	39	41	20
Larger states, Africa (N=20)	0	6	14
Larger states, Americas (N=20)	10	9	1
Larger states, Asia (N=20)	5	14	1
Larger states, Europe (N=20)	16	4	0

Note: See text for the meaning of High, Medium and Low.

from national statistical offices.[5] Again, the initial guiding ambition is to classify countries in three categories that reflect and summarize expectancy differences. The relevant cutting points have been decided on the basis of the fact that the average life expectancy at birth of the global population in 2015 was 71.4 years. Countries with expectancy values of 75 years or more are placed in a 'high' expectancy category. Countries that have values of 65 years or less are in a 'low' expectancy category, and countries that have values in the interval of 65–74 years are placed in an intermediate 'medium' category. The resulting distributions reported in Table 22.6 indeed show that there are great variations in life expectancy capacities between different parts of the world.

The overall picture again looks familiar: the difference between small and larger states is negligible and the overall profiles of the two groups resemble much each other. The implication of this is, of course, that the democracy advantage of small states over larger states is not to be derived from a corresponding advantage in regard to modernization in the form of life expectancy. It is also evident from the similarities that a potential inclusion of larger sets of small states in research settings would not alter much the overall validity of findings. The internal differences within both groups are considerable; the strength of the link between expectancy and democracy fluctuates in like manner. To give just two examples from the world of small states: tiny Monaco has the highest expectancy score (89.6 years) and is a democracy; so is Vanuatu with a much lower expectancy score (73.4 years); Andorra has an expectancy score of 82.6 years and is a democracy; so is St Vincent and the Grenadines with a much lower expectancy score (73.2 years). On the other hand, while Seychelles has the same expectancy score as St Vincent, Seychelles is not a democracy.

Also again: Europe and Africa are extreme regions. All European countries but four, namely Belarus, Moldova, Russia and Ukraine, are in the 'high' category and twelve countries report expectancy figures that indeed exceed the 80 years mark, Switzerland, Spain, Italy and Sweden even exceeding the 82-year mark. In contrast, 14 out of 20 African states are placed in the 'low' category, and not a single one is placed in the 'high' category, Morocco (74.3 years) and Egypt (70.9 years) being in top, and Angola (52.4 years) and Burundi (53.6 years), both plagued by intense ethnic and ideological conflict and violence (e.g. Bekink, 2007: 25–26; Mangu, 2007: 146–147) having the worst scores. Between the two extremes, America is closer to Europe and Asia is closer to Africa – half of the American states are in the 'high' category, and only one, namely Haiti (63.5 years), is in the 'low' category, whereas of Asian countries five are in the 'high' category, Japan (85.7 years), Israel (82.5 years) and South Korea (81.4 years) reporting top scores, and almost all other countries being in the 'medium' category. Several of these countries, however, like Laos (65.7 years), Pakistan (66.4 years), Myanmar (66.6 years) and India (68.3 years) have records that come quite near to the 'low' expectancy category.

Modernization IV: literacy rate

The next and final modernization component is the literacy rate, which may be regarded a key measure of a population's education. Of the many available lists of countries by literacy rate, the one used here reports figures collected by the UNESCO Institute for Statistics on behalf of the UNESCO.[6] The figures are 2015 estimates relating to people aged 15 or over who can read and write. In quite a few cases data are not reported by UNESCO; concerning these cases, *The World Factbook*[7] has been consulted. Based on the given estimates, in line with previous presentations, countries are placed in one of three categories, one denoting 'high' rate countries, one denoting 'medium' rate countries, and one denoting 'low' rate countries. Given that the global literacy rate for all people aged 15 and above is 86.3% (UNESCO), the cutting points used are the following: countries with 'high' literacy rates are those that represent rates of 95% or more, countries with 'low' literacy rates are those reporting rates of less than 85%, and countries with 'medium' rates are those reporting rates in the interval 85.0–94.9%.

Findings, arranged by the same structure and logic as in previous summations, are reported in Table 22.7, the main features of which again are variation, manifoldness and miscellany. Indeed, while there has been over time a global expansion of literacy (e.g. Roser and Ortiz-Ospina, 2016), differences between groups of nations and regions prevail. Concerning the essential divide between small and larger states, the finding is that a difference now comes forward between the two size groups. Surprisingly, however, the difference is by a relatively evident margin in favour of small states. No less than 13 out of the 40 small states score literacy rates of 99.0% or more, Andorra, Liechtenstein and Luxembourg even reporting, somewhat dubiously perhaps, rates of a full 100%. Bhutan (64.9%) and Djibouti (67.0%) are the two only explicit deviationists in the group. It appears to be the case, then, that disregarding small states, as far as this modernization component is concerned, besides distorting empirical democracy patterns also obscures the study of democratization patterns – small size implies satisfactory achievements as regards democracy as well as literacy and therefore suggests that there are links which could be reinforced between these two variables. Actually, a neglect of small states in research on political consequences of literacy implies an omission of countries that stand for considerable achievements in regards to the very factor that is investigated.

The profiles and internal positions of the various regions resemble once more the corresponding findings for other modernization components. Europe is a top region and in fact

Table 22.7 Literacy rate differences between small and larger states and between groups of larger states

Literacy rate level:	High	Medium	Low
Small states, % (N=40)	63	22	15
Larger states, % (N=80)	54	16	30
Larger states, Africa (N=20)	0	4	16
Larger states, Americas (N=20)	11	6	3
Larger states, Asia (N=20)	11	3	6
Larger states, Europe (N=20)	20	0	0

Note: See text for the meaning of High, Medium and Low.

scores full points, as all 20 countries are in the 'high' rate category, Portugal (95.7%) and Albania (97.6%) having bottom scores and no less than 15 countries having rates of 99% or more. Africa is again at the other extreme, 16 countries out of 20 being classified in the 'low' rate category. Some of these countries, like Guinea (30.4%) and Senegal (55.7%) represent particularly modest scores. The profiles of the Americas and Asia are fairly similar, both regions placing about a dozen countries in the highest category. American countries such as Haiti (60.7%) and Guatemala (79.3%) and Asian countries such as Afghanistan (38.2%) and Pakistan (56.4%) perform particularly poorly.

4 Smallness compared

The observations and findings presented so far are now set out in three tables. Table 22.8 compares the 40 small states and the 80 larger states that have been investigated above and uses two dichotomized dimensions, namely modernization and democracy. As already explained, democracies are countries classified by Freedom House in the category of 'Free' countries; the adequate listings have been reported in Tables 22.1 and 22.2. Concerning modernization, a summarizing calculation is now performed, the meaning of which is that countries classified above as 'high' quality performers in at least three of the four modernization components that have been used are classified as modernized, whereas other countries are classified as non-modernized. To give just one example: Iceland is classified as a 'high' performer in terms of all four components and is in consequence doubtless a modernized country. In contrast, Cape Verde is classified in a 'low' category as regards income and in a 'medium' category as regards employment, life expectancy and literacy, and is therefore, its epithet 'The Happy Islands' notwithstanding (Davidson, 1990), an evident case of non-modernization.

Table 22.9 introduces a correlation analysis that builds on Tables 22.3–22.8 in the previous analyses and confirms the main finding of this study, namely that there are marginal or no differences between small states and larger states when it comes to modernization, but noticeable differences in the level of democracy. Finally, Table 22.10, somewhat impressionistic but still aiming at systematizing findings, grades the overall modernization performance of the small states group as compared to the corresponding performances of the larger states group and the regionally defined groups. The grades that are used are B for 'better', W for 'worse', and EQ for 'about equal'. For example, the summation in the table as regards life expectancy is that while the small states are below European standard, they still perform, on the whole, about equally well as the remaining groups of larger states.

From these tables, three lessons are learned:

One. Indeed, modernization is associated with democracy. It is a rule with few exceptions that modernized countries are democracies, and this rule covers small states and larger states alike. Of 36 modernized states, no less than 31 are democracies, this meaning, then, that the

Table 22.8 Modernization and democracy linkages: small and larger states compared, number of countries

		Democracies?	
		Yes	*No*
Modernized?	Yes	SS: 10 LS: 21	SS: 3 LS: 2
	No	SS: 19 LS: 11	SS: 8 LS: 46

Note: SS=small states; LS=larger states.

Table 22.9 Size, democracy and modernization: a correlation analysis

Variables	Correlation (tau-c)	Significance	Table in text
Size/democracy	−0.297	0.000	3
Size/income	−0.004	0.965	4
Size/employment	−0.183	0.048	5
Size/life expectancy	0.063	0.473	6
Size/literacy	0.116	0.170	7
Size/democracy	−0.306 (tau-b)	0.000	8
Size/modernization	−0.093 (tau-b)	0.321	8

Table 22.10 Modernization performances of small states as compared to performances of groups of larger states

	Larger countries	African countries	American countries	Asian countries	European countries
Income	EQ	B	B	B	W
Employment	W	B	W	W	W
Life expectancy	EQ	B	W	EQ	W
Literacy	B	B	EQ	EQ	W

Note: B=better; W=worse; EQ=about equal.

two key variables link together in 86% of the cases and that modernization therefore can be considered as almost a sufficient condition for democracy. Of 23 modernized larger states, only two, namely China and education and health devoted Cuba (Ritter, 2004), are non-democracies. Of 13 modernized small states only three, namely Brunei, Seychelles, and the Vatican are non-democracies – let it be added that Brunei, an oil-inflated rich small sultanate with no democratic procedures (Hass, 1999: 145; Karvonen, 2008: 117–127) and Vatican, a most different and peculiar political entity (Murphy, 1974; Duursma, 1994: 413–466), are anomalous state formations that do not provide much fuel for meaningful comparison. And, of course: it follows from the similarity of the profiles of small and big states that the introduction of a number of small states in research settings does not on this point alter findings about the significance of the modernization factor. When present in larger states the factor promotes democracy, when present in small states, the outcome is the same.

Two. When and if modernization is a driving force behind democracy, it lies near at hand to believe that a lack of the same driving force provokes non-democracy. This thought, by the way, is congruent with the finding in the research literature that countries have in general democratized successfully only after economic growth but have come off less well when democratizing at lower levels of wealth (Peerenboom, 2008). The expectation, then, would be that a great majority of the non-modernized countries stand out as non-democracies. Indeed, in the case of larger states the expectation is met – of 57 non-modernized larger countries only 11 turn out to be democracies, whereas 46 are not.

Importantly, however, the situation is much different in regards to the small states. There are 27 non-modernized small states; of these states an evident majority of no less than 19 (amounting to 70%) are in the democracy camp. The minority cases do not represent regional or cultural similarity – African cases like Comoros, Djibouti and Equatorial Guinea are joined by Pacific cases like Fiji and Solomon Islands and Asian cases like Bhutan and Maldives. In the world of small states, therefore, while modernization spells democracy, so does non-modernization: it does not really appear to matter much whether the states are modernized or not. Obviously, they are democracies because they are small, not because they are modernized. It is also worth noting that the small group of non-modernized small nations that are also non-democracies, eight in all, is comprised almost entirely of the seven largest microstates, as reported in Table 22.1. In other words: internal size differences between microstates again appear to be important, recasting a link between non-modernization and non-democracy and thus in fact bridging the gap between small and larger states.

Summing up, then: If modernization is regarded as an independent and democracy as a dependent variable, an assumption which is far from self-evident but still dominates the research literature, our findings are that size makes a difference in regards to the dependent and to a lesser extent also in regards to the independent variable. Small states tend to be more democratic than larger states, but this does not necessarily follow from differences in the extent of moderniza-tion. In a manner of speaking, the small states category is a deviant case, the performance of which in terms of economy and wealth has limited correspondence only with its democracy performance. It follows, of course, that it makes good sense to include sets of small states in studies of modernization and democracy – they are omitted only at the risk of relating a too bright image of modernization to a dismal image of democracy.

Three. Already in the early 1990s, in a comparative study of 147 states, Tatu Vanhanen concluded that more than other regions, the Pacific region defies attempts at explaining democratization by means of resource distribution; therefore, according to Vanhanen, there must be local explanations for the success of democracy in the small Pacific countries (Vanhanen, 1990: 161–162). As evident from later research, the Pacific islands do indeed stand out as a dis-tinctive group, combining the incompatible factors of poverty and democracy (Anckar, 2002a: 218–219). However, as evident from the present study, when focusing the small states of the globe rather than the specific area of the Pacific islands, the overall picture stills remains the same – small states are different from larger states, and since this is true of small states in general, a valid explanation cannot be local in nature.

In fact, there is in Table 22.9 a pattern that suggests that the good democracy achievements of small states have in part at least a modernization background. In defence of this view, it is necessary to return to the reference to literacy rates inserted earlier in this presentation. The summation in Table 22.9 as regards this particular dimension is that while the small states cannot in full match the European standard, they still perform better or at least on the same level as their larger counterparts. Or, in other words, while modernization, taken as a lump category, is not very helpful in promoting an understanding why small states are more democratic than larger states, it is still possible that one particular aspect or dimension of modernization, namely education, in which small states have a particularly good record, may contribute to an under-standing. The thought is by no means daring or far-fetched. On the contrary, it is well supported by research findings that establish a link between education and democracy. In a large-scale empirical study of democracy in Third World countries, Axel Hadenius found an almost linear association of literacy and the level of democracy; indeed, Hadenius' conclusion reads: 'With reference to the development of democracy, this (literacy) seems to be the central factor in the modernization process' (Hadenius, 1992: 86–91). Diamond, similarly (as quoted in Lipset and Lakin, 2004: 167), found that education predicts a democratic political culture and does so universally rather than in specific regions only. Furthermore, the finding in this research that small states in general show higher literacy rates than larger states is well substantiated in previous research, which compared, in 2002, the then 43 microstates of the world with all remaining 147 other states. The comparison indicated that 60% of the microstates as against 39% of the larger states showed high literacy ratings (Anckar, 2002a: 221); also, the corresponding proportions of states with low literacy ratings were 23% in the microstate group as against 42% in the group of larger states (Anckar, 2002a: 221).

Of course, the identification of a correlation between two factors does not yet tell much about the chains of causation that are at play. Presently, our knowledge of mechanisms and mediations is clearly less than perfect – an important review of the literature that investigates the impact of education on democracy states that the literature is still 'relatively thin', and that the mechanism by which education may lead to more democratic attitudes 'is still poorly understood' (Lipset and Lakin, 2004: 168). These are no doubt apposite observations, and thorough and ramified future research on mechanisms and linkages is certainly called for. The contribution of this chapter in this regard may be considered as one of urging the necessity to pay more attention than hitherto to the small states, thereby possibly enriching and cultivating the research field.

Notes

1 www.systemicpeace.org/polity/polity4.htm/.
2 *World Population Prospects*, Population Division, United Nations. Available at https://esa.un.org/unpd/wpp/.
3 *The World Bank. GNI per capita, PPP*. Available at data.worldbank.org/indicator/NY.GNP.PCAP.PP.CD/.
4 International Labour Organization, ILOSTAT database. Available at http://data.worldbank.org/indicator/SL.UEM.TOTL.ZS/.
5 *The World Bank. Life Expectancy at Birth*. Available at data.worldbank.org/indicator/SP.DYN.LE00.IN.
6 *List of Countries by Literacy Rate*. Available at www.indexmundi.com/facts/indicators/SE.ADT.LITR.ZS/rankings.
7 *The World Factbook*, Central Intelligence Agency. Available at ein.gov/library/publications/the-world-factbook/fields/2103.html.

References

Anckar, C. (2008). 'Size, Islandness, and Democracy: A Global Comparison'. *International Political Science Review*, 29(2): 433–459.
Anckar, D. (2002a). 'Democratic Standard and Performance in Twelve Pacific Micro-states'. *Pacific Affairs*, 75(2): 207–225.
Anckar, D. (2002b). 'Why Are Small Island States Democracies?'. *The Round Table*, Issue 365: 375–390.
Anckar, D. (2008). 'Microstate Democracy Revisited: Developments in Time and Space'. *The Open Political Science Journal*, 1(1): 75–83.
Anckar, D.(2010a). 'Small is Democratic, But Who is Small?'. *Arts and Social Sciences Journal*, 2: 1–10.
Anckar, D. (2010b). 'Undemocratic Miniatures: Cases and Patterns'. *International Journal of Politics and Good Governance*, 1(1.2): 1–22.
Bekink, B. (2007). Angola. In Robbers, G. (ed.) *Encyclopedia of World Constitutions*, Vol. I: 25–29. New York: Facts on File.
Blanchard, O. J. (2004). Explaining European Unemployment. Available at nber.org/reporter/summer04/Blanchard.html. Accessed March 21, 2017.
Campbell, D. F. J. (2008). *The Basic Concept for the Democracy Ranking of the Quality of Democracy*. Vienna: Democracy Ranking.
Davidson, B. (1990). *Kap Verde: de lyckliga öarna*. Uppsala: Nordiska Afrikainstitutet.
Denk, T. and Silander, D. (2012). 'Problems in Paradise? Challenges to Future Democratization in Democratic States'. *International Political Science Review*, 33(1): 25–40.
Diamond, L. and Tsalik, S. (1999). Size and Democracy: The Case for Decentralization. In Diamond, L. (ed.) *Developing Democracy: Toward Consolidation*: 117–160. Baltimore, MD: Johns Hopkins University Press.

Duursma, J. (1994). *Self-Determination, Statehood and International Relations of Micro-States*. Leyden: University of Leiden.

Fleischhacker, H. (1999). Equatorial Guinea. In Nohlen, D., Krennerich, M. and Thibaut, B. (eds) *Elections in Africa. A Data Handbook*: 351–366. Oxford: Oxford University Press.

Foweraker, J. and Krznaric, R. (2000). 'Measuring Liberal Democratic Performance: An Empirical and Conceptual Critique'. *Political Studies*, 48(4): 759–787.

Hadenius, A. (1992). *Democracy and Development*. Cambridge: Cambridge University Press.

Hansen, S. (2007) Belarus. In Robbers, G. (ed.) *Encyclopedia of World Constitutions*, Vol. I: 85–88. New York: Facts on File.

Hass, J. K. (1999). State of Brunei. Home of Peace. In Kaple, D. A. (ed.) *World Encyclopedia of Political Systems and Parties*, Vol. I, 3rd edition: 145. New York: Facts on File.

Huntington, S. P. (1991). *The Third Wave: Democratization in the late Twentieth Century*. Norman: University of Oklahoma Press.

Karvonen, L. (2008). *Diktatur. Om ofrihetens politiska system*. Stockholm: SNS Förlag.

Lane, J-E. and Ersson, S. (1994). *Comparative Politics. An Introduction and New Approach*. Cambridge: Polity Press.

Lijphart, A. (1999). *Patterns of Democracy. Government Forms and Performance in Thirty-Six Countries*. New Haven and London: Yale University Press.

Lipset, S. M. (1959). 'Some Social Requisites of Democracy: Economic Development and Political Legitimacy'. *The American Political Science Review*, 52(1): 69–105.

Lipset, S. M. and Lakin, J. M. (2004). *The Democratic Century*. Norman: University of Oklahoma Press.

Mangu, A. M. (2007). Burundi. In Robbers, G. (ed.) *Encyclopedia of World Constitutions*, I: 146–149. New York: Facts on File.

Melber, H. (2010). 'Namibia's National Assembly and Presidential Elections 2009: Did Democracy Win?' *Journal of Contemporary African Studies*, 28(2): 203–214.

Murphy, F. X. (1974). 'Vatican Politics: Structure and Function'. *World Politics*, 26(4): 542–559.

Nagar, M. F. (2015). *Democratic Development States in Southern Africa: A Study of Botswana and South Africa*. Cape Town: University of Cape Town.

Osei-Hwedie, B. Z. and Sebudubudu, D. (2005). 'Botswana's 2004 Elections: Free and Fair?'. *Journal of African Elections*, 4(1): 27–42.

Ott, D. (2000). *Small is Democratic: An Examination of State Size and Democratic Development*. New York: Garland.

Peerenboom, R. (2008). *China Modernizes: Threat to the West or Model for the Rest*. Oxford: Oxford University Press.

Przeworski, A. and Limongi, F. (1997). 'Modernization. Theories and Facts'. *World Politics*, 49(2): 155–183.

Rich, T. S. (2014). 'Integrating Microstates into Cross-National Research'. *Journal of International and Global Studies*, 6(1): 1–13.

Ritter, A. R. M. (2004). The Cuban Economy in the Twenty-First Century: Recuperation or Relapse? In Ritter, A. R. M. (ed.) *The Cuban Economy*: 3–24. Pittsburgh, PA: University of Pittsburg Press.

Roser, M. and Ortiz-Ospina, E. (2016). Literacy. Published online at *OurWorldInData.org*. Available at http s://ourworldindata.org/literacy/. Accessed March 3, 2017.

Sartori, G. (1976). *Parties and Party Systems: A Framework for Analysis*. Cambridge: Cambridge University Press.

Srebrnik, H. (2004). 'Small Island Nations and Democratic Values'. *World Development*, 32(2): 329–341.

Teorell, J. (2010). *Determinants of Democratization. Explaining Regime Change in the World, 1972–2006*. Cambridge: Cambridge University Press.

Thibaut, B. (1999a). Comoros. In Nohlen, D., Krennerich, M. and Thibaut, B. (eds) *Elections in Africa. A Data Handbook*: 243–258. Oxford: Oxford University Press.

Thibaut, B. (1999b). Djibouti. In Nohlen, D., Krennerich, M. and Thibaut, B. (eds) *Elections in Africa. A Data Handbook*: 315–328. Oxford: Oxford University Press.

Vanhanen, T. (1990). *The Process of Democratization*. New York: Crane Russak.

Veenendaal, W. P. and Corbett, J. (2015). 'Why Small States offer Important Answers to Large Questions'. *Comparative Political Studies*, 48(4): 527–549.

Whitecross, R. (2007). Bhutan. In Robbers, G. (ed.) *Encyclopedia of World Constitutions*, I: 104–107. New York: Facts on File.

23

Challenges and opportunities for the health sector in small states

Natasha Azzopardi Muscat and Carl Camilleri

1 Introduction

Objectives

The purpose of this chapter is to explore the characteristics of the health sector in small states. It aims to identify any specific epidemiological challenges from the literature and provide an overview of the health system profiles in small states. It further aims to elucidate whether any specific challenges or opportunities affect health systems in small states in relation to country size. It aims to explore whether there are any associations between country size and a number of variables associated with health.

Background

The health sector is inextricably linked to socio-economic development. The third sustainable development goal set by the United Nations aims to ensure healthy lives and promote well-being for everyone at all ages (United Nations, 2015). In addition, health also features in several of the other Sustainable Development Goals. The concept of health in all policies (Ståhl *et al.*, 2006) requires an integrative approach to address health problems. Health is rising rapidly on the global agenda and has been discussed in meetings of the G7 and G20 (Cooper, 2016), (Gostin and Friedman, 2017). To date however, there have been few and sporadic research initiatives relating to the health sector in small states.[1] This is surprising given that health is an important component of socio-economic development.

Research questions

Specifically, this chapter aims to answer the following research questions:

- What do we know about health determinants and health outcomes in small states?
- What are the specific characteristics of health systems in small states?
- Is there a relationship between country size, health resources, health determinants and health outcomes?

A desktop literature review and correlation analyses are used to answer the research questions posed above.

Layout of the chapter

Following this introduction, Section 2. presents the literature review covering relevant aspects of the overarching theme, namely health sector characteristics in small states. This section opens with a discussion of the meaning of small country size and an overview of the main theoretical approaches that describe the special characteristics of small states. This is followed by a discussion, based on available literature, on issues related to public health and health systems in the main regions where small states are located. Section 3. presents a series of correlation analyses so as to assess whether there is an association between a number of health variables and country size. Section 4. draws some conclusions, sets out policy implications and charts an agenda for further research in the domain of health systems and public health in small states.

2 Literature review

Coverage of this review

This literature review will cover a number of topics associated with the main theme of this chapter. We introduce the chapter by referring to the meaning of small country size and the special constraints faced by these states as a backdrop to expand upon aspects related to public health and health systems with a focus on small population size. We also review the available literature on health status, access and quality of health care and specific characteristics (constraints or opportunities) faced by health systems in small states.

What is a small state?

Generally speaking, the size of a country is measured in terms of its population. However alternative indicators have been used notably territory size and GDP (Downes, 1988, Crowards, 2002, Thorhallsson, 2006). Population size is the most commonly used indicator, possibly because this variable is related to a major resource of a country, namely its labour force.

However, there is no general acceptance as to what in actual fact constitutes a small state, and there is therefore ongoing debate as to how one should define a small state (Maass, 2009) even when it is agreed that population is a good indicator of size. For example, the World Health Organization in the European region includes in its small countries network those countries with a population of less than one million[2] while the Commonwealth Secretariat[3] and World Bank[4] both take a cut-off point of 1.5 million population in their work on small states. The 1.5 million population threshold will be adopted in this chapter and therefore the analysis is based on 39 countries in the category of small states for which data was available (see Appendix 3).

Constraints and opportunities related to smallness

Whereas some authors contend that small states perform relatively well in terms of economic growth and that small size plays a less significant role than generally ascribed in determining outcomes (Easterly and Kraay, 2000), others emphasize the inherent constraints that characterize small states (Briguglio, 1995, Atkins et al., 2000). These constraints include limited ability to reap the benefits of economies of scale, their small domestic market and their limited natural resources endowments, all of which compel these countries to depend highly on international trade and therefore expose themselves highly to external shocks. In the case of small states that are remote such as those located in the Pacific and Indian Ocean, remoteness and high international transport costs are considered as additional constraints. Some small states located in the tropics are also prone to natural disasters and the severe impact of climate change. As expected this poses serious challenges relating to their economic development options.

Studies from the discipline of economics that focussed on the inherent economic vulnerabilities of small states admit that their performance at the global level is often very satisfactory and this has been attributed to their success in building resilience through good governance and the pursuit of appropriate economic and social policies (Briguglio *et al.*, 2009).

With regard to opportunities, several authors refer to the ability of many small states to respond to their special constraints. Baldacchino refers to the resourceful population (Baldacchino and Bertram, 2009) practically suggesting that this type of reaction is a spontaneous one among islanders. Briguglio (2016) on the other hand refers to policy induced resilience which enables these countries to reduce the negative effects of external shocks. Briguglio calls this the 'island' or 'Singapore' paradox, meaning that small countries can succeed economically in spite of and not because of their small size.

Whilst there may be disagreement about the extent to which small size constitutes a disadvantage in the global economy, small state scholars generally agree that good governance and social capital are particularly important for building resilience in small states (Briguglio *et al.*, 2009). In fact, many small countries that are not well governed tend to be almost 'failed' states.

The focus on health systems in small states is however relatively absent from the literature (Azzopardi-Muscat, 2016) and a principal scope of this study is to evaluate how special circumstances characterize health and health systems in small states.

Small states and health

A cursory scan of the literature indicates that there is very little published work on the connection between country size and health systems or outcomes. It is sometimes observed that a number of small states tend to be amongst the top performers in health indices. In the seminal benchmarking exercise carried out by the World Health Organization in the year 2000 several small countries including Andorra, Iceland, Malta, Monaco and San Marino[5] ranked amongst the top fifteen performers in terms of health outcomes and health systems (WHO, 2000). The methodology used in this benchmarking exercise has been critically appraised (Wait and Nolte, 2005), and over the past years, further refinements to the modelling approaches have been implemented primarily through the work undertaken by the Institute for Health Metrics through the Global Burden of Disease Collaboration.[6]

The Global Burden of Disease Collaboration regularly publishes studies for mortality and disability. Important publications include the Global Burden of Disease 2015 Study which provides a comprehensive assessment of all-cause and cause-specific mortality for 249 causes in 195 countries and territories from 1980 to 2015. These results informed an in-depth investigation of observed and expected mortality patterns based on socio-demographic measures (Feigin, 2016). In this publication, Andorra, Iceland, Cyprus and Malta feature in the top ten countries having the lowest years of life lost in relation to their socio-demographic index. At the other extreme, Swaziland is the only country included in this chapter which features in the lowest ten performers. The Maldives is an example of a positive outlier as it performs far better than the other middle-income countries.

The Health Care Access and Quality Index published for the first time in 2017, is based on mortality from causes amenable to personal health care in 195 countries and territories between 1990 and 2015 using data from the Global Burden of Disease study. Of the small countries included in this chapter, it is worth noting that Andorra, Iceland and Luxembourg feature amongst the top ten performers whilst none of the small countries included in this review feature amongst the lowest ten performers. The Maldives consistently emerges as a positive outlier, being one of five outlier countries having registered the most remarkable improvement in health care access and quality between 1990 and 2015. Notably Cape Verde is the highest performing health system on the Health Care Access and Quality Index in Sub-Saharan Africa as (Gregg and Shaw, 2017; Barber *et al.*, 2017). These two health systems have therefore been selected for more detailed reviewed below.

Another important issue meriting careful consideration is the prevalence of overweight people and obesity. This is a key health determinant, where small islands appear to face major problems. In an analysis of trends in the prevalence of overweight and obesity among children and adults between 1980 and 2015, many small islands featuring in this review, including Barbados, Dominica, Grenada, Malta, the Marshall Islands, Micronesia, Saint Lucia, Samoa, Solomon Islands and Tonga, were found to have an obesity prevalence above 30% (Barber *et al.*, 2017).

Briguglio and Azzopardi-Muscat (2016) attempted to place the health sector characteristics in small states in the context of the so-called vulnerability/resilience framework, developed by Briguglio *et al.* (2009). Briefly, the vulnerabilities and constraints of small states were considered to be associated with a small genetic pool, the inability to provide full range of specialized services, and a limited health workforce capacity. A highly relevant point made by the authors relates to the issue of indivisibilities of overhead costs which leads to higher cost per capita in the provision of certain health services. The authors also refer to the special problem of small domestic markets and the limited ability to negotiate good prices coupled with high transportation costs posing a problem of access to affordable medicines.

The authors, however, noting that some small states succeed in spite of these constraints, argued that these states often find ways to strengthen their resilience in the face of such vulnerabilities through community action and policy-induced measures. These resilience-enhancing factors include that a small jurisdiction makes it easier for the government to identify and address shortcomings in health care, policy makers tend to have a 'helicopter view' of health issues associated with implementation of health policy, rendering health-related policies more implementable. Social cohesion, often a characteristic of small states, may permit a more comprehensive population health surveillance. The small population size renders it easier to keep national registers and leads to a 'shorter distance' between research, policy and practice, enabling more rapid uptake of the policy intervention.

In connection with the issues featuring in the vulnerability/resilience framework just discussed, two issues appear to have received some attention in the literature, notably loss of the skilled health workforce (Connell, 2007) and access to medicines (Walker *et al.*, 2017). On the issues of governance, the literature seems to suggest that difficulties in the capacity to implement often arise (Greaves, 2016).

Major outcome documents of global conferences

There are three major documents relating to small states, all of which are outcomes of major conferences held under the auspices of the United Nations. The first of these documents hails from the 1994 Barbados conference on the sustainable development of SIDS where the outcome document was the Barbados programme of action (BPOA).[7] This document however does not make any particular reference to health.

The second major document resulted from the 2005 Mauritius international conference where the outcome document 'Report of the International Meeting to Review the Implementation of the Programme of Action for the Sustainable Development of Small Island Developing States'[8] includes a specific focus on the health sector. Recognition of the importance of health for continued socio-economic development is given. The fact that a number of SIDS in 2005 were facing the epidemiological challenge of communicable disease including HIV/AIDS, TB, Malaria as well as the rapid development of non-communicable diseases such as diabetes was highlighted as a specific concern. Key areas of priority action for health identified by SIDS in the 2005 document include:

- Strengthening the health management and financing systems;
- Arresting the HIV/AIDS epidemic;
- Prompt access to funds from the Global Fund to Combat HIV/AIDS, Tuberculosis and Malaria;
- Enhanced accessibility to effective pharmaceutical drugs at affordable prices;
- Effective prevention programmes in immunization, reproductive health, mental health and health education;
- Development and implementation of effective surveillance initiatives and early information-sharing on possible emerging outbreaks;
- Development and implementation of modern, flexible national public health legislation;
- Implementation of targeted environmental health programmes;
- Enhanced data collection on demographic and epidemiological trends.

The Samoa International meeting of 2014, produced the third major outcome document, commonly referred to as the Samoa pathway.[9] Here health features in the sections on food security and nutrition, chemical waste, sustainable transport as well as in a specific section on Health and Non-communicable diseases (NCDs). This document identifies universal health coverage as a priority in line with the developing narrative and discourse in the International health policy arena. Furthermore, it emphasizes the threat and severity of rising rates of non-communicable diseases, the re-emergence of tropical diseases and the need to improve maternal health. Whilst health appears to be rising on the policy agenda for SIDS, none of the above referenced documents explicitly pinpoint or link the specific health sector concerns listed with the small size of the country.

Regional aspects

Differences arising from different regional locations might be one reason why health systems and health outcomes differ between small countries.

Small developing states are often classified into three main regions namely the Pacific, the Caribbean and the Indian ocean/African regions. The European small states are among the most highly developed countries in the world and are not generally given major attention in global conferences on small states. Yet a short section on the European small states has also been included in this review.

The Caribbean region

One characteristic of the Caribbean small states is that they experience a particularly high burden of NCDs. According to Unwin et al. (2017), age standardized mortality rates from

NCDs in the English-speaking Caribbean countries range from 30% higher to over twice as high as those in North America. Underlying this high mortality rate are high levels of risk factors, particularly obesity, diabetes, and hypertension. The same authors state that a proactive approach has been taken through a conference organized in 2007 to address NCDs in the Caribbean which led to the Port of Spain Declaration on NCDs, in which governments committed to a range of multi-sectoral policy measures for NCD prevention and control. This resulted in a policy window of opportunity opening up with the potential to address NCDs in a holistic manner.

A number of governance issues relating to health policy implementation were identified for the Caribbean by Greaves (2016). Evidence-based management in decision-making is not a common approach taken by top officials of health systems because of internal and external barriers to its use. Indeed, the absence of a culture of decision-making based on evidence pervades the public services of Caribbean island states with a resultant impact on health outcomes and performance.

Furthermore, Caribbean countries have been vulnerable to out-migration, notably of nurses-who are well trained and speak English. In previous decades outmigration was principally to the UK. More recently it is now to USA and Canada..

The WHO produces country profiles on each Caribbean small state which show that the major health problems in these states relate to non-communicable diseases. Descriptive information on health systems was also obtained from the website of the Commonwealth Health[10] where applicable. In this review, we shall briefly refer to an example of what we consider to be the best and worst performers in the region.

Barbados had a life expectancy of 73 years for men and 78 years for women in 2015. Ischaemic heart disease, stroke and diabetes contributed around one third of the mortality with no change registered between 2000 and 2012 in the mortality rates from these causes. Obesity, particularly in women is a cause for concern.[11] However, Barbados performs relatively well in terms of health indicators when compared to the average of the region. Barbados has a national health service with an extensive network of district hospitals and polyclinics spread throughout the island delivering publicly funded health care.[12]

On the other end, Guyana had a life expectancy of 64 years for men and 68 years for women in 2015 with practically no increase in life expectancy having been registered between 2000 and 2012 and an increase in maternal mortality being recorded over this period. Ischaemic heart disease, stroke and diabetes accounted for more than one third of deaths and represent the commonest causes of death.[13] Health and medical care in Guyana is provided by both public and private suppliers. The private health care sector operates independently but is subject to regulations ensuring standards of care and practice. There is significant involvement of NGOs in service delivery related to HIV/AIDS. A small pharmaceutical industry exists in the country producing a range of medicines, including antiretroviral treatments for HIV.[14]

The Pacific region

In 1995, a first meeting of Pacific health ministers launched the Healthy Island initiative with a strong commitment to the health in all policies approach linking health with ecological balance and making reference to the oceans (Galea et al., 2000).

The 2015 Yanuca Island Declaration on health in Pacific island countries and territories is inspired by the WHO Healthy Cities network. (WHO, 2015) The Yanuca Island Declaration of 2015, recognizes progress made in addressing Hepatitis B and eliminating polio. It however acknowledges that mounting challenges facing the health of Pacific island communities including emerging disease e.g. chikungunya. The increasing prevalence of non-communicable diseases e.g. diabetes related to widespread availability of tobacco, alcohol and poor quality food are leading to shortened life expectancy in a number of Pacific countries. The increasing complexity of health services delivery presents opportunities but for these to be harnessed a whole of Government approach addressing access, transportation costs and trade needs to be in place (WHO, 2015).

Medicines shortages arise due to a combination of factors including almost entire reliance on foreign sources due to the absence of a domestic manufacturing and the consequent reliance on third party suppliers instead of manufacturers and the long transportation routes. These issues were captured in a paper that carried out an in-depth analysis on the situation in Fiji by Walker et al. (2017).

Many small island Pacific states are working towards achieving universal health coverage. For example, a study carried out in Fiji has shown that the system is achieving a moderate degree of vertical equity with attention given to ensure that out of pocket payments are progressively distributed (Asante et al., 2017).

Furthermore, cultural issues and geographical isolation have been identified as barriers in improving the delivery of modern health services. Young et al. (2016), in a study carried out in Vanuatu in 2016, found that Vanuatu faces deficits in surgical infrastructure, equipment and human resources, especially in the rural provinces. Geographic isolation, poverty and culture – including the use of traditional medicine and low health literacy – all act as barriers to patients accessing timely surgical care. Issues with governance, human resourcing and perioperative care were commonly identified as key challenges facing surgical services.

Such challenges are common to several Pacific island countries including archipelagos. For example, the Solomon Islands Government is dealing with the challenge of serving widely dispersed and often remote island communities with serious shortages of health workers, essential drugs, clinical equipment and medical supplies (Whiting et al., 2016). The top 20 causes of morbidity and mortality indicate the country is dealing with the 'double disease burden' of both communicable and non-communicable diseases, a situation typical of several Pacific Island countries.

Health services spread out over the rural communities such as remote atolls pose special challenges. These are often compounded by loss of skilled health workers due to migration from small Pacific islands (Connell, 2007). Whilst the medical workforce is set to increase due to agreements for overseas training of doctors, the absorption of these trained doctors also raises a series of challenges namely that there are limited positions available in the hospitals, the supervisory capacity to manage them all is also finite and the cost of paying them in the current fiscal environment may be difficult (Buchan et al., 2011).

Such workforce challenges are not limited to doctors and nurses. A recent publication (Homer et al., 2017) has shown that midwives are also in short supply in several Pacific Islands. This is of relevance considering the objective to improve maternal and infant mortality. The variation and the small number of midwives poses challenges for workforce planning. It has been suggested that consideration could be given to developing regional standards and potentially a shared curriculum framework. The issue of building leadership capacity in the health workforce in the Pacific for nursing and midwifery has been mentioned as an important element to ensure sustained health improvement in the region (Rumsey et al., 2017)

Again, the WHO and the Commonwealth Secretariat publish various country profiles for the Pacific region and here we shall briefly refer to an example of what we consider to be the best and worst performers in this region.

In 2015 Samoa had a life expectancy of 71years for men and 78 years for women. It is one of the best performing countries in the Pacific although obesity in women is a major problem for this island.[15] Despite its overall relatively good performance, Samoan tertiary care is limited and mainly provided through an arrangement with New Zealand's health care system.[16]

On the other hand, Kirbati had a life expectancy of 64 years for men and 69 years for women in 2015. Obesity and tobacco use are important risk factors leading to a reduction in healthy life expectancy. Per capita expenditure on health remains significantly lower than the average in the region.[17] According to the Commonwealth Secretariat[18] health care facilities in Kiribati are adequate for routine medical care, but extremely limited in availability and quality. Kiribati relies on obtaining medicinal supplies through a pooled procurement arrangement coordinated by Fiji, yet this arrangement itself also faces problems in ensuring secure and continuous supply (Walker *et al.*, 2017).

The Indian Ocean region

The Indian Ocean region is characterized by islands exposed to frequently harsh weather events. There is quite a large variability in terms of health outcomes registered. Using the WHO Country health profiles as well as descriptive information on the health systems obtained from the Commonwealth Health Online website where applicable, the variation between small countries in this region emerges clearly.

Mauritius has a comparatively well-developed health system for this region. Life expectancy in 2015 was 71 for men and 78 years for women. It successfully registered almost complete 100% vaccination against measles. Diabetes is a major problem and accounts for around a quarter of all deaths and tobacco use is higher than the average for the region.[19] According to the Commonwealth Health Organization, medical care standards in Mauritius are high with multiple public and private providers. Mauritius also has an institute for the training of its health professionals and has two local medicines manufacturers.[20]

The Maldives achieved its Millennium Development Goals (MDG) targets for health ahead of the 2015 deadline. Since 2000 life expectancy has increased by more than 10 years and reached 77/80 years for men and women respectively in 2015. Non-communicable diseases make up 80% of mortality.[21] The geography of The Maldives with its scattered islands makes health service provision a key challenge. The reorganization of the health system, with the introduction of atoll hospitals and placement of doctors at health centres, has enabled increased access to medical services for the island communities. The logistical problems include infrequent transport links and high operational costs. Accordingly, providing health care services to the outlying islands has almost doubled the cost of health services delivery and a relatively high proportion of GDP is spent on health.[22] Nonetheless, this investment appears to have yielded the desired results since multi country studies from the Global Burden of Disease are consistently showing The Maldives as a positive outlier for the rate of progress registered.

On the other end of the spectrum, Comoros had a life expectancy of 62 years for men and 65 years for women in 2015. Life expectancy only increased by three years over the period 2000–2012 whilst in the region the average increase was of a 7-year increase in the same period. Whilst child mortality and maternal mortality have declined, they still contribute significantly to the burden of disease unlike the better performing small countries in this region were NCDs now play the most important role in determining mortality and burden of disease.[23] According to the Commonwealth Health Organization, Comoros is characterized by a low uptake of health facilities by the population. This is thought to be due to the low public spending on health, inadequate and poor management of human resources, and poor health structures.[24]

African small states

The continent of Africa is often associated with the HIV/AIDS epidemic, and although declining, AIDS still claims many in different parts of Africa, notably in sub-Saharan Africa. On the positive side, WHO (2014) states that although diseases, such as malaria and tuberculosis are widespread in Africa, the continent has seen marked improvements in health outcomes during the 2000s. There has been a considerable decline in child, maternal and adult mortality rates, and substantial decreases in the burdens of several diseases. Recently however there was the Ebola outbreak in West Africa[25] which required emergency responses to control its further transmission.

WHO has published a series of country fact sheets for the region, covering the small states in the region, but space does not permit a discussion on each and every case, so here we will very briefly refer to just two examples relating to what we consider to be the best small state performer, namely Cape Verde and worst performer, namely Swaziland.

In the archipelago of Cape Verde, located on the Western coast of Africa, life expectancy was 71 years for men and 75 years for women in 2015 well above the average for the small states of Africa. Child and maternal mortality rates are significantly lower than those of neighbouring countries and continue to decline. Cardiovascular disease, diabetes and other NCDs account for the bulk of the burden of disease having overtaken deaths from communicable disease. Deaths from stroke are the commonest cause of death and deaths from NCDs are on the rise whilst deaths from TB and other communicable diseases decline.[26]

The Cape Verde health system is based on the models of the Welfare State, and the right to health is constitutionally enshrined and can be considered universal and tend to be free. Health promotion is viewed as a strategic investment, since it has a strong impact on the economic and social development of the country, as well as influencing the degree of inequality among citizens. This strategy has led to marked improvements in health outcomes and health care access being achieved. The lack of training facilities for the health workforce has been described as one of the vulnerable aspects of the health system in these islands.[27]

Swaziland had a life expectancy of 57 years for men and 51 for women in 2015. After a very difficult period in which life expectancy declined primarily due to the HIV epidemic, modest increases in life expectancy are again being registered with around 7 years increase between 2000 and 2015. Communicable diseases, particularly HIV remain of high importance and contribute significantly to the burden of disease with HIV being the leading cause of death.[28] The HIV epidemic and resurgence of TB have overstretched the health system, yet increases in the medical and nursing workforce have been registered in the recent past and health expenditure has increased significantly over the past decade.[29]

The European region

A number of small states in the European region are identified as being amongst the top performers in the world when it comes to health outcomes and quality of health systems (Gregg and Shaw, 2017; Barber et al., 2017). Nonetheless, a narrative literature review on European small states, which includes Cyprus, Estonia, Iceland, Latvia, Lithuania, Luxembourg and Slovenia and takes a population cut off point of 3 million (Azzopardi-Muscat et al., 2016b) identifies several challenges. Although some of the countries in this review do not specifically meet the criterion of having a population threshold of 1.5 million, the findings from this review are anyhow useful to shed light on some of the key policy challenges.

Lack of capacity is highlighted as an issue that gives rise to several other concerns. Health services research is comparatively weak in small countries (Delnoij and Groenewegen, 2007.

This gap arises primarily from limited technical and human capacity (Bero *et al.*, 2013). Another challenge identified is the limited capacity to provide highly specialized treatments for rare diseases. Small countries need to come to a decision as to whether such diseases are treated within the country (self-sufficient model) or if these patients should be treated abroad. The decision largely depends on the respective overall national plans for health care, the available funds and the number of patients. Successful bilateral cooperation programmes, for example the generic agreement between Malta and the UK (Saliba *et al.*, 2014), can lead to the development of a modified self-sufficiency model.

Measures affecting the pharmaceutical industry during a financial crisis affect the availability of medicines, an issue of special concern for small national markets in European countries (Vogler *et al.*, 2011). Despite the sporadic success in health system reforms in small EU member states, several publications provide examples that indicate a general inertia and difficulty in health system reform implementation. Lack of financial and technical resources, weak inter-sectoral cooperation, strong industry pressure, insufficient separation between policy development and policy execution, lack of leadership and institutional capacity are described as key barriers (O'Connor and Bankauskaite, 2008). On the other hand, the relatively short distance between research, policy-making and practice and the ability to generate a helicopter view have been identified as opportunities for innovation to be introduced in the health sector (Azzopardi-Muscat *et al.*, 2016a).

Some of these issues that are highlighted in this review have been well described in the reports relating to the three WHO High Level meetings of Small Countries.[30] In particular, two specific policy areas that have been examined as areas of good practice in small countries that may provide useful lessons for larger countries are those of inter-sectoral actions and building resilience (WHO, 2016, 2017).

Synthesis

This literature review shows that there are considerable differences in terms of health outcomes and health systems development between small states and this renders it difficult to treat small states as a homogenous entity.

The issue of the challenges related to the training and retention of a skilled health workforce however emerges as a common challenge associated with small country size as does the need to rely on larger countries for the provision of certain specialized services and the issue of ensuring a secure and affordable supply of medicines.

The special constraints faced by small states such as indivisibilities related to overhead costs, small numbers of players in the market leading to monopolistic and oligopolistic structures, a small genetic pool and other matters relating to health are very rarely discussed in the literature on health systems in small states, hence the small number of references to these matters in the review carried out above. These areas require further research to deepen the knowledge around the identified issues.

3 Health, country size and per capita income: empirical findings

Methodology and data

This section seeks to analyse the association between country size and a number of 'health' indicators, in an attempt to test whether small country size matters in this regard. The variables refer to three aspects of health, namely (i) health outcomes, (ii) health care resources and (iii) health determinants. Moreover, given the variation in income per capita levels across the countries under analysis, the relationship between size and each of the variables is studied across two broad groups of countries in terms of the GDP per capita variable. There will also be an attempt to find out whether there are differences in the regional location of small states.

The analysis carried out in this section is based on data pertaining to a cross-section of 184 countries[31] for the latest year of available data. Health care outcomes are represented by the life expectancy indicator, health resources are represented by health care expenditure per capita and health determinants are represented by the Body-Mass Index (BMI).

The size of the countries under analysis is measured by their population whilst the income per capita level is measured using the Gross Domestic Product per capita indicator in US dollars. This indicator is likely to be associated with the varying socio-economic conditions prevailing in the countries under study.

The analysis across countries seeks to find out whether there is a relationship between the mentioned health indicators and population size under different income per capita levels[32] primarily: (1) high and upper-middle income grouped together, here labelled as higher-income countries and (2) lower-middle income and low-income countries, here labelled as lower-income countries.

Details relating to the number of countries used in the empirical analysis, disaggregated into two major income groups, are given in Appendix 1. This Appendix also presents information about the sources of data pertaining to the variables used in all the figures presented below.[33]

Life expectancy as a health outcome

Life expectancy is often considered to be an important indicator of health outcomes. For example, the Human Development Index uses a Life Expectancy Indicator to measure health as one of its components.

Life expectancy and GDP per capita

Recent trends observed for life expectancy across countries indicate a positive and gradual increase in the life expectancy over time. Various reasons have been attributed to such an increase, including improvements in health care, better levels of education and enhanced socio-economic conditions. For these reasons, life expectancy is often highly associated with GDP per capita. Indeed, Figure 23.1, utilizing 2015 data for 184 countries confirms the well-known relationship referred to as the Preston curve (Mackenbach and Looman, 2013) whereby a county's economic conditions, measured by increases in national income are linked to improvements in life expectancy.[34]

Life expectancy and population size

Figure 23.2 illustrates the relationship between life expectancy and population size (measured in logs) using 2015 data on 184 countries. The figure shows a negative relationship between population size and life expectancy. This would seem to suggest that countries with a smaller population tend to have a population with a higher life expectancy. As shown in the graph, however, there is considerable variation of the observed data around the fitted trend line.

Interestingly, if the population is disaggregated in terms of income per capita, the relationship with life expectancy would differ between the different country income-groups. It can be seen from Figure 23.3 that when higher-income countries are considered, a positive relationship is registered, although, here again there is considerable dispersion around the fitted line. Conversely when lower-income countries are considered, the relationship turns negative as shown in Figure 23.4.

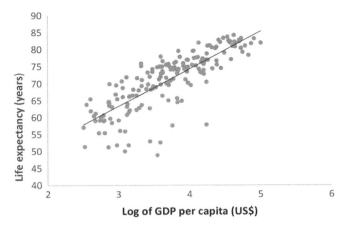

Figure 23.1 GDP per capita and life expectancy

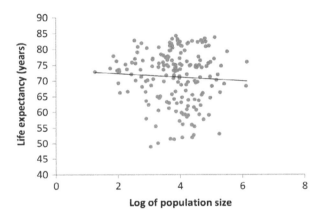

Figure 23.2 Life expectancy and population

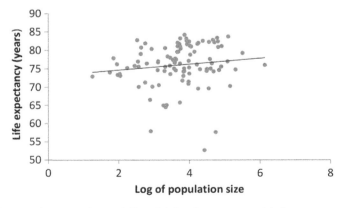

Figure 23.3 Life expectancy and population (higher-income countries)

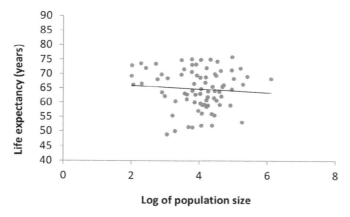

Figure 23.4 Life expectancy and population (lower-income countries)

It would be interesting to find an explanation for the tendencies shown in Figures 23.3 and 23.4. One possibility could be that smaller states that form part of the higher-income group tend to register a lower per capita income than larger ones in this same income category, as can be seen from Figure 23.5. Figure 23.6, shows the opposite tendency, namely that the smaller states that form part of the lower-income group tend to register a higher per capita income than larger ones in this income category. Again here, in both cases, there is considerable dispersion around the two fitted lines indicating that there are many exceptions. This life expectancy/ population relationship therefore to some extent, mirrors the income per capita relationship/ population relationship, suggesting that the major driver is income per capita, which itself, as stated, reflects the stage of development of the countries in question.

Life expectancy in small states

Life expectancy levels amongst small countries, defined as those with a population of 1.5 million or less, of which there are 39 included in this chapter, tended to decrease as country size increases, as shown in Figure 23.7[35] which is the same tendency observed when all countries are considered.

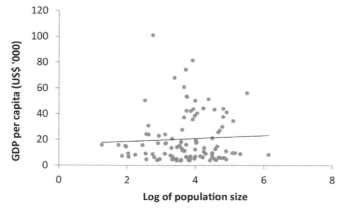

Figure 23.5 GDP per capita and population size (higher-income countries)

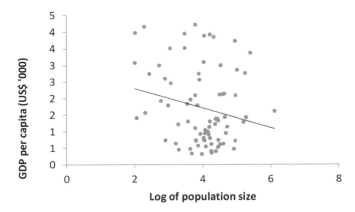

Figure 23.6 GDP per capita and population size (lower-income countries)

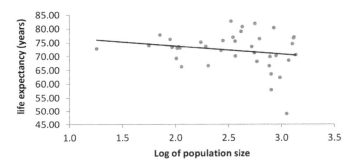

Figure 23.7 Life expectancy in small states (population up to 1.5 million)

A more detailed look at the group of small states reveals that four European small states registered the highest life expectancy (Iceland, Luxembourg, Malta and Cyprus), as shown in Figure 23.8. This is to be expected in view of their relatively high GDP per capita. Life expectancy in most Caribbean small states was generally lower than that of the European small states and generally higher than that of the Pacific small states, but there are exceptions as can be seen in Figure 23.8. Three African small states registered the lowest life expectancy (Djibouti, Equatorial Guinea and Swaziland) among this group of small states.

Health resources: expenditure on health per capita

As observed in the literature on the topic, the spending levels of a country directed towards health care related measures depends on historical, cultural, political, social and economic factors apart from the particular financing and organizational structures which make up the health care system.

Health expenditure and GDP per capita

Significant variations exist in expenditure on health[36] across countries, as presented in Figure 23.9, which shows that there is a positive relationship between health spending per capita and the income per capita of 180 countries for which data was available.

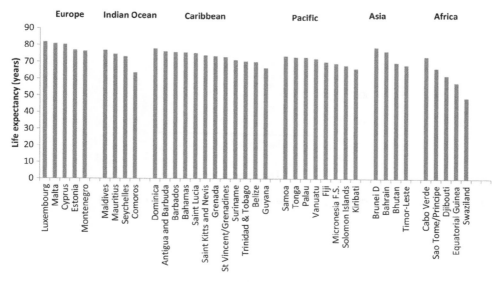

Figure 23.8 Life expectancy in small states in different regions

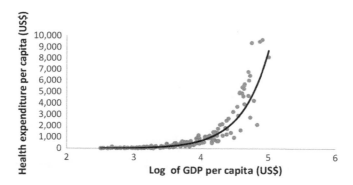

Figure 23.9 Health expenditure per capita and GDP per capita (all countries)

Health expenditure and population size

Figure 23.10 shows the relationship between expenditure on heath per capita in US$ and population size for 180 countries. It can be seen that the fitted line is practically horizontal, possibly suggesting that country size does not matter.

Interestingly, as displayed in Figures 23.11 and 23.12, if the population is disaggregated in terms of income per capita, the relationship between health expenditure per capita and population differs between the two income groups.[37] There is a positive relationship between health expenditure per capita and population size in higher-income countries, reflecting the higher GDP per capita and life expectancy patterns described above with regard to this income group. Conversely, with regard to the lower-income group of countries, the smaller countries tend to spend more per capita on health. Again this mirrors the life expectancy and GDP per capita patterns described above with regard to this income group of countries.

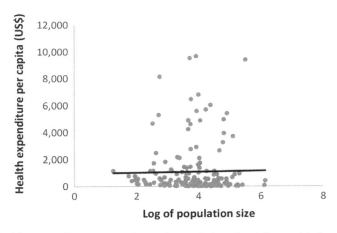

Figure 23.10 Health expenditure per capita and population size (all countries)

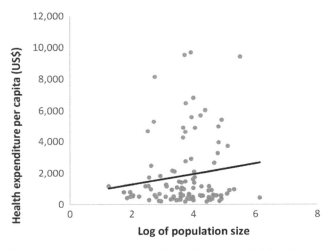

Figure 23.11 Health expenditure per capita and population size (higher-income countries)

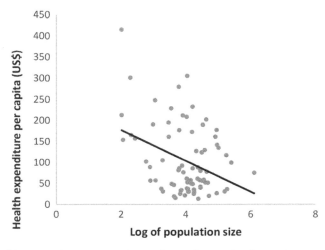

Figure 23.12 Health expenditure per capita and population size (lower-income countries)

Health expenditure and small states

When small states only are considered, the tendency would seem to be that larger small states spend a higher proportion on health care, as shown in Figure 23.13, although the slope of the line would seem to be 'pulled up' by four European small states, namely Luxembourg, Iceland, Malta and Cyprus.

A more detailed look at the group of small states reveals that four European small states registered the highest health expenditure per capita (Luxembourg, Iceland, Malta and Cyprus), as shown in Figure 23.14. Again, this is to be expected in view of their relatively high GDP per capita. Health expenditure in most Caribbean small states was generally lower than that of the European small states and generally higher than that of the Pacific small states, but there are

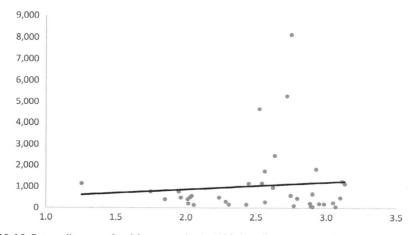

Figure 23.13 Expenditure on health per capita in US$ (small states, population up to 1.5 million)

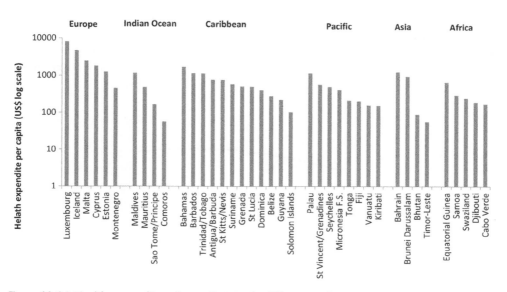

Figure 23.14 Health expenditure in small states in different regions

exceptions and can be seen in Figure 23.14. The African small states did not this time register the lowest health expenditure per capita, with Bhutan, Timor-Leste and Comoros coming last in this regard.

Health determinants: body mass index

Body mass index (BMI) is used as a health-determinant indicator in this study. BMI is a simple index of weight-for-height that is commonly used to classify overweight and obesity in adults. It is defined as a person's weight in kilograms divided by the square of his height in meters (kg/m^2). Various World Health Organization studies show that overweight and obesity lead to adverse metabolic effects on blood pressure, cholesterol, triglycerides and insulin resistance. Risks of coronary heart disease, ischemic stroke and type 2 diabetes mellitus increase steadily with increasing BMI. Thus, it can be considered as a suitable health determinant in a country, although there may be others.

BMI and GDP per capita

A cross sectional analysis of the BMI across 177 countries shows that there is a tendency for a higher BMI in countries with higher-income per capita levels (Figure 23.15). While richer countries have higher life expectancy and more health resources, they are associated with a higher BMI. Figure 23.15 suggests that the highest BMI is not found in the richest countries, generally speaking, since the best-fitting trend line is inverted U shaped. This may be due to the high-level of awareness relating to food intake in very rich countries.

BMI and population size

The relation between population size and the BMI index is shown in Figure 23.16. The trend line shows that there is a tendency for small states to register higher BMI scores, although the relationship is found to be rather weak.

Again, interestingly, as displayed in Figures 23.17 and 23.18, if the population is dis-aggregated in terms of income per capita, the relationship between BMI and population differs between the two income groups in that, although in both cases there is the tendency for the smaller states to register higher BMIs, this tendency is more pronounced when only lower-income countries are considered, as shown in Figure 23.18.

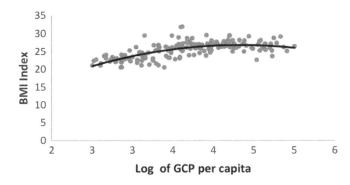

Figure 23.15 BMI and GDP per capita (all countries)

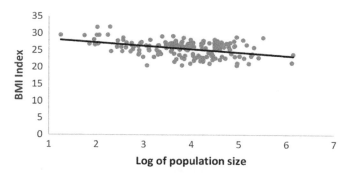

Figure 23.16 BMI and population (all countries)

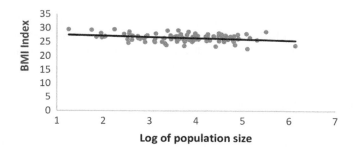

Figure 23.17 BMI and population (higher-income countries)

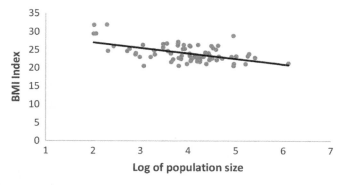

Figure 23.18 BMI and population (lower-income countries)

When only small states are considered the tendency would seem to be that the very small states register a higher BMI index, as shown in Figure 23.19.

A more detailed look at the group of small states reveals that many Pacific small states register high BMI scores and many African small states low values. The European small states lie somewhere in the middle. This would seem to suggest that among the small states, the relationship between BMI and income per capita is not a straight forward one. Probably the poorer countries of Africa are still characterized by low calorie intake and more physical activity. The Pacific and the Caribbean small states are mostly islands at the middle-income level, with a high dependence on imports and a higher calorie diet. Some pacific islands have gone from low to

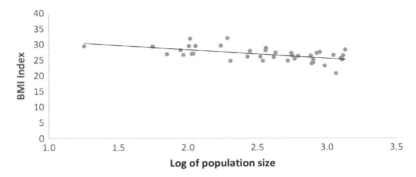

Figure 23.19 BMI and population in small states (population up to 1.5 million)

high BMI in a generation as diet has changed from domestically produced fish, vegetables and fruit, to imported high-carb, high-sugar, processed food. This could explain the tendencies shown in Figure 23.20. The European small states, generally speaking, can afford a high calorie intake but may be more aware of the dangers of obesity.

Life expectancy and health expenditure per capita

As shown, both life expectancy and health expenditure per capita are highly correlated to GDP per capita, and therefore likely to be correlated with each other. The test of such a correlation is

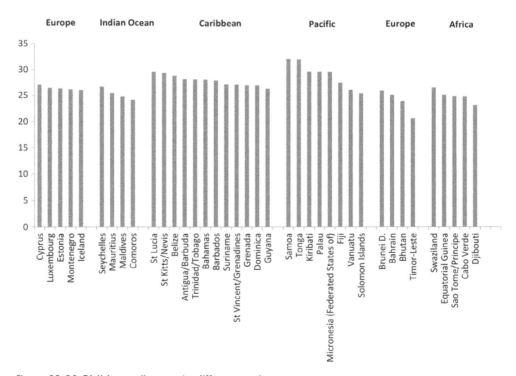

Figure 23.20 BMI in small states in different regions

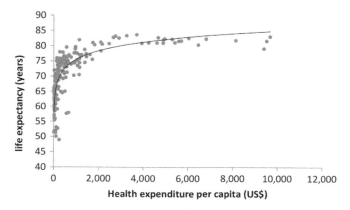

Figure 23.21 Life expectancy and health expenditure per capita (all countries)

shown as Figure 23.21, where the relation is non-linear, and where the correlation coefficient is on the high side. This confirms the established literature that health outcomes are related to health resources, and both these variables are related to the stage of development.

We found that this relationship also holds if the countries are disaggregated into the two broad income groups, as shown in Figures 23.22 and 23.23 and if the small states are considered separately as shown in Figure 23.24.

Comments on the overall results

The empirical analysis conducted in this section confirms that the main factor affecting health outcomes, health resources and health determinants, measured respectively by life expectancy, health expenditure per capita and BMI, is GDP per capita. GDP per capita is widely considered to capture the stage of development of the countries under analysis. This is to be expected, as such development is associated with higher financial resources, better institutional set ups and better government regulatory quality.[38]

However, there was an indication that country size may matter when countries were disaggregated in terms of two broad income-per-capita groups, in that the major health outcome, namely life expectancy, tended to increase with population size in the higher-income group of

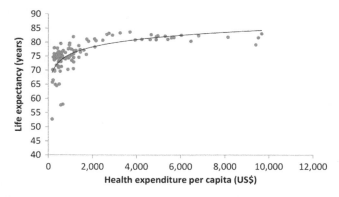

Figure 23.22 Life expectancy and health expenditure per capita (higher-income countries)

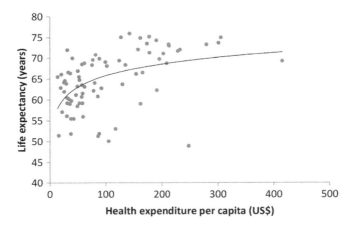

Figure 23.23 Life expectancy and health expenditure per capita

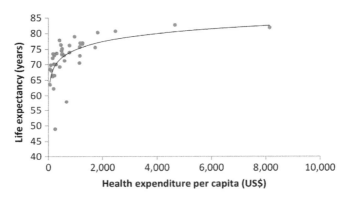

Figure 23.24 Life expectancy and health expenditure per capita (small states with a population of up to 1.5 million)

countries and to decrease with population size in the case of the lower-income group of countries. This tendency was replicated in the case of health expenditure per capita.[39] It was explained that this could possibly be due to the fact that for the smaller states in the higher-income country category there was a tendency for the larger countries to have a higher GDP per capita than the smaller ones, and the opposite was true with regard to lower-income countries.

It is pointed out here that the pair-wise correlations between population size and the three health variables reported in this section are not meant to capture causality, but to identify general tendencies. In most cases the correlation coefficients were on the low side (see Appendix 2) suggesting that the tendencies described above had many exceptions.

4 Conclusion

Main thrust of the literature

The literature, as shown in Section 2 of this chapter, points to the reality that most small states, notably those that are islands or a group of islands, face special constraints, logistically, economically and structurally. The main issues identified pertain to securing a skilled workforce, securing uninterrupted supply and access to affordable medicines and provision of comprehensive health services. For the latter, small countries, particularly islands often seek recourse to overseas arrangements with neighbouring larger states. Small countries that invest in health systems appear to achieve results over comparatively short periods of time, even if such investment comes at a relatively high cost.

It was pointed out however that the literature on health systems in small states does not adequately treat issues related to economies of scale limitations, market size and insularity. Particular challenges arise in view of the fact that small states may also be very different for example a highly densely populated island versus an archipelago of remote atolls pose very different challenges in terms of health services provision and delivery. Investment in health care systems within small states is particularly challenging in view of disadvantages related to economies of scale and scope. Problems related to the procurement of supplies, equipment and pharmaceuticals are also common amongst health care systems in small states. Small states have smaller supply requirements and this can be reflected in the higher per unit prices charged for products and services within such countries.

Whilst in terms of effective implementation, small countries are often reported to be in a position to act faster than large nations, particularly in countries with strong central governments and weak or absent civil society in other cases, it is often the case that small states lack capacity. These in turn have impacts on elements of health system governance, health services delivery and the ability to implement health system reforms effectively.

A number of studies on small states argue that these states can succeed in spite of the challenges they face. Briguglio and Azzopardi-Muscat (2016) contend that good governance is a major requisite for health resilience building, and this could enable these countries to withstand their specific vulnerabilities. One implication of the vulnerability/resilience framework for the health system is that small states need to adopt policies associated with good governance in order to have a strong public health system, an implication that would seem to be confirmed in the literature review where an explicit drive to invest in the health sector as shown by Cape Verde can yield significant benefits over a short period.

Main empirical findings

The empirical work produced in this chapter did not find a clear-cut indication that small states tend to be systematically different from large states in terms of health outcomes (as measured by life expectancy), health resources (as measured by health expenditure per capita) and health determinants (as measured by BMI).

However, the results clearly show that these variables are highly correlated with GDP per capita of countries, which is likely to capture their stage of development and their socio-economic conditions. Even among the small states themselves, income per capita plays a major role with regard to health outcomes and health resources.

Another finding is that regional factors play a role in matters relating to health in small states, with the European small states emerging with the best outcomes and highest resources, followed by those in the Caribbean, the latter generally performing better than the small states of the Pacific regions. The small states of Asia and Africa tended to register poorer results in terms of health outcomes and health resources although variation within each region exists. Again here, the stage of development in these regions is likely to be the major explanation for these differences.

Concluding remarks

Major health determinants, particularly for NCDs, are becoming increasingly subject to global forces and health systems are becoming ever more complex to manage and deliver. These developments are affecting small as well as large states, but given the constraints faced by small states these need to ensure that they do not fall behind in this regard. Several small states, particularly those in the European region are demonstrating their ability to lead in terms of health outcomes and health care access and quality, suggesting that size need not be a binding constraint in matters related to health.

Small states can strengthen their efforts by sharing of best practices, joint learning and joint lobbying within the international arena. As countries move towards implementation of the Sustainable Development Goals with the overall mantra of 'leaving no one behind', small states need to continue to ensure that their particular needs and concerns are identified, acknowledged and met.

There however remains an urgent need to plug the gap when it comes to the production of research on health systems and health outcomes in small states. This requires the input of scholars and practitioners from the small states themselves.

It has been noted earlier in this chapter that one of the main challenges faced by small states is their limited public health capacity and as part of this, their ability to generate comprehensive high quality health data. This may be a considerable limitation affecting the quality of the data analysed and thus impacting on the nature of the observed results through missing data amongst others.

Even here, the issue of limited resources in many small states could restrict research initiatives on this matter, and the support of international organizations for capacity building initiatives is called for. It is therefore a most welcome move by the WHO when it approved the setting up of a WHO Collaborating Centre at the University of Malta,[40] focussing on research and related initiatives associated with health in small states.

Notes

1 In 2014, the Regional Office for Europe of the World Health Organization launched the first Small Countries Network (REF). One of the main purposes of this network is to identify how small countries can serve as beacons for the development of the health in all policies approach at national level. The network also serves to highlight the specific issues that health policy makers in small states encounter.
2 www.euro.who.int/en/about-us/networks/small-countries-initiative/.
3 http://thecommonwealth.org/small-states/.
4 www.worldbank.org/en/country/smallstates/.
5 Andorra, Monaco and San Marino are not in the list of 39 small states listed in Appendix, mostly because data is often not available for such states. All three are often associated with nearby larger states.
6 www.healthdata.org/gbd/.
7 www.un.org/esa/dsd/dsd_aofw_sids/sids_pdfs/BPOA.pdf/.
8 www.un.org/ga/search/view_doc.asp?symbol=A/CONF.207/11&Lang=E/.
9 www.un.org/ga/search/view_doc.asp?symbol=A/CONF.223/10&Lang=E/.
10 www.commonwealthhealth.org/ Accessed several times during July 2017/.
11 www.who.int/gho/countries/brb.pdf?ua=1/.
12 www.commonwealthhealth.org/americas/barbados/health_systems_in_barbados/.
13 www.who.int/gho/countries/guy.pdf?ua=1/.
14 www.commonwealthhealth.org/americas/guyana/health_systems_in_guyana/.
15 www.who.int/gho/countries/wsm.pdf?ua=1/.
16 www.commonwealthhealth.org/pacific/samoa/health_systems_in_samoa/.
17 www.who.int/gho/countries/kir.pdf?ua=1/.

18 www.commonwealthhealth.org/pacific/kiribati/health_systems_in_kiribati/.
19 www.who.int/gho/countries/mus.pdf?ua=1/.
20 www.commonwealthhealth.org/africa/mauritius/health_systems_in_mauritius/.
21 www.who.int/gho/countries/mdv.pdf?ua=1/.
22 www.who.int/countries/mdv/en/.
23 www.who.int/gho/countries/com.pdf?ua=1/.
24 www.aho.afro.who.int/profiles_information/index.php/Comoros:Health_system_outcomes/.
25 www.cdc.gov/vhf/ebola/outbreaks/2014-west-africa/index.html/.
26 www.who.int/gho/countries/cpv.pdf?ua=1/.
27 www.aho.afro.who.int/profiles_information/index.php/Cape_Verde:Index/.
28 www.who.int/gho/countries/swz.pdf?ua=1/.
29 www.aho.afro.who.int/profiles_information/index.php/Swaziland:Index/.
30 www.euro.who.int/en/countries/malta/publications2/meeting-report-of-the-first-high-level-meeting-of-small-countries; www.euro.who.int/en/countries/malta/publications2/meeting-report-of-the-second-high-level-meeting-of-small-countries-soldeu,-andorra,-23-july-2015; www.euro.who.int/en/countries/malta/publications2/meeting-report-of-the-third-high-level-meeting-of-small-countries-2017/.
31 All sources of the data are presented in Appendix 1.
32 Based on the World Bank Atlas method: https://datahelpdesk.worldbank.org/knowledgebase/articles/378832-what-is-the-world-bank-atlas-method.
33 It should be noted that the fitted lines in the Figures presented in this chapter, with the exception of Figures 23.9, 23.15 and 23.21, 23.22, 23.23 and 23.24 are based on a linear equation with two variables. In the case of Figures 23.9, 23.15 and 23.21, 23.22, 23.23 and 23.24 non-linear specifications were used as these produced markedly higher correlation coefficients.
34 One reason why the GDP per capita and the population size are measured in logs is that this permits a neater representation of the relationship in a scatter diagram, given the wide range of GDP per capita and population sizes across countries. In addition, measuring the relationship in logs assumes that there is a diminishing marginal effect of the GDP and the population variables on the health variables. The sign of the gradient of the fitted line will be the same irrespective of whether logs or the actual figures are used.
35 The list of the 39 small states is given in Appendix 3.
36 Total health expenditure is the sum of public and private health expenditures as a ratio of total population. It covers the provision of health services (preventive and curative), family planning activities, nutrition activities, and emergency aid designated for health but does not include provision of water and sanitation. Data is in current U.S. dollars.
37 The positive relation between GDP per capita and health related resources was also found to exist with other health resources variables including number of physicians per 1,000 population and number of beds per 1,000 population.
38 A regulatory quality indicator sourced from the Worldwide Governance Indicators (http://info.worldbank.org/governance/wgi/#home) was highly correlated with GDP per capita.
39 A multiple regression analysis was carried out between life expectancy as dependent variable and population size and GDP per capita as explanatory variables. As expected, the GDP per capita variable was statistically significant at the 95% level whereas the population variable was not. Similar results were obtained when the dependent variable was replaced by health expenditure per capita.
40 The WHO Collaborating Centre on small states was set up at the Islands and Small States Institute of the University of Malta. The work plan of this centre includes conducting research on the so-called vulnerability/resilience framework, with a focus on small states.

Appendix 1

Table 23.A1 Data used in this study and their sources

Variable	Source	Year	URL	Number of countries			
				All	*Small[a]*	*H-I[b]*	*L-I[c]*
GDP per capita	IMF	2015	www.imf.org/ external/pubs/ft/ weo/2016/02/ weodata/index. aspx	184	39	106	78
Population size	IMF	2015	www.imf.org/ external/pubs/ft/ weo/2016/02/ weodata/index. aspx	184	39	106	78
Expenditure on health care per capita	World Bank based World Health Organization Data	2014	http://data. worldbank.org/ indicator/SH. XPD.PCAP	180	39	103	77
Life expectancy	UNDP – Human Development Report	2015	http://hdr.undp. org/en/2016-rep ort	184	39	106	78
Body Mass Index	World Health Organization	2014	http://apps.who. int/gho/data/ view.main. CTRY12461	177	39	102	75

Notes: [a] Small states are defined as those with a population of up to 1.5 million

[b] Higher-income counties comprise high-income and upper-middle income countries, as classified by the World Bank, grouped together.

[c] Lower-income countries comprise lower-middle income and low income countries, as classified by the World Bank, grouped together.

Appendix 2

Table 23.A2 Pair-wise simple correlation matrix

Figure	Correlation	Y Axis	X-Axis	Countries
Figure 23.1	0.807	Life expectancy	Log GDP PC	All countries
Figure 23.2	0.062	Life expectancy	Log pop	All countries
Figure 23.3	0.128	Life expectancy	Log pop	Higher-income countries
Figure 23.4	0.074	Life expectancy	Log pop	Lower-income countries
Figure 23.5	0.053	GDP PC	Log pop	Higher-income countries
Figure 23.6	0.210	GDP PC	Log pop	Lower-income countries
Figure 23.7	0.211	Life expectancy	Log pop	Small states
Figure 23.9	0.960	Health exp. PC	Log GDP PC	All countries
Figure 23.10	0.017	Health exp. PC	Log pop	All countries
Figure 23.11	0.139	Health exp. PC	Log pop	Higher-income countries
Figure 23.12	0.362	Health exp. PC	Log pop	Lower-income countries
Figure 23.13	0.096	Health exp. PC	Log pop	Small states
Figure 23.15	0.681	BMI	Log GDP PC	All countries
Figure 23.16	0.390	BMI	Log pop	All countries
Figure 23.17	0.276	BMI	Log pop	Higher-income countries
Figure 23.18	0.517	BMI	Log pop	Lower-income countries
Figure 23.19	0.586	BMI	Log pop	Small states
Figure 23.21	0.798	Life expectancy	Health exp. PC	All countries
Figure 23.22	0.704	Life expectancy	Health exp. PC	Higher-income countries
Figure 23.23	0.473	Life expectancy	Health exp. PC	Lower-income countries
Figure 23.24	0.628	Life expectancy	Health exp. PC	Small states

Appendix 3

Table 23.A3 Small states included in this study (population up to 1.5 million)

Country	GDP per capita (US$, 2015)	Population ('000, 2015)
Antigua and Barbuda	15155	89
Bahamas	24310	364
Bahrain	24058	1.294
Barbados	15808	28
Belize	4757	366
Bhutan	2603	779
Brunei Darussalam	30995	417
Cape Verde	3001	525
Comoros	736	799
Cyprus	23105	847
Djibouti	1788	966
Dominica	7312	71
Equatorial Guinea	17287	799
Estonia	17111	1.313
Fiji	4929	891
Grenada	9222	107
Guyana	4151	767
Iceland	50473	333
Kiribati	1410	114
Luxembourg	100950	563
Maldives	9178	348
Malta	23973	429
Mauritius	9115	1.263
Micronesia (Fed. States)	3079	102
Montenegro	6465	622
Palau	15907	18
Saint Kitts and Nevis	15766	56
Saint Lucia	8256	173
Saint Vincent/Grenadines	6706	11
Samoa	4159	193
Sao Tome and Principe	1567	203
Seychelles	14554	93
Solomon Islands	1923	588
Suriname	8768	556
Swaziland	3512	1.119
Timor-Leste	2462	1.167
Tonga	3974	104
Trinidad and Tobago	17322	1.36
Vanuatu	2747	269

Source: www.imf.org/external/pubs/ft/weo/2017/01/weodata/index.aspx/.

References

Asante, A. D., Irava, W., Limwattananon, S., Hayen, A., Martins, J., Guinness, L., Ataguba, J. E., Price, J., Jan, S., Mills, A. and Wiseman, V. (2017). 'Financing for universal health coverage in small island states: evidence from the Fiji Islands'. *BMJ Global Health*, 2(2).

Atkins, J. P. (2000). A commonwealth vulnerability index for developing countries: the position of small states. *Economic Paper*, No. 40. Commonwealth Secretariat.

Azzopardi-Muscat, N. (2016). *Europeanisation of health systems: a small state perspective*. Doctoral dissertation. Maastricht University.

Azzopardi-Muscat, N., Funk, T., Buttigieg, S. C., Grech, K. E., Brand, H. (2016b). 'Policy Challenges and reforms in small EU member state health systems: a narrative literature review'. *The European Journal of Public Health*, 26(6): 916–922.

Azzopardi-Muscat, N., Sorensen, K., Aluttis, C., Pace, R. and Brand, H. (2016a). 'Europeanisation of health systems: a qualitative study of domestic actors in a small state'. *BMC Public Health*, 16(1): 334.

Baldacchino, G. and Bertram, G. (2009). 'The beak of the finch: insights into the economic development of small economies'. *The Round Table*, 98(401): 141–160.

Barber, R. M., Fullman, N., Sorensen, R. J., Bollyky, T., McKee, M., Nolte, E., Abajobir, A. A., Abate, K. H., Abbafati, C., Abbas, K. M. and Abd-Allah, F. (2017). 'Healthcare Access and Quality Index based on mortality from causes amenable to personal health care in 195 countries and territories, 1990–2015: a novel analysis from the Global Burden of Disease Study 2015'. *Lancet*.

Bero, L. A., Hill, S., Habicht, J., Mathiesen, M. and Starkopf, J. (2013). 'The updated clinical guideline development process in Estonia is an efficient method for developing evidence-based guidelines'. *Journal of Clinical Epidemiology*, 66(2): 132–139.

Briguglio, L. (1995). 'Small island developing states and their economic vulnerabilities'. *World development*, 23(9): 1615–1632.

Briguglio, L. (2016). 'Exposure to external shocks and economic resilience of countries: evidence from global indicators'. *Journal of Economic Studies*, 43(6): 1057–1078.

Briguglio, L. and Azzopardi Muscat, N. (2016). *The Vulnerability and Resilience Framework applied to the Public Health System*. Presentation delivered at the WHO Third High Level Meeting for Small Countries, Monaco, October.

Briguglio, L., Cordina, G., Farrugia, N. and Vella, S. (2009). 'Economic vulnerability and resilience: concepts and measurements'. *Oxford Development Studies*, 37(3): 229–247.

Buchan, J., Connell, J., Rumsey, M. and World Health Organization (2011). *Recruiting and retaining health workers in remote areas: Pacific Island case-studies*. Geneva: World Health Organization

Connell, J. (2007). 'Local skills and global markets? The migration of health workers from Caribbean and Pacific island states'. *Social and Economic Studies*: 7–95.

Cooper, A. (2016). *Governing global health: challenge, response, innovation*. London: Routledge.

Crowards, T. (2002). 'Defining the category of 'small' states'. *Journal of International Development*, 14(2): 143–179.

Delnoij, D. M. and Groenewegen, P. P. (2007). 'Health services and systems research in Europe: overview of the literature 1995–2005'. *European Journal of Public Health*, 17(suppl_1): 10–13.

Downes, A.S. (1988). 'On the statistical measurement of smallness: a principal component measure of country size'. *Social and Economic Studies*: 75–96.

Easterly, W. and Kraay, A. (2000). 'Small states, small problems? Income, growth, and volatility in small states'. *World Development*, 28(11): 2013–2027.

Feigin, V. (2016). 'Global, regional, and national life expectancy, all-cause mortality, and cause-specific mortality for 249 causes of death, 1980–2015: a systematic analysis for the Global Burden of Disease Study 2015'. *The Lancet*, 388(10053): 1459–1544.

Galea, G., Powis, B. and Tamplin, S. A. (2000). 'Healthy Islands in the Western Pacific – international settings development'. *Health Promotion International*, 15(2): 169–178.

Gostin, L. O. and Friedman, E. A. (2017). 'Global health: a pivotal moment of opportunity and peril'. *Health Affairs*, 36(1): 159–165.

Greaves, D. (2016). 'Health Management/Leadership of Small Island Developing States of the English-speaking Caribbean: A Critical Review'. *Journal of Health Management*, 18(4): 595–610.

Gregg, E., Shaw, J. E. (2017). 'Global Health Effects of Overweight and Obesity'. *New England Journal of Medicine*, 377(1): 80–81.

Homer, C. S., Turkmani, S. and Rumsey, M. (2017). 'The state of midwifery in small island Pacific nations'. *Women and Birth* 30(2): 193–199.

Maass, M. (2009). 'The elusive definition of the small state'. *International Politics*, 46(1): 65–83.

Mackenbach, J. P. and Looman, C. W. N. (2013). 'Life expectancy and national income in Europe, 1900–2008: an update of Preston's analysis'. *International Journal of Epidemiology*, 42: 1100–1110.

O'Connor, J. S. and Bankauskaite, V. (2008). 'Public health development in the Baltic countries (1992–2005): from problems to policy'. *The European Journal of Public Health*, 18(6): 586–592.

Rumsey, M., Catling, C., Thiessen, J. and Neill, A. (2017). 'Building nursing and midwifery leadership capacity in the Pacific'. *International Nursing Review*, 64(1): 50–58.

Saksena, P. and Xu, K. (2011). *The determinants of health expenditure*. Working Paper December, World Health Organization.

Saliba, V., Muscat, N.A., Vella, M., Montalto, S.A., Fenech, C., McKee, M. and Knai, C. (2014). 'Clinicians', policy makers' and patients' views of pediatric cross-border care between Malta and the UK'. *Journal of Health Services Research and Policy*, 19(3): 153–160.

Ståhl, T., Wismar, M., Ollila, E., Lahtinen, E. and Leppo, K. (2006). *Health in all policies. Prospects and potentials*. Helsinki: Finnish Ministry of Social Affairs and Health.

Thorhallsson, B. (2006). 'The size of states in the European Union: Theoretical and conceptual perspectives'. *European Integration*, 28(1):7–31.

United Nations (2015). *Sustainable Development Goals*. Available at www.un.org/sustainabledevelopment/sustainable-development-goals.

Unwin, N., Samuels, T. A., Hassell, T., Brownson, R. C., Guell, C. (2017). 'The development of public policies to address non-communicable diseases in the Caribbean country of Barbados: the importance of problem framing and policy entrepreneurs'. *International Journal of Health Policy and Management*, 6(2): 71.

Vogler, S., Zimmermann, N., Leopold, C. and de Joncheere, K. (2011). 'Pharmaceutical policies in European countries in response to the global financial crisis'. *Southern Med Review*, 4(2): 69.

Wait, S. and Nolte, E. (2005). 'Benchmarking health systems: trends, conceptual issues and future perspectives'. *Benchmarking: An International Journal*, 12(5): 436–448.

Walker, J., Chaar, B. B., Vera, N., Pillai, A. S., Lim, J. S., Bero, L. and Moles, R. J. (2017). 'Medicine shortages in Fiji: A qualitative exploration of stakeholders' views'. *PloS one*, 12(6).

Whiting, S., Dalipanda, T., Postma, S., de Lorenzo, A. J. and Aumua, A. (2016). 'Moving towards Universal Health Coverage through the Development of Integrated Service Delivery Packages for Primary Health Care in the Solomon Islands'. *International Journal of Integrated Care*, 16(1).

World Health Organization (WHO) (2014). *African Regional Health Report*. Geneva: WHO.

World Health Organization (WHO) (2015). Yanuca Island Declaration on health in Pacific island countries and territories. Eleventh Pacific Health Ministers Meeting, 15–17 April.

World Health Organization (WHO) (2016). *Intersectoral action for health – Experiences from small countries in the WHO European Region*. Geneva: WHO.

World Health Organization (WHO) (2017). *Building resilience: a key pillar of Health 2020 and the Sustainable Development Goals – Examples from the WHO Small Countries Initiative*. Geneva: WHO.

World Health Organization (WHO) (2000). *The world health report 2000: health systems: improving performance*. Geneva: WHO.

Young, S., Perry, W., Leodoro, B., Nosa, V., Bissett, I. and Windsor, J. A. (2016). 'Challenges and Opportunities in the Provision of Surgical Care in Vanuatu: A Mixed Methods Analysis'. *World Journal of Surgery*, 40(8): 1865–1873.

24

Demographic transition and population ageing in small states

Philip von Brockdorff and Melchior Vella[1]

1 Introduction

Objective and background

The objective of this chapter is to test whether there are significant differences between small and larger countries in terms of their demographic transitions. The analysis also takes into account the magnitude and speed of ageing in different sized countries, classified by income per capita categories.

As is well known, the population changes are affected by birth and death rates and by net migration. As we shall show in the literature review, these factors have an impact on the age distribution of the population, and therefore on population ageing.

Population ageing refers to the process by which the share of older people become proportionately larger in respect of the total population. Ageing is often represented by the old-age dependency ratio, which gives the number of persons at 65 years of age or over expressed as a percentage of the working-age population (15–64). Movements in the ratio represents only demographic shifts and does not reflect any changes in the economic activity among those of working-age or pensionable age.

Population ageing is widely recognized as an emerging social challenge in many countries of the world. It is poised to have substantial effects on both social and economic transformations, including the labour, housing, financial markets, and the sustainability of public finance. The share of the number of persons aged 65 years or over per one hundred persons aged 15 to 64 years increased from 8% in 1950 to 12% in 2015 worldwide and it is projected to be 26% by 2050 (United Nations, 2016). While the ageing process will continue to advance amongst more developed regions, this process is expected to accelerate even faster in many developing regions and is likely to have a profound impact on various dimensions of society.

Layout of the chapter

The rest of the chapter is organized as follows: Section 2 presents a literature review on a number of topics related to the main theme of the chapter including the demographic transition and population aging in various categories of countries. Given that the focus of the chapter is on small states, a section of the literature review is dedicated to the main characteristics of small states. Section 3 looks at the drivers of the demographic transition and population ageing amongst different sized countries, categorized by their GDP per capita. Conclusions derived from the results and their implications are presented in Section 4.

2 Literature review

Demographic Transition Model

According the Demographic Transition Model, a country progresses over time from one stage to the next as social and economic forces act upon the birth and death rates. Every country can be placed within the Demographic Transition Model, but not every stage of the model has a country that meets its specific definition (Livi-Bacci, 1992; Caldwell *et al.*, 2006).

According to Livi-Bacci (1992), the Demographic Transition Model generally consists of four phases. The first phase marks the beginning of the transition and is characterized by high levels of fertility and mortality. The second phase marks the beginning of both mortality and fertility decline, and the third phase is characterized by further reductions in mortality and fertility. The fourth and final phase is characterized by very low levels of mortality and fertility.

This Model is based on the hypothesis that the process of falling fertility rates will continue until low rates are reached. As stated by Livi-Bacci (1992: 105), most European countries have had such an experience but the duration of the transition has differed. Mortality decline generally precedes that of fertility but there have been exceptions. In France, for instance, the downward trend in mortality and fertility levels moved in tandem.

Fertility rates

Lower fertility levels affect the number of persons feeding into the young segment of the population, or as described by Johnson and Falkingham (1992: 20) 'the population pyramid at its base'. To an extent, the number of births depend on the number of married couples and the time spent bearing children. Fertility control is largely voluntary but the traditional system of fertility regulation through marriage has long been replaced by contraception. This has proved to be highly efficient and in some European countries the fertility rates are well below the hypothetical level of generational replacement of about 2.1 children per woman of childbearing age (Demeny, 2015).

In many developing countries, irrespective of size, fertility has fallen rapidly over the past quarter century (Bongaarts, 2008). Projections typically assume that this trend will go on until the replacement level is reached. However, evidence shows that the fertility decline has slowed down or possibly stalled in sub-Saharan African countries. Around the year 2000, for instance, the average pace of decline in fertility was lower than in the mid-1990s. This demonstrates that the experience of demographic transition is not the same for all countries.

Some authors discuss the relationship between economic development and fertility (for example Mason and Kinugasa, 2008; Poot, 2008). This relationship is not always straightforward (Cleland, 1994). The empirical analysis by Bloom and Williamson (1998) suggests that population growth has a transitional effect on economic growth. The effect depends on whether the dependent and working-age populations are growing at different rates. The implication of this is that the accelerated demographic ageing will tend to slow down economic growth rates. However, the effect is not similar in all countries. For example, in the case of Asia (ibid.) some countries are experiencing a fall in the relative size of the working-age population while others in the same continent are still experiencing growth in this variable.

Ageing population

The transition to low fertility will eventually result in populations with a high level of old-age dependency. Most developed countries are in this phase of their demographic transition but the economic burden caused by ageing populations will depend to a significant extent on the social and economic structures in place. There is no question that developed countries are better placed to develop such structures than developing countries. And this gives them an edge over developing countries in dealing with ageing populations.

There is extensive literature that examines the ageing process in developed and developing countries (see for example Wise, 1989; Shrestha, 2000; Banik and Bhaumik, 2006; Bloom et al., 2010; Lee and Mason, 2011; Formosa, 2014; Aiyar and Ebeke, 2016). The increase in longevity at old age is generally seen to pose challenges on the size of the labour force and saving rate and higher reliance on health care, long-term care (Werblow et al., 2007; Zweifel et al., 1999), and pension benefits (*Ageing Report*, 2015; Bongaarts, 2004). By contrast, higher survival rates may induce persons to remain active in the labour market and to begin drawing down their savings at a later stage. Overall, the macroeconomic effects of ageing are mediated by changes in the labour and financial markets and the financing of the social welfare (Bloom et al., 2010).

Using 'National Transfer Accounts' and describing the age patterns of economic activity and the economic relations between generations, Lee and Mason (2011) quantified the economic lifecycle and economic flows across generations for several developed and developing countries and found that in countries with low levels of fertility, more financial resources can be devoted to raising human capital spending per child; more can be used to raise standards of living and to reduce poverty; and more can be saved and invested in the future. However, low fertility eventually results in populations with high rates of old-age dependency. In contrast, in those developing countries with high levels of fertility and therefore still young populations, Lee and Mason (2011) concluded that a large proportion of what the adult population produces goes to meet the material needs of their children with most intended for basic needs like food, clothing and housing. Very little remains for health and education for children. This would seem to indicate that in developing countries with high fertility and a young age structure, investment in human capital could be undermined by the economic burden placed on the working-age population.

As already explained, an ageing population may cause a shrinking in the relative size of the labour force that, keeping all other things constant, would generate a reduction of the economic growth rates. Increased longevity and a reduced birth rate has also been associated with a slower growth in capital stock and a weakened labour productivity (Aiyar and Ebeke, 2016; Feldstein, 2006), though the effect on the latter is inconclusive. Some find empirical evidence that the relationship between age, wage and productivity increases with age (Ilmakunnas and Maliranta, 2005; Hellerstein and Neumark, 2007), while others find little evidence (Van Ours and Stoeldraijer, 2011).

Some authors (e.g. Formosa, 2014) identify a number of economic opportunities associated with an ageing population, moving away from the traditional view of older persons as poor, frail, and unemployable. Such opportunities include older volunteerism, which can be a valuable economic and social resource, and the so-called 'silver market phenomenon' where older persons act as consumers as well as a major target for services such as finance, housing, vacations, and leisure activities (including education).

Migration

A factor, other than birth and death rates, which affects the demographic transition is emigration (Fargues, 2011). The effect of emigration for developing states is not clear-cut. Most migrants worldwide are of working-age (United Nations, 2016) and thus persistent negative net-emigration rate represents a fall in the working-age population, and labour supply. Considerable theoretical and empirical work devoted to this topic highlights that negative net-emigration has negative repercussions on the home country, including brain drain, lower return on human capital investment, loss of capital that emigrants possess, and limitations on scale economies in production (Lucas, 1981; Dayton-Johnson et al., 2009).

Some authors on the other hand, (e.g. Chand, 2008) argue that emigration provides incentives for workers to invest in human capital and generates remittances for the source nations. The effect also depends on various economic factors including whether (i) there is high unemployment, poverty and lack of economic growth; (ii) emigrants are high-skilled or low-skilled; (iii) emigrants send remittances; and (iv) emigration is temporary or permanent.

Experience of small states

There is no exact definition of a small state. The Commonwealth Secretariat considers a population threshold of 1.5 million people in its list of small states.[2] However, larger countries, including Lesotho, Papua New Guinea and Jamaica are included in this list, presumably because they share similar characteristics with the smaller states.

Despite the diversity with respect to the geographical location and the level of development of small states, small country size is likely to lead to similar traits and challenges. Small state economies are associated with several special characteristics (Briguglio, 1995; Atkins et al., 2000; Guillaumont, 2010), including high degree of trade openness, export concentration and a high degree of dependence on strategic imports – notably food and fuel which render them highly exposed to external shocks (Briguglio, 2016). In addition, small states face many economic disadvantages associated with small size, notably their limited ability to reap the benefits of economies of scale (Briguglio and Vella, 2015), due to, amongst other things, overhead cost indivisibilities and limited scope for specialization, leading to relatively higher per unit costs (Winters and Martins, 2004). These distinguishable features limit their competitiveness potential and their development options.

Issues relating to the demographic transition and the problems associated with an ageing population do not feature often in the literature on small states. It should be noted here that the outcome documents of the three major conferences dedicated to the sustainable development of small island developing states under the auspices of the United nations, respectively held in 1994 in Barbados, in 2005 in Mauritius, and in 2014 in Samoa,[3] recognized that population size and high population density pose a risk to vulnerability of small island developing states. However, these documents do not delve into the risks that ageing may have on sustainable development. Nor do they give sufficient prominence to the problem posed by emigration.

Possibly, as a result of the constraints relating to their economic development, many small developing states face higher rates of emigration per capita, particularly of high-skilled persons, relative to larger states (Chand, 2018).

Emigration, in small island developing states, is sometimes viewed as an 'escape valve' in times of large labour surpluses (Fitzgerald, 2004). One can argue that emigration is a requisite that reduces labour surplus, and in turn may be conducive to economic development. Even if emigration accelerates dependency ratios by the loss of people of working-age, this deterioration is to an extent compensated by remittances (Chand, 2008, 2017).

The literature convincingly shows that small states tend to have higher rates of emigration than larger ones. Docquier and Marfouk (2006), basing on census data, show that, in 2000, the average emigration rates are about seven times higher for small countries than for large countries. It appears that highest emigration rates are mostly observed in medium-income countries where people have both the incentives and means to emigrate. By way of example, small Caribbean economies have had significant demographic changes due to rising incomes in the proximity to large developed countries. Together with capital outlays, the small economies experienced shortage of skilled workers and high rates of unemployment (Banik and Bhaumik, 2006; Micklin, 1994). In likewise manner, the emigration rate in the Pacific for small island states is significantly higher than larger countries (Chand, 2008).

It is often contended that emigration rates of high-skilled workers exceed those of low-skill workers in virtually all countries (Docquier *et al.*, 2007, 2009), resulting also into potential substantial loss in human capital and permanent forgone output. This has been the case for Caribbean islands (Nurse, 2004). Nevertheless, Chand (2008) identifies positive factors associated with migration from small states arguing that emigration provides possibilities for workers to upgrade their skills – in an alternative scenario of restriction on emigration, the stock of skilled personnel would likely fall in source nations.

All in all, evidence on brain drain points that many small developing countries suffer substantial losses in terms of human capital (Beine *et al.*, 2008). By contrast, larger developing countries seem to experience fewer losses in relative terms, such that the largest developing countries all appear to have experienced a net gain.

Regarding fertility rates and population aging in small states, the literature on this matter is limited and to our best knowledge, little is known as to whether countries with a small population size face significant difference in terms of natural population changes. The figures shown in Table 24.1 of this chapter would seem to suggest that income per capita rather than country size is the main driver in this regard.

3 Methodology

In order to derive empirical tendencies relating to the demographic transition and ageing in different sized countries we use the following two identities:

$$CPCR \equiv CBR - CDR_{0-64} - CDR_{65-99} + CNMR \tag{1}$$

$$OADR \equiv OP_{65\text{and over}}/WAP_{15-64} \tag{2}$$

where CPCR is the crude population change rate (population change per 1,000 population), CBR is the crude birth rate (births per 1,000 population), CDR is the crude death rate (deaths per 1,000 population) for persons aged 0–64 and 65 years or over, and the CNMR is the crude net-migration rate (net-migration per 1,000 population). In Equation 2, OADR stands for old-age dependency ratio, $OP_{65\text{and over}}$ stands for older persons aged 65 or over and WAP_{15-64} stands for the working age population. Data is sourced from the World Population Prospects, published by the United Nations, and covers the historical period 1950–2015. For this study we consider 179 countries, for which data was available (see Appendix 1).

The decomposition of population change shown in equation (1) indicates that population changes are not only the outcome of declining fertility and mortality, but also migration flows. Equation (2) shows that the extent of the aging population may be measured by the so-called dependency ratio, comparing the number of persons of working age to the number of those aged 65 and over. In both equations, comparison across countries is possible. Consequently, we can evaluate whether systematic variability exists when evaluating demographic transition and ageing patters by country size, after controlling for the level of economic development.

Table 24.1 Main determinants of crude population change, average, 1950–2015 (rates per 1,000 population)

	1950–2015		
	Small	*Medium*	*Large*
Low Income			
CPCR	21.0	22.6	22.5
CBR	38.6	39.6	36.9
CDR (0–64)	−10.5	−12.6	−10.9
CDR (65–99)	−2.6	−2.8	−2.8
CNMR	−4.4	−1.7	−0.7
COADR	0.1	0.0	0.1
Medium Income			
CPCR	14.5	19.0	17.8
CBR	31.3	30.1	28.3
CDR (0–64)	−6.9	−6.8	−7.3
CDR (65–99)	−3.6	−3.6	−3.3
CNMR	−6.3	−0.7	0.2
COADR	0.1	0.3	0.3
High Income			
CPCR	12.9	14.4	7.1
CBR	20.5	18.4	15.0
CDR (0–64)	−3.6	−3.4	−2.9
CDR (65–99)	−5.1	−5.7	−6.4
CNMR	1.1	5.0	1.4
COADR	0.5	0.7	1.1
All income groups			
CPCR	16.5	19.3	16.9
CBR	30.4	31.0	28.4
CDR (0–64)	−7.2	−8.4	−7.7
CDR (65–99)	−3.7	−3.8	−3.9
CNMR	−3.0	0.5	0.1
COADR	0.2	0.3	0.4

Source: Authors' calculations. Data sourced from the World Population Prospects: the 2015 Revision (United Nations, Department of Economic and Social Affairs, 2015).

Note: CPCR is crude population change rate, CBR is crude birth rate, CDR is crude death rate, CNMR is crude net migration rate and COADR is the change in old age ratio.

In our study, small states are defined as countries with a population size of 2.0 million or fewer.[4] Medium-sized countries are considered as those with a population of 2 to 50 million, while large countries are considered as those with a population exceeding the 50 million. In addition, the World Bank classification is used to categorize countries by income group. Low-income economies are defined as those with a GNI per capita of $4,035 or less in 2015; middle-income economies are those with a GNI per capita between $4,035–$12,475; whereas high-income economies are those with a GNI per capita of $12,476 or more.[5]

4 Demographic determinants and of population ageing

Changing demographic determinants

As illustrated in Figure 24.1, the demographic tendencies between 1950 and 2015 show the post-World War II baby boom was followed by a steady decline in the fertility rate and the crude birth rate by approximately a half during this period.

It can be seen that even though the crude birth rate in small states was still above average, particularly amongst the high-income group, the declining births were experienced in both small and larger states. The gap in the high-income group between small states and the average crude birth rate has narrowed down at a fast pace from 4.5 to 1.6 per thousand over the period 1950–2015. Turning to the crude birth rate of small states by region, Africa has the highest rate across all income groups, followed by Asia, Oceania, Latin America and Caribbean, and Europe.

Significantly large and sustained increases in life expectancy at birth has also had an impact on the demographic composition, albeit with a considerable degree of diversity across countries. The

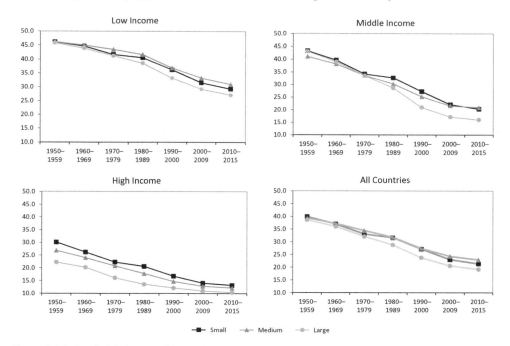

Figure 24.1 Crude birth rate, 1950–2015
Source: Authors' calculations, based on World Population Prospects: the 2015 Revision (United Nations, Department of Economic and Social Affairs, 2015).

reduction in mortality rate has also been sustained in smaller states and is marginally below that reported in larger states over the whole period. However, extension of average life at birth does not necessarily result in population ageing. Declines in the infant mortality rates alleviate the support ratio whereas increases in the proportion of older persons intensifies the speed of ageing.

Figure 24.2 shows that throughout the 1950–2015 period, the crude mortality rates for persons aged 65 years or over in low and middle-income countries have been similar across states with different size. Lower rates of mortality occurred in small states relative to larger states for the same income group. Meanwhile, the mortality rates for persons aged less than 65 in larger countries converged progressively to that recorded in small states across low- and middle-income groups; meaning that in 2010–2015 period, the gap was almost non-existent.

Small states among the high-income group category are endowed with lower old-age mortality rate, meaning that higher longevity at older ages is resulting in more persons in the older age categories relative to larger states.

Demographic changes are also affected by net migration flows. The first striking observation from Figure 24.3 is that net migration flows are characterized by high variability. Over the years small states registered significant outflows, particularly low- and medium-income countries. This means that net-migration has had a large negative effect on the demographic transition of these states, considering that the highest proportion of migrants are of working-age.

Furthermore, as expected, the largest number of net-arrivals occurred in high-income countries. The situation for small and high-income countries is less clear as the net-migration

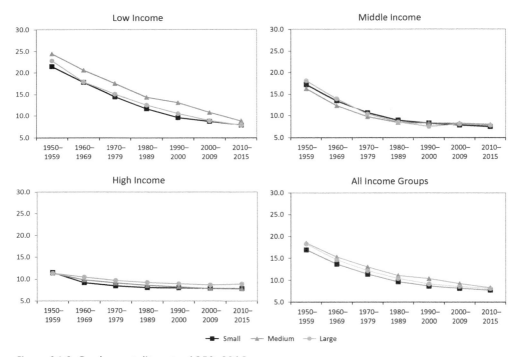

Figure 24.2 Crude mortality rate, 1950–2015
Source: Authors' calculations, based on World Population Prospects: the 2015 Revision (United Nations, Department of Economic and Social Affairs, 2015).

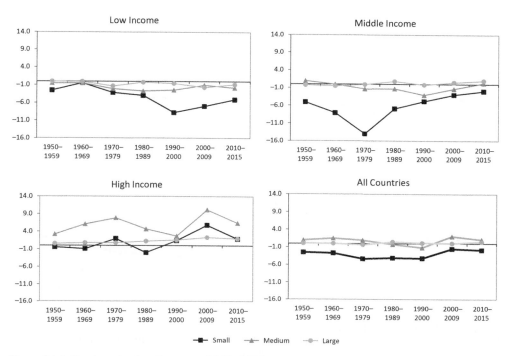

Figure 24.3 Crude net migration rate, 1950–2015
Source: Authors' calculations, based on World Population Prospects: the 2015 Revision (United Nations, Department of Economic and Social Affairs, 2015).

flow rates tended to fluctuate interchangeably, however bounded between −0.9% to an all-time-high of 5.9%.

Turning to the crude net migration rate by region, African and Oceania low-income, and Latin American and Caribbean middle-income small states registered consistent negative net migration rate throughout the historical period. Experience in Asia is less clear, though low- and middle-income groups also suffered from negative net-migration flows. Meanwhile, except for the mid-twentieth century, European small states have had positive net-migration flows, possibly reflecting their high level of development.

Turning to the mean age by country size and level of income, Figure 24.4 shows that the mean age in small states has been somewhat lower than the population average age of all countries, suggesting that ageing intensity is not severe. This is so even though the demography transition tends to be exacerbated by higher net migration outflow densities in smaller countries.

Likewise, evidence of old-age dependency ratio illustrated in Figure 24.5 reveals that there is a noticeable degree of disparity amongst the high-income group of countries. The ageing process of small and medium sized states has been slower than large countries, such that the transition did not converge. Indeed, the demographic old-age dependency ratio for large high-income countries increased from 13.6% to 25.7%, meaning that over the years there was a movement from 7 working-age people for every person aged 65 years or over to only 4 working-age persons by 2015. This process has been much slower for small high-income states, which saw the dependency ratio increasing to 16.0% in 2015 from 10.6% in 1950.

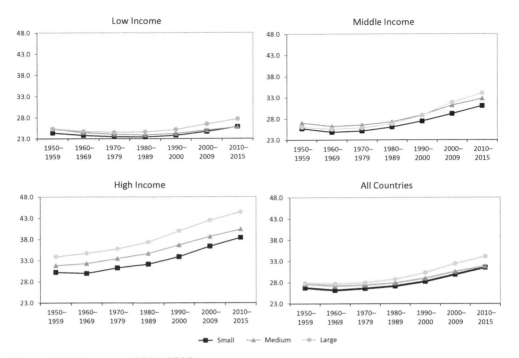

Figure 24.4 Mean age, 1950–2015
Source: Authors' calculations, based on World Population Prospects: the 2015 Revision (United Nations, Department of Economic and Social Affairs, 2015).

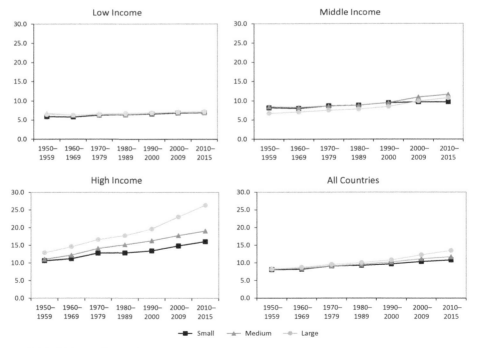

Figure 24.5 Old-age dependency (65+), 1950–2015
Source: Authors' calculations, based on World Population Prospects: the 2015 Revision (United Nations, Department of Economic and Social Affairs, 2015).

Small states exhibit more pronounced demographic changes due to higher crude emigration rates, that render them exposed to the ageing transition. Notwithstanding such exposure, small states, in general, register lower demographic old-age dependency.

Table 24.1 summarizes the main results of the population change decomposition for the period 1950 to 2015 with data averaged in terms of three categories of country size and three categories of country per-capita income, as explained above. Based on these classifications, the main tendencies that can be derived from the demographic decomposition are explained hereunder.

First, throughout the period under consideration, the average crude net-migration rate increases with population size for all income groups, indicating that larger nations, particularly the high-income ones, tend to attract migrants, whereas small countries, particularly in the medium income group are net senders of migrants.

Considering the whole period and all income groups taken together, it emerges that the drivers of ageing amongst countries with different size differ. The change in the old-age dependency ratio by country size for all income groups reveals that the speed of ageing in larger countries was somewhat faster than small states. While, the speed of ageing accelerated in larger states because of natural factors, small states faced a different experience. Notwithstanding higher migration outflows in small states, this effect has been to an extent cancelled out by the higher crude birth rate for all small states taken together. Nevertheless, this does not imply that the number of older people will not grow fast in the future. At the root of the ageing process is the higher birth rates experienced since 1950, as shown in Table 24.1.

When looking at medium and high-income groups, the tendency for higher outward net-migration rates and higher birth rates in small states remains. In the low income category, outward net-migration rates of small states are also relatively high, but interestingly the birth rate is somewhat lower than that of medium- sized countries but higher than that of large countries.

An accelerated speed of ageing was recorded for the high-income group across countries of different size; indicating that income per capita is one of the main drivers in this regard. The average increase in the ageing ratio, however, was higher for large than small states. Meanwhile, the demographic transition of medium income countries was slower for small states notwithstanding the outward net-migration rate size. As regards low-income countries, no marked differences emerged between different sized countries.

The results presented in this study are subject to certain caveats, which need to be acknowledged. Specifically, data constraints limit our efforts to disentangle the factors that lead to an ageing population, so we are only reporting the manifestation of the phenomenon rather than the cause, although income per capita and all that it brings with it was used to assess tendencies in this regard. Also, there is the usual problem with the accuracy of the data. For example, net migration flows are computed as a residual from the demographic balance and therefore incorporating all possible errors.

5 Conclusion

This study reveals differences between countries of different size and of different per capita income, in terms of their demographic changes. There is a clear negative relationship between emigration rates and country size, suggesting that this was a major factor affecting small countries during the period under consideration. According to the literature, as explained in Section 2 of this chapter, the heavy loss, through emigration, of people who are of working-age and educated, may have had a negative effect due to the loss of human resources, counterbalanced by, among other things, the sending of remittances by emigrants to their families back home.

The speed of ageing in larger countries is different from the experience of small countries. Higher migration outflows and higher fertility rates in small countries have shaped the demographic transition somewhat differently from larger countries. Consequently, the speed of ageing has been slower in smaller states, although there were marked differences when income per capita is taken into consideration.

The study also reveals that the stage and speed of ageing is heterogeneous particularly among less developed countries. Still population ageing is expected to unfold in low income countries. Such demographic transition could have adverse economic effects. In contrast, an increase in the share of working-age population provides a country with a window of opportunity, which if properly tapped can generate a 'demographic dividend' from higher growth. A direct implication of ageing in least developed countries is letting this window of opportunity pass by without any meaningful progress.

Notes

1   The views and opinions expressed in this article are those of the authors only.
2   See http://thecommonwealth.org/small-states/.
3   The three outcome documents are The Barbados Programme of Action for the Sustainable Development of Small Islands States (www.un.org/esa/dsd/dsd_aofw_sids/sids_pdfs/BPOA.pdf), the Mauritius Strategy for the Further Implementation of the Programme of Action for the Sustainable Development of SIDS (http://www.un.org/ga/search/view_doc.asp?symbol=A/CONF.207/11&Lang=E) and the SIDS Accelerated Modalities of Action [S.A.M.O.A.] Pathway (www.sids2014.org/index.php?menu=1537).
4   We did not restrict ourselves to the 1.5 million population threshold as some slightly larger countries in the literature are considered small due to similar characteristics.
5   Sourced from http://databank.worldbank.org/data/download/site-content/CLASS.xls. The per capita income used by the World Bank is calculated on the basis of the Atlas method, as explained here: https://datahelpdesk.worldbank.org/knowledgebase/articles/378832-the-world-bank-atlas-method-detailed-methodology/.

Appendix 1 Countries included in this study

Low-income countries

Small	Congo Rep	Tanzania
Bhutan	El Salvador	Togo
Cape Verde	Eritrea	Tunisia
Comoros	Ghana	Uganda
Djibouti	Guatemala	Ukraine
Gambia	Guinea	Uzbekistan
Guinea-Bissau	Haiti	Yemen
Kiribati	Honduras	Zambia
Lesotho	Kenya	Zimbabwe
Micronesia	Liberia	
Samoa	Madagascar	**Large**
Sao Tome and Principe	Malawi	Congo, Dem. Rep.
Solomon Islands	Mali	Egypt
Swaziland	Mauritania	Ethiopia
Timor-Leste	Moldova	Myanmar
Tonga	Mongolia	Vietnam
Vanuatu	Morocco	Bangladesh
	Mozambique	India
Medium	Nepal	Indonesia
Afghanistan	Nicaragua	Nigeria
Armenia	Niger	Pakistan
Benin	Papua New Guinea	Philippines
Bolivia	Rwanda	
Burkina Faso	Senegal	
Burundi	Sierra Leone	
Cambodia	Sri Lanka	
Cameroon	Sudan	
Central African Republic	Syria	
Chad	Tajikistan	

Middle-income countries

Small		Large
Small	Cote d'Ivoire	**Large**
Belize	Colombia	Iran
Equatorial Guinea	Costa Rica	South Africa
Fiji	Dominican Republic	Thailand
Gabon	Ecuador	Turkey
Grenada	Georgia	Brazil
Guyana	Iraq	China
Maldives	Jamaica	Mexico
Mauritius	Jordan	Russia
Montenegro	Kazakhstan	
St Lucia	Lebanon	
St Vincent and the Grenadines	Libya	
Suriname	Macedonia	
	Malaysia	
Medium	Namibia	
Albania	Panama	
Algeria	Paraguay	
Angola	Peru	
Argentina	Romania	
Azerbaijan	Serbia	
Belarus	Turkmenistan	
Bosnia and Herzegovina	Venezuela	
Botswana		
Bulgaria		

High-income countries

Small		
Small	Chile	Sweden
Antigua and Barbuda		Switzerland
Bahamas	**Medium**	United Arab Emirates
Bahrain	Croatia	Uruguay
Barbados	Czech Republic	
Brunei Darussalam	Denmark	**Large**
Cyprus	Finland	France
Estonia	Greece	Germany
Iceland	Hungary	Italy
Latvia	Ireland	Korea
Luxembourg	Israel	United Kingdom
Malta	Kuwait	Japan
	Lithuania	United States
	Netherlands	
	New Zealand	

Seychelles	Norway
Slovenia	Oman
St. Kitts and Nevis	Poland
Trinidad and Tobago	Portugal
	Qatar
Medium	Saudi Arabia
Australia	Singapore
Austria	Slovak Republic
Belgium	Spain
Canada	

References

Ageing Report (2015). *Ageing Report 2015*. Brussels: European Commission.

Aiyar, S. and Ebeke, C. H. (2016). The Impact of Workforce Aging on European Productivity No. 16/238. International Monetary Fund.

Atkins, J. P., Mazzi, S. and Easter, C. D. (2000). A Commonwealth vulnerability index for developing countries: The position of small states. *Economic Paper Series* 40. London: Commonwealth Secretariat.

Banik, A. and Bhaumik, P. K. (2006). 'Aging population, emigration and growth in Barbados'. *International Journal of Social Economics*, 33(11): 781–788.

Beine, M., Docquier, F. and Rapoport, H. (2008). 'Brain drain and human capital formation in developing countries: winners and losers'. *The Economic Journal*, 118(528): 631–652.

Bloom, D. E. and Williamson, J. G. (1998). 'Demographic transitions and economic miracles in emerging Asia'. *The World Bank Economic Review*, 12(3): 419–455.

Bloom, D. E., Canning, D. and Fink, G. (2010). 'Implications of population ageing for economic growth'. *Oxford Review of Economic Policy*, 26(4): 583–612.

Bongaarts, J. (2004). 'Population aging and the rising cost of public pensions'. *Population and Development Review*, 30(1): 1–23.

Bongaarts, J. (2008). 'Fertility transitions in developing countries: Progress or stagnation?' *Studies in Family Planning*, 39(2): 105–110.

Briguglio, L. (1995). 'Small island developing states and their economic vulnerabilities'. *World Development*, 23(9): 1615–1632.

Briguglio, L. (2016). 'Exposure to external shocks and economic resilience of countries: evidence from global indicators'. *Journal of Economic Studies*, 43(6): 1057–1078.

Briguglio, L. and Vella, M. (2015). 'Labour demand in the EU and returns to scale: A production function approach'. *The Journal of International Trade and Economic Development*, 24(8): 1103–1116.

Caldwell, John C., Caldwell, Bruce K., Caldwell, Pat, McDonald, Peter F. and Schindlmayr, Thomas (2006). *Demographic Transition Theory*. Dordrecht, the Netherlands: Springer: 239.

Chand, S. (2008). 'Skilled Migration and Brain Drain'. *Bank of Valletta Review*, 38: 1–7.

Chand, S. (2018). The Effects of Skilled Emigration on Small Island Nations in Briguglio, L., ed. *Handbook of Small States: Economic, Social and Environmental Issues*. New York: Routledge.

Cleland, J. (1994). A regional review of fertility trends in developing countries: 1960–1990. In W. Lutz (ed.), *The Future of the World: What Can We Assume Today*: 55–82.

Dayton-Johnson, Jeff, Pfeiffer, Antje, Schuettler, Kirsten and Schwinn, Johanna. (2009). Migration and employment. *Unclassified DCD/DAC (2009) 16/ADD*: 93.

Demeny, P. (2015). 'Sub-replacement fertility in national populations: Can it be raised?' *Population Studies*, 69(1).

Docquier, F. and Marfouk, A. (2006). International migration by education attainment 1990–2000. In C. Ozden and M. Schiff (eds), *International migration, remittances, and the brain drain*: 151–199. New York: Palgrave Macmillan.

Docquier, F., Lohest, O. and Marfouk, A. (2007). 'Brain drain in developing countries'. *The World Bank Economic Review*, 21(2): 193–218.

Docquier, F., Lowell, B. L. and Marfouk, A. (2009). 'A gendered assessment of highly skilled emigration'. *Population and Development Review*, 35(2): 297–321.

Fargues, P. (2011). 'International migration and the demographic transition: A two-way interaction'. *International Migration Review*, 45(3): 588–614.

Feldstein, M. S. (2006). The effects of the ageing European population on economic growth and budgets: implications for immigration and other policies. No. w12736. National Bureau of Economic Research.

Fitzgerald, D. (2004). Escape Valve or Hemorrhage? Mexican Emigration and the Politics of Labor Control, 1900–1964. Paper presented at the annual meeting of the American Sociological Association, August 14.

Formosa, M. (2014). 'Socio-economic implications of population ageing in Malta: risks and opportunities'. *Bank of Valletta Review*, 49: 79–98

Guillaumont, P. (2010). 'Assessing the Economic Vulnerability of Small Island Developing States and the Least Developed Countries'. *The Journal of Development Studies*, 46(5): 828–854.

Hellerstein, J. K. and Neumark, D. (2007). Production Function and Wage Equation Estimation with Heterogeneous Labor: Evidence from a new matched employer-employee data set. In *Hard-to-measure goods and services: essays in Honor of Zvi Griliches*: 31–71. Chicago, IL: University of Chicago Press.

Ilmakunnas, P. and Maliranta, M. (2005). 'Technology, Labour Characteristics and Wage-Productivity Gaps'. *Oxford Bulletin of Economics and Statistics*, 67(5): 623–645.

Johnson, P. and Falkingham, J. (1992). *Ageing and Economic Welfare*. London: Sage.

Lee, R. D. and Mason, A. (2011). *Population Aging and the Generational Economy: A Global Perspective*. Cheltenham: Edward Elgar Publishing.

Livi-Bacci, M. (1992). *A concise history of world population*. Sussex: John Wiley and Sons.

Lucas, R. (1981). International Migration: Economic Causes, Consequences, and Evaluation. In M. Kritz, C. Keely, and S. Tomasi (eds) *Global Trends in Migration: Theory and Research on International Population Movements*: 84–109. New York: Centre for Migration Studies.

Mason, A. and Kinugasa, T. (2008). 'East Asian economic development: two demographic dividends'. *Journal of Asian Economics*, 19(5): 389–399.

Micklin, M. (1994). 'Population policies in the Caribbean: Present status and emerging issues'. *Social and Economic Studies*: 1–32.

Nurse, K. (2004). Diaspora, Migration and Development in the Caribbean. *Focal Policy Paper*.

Poot, J. (2008). 'Demographic change and regional competitiveness: the effects of immigration and ageing'. *International Journal of Foresight and Innovation Policy*, 4(1–2): 129–145.

Shrestha, L. B. (2000). 'Population aging in developing countries'. *Health affairs*, 19(3): 204–212.

United Nations (2016). *World Population Ageing*. New York: United Nations.

Van Ours, J. C. and Stoeldraijer, L. (2011). 'Age, wage and productivity in Dutch manufacturing'. *De Economist*, 159(2): 113–137.

Werblow, A., Felder, S. and Zweifel, P. (2007). 'Population ageing and health care expenditure: a school of 'red herrings'?'. *Health Economics*, 16(10): 1109–1126.

Winters, L. A. and Martins, P. M. (2004). 'When comparative advantage is not enough: business costs in small remote economies'. *World Trade Review*, 3(03): 347–383.

Wise, D. A. (1989). *The Economic of Ageing*. Chicago, IL: NBER, University of Chicago Press.

Zweifel, P., Felder, S. and Meiers, M. (1999). 'Ageing of population and health care expenditure: a red herring?' *Health Economics*, 8(6): 485–496.

Part VI
Environmental issues

25

Environmental economics: special considerations for small states

Stefano Moncada, Spiteri Jonathan and Marie Briguglio

1 Introduction

The objective of this chapter is to identify the key tenets of Environmental Economics and discuss them within the context of small states. We focus our research on three broad environmental characteristics, namely a country's polluting activities, exposure of local population to pollution and governance in protecting the environment, with the purpose being to establish whether these characteristics are related to population size. We further aim at illustrating our findings via a case study that describes the situation in Malta with regard to its reliance on the natural environment, the challenges and issues that it faces as well as policy interventions aimed at protecting the environment.

The pursuit of economic prosperity through a linear economic system which entails extraction, production, consumption and disposal has had serious environmental implications – in the last 60 years, the rate of environmental degradation in terms of land exploitation, freshwater pollution and greenhouse gas emissions has accelerated at levels unprecedented over the last 10,000 years, with no sign of immediate abatement (Steffen *et al.*, 2015). The developments are particularly poignant as the myriad services provided by the natural environment are crucial to our way of life (de Groot, Wilson and Boumans, 2002), from the continued survival of our species, to the provision of resources which are critical inputs for the competitiveness of various economies around the world (Balmford *et al.*, 2002), and indeed to the direct contribution of the environment to the wellbeing of people (Prescott-Allen and IUCN, 2001).

It therefore comes as no surprise that a global consensus, especially within the international organizations, is emerging, one which recognizes that environmental protection is a pre-requisite for sustainable economic development (UNDESA, 2013). The long-term economic effects of ignoring this relationship are significant. For example, the global cost of land mismanagement and degradation is estimated at US$10.6 trillion a year (ELD Initiative, 2015), while climate change could have a net global cost equivalent to 5%–20% of global GDP (Stern, 2007).

Within this context, environmental economics has emerged as one of the pillars of modern-day mainstream economics. To the uninitiated, the phrase 'environmental economics' may at first glance sound like an oxymoron, given the contribution of economic growth to pollution and the continued degradation of natural resources worldwide. However, the fundamental premise of economics has always dealt with the problem of *scarcity*, which is a key contributor to most of the environmental problems evident today (Reuveny, 2002). Thus, managing the environment and its scarce resources can be considered a natural domain for economists, and one which has become increasingly more influential among policymakers.

The origins of academic Environmental Economics can be traced back to the 1960s, where rampant pollution and resource depletion led many to question the sustainability of pursuing economic growth and development at all costs (Pearce, 2002). This led to the development of a rich analytical approach, which recognizes the failure of free markets to adequately account for the vital contribution of environmental goods and services due to market failure and the absence of well-defined property rights (Hanley *et al.*, 2007). The establishment of the Journal of Environmental Economics and Management in 1974 further solidified the discipline's status, enabling researchers to publish their work in a specialized journal specifically designed to accommodate research in the field.

Many of the conceptual ideas underpinning the discipline actually pre-date the 1960s, with Pigou (1920; 1928) being the first economist to articulate the distinction between private and social marginal costs and benefits, thus setting the scene for the analysis of market failure. Similarly, earlier work by Jevons (1865) and Marshall (1890) underlined the potential scarcity problems associated with non-renewable resources, as well as the potential inefficiencies arising from a free market allocation of common pool resources like fisheries. In addition, Hotelling's (1931) seminal management rule for the optimal extraction of non-renewable resources over time contributed greatly to the formalization of natural resource economics, by considering these resources as capital with associated rents which must be discounted over time. Furthermore, Environmental Economics has pioneered the development of innovative techniques to assign monetary values to environmental services, enabling stakeholders to incorporate the environment within the context of economic, commercial, social, and political decision making (Bateman and Willis, 2001).[1]

Today, environmental economics is an established field of study with a thriving research agenda (Callan and Thomas, 2013). In addition, other seemingly unrelated fields of economics like industrial organization, development and behavioural economics have increasingly focused on environmental issues, helping to widen the scope of the research and analytical tools utilized (e.g. Arora and Gangopadhyay, 1995; Stern *et al.*, 1996; Shogren and Taylor, 2008). In providing a framework that considers the trade-offs and choices inherent in environmental policymaking, Environmental Economics has become a crucial tool for analysing and managing the most salient environmental problems of our time.

This chapter looks at the implications of Environmental Economics for small states, defined according to a population below 1.5 million inhabitants. We explore the notion that the analytical approach provided by Environmental Economics is particularly pertinent for small countries, due to the various peculiarities associated with these states (Briguglio L., 1995, 2004), notably because of a higher degree of market failure. The study also examines the relationship between country size and two broad environmental issues, namely negative externalities and governance. Throughout the chapter we emphasize the notion that small states are more likely to under-provide essential environmental public goods due to overhead cost indivisibilities in their provision. We further illustrate our argument by reference to a case study of one particular small state: Malta.

The chapter proceeds as follows: in the next section, we briefly synthesize the key insights from the environmental economics literature, making reference to some of the theoretical and empirical consistencies that have been derived over time. The section then proceeds to review the literature on small states, focusing on their key unifying characteristics, with special reference to their environmental peculiarities. In Section 3. we briefly outline the method which we employ in the chapter to associate a number of environmental variables with country size. In Sections 4. and 5. we present the findings of our cross-country data and those pertaining to the case study (Malta), respectively. We conclude the chapter in Section 6 with a discussion on the main findings and derive a number of implications associated with these findings.

2 Literature review

Insights from Environmental Economics

Environmental Economics as a field of research has come a long way since the 1960s, combining a variety of different approaches from classical economics along with more recent concepts like sustainability to provide a more holistic analytical framework (Pearce and Turner, 1990). The breadth of the field is reflected in the diversity of topics and issues covered in its expansive literature, including the oft-discussed, and critiqued, relationship between economic growth and pollution (Selden and Song, 1994), the impact of global warming on the agriculture sector (Mendelsohn et al., 1994) and the role of environmental standards and taxation to control negative environmental behaviour (Baumol and Oates, 1971).

Such a vast literature has predictably resulted in a plethora of findings, some of which may be contradictory in nature. For example, Selden and Song (1994) find that although increased economic growth may lead to higher levels of pollution initially, this pattern will eventually be reversed in the long run as countries grow further, thus implying that the focus of policymakers should be on accelerating current economic growth rates rather than explicit environmental protection, since the former will eventually lead to the latter, a claim that has been critiqued by the likes of Stern (2004). Nonetheless, away from specific empirical results, a number of more general tenets may be derived from the literature as a whole, which go to the heart of what modern-day Environmental Economics entails (Pearce, 2002). We can summarize these insights as follows:

1   Environmental and natural resources are scarce, and essential for economic wellbeing;
2   Unregulated economic activity leads to negative externalities, which harm the environment;
3   Economics can offer solutions to ensure optimal environmental regulation.

We start off with the first tenet. The natural environment provides a number of essential functions and services that are unaccounted for by market forces. Firstly, the environment is a source of a multitude of renewable and non-renewable resources, from freshwater and arable land to petroleum and precious metals (de Bruyn, 2012). The environment also acts as a sink that absorbs stores and processes human waste, like for example carbon dioxide and solid waste (OECD, 2005). The regenerative nature of the environment means that it can use the waste deposits in order to create new resources and thereby reinforce its 'source' role. For example, carbon dioxide emitted by humans can be converted into oxygen via photosynthesis, and biodegradable waste can be broken down by bacteria over time to produce compost which helps to fertilize soil (Odlare et al., 2011). In addition, the environment also provides a number of support services like climate regulation and disease control (MEA Board, 2005).

Recent evidence has also highlighted a direct relationship between the environment and wellbeing. Economists have long been interested in what determines individual happiness, and subjective wellbeing, typically focusing on economic prosperity as a key factor in this regard (e.g. Easterlin, 1974). However, authors like Smyth et al. (2008) and Ferreira et al. (2013) have identified a clear, causal link between environmental quality and self-reported measures of happiness among people, even after controlling for various other factors like income differences. Environmental protection does not simply provide direct benefits in terms of improved access to natural resources and amenity, but also indirect benefits through improved health, which itself is a key determinant of individual wellbeing (Dolan *et al.*, 2008).

This illustrative list of functions performed by the environment underscores its vital role in every aspect of human life. And yet the economic value of these important services is often overlooked (Pearce and Turner, 1990). Classical economic thought relies on the price of a good or service to determine its efficient allocation, since in a perfectly-competitive setting (which in itself is heavily stylized) the market price embeds information regarding both the product's costs and benefits, derived from the behaviour of market players. However, while certain environmental products like petroleum are traded, others like nature's sink function or its regenerative processes are not, meaning that we do not assign a price to these services that truly reflect the benefits they confer to society. In the absence of price, environmental economists have developed a number of tools in order to capture the economic value of these services.

The unifying characteristic of these tools is that they seek to determine the social costs and benefits of both environmental goods and services, as well as other products that may in some way have a tangible impact on the natural environment (Pearce, 1998). These tools include *stated preference methods* like the contingent valuation method (CVM), which involves surveying stakeholders in order to ascertain their willingness to pay for environmental services, or their willingness to accept compensation for losses (Hanemann, 1994), as well as *revealed preference methods* like the travel cost method (Shrestha *et al.*, 2002) which infers the value attributed to an environmental service from the costs incurred to enjoy the service (e.g. fuel costs, time, opportunity costs, etc.). Environmental valuation has become a crucial component of cost-benefit analysis (CBA) in appraising large-scale investment projects due to its focus on true economic value and welfare as opposed to financial analysis. In fact, the European Commission has drawn up a detailed set of guidelines for the implementation of CBAs, which must be conducted by all member states in appraising all major infrastructure projects over €50 million (European Commissaion, 2015). The manual explicitly refers to the importance of estimating *shadow prices* rather than market prices, which consider the opportunity costs to society associated with a particular good or service, including environmental costs and benefits, along with any externalities. For example, the guidelines recommend that the unit costs of carbon dioxide pollution from passenger transport should be set at €0.015 per passenger kilometre for road transport, and €0.007 per passenger kilometre for rail transport.

The second tenet of Environmental Economics is that economic activity, if left to its own devices, will result in too much environmental damage relative to what an economically efficient outcome would suggest. This is intimately-related to the previous discussion regarding the absence of pricing for environmental services. It follows that without a price the efficient allocation of environmental services is impossible to determine (Hanley *et al.*, 2007). This market failure stems primarily from the fact that everyone collectively 'owns' the environment, and thus no individual can in effect be excluded from enjoying its benefits. The absence of properly-assigned property rights is a well-established problem in Environmental Economics (Angelsen, 1999), and leads to two important market failures that damage the environment.

The first market failure is known as the *tragedy of the commons* (Hardin, 1968), and occurs when people over-exploit a natural resource or service by acting in their own individual self-interest without regarding the collective good. Since people cannot be excluded from enjoying the environment, they will utilize as much as they want while reducing the ability of others to enjoy these services. For example, the reported 97% reduction in Bluefin tuna stocks over the last few decades in the Northern Pacific Ocean (Nakatsuka *et al.*, 2017), can be traced back to rampant overfishing driven by soaring demand for Bluefin tuna, which has interfered with the species' natural reproductive cycles and led to a collapse in fish stocks, to the detriment of future consumers and fishermen alike (Myers and Worm, 2003).

The second type of market failure is related to the concept of *negative externalities* from production and consumption (Heller and Starrett, 1976). These externalities are by-products of economic activity, and are unaccounted for in market prices despite their adverse impact on others, leading to an inefficient allocation of resources. Pollution and environmental degradation fit squarely within this definition. The absence of property rights exacerbates the problem since those who are negatively-impacted by the polluting activities would not be able to seek recourse for the damages suffered, since the environment is collectively-owned. Therefore, without any incentive to 'internalize' these negative externalities, economic activity will continue to damage the natural environment. For example, Pope *et al.* (2002) estimate that exposure to fine particulate matter air pollution increases the risk of mortality by 4–8% due to various associated ailments like lung cancer and cardiopulmonary disease.

The third tenet of Environmental Economics is that economics is able to devise meaningful tools and policy solutions to manage the environment in an efficient manner. Briefly, a fundamental aim of Environmental Economics is to propose (i) the ideal level of environmental quality and protection, and (ii) the best way of achieving this objective (Gray and Shadbegian, 2004). A key concept in this regard is the idea of *optimal pollution control*, which recognizes the fact that environmental protection has both benefits as well as costs in terms of abatement (Kwerel, 1977). What this implies is that the complete elimination of pollution is likely to be socially-inefficient or undesirable. Pollution certainly generates costs (loss of amenity, health, recreational) but it also facilitates the production and consumption of goods and services at lower costs, in turn creating consumer and producer surplus. The optimal level of pollution (and by corollary pollution control) therefore implies a trade-off between the value of environmental services damaged by pollution and the value of production and consumption foregone (relative to free market levels), due to the abatement costs involved in reducing pollution.

Beyond the concept of an 'optimal' level of pollution (and attempts at identifying it using measurement tools), environmental economists have also proposed various policy instruments that can assist in reaching this objective. In contrast to other disciplines, economists generally shun regulatory measures based on command and control, arguing instead for market-based measures, particularly taxes, that incentivize a movement towards the optimum (Dasgupta *et al.*, 2000), due to their flexibility, dynamic incentive and lower compliance costs. In theory, so-called 'polluter pays' taxes should be set to equal the marginal cost of pollution (Pigou, 1920). As such they 'internalize the externality' to move the free market away from sub-optimal (excessively polluting) consumption and production levels, to levels that are socially optimal. In practise taxes have been called into question due to their perceived lack of efficacy in reining in pollution (Fankhauser *et al.*, 2010; Daugbjerg and Swinbank, 2007). Many argue that they exacerbate distortions in the tax system (Bovenberg and De Mooij, 1994), are regressive in nature (West and Williams, 2004) and highly unpopular among the general populace – a Flash Eurobarometer (2014) survey[2] shows that less than 3 out of every 10 people in Europe believe that improved resource efficiency can be achieved via increased taxation on resource usage, even if this is accompanied by a decrease in labour taxes, with similar aversion.

One of the more interesting policy instruments proposed in recent years is the so-called Cap and Trade mechanism, where polluters are allocated a fixed pollution allowance that in aggregate equates to the optimal level. These individual allowances are tradable, meaning that polluters can decide to either purchase additional pollution permits from others, or sell any excess allowance. Firms that have high costs in reducing pollution can buy permits from firms that can achieve reductions more cheaply. In this way, the system reduces the overall economic cost of achieving a given environmental outcome, while creating an incentive for polluters to rein in their pollution (Montgomery, 1972; Burton and Sanjour, 1967; Burtraw, 2016). Cap and Trade has been widely used in environmental protection, notably the EU's Emissions Trading Scheme (ETS) which established a pan-European market system to regulate greenhouse gas emissions emanating from some 11,000 firms across the continent (Ellerman and Buchner, 2007; Laing *et al.*, 2014). Perceptions of the ETS have been decidedly mixed – while some studies (e.g. Egenhofer *et al.*, 2011) show that greenhouse gas emissions in Europe have indeed fallen as a direct result of the scheme, others (e.g. Anderson and Di Maria, 2011) have criticized the scheme due to the volatility of permit prices resulting from thin markets as well as an over-allocation of pollution permits.

Recent criticism of environmental economics has also centred on the tendency of economists to disregard the psychological traits and biases inherent in human beings, which may not only be key to preventing people from reducing pollution but may also hinder the efficacy of interventions based on expected rational response (Frederiks *et al.*, 2015; Shogren and Taylor, 2008; Croson and Treich, 2014). Eschewing the neo-classical viewpoint of perfectly rational decision makers in favour of a more nuanced approach that acknowledges significant and systematic deviations in human behaviour (Kahneman, 2003a; Camerer *et al.*, 2011), behavioural economics insights strengthen the economists' toolkit, in various ways ranging from insights on how to frame taxes, to the prospect of tapping social preferences for voluntary compliance. In the field of waste management, Briguglio *et al.* (2016) show how political preferences may influence household cooperation in a voluntary recycling scheme, while Thøgersen and Nielsen (2016) show how the importance of reference points in interpreting information (Tversky and Kahneman, 1975) can be used to design more effective carbon footprint labels that encourage consumers to pick the more environmentally-friendly product. The insights shed by the literature in behavioural environmental economics may be particularly useful to guide policy in small communities. Nobel prize-winner Elinor Ostrom's work is indispensable in this regard, showing how communities can effectively manage common-pool resources on the basis of strong cultural norms and shared trust (Ostrom, 1992), without any state intervention, in varied ecosystem contexts like forestry management in India and Nepal (Agrawal and Ostrom, 2001), self-governing irrigation systems in Spain and fisheries in Indonesia (Dietz *et al.*, 2003), although this idea is not without criticism (e.g. Block and Jankovic, 2016).

There are also other insights from behavioural economics which can readily be applied within the scope of environmental economics and which can find particular resonance in small states. Work on bounded rationality (Kahneman, 2003b) shows the potential limitations of relying solely on information in order to bring about changes in environmental behaviour, due to people's limited cognitive resources, while self-control issues (Ariely and Wertenbroch, 2002) may also inhibit pro-environmental choices, particularly if prior behaviours are deeply-ingrained. Similarly, Venkatachalam (2008) considers how time inconsistencies in people's behaviour can severely underestimate future benefits from environmental protection, and place undue weight on short term benefits from current polluting behaviour, particularly since people generally are reluctant to alter their behaviour even in the presence of welfare-improving alternatives (status quo bias). What perhaps merits further inquiry is the idea of bounded self-interest within the scope of environmental behaviour (Shogren and Taylor, 2008), which posits that people are often willing to forgo their own personal gains for the greater good, since this may help to further encourage pro-environmental behaviour, particularly if understood in relation to social and moral preferences.

The characteristics of small states

Small states have been the subject of significant academic attention over the last few decades (Nurse *et al.*, 2014; Baldacchino, 2012; Commonwealth Secretariat, 2014). Although various measures exist, the majority of the literature in this field has sought to define 'smallness' on the basis of population. The Commonwealth Secretariat[3] and the World Bank[4] define small states as those with a population of about 1.5 million persons or less. Other variables used are land area and GNP (see Downes, 1988; Armstrong and Read, 2003).

Much of this research has sought to identify the various characteristics and features that are common to these countries, which can have a substantial impact on their economic prosperity (Briguglio, 1995; Guillaumont, 2010). The size of the domestic economy is perhaps the most apparent feature of these countries, which acts as a natural ceiling to both demand and supply, which in turn increases the importance of international trade and thus exposure to external economic shocks (Armstrong and Read, 1998; Briguglio *et al.*, 2016). Smallness also prevents firms from reaping important economies of scale when it comes to production and sourcing of raw materials, which coupled with market imperfections and a limited pool of domestic talent, help to raise operating costs and may hamper external competitiveness (Briguglio, 1995).

Environmental and resources problems are themselves a feature of small countries. In spite of an often vast availability of oceanic resources, many small countries still have limited natural resource endowments, and risk sustainability implication with considerable extraction and usage (Collier, 2012). In small island states, coastal areas and habitats face pressures due to tourism and residential property demand (Briguglio, 1995), and several face risks of natural hazards like floods and hurricanes due to their location (Briguglio, 1995; Formosa *et al.*, 2017). Small, land-locked countries may be more prone to trans-boundary pollutants like sulphur dioxide and nitrogen oxides which are emitted by other (larger) countries and travel across borders – Bhutan's ambient air quality is a case in point with air pollution from India and China (Pannozzo, 2015).

The peculiarities of small states also extend to the size and operation of the public sector. Certain expenditures on the provision of non-rivalrous goods like running a public administration and road networks are by nature fairly indivisible, meaning that the cost per capita of providing these goods should fall as population size increases (Lewis, 1947; Briguglio, 1998; Alesina and Spolaore, 2005). Similarly, many overhead costs associated with public administration are also indivisible, like for example tax collection (Lewis and Frank, 2002; Briguglio *et al.*, 2016). As a result, small countries are often characterized by relatively large governments with higher per capita public expenditure levels (Natella and O'Sullivan, 2014) and elevated levels of bureaucracy (Brown, 2010). Smallness also breeds familiarity between private and public officials, leading to conflicting pressures in the pursuance of the latter's work (Farrugia, 1993), exacerbated by a restricted talent pool (Streeten, 1993), which may lead to further inefficiencies in government administration. Insights from behavioural economics suggest that such inefficiencies may be even stronger. Gift exchange, favours and promises are more credible among incumbents and familiar candidates, since their promises are perceived as being more credible (Wantchekon, 2003). A bias against change (status quo bias) further exacerbates the power of incumbency (Bernhardt and Ingerman, 1985). Population size can also be a key factor for countries when considering their stages of development, especially in SIDS. Roberts and Ibitoye (2012) clearly show an association between population size and progress toward the achievement of the Millennium Development Goals (MDGs), with states under 100,000 population presenting the poorest performance. This has evident policy repercussions, especially in the area of allocation of development aid.

Apart from the canonical features of small states that have been widely cited in the literature, more recent work has sought to focus on the social peculiarities present in these countries.

More specifically, there is some evidence that social preferences like trust and altruism play a key role in small states, and may have a significant impact on various outcomes like the provision of environmental protection by government and the propagation of pro-environmental norms in society (Briguglio and Spiteri, 2017). Such insights include the strong potential for nurturing voluntary cooperation and the role of nudge-based intervention both among households as well as firms (Briguglio *et al.*, 2016; Baldacchino, 2005).

Synthesis

Environmental Economics offers important insights in the global drive towards improved environmental quality and protection. Its strength lies not only in the clarity of its analytical insights, but also in the multitude of tools that have been developed to value the environment and encourage pro-environmental behaviour. We can summarize the key take-away messages from our cursory overview of the extensive literature as follows:

1   Economics is premised on the idea of scarcity, a notion that increasingly fits the demand and supply for natural resources and environmental quality.
2   Environmental Economics uses the concept of market failure to explain the persistence of environmental damage from economic activity, and proposes a multitude of policy interventions to deal with such issues;
3   Small states are characterized by a number of peculiarities related to their economic size, governance and natural environment, all of which can have important implications for the implementation of Environmental Economic policies in these countries;
4   In particular, small states may be more prone to natural resource degradation and pollution due to their size and population density, while problems related to indivisibilities and governance issues may severely hamper environmental protection efforts;
5   Emerging fields like Behavioural Economics can play an important role in expanding the scope of Environmental Economic policy, and may be particularly relevant to small states due to the importance of social preferences in economic interactions within such countries.

3 Method

We now seek to evaluate any potential relevance that key theoretical underpinnings of environmental economics can have for small states. It must be emphasized that the object of this exercise is not to establish causation, but to assess whether there is an association between population size and some relevant environmental variables. The exercise carried out in this chapter can be considered an initial step ahead of a more sophisticated study using various specialized methodologies like field experiments in order to properly tease out causality.

We first examine the extent of market failure both in terms of pollution per capita as well as exposure. Following this, we explore government intervention, examining the extent and cost of provision of public goods in the context of small states. We employ data from two key sources, namely the Environmental Performance Index[5] and the World Bank, which we selected not only because of the comprehensive coverage of countries across the world, but also because they are open source databases available to other researchers who may wish to take this research agenda further. The databases also capture environmental statistics in various fields. Information about the data sources is given in Appendix 1. While other databases, such as the OECD, are perhaps richer in terms of environmental statistics, they do not to cover the majority of existing small states and were not, as such, suitable for this review.

Exposure to environmental pressures, and externalities, was measured by looking at established factors used as predictors of market failures, or more generally at factors affecting trajectories of development, in environmental economics literature, such as greenhouse gases (Stern, 2007), extreme events (Loayza et al., 2012), and polluted environment (Muller and Mendelsohn, 2007).

Indicators for government intervention included all those actions believed to be capturing changes in policy that would internalize the cost of market failures. These include reduction in CO2 emissions, terrestrial and marine protected areas, improvements in wastewater treatment rates, and investments in infrastructure, R&D and health. This too, is in line with existing literature assessing the role of government intervention in addressing market failures (Stiglitz, 1989, Engel et al., 2008).

We relate the variables of interest to population size, which is considered as an appropriate measure of country size in this regard. This attribute of smallness is in line with existing literature defining small states as well as its application in environmental and resource economics (Nath et al., 2010). We examine small countries within a continuum of all countries.[6]

4 Results and analysis

Environmental exposures, externalities and smallness

An important research question set in this chapter is whether small countries suffer greater environmental pressures, exposure or externalities. Here we run pairwise correlations between population size and a number of proxy variables, namely:

a   percentage of total population exposed to extreme events from 1990 to 2009;
b   percentage of total population exposed to PM2.5 above WHO thresholds;
c   total GHG in CO2 equivalent per capita;
d   percentage of cropland's excess nitrogen;
e   change in CO2 emissions from electricity and heat production;
f   change in forest cover from 2001–2014;
g   cubic meters of water as a ratio of GDP in US dollars.

The results are reported in Table 25.1.

The correlation coefficients reported in Table 25.1 send mixed messages. For example, there is a strong positive correlation between population size and total emissions of CO_2 per capita, $r = 0.745$, $p < 0.01$, showing that smaller countries tend to have less per capita CO_2 emitted. It should be emphasized that the test of significance has to be interpreted with caution, and that it does not strictly measure causation, as already indicated in Section 3. The smaller quantity of CO_2 equivalent per capita (in tonnes) emitted by smaller countries, however, does not suggest lower exposure given the transboundary nature of pollution (Bindoff et al., 2013). We also find a positive correlation with the percentage of population exposed to PM2.5 above WHO acceptable thresholds, $r = 0.304$, $p < 0.01$, indicating that small states tend to be less exposed to PM2.5, as shown by Figure 25.1. This would seem to suggest that small states tend to be less exposed to environmental externalities than larger ones.

On the other hand, negative correlations with population size are reported with regard to the percentage of cropland's excess nitrogen, change in CO2 emissions from electricity and heat production, change in forest cover 2001–2014, cubic meters of water as a ratio of GDP in US dollars and percentage of total population exposed to extreme events 1990 to 2009. These

Table 25.1 Pairwise correlation between exposure/externalities and population size

Variable	Correlation coefficient all countries	Countries sampled	Small countries included
Percentage of total population exposed to extreme events 1990 to 2009	−0.032	129	31
Percentage of total population exposed to PM2.5 above WHO thresholds	0.304★	194	49
Total GHG in CO_2 equivalent per capita	0.745★	169	32
Change in CO_2 emissions from electricity and heat production	−0.010	126	11
Percentage of cropland's excess nitrogen	−0.025	164	30
Change in forest cover 2001–2014	−0.016	177	38
Cubic meters of water as a ratio of GDP in US dollars	−0.061	167	42

Note: * statistically significant at the 99% level.

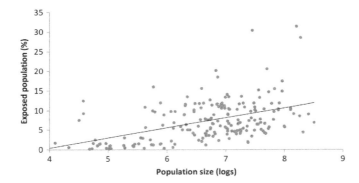

Figure 25.1 Population percentage exposed to PM2.5 above WHO thresholds and population size (2014)
Source: Environmental Performance Index, Yale University, http://epi.yale.edu/sites/default/files/2016EPI_Raw_Data.xls/.

correlations indicate, albeit being very weak, that small states tend to be more exposed to environmental externalities that larger states.

Government intervention and smallness

We now examine whether small countries have more constraints in intervening in terms of policy. Once again, we perform pairwise correlations between population size, and a set of relevant variables we identify for this purpose, namely:

a   terrestrial domestic protected area as a percentage of total land area;
b   marine protected areas as a percentage of total marine area;
c   per capita public expenditure on health in US dollars;
d   score of quality of port infrastructure;

e   per capita public research & development expenditure in US dollars;
f   renewable energy as a percentage of total energy;
g   disaster risk reduction progress score; and
h   wastewater treatment level as a percentage of total.

Table 25.2 shows the correlation coefficients, and the number of countries sampled.

Again, here the correlation results send mixed messages. We find a positive correlation between population size and the disaster risk reduction score, r = 0.300, p<0.01, possibly because small states tend to have higher per capita administrative and financial costs, and thus may have a lower capacity to reduce risk from natural and man-made events. This tendency is illustrated by Figure 25.2, where the risk reductions score represents the degree to which countries have prioritized disaster risk reduction and the strengthening of relevant institutions. This is in line with arguments put forward in existing literature, especially on the economics of

Table 25.2 Pairwise correlation between government intervention and population size

Variable	Correlation coefficient all countries	Countries sampled	Small countries included
Terrestrial domestic protected area (% of total land area)	0.120	142	36
Marine protected areas (% of total marine area)	−0.036	145	41
Per capita public health expenditure (US$)	0.082	179	44
Score of quality of port infrastructure (1–7 rate)	−0.076	154	39
Per capita public research & development expenditure (US$)	0.071	53	7
Renewable energy of total energy (% of total energy)	−0.005	196	47
Disaster risk reduction progress score (1–5 score)	0.300*	80	14
Wastewater treatment level (% of total wastewater)	−0.011	160	19

Note: * statistically significant at the 99% level.

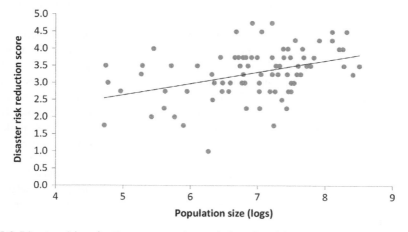

Figure 25.2 Disaster risk reduction score and population size, 2011
Source: World Bank, 2015, http://data.worldbank.org/indicator/EN.CLC.DRSK.XQ.

climate change adaptation (Mercer, 2010, Kelman, 2010), that indicates higher burdens for small states.

In the case of the other tests, the correlation was very weak. It was positive for terrestrial domestic protected area as a percentage of total land area, per capita public expenditure on health and per capita public research & development expenditure, suggesting that environmental governance in small states tends to be better than that of larger states, although there are many exceptions, as indicated by the low correlation coefficient.

On the other hand, the correlation coefficients were found to be negative in the case of marine protected areas as a percentage of total marine area, the quality of port infrastructure, renewable energy as a percentage of total energy and percentage of wastewater treated. This suggests that, in these specific realms, environmental governance in small states tends to be worse than that of larger states, again with many exceptions.

On the basis of the correlation exercises, reported in Tables 25.1 and 25.2, therefore, it appears that the results do not support the contention, often held, that small states are more exposed to environmental negative externalities or that small states tend to be better environmentally governed than larger ones. As already indicated, the results send mixed messages on some specific tendencies.

However, on the basis of the same results, it cannot be said that the opposite is true, i.e. that smaller states are less at risk or that their governance is worse. At best one can state that size does not seem to matter in this regard.

It is pertinent, in this context, to refer to the vulnerability-resilience framework developed by Briguglio et al. (2009). In fact, one implication of this framework is that it may be possible that the variables we chose for our analysis may be capturing the net effect of vulnerability and resilience. This means that small states may be inherently highly environmentally vulnerable, but pro-environmental government policies and community measures may be totally or partially cancelling out this tendency, possibly because these policies and measures could be more effective in small countries, particularly in small island states, where the proximity of nature to human life is more immediate than in larger countries, rendering the population more aware of environmental issues, and where tourism is critical to development and conditional on ecologically quality. This does not of course explain all the seeming contradictions in Tables 25.1 and 25.2, but it may shed light as to why small states tend to spend more per capita on health expenditure and tend to have a higher percentage of protected areas than larger states.

A key result that emerges from this analysis is the positive correlation between governance indicators of disaster risk reduction and population size. This emphasizes the indivisibilities problem inherent in both public administration and intervention (Briguglio, 1995), only in this case within the context of environmental policy. This is where the various tools proposed in environmental economics may prove to be vital, since they shift the focus away from command and control, regulations and standards (which may entail significant overheads) towards a carrot and stick approach rooted in incentives and, more recently, people's behavioural quirks.

We must point out that the correlation exercises presented in this study have a number of limitations mostly due to the fact that we have only looked at simple correlations between various environmental indicators. There may be various factors, left uncontrolled in the analysis that may have affected the dependent environmental variables examined. Correlation is an insufficient condition for causality, although it certainly serves its purpose in flagging the potential for further investigation.

In addition, data for a number of small states is missing, again suggesting that the results should be interpreted with caution. This problem is a pervasive one and in many studies (e.g.

Roberts in this volume) the authors indicate this as a major problem when it comes to comparing large states to smaller ones, particularly in matters relating to the environment.

5 Malta: a case study

Background

We now illustrate the findings described in the previous section by describing the environmental economic issues prevalent in Malta. The purpose is to provide a more practical context to the propositions drawn from the data, and look at both the environmental challenges that exist in Malta as well as the measures taken to overcome these problems, and the main drivers behind such initiatives.

Malta is an archipelago in the Mediterranean Sea covering 316 km^2 of land area with a population of approximately 430,000 inhabitants (World Bank, 2016).

Environmental endowments and economic contribution

As with many other small countries, the natural environment is of vital importance to the Maltese economy. The environment's direct contribution to Maltese economic prosperity is significant; a 2010 report by the Malta Environment and Planning Authority (MEPA, 2010) estimated that it is directly involved in producing around 20% of employment and 17% of value added. It provides an invaluable contribution to one of Malta's key economic sectors, namely tourism, which reaches its peak during the summer months due to the island's plentiful supply of sun and sea activities.

The environment also serves as an invaluable sink for waste, both in terms of landfills for municipal waste as well as the sea for construction debris. It plays a role in supporting recreation and health in Malta, which is particularly important given its small size and high population density. Recreation is an essential contributor to subjective wellbeing and happiness (Diener, 2006), which in turn has been shown to be intimately-related to employee performance and productivity (Oswald et al., 2015). In addition, the environment's important contribution to health in Malta cannot be underestimated (WHO, 2009), and various studies have shown a strong causal link between pollution and the incidence of various heart and respiratory diseases (Brook et al., 2010) which of course is a key determinant of subjective wellbeing (Briguglio, 2016).

While environmental services are important, mineral extraction is low (mainly softstone, hardstone and gravel) and raw materials are often sourced from abroad. Furthermore, almost 50% of domestic water consumption is drawn from the sea via reverse osmosis plants (Sapiano, 2013), which in turn requires electricity generated primarily from fossil fuels, as does 95% of energy consumed in Malta (NSO, 2015b).

Environmental exposure and externalities

Despite this evident importance, the environment in Malta is vulnerable to a variety of negative externalities and challenges which may have serious repercussions for economic and social wellbeing. Resource productivity, which measures the extent to which natural resources are used efficiently in an economy, has fallen by 7.6% from 2000 to 2015 and in 2016 stood at €1.44 per kilogramme, below the EU average of €2 per kg (Eurostat, 2016).[7] Despite efforts to promote waste separation and recycling, over 90% of municipal waste generated domestically is

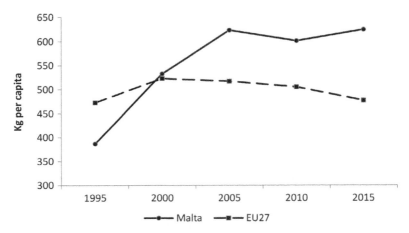

Figure 25.3 Municipal waste generated per capita (in kg) in Malta and the EU, 1995–2015
Source: Eurostat, http://ec.europa.eu/eurostat/statistics-explained/index.php/Municipal_waste_
statistics.

landfilled (NSO, 2015a), and Malta ranks among the top five generators of municipal waste in
the EU (Eurostat, 2016).[8] This is shown in Figure 25.3 where we can see that although the
average level of municipal waste per head generated in the EU has tended to fall between 2000
and 2015, the opposite is true for Malta.

Air pollution is another major concern. Although greenhouse gas emissions per capita are
below the EU average (Malta Resources Authority, 2013), median particulate matter levels are
higher than those recommended by the World Health Organization (WHO, 2006). The main
source of such pollution is motor vehicle traffic, with Malta having 608 passenger cars per 1,000
inhabitants (Eurostat, 2015).[9] Traffic congestion has been estimated to cost the Maltese economy some €274 million per year in terms of lost productivity, accidents, air pollution and
contribution to climate change (Attard *et al.*, 2015).

As one of the smallest nations in the world, effective management of land resources is predictably one of the key challenges faced in Malta. As seen in Figure 25.4, an estimated 18.7% of
Malta's total land area is built up, by far the highest in Europe where the average is a mere
1.5%. Over-development has various environmental implications, from the non-recoverable
destruction of eco-systems and biodiversity (MEPA, 2012) to air pollution and increased waste.
In addition, freshwater availability is also under severe pressure Malta currently has the lowest
quantity of freshwater resources in Europe (Eurostat, 2016)[10], under pressure from both
unregulated boreholes and excessive fertilizer usage (Spiteri *et al.*, 2015).

Governance and engagement

Given the vital role of the environment in the domestic economy and the high level of exposure to negative environmental externalities, it should come as no surprise that the Maltese
population is acutely aware of the environmental problems. A recent survey found that 25% of
the Maltese population mentioned the environment as the greatest concern facing the country
today, second only to immigration (InsightPolls, 2015).[11] Furthermore, 88% of people in Malta
believe that resource efficiency is 'very important', and 86% recognize that this would both
improve the quality of life within the country as well as boost economic growth (Flash Eurobarometer, 2014).[12] In addition, 95% of small and medium-sized enterprises in Malta reported

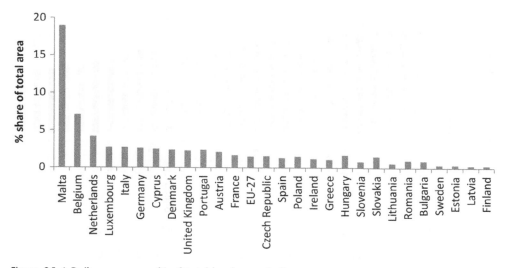

Figure 25.4 Built-up area, as % of total land area, in Europe
Source: Eurostat, http://ec.europa.eu/eurostat/statistics-explained/index.php/Land_cover,_land_use_and_landscape.

some involvement in waste minimization (recycling, reuse, etc.), re-planning energy use, and reduced usage of materials (Flash Eurobarometer, 2016).[13]

Amid increased concern and awareness regarding the importance of the natural environment, a number of measures have been implemented to address the situation. Firstly, as a member state of the EU Malta must abide by the regulations and targets set by the Commission in various areas, including waste management, greenhouse gas and renewable energy targets. The Maltese government has also undertaken various policy measures, notably in the energy sector where the recent de-commissioning of the heavy fuel oil power station in favour of a gas-powered installation, coupled with the construction of an interconnector to Sicily, should lead to a significant reduction in air pollution from electricity generation. Various subsidies and incentives have been introduced over the years to encourage the installation of roof insulation, electric cars, solar water heaters and photovoltaic cells, with the introduction of feed-in tariffs for excess electricity further encouraging uptake. Green taxation also plays a role in Maltese environmental policy, with revenues constituting 9.1% of total tax and social security contribution receipts (Eurostat, 2016).[14]

Figure 25.5 shows the different categories of environmental taxes in the EU. As seen from the diagram, the bulk of environmental taxes in Malta (51.3%) are related to energy consumption, which also includes taxes on fuels, although this figure is the lowest in the EU. By contrast, Malta has the highest proportion of environmental taxes emanating from transportation (40.3%), which includes car registration taxes and licence fees, reflecting the ever-increasing number of cars on Maltese roads. Direct pollution taxes only make up 8.3% of total environmental tax revenue, and no taxes are levied on resource use. This is somewhat surprising given the scarcity of natural resources and concerns regarding over-exploitation of limestone (MEPA, 2012), while less than 50% of registered agricultural boreholes are fitted with meters to calculate water charges, meaning that in most cases freshwater extraction is completely free of charge, let alone tax-free (Roberts *et al.*, 2015).

Clearly, although efforts to address the environmental challenges in Malta have increased significantly over time, there is still much scope for further intervention, particularly with regard to waste management and traffic congestion (Briguglio and Moncada, 2015).

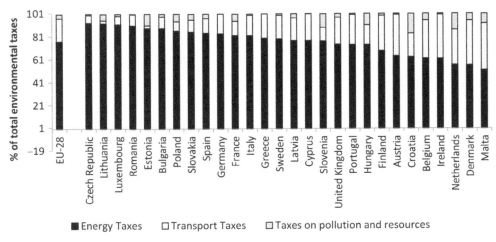

Figure 25.5 Environmental taxes in the European Union by category, 2015, % of total environmental taxes

Source: Eurostat, http://ec.europa.eu/eurostat/statistics-explained/index.php/Environmental_ta x_statistics.

In addition, recent work has shown the potential importance of behavioural economic interventions in encouraging pro-environmental behaviours among Maltese households. The bulk of this nascent literature has focused on the potential role of people's political allegiances in encouraging or even hindering government efforts to promote environmental protection.[15] For example, evidence suggests that pro-government sentiment in Malta increases uptake of schemes like voluntary recycling and the installation of photovoltaic cells (Briguglio *et al.*, 2016; Briguglio and Formosa, 2017). Social norms and pro-social behaviour may play an important role in promoting environmental protection among people in small states more generally (Briguglio and Spiteri, 2017).

Given the importance of governance in enacting appropriate environmental policies, and the challenges faced by small countries in this regard, it is worth considering Malta's experiences. Insights on the peculiarities of environmental regulation can be gleaned by referring to negotiations in this area in the run-up to Malta joining the European Union in 2004. As outlined in Briguglio and Mercieca (1988, 1997) the key concern was that regulations pertaining to the environment at the EU level may have been inappropriate within the Maltese context due to its unique environmental, economic and administrative realities, which are a direct result of Malta's population density and stage of development (Briguglio and Mercieca, 1988; 1997). The authors illustrate this by referring to the EU's waste policy, arguing that a literal transposition of these regulations would have imposed a number of significant costs on the country due to various factors like its high dependency on imported goods and technologies, which reduces its ability to influence product design and packaging, and the limited market size (and space) for recycling. This reflects the indivisibilities problem inherent in the governance of small states.

Thus, Malta's experience in negotiating its EU accession agreement highlights the double-edged sword of environmental issues in small states, namely that they can benefit highly from regulations in this regard, while at the same time they are also likely to incur higher costs per capita significant costs when implementing these regulations.

6 Discussion and conclusion

This chapter sought to identify the key tenets of Environmental Economics and to analyse them within the context of small states. The findings emanating from our study, coupled with those derived from the literature, clearly underscore the importance of Environmental Economics insights for small countries. The major implication of this study is that the tools and techniques proposed by environmental economists are highly relevant to small states, when devising environmental policy. This study also assigned importance to the need for incorporating behavioural economic insights in environmental policy for small states.

The study attempted to analyse the relationship between country size and two broad environmental issues, namely negative externalities and governance. The results obtained produced mixed results and did not confirm that small country size matters significantly in such matters. It was argued that this does mean the small states are not inherently at higher environmental risk than larger states, as it may be possible that the variables we chose for our analysis may have captured the net effect of vulnerability and resilience, meaning that small states are in reality highly environmentally vulnerable, but pro-environmental community measures may be more effective in a small country, particularly small island states, where the proximity of nature to human life is more immediate than in larger countries.

As has been pointed out the correlation exercises presented in this study have a number of limitations although they could serve for the purpose in flagging the potential for further investigation. Future research on the relationship between country size and environmental risk as well as environmental governance can attempt more sophisticated analysis, so to identify the mechanisms at play in small countries that may be responsible for the observed results, an exercise similar to the economic/vulnerability nexus developed in Briguglio *et al.* (2009).

We also presented a case study by describing the situation in Malta with regard to environmental negative externalities and the governance challenges it faces in view of its population density and stages of development. The Malta case-study served to investigate further the constraints faced by a small state in terms of attenuating negative externalities and environmental governance.

When discussing the issues of governance this chapter highlighted the relative constraints faced by small states when it comes to environmental governance. This may be considered a consequence of the well-documented public sector issues that characterize small states, mainly related to indivisibilities in overhead expenditures which hamper public good provision. It is also possible that, since some small countries are still developing, their policy priorities lie elsewhere, meaning that initially economic growth will result in greater environmental degradation (Selden and Song, 1994). Given the current state of affairs, further applied research focusing on assigning an economic cost of pollution and value to the environment in small states might help make the case for increased government intervention in this field, particularly given the importance of the environment to small economies and the various benefits to health and wellbeing that it offers.

Notes

1 Environmental Economics is somewhat distinct from the related subfield of Ecological Economics, in that Ecological Economics considers the economy to be a subsystem of the natural ecosystem, emphasising the importance of preserving the stock of natural assets while questioning the role of environmental valuation techniques.
2 https://data.europa.eu/euodp/en/data/dataset/S1102_388/.
3 http://thecommonwealth.org/small-states/.
4 http://www.worldbank.org/en/country/smallstates/.

5 The Environmental Performance Index (EPI) is a method of quantifying and numerically marking the environmental performance of a state's policies. The EPI ranks countries' performance on high-priority environmental issues in two areas: protection of human health and protection of ecosystems.

6 The correlation exercises were carried out with two country size outliers, namely China and India. When they were introduced the results only changed minimally.

7 http://ec.europa.eu/eurostat/statistics-explained/index.php/Municipal_waste_statistics.

8 http://ec.europa.eu/eurostat/statistics-explained/index.php/Municipal_waste_statistics.

9 http://ec.europa.eu/eurostat/statistics-explained/index.php/Passenger_cars_in_the_EU/.

10 http://ec.europa.eu/eurostat/statistics-explained/index.php/Municipal_waste_statistics/.

11 http://corporateidentities.eu/traffic-corruption-and-immigration-are-seen-as-the-main-issues-of-concern-in-malta/.

12 https://data.europa.eu/euodp/en/data/dataset/S1102_388/.

13 https://data.europa.eu/euodp/en/data/dataset/S2088_426_ENG/.

14 http://ec.europa.eu/eurostat/statistics-explained/index.php/Municipal_waste_statistics.

15 Malta's political landscape is dominated by two parties (the Nationalist party and the Labour party), with allegiances almost evenly-split between the two. In addition, voter turnout in general elections is on average 95%, one of the highest in the world, reflecting a strong sense of domestic political engagement.

Appendix 1

URL of each variable source

Smallness

(a) Total population
http://data.worldbank.org/indicator/SP.POP.TOTL

Environmental exposures and externalities

(a) Percentage of the population exposed to air pollution
http://epi.yale.edu/sites/default/files/2016EPI_Raw_Data.xls

(b) Percentage of total population exposed to extreme events from 1990 to 2009
http://data.worldbank.org/indicator/EN.CLC.MDAT.ZS

(c) Percentage of total population exposed to PM2.5 above WHO thresholds
http://epi.yale.edu/sites/default/files/2016EPI_Raw_Data.xls

(d) Total GHG in CO_2 equivalent per capita
http://data.worldbank.org/indicator/EN.ATM.GHGT.KT.CE

(e) Percentage of cropland's excess nitrogen
http://epi.yale.edu/sites/default/files/2016EPI_Raw_Data.xls

(f) Change in CO_2 emissions from electricity and heat production
http://epi.yale.edu/sites/default/files/2016EPI_Raw_Data.xls

(g) Change in forest cover from 2001–2014
http://epi.yale.edu/sites/default/files/2016EPI_Raw_Data.xls

(h) Cubic meters of water as a ratio of GDP in US dollars
http://data.worldbank.org/indicator/ER.GDP.FWTL.M3.KD

Government intervention

(a) Terrestrial domestic protected area as a percentage of total land area
http://epi.yale.edu/sites/default/files/2016EPI_Raw_Data.xls

(b) Marine protected areas as a percentage of total marine area
  http://epi.yale.edu/sites/default/files/2016EPI_Raw_Data.xls
(c) Per capita public expenditure on health in US dollars
  http://data.worldbank.org/indicator/SH.XPD.PCAP
(d) Score of quality of port infrastructure
  http://data.worldbank.org/indicator/IQ.WEF.PORT.XQ
(e) Per capita public research & development expenditure in US dollars
  http://data.worldbank.org/indicator/GB.XPD.RSDV.GD.ZS
(f) Renewable energy as a percentage of total energy
  http://data.worldbank.org/indicator/EG.ELC.RNEW.ZS
(g) Disaster risk reduction progress score
  http://data.worldbank.org/indicator/EN.CLC.DRSK.XQ
(h) Wastewater treatment level as a percentage of total
  http://epi.yale.edu/sites/default/files/2016EPI_Raw_Data.xls

References

Agrawal, A. and Ostrom, E. (2001). 'Collective action, property rights, and decentralization in resource use in India and Nepal'. *Politics and Society*, 29(4): 485–514.
Alesina, A. and Spolaore, E. (2005). *The size of nations*. Cambridge, MA: MIT Press.
Anderson, B. and Di Maria, C. (2011). 'Abatement and Allocation in the Pilot Phase of the EU ETS'. *Environmental and Resource Economics*, 48(1): 83–103.
Angelsen, A. (1999). 'Agricultural expansion and deforestation: modelling the impact of population, market forces and property rights'. *Journal of Development Economics*, 58(1): 185–218.
Armstrong, H. W. and Read, R. (1998). 'Trade and growth in small states: the impact of global trade liberalisation'. *The World Economy*, 21(4): 563–585.
Armstrong, H. W. and Read, R. (2003). 'The determinants of economic growth in small states'. *The Round Table*, 368: 99–124.
Ariely, D. and Wertenbroch, K. (2002). 'Procrastination, deadlines, and performance: Self-control by precommitment'. *Psychological science*, 13(3): 219–224.
Arora, S. and Gangopadhyay, S. (1995). 'Toward a theoretical model of voluntary overcompliance'. *Journal of Economic Behavior and Organization*, 28(3): 289–309.
Attard, M., Von Brockdorff, P. and Bezzina, F. (2015). *The external costs of passenger and commercial vehicles use in Malta*. Msida: Institute for Climate Change and Sustainable Development University of Malta.
Baldacchino, G. (2005). 'The contribution of 'social capital' to economic growth: lessons from island jurisdictions'. *The Round Table*, 94(378): 31–46.
Baldacchino, G. (2012). 'Islands and despots'. *Commonwealth and Comparative Politics* 50(1): 103–120.
Balmford, A., Bruner, A., Cooper, P., Costanza, R., Farber, S., Green, R. E., Jenkins, M., Jefferiss, P., Jessamy, V., Madden, J. and Munro, K. (2002). 'Economic reasons for conserving wild nature'. *Science*, 297(5583): 950–953.
Bateman, I. J. and Willis, K. G. (2001). *Valuing environmental preferences: theory and practice of the contingent valuation method in the US, EU, and developing countries*. Oxford: Oxford University Press.
Baumol, W. J. and Oates, W. E. (1971). 'The use of standards and prices for protection of the environment'. *The Swedish Journal of Economics*: 42–54.
Bernhardt, M. D. and Ingerman, D. E. (1985). 'Candidate reputations and the 'incumbency effect'. *Journal of Public Economics*, 27(1): 47–67.
Bindoff, N. L., Stott, P. A., AchutaRao, K. M., Allen, M. R., Gillett, N., Gutzler, D., Hansingo, K., Hegerl, G., Hu, Y., Jain, S., Mokhov, I. I., Overland, J., Perlwitz, J., Sebbari, R. and Zhang, X. (2013). 'Detection and Attribution of Climate Change: from Global to Regional'. In Stocker, T. F., Qin, D., Plattner, G.-K., Tignor, M., Allen, M. K., Boschung, J., Nauels, A., Xia, Y., Bex, V. and Midgley, P. M. (eds), *Climate Change 2013: The Physical Science Basis*. Contribution of Working Group I to the Fifth Assessment Report of the Intergovernmental Panel on Climate Change. Cambridge and New York: Cambridge University Press.

Block, W. and Jankovic, I. (2016). 'Tragedy of the Partnership: A Critique of Elinor Ostrom'. *American Journal of Economics and Sociology*, 75(2): 289–318.

Bovenberg, A. L. and De Mooij, R. A. (1994). 'Environmental levies and distortionary taxation'. *The American Economic Review*, 84(4): 1085–1089.

Briguglio, L. (1995). 'Small island developing states and their economic vulnerabilities'. *World development*, 23(9): 1615–1632.

Briguglio, L. (1998). 'Small country size and returns to scale in manufacturing'. *World Development*, 26(3): 507–515.

Briguglio, L. (2004). Economic Vulnerability and Resilience: Concepts and Measurements. In Briguglio, L. and Kisanga, E. J. (eds), *Economic Vulnerability and Resilience of Small States*. Malta and London: Islands and Small States Institute, University of Malta and Commonwealth Secretariat.

Briguglio, L., Cordina, G., Farrugia, N. and Vella, S. (2009). 'Economic vulnerability and resilience: concepts and measurements'. *Oxford Development Studies*, 37(3): 229–247.

Briguglio, L. (2016). 'Exposure to external shocks and economic resilience of countries: evidence from global indicators'. *Journal of Economic Studies*, 43(6): 1057–1078.

Briguglio, M., and Formosa, G. (2017). 'When households go solar: Determinants of uptake of a Photovoltaic Scheme and policy insights'. *Energy Policy*, 108: 154–162.

Briguglio, M., Delaney, L. and Wood, A. (2016). 'Voluntary recycling despite disincentives'. *Journal of Environmental Planning and Management*, 59(10): 1751–1774.

Briguglio, M. and Mercieca, K. (1988). Solid waste management policy in the EU and the Euromed process: Some reflections on the way forward for Malta. In Xuereb, P. S. (ed.), *Malta, the European union and the Mediterranean: Closer relations in the wider context*. Malta: European Documentation and Research Centre, University of Malta: 275–304.

Briguglio, M. and Mercieca, K. (1997). 'The economics of waste management in small island states'. *Bank of Valletta Review*. Spring: 13–46.

Briguglio, M. and Moncada, S. (2015). Environmental challenges in Malta. In Gale de Oliveira, M. S., Kennet, M., Amaral, S. E., Tezza, S., Briguglio, M. and Salman, D. (eds) *The greening of the Mediterranean*. Oxford: The Green Economics Institute: 52–57.

Briguglio, M. and Spiteri, J. (2017). Behavioural economics and small states: A focus on social preferences. *Handbook of Small States*. London: Routledge.

Brook, R. D., Rajagopalan, S., Pope, C. A., Brook, J. R., Bhatnagar, A., Diez-Roux, A. V., Holguin, F., Hong, Y., Luepker, R. V., Mittleman, M. A. and Peters, A. (2010). 'Particulate matter air pollution and cardiovascular disease'. *Circulation*, 121(21): 2331–2378.

Brown, D. R. (2010). 'Institutional development in small states: Evidence from the Commonwealth Caribbean'. *Halduskultuur–Administrative Culture*, 11(1): 44–65.

Burton, E. and Sanjour, W. (1967). An Economic Analysis of the Control of Sulphur Oxides Air Pollution. *DHEW Program Analysis Report* No. 1967–1969. Washington, DC: Ernst and Ernst.

Burtraw, D. (2016). *Why California's Cap-and-Trade Program Works*. Washington, DC: Resources for the Future.

Camerer, C. F., Loewenstein, G. and Rabin, M. (eds) (2011). *Advances in behavioral economics*. Princeton, NJ: Princeton University Press.

Callan, S. J. and Thomas, J. M. (2013). *Environmental economics and management: Theory, policy, and applications*. United States: Cengage Learning.

Collier, P. (2012). 'Small Countries and Big Resources: Harnessing Natural Resources for Development in the g7+ Countries'. *G7+ high level ministerial retreat Nov (2012)*: 13–14.

Commonwealth Secretariat (2014). *Small States: Economic Review and Basic Statistics*. Volume 17. London: Commonwealth Secretariat.

Croson, R., and Treich, N. (2014). 'Behavioral environmental economics: promises and challenges'. *Environmental and Resource Economics*, 58(3): 335–351.

De Bruyn, S. M. (2012). *Economic growth and the environment: An empirical analysis*, Vol. 18. Berlin: Springer Science and Business Media.

De Groot, R. S., Wilson, M. A. and Boumans, R. M. (2002). 'A typology for the classification, description and valuation of ecosystem functions, goods and services'. *Ecological economics*, 41(3): 393–408.

Dasgupta, S., Hettige, H. and Wheeler, D. (2000). 'What improves environmental compliance? Evidence from Mexican industry'. *Journal of Environmental Economics and Management*, 39(1): 39–66.

Daugbjerg, C. and Swinbank, A. (2007). 'The politics of CAP reform: trade negotiations, institutional settings and blame avoidance'. *JCMS: Journal of Common Market Studies*, 45(1): 1–22.

Diener, E. (2006). 'Guidelines for national indicators of subjective well-being and ill-being'. *Applied Research in Quality of Life*, 1(2): 151–157.

Dietz, T., Ostrom, E. and Stern, P. C. (2003). 'The struggle to govern the commons'. *Science*, 302(5652): 1907–1912.

Dolan, P., Peasgood, T. and White, M. (2008). 'Do we really know what makes us happy? A review of the economic literature on the factors associated with subjective well-being'. *Journal of Economic Psychology*, 29(1): 94–122.

Downes, A. S. (1988). 'On the Statistical Measurement of Smallness: A Principal Component Measure of Country Size'. *Social and Economic Studies*, 37(3): 75–96.

Easterlin, Richard A. (1974). 'Does economic growth improve the human lot? Some empirical evidence'. *Nations and households in Economic Growth*: 89–125.

Egenhofer, C., Alessi, M., Georgiev, A. and Fujiwara, N. (2011). *The EU Emissions Trading System and Climate Policy towards 2050: Real incentives to reduce emissions and drive innovation?* Brussels: Centre for European Policy Studies.

ELD Initiative (2015). The value of land: Prosperous lands and positive rewards through sustainable and management. Available at www.eld-initiative.org.

Ellerman, A. D. and Buchner, B. K. (2007). 'The European Union emissions trading scheme: origins, allocation, and early results'. *Review of Environmental Economics and Policy*, 1(1): 66–87.

Engel, S., Pagiola, S., and Wunder, S. (2008). 'Designing payments for environmental services in theory and practice: An overview of the issues'. *Ecological Economics*, 65(4): 663–674.

European Commission (2015). *Guide to cost-benefit analysis of investment projects: Economic appraisal tool for cohesion policy, 2014–2020.* Brussels: Directorate-General Regional and Urban Policy.

Fankhauser, S., Hepburn, C. and Park, J. (2010). 'Combining multiple climate policy instruments: how not to do it'. *Climate Change Economics*, 1(3): 209–225.

Farrugia, C. (1993). 'The special working environment of senior administrators in small states'. *World Development*, 21(2): 221–226.

Ferreira, S., Akay, A., Brereton, F., Cuñado, J., Martinsson, P., Moro, M. and Ningal, T. F. (2013). 'Life satisfaction and air quality in Europe'. *Ecological Economics*, 88(1): 1–10.

Formosa, S., Briguglio, L. and Moncada, S. (2017). Assessing the Vulnerability of Small Island Developing States to Sea-Level Rise. Occasional Papers on Islands and Small States. Islands and Small States Institute, University of Malta. ISSN 1024-6282.

Frederiks, E. R., Stenner, K. and Hobman, E. V. (2015). 'Household energy use: Applying behavioural economics to understand consumer decision-making and behaviour'. *Renewable and Sustainable Energy Reviews*, 41: 1385–1394.

Gray, W. B. and Shadbegian, R. J. (2004). '"Optimal' pollution abatement – whose benefits matter, and how much?'. *Journal of Environmental Economics and management*, 47(3): 510–534.

Guillaumont, P. (2010). 'Assessing the economic vulnerability of small island developing states and the least developed countries'. *The Journal of Development Studies*, 46(5): 828–854.

Hanley, N., Shogren, J. and White, B. (2007). *Environmental Economics in Theory and Practice*. London: Palgrave.

Hanemann, W. M. (1994). 'Valuing the environment through contingent valuation'. *The journal of economic perspectives*, 8(4): 19–43.

Hardin, G. (1968). 'The tragedy of the commons'. *Science*, 162(3859): 1243–1248.

Heller, W. P. and Starrett, D. A. (1976). On the nature of externalities. *Theory and measurement of economic externalities*: 9–22.

Hotelling, H. (1931). 'The economics of exhaustible resources'. *Journal of Political Economy*, 39(2): 137–175.

Hsu, A. *et al.* (2016). *Environmental Performance Index*. New Haven, CT: Yale University. Available at www.epi.yale.edu.

InsightPolls (2015). Traffic, corruption and immigration are seen as the main issues in Malta. *MISCO International Ltd. and Corporate Identities Ltd. Survey*. Available at http://corporateidentities.eu/traffic-corruption-and-immigration-are-seen-as-the-main-issues-of-concern-in-malta/. Accessed 1 June 2017:

Jevons, W. S. (1865). *The coal question: An inquiry concerning the progress of the nation, and the probable exhaustion of the coal-mines*. London: Macmillan.

Kahneman, D. (2003a). 'A perspective on judgment and choice: mapping bounded rationality'. *American psychologist*, 58(9): 697.

Kahneman, D. (2003b). 'Maps of bounded rationality: Psychology for behavioral economics'. *The American economic review*, 93(5): 1449–1475.

Kelman, I. (2010). 'Introduction to climate, disasters and international development'. *Journal of International Development*, 22(2): 208–217.

Kwerel, E. (1977). 'To tell the truth: Imperfect information and optimal pollution control'. *The Review of Economic Studies*: 595–601.

Laing, T., Sato, M., Grubb, M. and Comberti, C. (2014). 'The effects and side-effects of the EU emissions trading scheme'. *Wiley Interdisciplinary Reviews: Climate Change*, 5(4): 509–519.

Lewis, W. A. (1947). *Overhead Costs*. London: George Allen And Unwin Ltd.

Lewis, G. B. and Frank, S. A. (2002). 'Who wants to work for the government?'. *Public Administration Review*, 62(4): 395–404.

Loayza, N. V., Olaberria, E., Rigolini, J. and Christiaensen, L. (2012). 'Natural disasters and growth: going beyond the averages'. *World Development*, 40(7): 1317–1336.

Marshall, A. (1890). *Principles of Political Economy*. New York: Macmillan.

Malta Resources Authority (2013). Malta's Biennial Report on Policies and Measures and Projected Greenhouse Gas Emissions. Marsa: Climate Change and Policy Unit.

MEA Board (2005). A framework for assessment. Washington, DC: Island Press.

Mendelsohn, R., Nordhaus, W. D. and Shaw, D. (1994). 'The impact of global warming on agriculture: a Ricardian analysis'. *The American Economic Review (1994)*: 753–771.

MEPA (2010). *The Environment Report 2008*. Floriana: MEPA.

MEPA (2012). *State of the Environment Report 2012*. Floriana: MEPA.

Mercer, J. (2010). 'Disaster risk reduction or climate change adaptation: Are we reinventing the wheel?'. *Journal of International Development* 22(2): 247–264.

Montgomery, W. D. (1972). 'Markets in Licenses and Efficient Pollution Control Programs'. *Journal of Economic Theory*, 5: 395–418.

Myers, R. A. and Worm, B. (2003). 'Rapid worldwide depletion of predatory fish communities'. *Nature*, 423(6937): 280–283.

Muller, N. Z. and Mendelsohn, R. (2007). 'Measuring the damages of air pollution in the United States'. *J .Environ. Econ. Manage.*, 54(1): 1–14.

Nakatsuka, S., Ishida, Y., Fukuda, H., and Akita, T. (2017). 'A limit reference point to prevent recruitment overfishing of Pacific bluefin tuna'. *Marine Policy*, 78: 107–113.

Nath, S., Roberts, J. L., Madhoo, Y. N. (2010). *Saving Small Island Developing States: Environmental and Natural Resource Challenges*. London: Commonwealth Secretariat.

National Statistics Office (NSO) (2015a). *Municipal Waste Statistics, 2015*. Floriana: NSO.

National Statistics Office (NSO) (2015b). *Electricity Generation: 2006–2015*. Floriana: NSO.

Natella, S. and O'Sullivan, M. (2014). *The success of small countries*. Zurich: Credit Suisse Research Institute.

Nurse, L. A., Sem, G., Hay, J. E., Suarez, A. G., Wong, P. P., Briguglio, L. and Ragoonaden, S. (2001). 'Small island states'. *Climate change*: 843–875.

Nurse, L., McLean, R., Agard, J., Briguglio, L., Duvat-Magnan, V., Pelesikoti, N., Tompkins, E. and Webb, A. (2014). 'Small islands'. In Barros, V., Field, C., Dokken, D., Mastrandrea, M., Mach, K., Bilir, T., Chatterjee, M., Ebi, K., Estrada, Y., Genova, R., Girma, B., Kissel, E., Levy, A., MacCracken, S., Mastrandrea, P. and White, L. (eds), Climate Change 2014: Impacts, Adaptation, and Vulnerability Part B: Regional Aspects. Contribution of Working Group II to the Fifth Assessment Report of the Intergovernmental Panel on Climate Change. Cambridge and New York: Cambridge University Press: 1613–1654.

OECD (2005). 'Sink functions of the natural capital'. *Environmental Statistics: Glossary of Statistical Terms*. Paris: OECD.

Odlare, M., Arthurson, V., Pell, M., Svensson, K., Nehrenheim, E. and Abubaker, J. (2011). 'Land application of organic waste—effects on the soil ecosystem'. *Applied Energy*, 88(6): 2210–2218

Ostrom, E. (1992). *Crafting institutions for self-governing irrigation systems*. Ann Arbor, MI: ICS Press University of Michigan.

Oswald, A. J., Proto, E. and Sgroi, D. (2015). 'Happiness and productivity'. *Journal of Labor Economics*, 33(4): 789–822.

Pannozzo, L. (2015). 'In with the bad: Ambient air quality and transboundary pollution in Bhutan'. *Journal of Bhutan Studies*, 23: 118–126.

Pearce, D. (1998). 'Cost benefit analysis and environmental policy'. *Oxford review of economic policy*, 14(4): 84–100.

Pearce, D. (2002). 'An intellectual history of environmental economics'. *Annual review of energy and the environment*, 27(1): 57–81.

Pearce, D. W. and Turner, K. T. (1990). *Natural resource and environmental economics*. Baltimore: Johns Hopkins University Press.

Pigou, A. C. (1920). *The Economics of Welfare*. London: Macmillan.

Pigou, A. C. (1928). *A study in public finance*. London: Macmillan.

Popo III, C. A., Burnett, R. T., Thun, M. J., Calle, E. E., Krewski, D., Ito, K. and Thurston, G. D. (2002). 'Lung cancer, cardiopulmonary mortality, and long-term exposure to fine particulate air pollution'. *Jama*, 287(9): 1132–1141.

Prescott-Allen, R. and Union internationale pour la conservation de la nature et de ses ressources (IUCN) (2001). *The wellbeing of nations: a country-by-country index of quality of life and the environment*. Washington, DC: Island Press.

Reuveny, R. (2002). 'Economic growth, environmental scarcity, and conflict'. *Global Environmental Politics*, 2(1): 83–110.

Roberts, J. L. and Ibitoye, I. (2012). *The Big Divide – A Ten Year Report on Small Island Developing States and the Millennium Development Goals*. London: The Commonwealth Secretariat.

Roberts, J. L. (2017). SIDS and SDGs: Curse or Cure. *Handbook of Small States*. London: Routledge.

Roberts, L., Cremona, M. and Knox, G. J. (2015). *Why Malta's national water plan requires an analytical policy framework*. Valletta: The Today Public Policy Institute.

Sapiano, M. (2013). *Water consumption in the domestic sector in Malta*. Valletta: Ministry for Energy and the Conservation of Water.

Selden, T. M. and Song, D. (1994). 'Environmental quality and development: is there a Kuznets curve for air pollution emissions?'. *Journal of Environmental Economics and Management*, 27(2): 147–162.

Shogren, J. F. and Taylor, L. O. (2008). 'On behavioral-environmental economics'. *Review of Environmental Economics and Policy*, 2(1): 26–44.

Shrestha, R. K., Seidl, A. F. and Moraes, A. S. (2002). 'Value of recreational fishing in the Brazilian Pantanal: a travel cost analysis using count data models'. *Ecological Economics*, 42(1): 289–299.

Smyth, R., Mishra, V. and Qian, X. (2008). 'The environment and well-being in urban China'. *Ecological Economics*, 68(1): 547–555.

Spiteri, D., Scerri, C. and Valdramidis, V. (2015). 'The current situation for the water sources in the Maltese Islands'. *MJHS*: 22.

Spiteri, J. (2017). Transboundary pollution, trade and the Environmental Kuznets Curve. Unpublished manuscript.

Steffen, W., Richardson, K., Rockström, J., Cornell, S. E., Fetzer, I., Bennett, E. M. and Folke, C. (2015). 'Planetary boundaries: Guiding human development on a changing planet'. *Science*, 347(6223).

Stern, D. I. (2004). 'The rise and fall of the environmental Kuznets curve'. *World development*, 32(8): 1419–1439.

Stern, N. H. (2007). *The economics of climate change: The Stern review*. Cambridge: Cambridge University Press.

Stern, D. I., Common, M. S. and Barbier, E. B. (1996). 'Economic growth and environmental degradation: the environmental Kuznets curve and sustainable development'. *World Development*, 24(7): 1151–1160.

Stiglitz, J. E. (1989). 'Markets, market failures, and development'. *Am. Econ. Rev.*, 79(2): 197–203.

Streeten, P. (1993). 'The special problems of small countries'. *World Development* 21(2): 197–202.

Thøgersen, J. and Nielsen, K. S. (2016). 'A better carbon footprint label'. *Journal of Cleaner Production*, 125: 86–94.

Tversky, A. and Kahneman, D. (1975). Judgment under uncertainty: Heuristics and biases. In *Utility, probability, and human decision making*. Netherlands: Springer: 141–162.

United Nations Department of Economic and Social Affairs (UNDESA) (2013). *The World Economic and Social Survey 2013*. New York: United Nations.

Venkatachalam, L. (2008). 'Behavioral economics for environmental policy'. *Ecological Economics*, 67(4): 640–645.

Wantchekon, L. (2003). 'Clientelism and voting behavior: Evidence from a field experiment in Benin'. *World Politics*, 55(03): 399–422.

West, S. E. and Williams, R. C. (2004). 'Estimates from a consumer demand system: implications for the incidence of environmental taxes'. *Journal of Environmental Economics and management*, 47(3): 535–558.

World Bank Group (2016). *Population Estimates and Projections: Population Statistics*. Washington, DC: World Bank.

World Health Organization (WHO) and UNAIDS (2006). *Air quality guidelines: global update 2005*. Geneva: World Health Organization.

World Health Organization (WHO) (2009). *Environment and health performance review: Malta*. Copenhagen: World Health Organization.

26

Small island developing states and Sustainable Development Goals: curse or cure

John Laing Roberts

1 The burden of SDGs

The UN produced in 2016 the Sustainable Development Goals (SDGs)[1] to provide an improved and more elaborate basis for monitoring country progress to sustainable development and provide reports to the UN General Assembly. The shift from the eight MDGs[2] with some 48 indicators to the new SDG system with 17 Goals, 169 Targets and 242 listed indicators,[3] and with only 105 of the indicators set to be achieved by 2030,[4] presents SIDS, especially micro SIDS, with what will seem an unsupportable task for many in reporting the data and establishing a strategy for responding to the targets and goals. *The Economist* has called them a distraction[5] and suggested cutting these commandments down to ten. William Easterly, in the *Foreign Policy* magazine[6] has suggested SDG should stand for 'senseless, dreamy and garbled'.

Moreover, whilst the SDG system includes indicators for inputs, processes and outcomes it is not supported by an economics framework for the pursuit of targets and goals, nor a model for distinguishing between inherent vulnerability and nurtured resilience. There is a critical absence of any systematic attention to the issues of allocative and technical efficiency in guiding investment policies. In addition, whilst there are nominal regional forums for SIDS, they do not position themselves to address the issues of regional or global inequity in the pursuit of targets, despite the wide variation in proximity to target.

Many factors affect decisions on investment in the three SIDS regions (Caribbean, AIMS[7] and Pacific) to pursue the SDGs. First there is an increasing marginal cost of investment as SIDS move towards the defined targets; second even in the redefined 28 SIDS used for this chapter, there are important differences in the population size and wealth of the countries[8] which affect the size of the costs and the benefits in making progress; third there are large differences in the economic and technical capacity of the countries and their prospects for economic growth that serve as variable constraints to progress and affect the assessment of trends and future prospects. Finally, whilst all the 28 defined SIDS are sovereign state members of the UN there is clearly a variation in the political commitment to the SDGs, as there was for the MDGs and few include specific plans and budget allocations linked to progress with targets based upon explicit assessments of the resource requirements for making progress.

The flexibility given to countries to define their own targets and indicators within the SDG system makes more indeterminate the ways in which inter-country comparisons of status and progress can be made. Overall for some, especially the micro SIDS, the official commitment to the SDG system may seem more of a curse than a cure to their development challenges.

The unsustainable pathway of SIDS

There is a continuing tendency for those SIDS with a high level on the UNDP Human Development Index to have a raised level of material footprint per capita (SDG Indicator 12.2.1). In a comparison of SIDS with other benchmark countries, including the island of Singapore and the small state of Liechtenstein, there appears the risk that SIDS could follow such a pathway adding to the burden on their scarce natural resources as they seek higher levels of economic and social development. Recent data indicate that this is being avoided in certain Caribbean SIDS, though the specific mechanisms and policies promoting this trend yet need to be identified.

The SDG system is a heavy weight to carry for SIDS. Evidence shows the high levels of missing data arising from the very limited statistical and analytical capacities of SIDS. Whilst the new SDG system appears to provide complete reports from every country, with even a special line for SIDS, closer examination shows the system is still in an early stage of development, with results based on scant source data.

There is evidently room for a simpler core system of fundamental sustainable development indicators for SIDS. This is necessary to provide a realistic assessment of their problems and their potential for targeting investment to improve nurtured resilience, on those aspects of sustainable development that, on an evidence base, are likely to yield the best results. Then they can pursue more confidently the further implementation of the UN 2005 SIDS Mauritius Strategy and make progress with Rio + 20 the Future We want.

MDGs and SDGs: relevance to SIDS strategy

The Millennium Development Goals (MDGs) statistical monitoring system agreed by the UN in 2000[9] consists of eight goals, 21 targets and an original set of 48 indicators, which was later extended to 58–62 indicators, not all of which apply to all countries. The Sustainable Development Goals (SDGs)[10] statistical monitoring system announced by the UN in 2016 consists of 17 Goals, 169 targets and over 240 indicators. The whole set is still subject to further amendment although it was endorsed in principle by the UN as part of the Global policy document Transforming Our World in 2015.[11] The data base for the SDGs is maintained by the UN statistics unit.[12] The entries are primarily based on reports from countries in accordance with guidelines which define each indicator and the methods for measurement and reporting. Other sources that are used are from other UN agencies and the World Bank.

The database is provided in various forms showing the data for each country by year, but also for international comparative purposes, where data are missing, the UN estimates values and inserts those in a parallel set of data for what it terms global monitoring. The database is presented by country by region from 1990–2015 and this will be continued up to 2030.

The data tables are available in Excel format showing a line for each indicator, for each country and for each year, in many cases going back to 1990 which was the base year for the MDGs. Each country row has a column for the source of the data and one column for each of the years reported. At present for many of the country entries the data source is indicated as not available (NA), and the value is noted as estimated value (E) without any other note on its provenance. It is necessary to scan 149 footnotes in the main metadata notes for the SDG system to identify the origin of the entries.

In addition, there are footnotes for each statistical table for each indicator, although these are not available in the Excel table format. The whole system was designed to track progress in preparation for the annual report by the Secretary General of the UN on progress towards sustainable development.

For the SIDS, the UN presents data for each country separately but also defines a special region consisting of 51 UN defined SIDS countries, presenting the data for this so called region in one line (see Appendix 1 setting out the list of 51 countries in the UN defined SIDS.)

Where the data for the 51 UN SIDS are percentages, the regional value consists of data from those countries with either submitted data or values estimated by the UN statistics unit, each value is then adjusted by the appropriate denominator, such as population or births or land space etc., as the basis for the regional figure. Where there are missing data from the countries or no estimates of the missing values, there is no indication on how many entries, from the 51 countries, the regional figure is based.

The UN Statistics division does not provide a disaggregated table for the 51 SIDS separately across the 17 Goals and 242 indicators. So to examine the distribution of SIDS data for SDGs it would be necessary to compile a matrix consisting of over 300,000 entries (51 countries x 240 indicators x 25 years). That would be a major project and is not attempted here.

This chapter therefore critically examines a selection of entries across the seventeen goals in the UN SDG data base downloaded in January 2017. The review identifies major shortcomings in the system which serve to underline the weaknesses in an over-elaborate design, which fails to take account of both the cost of producing accurate data and the likely cost-effectiveness of the results in aiding decision making and monitoring progress.

2 Which countries are SIDS?

The 51 countries in the UN defined regions of SIDS include some that are not small (such as Haiti, 9.8 million population; Cuba, 11.2 million; and Papua New Guinea, 6.6 million); some that are not islands (such as Guyana, Guinea-Bissau and Belize), one that that is not a developing country (Singapore GDP US$ 49,700 per head: with a Human Development Index global rank of 11 and a, Human Development Index score of 0.912, in 2014); and some that are not sovereign states (such as American Samoa, Aruba, Cook Islands, Guam and the Netherlands Antilles).[13] The review in this chapter excludes those in the UN definition of the region of SIDS that are not small island developing States and thus examines just the 28 Sovereign States shown in Appendix 1.[14]

The United Nations has a special office (OHRLLS)[15] for promoting the interests of SIDS in conjunction with Least Developed Countries (LDCs) and Land Locked Countries. There are 48 LDCs on the UN list of which 10 are also listed as SIDS and seven of these SIDS are within the 28 examined in this chapter, (see Appendix 1).

The LDCs are a category of country recognized by the UN as in need of special support for development. They are economically vulnerable with a small range of exports of primary goods, weak human development and inadequate institutional capacities, low income, heavy debt and dependence on key strategic imports such as energy, food, clothing and transport. They suffer from low investment and low productivity.

SIDS have also been recognized by the UN as a special category for development support through the OHRLLS based on their inherent economic, social and environmental vulnerabilities. They lack economies of scale in production, have small internal markets, their remoteness ensures high import coats and high costs for transporting exports. They are especially vulnerable to natural catastrophes, have limited private sectors for driving development and weak undifferentiated public sector development. Those SIDS that are also LDCs (Comoros, Kiribati, Sao Tome and Principe, Solomon Islands, Timor Leste, Tuvalu and Vanuatu) tend to be subject to overwhelming disadvantages for development.

Goals and targets

Whilst the Millennium development goals consisted of eight goals, the SDGs are now expanded to 17 (see Appendix 2). These add to the range of performance covered in line with the UN Agenda 2030. Some of the goals and targets specified are to be achieved by 2030, others with a specified target date of 2020 and others with no specific date set at all. Fewer of the SDGs have specified levels set for the targets, than the MDGs, where more specific dates and levels were defined. This all adds to the vagueness of the strategy, leaving too many loopholes for the uncommitted.

Performance of SIDS on MDGs against benchmarks

In a review 2012 review of progress with MDGs the performance of 46 small states including 39 then classified as SIDS and five Commonwealth other small states, it was found that 19% of their targets had been achieved, by comparison with 28% achievement of targets by larger benchmark states (Roberts and Ibitoye, 2012). Broadly, progress with MDGs (defined as targets achieved plus those where progress was being made towards the targets) was less in smaller states and markedly less in micro states of under 100,000 population.

Small states however had clearly more difficulty than others in collecting and reporting the MDG data. Even with a flexible definition of the baseline and the latest values[16], missing data (where either a baseline value was missing or a latest value was missing) were found to be 44% for the small states and SIDS and 27% in the benchmark states. For the small states and SIDS across the eight MDGs there were 71% missing data on MDG1 1 Poverty reduction and 1% on MDG 4 Child Health. For the ten benchmark states there were 59% missing data for MDG 6 Disease control and 0% missing data for MDG 4 (Child Health).

For the Small states and SIDS, in the 2012 review, there were six MDGs for which more than 33% of the data were missing and for the larger bench mark states there were 4 MDGs for which more than 33% of the data were missing. Clearly for the MDG system missing data has been a major obstacle to detailed analysis though some broad comparisons can still be extracted as the Commonwealth Secretariat report (Roberts and Ibitoye, 2012) demonstrates.

In a later report (Roberts, 2014), for the Indian Ocean Commission, on progressing Rio +20 outcomes in the AIMS region, for the eight SIDS reviewed there was 32% missing data, with 44% missing on MDG1 Poverty reduction and 0% missing data on MDG 4 Child Health. Overall by the latest assessment for each country 30% of the targets had been achieved overall, and progress with targets (countries with targets achieved plus countries with progress towards targets) had been attained by 53% after 20 years.

Angeon and Bates (2015) in their paper reviewing the selection of data sources for measuring vulnerability and resilience, claim from their analysis that 'contrary to the conclusion generally shared by scholars in development economics, Small Island Developing States are not specifically more prone to vulnerability than other countries'. It is difficult to share this view in the light of the small number of SIDS, six out of the UN list of 51, included in their data.

3 Overall assessment of the pursuit of MDGs

Such evidence as exists from analysis of the MDGs for SIDS and small states shows that in general:

- They have a low level of achievement on MDGs compared with benchmark countries;
- there is a large divide between the best and the worst performing states;
- the closer to target the more difficult it is to progress;
- the technology for making progress varies in distance from target;
- the marginal costs become progressively greater as the distance from target decreases;
- progress towards target is directly associated with population size, the micro SIDS of less than 100,000 population, making the least progress with MDGs and having greater difficulty measuring and compiling the data reports;
- using numbers instead of percentages, the 80–5 rule generally applies – that is a large majority of the deprived people in SIDS who come from a very small number of the SIDS themselves, thus justifying a focus not on the percentage deprived but on the total population of the deprived people in those SIDS where they are concentrated (Roberts and Ibitoye, 2012).

The scope of SDGs as a planning and policy tool

The SDG system consists of 17 goals with 169 targets and 242 indicators. In addition, there is a call for reporting on disaggregated elements of relevant indicators by income, sex, age, race, ethnicity, migratory status, disability and geographical location. Thus the full matrix for some 200 countries adopted in the system, with planned annual entries until 2030, will consist of over one million data cells for which reports have to be captured, checked, edited, and stored for retrieval and analysis. The present storage system has been set up with a comprehensive system of meta-data of concepts, methods of measurement and reporting for each of the 242 indicators and has 149 footnotes of explanation for the overall matrix plus additional footnotes and commentaries for each of the indicators.

It is a Byzantine system dedicated to the task of providing a counting system for monitoring progress with the Agenda 2030, apparently unconstrained by advice from policy makers, budget holders, other related disciplines, such as economists and accountants, nor with the realism that normally emerges from common sense. And for refinements it seems that the international expert group that devised the unwieldy system is likely to extend it further, rather bringing some realism to the task and cutting it down to workable size.

It is evident that the system is exhausting the process for country reporting and overwhelming the central system of editing and storage.

Preliminary assessment of progress with SDGs

A detailed review of selected SDG indicators (available from the author on request) sets out results of the data assembled between January and March 2017 for the 28 SIDS defined for this chapter. The review shows that there are serious flaws in the data presented. There are large amounts of data missing; a high level of the use of estimates and interpolation of numbers to cover where none exist, certain design features that inhibit access to data for selected countries[17]; there is no supplementary technical evidence base to guide decision makers on action to be taken where results are poor; the system lacks economic appraisal critically reviewing the cost effectiveness of increasing the number of goals, targets and indicators and how far they illuminate aspects of sustainable development. So the time is ripe for a radical review of the future needs of SIDS for a realistic short list of indicators that really assist planning and the implementation of policies and programme for development.

The review mentioned above illustrates a series of weaknesses in the SDG data system applied to the 28 SIDS:

- On poverty, indicator 1.1.1 there are 10 of the 28 SIDS with no data.
- On the rate of renewable energy used, indicator 7.2.1, there are some bizarre records: Tonga is reported to have had a fall from 100% renewables in 1990 to 1.16% in 1991. In four other SIDS there are reported also major falls in the rate, including Mauritius with a fall from 50.96% to just 7.22% in the period under review.
- On youth unemployment, indicator 8.6.1, 23 of the 28 SIDS have no recorded data.
- On road access in rural areas, indicator 9.1.1, there were no data recorded for any of the 28 SIDS.
- On the growth rates of income for the bottom 40% of the population, there were no recorded data for 27 of the 28 SIDS.
- On urban slums, indicator 11.1.1, there were no data for 23 of the 28 SIDS.
- On the material footprint, indicator 12.2.1, there were no recorded data for 15 of the 28 SIDS.
- On the existence of disaster reduction strategies, indicator 13.1.1, there were no data for 15 of the 28 SIDS.
- On coverage of marine protected areas, there were data for 24 of the 28 SIDS but in 16 of these SIDS the values were recorded as zero.
- On the existence of national fully funded statistical strategies, indicator 17.18.3, for 11 of the 28 SIDS there were no data recorded.
- More worrying is the report on indicator 17.9.2 that five of the 28 SIDS had not even had a population household census in the past ten years.

In the face of this dearth of hard data the elegantly produced UN report of 2016 (UN, 2016) is uncomfortably unreliable. It is true that it signals that the report is based upon available data, but it fails to reveal that the considerable number of tables setting out results for each region purportedly on the full scope of the SDGs, only present data for 128 of the 242 indicators across all regions, and for the 51 UN so defined SIDS, it manages to report on just 87 of the 242 indicators. This in itself should be a warning of the problems ahead for the whole system.

It is all the more of concern that for example on SDG 13 on climate change, there are no data reported; on SDG 10 on reducing inequality, it reports on only one of the 11 indicators; on SDG 12 on consumption and production, it reports on only one out of 13 indicators. Worse still on SDG 17 only two of the 51 UN so defined SIDS were recorded as having fully funded plans for improving national statistics.

4 An economics framework for investment

Moving from curse to cure

The current SDG system is too long and complex. For the needs of SIDS it is unwieldy. It would be better to close in on the fundamentals of sustainable development and to adopt only those for which there are reliable data and which directly link to key areas of decision making for SIDS. A shorter list would need to be carefully assessed in close consultation with the SIDS themselves and taking into account issues of economics and effectiveness of the indicators as tools for analysis and action,[18] and the big divide in stages of development and performance of SIDS.

But what is essential is that the framework succinctly addresses the core issues of the inherent economic and environmental vulnerabilities of SIDS and the action to be taken to promote greater nurtured resilience to the inherent threats to sustainability. Moreover, since for SIDS by their nature, technical capacity for the capture and analysis of data is a scarce resource, it is essential to focus any system of monitoring, on the fundamentals of sustainable development. If this is done then rather than try to collect data over the vast range of 242 indicators, SIDS can concentrate on a set of seven. The criteria for these should be that they are relevant, can be captured, illuminate diversity in performance and in tandem with a technical evidence base, throw light on points for policy making and action.

Implementation, target dates and specified target levels on the indicators should also relate to the varied stages of social and economic development of the SIDS concerned (Roberts and Ibitoye, 2012) which affect the technical interventions required, the resource requirements to make progress and the timescale for achievement. Global reports should clearly state the limitations of quality and quantity of data on which UN reports are based and the extent of missing data.

Cutting SDGs down to size

A revised system for SIDS should start with the core of the Briguglio data set for assessing economic vulnerability and resilience (Briguglio *et al.*, 2009 and Briguglio, 2016). Table 26.1 presents a set of indicators that can be used for this purpose. The vulnerability indicators would describe the state of the SIDS in terms of exposure to external shocks and the resilience indicators would point to the weaknesses for which many of the 28 SIDS would require evidence based plans and technical support from international donors to address their vulnerabilities.

Whilst the 2005 UN SIDS Mauritius Strategy[19] and the outcome of the UN 2014 SIDS Samoa conference,[20] provide a host of elements for a wide ranging programme of action, this short list of under ten indices and indicators would avoid the overload of the SDG system for SIDS and sharpen the focus of their limited resources for data capture and analysis on the most essential elements for decision making.

5 Conclusion and points for action and research

The scheme of SDGs, is a Byzantine system that has little hope of being of use to SIDS, if it is to anyone else. It is replete with missing data, shows signs of ineffective audit and is undermined by the interpolation of estimated values. The SDG system might be considered a data management curse devised by a synconium[21] of 'experts' devoid of constraints of practicality or concern for the cost and value of the elements for revealing differences, illuminating change and aiding decision making.

This chapter proposes cutting down the number of SIDS from the 51 in the UN book to just 28 excluding those that are not sovereign states, not small islands and not developing. It exposes flaws and weaknesses in the proposed UN system of sustainable

Table 26.1 Proposed list of indicators for sustainable development for the 28 SIDS showing the current availability of data and possible sources

Possible indicator	*Possible source*
Economic vulnerability	
Trade openness	This can be measured by the average of imports and exports as a ratio of GDP. Data are available from the UNCTAD: http://unctadstat.unctad.org/wds/ReportFolders/reportFolders.aspx Data is available for all the 28 SIDS.
Export concentration	A possible source of the data is the UNCTAD database: http://unctadstat.unctad.org/wds/ReportFolders/reportFolders. aspx/, which contains data on export concentration, but this only covers merchandise. Briguglio (2016) http://emeraldinsight.com/doi/abs/10.1108/JES-12-2014-0203?af=R uses an export concentration index which covers services. This is more meaningful, given that many small states have a high dependence on tourism and/or financial services. All of the 28 SIDS are covered in this index.
Proneness to natural disasters	The CRED database is a very good source of disaster statistics, and covers most of the 28 SIDS. http://www.emdat.be/database/.
Economic resilience	
Political governance	A possible source of governance indicators are the Worldwide Governance Indicators: http://info.worldbank.org/governance/wgi/#home/. All of the 28 SIDS are covered in this index.
Competitiveness	A possible source of competitiveness indicators is the Global Competitiveness Report: http://reports.weforum.org/global-competitiveness-index/. Not all of the 28 small island developing states are not covered in this index.
Social development	A possible source is the non-income components of the Human Development Index, covering health and education: http://hdr.undp.org/en/data/. Almost all the 28 small island developing states are covered in this index.
Environmental management	Possible environmental management indicators can be obtained from the Environmental Performance Index, available at: http://epi.yale.edu/reports/2016-report/. Almost all of the 28 SIDS are covered by this index.

development goals, targets and indicators. It recommends a short list of seven elements that can link the model of building nurtured resilience to the inherent economic and environmental vulnerabilities of SIDS, within a framework of technical evidence based interventions.

SIDS should now put together fresh strategies for implementation of sustainable development, with clear target dates and target levels on each of the fundamental indicators, the resources required and the technical interventions proposed, related to their stages of development and an evidence base of the expected cost effectiveness of planned action. Support should be provided for SIDS to reduce missing data and estimated data and reports should be independently audited. Table 26.2 presents the key issues for SIDS for the pursuit of sustainable development with recommendations for action.

Table 26.2 SDGs the key issues, recommendations and action needed

Key issues	Recommendations	Action needed
Weak UN definition of SIDS	The UN should review their list of SIDS and exclude from their list those SIDS that are not small, not islands, not developing and not sovereign states.	The 28 real SIDS reviewed in this chapter should promote the case for revision of UN practice to establish a more realistic short list that can help in advocacy to secure special consideration and technical support. A supplementary quite separate list of other associated entities that suffer from similar problems of vulnerability and weak resilience could be mooted.
Too many goals, targets and indicators beyond the capacity of SIDS to capture and report data.	SIDS should focus on a a few (say seven) fundamental data fields for monitoring their progress in sustainable development	SIDS regions should raise the issue with UNDESA and UNOHRLLS to reach agreement on fundamental data sets.
Unwarranted and confusing variation in target dates and target levels lacking relevance to differing stages of development and performance.	SIDS should tighten up the specification for target dates and action related to their stages of development and current achievements.	UN SDG Commission should review the target dates and rationalize the system to avoid confusion and more closely link the programme to the different stages of SIDS' development and their performance.
Too much missing data	SIDS should reduce the extent of missing data to ensure coverage of the fundamental data fields for monitoring sustainable development.	Global and regional support should be given to SIDS to improve the collection and reporting of data for SDGs with the introduction of independent audit to improve quality and timeliness.
Absence of economic framework for the pursuit of SDGs.	SIDS should promote at national, regional and global levels the review of strategic development models and the assimilation of evidence for cost-effective intervention to secure sustainable development.	Global and regional networks should be coordinated to test development models for SIDS and to establish an evidence base on cost effective intervention for securing progress with SDGs at their varying levels of performance.
Weak focus on action to improve responsiveness to inherent economic, social and environmental vulnerability	SIDS suffer from inherent social, economic and environmental vulnerability: for each area they should focus attention on responsiveness and planned, funded, action to improve resilience.	Special Global and regional technical support should be offered to SIDS to improve analysis and action programmes to increase resilience to inherent vulnerability.

Notes

1 UN (2017) Statistics SDG data base, available at https://unstats.un.org/sdgs/indicators/database/.
2 UN Statistics MDG Data base 2017, available at http://unstats.un.org; http://mdegs.un.org .
3 Inexplicably 9 of the 242 Indicators are repeated e.g. 8.4.1 and 12.2.2 Material footprint, which reduces the net total Indicators to 234.
4 105 by 2030; 1 by 2025; 16 by 2020 and 47 with no set date.
5 'The 169 commandments: the proposed sustainable development goals would be worse than useless', March 26, 2015. Available at www.economist.com/news/leaders/21647286-proposed-sustainable-development-goals-would-be-worse-useless-169-commandments/.
6 *Foreign Policy* Sep. 28, 2015. Available at http://foreignpolicy.com/2015/09/28/the-sdgs-are-utopian-and-worthless-mdgs-development-rise-of-the-rest/.
7 The AIMS SIDS region was originally defined as those UN SIDS in the marine areas of the Atlantic, Indian Ocean, Mediterranean and South China Seas. Subsequently Malta and Cyprus on entering the EU withdrew, so the AIMS SIDS region now consists of eight countries Cape Verde, Sao Tome and Principe, and Guinea-Bissau, from the Atlantic; Comoros, Maldives, Mauritius and Seychelles from the Indian Ocean, and Singapore from the South China Seas. The title AIMS nevertheless persists.
8 In the 28 defined SIDS population ranges from Tuvalu in the Pacific region with a population of 12,000 to Jamaica in the Caribbean with a population of 2.7 million, over 200 times as big: whilst GDP per capita per day ranges from US$ 3 in the Comoros in the SIDS AIMS region, to US$ 64 in Trinidad and Tobago in the Caribbean.
9 http://unstats.un.org; http://mdegs.un.org/.
10 https://sustainabledevelopment.un.org/post2015/transformingourworld/.
11 *Transforming out World, UN 2030 Agenda for Sustainable Development.* Available at https://sustainabledevelopment.un.org/post2015/transformingourworld/.
12 https://unstats.un.org/sdgs/indicators/database/.
13 There is clearly a case for the UN to review the current UN definition of SIDS and consider excluding from their list of those that are not small, not islands, not developing and not sovereign states. This would avoid confusion and promote more convincing advocacy for their support.
14 This list of 28 SIDS is the same as that defined in the UNCTAD analytical (non-official) list of SIDS, with the exception that the list used in this chapter excludes Papua New Guinea. All the 28 sovereign states reviewed in this chapter are islands with populations under 5 million and GDP per capita of less than US$ 30,000 per year at Purchasing Power Parity and a 2016 Human Development Index of < 0.802.
15 Office of High Representative for Least Developed Countries, Landlocked Countries and Small Island Developing States (OHRLLS). Information available at http://unohrlls.org/.
16 In the absence of values for 1990, reported values from 1990–2003 were accepted as baseline values: in the absence of values for 2010, values from 2000–2008 were accepted as latest values.
17 The Excel tables of results by country are listed in a bafflingly non alphabetical order, instead of the strict alphabetical order as for MDGS; there are some 149 footnotes qualifying the validity of the data; mixing rates and numbers in the same table can also be confusing; whilst the so called region of SIDS of 51 countries has one line in each table as a summary of the SIDS data, there is no provision for disaggregation of this line to the individual countries themselves, nor is the procedure used for summarizing the data explicitly defined.
18 Much work has been done in the field of cost-effectiveness of interventions, which might be used as a model for the better development of policy analysis in the wider field of sustainable development; see for example (Marseille *et al.*, 2015).
19 'Mauritius Strategy of Implementation', available at: https://sustainabledevelopment.un.org/conferences/msi2005.
20 'SIDS Accelerated Modalities of Action (S.A.M.O.A) Pathway', available at www.sids2014.org/index.php?menu=1537.
21 A synconium is a seed that spontaneously develops into multiple fruits, as a fig.

Appendix 1

Table 26.A1 List of 51 countries in the UN-defined SIDS regions showing their deficiencies as SIDS with a list of 28* real SIDS countries under review

UN list of 51 SIDS used in SDG tables	Not small	Not island	Not developing$	Not sovereign	28 real SIDS
American Samoa				x	
Anguilla				x	
Antigua and Barbuda					**x**
Aruba				x	
Bahamas					**x**
Barbados					**x**
Belize		x			
British Virgin Islands				x	
Cape Verde					**x**
Comoros					**x**
Cook Islands				x	
Cuba	x				
Dominica					**x**
Dominican Republic	x				
Fiji					**x**
French Polynesia				x	
Grenada					**x**
Guam				x	
Guinea-Bissau		x			
Guyana		x			
Haiti	x				
Jamaica					**x**
Kiribati					**x**
Maldives					**x**
Marshall Islands				x	**x**
Mauritius					**x**
Micronesia (Federated States of)					**x**
Montserrat				x	
Nauru					**x**
Netherland Antilles				x	
New Caledonia				x	

UN list of 51 SIDS used in SDG tables	Not small	Not island	Not developing$^{\$}$	Not sovereign	28 real SIDS
Niue				x	
Northern Mariana Islands				x	
Palau					**x**
Papua New Guinea	x				
Puerto Rico				x	
St Kitts and Nevis					**x**
St Lucia					**x**
Samoa					**x**
Sao Tome and Principe					**x**
Seychelles					**x**
Singapore			x		
Solomon Islands					**x**
St Vincent and the Grenadines					**x**
Suriname					
Timor-Leste					**x**
Tonga					**x**
Trinidad and Tobago					**x**
Tuvalu					**x**
U.S. Virgin Islands				x	
Vanuatu					**x**
Grand total					**51**
Countries with missing elements	4	3	1	15	**23**
Real SIDS					**28**

$^{\$}$ Not developing is defined here as a value on the UNDP Human Development Index < 0.802 and in the very high development category.

Appendix 2 Official list of SDGs

Goal 1.   End poverty in all its forms everywhere.

Goal 2.   End hunger, achieve food security and improved nutrition and promote sustainable agriculture.

Goal 3.   Ensure healthy lives and promote well-being for all at all ages.

Goal 4.   Ensure inclusive and equitable quality education and promote lifelong learning opportunities for all.

Goal 5.   Achieve gender equality and empower all women and girls.

Goal 6.   Ensure availability and sustainable management of water and sanitation for all.

Goal 7.   Ensure access to affordable, reliable, sustainable and modern energy for all.

Goal 8.   Promote sustained, inclusive and sustainable economic growth, full and productive employment and decent work for all.

Goal 9.   Build resilient infrastructure, promote inclusive and sustainable industrialization and foster innovation.

Goal 10.   Reduce inequality within and among countries.

Goal 11.   Make cities and human settlements inclusive, safe, resilient and sustainable.

Goal 12.   Ensure sustainable consumption and production patterns.

Goal 13.   Take urgent action to combat climate change and its impacts.

Goal 14.   Conserve and sustainably use the oceans, seas and marine resources for sustainable development.

Goal 15.   Protect, restore and promote sustainable use of terrestrial ecosystems, sustainably manage forests, combat desertification, and halt and reverse land degradation and halt biodiversity loss.

Goal 16.   Promote peaceful and inclusive societies for sustainable development, provide access to justice for all and build effective, accountable and inclusive institutions at all levels.

Goal 17.   Strengthen the means of implementation and revitalize the Global Partnership for Sustainable Development.

References

Angeon, V. and Bates, S. (2015). 'Reviewing composite vulnerability and resilience indexes: a sustainable approach and application'. *World Development*, 72: 140–162.

Briguglio, L. (2016). 'Exposure to external shocks and economic resilience of countries: evidence from global indicators'. *Journal of Economic Studies*, 43(6): 1057–1078.

Briguglio, L., Cordina, G., Farrugia, N. and Vella, S. (2009). 'Economic vulnerability and resilience: concepts and measurements'. *Oxford development studies*, 37(3): 229–247.

Marseille, E., Larson, B., Kazi, D., Kahn, J. and Rosen, S. (2015). Thresholds for the cost effectiveness of interventions. *Bulletin of WHO*, 93: 118–124

Roberts, J. L. (2014). *The Divided Region, Progressing RIO+20 Outcomes in the AIMS Region*. Indian Ocean Commission.

Roberts, J. L. and Ibitoye, I. (2012). *The Big Divide, a Ten Year Report of Small Island Developing States and the Millennium Development Goals*. London: Commonwealth Secretariat.

UN (2016). *Global Sustainable Development Report*. Geneva: United Nations.

UNCTAD (2004). Is a Special treatment of small island developing States possible?, *UNCTAD/LDC/ 2004/1*. Geneva: United Nations.

27

Small island developing states and the ocean economy: widening the development frontier

Bonapas Francis Onguglo and David Vivas Eugui[1]

1 Introduction

This chapter discusses the realization of economic benefits from the oceans for SIDS and small scale artisanal fishers which comprise the bulk of fishers in SIDS. A United Nations working paper on SDG 14.7 notes that 'Target 14.7 focuses on enhanced benefits to SIDS and LDCs from the sustainable use of marine resources, including through sustainable management of fisheries, aquaculture and tourism'. For many lower and lower-middle-income island countries, much of the areas over which they exercise jurisdictional rights are oceans. Oceans and their marine resources are thus the base upon which the economies of many SIDS are built, and are central to their sustainable development, to poverty reduction and to delivering the Sustainable Development Goals' (World Bank and United Nations, 2017).

The rest of this chapter is organized as follows. Section 2 of this chapter discusses the particular position of SIDS and their special relation with oceans. Section 3 points to the oceans as a common resource available to all SIDS and its vast size in comparison to land size and resources of SIDS, and Section 4 discusses strategies needed to harness such potential force for inclusive development. Section 5 provides an overview of export of fish and fisheries products as a key sector for SIDS, and Section 6 explores the relevance of marine genetic resources as inputs for R&D and value addition. The need for SIDS to develop and implement ocean strategies is highlighted in the concluding section.

2 SIDS and the oceans goal

Sustainable Development Goal 14 is often referred to as the '*oceans goal*' dealing with *life on, and below water* (see https://sustainabledevelopment.un.org). SDG 14 sets out an ambitious set of targets. These include addressing the impact of pollution and land-based activities; protection of marine ecosystems; the reduction of acidification; the regulation of harvesting of fish; the introduction of special and differential treatment in WTO fisheries subsidies negotiations for developing countries and LDCs; improved sustainable management of fisheries, providing access to small-scale artisanal fishermen to marine resources and markets; and improving scientific knowledge to advance ocean health. Furthermore, SDG 14 makes specific references to the needs of SIDS, aiming 'by 2030, [to] increase the economic benefits to SIDS and LDCs from the sustainable use of marine resources, including through sustainable management of fisheries, aquaculture and tourism'.

Taken together, the achievement of these targets would support meaningful progress on the three main pillars of sustainable development. It would also contribute to achieving other SDGs and other internationally agreed development goals. The latter includes, for example, the SIDS Accelerated Modalities of Action (SAMOA) Pathway, the outcome of the 2014 Third International Conference on SIDS. The implementation and realization of SDG 14 can also contribute to the achievement of national and regional development goals pertaining to oceans and development, such as the blue economy goals contained in Africa's Agenda 2063, the continental development strategy endorsed by African governments.

The 2030 Agenda for Sustainable Development and the Samoa Pathway build upon the Outcome of the Rio+20 Summit on Sustainable Development, 'The Future We Want'. Therein an entire section is devoted to issues related to oceans and seas. Oceanic economic sectors can be harnessed for development purposes only by keeping seas and oceans healthy, resilient and safe which in itself is a significant challenge as oceans are currently endangered by many factors including climate change and the deposit of pollutants, fertilizers and plastics in oceans. SDG 14 targets dealing with ocean conservation are 14.1, 14.2, 14.3, 14.5, and 14.a; those that address sustainable use of marine resources and trade-related aspects of fisheries are targets 14.4, 14.6, 14.7, and 14.b; and target 14.c addresses both conservation and sustainable use of marine resources as well as concerns of small scale and artisanal fishers and the need for policy coherence with the law of the sea regime.

3 SIDS and oceans

SIDS comprises a group of developing countries with a common set of defining development characteristics (social, economic, environmental). However, there is no official United Nations or other internationally agreed list of SIDS. As a result, various international organizations have developed their own lists of SIDS for working purposes. For example, UNCTAD, for analytical purposes, lists 29 SIDS (Antigua and Barbuda, Bahamas, Barbados, Cabo Verde, Comoros, Dominica, Fiji, Grenada, Jamaica, Kiribati, Maldives, the Marshall Islands, Mauritius, Micronesia (Federated States of), Nauru, Palau, Papua New Guinea, Samoa, São Tomé and Príncipe, Seychelles, Solomon Islands, St Kitts and Nevis, St Lucia, St Vincent and the Grenadines, Timor-Leste, Tonga, Trinidad and Tobago, Tuvalu and Vanuatu.[2]

The developmental state of SIDS is discussed extensively in the literature.[3] SIDS face similar development challenges, as other developing countries, in promoting sustainable development and eradicating poverty amid growing populations. SIDS are island countries, with mostly small population, surrounded by large oceans and seas which tends to isolate and insulate them from the wider world and with narrow based of commodity and/or services economy. They have high levels of economic dependency, a narrow terrestrial natural resource base, are subject to environmental and climatic vulnerability, and as sea-locked countries they are remotely located from their major markets. All these impose formidable constraints on their capacities and capabilities to manage their development.

SIDS are not homogenous and have diverse economic structures. For example, certain SIDS possess natural resource or commodities driven economies – such as Trinidad and Tobago, Papua New Guinea and Nauru which rely heavily on oil, gas, phosphate, timber and fish exports. Others are more services oriented – such as Barbados, Saint Lucia and Seychelles which rely heavily on services exports including tourism and financial services. Others such as Fiji and Tonga are highly dependent on migrants' remittances as many of their citizens work abroad. Many SIDS face a generally high level of migration of citizens with training and skills, and this has implications for addressing their development challenges, including that of harnessing the potential of the blue economy.

For SIDS, their surrounding oceans constitutes a much larger geographic area than their land area, thus offering potentially wider development opportunities beyond the limits imposed by their small land mass. The ocean space available to SIDS, or for that matter many coastal countries, is defined by their territorial waters and exclusive economic zones (EEZs) under the United Nations Convention on the Law of the Seas (UNCLOS).[4] An EEZ is the sea area over which a State has exclusive rights regarding the exploration and use of marine resources. It stretches from the baseline out to 200 nautical miles from the country's coast.

The EEZs of SIDS is estimated to represent about 30% of all oceans and seas.[5] The EEZs of these countries exceed by far the SIDS total terrestrial space in all cases. For example, the Bahamas has an EEZ of an estimated 629,292 sq km compared to a land area of 13,942 sq km. Additionally, several SIDS have submitted requests for an extended continental shelf surface area which would further increase the development potential of their oceans. These include, for example, Barbados, the Federated States of Micronesia, Mauritius, Palau, Papua New Guinea, Solomon Islands, and Seychelles (UNEP-GRID, 2009).

The special development circumstances of SIDS have led to the creation of a SIDS work programme in the UN development system and other international organizations. Recognition of SIDS' special development circumstance is also seen in international diplomacy and in inter-governmental processes where SIDS have issues of common interest such as in negotiations on climate change through the Conference of the Parties (COP) of the United Nations Framework Convention on Climate Change (UNFCCC) and multilateral trade negotiations in the World Trade Organization (WTO). Within the broader context of the United Nations Sustainable Development Agenda, SIDS collectively played a significant role in securing a standalone outcome on oceans. This is an issue of not only developmental significance but also of existential significance to SIDS.

SIDS have been particularly strong in articulating negotiating positions that focus international attention on their development concerns. For example, in global negotiations on the SDGs under the UN General Assembly, focus was placed on the economic importance of oceans to their economies. The inclusion of an oceans goal in the SDGs could not have been possible without the strong and persistent involvement of SIDS.

4 The ocean economy for SIDS

In implementing and realizing the SDGs, SIDS must identify, develop and sustain dynamic economic sectors that can be developed locally and sustainably, and produce goods and services that can be traded nationally, regionally and internationally to stimulate growth, create decent jobs and provide alternative sources of income, as well as secure development of SIDS, while preserving and protecting their fragile terrestrial and marine ecosystems. In this search for new avenues for growth, the ocean space stands out, to a large extent, due to the previous lack of attention accorded to its potential, which some have referred to as 'sea-blindness'.

The ocean or blue economy

The ocean economy, or the blue economy, is a relatively new economic concept and approach to sustainable development[6] and as such many countries including some SIDS are not yet fully sensitized to the concept or its implication. There is also no internationally agreed definition of an ocean or blue economy. One of the first references to the concept of economic use of oceans in a sustainable manner was in 2007 as 'living with the ocean and from the ocean in a sustainable relationship' that generates prosperity (Behnam, 2013). In 2010 Gunter Pauli's book on 'The Blue Economy: 10 years, 100 innovations, 100 million jobs' articulated further the potential contribution of the oceans economy to sustainable development as opposed to a conventional economy or in addition to a green economy (Pauli, 2010).

For some the blue economy is a subset of, and complement to, the green economy concept that came to the fore of international attention at the Rio+20 UN Conference on Sustainable Development (see Onguglo and Vivas Eugui, 2014; Economist Intelligence Unit, 2015). Other definitions specify that blue growth decouples socio-economic growth based on marine resources from environmental and ecosystem degradation associated with oceans, coining the notion of promoting ocean-based economic growth while maintaining healthy and resilient oceans (World Bank and United Nations, 2017; FAO Blue Growth Initiative). The term 'blue' signifies both the oceans (waters) and the sustainable management of ocean resources just as the term 'green' signifies the earth (land) and the environmentally friendly management of earth's resources.

The common feature of the various definitions of the blue economy is the sustainable use of marine resources to promote economic growth. In this perspective, the ocean, and in particular the EEZs in the case of SIDS, constitute an economic resource that is under-utilized relative to its full potential. Moreover, given the limited land area of many small island states, the ocean presents a unique opportunity to sustainably scale-up economic output. Island and coastal States, can therefore approach marine resources as a new development frontier.

For Small Island States, the ocean economy provides the platform for a paradigm shift in development philosophy. Transitioning from the limits of smallness, isolation and dependency, to a paradigm of substantial size based on the geographical area of their oceans and the value locked within. This new perspective was articulated by Jean-Paul Adam, Minister of Finance, Trade and Blue Economy of Seychelles, in the following terms: 'While we may be small in terms of landmass and population, when you look at the ocean we are a very big country.'[7]

This novel view of 'Small Island' States as 'Large Ocean' States signals a new approach to development that encourages SIDS to take ownership on their own development, and mobilize the financial resources, skills and institutions to promote sustainable development by harnessing resources available to them on and under their seas. As articulated by Onguglo and Vivas Eugui (2015), for SIDS, the ocean economy is premised on expanding the economic, production and trade frontiers beyond their land territories to encompassing their oceans-based marine environment, related biodiversity, ecosystems, species and genetic resources including marine living organisms (from fish and algae to micro-organisms) and mineral resources in the seabed, while ensuring their sustainable use and conservation.

UNCTAD has proposed an ocean economic space approach that can provide an avenue to SIDS for the co-management and co-benefit sharing of joint marine resources. The approach seeks to combine national EEZs into regionally integrated ocean spaces that allow more economic opportunities under regional cooperation schemes. This concept of enlarged economic spaces through combing EEZs becomes a truly monumental step forward for small economies, although matters relating to ceding of national sovereignty has and can be a major hurdle. This approach is also in step with current efforts, in response to continuing difficult international economic environment, by many developing countries with small economies, to build and strengthen regional economic spaces in the form of economically integrated markets or free trade areas and customs unions. SIDS are already involved in many such efforts as part of their broader development strategies, such as evidenced by the Caribbean Community (CAR-ICOM), Indian Ocean Commission (IOC), and the Pacific Islands Forum (PIF). There are also attempts to pool the management and development of economic zones through zone based management techniques such as Marine Spatial Planning (MSPs). The ocean economic space is another logical aspect of the formation of new regional growth poles.

Within such regional economic groupings, SIDS can combine and consolidate their oceanic economic space bearing in mind the hurdle of national sovereignty as noted above. Resources could be pooled under cross-sectoral or sectoral oceans regulatory and institutional frameworks at the regional level. These can be particularly relevant when:

- The EEZs are connected;
- Capital or knowledge in any one country alone in the region is not adequate to ensure commercial oceans resource exploitation;
- There is a need for common infrastructure when countries share common migratory species flows or seaways;
- There is a need to sustainably manage common living and non-living resources;
- There is a need for regional coordination as there are too many national authorities involved with limited capacity to monitor and implement policies;
- There are no linkages between public authorities managing the oceans resources, like fisheries, and those authorities responsible for trading in these same resources.

Recent studies as noted below indicate that the oceans economy could provide a huge stimulus to sustainable economic growth and extend the frontiers of development. It is timely to view the consideration of the oceans economy as an extension of the frontier of development towards marine based sectors, derived from living resources, non-living resources, marine biodiversity and ecosystems, the seas as transportation routes, and ocean conservation and resilience (see Table 27.1).

A recent study (OECD, 2016) estimates that the ocean economy offers high potential for ocean-based industries. It conservatively values the ocean economy value added output in 2010 at US$1.3 trillion which is about 2.5% of world gross value added, with an employment level of 31 million jobs. It further estimates that this contribution to world gross value added would double to over US$3 trillion between 2010 and 2030 (see Figure 27.1), and provide over 40 million full time jobs, under a business as usual scenario. The industries sustaining this growth are expected to be marine aquaculture, offshore wind energy, fish processing, shipbuilding and repair and port activities. Ecosystem services could further expand the expected benefits.

Another study the World Wildlife Fund (Hoegh-Guldberg, 2015) conservatively estimates the value of goods and services from oceans is about US$2.5 trillion annually and its long-term asset value is worth US$24 trillion, which is far larger than any of the largest sovereign wealth funds. Thus ocean-based economies like SIDS could benefit from such huge growth potential in ocean-based sectors by 2030 and beyond.

National and regional ocean economy strategies

A review of current and proposed ocean economy policies at national and regional levels shows that few strategies have actually been adopted and that many existing blue economy initiatives operate without an overall policy framework. Only a few coastal States, including some SIDS, have actually started to investigate, analyze, elaborate and implement national and regional policies for the conservation and sustainable use of the oceans and seas and their resources.

Table 27.1 Components of the blue economy

Type of activity	Activity sub-categories	Related industries/sectors	Drivers of growth
Harvesting and trade of marine living resources	Seafood harvesting	Fisheries (primary fish production)	Demand for food and nutrition
		Secondary fisheries related activities (e.g. processing, net and gear making, ice production and supply, boat construction and maintenance, manufacturing of fish- processing equipment, packaging, marketing and distribution)	Demand for food and nutrition
		Trade of seafood products	Demand for food, nutrition and protein
		Trade of non-edible seafood products	Demand for cosmetic, pet and pharmaceutical products
		Aquaculture	Demand for food, nutrition and protein
	Usage of marine living resources for pharmaceuticals and chemicals	Marine biotechnology and bioprospecting	R&D and usage for healthcare, cosmetic, enzyme, nutraceutical and other industries
Extraction and use of marine non-living resources and use of renewable, non-exhaustible natural forces (wind, wave and tide energy)	Extraction of minerals	(Seabed) mining	Demand for minerals
	Extraction of energy sources	Oil and gas	Demand for (alternative) energy sources
	Generation of (off-shore) renewable energy	Renewables	
	Fresh water generation	Desalination	Demand for fresh water

Type of activity	Activity sub-categories	Related industries/sectors	Drivers of growth
Commerce and trade in and around the oceans	Transport and trade	Shipping and shipbuilding; Maritime transport; Ports and related services	Growth in seaborne trade; transport demand; international regulations, maritime transport industries (shipbuilding, scrapping, registration, seafaring, port operations, etc.)
	Coastal development	National planning ministries and departments, private sector	Coastal urbanization, national regulations
	Tourism and recreation	National tourism authorities, private sector, other relevant sectors	Global growth of tourism
Ocean monitoring and surveillance	Land-, water-and air-based monitoring, control and surveillance activities	Technology and R&D	(Advancements in) R&D in ocean technologies
Coastal and marine area management, protection and restoration	Activities supporting carbon sequestration	National ministries and institutions, local communities	Growth in coastal and ocean protection and conservation activities
	Coastal and marine area management, protection and restoration activities	National ministries and institutions, local communities	National sustainable strategies
	Waste disposal management	Assimilation and sustainable disposal of nutrients and wastes	National sustainable strategies

Source: World Bank and United Nations (2017) and the Economist Intelligence Unit (2015).

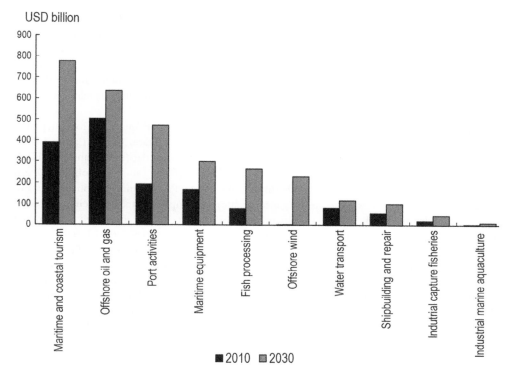

Figure 27.1 Overview of industry-specific value-added, 2010 and 2030
Source: OECD (2016), The Ocean Economy to 2030.

The ocean economy development paradigm is still in its infancy in terms of specific implementing strategies in most countries. While this is the case for cross-sectoral planning, at the sectoral level, such as fisheries, much work has been undertaken. It is also too early to point to concrete results of ocean economy policy frameworks, but a shift in mind-set towards a 'common oceans space' is starting to emerge and programmes have been developed that will achieve results in the years to come. Countries have traditionally focused on collective fisheries agreements for their common benefit. Such agreements could also be applicable to the management of other living and non-living ocean resources. Also SIDS would need to consider broader regional ocean agreements complementing national policies in order to sustainably manage the marine natural resources of their common ocean space and to bolster the basis for their economic development. Some blue economy strategies developed are considered below.

The European Union has a blue growth strategy which is part of its Integrated Maritime Policy based on the Limassol Declaration on an EU 'Marine and Maritime Agenda for growth and jobs', adopted in October 2012. This strategy involves, inter alia developing dynamic ocean sectors for jobs creation and economic growth including sustainable fisheries, aquaculture, coastal tourism, marine biotechnology, and tidal energy.

The African Union (AU) Heads of State and Government adopted in January 2014 the 2050 Africa Integrated Maritime (AIM) Strategy and Plan of Action based on the theme of 'Harnessing the Blue Economy in Achieving the African Union Agenda 2063'. The objective of strategy is 'to foster more wealth creation from Africa's oceans, seas and inland waterways by developing a thriving maritime economy and realizing the full potential of sea-based activities in an environmentally sustainable manner'. It focuses, inter alia, on fostering a Combined Exclusive Maritime Zone of Africa (CEMZA) as a key driver to benefit from Africa's integrated maritime space. Key areas covered include fisheries and aquaculture; environmental and biodiversity monitoring; marine tourism; disaster risk management; handling and shipment of hazardous materials and dangerous goods; maritime governance; flag State responsibility and port State control; and action to tackle illegal activities, including money laundering, piracy, maritime terrorism and human trafficking and smuggling by sea.

The Pacific Islands Regional Ocean Policy (PIROP), with its Framework for Integrated Strategic Action, was endorsed in 2002 comprising the member States of the Pacific Islands Forum and several Pacific island territories. The Framework for a Pacific Oceanscape (FPO, 2010), the Palau Declaration – the Ocean: Life and Future (2014), and the Pohnpei Ocean Statement – a Course to Sustainability (2016) all gave life to Pacific priorities on the oceans. The Palau Declaration stresses the convergence of efforts to improve the well-being of Pacific people through sustainable ocean management, and the need for 'integrated and mixed management approaches' which takes a holistic vision including jurisdictional rights, ocean governance, sustained action and adaptation to a rapidly changing environment.[8] Furthermore, the FPO called for a strengthening of the regional institutional framework for ocean governance and policy coordination by establishing a Pacific Ocean Commissioner (POC) to provide the necessary high level representation, ensure cooperation, and dedicated advocacy and attention to ocean priorities, decisions and processes at all levels. The POC is supported by the Office of the Pacific Ocean Commissioner (OPOC) which was set-up in late 2014. The Pohnpei Ocean Statement: A Course to Sustainability reinforced the coordinating role of the POC and calls on OPOC to provide the necessary technical, financial and administrative support to Pacific countries' implementation of SDG14.

The notion of a regional ocean governance policy for the Caribbean States, including among CARICOM and OCES member States, has been assessed and discussed for many years, and various projects and initiatives have been undertaken.[9] The scope of harnessing the oceans or blue economy has featured prominently in these discussions. The concrete elaboration and adoption of a policy to implement the concept remains outstanding.

National level ocean development strategies are being considered and/or embraced by a many SIDS however progress towards implementation remains uneven. Mauritius launched its first oceans economy roadmap in 2013, which seeks to take advantage of the immense economic potential of oceans.[10] The road-map places emphasis on the need to make use of the untapped value locked up in the EEZ by ensuring sustainable and coordinated utilization of living and non-living resources. Economic clusters or sectors of interest include seafood-related activities, seaport facilities and related services, and coastal tourism (UNCTAD, 2014).

In Seychelles, its Blue Economy Strategy[11] explicitly seeks to 'promote the sustainable and responsible fisheries development and optimization of the benefits from this sector for the present and future generations'. More specifically, it aims at maximizing revenue from fisheries and other related activities. The areas of intervention to advance these goals are: economic diversification, creation of high value jobs, ensuring food security, and the management and protection of the marine environment in a sustainable and responsible manner. Particular emphasis has been placed on small scale and artisanal fisheries.

In 2015, Cabo Verde adopted its Blue Growth Charter, aimed to support for sustainable growth in the marine and maritime sectors (FAO, 2016). The Charter targets key sectors, such as fishing and aquaculture, seafood value chains, marine and coastal tourism, scientific research, and responsible management of coastal areas and maritime transportation.

5 Exports of fish and fish products

Due to rapid global population growth, estimated at about 2.3% annually from 2015 to 2030, total food fish consumption demand could increase by 30% by 2030 (World Bank, FAO, IFPRI and AES, 2013) to about 144 million tons. While it is foreseen that the wild harvest of fish will remain relatively steady and could reach the 93 million tons annually, the gap in meeting the demand will be mostly filled by an augmentation of farmed fish production. This can potentially raise prices for 'wild marine' products and, as these become scarcer, they may become 'specialties' and value added exports.

Currently, exports of fish and fish products can contribute between 0.2 and 2.2% of gross domestic product (GDP) of different country groupings. SIDS and LDCs are the two country groups where the contribution to GDP of fisheries is highest. In the case of SIDS, the contribution of fish exports to GDP is 2.2% illustrating the key role these exports have for national income, foreign currency earnings, jobs and livelihoods (see Figure 27.2). This is almost four times more than in the next country grouping, the LDCs, where fish exports represent 0.6% of their GDP. In individual SIDS, fisheries can be even more important as they contribute to as much as 10% or more of GDP and may account for up to 90% of animal protein in their populations' diet, where national fish consumption can be as much as 4 times higher than the global per capita average (UNEP, UNDESA and FAO, 2012).

UNCTAD data demonstrate that in 2015 SIDS exports of fish products reached US$1.6 billion, some 6% of their total exports. When comparing fish and sea food exports to other food item exports, the former represent a significant 43% share (see Figure 27.3). Exports of fish and fish products have shown a growth rate of close to 20% over the last five years. The increase in exports has been mostly driven by an increase in fish demand in Asia. However, more recently the sustainability of these exports has become threatened by a variety of factors including illegal, unreported and unregulated (IUU) fishing, overfishing, unfair competition based on subsidies,

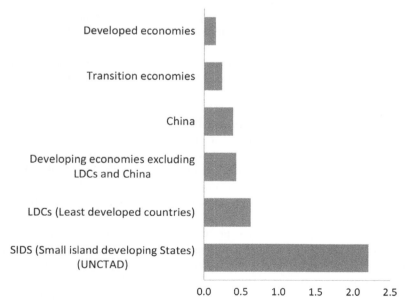

Figure 27.2 Exports of fish and fish products as a share of GDP, 2014
Source: UNCTAD (2017), see http://unctadstat.unctad.org/EN/.

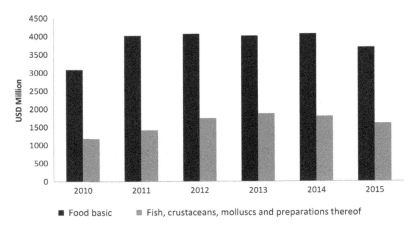

Figure 27.3 Export comparison: all basic food vs fish, crustaceans and molluscs and preparations by SIDS, 2010–2015
Source: UNCTAD (2017), see http://unctadstat.unctad.org/EN/.

climate change, micro-plastics, oceans acidification and pollution, and an increasing number of non-tariff measures (NTMs) in key markets.

When looking at the regional composition of SIDS exports during the period 2010–2015, approximately 70% of fish exports were destined for developed countries (see Table 27.2). Close to 26% went to developing countries while exports to other SIDS and LDCs were marginal. This illustrates the high reliance of SIDS on developed country markets for their fish exports, especially Japan and the EU. These tend to be well regulated markets with stringent compliance measures, especially owing to a variety of non-tariff measures (NTMs) including technical barriers to trade (TBT) and sanitary and phytosanitary (SPS) measures.

Currently, farmed fish account for 49% of global seafood consumption; and this share is expected to increase to 62% by 2030 (World Bank, 2013). Fish farming has greatly diversified over the past decade to now include not only fish but also crustaceans and molluscs, and algae among other marine species. Most aquaculture production is meant for human consumption, but there are also other uses such as aquariums, fashion inputs, animal feed, and production of pharmaceuticals and perfumes.

While disaggregated statistics specific to aquaculture for SIDS are not readily available, total aquaculture production in the Caribbean and Oceania (islands of the tropical South Pacific Ocean) together represented less than 1% of global aquaculture production in 2012 (FAO, 2012). SIDS in Oceania, led by Fiji, Papua New Guinea and Vanuatu, account for about 10% of the region's total aquaculture production. In all regions of the world including Africa and the Caribbean, aquaculture production is showing upward trends in order to meet a growing demand for fish. This is not the case in Oceania where its share of global production has declined in the last three years.

In terms of value addition, SIDS are exporting approximately US$100 million in fish fillets and fish preparations, to high-income countries (see Figure 27.4). This is encouraging and shows there is not only a market for raw fish and frozen fish but also for intermediate and final processed fish products. These latter two sets of products represent about 12% of total exports, which illustrates that there is a market for developing and exporting more value-added products by SIDS. For SIDS and small coastal economies this is a clear opportunity that needs to be consolidated, especially by setting appropriate policies to ensure that domestic

Table 27.2 Exports from SIDS: exports regional composition

	Developed			Developing			LDCs			SIDS		
	All food items	Basic food	Fisheries	All food items	Basic food	Fisheries	All food items	Basic food	Fisheries	All food items	Basic food	Fisheries
2010	70%	72%	74%	29%	28%	26%	2%	2%	1%	10%	8%	2%
2011	67%	69%	73%	33%	31%	27%	2%	2%	1%	9%	7%	1%
2012	70%	71%	75%	30%	28%	24%	2%	2%	1%	10%	8%	2%
2013	69%	71%	75%	30%	29%	25%	3%	2%	1%	11%	9%	3%
2014	69%	71%	74%	31%	29%	26%	2%	2%	1%	9%	8%	2%
2015	65%	67%	71%	34%	33%	26%	2%	2%	1%	11%	9%	2%

Source: UNCTAD (2017), see http://unctadstat.unctad.org/EN/.

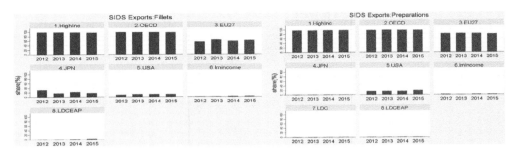

Figure 27.4 SIDS exports of fish fillets and preparations to main destinations
Source: UNCTAD (2017), based on FAO data (2017).

firms catch and process the fish domestically or regionally, using sustainable fishing and processing methods.

The economic importance of fisheries and seafood production for SIDS is undeniable. Expected growing demand and potentially higher prices for wild fish and for value added seafood products, especially in Asia, represent unique opportunities for SIDS. Most SIDS exports go to developed country markets that usually have more stringent market access conditions (unless there are preferences) as well as burdensome non-tariff measures.

With about 12% of value added fish exports in certain segments, there is ample scope for SIDS to move up in Global Value Chain integration by specializing in certain phases of the manufacturing process or by encouraging national and regional vertical integration, thus capturing more value locally. Some measures to develop the fisheries and seafood sector in SIDS could include the following:

1   fight against illegal, unreported and unregulated (IUU) fishing activities and ensure that illegal products do not reach markets;
2   develop local capacities to directly harvest fish and rely less on fish access agreements and consequential income;
3   engage in the WTO debate on fish subsidies to prohibit harmful subsidies while securing special and differential treatment for SIDS;
4   provide for the necessary infrastructure and finance for sustainable management of stocks;
5   determine capture limits where industrial fleets, so resources are also kept for local fishers and to sustain livelihoods;
6   address relevant market access barriers for SIDS;
7   make effective use of certification to secure a premium price and market access;
8   leverage the markets for the processing and canning of low-value but highly protein-based seafood.

6 The potential of Marine Genetic Resources for SIDS

The value of Marine Genetic Resources (MGRs)

Oceans and seas contain the largest portion of biodiversity on the planet for both macro-species (e.g. plants and animals) and microorganisms. Marine species have the longest evolutionary path of all life forms, compared with terrestrial species. The variety in marine biodiversity results from a widely diverse set of oceans habitats with varied temperature, sunlight, depth, currents, chemistry such as levels of acidity, and types of surrounding ecosystems where these lifeforms interact. The number of marine species has been estimated to range from 0.7 to 1 million of which about only 230,000 (less than a quarter) have been described in the taxonomic literature (Appeltans et al., 2012).

According to the Convention on Biological Diversity (CBD), genetic resources are defined as 'genetic material of actual or potential value'. This definition includes resources from any ecosystem, and it applies to all genetic resources whether from marine or terrestrial origin. The difference between marine and terrestrial genetic resources is basically the environment and ecosystem where species live and develop. While there are many macro-species in the oceans (from whales to algae), about 95% of all marine life is microscopic[12], showing where the lion share of interest in MGRs rests.

Living marine resources provide huge potential for developing new food, biochemical, pharmaceutical and cosmetic products, biomaterials, bioenergy applications, as well as pests control and fertilizers. About 18,000 natural products have been developed to date from about 4,800 marine organisms, and the number of natural products from marine species is growing at an annual rate of 4% (Global Oceans Commission, 2013). Moreover, the global market for marine biotechnology is projected to reach US$4.9 billion by 2018 (Global Industry Analysts Inc., 2013), driven by increased investments in marine biotechnology research and growing demand for natural marine ingredients due to changes in consumer preferences for the 'natural' products.

As an example, in 2011 there were over 36 marine delivered drugs in clinical development, including 15 with potential for cancer treatment (OECD, 2016). Among all MGRs, extremophiles have been considered as particularly interesting for the industry due to their particular capacity to survive and reproduce in extreme environments. This feature could translate into specific product applications, especially in biotechnology. Additionally, as the world reaches a ceiling in terms of wild capture fish of about 90 million tons (UNCTAD, 2015), it is expected and confirmed by current trends that in the near future gaps in supply will be filled by aquaculture development. Therefore, there will be important research and development needs on macro-species (and their genetics) in order to scale-up the development of the aquaculture.

Jurisdictional issues and applicable international law

Marine genetic resources are found throughout the oceans although species richness and diversity tend to be higher closer to the land and sea surface due to these areas having higher levels of photosynthesis and the interaction with coastal and terrestrial ecosystems among other factors. MGRs found within territorial waters, the EEZs (applicable to living organisms found in included waters, soils or subsoil) and in the extended continental shelf (only applicable to sedentary living species within the soil and subsoil) are subject to national jurisdiction of States (UNCLOS, Articles: 2, 56.1 and 77.4). States have full exclusive right to regulate, authorize and conduct marine scientific research in their territorial seas (UNCLOS, Article 245) under conditions they consider adequate and respecting international commitments.

In their EEZs, coastal States have sovereign right for the purpose of exploring, exploiting, conserving and managing the natural resources, whether living or non-living, of the waters superjacent to the seabed and in the seabed and its subsoil (UNCLOS, Article 56.1). Jurisdiction by States to regulate, authorize and conduct marine scientific research within their EEZs is explicitly mentioned in the UNCLOS (Article 56.2). However, this exclusive right is subject to a series of principles and obligations under UNCLOS. The most important in this regard is the obligation to grant, in normal circumstances, consent for marine scientific research projects by other States or competent international organizations to be carried out in accordance with this

Convention and exclusively for peaceful purposes and in order to increase scientific knowledge of the marine environment for the benefit of all mankind. Additionally, under UNCLOS, States shall introduce measures to protect and preserve the marine environment and conserve and manage living marine resources.

Activities in areas beyond national jurisdiction (ABNJ) have been mostly subject to general principles applicable to the high seas, the Area[13] and relevant authorities under UNCLOS. An important number of MGRs can be found in areas beyond national jurisdiction. Natural resources in the high seas tend to be considered as 'common heritage of mankind'. However, there is not yet full clarity on rights and conditions for access and use. Specialized access and benefit sharing (ABS) rules for marine resources in the high seas have not yet been developed (Arico and Salpin, 2005). Nevertheless, the UN Ad Hoc Open Ended Informal Working Group relating to the Conservation and Sustainable Use of Marine Biological Diversity is currently considering the issue in order to agree on a new international instrument under the UNCLOS framework[14]

Right to undertake marine scientific research

Under UNCLOS, all States have the right to conduct and promote marine scientific research. Such research is subject to the following principles (UNCLOS, Article 238 and 239):

1   it shall be conducted exclusively for peaceful purposes;
2   it shall be conducted with appropriate scientific methods and means compatible with this convention;
3   marine scientific research shall not unjustifiably interfere with other legitimate uses of the sea compatible with this convention;
4   marine scientific research shall be conducted in compliance with all relevant regulations adopted in conformity with UNCLOS (UNCLOS, Article 240).

Interestingly, according to the UNCLOS (Article 241), marine scientific research activities can not (underlined text by the authors) constitute a legal basis for any claim to 'any part of the marine environment or its resources'. This UNCLOS principle can have interesting implications vis-à-vis potential claims in patent applications for inventions based on MGRs. The potential scope of what is considered as 'resources' in this article is not entirely clear for the purposes of understanding potential implications for intellectual property, as there is no definition of resources in UNCLOS. However, when looking at the UNCLOS, for the purposes of assessing national jurisdiction, it clearly covers both living resources and non-living resources found territorial waters and EEZs, and it also applies to sedentary living species within the soil and subsoil of the extended continental shelf. It can also cover living resources as 'such' and 'to any part of the marine resources'. This principle may have important implications for patent applications based on marine research unless modifications or improvements in existing law are introduced.

A quick overview on the use of marine genetic resources in patent applications

The patents leading to inventions that have benefitted from direct or indirect use of MGRs in research and development have grown significantly over the past 10 years. Patents are an important indicator, but not the only one, for the use of MGRs in research and development. Usually, patent filing is the consequence of successful research and development. MGRs can be important inputs for research and development as terrestrial lifeforms have already been extensively studied over the centuries. This is not the case for marine species, which have only become the subject of serious scientific analysis less than a century ago.

According to Oldham *et al.* (2013) about 10,000 patents on MGRs have been published in peak years from 1976 to 2000. It is highly probable that most cases of access to and use of these resources may have not been granted by national authorities when falling within waters under national jurisdiction, probably leaving the patent applicant as the sole collector of benefits. This is confirmed by the fact that there are very few cases of Access and Benefit Sharing (ABS) contracts on genetic resources[15] and even less ABS laws specifically dealing with marine genetic resources.

A map produced in Oldham *et al.* (2013) shows the geographical origin of marine species used in patent applications over the past 10 years. This map gives an idea of the number of samples that have been used for marine bioprospecting and research and development globally. It shows that in most cases the geographical origin is close to coasts and almost certainly subject to the national jurisdiction of States. So far there is no clear evidence of many cases of legal access and benefit sharing on MGRs under these patents. This situation shows there are untapped sources of benefits for SIDS and coastal States and the potential space for research and value addition by SIDS.

A preliminary look at potential opportunities and challenges for SIDS

The oceans of many SIDS contain rich sources of MGRs for local and international R&D as well as related product development. The number of undiscovered species with unknown economic value potential in areas within national jurisdiction (territorial waters, EEZs and extended continental shelf) could be immense when looking at recent user trends. While there could also be a potential for SIDS in areas beyond national jurisdiction, due to their weak capacities to already regulate and make use of MGRs within national jurisdiction, they should focus on national jurisdiction in order to better capture the inherent value of such marine resources.

Capturing the value of genetic resources is not easy, whether from marine or terrestrial sources. While there is a widespread use of genetic resource among large companies worldwide, many businesses in large countries, especially in States that are not Parties to the CBD, have been particularly reluctant to disclose the origin, source of, and means of legal access to, genetic material used as inputs in their research, patent applications or in product development. Fully capturing this value can only be effectively done by regulating access to the resources in coordination with other biodiversity rich countries; by securing benefit sharing from foreign researchers and prospectors; and by undertaking direct research for practical applications that could respond to current and future needs of SIDS. The practical experience of many biodiversity rich countries trying to obtain monetary and non-monetary benefits from the use of biological resources illustrates that, when a national research centre or a university is involved in the ABS project or contracts, the technical bargaining capacity of the country is stronger and the benefits, especially non-monetary benefits, are much higher and can be better absorbed (Vivas Eugui, 2012).

In areas within national jurisdiction, conservation, access and use of MGRs is governed by the CBD and the Nagoya Protocol on Access to Genetic Resources and the Fair and Equitable Sharing of Benefits Arising from their Utilization (Nagoya Protocol) as well as by other relevant multilateral environmental agreements. At the national level, access and use is defined by national implementing Access and Benefit Sharing (ABS) regulations, and by other environmental laws and R&D regulations. Both SIDS policy makers and interested researchers and prospectors need to understand and internalize that not all MGRs are openly available and free for access and use. States have the right to regulate access and downstream use of MGRs within their national jurisdiction based on the objectives, principles and obligations under CBD and Nagoya Protocol. Users of MGRs within national jurisdiction have to obtain prior informed consent from competent national authorities and there must be mutually agreed terms on ABS of benefits arising from their use in complying with the CBD and Nagoya Protocol obligations.

Almost all SIDS are parties to the CBD and 12 SIDS have already ratified or acceded to the Nagoya Protocol.[16] Nevertheless, no small Island State has notified implementing legal, administrative or policy measures related to access and benefit sharing applicable to genetic resources, whether marine or terrestrial, to the CBD ABS clearing House mechanism.[17] This makes it difficult for SIDS to regulate scientific marine research or bio-prospecting activities or to obtain any benefits derived from their use, whether inland, in territorial waters or within their EEZs.

The implementation of CBD and Nagoya principles in the marine environment can prove to be challenging as it does not only require adequate ABS regulations but also the capacity to regulate, monitor and to understand R&D models. SIDS can engage in establishing a public policy framework to support potential economic development in marine bio-prospecting and ensure mutual benefits. There are not many specific laws dealing with ABS on MGRs as most countries cover both terrestrial and marine biodiversity in the ABS laws and regulations. However, some countries have specific rules. One salient example of a law specifically regulating marine bio-prospecting is the case of the Norwegian Marine Resource Act of 2009 (Frogner, 2009). It could serve as a model for legal ABS development for marine bio-prospecting in SIDS. Another example is Peru, which has assigned to the Ministry of Production exclusive competence on ABS for hydro-species (both on sea and fresh water)[18] as it also has competences on fisheries and aquaculture and can better respond to access requests in these sectors.

For SIDS to be in a better position to regulate and obtain benefits from MGRs, certain conditions need to be in place including the following:

1   mapping of the geographical areas, with biological value and list species with highest economic potential value;
2   consider how ABS measures can be designed to recognize and enhance the social, economic, ecological and cultural value of MGRs;
3   introduce a national ABS regulatory framework that can encompass the particularities of both terrestrial and marine genetic resources;
4   ensure integration of ABS measures in existing strategies for poverty alleviation, sustainable use and conservation of biodiversity, oceans/blue economy, R&D, local development and technology transfer, among other policies and policy goals;
5   consider dimensions and elements of R&D models in products derived from marine genetic resources, their biochemical, derivatives and biodiversity in general.

In sum, scientific marine research and bio-prospecting offer interesting opportunities for growth, benefit sharing, value addition and creation of scientific capacities in SIDS. MGRs within national jurisdiction are subject to a three-layer regime embodied in rights over territorial waters, EEZs and on the continental shelf. There are no examples of ABS laws notified by SIDS to the CBD ABS clearing House Mechanism that could regulate access and benefit sharing of genetic resources, whether marine or terrestrial. Hence introducing national or regional ABS laws and framework is essential in order for countries to be able to regulate access to, and use of, MGRs. There is a need for technical assistance to develop such national/regional ABS regulatory systems, especially on MGRs where the potential could be higher for SIDS. Partnerships to support the creation of regional regulatory and institutional ABS frameworks seem to be lacking.

7 Conclusions

SIDS face important climate, economic and geographical challenges and many of them are also large oceans States in terms of their vast ocean space and marine natural resources. These provide significant opportunities for these SIDS to harness and foster new development enhancing options that can provide a stable and dynamic source of income, growth and sustainable development. The ocean or blue economy however constitutes a new frontier of development that most SIDS have yet to fully explore and harness, without undermining environmental sustainability. Furthermore, the oceans blue/economy recognizes the economic opportunities in ocean-based sectors as well as the key stewardship role of SIDS as 'custodians' of large marine areas under their EEZs in the surrounding high seas. The notion of SIDS as 'great ocean states' means that attention should be paid to the role SIDS are playing, and must necessarily play in the conservation and preservation of the oceans and oceans resources (i.e. as stewards), and thus not just in regard to the sustainable use of marine resources. These two roles – conservation and preservation, and sustainable use – are the two 'intertwined aspects' of SDG14.

The 2030 Sustainable Development Agenda and SDG 14 in particular provides a wakeup call for SIDS and the international community to consider more fully the potential of the ocean economy in realizing economic growth and promoting prosperity of SIDS. Various sectors of the ocean economy can be galvanized to foster growth, economically diversify and add value, as shown by the discussion in this chapter on fish trade and marine genetic resources. Fish and sea food export can be harnessed to generate high levels of value addition and expand SIDS integration into seafood GVCs. MGRs can be better regulated and mainstreamed into national innovation systems so their significant value can be captured and potential for developing new foods, drugs and cosmetic products can be developed. Direct and in-direct links can also be strengthened between sustainable fish and seafood production and marine resources development with other oceans economy sectors with growth potential such as port services, tourism, food processing, and research and development.

To that end, national and regional oceans or blue economy strategies should be developed, as is being considered and implemented by a few countries. This is a nascent area despite the importance of oceans. Thus the particular attention of SIDS is required, drawing upon some initial steps in some countries, such as Mauritius and the Seychelles, and some regions that have done so. In this regard, templates provided by international organizations such as UNCTAD on the ocean economy can be used by SIDS and adapted to their specific localities and requirements.

Oceans will provide a setting within which SIDS can pursue their ambitions for economic transformation and welfare improvement, and strive to achieve the SDGs. There is hence a need for permanent advocacy on oceans to build up expertise, knowledge and support for ocean strategies. There is need to continue developing ocean ambassadors and experts that would possess the knowledge and skills needed to transform oceans into a formidable asset for sustainable development. There is a need to develop ocean or blue economy and trade strategies at national and regional levels by SIDS and coastal States to harness the inherent economic potential of oceans and marine resources for current and future generations.

An irony of sorts, is that while SIDS may be in reality, taking into account their expansive EEZs, i.e. great ocean States, they are severely handicapped in accessing and developing on a sustainable basis their huge potential marine resources by lack of skills, technology, capital and by the absence or weakness of institutional and regulatory frameworks. The chapter is a contribution to the necessary dialogue on remedying this.

SIDS governments and populations have been shaped by their unique development experiences and vulnerability, as expressed in their isolation and fragile nature, to be resilient, to appreciate community, good neighbourliness, to value people and nature, and to work in partnership with the international community. These experiences will help SIDS to carve out their destinies in moving ahead in promoting inclusive economic growth and sustainable development in what appears to be a difficult global economic period. In particular, putting into practice this notion of large ocean States is a unique and important opportunity for SIDS in the period ahead as they set their sails to navigate the vast seas and resources under these waters, to bring their populations to safe, secure, prosperous, resilient and sustainable shores.

Notes

1 The authors would like to thank Mr Ransford Smith, Former Deputy Secretary-General of the Commonwealth and Permanent Representative of Jamaica to the UN, and Mr Stephen Fevrier, Adviser, Office of the Pacific Commissioner and Mr Marco Fugazza, Economic Affairs Officer, UNCTAD for their comments on an earlier version of this paper. The views expressed here, however, are solely those of the authors and do not reflect the views of UNCTAD or the reviewers.
2 See http://unctad.org/en/pages/aldc/Small%20Island%20Developing%20States/UNCTAD%C2%B4s-unofficial-list-of-SIDS.aspx). In this chapter, the UNCTAD list is used when referring to SIDS.
3 See for example, UNCTAD, 2014. Santos-Paulino *et al.*, 2011; Soobramanien and Gosset, 2015.
4 www.un.org/depts/los/convention_agreements/texts/unclos/unclos_e.pdf/.
5 SIDS Global Business Network, *The ocean economy and SIDS*, https://sidsgbn.org/oceans/, accessed July 2017.
6 For a discussion on the concept of the blue economy and its operationalization see, for example, Economist Intelligence Unit (2015).
7 Reported in *The WorldFolio* (12 October 2016). See www.theworldfolio.com/news/blue-economy-pioneer-sets-global-example/4194/.
8 Statement by the Pacific Oceans Commissioner at the UN Oceans Conference.
9 See for example Patil *et al.* (2016).
10 Mauritius Prime Minister's Office (2013), 'The ocean economy: A Road Map for Mauritius'.
11 Commonwealth Secretariat and Government of Seychelles (2016), Seychelles Blue Economy Strategic Roadmap and Implementation. See http://thecommonwealth.org/project/seychelles-blue-economy-strategic-roadmap-and-implementation/.
12 UNDESA, 'The role of Oceans and Seas for our future: Expert Voices', www.un.org/development/desa/undesavoice/expert-voices/2017/01/30707.html/.
13 The Areas is defined as the seabed and ocean floor and subsoil thereof, beyond the limits of national jurisdiction (UNCLOS, Article 1).
14 Paragraph 162 of the Rio+20 outcome document: *The future we want*.
15 Only about 51 ABS contracts have been notified to the CBD Clearing House Mechanisms by four countries. See https://absch.cbd.int/search/nationalRecords?schema=absPermit (accessed April 2017).
16 This number applies only to the UNCTAD list of SIDS. It includes Antigua and Barbuda, Comoros, Fiji, the Marshall Islands, Mauritius, Federated States of Micronesia, Samoa, Sao Tome and Principe, Samoa, Seychelles, Togo and Vanuatu. For an updated list of Parties to the Nagoya Protocol see https://absch.cbd.int/countries/status/party (accessed April 2017).
17 See https://absch.cbd.int/.
18 Article 15(c) of the 'Reglamento de Acceso a los Recursos Genéticos de Perú (Resolución Ministerial N° 087–2008-MINAM del 31 de Diciembre del 2009)'.

References

Appeltans, W., Ahyong, S. T., Anderson, G., Angel, M. V., Artois, T., Bailly, N., Bamber, R., Barber, A., Bartsch, I., Berta, A. and Błażewicz-Paszkowycz, M. (2012). 'The magnitude of global marine species diversity'. *Current Biology*, 22(23): 2189–2202.

Arico, S. and Salpin, C. (2005). *Bioprospecting of genetic resources in the deep seabed: Scientific, legal and policy aspects*. Yokohama: United Nations University – Institute of Advanced Studies.

Behnam, A. (2013). *Tracing the blue economy*. Malta: Fondation de Malte.

Economist Intelligence Unit (2015). The blue economy: Growth, opportunity and a sustainable ocean economy. An Economist Intelligence Unit briefing paper for the World Ocean Summit 2015.

FAO (2012). *State of World Fisheries and Aquaculture*. Rome: FAO.

FAO (2016). *Cabo Verde and FAO: partnering for resilience and sustainable rural development*. Rome: FAO.

Frogner, D. (2009) *The Norwegian Marine Resources Act*. Norway: Ministry of Fisheries and Coastal Affair.

Global Industry Analysts Inc. (2013). *Marine Biotechnology – A Global Strategic Business Report*. San Jose, CA: Global Industry Analysts Inc.

Global Oceans Commission (2013). Bioprospecting and marine genetic resources in the high seas. *Policy Options Paper 4*. Oxford: Global Oceans Commission.

Hoegh-Guldberg, O. (2015). *Reviving the Ocean Economy: the case for action – 2015*. Switzerland: WWF.

OECD (2016). *The Ocean Economy in 2030*. Paris: OECD Publishing.

Oldham, P., Hall, S. and Barnes, C. (2013). *Marine Genetic Resources in Patent Data*. New York: United Nations University and One World Analytics.

Onguglo, B. and Vivas Eugui, D. (2014). 'The Oceans Economy for Small Island Developing States'. In *Commonwealth Trade Hot Topics*, No. 110. London: Commonwealth Secretariat.

Onguglo, B. and Vivas Eugui, D. (2015). The Ocean Economy and Small Island Developing States: Oceans and Seas Matter for Sustainable. *Ministers Reference Book Commonwealth 2015*: 126–128.

Patil, P.G., Virdin, J., Diez, S. M., Roberts, J., Singh, A. (2016). *Toward A Blue Economy: A Promise for Sustainable Growth in the Caribbean: An Overview*. Washington, DC: The World Bank.

Pauli, G. (2010). *The Blue economy: 10 years, 100 innovations, 100 million jobs: A report to the Club of Rome*. Taos, NM: Paradigm Publications.

Santos-Paulino, A. U., McGillivray, M. and Naudé, W. (2011). *Understanding Small-Island Developing States: Fragility and External Shocks*. New York: Routledge.

Soobramanien, T. Y. and Gosset, L. (2015). *Small States in the Multilateral Trading System*. London: Commonwealth Secretariat.

UNCTAD (2015). *Sustainable Fisheries: International Trade, Trade Policy and Regulatory Issues*. Geneva and New York: United Nations.

UNCTAD (2014). *The Ocean Economy: Opportunities and Challenges for Small Island Developing States*. Geneva and New York: United Nations.

UNEP-GRID (2009). *Continental Shelf: The Last Maritime Zone*. UNEP/GRID-Arendal.

UNEP, UNDESA and FAO (2012). *SIDS-FOCUSED Green Economy: An Analysis of Challenges and Opportunities*. United Nations Environment Programme.

Vivas Eugui, D. (2012). Bridging the Gap on Intellectual Property and Genetic Resources in WIPO's Intergovernmental Committee (IGC). *Issue Paper* No. 34. International Centre for Trade and Sustainable Development (ICTSD).

World Bank, FAO, IFPRI and AES (2013). Fish to 2030: Prospects for Fisheries and Aquaculture. *World Bank Report* Number 83177-GLB.

World Bank and the United Nations (2017). *The Potential of the Blue Economy: Increasing Long-term Benefits of the Sustainable Use of Marine Resources for Small Island Developing States and Coastal Least Developed Countries*. Washington, DC: World Bank.

28

The fiscal consequences of natural disasters: does country size matter?

Reginald Darius, Travis Mitchell, Sanjana Zaman and Charumathi Raja

1 Introduction

The few studies assessing the fiscal consequences of natural disasters suggest that natural disasters induce a pro-cyclical fiscal response in developing countries, and conversely, a countercyclical fiscal response in advanced countries, respectively. These results are intuitive. Countries with higher incomes usually have stronger institutions, and are better able to preserve a desirable level of fiscal space. On the other hand, in lower-income countries, preserving fiscal space tends to be more difficult, given the political costs of decreasing development spending and other key expenditures. Additionally, automatic stabilizers in low-income countries are often weak, and may sometimes be non-existent.

The general finding that developing countries respond pro-cyclically to shocks is worth further investigation. There exist a substantive body of literature which alludes to the significant disadvantage of small size to developing countries (Commonwealth Secretariat, 2013; Briguglio, 1995; Alesina and Spoalare, 1997; Easterly and Rebelo, 1993; Streeten, 1993; Milner and Westaway, 1993), and giving reason to believe that fiscal policy may be impacted more acutely by disasters occurring in smaller states.

Small states suffer from higher institutional costs on average, due primarily to their smaller populations. Output is hampered by economies of scale constraints and is highly volatile (IMF 2013; 2015; 2016), whilst locations of small states render them disproportionately susceptible to the impact of natural disasters. Consequently, there is high volatility in revenue collections, and expenditures are highly rigid. Together, these factors seem to suggests that the likelihood of pro-cyclicality in fiscal policy following natural disaster shocks, should be higher in smaller states.

To test whether country size is an important determinant of the impact of natural disasters on fiscal policy, this paper distinguishes between small and large countries, and controls for countries' levels of income. This is partially accomplished by restricting the sample to developing countries. Developed countries are high income, so drawing a distinction between large and smaller developed countries, or between large developed and small developing countries is less interesting in this context. The average income difference between developed and developing countries is relatively substantial. In comparison, developing countries have income levels that are much closer in magnitude, so that the role of income in distinguishing the difference in impact from disasters in larger and smaller developing countries is less pronounced. This could explain why empirical studies have found income to be a delineating factor with regard to the fiscal impact of disasters, as measured in developed and developing economies.

Beyond the question of size, the paper adds to the limited number of papers exploring the fiscal consequences of natural disasters. As commented by Noy and Nualsri (2011), it is surprising that there has not been much work investigating the topic. Natural disasters are said to represent one of the greatest risks to the future development of small states, especially in the context of climate change. With the tax bases in these countries already narrow, exogenous shocks to output and revenue could have deleterious fiscal effects.

Acevedo (2016) attributes the dearth of research on the topic to the absence of readily available disaster data. The recent development of EM-DAT – the world's most comprehensive disaster database has provided a unique set of disaster data for empirical analysis.[1] Following the introduction of EM-DAT, research on disasters has increased, with the bulk of it focusing on natural disasters' impact on growth, and on the differential impact of disasters on advanced and developing countries (see Cavallo and Noy, 2009; Crespo Cuaresma et al., 2008; Noy, 2009; and Skidmore and Toya, 2002).

Using this data and the panel vector autoregression framework developed by Noy and Nualsri (2011), the paper seeks to analyze the impact of natural disasters on fiscal policy in large and small developing countries. However, this paper extends the analysis beyond the impact on aggregate fiscal policy and explores the impact of disasters on individual revenue and expenditure components, in order to better understand differences in the fiscal impact of disasters.

The remainder of the paper is organized as follows: Section 2 reviews the literature on fiscal policy and the impact of natural disasters. In Section 2, the data is discussed and the paper takes an initial look at the above questions via a preliminary data analysis. The main results are presented and discussed in Section 3, where the panel vector autoregressive approach is briefly presented. Policy conclusions are provided in Section 5.

2 Literature review

Noy and Nualsri (2011) estimated the fiscal consequences of natural disasters for a large panel of countries. Their results suggest that in the aftermath of natural disasters, developed countries adopt counter-cyclical policies while developing countries adopt a pro-cyclical stance. They also conclude that the pro-cyclical fiscal dynamics are likely to worsen the adverse consequences of natural disasters on middle- and low-income countries.

In exploring the implications of large scale extreme weather events on fiscal policies, Lis and Nickel (2009) estimate that such events have a budgetary impact ranging between 0.23% and 1.1% of GDP, depending on the country group. The authors show that developing countries, particularly those near the equator, face a much larger effect on budget balances following an extreme weather event, than do advanced economies. As a consequence, Lis and Nickel (2009) recommend maintaining sound fiscal positions in developing countries, given that climate change is expected to cause an increase in the frequency and severity of natural disasters. Raddatz (2009) also shows that smaller and poorer countries are more vulnerable to climatic shocks.

Melecky and Raddatz (2011) dissected the fiscal impact into the impact on revenue and expenditures. Specifically, they estimate the impact of geological, climatic, and other types of natural disasters on government expenditures and revenues for high and middle-income countries. They also find that natural disasters have a significant negative impact on the fiscal position. This is driven in particular by a fall in revenue collections due to negative output effects, a phenomenon which they conclude is highly prevalent in lower-middle-income countries. These authors also explore whether having elevated government debt increases the fiscal impact. Their results suggest that disasters do not generate larger changes in the deficit or higher output declines in countries with elevated initial government debt. Additionally, in terms of output declines, they find that countries with more developed financial or insurance markets suffer less from disasters.

Fidrmuc *et al.* (2016) analyze the fiscal consequences of an exogenous fiscal shock for the United States, as identified by natural disasters. The author uncovers a hump-shaped increase in government expenditure which peaks in the second year and remains significantly positive for 10 years. In addition, he illustrates that revenue increases on impact, peaking during the first year before income increases. This the author suggests demonstrates that the post-disaster increase in revenue is not from an increase in taxes (or borrowing) but emanates from federal transfers to the local government.[2]

Regarding the broader impact of natural disaster shocks related to the resulting effects from fiscal and non-fiscal reactions, Noy (2009) shows that natural disaster impacts are less pronounced in countries that have a higher literacy rate, better institutions, higher per capita income, higher degree of openness to trade, higher levels of government spending, more foreign reserves and higher levels of domestic credit.

Skidmore and Toya (2002) suggest that a higher frequency of natural disasters is associated with higher growth rates in the long-run. This they term creative destructions – the case where older physical assets and technologies tend to be more prone to destruction during natural disasters, and therefore more likely to be replaced by more advanced assets and technologies.

3 Data and stylized facts

In this paper, small states are as defined by the Commonwealth Secretariat and the World Bank criterion which sets a population ceiling of 1.5 million. The chapter makes exceptions for Jamaica, Lesotho, Namibia and Papua New Guinea, who share similar characteristics with small states but have larger populations. Small states are compared with larger developing and emerging countries, for which data is readily available. Conflict affected states are excluded from the large developing country dataset, termed 'larger countries'. In total, the study sample comprises 53 countries, of which 22 are small states.[3] Data on disasters and a range of fiscal and control variables are analyzed over the period 1972 to 2014 for the two country categories.

Data on natural disasters are derived from EM-DAT, the most comprehensive and reliable disaster database. In particular, the disaster data encompass damages from storms, floods, earthquakes, extreme temperatures, landslides and wild fires, which are aggregated and expressed as a percentage of GDP. The data is fairly reliable for the period under review. However, it is worthwhile to note its shortcomings. EM-DAT may underreport the number of disasters because of (i) inadequate recording coverage prior to 1988 and (ii) elimination of events that do not satisfy the threshold for classification of a natural disaster. In the EM-DAT database to be recorded as a natural disaster requires at least 100 people affected, at least 10 people killed, or a state of emergency declared. Further, disaster damages may also be underreported (Acevedo, 2016).

The fiscal impact of natural disasters is assessed on the basis of changes in the overall primary balance, total revenue, total expenditure and their individual components.[4] To control for other fiscal influences, a set of control variables are included, namely the degree of openness, the external debt to GDP ratio and real gross GDP. Openness is measured as the total of exports and imports of goods and services to nominal GDP. External debt is used in place of central government debt to proxy resource constraints, primarily because of the non-stationarity of the

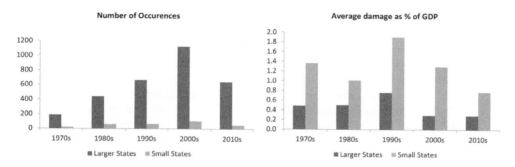

Figure 28.1 Frequency and damage from natural disasters by decades
Source: The CRED/OFDA International Disaster Database (EM-DAT) (developing countries only).

central government debt to GDP ratio. The sources and descriptions of the data set is detailed in Appendix 2.

Trends in the disaster data are depicted in Figure 28.1 for smaller and larger states. For in the period under consideration, the frequency of disasters in both small and larger developing countries increased steadily during the first four decades, before dipping in 2010. In absolute terms, larger developing countries experience a much greater number of natural disaster events. This reflects the rarity of events such as landslides, wild fires, and extreme temperatures in smaller developing countries.

Damages from natural disasters measured as a ratio to GDP were highest in the 1990s but displayed a more random trend, particularly in small countries. In contrast, despite the higher frequency of disasters in larger developing countries, damages from disasters were approximately three times larger in small states. The relative impact of storms, which are much more frequent in small states (Figure 28.2), probably accounts for the difference between the frequency of and damage from natural disasters.[5]

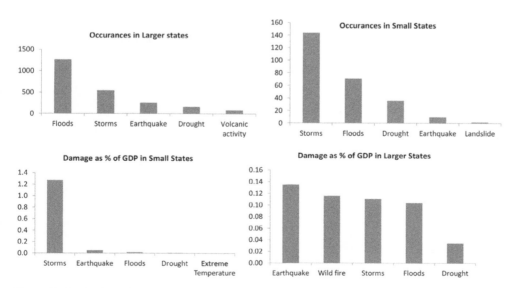

Figure 28.2 Number of occurrences and damage as % of GDP
Source: The CRED/OFDA International Disaster Database (EM-DAT) (developing countries only).

Comparing the occurrence of the different types of natural disasters, storms and floods appear more frequent in both small and large countries, but floods are more consistent in the latter. The third most frequent disaster in small states is drought. Whereas earthquakes are the next most frequent in larger developing countries. In terms of damages, small states' costs are largely due to storms, whereas earthquakes, and similarly: wild fires, storms and floods, all have almost equal impact in larger states, when assessed as a ratio to GDP (Figure 28.2).

Figure 28.3 depicts natural disaster effects on total expenditure and total revenues as a percent of GDP for small and large developing countries. Note, while caution should be exercised in using this type of analysis to assess the effects of natural disaster shocks, the figure suggests that variations in revenue and expenditure in small states, post disasters, are larger in small states compared to that recorded for larger countries. This signals a larger voluntary or involuntary shift in small states fiscal policy, post disaster.[6] Also worthy of note is that the majority of variation seems to be in government expenditures, which appears to increase in the aftermath of disasters. In larger states, with the exception of a few outliers, the impact on revenue and expenditure seems fairly negligible.

Note: The 45-degree line represents zero change in revenues and expenditures. Values to the left of the line represent a contraction post-disaster, while values to the right of the line signify and increase. The figures on the vertical and horizontal axes indicate the specific changes.

In Figure 28.4, total revenue and expenditures are further disaggregated. The data suggests that in small states, the larger post-disaster variation in revenues and expenditures is underpinned by deviations in subsidies and transfers, goods and services revenue, grants, and taxes on trade. In larger states, there is similar but smaller movements in these categories, with the exception of goods and services tax and grants.

The stylized facts support the view that the impact from natural disasters on smaller states is more substantial. However, as to the shape of the resulting fiscal policy, the analysis is somewhat inconclusive. There is hardly any variation in revenue and expenditure balances in larger developing countries, during the year following a natural disaster. And whereas one would expect a fall in revenue and output contraction, revenues in small states appear stable on average.

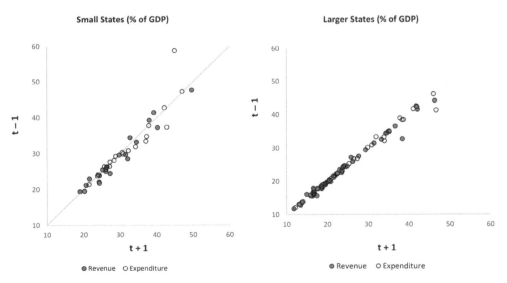

Figure 28.3 Expenditure and revenue post-disaster changes (% of GDP)

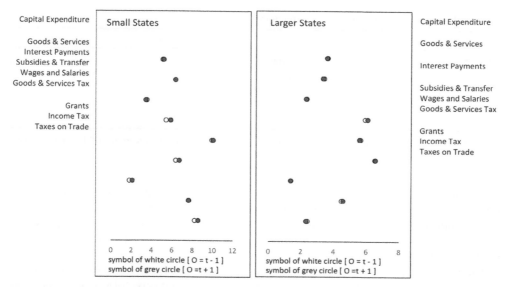

Figure 28.4 Expenditure and revenue components (% of GDP)
Source: World Development Indicators and the IMF World Economic Outlook.

4 Response of fiscal policy to natural disaster shocks

The impact of natural disaster shocks on fiscal policy

The empirical analysis presented in this section is based on panel vector autoregressions (PVAR). A panel framework is useful given existing data gaps, particularly within the small states' fiscal data set. The vector autoregressive component of the methodology allows for feedback between variables. For example, whilst GDP growth will have an effect on the primary balance, growth will simultaneously be affected by changes in fiscal policy. Accounting for these feedback effects increases confidence that the observed changes in revenues and expenditures are net effects, and not driven by the business cycle, other external disturbances or public sector credit constraints, for example. These controls are represented in the model by the trade openness and external debt variables (see Tanzi (1998) and Halland and Bleaney (2011)), respectively. The only variable in the model treated as purely exogenous is damage from natural disasters. Details of the PVAR models are summarized in Appendix 3.

The model is estimated to assess changes in (a) the primary balance, (b) total revenue, and (c) total expenditure due to shocks from natural disasters. The impulse responses from these regression exercises are presented in Appendix 5. Cumulative responses calculated from the impulse responses are discussed in the text below.

Benchmark model: the primary fiscal balance

The benchmark model captures the reaction of the primary fiscal balance to natural disaster shocks, controlling for the business cycle and government's credit constraints. Benchmark models are estimated for small states and for larger developing countries, respectively. The results from these estimations are presented in Figures 28.A1–28.A3 of Appendix 5.

Table 28.1 Five-year cumulative shocks on the primary fiscal balance*

Model	Variables	Small states	Larger states
Benchmark model	International trade	1.90	1.21
	External debt	1.26	0.05
	Gross output	1.00	1.00
	Primary balance	5.07	−1.54

Note: * Variables are estimated in real values but in Table 28.1 are all expressed as a ratio to GDP for easier comparability. Therefore, the cumulative output change is normalized to 1.

The model estimates suggest that natural disaster shocks invoke different fiscal responses. This is reflected more clearly in the five-year cumulative response estimates presented in Table 28.1. Here cumulative responses are the sum of variable estimates from time t to t+1, expressed as ratios to GDP. A negative cumulative fiscal estimate reflects a pro-cyclical response, whilst a positive estimate signals a countercyclical fiscal reaction.

The results suggest that small states react pro-cyclically, whilst larger countries respond in a countercyclical fashion.[7] Of note, the improvement in the primary balance in small states extends over two years, before reaching a small surplus position. In contrast, larger countries generate a comparably weaker countercyclical response which occurs in year one, and which is fully dissipated in one period. These results indicate a greater and more sustained impact on smaller states' fiscal balances, reflected in the size of the required fiscal contraction vis-a-vis the fiscal expansion in larger countries.

Output growth in small states stagnates immediately following disasters, but expands fairly rapidly in the large country case (as shown in Figures 28.A1 and 28.A2 of Appendix 5). These growth effects both dissipate at year 5. Despite growth's stagnation in the aftermath of disaster shocks, a reduction in the external debt to GDP ratio is observed. This supports the observed large fiscal retrenchment. In the case of larger states, external debt remains fairly benign but there is a v-shaped swing in the traded sectors, captured by the change in the degree of openness.

As Figure 28.2 indicates, larger developing country damages stem from various types of disasters, including earthquakes and wild fires, in addition to storms and floods. It suggests that the impact of disasters on main exports such as agriculture and commodities would be relatively more affected than in small states, which suffer almost solely from the impact of storms. The quick rebound is probably due to these countries countercyclical response. In contrast, the fiscal contraction in small states corresponds with a marginal improvement in their traded sectors, a result that is likely to be underpinned by a contraction in imports.

Revenue and expenditure changes

The fiscal impact on revenues and expenditures is estimated by way of a disaggregation of the primary fiscal balance into revenue and expenditures, and their respective individual components. These are regressed against disaster shocks and the control variables. Revenue and expenditure, and component effects, are estimated separately due to sample size. The impulse responses from these models are presented in Figures 28.A3–28.A6 for small and larger developing countries, respectively.

The estimates from these models corroborate the results in the benchmark models. In the case of small states, the pro-cyclical response is induced both by a reduction in expenditure and a decrease in revenue in the year following a natural disaster. This initial contraction in spending falls mainly on public investment and transfers and subsidies. An outcome which likely reflects small states' liquidity constraints and limited fiscal buffers. The fall in capital expenditure in small states could also reflect capacity constraints for engineering works, project design and implementation for the significant reconstruction effort required.

However, there is a relatively rapid reversal in the path of expenditure and revenues. This is reflected in a relatively sharp increase in expenditure, and a large and sustained increase in revenues, post disaster. It would appear therefore, that tax increases are used to finance the fiscal response.

The rise in expenditure in year 2 is fuelled in large part by a steep increase in wages and salaries, and to a lesser extent by increases in goods and services, and interest expenditure. The rise in wages and salaries possibly reflects hired help to assist with clean up and reconstruction efforts, or government attempts to stimulate growth via short-term employment programmes.

The large state countercyclical response is facilitated via an increase in expenditure. This is undertaken by way of higher but temporary expansions in wages and salaries and sustained spending on goods and services. There is no change in transfers and subsidies during the countercyclical period. This component only begins to rise two years later, suggesting weak automatic stabilizers. Investment expense in larger countries also contracts post disaster, though less steeply and for a shorter time period.

Given the rise in output growth and the fall in investment expenditure observed among larger countries, it is fair to assume that the reduction in goods and services revenue observed, is due to tax reductions.[8] The other components – income and profits, trade and other revenue – all increase in year one, with the effects beginning to dissipate by year 3.

Table 28.2 provides the cumulative fiscal responses by disaggregated revenue and expenditure categories in small and larger states, over a five-year horizon post disaster. Pro-cyclicality in small states is achieved through broad based increases in all but one component – income and profits. The decline in income and profits over the period shows the impact of the business cycle. Other revenue reflects the largest post-disaster increase, implying that small government's

Table 28.2 Five-year cumulative shocks on revenue and expenditure

Model	Variables	Small states	Larger states
Revenue	Total revenue	4.34	−0.02
	Goods and services	0.76	−0.01
	Income and profits	−3.07	−0.01
	International trade	0.03	−0.08
	Other revenue	5.83	0.05
Expenditure	Total expenditure	2.66	−0.01
	Wages and salaries	2.97	0.04
	Transfers and subsidies	−0.19	−0.02
	Interest	2.69	−0.02
	Goods and services	2.86	0.04
	Investment	−1.74	0.01

resort to non-traditional tax measures to shore up their revenue bases, and to finance increases in expenditure post disaster. The cumulative changes in expenditure confirm that revealed in the former discussion.

In larger states, counter-cyclicality is executed through traditional tax policies, whilst wages and salaries, goods and services, and public investment help to propel countercyclical efforts. Despite the observed pick up in transfers and subsidies noted earlier, on a cumulative basis, again transfers and subsides does not reflect the behaviour expected from automatic stabilizers.

The impact of large disaster shocks

The literature finds that there is a difference between the impact of small and large disaster shocks. This follows from work by Noy and Nualsri (2011) and others, who find that larger shocks drive the observed changes in output and the fiscal balances.

Large shocks are defined here as those that are greater than the 75th percentile of average disaster damages in small and larger developing countries, respectively. This measure of disasters intensity differs from that employed by other authors, namely, Fomby *et al.* (2013) and Acevedo (2014). Fomby *et al.* (2013) considers large shocks to be those where total fatalities plus total affected as a percentage of the population, is greater than 0.01 percent. Acevedo (2014), on the other hand, uses damages as a percentage of the population but employs the same threshold.

The threshold of 0.01% is fairly subjective and may not be appropriate, particularly for use with larger countries. Larger countries have bigger land masses and therefore, it is less likely for disasters to affect a significant portion of the population. Hence Fomby *et al.* (2013) method could rule out destructive disasters which may have affected only one region or community. Further, the choice of 0.01% as a disaster threshold is quite arbitrary. The percentile method, disaggregated by small and larger states, allows disaster intensity to be measured relative to the history of disasters experienced by these groups. Results with the percentile intensity indicator are generated using the benchmark models for small and larger developing countries. The impulse response responses generated from these models are presented in Figures 28.A7–28.A8 of Appendix 5.

The primary fiscal balance in small states shows only marginal signs of improvement when disasters are restricted to larger shocks. There is a similar trajectory in output and the trade balances decline, reflecting a turnaround from the benchmark case. External debt falls as well in the aftermath of larger shocks, but only temporarily. Small states seem to finance their rehabilitation via international loans in years 2 and 3, and appear to benefit from a moratorium since the primary balance in these years remain fairly unchanged. This implies that loans for disaster relief are contracted from the multilateral sector, possibly via IMF or World Bank disaster relief windows.

Over the five-year horizon, Table 28.3 shows that fiscal policy in small states and in larger states are both counter-cyclical. The difference is, as inferred, is that in small states this

Table 28.3 Five-year cumulative large shocks on the primary fiscal balance

Model	Variables	Small states	Larger states
Adjusted baseline (Large shocks)	International trade	0.44	0.93
	External debt	0.24	−0.12
	Gross output	1.00	1.00
	Primary balance	−0.27	−0.61

countercyclical reaction is financed by an increase in external debt, where in larger states the response is implemented through revenue and expenditures adjustments.

These results contradict the literature but they too are intuitive. Large disaster shocks, especially from storms, create the greatest damage in small states. For example, when a small state is affected by a large storm, there is likely to be significant infrastructural damage. Given that these countries normally lead a pro-cyclical fiscal policy, it is unlikely that at the time of impact, small states would have accumulated enough fiscal space to mitigate the negative impact of the disaster. Borrowing would be necessary to help with reconstruction, and this is reflected in the worsening primary balance and overall counter-cyclical response.

The finding that governments of larger developing countries respond counter-cyclically when faced with normal and large disasters gives credence to the hypothesis that size is a critical factor in determining fiscal effects from disasters. Larger developing countries have much greater land masses, implying that disaster damage in these countries could well be localized. It is therefore less likely that disasters would require the involvement of federal government.

5 Policy conclusions

Up to this point, the conventional wisdom has been that developing countries respond pro-cyclically to the business cycle and to shocks – including natural disasters. This chapter finds evidence of a difference between the response of smaller and larger developing countries to natural disasters. Small states do respond pro-cyclically to natural disasters but larger developing countries tend to respond counter-cyclically. However, in the context of larger shocks, the results reveal counter cyclical responses in both small and large developing countries, respectively, measured cumulatively over a five-year horizon. The counter-cyclical response in small states is assumed to be financed by an increase in external debt.

The relative sizes of small and larger developing country fiscal responses also lead to the conclusion that studies which neglect to take account of country size, are likely to produce inaccurate results. The evidence in this chapter shows that small states respond to disasters with a large fiscal contraction, whereas policy makers in larger states tend to respond via weaker fiscal expansions. Lumping the small and large country samples in this study, the results would imply that the fiscal impact of disasters in developing countries is pro-cyclical.[9] The primary conclusion therefore is that size matters.

From a policy perspective, the analysis suggests that small states should be mindful of the composition of their disaster responses, which is found to largely comprise of increases in spending on wages and salaries, an equivalently large fall in investment expenditure, and higher taxation. Combined, this policy mix negatively affects growth performance.

Further, given the vulnerability to disaster shocks and the growth effects of such occurrences, small states should seek to strengthen their fiscal position and build buffers to allow for an effective response to shocks, and disaster perturbations in particular. Improving the fiscal framework to build buffers would help dampen the immediate impact of disaster shocks by inducing a less procyclical policy stance. In addition, buffers can be effective in catalyzing additional international support in the aftermath of disasters. Building buffers would entail improving fiscal systems, particularly financial management systems, which are often tested in a disaster's aftermath. These systems would improve the effectiveness of the post disaster strategy and improve long term resilience, as shown by the impulse response functions.

In the face of large disaster shocks, small states are unlikely to build sufficient buffers to effectively respond to the negative effects of such disturbances. This is especially the case given that markets tend to be reluctant to increase credit in the aftermath of disasters, even when debt ratios are relatively low. Therefore, it is important that there continue to exist effective international mechanisms to help small states deal with the efforts towards rehabilitation.

In that regard, a number of facilities have been introduced by the IFI's to aid countries following disasters. While these facilities, particularly if augmented by domestic buffers are helpful, they can in the instance of large disaster shocks be inadequate. The international shock response architecture should be enhanced to deal with such instances and help support a more counter-cyclical stance. Assistance under such frameworks should be provided in a manner which limits the build-up of debt and supports the building of long term resilience to better respond to future shocks.

Notes

1 EM-DAT: The CRED/OFDA International Disaster Database, Université Catholique de Louvain, Brussels, Belgium. Available at www.emdat.be/.
2 This paper, although only indirectly related, is among the one of the most recent contributions to a limited body of research on the fiscal impact of natural disasters. The few others consist of earlier studies by Lis and Nickel (2009), Melecky and Raddataz (2011) and Noy and Nualsri (2011).
3 A list of these countries is provided in Appendix 1.
4 These variables are expressed in real terms through deflation by the consumer price index. Note that the disaggregated expenditure data may suffer from misclassification issues arising from changes in the methodology of compilation in Government Financial Statistics.
5 It should be pointed out, however, that adjust per head of population, the frequency of natural disasters is higher in small states.
6 The changes are calculated as the absolute difference between these values from t-1 to t+1 where t is the year of a disaster.
7 It should be noted that it is not possible to say whether the fiscal reaction is voluntary or involuntary. The results only present evidence on the direction of fiscal policy post-disaster.
8 The fall in investment expenditure implies that growth is not fuelled by investment post disaster. Hence with an acceleration in growth and lower goods and services revenues, the plausible explanation is a tax break.
9 Using Table 28.1, and adding the cumulative responses of small states and larger states gives 3.53 (5.07 -1.54).

Appendix 1

Table 28.A1 List of countries included in the analyses

Small states	*Larger states*
Antigua and Barbuda	Algeria
Bahrain	Bolivia
Barbados	Brazil
Belize	Bulgaria
Bhutan	Costa Rica
Botswana	Croatia
Cyprus	Dominican Republic
Dominica	El Salvador
Fiji	Ethiopia
Grenada	Guatemala
Jamaica	Indonesia
Lesotho	Jordan
Maldives	Kenya
Mauritius	Lithuania
Namibia	Madagascar
Sao Tome and Principe	Malaysia
Seychelles	Moldova
St Kitts and Nevis	Mongolia
St Lucia	Morocco
Suriname	Nepal
Swaziland	Pakistan
Trinidad and Tobago	Peru
	Philippines
	Romania
	Singapore
	Sri Lanka
	Thailand
	Tunisia
	Uganda
	Uruguay
	Zambia

Appendix 2

Table 28.A2 Data sources and descriptions

Variable	Details	Source
Natural disasters – occurrence	Natural disasters are divided in 5 sub-groups (geo-physical, meteorological, hydrological, climatological, biological and extra-terrestrial) covering 15 disaster types and over 30 sub-types. Droughts, epidemics, earthquakes, extreme temperature incidents, flooding, insect infestations, landslides, mass movement (dry), storms, volcanic activity, wildfires were focused on. The disasters recorded meet at least one of the following requirements: a) 10 or more people reported as killed; b) 100 or more people reported as affected; c) State of emergency declared; d) International assistance called for.	EM-DAT The International Disaster Database
Natural disasters – estimated damage	The total amount of damage to property, crops and livestock – in US$, figures corresponding to the damage value at time of disaster.	EM-DAT The International Disaster Database
Real GDP	GDP at market prices (constant 2010, US$)	World Development Indicators, 2017
Real GDP growth	Annual percentage GDP growth at market prices based on constant local currency	World Development Indicators, 2017
Consumer Price Index	2010 used as the base year	World Development Indicators, 2017
Inflation	Consumer prices, annual %	World Development Indicators, 2017
External debt	a) Real external debt stocks, total (DOD, current US$) as a percentage of GDP; b) External debt stocks, public and publicly guaranteed (PPG) (DOD, current US$).	World Development Indicators, 2017
Trade openness	Real total exports and imports of goods and services (BOP, current US$) as a percentage of GDP	World Development Indicators, 2017
Net official development assistance and official aid received	Current US$	World Development Indicators, 2017
Government revenue	Revenue, excluding grants (% of GDP)	World Development Indicators, 2017
General government revenue	% of GDP	IMF World Economic Outlook – October 2016

Variable	Details	Source
Government expenditure	Expense (% of GDP)	World Development Indicators, 2017
General government total expenditure	% of GDP	IMF World Economic Outlook – October 2016
General government budget balance	General government net lending/ borrowing (% of GDP)	IMF World Economic Outlook – October 2016
Primary balance	Authors' calculations. Estimated as Government revenue – Expenditure – Interest payments.	World Development Indicators, 2017
Taxes	a) on exports (% of GDP); b) on goods and services; c) on international trade; d) on income, profits and capital gains; e) other.	World Development Indicators, 2017
Capital expenditure	Net investment in non-financial assets (% of GDP)	World Development Indicators, 2017
Compensation of employees	Current LCU	World Development Indicators, 2017
Customs and other duties	Current LCU	World Development Indicators, 2017
Interest payments	Current LCU	World Development Indicators, 2017
Goods and services expense	Current LCU	World Development Indicators, 2017
Subsides and other transfers	Current LCU	World Development Indicators, 2017
Output gap	Authors' calculations. Potential and actual output estimates using GDP at market prices (constant 2010 US$). Estimating output gaps are subject to a significant level of uncertainty (IMF World Economic Outlook, 2017).	World Development Indicators, 2017
Fiscal impulse	Authors' calculations. Year-on-year difference between cyclically-adjusted primary balances using general government primary net lending/ borrowing (% of GDP).	IMF World Economic Outlook – October 2016

Appendix 3 The panel vector autoregression models (PVAR)

The PVAR models utilized in this paper build on the studies by Noy and Nualsri (2011); Fatas and Mihov (2012) and Fridmuc et al. (2016). However, it is closer in nature to the model developed in Noy and Nualsri (2011).

In their attempt to describe the typical fiscal response following a large exogenous shock, Noy and Nualsri (2011) estimate a PVAR model and corresponding impulse response functions. The PVAR model features standard panel components (fixed effects and time effects) and encompasses a bivariate vector containing disaster and fiscal variables (government consumption, revenue, payments, primary surplus and debt). In its reduced form, the PVAR is expressed by five model specifications, each containing a measure of disasters captured by the aggregate amount of disaster damage in any one quarter.

Following Fatas and Mihov (2012), Noy and Nualsri's (2011) specification is adapted to include individual revenue and expenditure components.[10]

$$X_t = A1_{it}X_{t-1} + A1_i + A1_t + \mu1_{it} \tag{1}$$

$$Y_t = A2_{it}Y_{t-1} + A2_i + A2_t + \mu2_{it} \tag{2}$$

$$Z_t = A3_{it}Z_{t-1} + A3_i + A3_t + \mu3_{it} \tag{3}$$

However, the PVAR is partitioned into three separate models, where X_t, Y_t and Z_t are {fiscal, disaster, controls} trivariate vectors comprising fiscal, disaster and control variables, respectively.[11] Equation (1) is the benchmark model. Partitioning into three separate models is necessary because of the data limitations. The only disadvantage of this approach is that it excludes interactions between revenue and expenditure and the components.

The fiscal variable in X_t is the primary balance. Y_t comprises: total revenue, revenue from income and profits, goods and services revenue, revenue from international trade and other revenue. Vector Z_t is made up of total expenditure, expenditure on wages and salaries, transfers and subsidies, goods and services expense, investment, interest and other expense. All these vectors comprise the control variables trade openness, gross output and external debt. A_{kit}, where k represents models 1 through 3, are matrices of coefficients capturing fiscal responses, panel fixed effects and time effects, whereas μk_{it} are white noise error terms.

The inclusion of trade openness and debt as control variables follows from Tanzi (1998), who comments that in developing countries, the impact of external shocks on the fiscal accounts are largely linked to changes in the foreign sector. The reason is the high proportion of foreign trade taxes in total revenue; domestic sales taxes collected from imports; heavy reliance on corporate income taxes from exports of mineral products; and the reliance on the part of the public sector on foreign borrowing or foreign grants, etc. As a consequence, Tanzi (1998) claims that it is very difficult when dealing with these countries to isolate the changes in fiscal variables that reflect genuine policy responses from those that reflect automatic effects.

With the above in mind, Gross output is included to control for changes in revenue and expenditure due to the business cycle, whilst external debt also accounts for credit constraints. In a related paper, Fidrmuc et al. (2016) explain the importance of controlling for changes in the business cycle on spending due to the presence of automatic stabilizers (for example: progressive taxes, unemployment benefits, welfare spending etc.).

The credit constraints hypothesis suggests that developing countries are less able to smooth the business cycle because of limited access to international credit markets, which prevents them from borrowing during bad times (Halland and Bleaney, 2011).

Data are annual and fiscal variables are expressed in real terms, while control variables are in ratios to GDP. The fisher panel unit root tests confirm stationary of all variables in first differences using the Phillips-Perron specification at two lags (see Appendix 4). Moreover, the Akaike Information Criteria (AIC), Bayesian Information Criteria (BIC) and the Hannan-Quinn Information Criteria (HQIC) suggest a PVAR(1) model specification. The PVAR models are estimated using the GMM/IV first difference estimator. Impulse response functions for each model are then generated with 500 repetitions of Monte Carlo Simulations.

Notes

10 Fatas and Mihov (1999) attempt to identify different measures of automatic stabilizers by decomposing the government expenditures and revenues to their primary components.
11 Baseline model.

Appendix 4

Table 28.A4 Unit root tests

Variables (levels)	Small states		Larger states	
	p-value for Z statistic	p-value for P statistic	p-value for Z statistic	p-value for P statistic
Trade openness	0.00	0.00	0.00	0.00
Revenue, excluding grants (real)	0.00	0.00	0.00	0.00
Taxes on goods and services (real)	0.02	0.00	0.00	0.00
Taxes on international trade (real)	0.08	0.00	0.00	0.00
Other taxes (real)	0.00	0.00	0.00	0.00
Taxes on income, profits and capital gains (real)	0.00	0.00	0.00	0.00
Compensation of employees (real)	0.24	0.00	0.00	0.00
Interest payments (real)	0.00	0.00	0.00	0.00
Expense (real)	0.00	0.00	0.00	0.00
Subsidies and other transfers (real)	0.00	0.00	0.00	0.00
Goods and services expense (real)	0.01	0.00	0.00	0.00
Net investment in non-financial assets (Real)	0.29	0.03	0.00	0.00
Natural disasters – total estimated damage	0.00	0.00	0.00	0.00
Real GDP	1.00	1.00	1.00	1.00
Primary balance (real)	0.00	0.00	0.00	0.00
External debt	0.54	0.47	0.37	0.70

Variables (first differences)	Small states		Larger states	
	p-value for Z statistic	p-value for P statistic	p-value for Z statistic	p-value for P statistic
Trade openness	0.00	0.00	0.00	0.00
Revenue, excluding grants (real)	0.00	0.00	0.00	0.00
Taxes on goods and services (real)	0.00	0.00	0.00	0.00
Taxes on international trade (real)	0.00	0.00	0.00	0.00
Other taxes (real)	0.00	0.00	0.00	0.00
Taxes on income, profits and capital gains (real)	0.00	0.00	0.00	0.00
Compensation of employees (real)	0.00	0.00	0.00	0.00
Interest payments (real)	0.00	0.00	0.00	0.00
Expense (real)	0.00	0.00	0.00	0.00
Subsidies and other transfers (real)	0.00	0.00	0.00	0.00
Goods and services expense (real)	0.00	0.00	0.00	0.00
Net investment in non-financial assets (real)	0.00	0.00	0.00	0.00
Natural disasters – total estimated damage	0.00	0.00	0.00	0.00
Real GDP	0.00	0.00	0.00	0.00
Primary balance (real)	0.00	0.00	0.00	0.00
External debt	0.00	0.00	0.00	0.00

Note: P values for the Z statistic (Inverse normal) and P statistic (Inverse chi-squared) are from Fisher-type panel-data unit-root tests with two lags.

Appendix 5 Impulse response functions

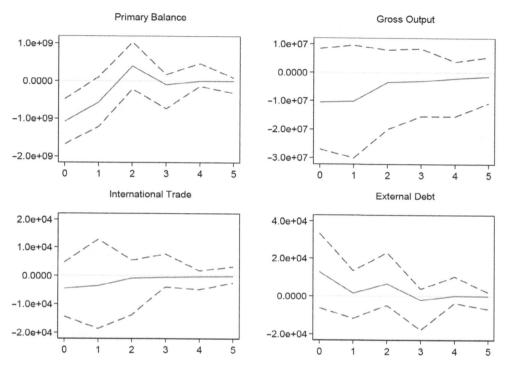

Figure 28.A1 Baseline: small states

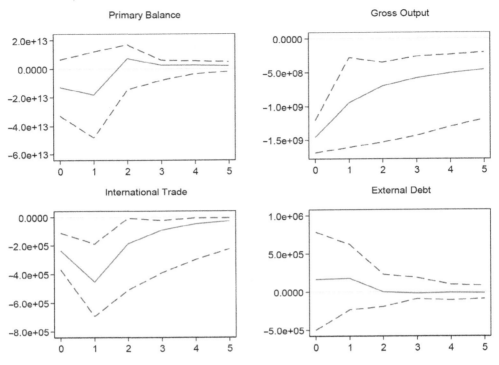

Figure 28.A2 Baseline: larger states

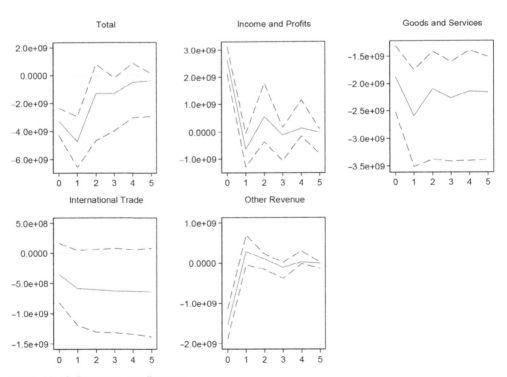

Figure 28.A3 Revenue: small states

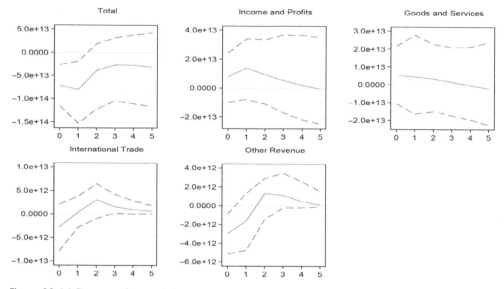

Figure 28.A4 Revenue: larger states

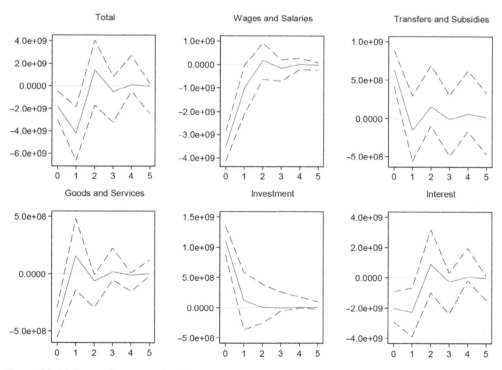

Figure 28.A5 Expenditure: small states

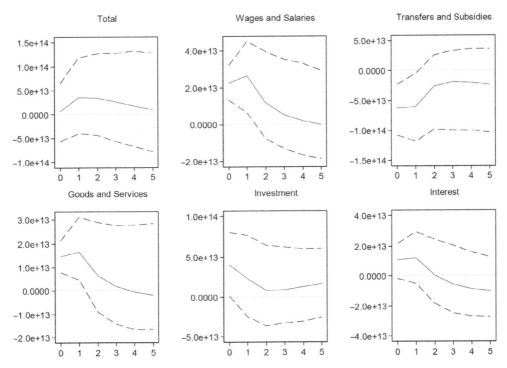

Figure 28.A6 Expenditure: larger states

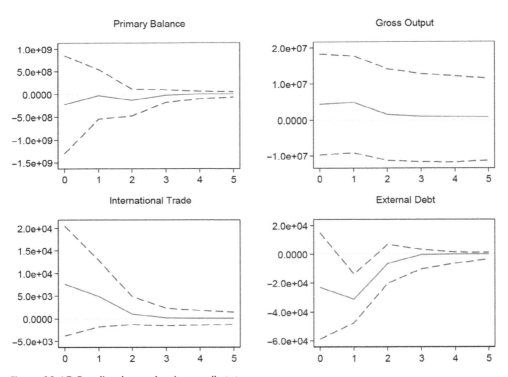

Figure 28.A7 Baseline large shocks: small states

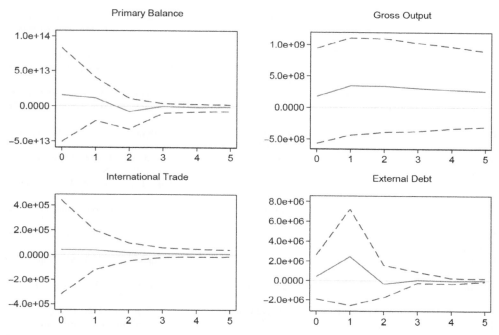

Figure 28.A8 Baseline large shocks: larger states

References

Acevedo, S. (2014). Debt, Growth and Natural Disasters: A Caribbean Trilogy. IMF, *WP/14/125*.

Acevedo, S. (2016). Gone with the Wind: Estimating Hurricane and Climate Change Costs in the Caribbean. IMF, *WP/16/99*.

Alesina, A. and Spoalare, E. (1997). 'On the Number and Size of Nations'. *Quarterly Journal of Economics*, 112(4): 1027–1056.

Briguglio, L. (1995). 'Small Island Developing States and Their Economic Vulnerabilities'. *World Development*, 23(9): 1615–1632.

Cavallo, E. A. and Noy, I. (2009). The Economics of Natural Disasters: A Survey. *IDB Working Paper*, No. 35.

Commonwealth Secretariat (2013). A Time to Act: Addressing Small States Financing and Debt Challenges. *Background Paper, Commonwealth High-Level Advocacy Mission*. Washington, DC.

Crespo Cuaresma, J., Doppelhofer, G. and Feldkircher, M. (2008). The Determinants of Economic Growth in European Regions. *Working Paper 2008-26*. Faculty of Economics and Statistics, University of Innsbruck.

Easterly, W. and Rebelo, S. (1993). Fiscal Policy and Economic Growth. *NBER Working Paper Series*, 4499.

Fatas, A. and Mihov, I. (1999). Government Size and Automatic Stabilizers: International and International Evidence. *CEPR Discussion Papers*, 2259.

Fatas, A. and Mihov, I. (2012). 'Fiscal Policy as a Stabilization Tool'. *The B.E. Journal of Macroeconomics*, 12(3).

Fidrmuc, J., Ghosh, S. and Yang, W. (2016). Natural Disasters, Government Spending, and the Fiscal Multiplier. *CESifo Working Paper* Series, No. 5665.

Fomby, T., Ikeda, Y. and Loayza, N. (2013). 'The Growth Aftermath of Natural Disasters'. *Journal of Applied Econometrics*, 28(3): 412–434.

Halland, H. and Bleaney, N. (2011). Explaining The Procyclicality of Fiscal Policy in Developing Countries. *CREDIT Research Paper*, 11/09. Centre for Research in Economic Development and International Trade, University of Nottingham.

International Monetary Fund (IMF) (2013). Macroeconomic Issues in Small States and Implications for Fund Engagement. Prepared by the *Strategy, Policy, and Review Department, in collaboration with other IMF Departments.*

International Monetary Fund (IMF) (2015). Macroeconomic Developments and Selected Issues in Small Developing States. *Staff Report on Macroeconomic Developments and Selected Issues in Small Developing States,* prepared by IMF staff and completed on March 9, to brief the Executive Board.

International Monetary Fund (IMF) (2016). Small States' Resilience to Natural Disasters and Climate Change- Role for the IMF. *Staff Report,* prepared by IMF staff and completed on November 7, 2016 for the Executive Board's consideration on December 1, 2016.

Lis, E. and Nickel, E. (2009). The Impact of Extreme Weather Events on Budget Balances and Implications for Fiscal Policy. *European Central Bank Working Paper Series,* No. 1055.

Melecky, M. and Raddatz, C. E. (2011). How Do Governments Respond After Catastrophes? Natural-Disaster Shocks and the Fiscal Stance. *World Bank Policy Research Working Paper,* No. 5564.

Milner, C. and Westaway, T. (1993). 'Country Size and The Medium-Term Growth Process: Some Cross-country Evidence'. *World Development,* 21(2): 203–211.

Noy, I. (2009). 'The Macroeconomic Consequences of Disasters'. *Journal of Development Economics,* 88(2): 221–231.

Noy. I. and Nualsri, A. (2011). 'Fiscal Storms: Public Spending and Revenues in the Aftermath of Natural Disasters'. *Environment and Development Economics,* 16(1): 113–128.

Raddatz, C. (2009). The Wrath of God: Macroeconomic Costs of Natural Disasters. *World Bank Policy Research Working Paper,* No. 5039. The World Bank.

Skidmore, M. and Toya, H. (2002). 'Do Natural Disasters Promote Long-Run Growth?' *Economic Inquiry,* 40(4): 664–667.

Streeten, P. (1993). 'The Special Problems of Small Countries'. *World Development,* 21(2): 197–202.

Tanzi, V. (1998). Corruption Around the World: Causes, Consequences, Scope, and Cures. *IMF Staff Papers,* 45: 559–594.

29

Natural disasters and tourism-led economic growth: a case study of Fiji: 1980–2014

T. K. Jayaraman, Chee Keong Choong, Cheong Fatt Ng and
Markand Bhatt

1 Introduction

Fiji's tourism industry has emerged to be the engine of growth in recent years. Its international airport at Nadi has been the gateway to South Pacific ever since the 1960s and continues to remain the main hub for airline connections between passengers flying out of Australia and New Zealand as well as for passengers from North America to other Pacific Island Countries (PICs)[1]. The air traffic is being catered to by airlines of Australia and New Zealand and by Fiji Airways, formerly known as Air Pacific, which was once owned by major PICs but now fully owned by Fiji.

Due to the fact that foreign direct investment flowed in the tourism sector over last five decades in preference to manufacturing because of very small size of domestic market, Fiji has now world-class tourist resorts and hotels which are mostly owned by well-known international hotel and resort chains. These resorts and hotels are concentrated close to Nadi, the international airport tapering down to the area around the banks of the river Sigatoka, all in the Western Division, which receives less rainfall and hence is sunnier than Central Division where the capital city, Suva is situated. However, as cyclonic disturbances during the cyclone season, November to April affect mostly the Western Division, overseas investors have seen the need for locating their new resorts and hotels in other less cyclone prone areas including small islands.

Most of the tourist arrivals until mid-2002 were by air from overseas. Since the mid-2000s travel by cruise ship has become attractive and more frequent. The growing popularity of cruise ship travel among the affluent senior citizens in Europe as well as in Australia and New Zealand has proved beneficial for Fiji. These ships arrive only at the country's two sea ports, Suva and Lautoka in the Western Division. Their visits do not extend beyond a day and they do not utilize any hotel facilities on land. However, they make short trips to places of historical interest and museums and return to their ships.

Empirical studies in the past, including those by Narayan *et al.* (2010) for Fiji and the most recent survey on small island developing states, commissioned by Commonwealth Secretariat and the World Bank (Hampton and Jeyacheya, 2013), focused on the connection between tourism and growth hypothesis in the South Pacific region. However, the impact of natural disasters on tourism and growth were not examined in detail. This chapter makes an attempt to go beyond the past studies by specifically including cyclone as a variable besides the conventional variables, which are employed in the tourism-led growth studies. This chapter is organized on the following lines: Section 2. reviews trends in tourism besides presenting a brief literature survey of tourism and growth; Section 3. describes the trend in Fiji's tourism sector. Section 4. lists the past annual occurrences of cyclones with estimates of damages and other details. Section 5. outlines the modelling and methodology procedures and presents results; and the final Section 6. presents a summary with some policy conclusions

2 Brief review of studies on tourism and growth

Tourist expenditure

Hampton and Jeyacheya (2013), while presenting a brief survey on tourism and inclusive growth, reminds us that tourism is not an industry within the UN SIC system, but it is a form of expenditure, part of final demand (Benyon et al., 2009), and therefore includes an import content. Such expenditure has many components, which include accommodation, meals, tours and entertainment such as local cultural shows (Jones, 2010). Younger groups who prefer to undertake more adventurous trips are also those who cannot afford high costs of accommodation often seek inexpensive stays and meals besides trips away from beaches and urban centres. Greater availability of inexpensive boarding services such as home stays and inns have sprung up in PICs to cater to the needs of back-pack youth groups.

In the context of constraints to growth posed by factors such as low physical endowments in term of land area and poor quality of soil, often subject to land tenure difficulties, which limit the range and possibilities of exports of agricultural commodities, the unique combination of sun, surf and offer greater scope for earnings from tourism as an export. Table 29.1 presents data on the share of tourism earnings in the respective gross domestic products of PICs.

It has been well recognized that tourism encouraged by both domestic investor friendly and liberal foreign direct investment policies (Jayaraman et al., 2014) creates additional jobs and

Table 29.1 Pacific island countries: contribution of tourism to GDP (%)

Year	Fiji	PNG	Samoa	Solomon I.	Tonga	Vanuatu
1995–99 (ave.)	18.4	0.3	15.1	2.3	5.5	22.5
2000–04 (ave.)	20.0	0.1	15.5	1.0	4.3	25.4
2005–09 (ave.)	23.6	0.1	17.7	5.3	5.3	28.8
2010	26.3	0.0	18.7	7.6	7.3	34.5
2011	25.3	0.0	17.6	7.4	6.8	31.4
2012	24.9	0.0	18.4	6.4	9.6	34.3
2013	23.1	0.0	17.1	6.7	10.4	39.2
2014	–	0.0	18.1	5.5	–	34.8

Source: United Nations World Tourism Organization (2016).

generates additional income. Tourism also has a multiplier effect through increasing business activity in both formal and informal sectors and improving the livelihoods of people in agriculture and retail trade. However, much of the tourism earnings are not retained in the country and are leaked by way of imports from rest of the world, as PICs have to import a variety of consumer goods ranging from toilet paper to food and beverages to satisfy the high-ended tourists from advanced countries. While foreign trade is part of open economy policies pursued by PICs, policy makers have been focusing their attention on how to strengthen the backward linkages from tourism to agriculture and other support services by shifting their emphasis from small family run farms to large, mechanized and irrigated farming. It is expected that commercial farming would ensure high quality as well consistent supplies to hotels and resorts as well as encouraging domestic processed consumer goods (Chand, 2015).

The tourism and growth nexus

Tourism, as an export of service, enables the country to earn valuable foreign exchange. Furthermore, tourism earnings can be devoted to fund public expenditures, aimed at speeding up growth and development in the economies of island nations. There are a large number of empirical studies that are available to confirm the contribution of tourism to growth.[2]

Figini and Vici (2009) have categorized the empirical studies in two broad groups: (i) multiplier approach, where tourism is treated as an exogenous variable, being a component of aggregate demand with an impact of positive nature, when it is given a boost; and (ii) application of trade and endogenous growth theories to tourism sector's role. The first group of studies has been criticized as being static and that they do not explain the long run impact of tourism.

One of the earliest studies was by Balaguer and Cantalvella-Jorda (2002) falls into the first group. The two authors employed a double log model with two explanatory variables in their study on Spain for investigating tourism impact on real gross domestic product (RGDP) growth. They used the elasticity estimates of tourism earnings and real exchange rate on RGDP, which were found both positive and significant. The second approach of two sector endogenous growth models, where productivity is a major ingredient, is employed by Lanza and Pigliaru (1995). The two authors argue that if technological progress is higher in the manufacturing sector than in the tourism sector, tourism specialization is growth enhancing if and only if the change in the terms of trade between tourism and manufacturing goods more than balances the technological gap in the tourism sector.

Following Lanza and Pigliaru (1995) model in their studies on small economies, Candela and Cellini (1997) showed that in small island economies it is easier for the terms of trade offsetting the technology gap, as the opportunity cost of specialization is small. In a subsequent paper, Lanza and Pigliaru (2000) picked up the idea and argued that since in small island economies, the natural resources endowments related tourism sector is more dominant than the almost absent or negligible manufacturing sector, ' the tourism dependent country can take advantage of the presence of natural resources even when the increase in the terms of trade does not balance the technological gap, the exploitation rate of tourism resources can increase sufficiently to correct the technological gap and to enhance growth'.

Leading empirical studies on tourism-growth nexus in island countries include Dritsakis (2004), Durbarry (2002, 2004) Gunduz and Hatemi (2005), Kim *et al.* (2006), Noriko and Mototsugu (2007). They have convincingly shown the existence of a long – run relationship between tourism and economic growth. Besides these studies, which were on specific countries, there are two panel studies, one by Narayan *et al.* (2010) and another by Seetanah (2011).

Narayan *et al.* (2010) studied impact of tourism on growth in four PICs, namely Fiji, Papua New Guinea (PNG), Solomon Islands and Tonga covering a period of 17 years (1988–2004). Only two variables were employed: the dependent variable, log of real GDP and log of tourist arrivals. In his panel study of 19 countries, comprising Fiji and Papua New Guinea from the Pacific region, Mauritius and Seychelles from the Indian Ocean region and the rest being from the Caribbean, covering a 13-year period (1990–2007), Seetanah (2011) unlike Narayan *et al.* (2010) adopted an augmented Solow growth model by including investment in physical capital, in the absence of a consistent times series of capital stock for all 19 countries. This approach is along the lines of Durbarry (2004), and Eugenio-Martin *et al.* (2004). Seetanah (2011) employed a double logarithmic model with the dependent variable per capita; and the explanatory variables, besides investment, secondary school enrolment representing human capital, exports and imports as% of GDP representing the openness of the economy and tourist arrivals and economic freedom index. Being a double logarithmic model, the coefficients indicate output elasticities. The Seetanah study (2011) remains the most up-to- date study on the tourism-led growth hypothesis.

3 Trends in Fiji's tourism

Fiji is one of the leading economies amongst the Pacific island nations. Key indicators relating to economy of Fiji are given in Table 29.2. The population of Fiji is less than a million. It possesses no oil, gas or major mineral resources. In spire of its limited natural resources endowments, Fiji is the only upper middle income country in the region with its per capita GNI at US$4,830 as per the World Bank 2015 classification of countries and is ranked 104 among 115 upper middle-income countries. Its traditional export earning sugar has now been replaced by tourism.

Table 29.2 Fiji: selected key indicators

Land area (sq. km)	18,270
Population in '000 (2015)	892
Per capita GNI (US$) (2015)	4,830
Aid per capita in US$ (2010–14)	105
Aid as percentage of GDP (2011–14)	2.3
Human development ranking (2015)	90/188
Annual average growth rate (%) (2011–15)	3.6
Annual average inflation (%) (2011–15)	3.1
Overall budget balance (% of GDP)(2010–14)	−2.4
Current account balance (% of GDP) (2011–15)	−5.5

Source: Reserve Bank of Fiji (2016), United Nations Economic and Social Commission for Asia and Pacific (2016), World Bank (2016a).

Table 29.3 Fiji's major sources of foreign exchange earnings (% of GDP)

	1996–00	*2001–05*	*2006–10*	*2011*	*2012*	*2013*	*2014*	*2015*
Sugar	7.6	5.1	3.3	1.7	2.5	1.8	2.4	1.6
Gold	2.3	1.7	0.9	2.1	1.9	1.3	1.1	1.0
Garments	8.2	5.3	1.7	1.4	1.3	1.4	1.2	1.2
Fish	1.8	1.9	2.4	1.5	0.8	1.2	0.9	1.1
Lumber	1.3	0.9	0.9	0.9	1.0	1.1	1.1	1.0
Molasses	0.4	0.2	0.3	0.4	0.2	0.2	0.2	0.2
Coconut oil	0.2	0.1	0.1	0.1	0.1	0.0	0.1	0.05
Others	4.7	6.0	6.7	7.0	6.9	6.2	6.1	6.3
Total	26.5	21.3	16.3	15.1	14.7	13.3	12.9	12.4
Tourism earnings	13.8	14.5	16.5	19.0	18.3	17.2	16.4	17.1
unrequited transfers								
Aid	1.9	2.0	1.8	2.1	2.7	2.2	2.0	N/A
Remittances	1.7	5.8	5.5	4.2	4.8	4.9	4.6	N/A
Capital flows								
Foreign direct investment	1.1	4.1	9.8	11.0	6.7	3.8	7.6	7.6

Source: Reserve Bank of Fiji (2016), United Nations Economic and Social Commission for Asia and Pacific (2016), World Bank (2016a).

Table 29.3 shows that tourism in Fiji is the most dominant foreign exchange earner. With its earnings at F$1,560 million, being 17.1% of GDP, tourism replaced sugar (with its earnings at F$144 million, being 1.6% of GDP). Substantial foreign direct investment by well-known international chains of resorts and hotels and domestic investors, have made Fiji a popular, attractive and safe tourist destination in the South Pacific for all categories of tourists, most importantly families travelling with children during the vacation periods in Australia, New Zealand and North America during Christmas and Easter holiday season. Its close proximity to Australia and New Zealand (ANZ) as well as direct non-stop flights by Fiji Airways from Los Angeles, Seoul, Hong Kong, China and Singapore have contributed to tourism growth. The emergence of Nadi, the country's premier international airport is now the Pacific hub for making connections to Solomon Islands, Samoa and Vanuatu by all international business travellers.

From the late 1990s, introduction of cruise ship trips to Fiji for holiday makers as well as for the rich retirees from Europe, which were only confined to Vanuatu and New Caledonia in the past years, have boosted tourism to new heights. Cruise ship passengers arriving in the two ports of Fiji, namely Lautoka and Nadi normally spend just a day, arriving in the early hours of the day and leaving around sunset visiting places of historical interest of colonial heritage in and around Suva and sugar city of Lautoka. These trips have become increasingly popular and as a result during the non-cyclone months, May to October, cruise ships have increased their weekly trips to Fiji, one arrival a day alternating between Suva and Lautoka[3].

The annual data series of tourist arrivals are reported for Fiji for the first time since January 2016 by International Monetary Fund (IMF) as part of *International Financial Statistics* in the form

Table 29.4 Tourist arrivals

Averages	Fiji ('000)	PNG ('000)	Samoa ('000)	Soloman I. ('000)	Tonga ('000)	Vanuatu ('000)
1995–99	520.0	60.6	74.4	12.9	34.4	88.0
2000–04	461.0	56.2	91.0	5.8	45.6	102.4
2005–09	580.3	97.2	113.8	13.8	63.7	173.8
2010	692.0	140.0	122.0	20.5	65.0	237.7
2011	734.0	158.0	121.0	22.9	68.4	248.9
2012	741.0	168.0	126.0	23.9	57.1	321.0
2013	768.0	174.0	116.0	24.4	56.7	357.0
2014	781.0	182.0	120.4	20.1	NA	329.0

Source: United Nations World Tourism Organization (2016).

Table 29.5 Number of cruise passengers for Fiji

Year	Cruise passengers
Avg. 1996–2000	14,200
Avg. 2001–2005	8,800
Avg. 2006–2011	45,200
2012	80,000
2013	110,000
2014	88,000

Source: United Nations World Tourism Organization (2016).

of index (Table 29.4), in addition to being reported by UNWTO.[4] The cruise ship arrivals are given in Table 29.5.

A recent study by World Bank (2016a) reports that in 2013 tourism receipts for all PICs amounted to US$1.4 billion, which happens to be a record not only in terms of earnings but also in terms of tourist arrivals at 1.37 million over-night visitors which arrived in 2014 for all 11 PICs. Fiji, Papua New Guinea, Palau, Samoa and Vanuatu emerged as top five destinations in the region. Two thirds of visitors arriving in PICs are from Australia and New Zealand, while the United States, China, Japan and Europe have shown significant growth potential. The World Bank estimates PICs can gain as much as US$1.8 billion per year from additional revenues and create up to 128,000 additional jobs by 2040.

4 Cyclones and other natural disasters

Bonte and Cook (2013) report that ten out of top thirty countries experiencing damages from natural disasters are in the Pacific region.[5] This is based on estimated average annual losses from natural disasters, as percentages of respective GDPs. Estimates by the United Nations Office for Disaster Risk Reduction[6] reveal that annual average damage has been around US$50 million per year over a recent ten-year period in Fiji alone. Hsiang and Jina (2014) estimated that annual catastrophic cyclones can reduce per capita income

Table 29.6 Fiji: estimates of the cyclone damages, 1980–2016

Year	Names of cyclone	Category of cyclone	Number of deaths	Damages in F$ million
1980	Wally	1	16	n/a
1982	Mark	3	n/a	n/a
1982	Oscar	5	n/a	n/a
1985	Erick	3	23	132.09
1985	Nigel	3	n/a	n/a
1985	Gavin	4	7	n/a
1985	Hina	3	3	n/a
1986	Martin	3	2	n/a
1986	Rajah	3	1	43.97
1990	Rae	2	3	91.95
1990	Sina	3	n/a	34.45
1990	Mike	n/a	n/a	n/a
1992	Fran	5	n/a	n/a
1992	Joni	4	n/a	5.27
1993	Kina	3	23	324.83
1994	Thomas	4	n/a	n/a
1995	Gavin	4	25	50.13
1997	June	2	0	156
1999	Dani	4	12	6.56
2001	Paula	4	1	2.8
2003	Ami	3	19	59.6
2006	Jim	3	4	0.03
2008	Cliff	3	0	6.1
2008	Daman	4	0	0.62
2008	Gene	3	8	65.25
2009	Mick	2	3	68.25
2010	Thomas	4	2	93.37
2012	Evan	4	0	n/a
2016	Winston	5	44	n/a
2016	Zena	3	n/a	n/a

Source: Pole and Bola (2012).

Note: n/a = not available

significantly by as much as 7.4% to 14.9% in PICs. Table 29.6 shows the estimates of the cyclone damages from 1980 to 2016.

Economic costs of natural disasters

A recent study by World Bank (2016b) estimates that natural disasters of all kinds including earthquakes and cyclones during 1950–2014 affected about 9.2 million people in the South

Pacific region, causing approximately 10,000 reported deaths, and resulting in US$5 billion in associated damage costs. The most comprehensive single country study to date on the economic costs of natural disasters is in regards to Fiji, which was undertaken, nearly two decades ago by Benson (1997). Economic costs are divided into three categories: direct costs, indirect costs and secondary effects (Andersen, 1991; Bull, 1992; Otero and Marti, 1995)[7]. Focusing on impact of natural disasters on tourism, Benson (1997) observed that little attention appeared to have been paid to the hazard vulnerability of the sector. The situation continues to remain the same. Many of Fiji's tourist resorts are located in coastal areas, 'often positioned at vantage points to ensure the best views'. Thus, most of the tourist resorts are particularly vulnerable to cyclones and sea surges and to the extent that they are built on reclaimed land.

Tourist resorts and hotels are located along the southwest coastal line of about 150 kilometres of Viti Levu. Cyclones each year are unpredictable. As long the cyclones do not affect the Viti Levu's coastal areas, which have the highest concentration of tourist infrastructures, damages to the economy and loss of lives are relatively low.

A highly destructive cyclone, prior to the Tropical Cyclone Winston (TCW) of February 2016, was in 1984 when Cyclone Oscar destroyed much of the tourist infrastructure in the Western Division. It resulted in about F$12 million damage to the Regent of Fiji hotel in Nadi as well as damaging other hotels in the Nadi area and on the Coral Coast. The cyclone Sina of 1990 destroyed the Warwick Hotel to a substantial extent; which was followed by Cyclone Joni in December 1992 causing considerable damage to tourist resorts (Benson, 1997).

The most destructive cyclone faced by Fiji to date is TCW of February 2016. Fortunately, the tourist areas were spared. It affected the sparsely populated eastern islands first; and after making the landfall on the main island, Viti Levu, it blew over the northern coastal line across Viti Levu. The Nadi international airport and tourist resorts and hotels in the Western Division remained mostly unaffected. The TCW of February 2016 is considered to be most devastating disaster with damages of more than F$1 billion. The damages inflicted were upon farm lands in the populated areas depending on sugar and other crops as well as communications, including bridges and roads.

Adverse publicity in the media soon after tropical cyclones has now come to be seen as a major destructive fallout, possibly more than direct damages. The economic costs tend to linger on as they are reflected in the cancellation of air travel, hotel bookings and car rentals and the like for the next three or more months.[8] For this reason, soon after evaluation of damages inflicted by TCW of February 2016, the government undertook a major campaign during the months of April to June in 2016 in the tourism markets including Australia, New Zealand and North America to assure the world that the tourist infrastructure and Nadi airport were all intact and Fiji Tourism was back in the business. However, domestic press reports of spread water borne diseases and airborne illnesses such as eye infection in the wake of TCW of February 2016, kept tourists at bay for a while. Tourist arrivals dipped in March to May 2016 as well,[9] although recovery of sorts began in late July 2016.

As noted by Benson (1997), the tourism industry is vulnerable to natural disasters although less so than other sectors, development of tourism which has proven to be the number one foreign exchange earner, offers immense opportunities to mitigate the overall impact of disasters on the country's foreign-exchange earnings. In this context, the latest study on *Climate and Disaster Resilience*, by the World Bank (2016b) estimates the highest adaptation costs for PICs will be in regard to coastal protection. The main components are beach nourishment in areas with high tourism revenue, besides sea and river dike construction and port upgrade. Further, existing buildings in the coastal regions, cyclone wind retrofitting options are needed which would reduce expected losses by 35%–50%. All new constructions would need to incorporate the code improvements necessary to ensure greater resilience to the current and future distribution of cyclone risks. No doubt, the retrofitting expenditures of public buildings will be the responsibility of the government and funds have to be sourced from within or foreign sources, aid or loan assistance from international funding agencies. On the other hand, expenditure on retrofitting and construction of new structures of hotels and resorts and restaurants and other entertainment joints have to be in accordance with the approved codes which will have to be borne by the owners in the private sector.

Specifically focusing on Fiji, the World Bank (2016b) has estimated that Fiji would have to spend US$ 329 million per year by 2040 and it would be at least US$ 229 million per year by 2020. The annual cost is estimated to be 3% of GDP, which is higher than the cost of coastal adaptation estimated in other regions of the world: 0.8% for Sub-Saharan Africa and 0.4% for other regions. The higher costs are attributed to greater need for components such as construction and maintenance of seawalls. As funding requirements for these components are substantial, PICs would be seeking assistance from international funding agencies. Fiji and other PICs have already started working on the next steps in this regard in consultation with other stakeholders.[10]

5 Modelling, methodology and results

In order to undertake an econometric analysis of the role of cyclones in the tourism-led growth analysis, we employ a production function approach with conventional variables of real GDP and capital stock and labour as explanatory variables. Besides these we include others as shift variables, which are also considered as policy variables specifically affecting growth process. As we do not have adequate data base for cyclone damages, we use a dummy variable for cyclone.

The model

Our choice of the model stems from the Cobb-Douglas production function and is along the lines employed by Luintel et al. (2008) and Rao et al. (2008) with constant returns and Hicks – neutral technical progress.

$$y_t = A_t k_t^{\alpha}, \quad 0 < \alpha < 1 \tag{1}$$

Where:

y = per capita output;

A = stock of technology;

k = capital stock per capita.

Our objective is to study the impact of tourism (tourism arrivals, TA represented by an index) on per capita output (y). Additionally, two policy variables are added. One is the real exchange rate index (REER), with nominal exchange rate being defined as units of Fiji dollar per unit of US dollar; and the other is OPEN, (sum of exports and imports as percent of GDP). The REER which is the product of nominal exchange rate and ratio of foreign price index to domestic price index would reflect the impact of fiscal and monetary policies pursued by the country authorities.

The other policy variable, *OPEN* would represent the degree of liberalization policies pursued by government in regard to exports and imports.

It is therefore plausible to assume shifts in growth can be influenced by the changes in variables such as policy changes. The variables which are considered include tourism arrivals, real exchange rate and openness of the economy.

$$A_t = f(TA_t, REER_t, OPEN_t) \tag{2}$$

Where:

TA = index number representing tourist arrivals;

$REER$ = real exchange rate index; and

$OPEN$ = ratio of trade to GDP in percent.

We enter *TA, REER and OPEN* as shift variables into the production function, noting capital per capita as the fundamental and conditioning variable explaining output per capita:

The Cobb-Douglas production model is modified as:

$$A_t = A_0 e^{gT} \, TA_t{}^\beta \, REER_t{}^\delta \, OPEN_t{}^\theta \tag{3}$$

$$y_t = (A_0 e^{gT} \, TA_t{}^\beta \, REER_t{}^\delta \, OPEN_t{}^\theta) \, k_t{}^\alpha \tag{4}$$

For the purpose of econometric estimation, the above model can be written as:

$$Ly_t = \alpha_0 + \alpha_1 Lk_t + \alpha_2 LTA_t + \alpha_3 LREER_t + \alpha_4 LOPEN_t + \sum \beta_m dum_{mt} + e_t \tag{5}$$

where:

Ly_t = natural logarithm of real gross domestic product per capita (in US dollars in 2005 prices);

Lk_t = natural logarithm of real capital stock per capita (in US dollars in 2005 prices);

LTA_t = natural logarithm of TA as percent of GDP;

$LREER_t$ = natural logarithm of real exchange rate;

$LOPEN_t$ = natural logarithm of openness [(X+M)/GDP].

dum_{mt} is a vector of dummy variables (dum_{1t}, dum_{2t} dum_{3t}) to capture effects of three coups in 1987, 2000 and 2006; currency devaluation in 2009; and cyclone affecting the country periodically; and e_t is the random error term.

The hypotheses to be tested are: (i) *Lk* is directly associated with Ly; (ii) LTA positively influences Ly;(iii) *LREER* is positively associated with Ly; (iv) *LOPEN* is positively associated

Table 29.7 Summary statistics of the variables

Period/Year	GDP per capita (constant US$)	Capital stock per capita (constant US$)	TA Index	REER (FJ$/US$) (Index)	OPEN (%) [(X+M)/GDP]
1980–89 (ave.)	2721	7936	34	157.5	95.9
1990–99 (ave.)	3054	8468	51	119.7	118.3
2000–04 (ave.)	3438	9364	63	109.5	128.5
2005–09 (ave.)	3637	10325	87	113.8	117.3
2010	3622	10861	100	100.0	121.7
2011	3688	11059	107	103.4	128.2
2012	3726	12100	105	106.6	128.9
2013	3828	12375	104	107.6	136.4
2014	3946	12656	110	106.6	129.4

Source: Capital stock from the Federal Reserve (2015); TA index series is from IMF (2016) and other data series from World Bank (2016a)

with Ly; (v) the dummy variable for coup is negatively associated with Ly; (vi) dummy variable for devaluation is directly associated with Ly and (vii) dummy variable for cyclone is negatively associated with Ly.

Data

The period included in this study is from 1980 to 2014. We utilize the data series of capital stock of Fiji in constant prices released from Penn Tables (Federal Reserve, 2014). All the other data series are sourced from World Development Indicators.[11] Table 29.7 presents summary statistics of variables used in the analysis.

6 Results and interpretation

Since the number of observations is not large enough, we resort to the autoregressive distributed lag (ARDL) procedure, developed by Pesaran *et al.* (2001). The Technical Appendix presents a brief exposition of the stationarity and unit root testing utilized in connection with the variables used in equation (7).

While estimating equation (5) we found the dummy variable for cyclone emerged with significance. Hence, the two non-significant dummy variables for coup and devaluation were dropped. The final estimated equation is shown as equation (7):

$$Ly = 0.309Lk^{**} + 0.253LTA^{***} + 0.339LREER^{***} + 0.199LOPEN^{**} - 0.022\ D3^{*} + 1.678 \qquad (7)$$
$$\quad\ (2.029) \qquad (5.067) \qquad\quad (3.346) \qquad\qquad (2.629) \qquad\qquad (-1.722) \qquad (0.98)$$

Adj. R^2 =0.885
S.E. of Regression =0.046
Sargan test p-value = 0.988
Note: The figures in brackets denote the t- statistic values, $*$, $**$, and $***$ indicate the variable is significant at 10%, 5%, and 1% respectively.

From the above equation, all the coefficients are found statistically significant at the 95% level. The coefficients of *Lk, LTA,* LREER and *LOPEN* have the expected positive signs, confirming that they are positively associated with the dependent variable, *Ly*. The dummy for cyclone has a significant and negative impact on Ly. The share of capital stock is 0.31 which is consistent with the stylistic values obtained in similar production function studies for developing countries (Rao *et al.*, 2008; Rao and Takirua, 2010).

Diagnostic tests were performed on equation (7), namely the Sargan test of over-identifying restrictions. Additionally, the VECM Granger causality test was performed to determine the direction of causality. The results of these tests are reported in the Technical Appendix, and the interpretation of the results are subject to the caveats indicated in this appendix.

7 Conclusions and policy recommendations

Although tourism has now emerged as an engine of growth in PICs, there are growing uncertainties in regard to its future. There are increasing concerns relating to impacts of cyclones, as they now appear to have become regular, annual occurrences, causing immense loss of lives and damages to infrastructure.

This chapter undertook a study on tourism led growth nexus in Fiji. The results show that the variable representing cyclones, along with other conventional explanatory variables in a production function model, emerged statistically significant and negative. This indicates that the there is a need to put in place corrective mechanisms to counteract the negative effects of cyclones.

One of the effective ways to reduce adverse effect of natural disasters is to prioritize efforts in building resilience to natural disasters rather than just focusing on emergency responses (Ramos, 2016). One example of building resilience is to invest in introduction of an early warning system since the benefits of early warning systems have been recognized to be much higher than the costs. Building resilience is crucial as more number of natural disasters of greater intensive nature have now come to be predicted with greater accuracy than in the past, which reflect the rapid rate of unprecedented occurrences of disasters due to climate changes (Mei and Xie, 2016).

Secondly, there is also urgent need to build buildings, roads and other communication facilities cyclone resistant (Prevatt *et al.*, 2010). It is essential for private sector to ensure new construction development activities are cyclone resistant to mitigate future risks.

Thirdly, South Pacific region is not new to experiencing natural disasters over centuries. Thus, systematic collection and documentation of useful indigenous knowledge are needed so as to utilize the past experiences in this regard. Hence, it is recommended to use indigenous knowledge integrating with contemporary tools in the process of disaster risk reduction (Mercer *et al.*, 2007).

Fourthly, there is an urgent need to recognize and investigate natural disasters as an economic event. The costs of damages from natural disasters are largely determined by economic policies and conditions of the countries concerned, as it was evident in case of earthquakes in Haiti and Chile. Although Chile had experienced occurrences of earthquake of much stronger intensity, compared to those experienced by Haiti, Chile had incurred lower damages. Hence, there is important role of economic analysis and policies in Disaster Risk Reduction (DRR) (Cavallo and Noy, 2011).

Finally, as the expenditure estimates over a 20-year period (World Bank, 2016b) for undertaking retrofitting of current public sector buildings and facilities together with re-construction of roads and other communication networks are beyond the financial capacity of national governments, the island nations are now making regional and collective efforts to seek assistance with a mix of aid from advanced countries and loans on a concessional basis from international funding agencies. The international donors should be more generous than ever before and come forward to assist the region.

Technical appendix

Stationarity and unit root testing

From Table 29.A1, it is seen that variables employed in the study are not found stationary at level but they are stationary at first difference. Though unit root tests are not needed for bound tests, test results confirm the results obtained for cointegration relationship are robust and free from bias.

The results obtained from Table 29A.2 confirm that there is only one cointegration equation after ensuring that the linkage is in only one direction and the relationship runs from all explanatory variables only to Ly. In other words, the variables are cointegrated in the long run when Ly is the dependent variable.

Table 29.A1 Unit root test results

Variables	ADF test		Ng and Perron test, MZa	
	Level (constant with trend)	1st difference (constant without trend)	Level (constant with trend)	1st difference (constant without trend)
Ly	−2.29	−7.46**	−8.40	−15.83**
Lk	0.31	−4.16**	−0.40	−13.11**
LTA	−2.65	−7.83**	−15.21	−17.90**
LREER	−1.58	−4.14**	−4.79	−14.53**
LOPEN	−2.55	−5.98**	−9.57	−16.42**

Note: The critical values for ADF test are based on MacKinnon (1996). The optimal lag is selected on the basis of Akaike Information Criterion (AIC). The Ng and Perron critical value is based on Ng and Perron (2001), and the optimal lag is selected based on Spectral GLS-detrended AR based on SIC. The null hypothesis of the test is: a series has a unit root. ** denotes the rejection of the null hypothesis at the 5% level of significance.

Table 29.A2 Results of bounds test for cointegration

Dependent variable	Computed F-statistic
Ly	9.73***
Lk	1.80
LTA	2.00
LREER	2.02
LOPEN	1.23

Critical value	Pesaran et al. (2001)		Narayan (2005)	
	Lower bound	Upper bound	Lower bound	Upper bound
1%	3.74	5.06	4.590	6.368
5%	2.86	4.01	3.276	4.630
10%	2.45	3.52	2.696	3.898

Note: *, ** and *** indicate significance at 10%, 5% and 1%, respectively.

Having confirmed the existence of a long-run relationship between the variables from the bounds tests, we resorted to the Generalized Method of Moments (GMM) estimation procedure for eliminating any bias due to potential endogeneity problem in explanatory variables. The long run equation was arrived at by using instrumental variables estimators. Instrumental variables employed in the estimation procedure include the differenced of the level of explanatory variables and the differenced of lagged of the explanatory variables.

A brief note on the ARDL bounds test

The ARDL bounds testing model is a general dynamic specification, which applies lags of the dependent variable and the lagged and contemporaneous values of the explanatory variables, through which short-run impacts can be directly assessed and long-run relationship indirectly estimated. The use of this technique is also based on its advantages over the conventional cointegration procedure. See, for example, Pesaran *et al.* (2001), Narayan and Smyth (2005), Akinlo (2006), among others for the advantages and applications of ARDL

An ARDL model of equation (5) is constructed as follows:

$$\Delta Ly_t = \alpha_0 + \beta_0 Ly_{t-1} + \beta_1 Lk_{t-1} + \beta_2 LTA_{t-1} + \beta_3 LREER_{t-1} + \beta_4 LOPEN_{t-1} +$$

$$\sum_{i=1}^{p} \beta_{0i}\Delta Ly_{t-i} + \sum_{i=0}^{p} \beta_{1i}\Delta Lk_{t-i} + \sum_{i=0}^{p} \beta_{2i}\Delta LTA_{t-i} + \sum_{i=0}^{p} \beta_{3i}\Delta LREER_{t-i} +$$

$$\sum_{i=0}^{p} \beta_{4i}\Delta LOPEN_{t-i} + \mu_t \tag{6}$$

The bound test is carried out by using equation (6). For simplicity, the dummy variables which are included in the analysis, which capture the effects of coup, currency devaluation and cyclones are not shown in the ARDL model. The bounds test equation (6) is repeated by using other explanatory variables as dependent variable to determine the number of cointegrating vectors in the model.

There are two steps in the ARDL bound testing approach. First, we estimate equation (6) by ordinary least squares techniques. Second, the existence of a long-run relationship can be traced by imposing a restriction on all estimated coefficients of lagged level variables equal to zero. Hence, bounds test is based on the F-statistics (Wald statistics) with the null hypothesis of no cointegration (H_0: $\beta_0 = \beta_1 = \beta_2 = \beta_3 = \beta_4 = 0$) against its alternative hypothesis of a long-run cointegration relationship (H_1: $\beta_0 \neq \beta_1 \neq \beta_2 \neq \beta_3 \neq \beta_4 \neq 0$).

Since the F-statistics used for this test has a nonstandard distribution, Pesaran *et al.* (2001) have generated two different sets of critical values for given significance levels. The first set assumes that all variable are integrated of order zero, *I(0)*, and the second set assumes all variables are integrated of order one, *I(1)*. If the computed F-statistic is greater than the upper critical bounds value, then the null hypothesis is rejected. In contrast, if the computed F-statistic is smaller than lower critical bounds value, it indicates no long-run relationship between variables. If the computed F-statistic lies between lower and upper bounds values, then the test becomes inconclusive. To enhance the robustness of results, the computed F-statistic is also compared with the critical values provided in Narayan (2005) which consider the properties of small sample size.

The Sargan test

Sargan test of over-identifying restrictions is applied to check on the validity of instruments used. The test examines the possibility of a correlation between the residuals and the instrument variables. There is no instrument misspecification if null hypothesis of the Sargan test cannot be rejected. From the Sargan test result, there is no instrument misspecification. This implies that the instruments are valid.

Granger causality test

Table 29.A3 shows the results of VECM Granger causality test. The error correction term (ECT) is significant only in the equation with Ly as the dependent variable. This is consistent with the bound test where there is only one long run relationship between the variables. In other words, Lk, LTA, LREER and LOPEN Granger cause Ly in the long run. The negative sign of the ECT which is in conformity with theoretical expectations indicates the existence of long run restoration in the equilibrium, when there is a short run shock in the model.

In terms of short run causality, we observe that there is bidirectional causality between Ly and LTA. This implies there is a feedback effect between growth and tourism and they are interdependent on each other. Other than bidirectional causality, unidirectional or one-way causality is found running from Lk, LTA, LREER and LOPEN to Ly, from LOPEN to Lk and from LREER to LTA.

Table 29.A3 VECM Granger causality

Dependent variable	ΔLy	ΔLk	ΔLTA	ΔLREER	ΔLOPEN	ECT(-1)
ΔLy	–	5.381**	21.911***	3.276*	7.339**	−0.105* (−1.825)
ΔLk	1.432	–	1.860	1.346	14.996***	−0.082 (−0.791)
ΔLTA	3.613*	1.754	–	4.387*	0.436	−0.024 (−0.067)
ΔLREER	2.371	2.261	1.744	–	1.255	−0.114 (−0.826)
ΔLOPEN	0.168	0.957	0.172		–	−0.049 (−0.312)

Note: Figures without bracket indicate the F-statistic value and coefficient for the ECT(-1). Figures in brackets are the t-statistics for the ECT. *, ** and *** denote significance at 10%, 5% and 1%, respectively.

Notes

1 The 14 Pacific island nations are Cook Islands, Fiji, the Marshall Islands, Nauru, Niue, Palau, Papua New Guinea, Samoa, Solomon Islands, Tonga, Tuvalu and Vanuatu.
2 See Seetanah (2011) for comprehensive survey on this subject.
3 The data series of cruise ship passenger arrivals, assembled as an independent series are available only from 1995.
4 Tourism Statistics Database. Available at www2.unwto.org/content/data/.
5 The ten PICs are: Cook Islands, Fiji, the Marshall Islands, Micronesia (Federal States), Niue, Palau, Samoa, Tonga, Solomon Islands and Vanuatu.

6   United Nations Office for Disaster Risk Reduction (UNISDR). (2012) Annual Report 2012. Retrieved from www.unisdr.org/files/33363_unisdrannualreport2012.pdf/.

7   Direct costs cover physical damage to capital assets, including buildings and infrastructure, inventories of finished, intermediate and raw materials, destroyed or damaged by the actual impact of a disaster. Indirect costs include damage to flow of goods and services including lower output from damaged or destroyed assets and infrastructure; loss of earnings due to damage to marketing infrastructure such as roads and ports and to lower effective demand; and the costs associated with the use of more expensive inputs following the destruction of cheaper usual sources of supply. They also include the costs in terms of both medical expenses and lost productivity arising from increased incidence of disease, injury and death. Secondary effects concern both the short- and long-term impacts of a disaster on overall economic performance, such as deterioration in trade and government budget balances and increased indebtedness as well as the impact on the distribution of income or the scale and incidence of poverty.

8   For example, in the wake of Cyclone Kina of January 1992, which struck the Western Division, visitors from Australia declined by 2.1% year on year in the January and by 20% in February whilst visitors from New Zealand and other Pacific islands fell by 9.1% and 5.8%, respectively, year on year in the same month. Earnings per head of tourist were also estimated to fall by about half in January 1993 as many tourist activities were cancelled.

9   Tourist arrivals were in the last quarter (October to December) of 2015 were 194,656 and in the first quarter of 2016 (January to March) were 158,069 (Reserve Bank of Fiji, 2016).

10 One of the proposals which have been agreed to by PICs in a workshop on 'Climate Change Financing Initiatives' sponsored by UN Economic Commission for Asia and Pacific (UN ESCAP), held in Fiji in August 2016, was to work on a regional level to formulate bankable projects for seeking funds from international agencies (*Fiji Times* 2016).

11 Available at https://data.worldbank.org/data-catalog/world-development-indicators/.

References

Akinlo, A. (2006). 'The stability of money demand in Nigeria: An autoregressive distributed lag approach'. *Journal of Policy Modeling*, 28(4): 445–452.

Andersen, M. B. (1991). Which Costs More: Prevention or Recovery?, In Kreimer, A. and Munasinghe, M. (eds), *Managing Natural Disasters and the Environment: Selected Materials from the Colloquium on the Environment and Natural Disasters Management*. Washington, DC: the World Bank.

Balaguer, J. and Cantalvella-Jorda, M. (2002). 'Tourism as a Long-Run Economic Growth Factor: The Spanish Case'. *Applied Economics*, 34(7): 877–884.

Benson, C. (1997). *The Economic Cost of Natural Disasters in Fiji*. Overseas Development Institute Working Paper, 97. London: Overseas Development Institute.

Benyon, M., Jones, C. and Munday, M. (2009). 'The Embeddedness of Tourism-related Activity: A Regional Analysis of Sectoral Linkages'. *Urban Studies*, 46(10): 2123–2141.

Bull, R. (1992). *Disaster Economics*. Disaster Management Training Programme. New York and Geneva: United Nations Development Programme and United Nations Disaster Relief Office.

Bonte, M. and Cook, S. (2013). 'Regional Disaster Risk Assessment and Pooling'. *Pacific Economic Monitor*. December. Manila: ADB.

Candela, G. and Cellini, R. (1997). 'Countries' size, consumers' preferences and specialisation in tourism: a Note'. *Rivista Internazionale di Scienze Economiche e Commerciali*, 44: 451–457.

Cavallo, E. and Noy, I. (2011). 'The Economics of Natural Disasters – A Survey'. *International Review of Environmental and Resource Economics*, 5: 63–102.

Chand, S. (2015). *Fiji: policies for growth*. School of Economics Working Paper, No. 4. Suva: School of Economics, the University of the South Pacific.

Dritsakis, N. (2004). 'Tourism as a long run economic growth factor: an empirical investigation for Greece using causality analysis'. *Tourism Economics*, 10: 305–316.

Durbarry, R. (2002). 'The economic contribution of tourism in Mauritius'. *Annals of Tourism Research*, 29(3): 862–865.

Durbarry, R. (2004). 'Tourism and economic growth: the case of Mauritius'. *Tourism Economics*, 10: 389–401.

Eugenio-Martin, J. L., Morales, N. M. and Scarpa, R. (2004). *Tourism and economic growth in Latin American countries: A Panel Data approach*. FEEM Working Paper, No. 26.

Federal Reseve, St. Louis (2014). Capital Stock of Fiji at Constant National Prices. (accessed December 10, 2015).

Figini, P. and Vici, L. (2009). Tourism and growth in a cross-section of countries. *RCEA Working Papers*, Rimini: The Rimini Centre for Economic Analysis.

Fiji Times (2016). 'Pacific countries discuss climate change financing initiatives', August 8, 2016.

Gunduz, L. and Hatemi, A. (2005). 'Is the tourism-led growth hypothesis valid for Turkey?'. *Applied Economics Letters*, 12(8): 499–504.

Hampton, M. P. and Jeyacheya, J. (2013). *Tourism and Inclusive Growth in Small Island Developing States*. London: Commonwealth Secretariat.

Hsiang, S. and Jina, A. (2014). The Causal Effect of Environmental Catastrophe on Long-Run Economic Growth: Evidence from 6,700 Cyclones. *NBER Working Paper*, No. 20352.

International Monetary Fund (IMF) (2016). *International Financial Statistics*, January 2016. Washington, DC: IMF.

Jayaraman, T. K.Chen, H. and Bhatt, M. (2014). 'Research note: Contribution of Foreign Direct investment to the Tourism Sector in Fiji: an Empirical Study'. *Tourism Economics*, 20(6): 1357–1362.

Jones, S. (2010). 'The Economic Contribution of Tourism in Mozambique: insights from a Social Accounting Matrix'. *Development South Africa*, 27(5): 679–696.

Kim, H. J., Chen, M. H. and Jang, S. S. (2006). 'Tourism expansion and economic development: the case of Taiwan'. *Tourism Management*, 27(5): 925–933.

Lanza, A. and Pigliaru, F. (1995). Specialization in tourism: the case of small open economy. In Coccossis, H. and Nijkamp, P. (eds), *Sustainable Tourism Development*. Aldershot: Avebury.

Lanza, A., and Pigliaru, F. (2000). 'Tourism and economic growth: Does country's size matter?'. *Rivista Internazionale di Scienze Economiche e Commerciali*, 47(1): 77–86.

Luintel, K., Khan, M., Arestis, P. and Theodoridis, K. (2008). 'Financial Structure and economic growth'. *Journal of Development Economics*, 86(10): 181–200.

MacKinnon, J. (1996). 'Numerical distribution functions for unit root and cointegration tests'. *Journal of Applied Econometrics*, 11(6): 601–618.

Mei, W., and Xie, S. P. (2016). 'Intensification of land falling typhoons over the northwest Pacific since the late 1970s'. *Nature Geoscience*, 9(10): 753–757.

Mercer, J., Dominey-Howes, D., Kelman, I., and Lloyd, K. (2007). 'The potential for combining indigenous and western knowledge in reducing vulnerability to environmental hazards in small island developing states'. *Environmental Hazards*, 7(4): 245–256.

Narayan, P. K. (2005). 'The Saving and Investment Nexus for China: Evidence from Cointegration Tests'. *Applied Economics*, 37: 1979–1990.

Narayan, P. K. and Smyth, R. (2005). 'Electricity consumption, employment and real income in Australia evidence from multivariate Granger causality tests'. *Energy Policy*, 33(9): 1109–1116.

Narayan, P. K., Narayan, S., Prasad, A. and Prasad, B. C. (2010). 'Tourism and Economic Growth: A Panel Data Analysis for Pacific Island Countries'. *Tourism Economics*, 16(1): 169–183.

Ng, S. and Perron, P. (2001). 'Lag Length Selection and the Construction of Unit Root Tests with Good Size and Power'. *Econometrica*, 69(6): 1519–1554.

Noriko, I. and Mototsugu, F. (2007). 'Impacts of tourism and fiscal expenditure to remote islands: the case of the Amami islands in Japan'. *Applied Economics Letter*, 14: 661–666.

Otero, R. C. and Marti, R. Z. (1995). The Impacts of Natural Disasters on Developing Economies: Implications for the International Development and Disaster Community. In Munasinghe, M. and Clarke, C. (eds), *Disaster Prevention for Sustainable Development: Economic and Policy Issues*. Washington, DC: The International Decade for Natural Disaster Reduction (IDNDR) and the World Bank.

Pesaran, H., Shin, Y. and Smith, R. (2001). 'Bound testing approaches to the analysis of level Relationships'. *Journal of Applied Econometrics*, 16: 289–326.

Pole, R. and Bola, J. (2012). *Training Manual on Earthquake, Cyclone, Flood and Tsunami Safe Construction in Fiji: Masons, Carpenters, Technicians*. UNDESA/UNCRD/NDMO.

Prevatt, D. O., Dupigny-Giroux, L. A., and Masters, F. J. (2010). 'Engineering perspectives on reducing hurricane damage to housing in CARICOM Caribbean Islands'. *Natural Hazards Review*, 11(4): 140–150.

Ramos, R. (2016) The Future Resilience of the Philippines and South-East Asia's Tropical Cyclones. Available at www.futuredirections.org.au/publication/12817/.

Rao, B., Singh, T. A., Singh, R. and Vadlamannati, K. C. (2008). *Financial developments and the rate of growth of output: An alternative approach*. MPAR Paper, No. 8605.

Rao, B. and Takirua, T. B. (2010). 'The Effects of Exports. Aid and Remittances output: The Case of Kiibati'. *Applied Economics*, 42(11): 1387–1396.

Reserve Bank of Fiji (2016). Quarterly Economic Review, Various Issues. Suva: RBF.

Seetanah, B. (2011). 'Assessing the dynamic economic impact of tourism for island economies'. *Annals of Tourism Research*, 38(1): 291–308.

United Nations Economic and Social Commission for Asia and Pacific (2016). Statistical Database. Available at www.unescap.org/stat/data/.

United Nations World Tourism Organization (UNWTO) (2016). Tourism Statistics Database. Madrid, Spain.

World Bank (2016a). *Pacific Possible: Tourism*. Washington, DC: The World Bank.

World Bank (2016b). *Pacific Possible: Climate and Disaster Resilience*. Washington, DC: The World Bank.

Index

For Product Safety Concerns and Information please contact our EU
representative GPSR@taylorandfrancis.com Taylor & Francis Verlag GmbH,
Kaufingerstraße 24, 80331 München, Germany

Printed and bound by CPI Group (UK) Ltd, Croydon, CR0 4YY
08/05/2025
01864310-0003